ADULT DEVELOPMENT AND AGING

ADULT DEVELOPMENT AND AGING

Marion Perlmutter
University of Minnesota

Elizabeth Hall

John Wiley & Sons
New York
Chichester
Brisbane
Toronto
Singapore

Cover Photo: Benn Mitchell, Image Bank

Library of Congress Cataloging in Publication Data:

Perlmutter, Marion.
    Adult development and aging.

    Bibliography: p.
    Includes index.
    1. Adulthood.   2. Aging.   3. Life cycle, Human.
4. Death—Social aspects.   I. Hall, Elizabeth, 1929–
II. Title.
HQ799.95.P47   1985   305.2'6   84–19611
ISBN 0-471-88217-8

Printed in the United States of America

10 9 8 7 6 5 4 3

For my parents, Eleanor Lifschutz Perlmutter and Frank Perlmutter, whose lives have been my primary model of adulthood and whose continued growth and development I look forward to sharing.

Marion Perlmutter

For my grandfather, Robert Norman Hall, whose life first made me question the stereotypes of aging, and for Scott O'Dell, whose example daily demolishes them.

Elizabeth Hall

PREFACE

The rapidly changing population balance in the United States has focused the attention of researchers and the general public on adult development and aging. As members of the postwar baby boom edge closer to middle age and their parents and grandparents develop a style of life that fits none of the cultural stereotypes of old age, a concept of development that stops at maturity clearly no longer fits the adult experience. It has become increasingly obvious that aging is not simply a process of decline, nor is development exclusively a process of growth.

In this book, we have adopted a life-span view of development, stressing growth and development during adulthood as well as tracing aging and decline. The developing individual is picked up at maturity and followed through middle age, early old age, late old age, and death. Both change and stability are considered, and we look at changes and continuities within the individual (intraindividual differences) as well as between individuals (interindividual differences). In the process, we have tried to offer a more optimistic view of the last few decades of life than has often been presented, one that we believe is warranted by research and example.

The concept of life-span development has been supported by research in the fields of biology, medicine, psychology, sociology, anthropology, economics, and history. Believing that an understanding of development over the life span requires a wider perspective than can be provided by a single discipline, we have adopted a multidisciplinary coverage, drawing on all levels of explanation. The book thus takes a topical organization. After establishing basic concepts of development and its study (Section I), we view adult development and aging at the level of biology and health (Section II), move on to individual psychological functioning (Section III), and then consider the adult within a social context (Section IV). The book closes with an exploration of death, looking at the survivors as well as the dying individual. The discussions take a spiral form, avoiding the compartmentalization of development by providing frequent examples of the ways in which various levels of development and aging interact.

Our presentation is not limited to a detailing of currently known facts about development: we also stress analytic skills that will allow the student to interpret age differences. Throughout the book runs an awareness that development and aging are open to cultural and environmental influence and that age differences reflect cohort and historical factors as well as developmental factors. This emphasis allows us to anticipate ways in which the path of adulthood in the future is likely to differ from its course today.

We have tried to remain sensitive to gender, ethnic, and cultural differences in our discussions, in the hope that the student will not fall into the trap of assuming that traditional studies of white, middle-class males can tell us all about development and aging in women, in other ethnic groups, and in other cultures. We have provided material on sex differences in biological and health status (Section I), cognition and personality (Section II), and the way relationships within and outside the family are experienced and the course of career development (Section III). Ethnic and cultural differences are noted throughout the book, with Chapter 15 entirely devoted to this topic.

Our goal was to produce a text that is clear and interesting, one can be followed by a student with little background but at the same time yields richer meaning to the student who has completed an introductory course in one of the behavioral sciences. To that end, we introduce each chapter with an illustrative example drawn from life and, where possible, include observations that demonstrate the major points, in the form of quotes from individuals who were interviewed by researchers or journalists.

Each chapter also contains the following special features that we hope will ease the student's path:

- Each chapter begins with an outline showing the logical arrangement of the text.
- Following each opening anecdote is a brief overview of the chapter.
- Each chapter contains a box that highlights a topic discussed in the text. Some boxes present a single study in detail, such as the discussion of sexual satisfaction in marriage (Chapter 11); some look at a controversial issue in depth, such as the consideration of midlife crisis (Chapter 10); some explore an aspect of development not usually considered, such as the problems faced by a stepparent (Chapter 12); and others provide a case history, such as B. F. Skinner's personal methods for outwitting an aging memory (Chapter 8).
- At the end of each chapter is a narrative summary of the material covered.
- Following the summary is a listing of key terms introduced in the chapter that appear in the glossary.
- The end-of-book glossary defines terms used in the book.
- The extensive bibliography at the end of the book enables students to explore any topic more deeply or instructors to expand course coverage.

A complete *Instructor's Manual* is also available for the text. This manual contains approximately 1,000 test items, lecture outlines, suggested paper topics, and recommended readings.

ACKNOWLEDGMENTS

The guidance and assistance of many people were necessary to bring this book into existence. Carol Luitjens, Executive Editor/Publisher of the Social Sciences Publishing Group at Wiley, who approached us to collaborate on the project; Mark Mochary, psychology editor, whose enthusiasm for the book's approach kept us going; Pamela Bellet-Cassell and Susan Goodall, who saw that it got done; Susan Giniger, who shepherded us through the editing process; Cecil Golann, whose copy editing caught our dangling participles; and Maryellen Costa, who saw that the book finally came off the presses. We are also grateful to Linda Gutierrez, who found just the right photographs for the book and Ann Marie Renzi, whose design captured its spirit.

We would also like to thank those reviewers who caught us when we slipped and suggested additional points that vastly improved the final manuscript. They included:

Dr. Irene Hulicka
State University of New York, Buffalo

Dr. Andrew Coyne
The Ohio State University

Professor Pamela Roberts
California State University—Long Beach

Professor Louis Heller
University of Minnesota—Duluth

Dr. Sandra Fiske
Onondaga Community College

Dr. Ilene Siegler
Duke University Medical Center

Professor Terry Allen
University of Texas at El Paso

Dr. Janet Johnson
University of Maryland

Dr. Gari Lesnoff-Caravaglia
Executive Director
University of Massachusetts, Center on Aging

Professor Paul S. Kaplan
Suffolk County Community College

Marion Perlmutter
Elizabeth Hall

CONTENTS

BOXES

PART ONE

INTRODUCTION TO THE STUDY OF ADULT DEVELOPMENT AND AGING

1

ADULTHOOD: DEVELOPMENT AND AGING

"**T**o enter the country of age is a new experience, different from what you supposed it to be. Nobody, man or woman, knows the country until he has lived in it and taken out his citizenship papers," explained critic Malcolm Cowley in *The View from 80* (1980). Impatient with the descriptions of aging produced by those of us who had not even reached a comparatively youthful 70, he described old age without sentiment, recounting its triumphs and sorrows.

A member of Harvard's class of 1919, Cowley recounted the activities of some of his octogenarian classmates. Most of them seemed active and busy. Some were still in the occupations they had pursued all their lives—journalism, the ministry, business. Others had started new businesses. One classmate was now manufacturing cross-country skis; another was running a gardening firm; yet another had begun a service to sell out-of-print books by mail. A retired banker had become a successful painter, exhibiting and selling his watercolors.

Harvard graduates are a privileged group, with incomes far above the national average, but these men, who were born in the nineteenth century, may give us a preview of what aging is likely to become for more and more people. A famous Spanish toast wishes us *salud y pesetas y tiempo para gastarlas*: health and money and the time to use them. As we will discover in this book, general improvements in health and increased income among older adults indicate that this prospect may now be within the grasp of many people.

The study of adulthood leads us inevitably to the study of aging and ultimately to death. But the quality of our passage to that far country has changed in the past few decades. Although physical aging may place some limits on our activities and economic constraints still hamper far too many of us, the reports from researchers who study adulthood and aging are much more encouraging than the stereotypes most of us hold. New findings indicate life is closer to Cowley's picture than to the gloomy portrait that haunts some people, and they hold the promise of continued improvement.

We begin this chapter by examining the meaning of maturity and the changing experience of adulthood in American society. This leads us to consider the concepts of adult development and aging and the value of using a person's age as a guide to his or her life. After looking at the factors that lead to change, we ask just how much consistency we can expect to find in a person's life. The chapter closes with a brief historical survey of researchers' attempts to study adulthood and aging.

ADULTHOOD

It is easy to describe an adult as a person who has grown up, one who has reached maturity; **adulthood** is the portion of the life span after maturity. The problem is deciding just when a person reaches maturity and how to define the concept. Maturity has been defined in biological, psychological, social, and legal terms.

MATURITY

Biological maturity is attained when a person is able to reproduce. Yet few would call a 13-year-old girl or a 15-year-old boy an adult. Psychological maturity comes when a person reaches a certain mental and emotional level. The adult can adapt to new situations; think about the future and about hypothetical situations; plan for tomorrow, for next month, and for next year. On the emotional level, the adult can commit himself or herself to intimate relationships (Erikson, 1980a). When measured by the psychological yardstick of maturity, some people in their thirties would be immature.

Social maturity is reached when a person assumes family and work roles. The adult generally marries, establishes a family, and becomes self-supporting. If childhood is a time of dependence, adulthood is a time of responsibilities. Yet many 25-year-old graduate students are still financially dependent and have not yet assumed family or occupational responsibilities. Finally, legal maturity comes when a person receives various legal rights: An adult can vote, drive a car, drink alcoholic beverages, or serve in the armed forces. The point of legal maturity varies, depending on the right specified and the country—or even state—of residence.

None of these definitions produces a satisfactory definition of adulthood, and for most of us each comes at a different time. Society recognizes this disparity in an unofficial way when it regards adolescents as sexually mature but socially and psychologically immature (Miller and Simon, 1980). The recognition has led to

Social maturity generally comes after biological and legal maturity has been reached. For many people, social maturity is marked by marriage and parenthood.

such practices as the states' establishment of legal ages for sexual consent and the federal government's attempt to require family planning clinics to notify the parents of any adolescent woman who requests birth control devices. When the government grants individuals the right to vote in national elections, it assumes that, by the age of 18, people are psychologically mature. But the Constitution sets up a different standard of maturity; it withholds the right to represent other voters in the House of Representatives until the age of 25 and in the Senate until the age of 30, and the office of president is restricted to individuals who are at least 35.

Because there is no age at which everyone automatically becomes an adult, we will arbitrarily set the age of maturity at age 20, when all are biologically and legally mature and many meet the requirements for psychological and social maturity. It is likely, however, that maturity is so broad and subjective that each person's sense of having crossed the border between adolescence and adulthood is much more ambiguous and that the sense of maturity undergoes many reassessments.

THE CHANGING EXPERIENCE OF ADULTHOOD

Not only do we have multiple definitions of maturity, but over historical time the experience of adulthood has changed as well. Two thousand years ago, half the Romans born in any year would be dead within 22 years; only a handful would live until their sixty-fifth birthday. By 1900, 4 out of every 100 Americans were 65 or older; half of those born during 1900 would be dead within 49 years. Today more than 11 out of every 100 Americans are at least 65, and by the year 2000, 13 out of every 100 will be that old (U.S. Bureau of the Census, 1982). It is estimated that half the people born in 1983 will still be alive 74 years later (Walford, 1983). This dramatic change in survival rates has affected adulthood in at least three ways: The structure of the population is getting older; a greater proportion of each person's life is spent as an adult; a greater proportion of adulthood is spent in retirement.

Age Structure of the Population

Greater survival and a reduced birth rate have changed the United States from a young society to an aging society—and one that is getting older (Fig. 1.1). Only a few years ago, more than half the population was under 30 years old. Babies were big business; schools were expanding; homes for young, growing families were under construction; the wants and needs of adolescents were a primary concern of most manufacturers. The middle-aged were slighted, and the elderly were largely ignored.

Babies, children, adolescents, and adults under 30 are now a minority. People are having fewer children, and members of the baby boom that followed World War II are in their thirties, with some facing their fortieth birthdays. At the far end of the scale, the number, as well as the proportion, of older adults is increasing. In 1900 about 3 million people, or about 4 percent of the population, were

1960	29.4 years
1970	27.9 years
1975	28.7 years
1980	30.0 years
1981	30.3 years

FIGURE 1.1   The aging of America: U.S. population—median age. The median age of Americans has been steadily increasing since 1970. Today more than half of the population is older than 30.

Source: U.S. Bureau of the Census, 1982.

aged 65 and over; by 1970 about 20 million had reached 65; by 1990, we can expect 28 million; and by 2000, 35 million Americans, or about 13 percent of the population, will have passed their sixty-fifth birthdays (U.S. Bureau of the Census, 1982).

As the structure of the population has changed, society has taken on a new look (Fig. 1.2). Many elementary classrooms are empty and schools have closed; new houses have fewer bedrooms; retirement communities have sprung up across the land. Manufacturers of cars, appliances, furniture, fashions, cosmetics, and sporting equipment are more attentive to the wants and needs of middle-aged and old people. For example, as the market for baseball bats shrinks, the market for golf clubs and tennis rackets grows. We should see fewer station wagons and vans on the highway and more full-size and luxury cars. One of the first manufacturers to shift marketing strategy to match population changes was Johnson & Johnson, whose Baby Shampoo is now widely advertised as an ideal product for adults. In the 1970s, models in Coca-Cola and Pepsi ads grew older whereas models in ads

Age	1960	1970	1980	1981
under 5 years	11.3	8.4	7.2	7.4
5 to 13 years	18.2	17.9	13.7	13.3
14 to 17 years	6.2	7.8	7.1	6.8
18 to 21 years	5.3	7.2	7.7	7.6
22 to 24 years	3.6	4.9	5.6	5.7
25 to 34 years	12.7	12.3	16.5	17.0
35 to 44 years	13.4	11.3	11.4	11.5
45 to 54 years	11.4	11.4	10.0	9.8
55 to 64 years	8.6	9.1	9.6	9.5
over 64 years	9.2	9.8	11.3	11.4

FIGURE 1.2   Changes in population structure, 1960–1981 (percent). The age structure of the population reflects changes in birth rates and mortality. Members of the baby boom now swell the young adult groups whereas the middle-aged groups reflect the lower birth rate during the Great Depression. Growth in the oldest groups reflects increases in survival.

Source: U.S. Bureau of the Census, 1982.

for Geritol and hair color grew younger (Jones, 1980). In the future we can expect to see advertising aimed toward the last part of the life span; people who are 65 or older now hold about 30 percent of the discretionary spending power in the United States (Eisdorfer, 1983).

This shift in the structure of the population has major implications for society. The looming increase in retired people means a corresponding growth in the **old-age dependency ratio**—which is the number of people over 65 divided by the number between 18 and 64. Although many people over 65 are employed and a good many people over 18 are in school, this ratio is used as a guide to the number of workers whose Social Security contributions will be available to pay retirement benefits. In 1930 the ratio was .09; there were nearly 10 people of working age for each person who had reached the age of retirement. By 1981 the old-age dependency ratio had risen to .19; there were only about 5 workers for each retiree. The ratio is expected to reach .29 by 2030, leaving only 3½ workers to support each retired person (U.S. Bureau of the Census, 1982). Fears that the increased dependency ratio would bankrupt the Social Security system led to a reorganization of the system in 1983 that will gradually extend the average person's working life. The caution with which politicians handled this issue indicates the growing political power of older adults.

Length of Adulthood

Increased survival rates mean that most people can look forward to a longer adulthood. Although the greatest drop in the death rate has been among infants and young children, adults have also benefited. The great killers of nineteenth century adults, such as tuberculosis, have been almost eliminated. Recent advances in the treatment of cancer and a better understanding of the relationship between life-style and heart disease have also reduced deaths among older people. As a result, Americans can expect to spend 50 to 60 years as adults. In the past, children and adolescents prepared for adulthood, but few adults prepared for an old age they doubted they would ever attain.

When we believe that we are likely to die young, physical risks may seem acceptable, and there may seem little need to save for the future. A Roman soldier who expected to die from cholera or dysentery may have found the risks of combat acceptable. The gladiator may have seen the financial reward that accompanied victory well worth the chance of dying in the Colosseum. But when we believe that we still will be alive at 80 or 90, we may become more cautious in all areas of life. Pensions become an important consideration to job applicants, physical risks become unacceptable, and health becomes a prime concern. Perhaps the popularity of jogging and attention to dietary fiber and cholesterol is partly due to the realization that our chances of living to a ripe old age have increased. As one octogenarian said, "If I had known I was going to be this old, I would have taken better care of myself."

Adulthood has changed in other ways. In 1900 a young couple could expect about 25 years of married life before tuberculosis, cholera, pneumonia, influenza, or accident ended the relationship. Today, unless they part voluntarily, a young couple can expect their marriage to last more than half a century. It has been suggested that the prospect of being married to the same person for 50 years may have contributed to the acceptance of divorce in American society (Erikson and Hall, 1983).

The experience of aging has also changed. Older adults today are more vigorous than the elderly of past generations. Sanitation, better nutrition, and medicine have combined to create a group of older Americans who are in relatively good health. Today's older adults are more likely to be active in a political campaign, a civic group, a charitable organization, out on the golf course, or attending college than sitting in a rocking chair. They are also better educated and in a far better economic position than their parents were. The elderly seem more youthful than they once did. When researchers interview older adults, 60- and 70-year-olds often say, "I am much younger than my mother—or my father—was at my age." (Neugarten and Hall, 1980).

Leisure in Adulthood

Over the past century, the amount of free time has increased. Working hours are shorter, vacations are longer, and automation and computers have made most jobs—whether in or out of the home—easier and faster. The 40-hour work week has become standard, and in some places flexible hours are resulting in a workweek of 4 days. Throughout adulthood we have more time to spend as we wish—in sports, travel, hobbies, or education; in cultural, political, or civic activities; and in loafing or in front of the television set.

This increased freedom in the way we use our time has led to a corresponding increase in our potential for growth and fulfillment. Greater concern and more resources can be directed to enriching the years of adulthood. For some, of course, the new leisure of adulthood seems only a dream. As we will see in Chapter 12, the employed mother of small children may find that shorter working hours and automation have merely made it possible for her to take on twice as many responsibilities.

The new leisure becomes especially apparent among older adults. Our great-grandparents worked as long as they were physically able to do so; in 1890, 68 percent of all men 65 and older were gainfully employed (Zubin, 1973). There was no Social Security, and neither unions nor businesses provided pensions. A company's responsibility ended when it presented a gold watch to the employee who had—in the company's eyes—outlived any usefulness. Today only 18 percent of the men and 8 percent of the women who are 65 or older are employed (U.S. Bureau of the Census, 1982). Most people retire by the time they are 65, their life savings bolstered by pensions or Social Security—or both.

Because the average 65-year-old can expect to live for another 16 years (U.S. Bureau of the Census, 1982), preparation for later adulthood becomes important. The retiree who has developed outside interests during early life will have more time to pursue them whereas the retiree whose life has centered around work may find the retirement years bleak and empty. As the educational level of retired men and women rises, there may be a shift in their activities and interests. The success of any person's preparation for later adulthood depends on the course of development during the adult years.

THE CONCEPT OF HUMAN DEVELOPMENT

Only a few years ago, the consideration of adult development—let alone courses in the subject—was rare. Social scientists, zoologists, physicians, and the general public agreed that development consisted of age-related changes in body and behavior from conception to maturity. Nearly 30 years ago, asked to describe development, researchers replied by saying that it was a "moving forward in time by growing in complexity and size" (Anderson, 1957, p. 25), a process of "progressive changes from a more simple to a more complex structure or organizational pattern" (Hamburger, 1957, p. 49), or sequential changes that produce permanent but novel increments in a system's structure and operation (Nagel, 1957). Development was generally considered in the fetus, infant, child, and adolescent. It was characterized by growth and improvement in structure and function and by the individual's increasing adaptation to the environment, even by those few researchers who saw it as possible through the life span (Schneirla, 1957). Development was obviously a good thing.

For the most part, adults were not assumed to develop; they aged. Aging consisted of age-related changes in body and behavior after maturity. It was characterized by decay and deterioration of structure and function and perhaps by the individual's increasing compensation for that decay. Aging was obviously a bad thing, made up of wrinkles, falling hair, slowed movements, dimming vision, increasing deafness, and failing memory.

DEVELOPMENT AND AGING

That old view of human development and aging is still held by many in the general public, but it is fading among researchers, its reality smudged by studies of age change. As more is discovered about growth before maturity, it becomes clear that aging, in the sense of decay, begins early in life. For example, the fetal brain contains many more cells, or neurons, than it will ever use. As the brain develops, cells that do not make connections with other cells die (Cowan, 1979).

Studies at the later end of the life span show that not all the changes after maturity involve decay or deterioration. Sometimes we get better as we get older. We may come to accept and understand ourselves and others better (Erikson, 1983). Many of us will show continued improvement in some aspects of intellectual functioning until at least 55 or 60, with little apparent decline until we are into our seventies or beyond (Schaie, 1982). Some of us will make important contributions when we are well into old age. Few people realize that Tolstoy was in his seventies when he wrote *Resurrection*, that photographer Imogen Cunningham was doing

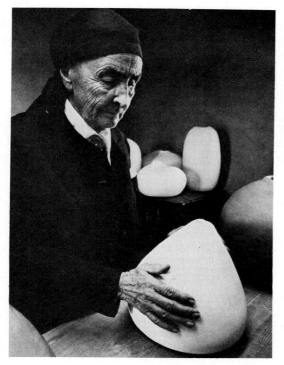

Many individuals continue to make creative contributions long after most people have retired. Artist Georgia O'Keeffe was still painting and sculpting when she was well past 80.

important work when she was in her nineties, that Benjamin Franklin invented bifocals when he was 78, or that Pablo Picasso and Georgia O'Keeffe were still creating important works of art when they were in their eighties.

Faced with a series of such findings, researchers revised their assumptions. They concluded that age-related changes before maturity sometimes fit the old definition of aging whereas age-related changes after maturity are sometimes improvements and fit the old definition of development, making old definitions unworkable. Today **development** is defined as any age-related change in body or behavior from conception to death. The direction of that change can be positive (toward improved functioning), negative (toward deterioration), or neutral (showing neither improvement nor deterioration, but simply a difference). Because development is a lifelong process, it is no longer regarded as moving toward any state of maturity (Baltes, Reese, and Lipsitt, 1980). Development and aging have become virtually synonymous (Featherman, 1981).

When researchers study development after maturity, however, their concept of the aging process may vary. It has been suggested that most developmentalists use either a stability model of aging, an irreversible decrement model, or a decrement with compensation model (Schaie, 1973). Some researchers view adult functioning as more or less stable from maturity until death. This "stability model" of aging recognizes that changes may occur but that decline is not inevitable. Decline is presumed to be the result of disease or some other unnatural condition. Some aspects of intelligence fit this model of aging.

Other researchers see adult functioning as irreversibly declining from a peak performance in young adulthood. In this "irreversible decrement" model, decline is inevitable even among healthy adults. The ability to focus the eye at close distances and tasks involving rapid hand-eye coordination seem to fit this model of aging. Finally, some researchers see adult function as involving phases of growth and decline but believe that environmental conditions can allow the individual to compensate for the declining function. In this "decrement with compensation" model, a person's situation, including health, educational level, and interests, will affect the level of compensation. Aspects of intelligence that do not fit the stability model may fit this model of aging.

THE PHASES OF LIFE

Divisions of the life span are arbitrary. They differ from one society to the next and change from one time in history to another. There are no clear physical benchmarks that guide the Western division of life into the main phases of infancy, childhood, adolescence, and adulthood. For example, some people see infancy as ending at about one year, when the baby begins to walk. Others see it as lasting until two, when youngsters are beginning to put several words together to form sentences.

The period of childhood did not officially exist until the seventeenth century (Aries, 1962). In medieval Europe, individuals went from infancy into the general population. Around their seventh birthday they were apprenticed and left their families to mix with people of all ages in work and play. Because no one believed children had any special needs or characteristics, they were generally treated as if they were small adults.

Because of the high mortality rate, infancy itself was regarded as a tentative phase of life, and parents did not become greatly attached to babies. The death of a baby was such a usual thing that it probably occasioned much less distress than would be felt today. The sorrow was soon over (Aries, 1962). Other societies with high infant mortality rates seem to make similar adjustments; the Hindu life cycle does not even have a place for infancy. The first part of the official Hindu life span begins with school entrance and lasts until young adulthood; it includes the period we call adolescence (Kakar, 1978).

Adolescence as we know it today was recognized only in the nineteenth century, when technological societies required educated workers and increasing wealth made it possible to excuse young people from work requirements. In many tribal societies, adult roles are assumed at puberty, and the passage from childhood to adulthood is brief and often marked by intense community rites.

Adulthood itself is often subdivided into the periods of **young adulthood, middle adulthood**, and **later adulthood**. As we have seen, deciding just when a person enters young adulthood is difficult; the border between young and middle adulthood is also fuzzy. In the United States, the dividing line varies by social class. When asked, members of the working class are likely to say that a person is "middle-aged" at 40 and "old" at 60; members of the middle class often say that a person reaches "middle age" at about 50 and is not "old" until 70 (Neugarten, 1968).

This ten-year difference in the way social classes divide the life span probably arises in part from the nature of their respective occupations and in part from differences in life expectancy. Many working-class jobs, especially in the past, have required physical strength and endurance. As reflexes slow and strength begins to diminish, work in mines, steel mills, building construction, and railroad repair becomes more difficult. Work that depends on intellectual rather than physical agility can be continued for a much longer period. Because people in the middle class also tend to live longer, the realization that they have more years ahead of them may lead to their extension of young and middle adulthood.

In this book, we will consider young adulthood as the years between 20 and 40 middle adulthood as the years between 40 and 60 and later adulthood as that portion of the life span past 60. We will also subdivide later adulthood to reflect the nature of aging in the United States during the 1980s. Older adults who are healthy and vigorous will sometimes be referred to as "young-old"—a period that roughly covers the years between 60 and 75. Older adults who are frail and ill will sometimes be called "old-old"—a period that generally begins after 75. But **chronological age**, or the elapsed time since birth, is not an infallible guide to this division. Bernice Neugarten (1980), who first suggested these terms, has stressed that physical and mental condition, not chronological age, determines whether a person belongs with the young-old or the old-old. A vigorous, healthy 85-year-old would be young-old, and a frail 65-year-old would be old-old.

Knowing a person's age tells us much about development in a young person, because age-related changes early in life tend to be canalized. **Canalization** is a genetic predisposition that guides development in a direction that is difficult to deflect. Because the predisposition is expressed in any natural human environment, canalized changes among people are fairly similar (Scarr, 1981). For example, a 12-month-old is likely to be learning to walk steadily; a 2-year-old, to be acquiring language; and a young adolescent, to be coming to terms with a developing body.

But what does the information that a person is 45 tell us? Not much except that he or she has lived for 45 years. An adult's age tells us little about economic or marital status, style of life, or health. Development in later life is much less canalized and more open to environmental influences. Human lives are like the spreading of a fan; the longer people live, the greater the differences between them (Neugarten and Hall, 1980). Some 55-year-olds may already seem elderly whereas some 90-year-olds are vital and very much alive. Among the elderly, age-related changes tend to differ more than at any other time of life. In fact, differences among 65- to 90-year-olds are often greater than differences between 40- to 64-year-olds and adults over 65 (Weg, 1983). There is not only an enormous variability in health and cognitive function but also considerable discrepancies in the ways in which old people view themselves.

THE MEANING OF AGE

Aware of the variability among people, researchers (Salthouse, 1982) have criticized the use of chronological age as a guide to development on three counts: (1) individuals age at different rates, so that knowing a person's date of birth tells us little about mental or physical capabilities; (2) various aspects of the individual age at different rates; and (3) the "meaning" of a given number of years changes across the life span. For example, age-related changes between birth and age 1 are widespread and impressive, but age-related changes between ages 65 and 66 are probably imperceptible. Thus, although time since birth may be closely linked to such developments as walking, talking, and sexual maturity, chronological age can be a misleading measure at any time of life. If most people in a society tend to have similar experiences, changes related to those experiences are easily confused with changes of development.

For example, children's ability to recall word lists increases steadily with age. Three- and 4-year-olds are very poor at memorizing word lists, but 8-year-olds do fairly well, and 12-year-olds are efficient memorizers. Our first assumption is likely to be that the ability to store and retrieve items from memory is an age-related skill that develops through maturation. But we might be wrong. During childhood, chronological age and schooling are highly correlated; the older the child, the more years of schooling she or he has. From the age of six, children spend their days in a situation where memorization is required, so that they learn various strategies that help them to remember. In this case, the effect of schooling may be more important than developmental effects of age (Hall, Lamb, and Perlmutter, 1982).

Among adults, similar situations can obscure attempts to understand development, and changes that become more prevalent with age are mistakenly believed to be caused by age. During middle adulthood, for example, income functions in a way that is similar to the effects of schooling during childhood. Most individuals start adult life with relatively modest financial resources, but their income increases throughout early and middle adulthood. Some aspects of adulthood, such as self-concept, are highly correlated with income. Because of this relationship, apparent age-related changes in self-concept may really reflect the effect of increases in financial resources that occur with age.

Among older adults, disease is highly correlated with chronological age, so that the effects of disease have often been mistaken for age-related changes in mental or physical functioning. For example, the incidence of serious memory loss increases with age, leading many people to believe that all old people are confused and forgetful and eventually become what is commonly called "senile." But severely impaired mental functioning is not a consequence of normal aging; it may be due to any number of conditions (all of which we will discuss in Chapter 5): Alzheimer's disease, heart disease, drugs, or simply a lack of motivation (Hickey, 1980). Some cases of apparently severe deterioration can be arrested or even reversed, and none are the inevitable result of chronological age.

Chronological age is only one way of looking at development. Depending on the purpose, another sort of measure may often be more helpful (Wohlwill, 1973). For example, most dimensions of maturity discussed earlier lend themselves to ways of viewing a person's development. Thus, developmentalists sometimes use estimates of a person's development in various areas, looking at biological age, psychological age, social age, or functional age (Birren and Renner, 1977).

Biological age refers to the individual's position on his or her own potential life span and is closely connected with physical health. A woman with a chronological age of 65 and a much younger biological age would show fewer of the physical appearances of aging that we have come to expect, would display a slighter-than-expected decrease in physiological functioning, and would be likely to live longer than the average 65-year-old woman.

Psychological age refers to a person's adaptive ability and reflects intellectual skills, emotions, and motivation. A 35-year-old man who was unable to establish intimate relationships would function at a much younger emotional age, and a 50-year-old who was suffering from Alzheimer's disease might have the cognitive functioning of a very old person.

Social age refers to the person's roles and habits relative to those expected by society for particular ages. A woman who became a grandmother at 40 was older, in terms of social age, than average whereas a woman who bore her first child at 40 was younger than average. Similarly, a 35-year-old man who assumed the role of head of an extended family clan would have a social role that was older than his chronological age, and a 55-year-old man who assumed a position at the bottom of a corporate hierarchy would have a social role that was younger than his chronological age.

Functional age refers to a person's ability to function in society and probably reflects biological, psychological, and social age. An 85-year-old man who lives alone, drives a car, and attends night classes is much younger, in terms of functional age, than the average 85-year-old. He is probably healthier, sharper, and more involved than most of his peers. Yet gerontologists would be unlikely to assign a functional age label to this man. Instead, most would evaluate various aspects of his functioning separately, for example, using vision and reaction time to evaluate his functional ability to operate a car at an age when many people no longer are capable of driving safely.

Some researchers believe that the concept of age is steadily becoming less useful. Neugarten (1975; 1980) proposed that the United States is becoming an **age-irrelevant society,** in which chronological age, already a relatively poor predictor of the way an adult lives, is losing much of whatever meaning it once had. She

AGEISM: DISCRIMINATION AGAINST OLDER PEOPLE

Thirty-year-old Pam Moore, an industrial designer, recently declared, "I know what it's like to be old. There really is age segregation and discrimination" (Halstead, 1983). For three and a half years, Moore spent up to 14 hours each week masquerading as an 80-year-old woman. It took her 4 hours to transform herself into a convincing octogenarian. Her portrayal was so persuasive that she was twice mugged and robbed. Most often, however, she found herself dismissed or condescended to.

For some years researchers have been concerned about **ageism**, or discrimination against older adults (Butler, 1975). People who engage in ageism see elderly people as all alike: unattractive, incompetent, feeble, sexless, and senile. Ageism certainly exists in the field of employment, and we will discuss its implication in Chapter 13, but attempts to discover the prevalence of ageism among the general public have had conflicting results.

When students in a college course in aging were asked to respond to stereotypical beliefs about older people, their agreement with the stereotypes ran from a low of 20 percent to a high of 77 percent. Yet when these same students were asked whether all old people fit the stereotypes, most agreed that there were many exceptions, and fewer than one in five students thought that the stereotypes described as many as 80 percent of older people (Schonfield, 1982).

Sometimes ageism fails to appear. When elementary schoolchildren wrote stories about old men, they portrayed them as good and wise (Thomas and Yamamoto, 1975). But older men are not always seen in a positive light, and ageism can be especially destructive when it affects employment. Asked to rate job applications, students at one university discriminated against older men, but not older women (Walsh and Connor, 1979). Told they were to rate applicants for the position of part-time art columnist on a local newspaper, the students read sample articles supposedly submitted by applicants. When students believed that the applicant was a 64-year-old man, most were unwilling to publish the article or to ask the author's advice about art; but when they believed that the applicant was a 64-year-old woman, they were both willing to publish and to take advice about art from the author. (The articles were identical.) Whether students value older women more highly than older men, whether they believe women are generally more knowledgeable about art than men, or whether they simply felt the female applicant rose above stereotypes is uncertain. But the discrimination against older men was clear.

In an attempt to see what kind of message about the elderly came

When a young woman disguised herself as an 80-year-old, she found herself discriminated against, segregated from the young, mugged, and condescended to.

across in daily newspapers, researchers (Buchholz and Bynum, 1982) studied the content of *The New York Times* and the *Daily Oklahoman* for 1970 and 1978. They discovered that the picture presented in both papers was generally favorable. Older men and women in the news stories were more likely to be active than passive and to be seen in a favorable light. Only 14 percent of the stories conveyed a negative image of old age.

Where then does ageism surface? Perhaps less in overt discrimination than in an attitude that dismisses old people by regarding their actions as "cute." A story about a pair of 80-year-old lovers who finally marry or a 75-year-old who runs a marathon may evoke the same kind of indulgent smile we give a 3-year-old who dresses up in Mother's clothing and staggers through the house in her high-heeled shoes. This sort of ageism is the hardest to dispel. It is similar in its condescension to the sexist remark made by the eighteenth-century man of letters Samuel Johnson. Told about a woman who preached at a Quaker meeting, Johnson said, "A woman preaching is like a dog's walking on his hind legs. It is not done well, but you are surprised to find it done at all" (Boswell, 1791, p. 328).

points out that there is no longer a particular decade in which a woman or man marries, has children, enters the labor market, or goes to school. Today there are 22-year-old mayors, 15-year-old presidents of computer software companies, 35-year-old grandmothers, 50-year-old retirees, and 70-year-old college students. Society is becoming more fluid, making social expectations misleading and public policies that are based solely on age, such as compulsory retirement, illogical.

No matter what measure of age is used, it is no more than a rough estimate, a convenient way of referring to changes that, in a society like ours, generally come in a certain part of the life span. Age should not be considered the *cause* of the change, merely an index of it.

INFLUENCES ON CHANGE

Age-related changes during any phase of life are a complicated process that comes about when the individual interacts with various influences. In fact, many believe that unless the individual interacts with the physical and social environment, there will be no development (Piaget, 1971; Vygotsky, 1978; Gelman, 1982). Paul Baltes, Hayne Reese, and Lewis Lipsitt (1980) have proposed that development and aging are best understood as the result of either age-normative, history-normative, or nonnormative influences.

AGE-NORMATIVE INFLUENCES

Some influences affect almost every person in a particular culture at about the same point in the life span. These are known as **age-normative influences**; they are the most general factors in development, and they are highly correlated with age. Age-normative influences are the factors traditionally studied by developmentalists. They can be biological or social. Walking, talking, puberty, and education are age-normative events encountered by almost every member of the society. They change a person's capabilities and, therefore, result in differences between age groups. Marriage, parenthood, and retirement affect fewer people, but they are still so widespread and so closely correlated with age as to be considered age-normative. Age-normative events that are social in nature involve roles, such as student, spouse, parent, or worker. Assuming the role of parent, for example, is likely to make a person feel more responsible and nurturant. The care of an infant demands changes in the priorities and behavior of the parents. The expectations of others about the behavior of parents also are part of such age-normative events.

HISTORY-NORMATIVE INFLUENCES

Some influences are the result of circumstances that exist at a particular historical moment. These influences are **history-normative**. As they affect everyone who is alive at the time, they are not correlated with age. The same history-normative event often has very different effects on people of different ages, but the influence of history-normative events tends to be general across each **cohort**, or generation of people born at the same time. No two birth cohorts experience the same set of events in the same way.

The computer, for example, is a history-normative influence that affects people of different ages in different ways. Eighty-year-olds who are approaching the end of the life span might find its influence slight, regard it as a nuisance, and never become comfortable with it. But 5-year-olds will grow up in a world changed by computers and, as adults, will interact easily with them, finding it hard to visualize a world without computers. Among other technological advances that have had history-normative effects on the present population are television and space exploration. For earlier generations, the automobile, the railroad, and the printing press were history-normative events.

Medical improvements, such as vaccines, can also produce a history-normative influence. For example, people now in their forties and fifties grew up before polio vaccine was developed. They generally knew of children whose legs were encased in metal braces or who lived in an iron lung, unable to breath without assistance. Their childhood summers were filled with warnings about the dangers of polio, or "infantile paralysis," as it was commonly called. As cases of polio began to mount, some children were not allowed to swim in public pools. The children lived under one set of restrictions and fears. Their parents lived with a different kind of fear. Today's 70-year-olds, who were their parents, spent their summers worrying about their children's health and were filled with apprehension each time a child complained of an ache or pain.

International events, such as wars, may lead to important history-normative changes in a population. The war in Vietnam is a recent example of a history-normative event with wide—and varying—effects on people's lives. Economic events can also exert a powerful influence. The Great Depression of the 1930s affected the lives of those who lived through it. Its immediate impact on family relationships, the peer group, personality, motivation, and attitudes toward work were obvious; but researchers have discovered that the depression had lasting influence on those who lived through it. What is more, its lifelong effects on those who were children at the time were different from the effects on those were were adolescents or adults (Elder, 1974).

NONNORMATIVE INFLUENCES

The developmental factors most restricted in scope are known as **nonnormative influences**, for they are specific to individuals. They do not affect all members of a society or all members of any cohort. Age bears little relation to their appearance. Winning the grand prize in a state lottery, for example, is clearly a nonnormative event. It happens to few people, but when it occurs, it can have a profound influence on the winner's life and development.

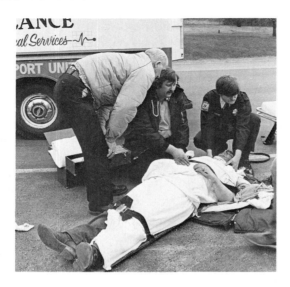

Nonnormative influences, which have little connection with age, can profoundly influence the course of a person's development. Winning a lottery or being seriously injured in an automobile accident can turn a life in a new and unexpected direction.

Some nonnormative influences are physical. Serious disease, such as diabetes or cancer, is nonnormative, as is having a major accident. Losing a leg in a car crash, for example, can affect many areas of life. Other nonnormative influences are social: divorce, losing a job, emigrating to another country, going to prison, or winning a professional award. None of these things happen to most of us at a particular age, but any of them can have a significant effect on a person's life.

INFLUENCE OVER THE LIFE SPAN

According to Baltes, Reese, and Lipsitt (1980), each of the three types of effects may follow a different course of influence over the life span (see Fig. 1.3). Age-normative influences appear to be strongest in childhood and again in advanced old age. Their strength during childhood is probably due to the relative power of genetic influences on the infant and young child. Earlier we saw that age-related changes are most similar among children. Although the reason for their revived strength toward the end of life is not yet known, it may be the result of a genetic program that limits the life span.

History-normative events may exert the greatest power on adolescents and young adults. It is during these years that major decisions are made on career, desired style of life, and family; and these kinds of decisions are heavily influenced by social, cultural, and economic factors.

Nonnormative events are believed to increase in power over the life span. As we saw earlier, individual's lives are like the spreading of a fan, and this widening of differences may reflect both the cumulative influence of nonnormative events and the decline in power of age-normative factors.

Each person's development is the result of interaction among the three classes of influence and the individual. A question that immediately arises is whether the course of that development is predictable from an early age or whether human be-

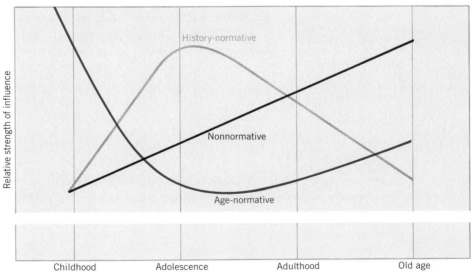

FIGURE 1.3   Developmental influences across the life span. The relative impact of various influences is believed to shift over the life span as shown in this hypothetical profile. Age-normative, history-normative, and nonnormative influences interact to produce age-related changes in development.

Source: P. B. Baltes, H. W. Reese, and L. P. Lipsitt, 1980, p. 77.

ings are likely to show unexpected, perhaps radical, changes in physical well-being, personality, and intellectual functioning.

CHANGE AND CONSTANCY

The answer to questions about the predictability of development depends on whether we talk about changes within the individual or changes across individuals. Changes within the individual, in which a person's behavior is compared with his or her own earlier behavior, are known as **intraindividual changes**. Differences in patterns of change across individuals are known as **interindividual differences**. Developmentalists are interested in understanding both kinds of change.

INTRAINDIVIDUAL CHANGE

When we ask about intraindividual predictability, we are asking whether knowing about a person at one time allows us to make predictions about that person at a later time. Does knowing that a man is a stockbroker, married, and the father of five children at age 35 allow us to predict his profession and family status eight years later? Not always. If the year is 1883, the place is Paris, and the stockbroker is Paul Gauguin, in 1891 he will be alone in Tahiti, devoting himself to painting.

Most of us expect people to change in minor ways, finding a new job, a new house, a new hobby, or a new hair color. But we do not expect people to change in their personality, attitudes, beliefs, or intelligence; nor do we expect them to desert their families and head for Tahiti. Many researchers have held the same view, assuming that human development is characterized by constancy, not change (Brim and Kagan, 1980). Childhood experiences are supposed to chart the course of adult development, and few of us are expected to stray from the charted path.

Some aspects of personality do seem to be formed by middle childhood. Studies in which people have been followed from childhood into middle adulthood have shown that several areas of adult personality can be predicted from personality at about 8 or 10 years of age (Moss and Susman, 1980). A good deal of this constancy is in characteristics that have been encouraged by society. Achievement, generally regarded as a good thing, remains stable for both men and women. Other characteristics that depend on traditional sex roles show different patterns of constancy in women and men. Dependency, for example, has tended to be more stable in women; and aggression, more stable in men. Some characteristics tend to predict differently for men and women. In one study (Bronson, 1967), a placid and controlled boy was likely to be a rigid, constricted, and humorless 30-year-old whereas a placid and controlled girl was likely to be calm, open, and dependable at 30.

Despite such predictability, people do change. Developmentalists emphasize that constancy and change are both present throughout life (Baltes and Goulet,

People may change in unpredictable and radical ways. Therapy groups and halfway houses have enabled drug addicts to kick their habit and former prisoners to lead exemplary lives.

1970). When change appears, it may be predictable, or it may take a totally unexpected form.

People may change in fairly predictable ways as they take on new social roles. Far from being stable and rigid, they adapt to the social demands of being a spouse, parent, worker, grandparent, or retiree. Most are flexible enough to handle considerable stress. A study of German adults who were in middle and later adulthood after World War II showed that they adjusted to changing social, political, and economic demands. Had they not been able to change, they would probably not have survived (Thomae, 1979).

People may also change in unpredictable ways although few show changes as radical as those made by Gauguin. Alcoholics stop drinking; teetotalers start to drink. Political liberals become conservative; conservatives become liberals. Agnostics embrace the church; religious zealots become agnostic. Convicted criminals lead exemplary lives; pillars of the community embezzle company funds. The existence of psychotherapy, organizations like Alcoholics Anonymous, half-way houses, drug education, occupational counseling, and affirmative action programs testifies to the possibility of change (Brim and Kagan, 1980). Such efforts are successful often enough to keep the organizations in business.

People vary considerably in the amount of constancy and change they display. Constancy is most likely to be found in characteristics that are valued by society, and change is most likely to be found in attitudes, for attitudes often change as the culture's values change (Moss and Susman, 1980).

Sometimes people are more stable than they think. Middle-aged adults in one study (Woodruff and Birren, 1972) tended to believe that their own personality had changed a good deal more since adolescence than it actually had. When they were nearly 20, these adults took a personality test; 25 years later they retook the same test. Their scores on the two tests were fairly similar, indicating little personality change in a quarter of a century. But these men and women believed that they had changed considerably. As 45-year-olds they had filled out the test twice: once to describe their present personalities and the second time to answer as they probably had as adolescents. Most believed that they had been much less competent as adolescents and less well-adjusted than they actually had been. Although their personalities had been fairly constant, they perceived a large change.

These adults may, of course, have changed in ways the test failed to measure. Or perhaps their experiences over 25 years led them to judge their adolescent selves more harshly than they actually judged themselves at the time. Memory is tricky, however, and a middle-aged adult's memory of adolescence may not always be trustworthy.

Cognitive functioning is also supposed to remain constant over most of the adult years; between the ages of 25 and 65 mental abilities tend to remain on a plateau or to decline slightly. But researchers have found that some people stay on the plateau, some show declines, and others show increases in certain functions. Whether constancy or change prevails in cognitive functioning appears to depend on the various influences on change discussed earlier. Health, education, socioeconomic status, and various nonnormative or historical-normative influences can lead to change (Thomae, 1979).

INTERINDIVIDUAL DIFFERENCES

As we saw earlier, people tend to become less alike as they grow older. The amount of interindividual difference in each cohort increases as the number of nonnormative experiences pile up. Pleasant influences (inheriting a fortune, writing a best-seller, entering a happy marriage, or earning great distinction in a profession) increase the amount of interindividual difference just as unpleasant influences (disease, accident, divorce, death of a loved one, losing a job) do.

Although age-normative influences are believed to affect extreme old age, they are unlikely to exert a strong influence in adulthood until the life span is almost over. Because people die over such a wide span of ages (another interindividual difference), age-normative influences on a group of 70 year olds, for example, would be affecting mainly those likely to die in the near future. Those who will live until 80 or 90 or longer would not yet be strongly affected by any genetic program that limits the life span.

Studies of older adults have found wide differences in every aspect of life, from blood pressure and cognitive functioning to personality and satisfaction with life (Thomae, 1979). The factors that seem to be closely related to interindividual differences are socioeconomic status and physical health.

Looking at interindividual differences across cohorts can be misleading. History-normative events can have such a strong influence that differences may not be the result of aging, but simply a cohort effect. For example, in 1972, 52 percent of adults over 50 believed that premarital sexual intercourse was always wrong; 41 percent of those between 30 and 49 believed that it was always wrong; and 18 percent of those under 30 believed that it was always wrong (Glenn, 1980). One way to interpret those figures would be to say that people become increasingly conservative about sexual matters as they age. It is more likely, however, that social standards at the time of sexual initiation are the key to the difference. People in the two older groups entered adulthood before the 1960s, when American sexual attitudes were fairly conservative. Those in the youngest group became adults in the 1960s and 1970s, when public attitudes were undergoing profound change.

The relationship between intraindividual change and interindividual differences is complicated. If everyone were exactly alike at conception, interindividual differences among adults would be the results of previous intraindividual change (Baltes, Reese, and Nesselroade, 1977). But we are not alike at conception. Each of us—unless we have an identical twin—has a unique genetic background, guaranteeing that interindividual differences will always be with us.

ADULT DEVELOPMENT AND AGING— A HISTORICAL VIEW

The developmental study of adulthood and aging went into high gear after World War II, but the tradition of writing and thinking about the human life span can be traced back more than 2000 years, when Greek philosophers gave considerable thought to human development. However, little progress was made until the late eighteenth century, when Johannes Nikolaus Tetens (1736–1807), a professor of philosophy in Kiel, set forth the basic goals of today's developmentalists. Tetens emphasized the need to search for general developmental laws, urged the use of scientific research to discover them, stressed the lifelong course of development, and noted the role of environmental influences on the development of interindividual differences (Reinert, 1979).

The next major figure to look at the entire life span was another philosopher, Friedrich August Carus (1770–1808), a professor at Leipzig, who described the interaction between the individual and environmental influences and noted that chronological age was not itself the cause of development (Reinert, 1979). The third major figure in the early history of adult development was Adolphe Quetelet (1796–1874), a mathematician, sociologist, and psychologist, who is considered the first scientist to study aging. He charted development from birth to old age, using empirical data on physical, moral, and intellectual development (Quetelet, 1842). In addition to presenting the first comprehensive account of the life span, Quetelet noted the effect of history-normative influences on age-related change (Baltes, 1979).

The foundation was now laid for a science of human development, but for nearly a century most scientists concentrated on children. However, some of the child-centered research that was begun in the 1920s and 1930s later shed light on adulthood and aging. At several places in the United States, groups of children were studied and then followed for decades. At Stanford University, Lewis Terman began the study of 1500 gifted children who are now in their seventies. At the University of California, three separate studies were begun; each has been in progress for more than 50 years. Children in a study at Fels Institute in Ohio are now in their mid-forties. As their subjects aged, researchers who began by studying development in infants and children found themselves studying development in adults (Charles, 1970).

But for decades, little research was done in the field of adult development. While one group of researchers was studying children, another group was looking at the last part of life. A new field, **gerontology**, or the scientific study of aging, slowly developed.

Medical research into aging was first. Before the twentieth century was a decade old, researchers were publishing material on the determinants of longevity and speculating about changes at the cellular level that might be responsible for the aging process (Riegel, 1977). The psychological study of aging was spurred by the publication of G. Stanley Hall's *Senescence, The Last Half of Life* (1922). Hall, who was an important figure in the study of children and adolescents, wrote his book while he was in his seventies, combining retrospection, statistics, theory, literature, and research (Charles, 1970).

Most early research on aging concentrated on cognitive functioning. The Army Alpha Test, an intelligence test developed to screen recruits during World War I, was used to explore changes in intelligence with age. Other researchers studied the relationships between education, socioeconomic level, and the growth and decline of intelligence over the life span. (Riegel, 1977). Psychomotor skills were the focus at Stanford University, where a research unit was established in 1928 to study the problems of workers over 40 who were having trouble obtaining jobs in industry.

In Germany, research on aging also began in the 1920s. By the early 1930s, Charlotte Buhler, who had been studying child and adolescent development, expanded her work to cover adulthood (Grofmann, 1970). At a time when most researchers were studying only a portion of the life span, she proposed a theory of life span development and attempted to discover regularities in human development.

Another important step in the study of adult development was taken when the University of Chicago established the Committee on Human Development. Its program, which combined sociological, anthropological, and psychological study, was the first of its kind in the United States. It awarded its first Ph.D. degree in 1943.

During World War II, research on aging diminished. With hostilities over, two major research centers were set up to investigate aging. In England, the Nuffield Research Center at Cambridge focused on the aging worker. In the United States, the National Institutes of Health founded a gerontological unit under the direction of Nathan Shock (Riegel, 1977). It was at this time, in 1946, that the new Gerontological Society began publishing the *Journal of Gerontology*.

Most of the early work on aging had been spurred by the practical problems of welfare and health among older adults. Then in 1948, with the Social Science Research Council's publication of *Social Adjustment in Old Age*, the interest of researchers broadened. Studies began to explore all aspects of the aging process (Maddox and Wiley, 1976).

Nonaging aspects of adult development also began to receive more attention. In 1950, Erik Erikson proposed the first coherent theory of personality development that covered the entire life span. Erikson, who is a psychoanalyst, stressed the importance of history-normative influences on development. Although he saw development as moving through the same stages in all societies, he believed that culture and history affected the way developmental tasks were resolved.

In the past 40 years, as the proportion of older adults in society has grown, interest in adult development and aging has increased steadily. Today there are centers for the study of aging at a number of universities. Research is carried on in many countries, and more than 30 journals devoted to gerontology are published. Since 1950 the International Association of Gerontology has brought together researchers from all disciplines in all parts of the world (Poon and Welford, 1980).

In the next chapter, we will see how each discipline has approached the study of adult development, and examine the methods that have been devised to separate age-normative effects, cohort influences, and the effects of historical time on development.

SUMMARY

Although **adulthood** is the portion of the life span after maturity, maturity can be defined in biological, psychological, social, or legal terms. Most people attain these various aspects of maturity at different times, leading to the arbitrary adoption of age 20 as maturity for the purposes of this book. As life expectancy has increased, it has affected adulthood in three major ways. First, the aging population structure has resulted in a change in the **old-age dependency ratio**, leaving fewer workers to support each retired person. Second, a longer adulthood may have made us more cautious and increased the possible length of marriages, and it has also increased the likelihood of a healthy, vigorous old age. Third, the retirement of healthy adults, combined with shortened working hours, longer vacations, and laborsaving technology has given adults more leisure throughout adulthood.

Development is any age-related change in body or behavior from conception to death. It can involve improved functioning, deterioration, or simply a difference. When studying aging, developmentalists use a stability model, in which changes in functioning may occur but decline is not inevitable; an irreversible decrement model, in which decline is inevitable even among healthy adults; or a decrement with compensation model, in which a person's situation affects the level of compensation. Some aspects of aging appear to follow each of these models.

Societies divide the life span in various ways; in the United States, life is seen as progressing through the stages of infancy, childhood, adolescence, adulthood, and old age. Adulthood is often arbitrarily subdivided into **young adulthood** (from about 20 to 40), **middle adulthood** (from about 40 to 60) and **later adulthood** (from about the age of 60). In later adulthood, healthy, vigorous people may be considered ''young-old'' and frail, ill people may be considered ''old-old.'' Knowing an adult's **chronological age** is not a very useful guide to development because individuals age at different rates, various aspects of each individual age at different rates, and the ''meaning'' of a given number of years changes across the life span. Depending on the purpose, it is sometimes helpful to assess a person's functioning by estimating **biological age**, the position on an individual's potential life span; **psychological age**, the level of adaptive ability; **social age**, the individual's roles and habits; or **functional age**, the abilty to function in society. As society becomes increasingly **age-irrelevant**, the concept of age steadily becomes less useful.

Ageism, or discrimination against older adults, arises when people see elderly adults as unattractive, incompetent, feeble, sexless, or senile. Although ageism in employment is widespread, its appearance among the general public is more likely to take the form of condescension and a failure to take older adults seriously than to appear as overt discrimination.

Age-related changes are the result of interaction between the individual and the environment, and such changes may be seen as composed of three major influences. **Age-normative influences** affect almost every person in the culture at about the same point in the life span; they seem to be strongest in childhood, when **canalization** guides development in a direction that is difficult to deflect, and again in advanced old age. **History-normative influences** affect every person in the culture at the same historical moment but at different points in the life span; they may have the greatest effect on adolescents and young adults. The effect of history-normative influences is likely to differ according to a person's age but to influence those within each **cohort,** or generation of people born at the same time, in a similar fashion. **Nonnormative influences** affect specific individuals with no regard to their age; however, these influences are believed to increase in power over the life span.

Researchers are interested in the predictabilty of human development in the areas of physiological functioning, intellectual functioning, and personality. Development is characterized by a certain amount of constancy, with some aspects of personality formed by middle childhood. Constancy is especially likely to be found in characteristics that are valued by society. **Intraindividual change**, in which a person's behavior changes compared with his or her own earlier behavior, may be predictable, as when people take on new social roles, or unpredictable, as when life-style changes radically. **Interindividual differences** increase as people grow older and nonnormative influences accumulate. When interindividual differences appear across cohorts, they may not be true age difference but simply cohort effects.

The basic goals of the study of adult development were set forth in the eighteenth century, and by the nineteenth century, the effect of history-normative influences was recognized. In the twentieth century, **gerontology**, or the scientific study of aging, began with the field of medicine, as researchers studied the aging process. Soon afterward, research began on age-related changes in cognitive functioning. After World War II, interest in all aspects of adult development grew: Life-span theories of personality were developed, people whose development had been followed from early childhood reached maturity, and centers for the study of adult development and aging were established at universities.

KEY TERMS

adulthood	**history-normative influence**
ageism	**interindividual difference**
age-irrelevant society	**intraindividual change**
biological age	**later adulthood**
canalization	**middle adulthood**
chronological age	**nonnormative influence**
cohort	**old-age dependency ratio**
development	**psychological age**
functional age	**social age**
gerontology	**young adulthood**

2

APPROACHES AND METHODS IN THE STUDY OF ADULT DEVELOPMENT AND AGING

There was once a city inhabited entirely by the blind. At its gates appeared an army headed by a king, who brought with him an enormous elephant. The elephant's sound struck fear into the people's hearts, and its mighty tread shook the ground beneath their feet.

The people wondered about this strange animal, and a group of men ran from the city gates to find out about it. They gathered around the beast, and each ran his hands over some portion of the elephant's body.

When the blind men returned to the city, their fellow citizens clustered around them, begging to be told of the awesome elephant. "What was it like?" they said.

The man who had felt the ear said, "It is simple; the elephant is like a great fan."

The man who had felt the tail said, "No, the elephant is like a tough rope."

The man who had grasped the trunk said, "You are both wrong; the elephant is like an enormous pipe."

"Never," said the man who had felt a leg. "The elephant is like a living pillar."

"Even you are mistaken," said the man who had touched its back, "the elephant is like an emperor's throne."

"You fools!" shouted the man who had touched a tusk, "The elephant is like a sharpened stick that will impale us all."

Each blind man had perceived a part of the elephant, but none had understood the entire animal. Their reliance on isolated information ensured that all would be wrong (Shah, 1979).

This Afghan folk tale from the thirteenth century is like an understanding of adulthood and aging that relies on the understanding of only a single discipline. Developmentalists are aware of the dangers of isolated information, and most draw on insights and research from several disciplines. As we will see in this chapter, the study of adult development is carried on by biologists, psychologists, sociologists, anthropologists, and historians. Researchers who study development use standard methods of studying people, but the nature of development has led to special research designs that take into account the time and cohort effects produced by history-normative events.

PERSPECTIVES ON DEVELOPMENT

Developmentalists in all disciplines focus on age-related changes in behavior, but the level of analysis varies from one discipline to the next. Some look at the biological bases of development, some at changes in individual function; some, at social interaction and social roles; and others, at sociocultural forces. It is gener-

TABLE 2.1   LEVELS OF DEVELOPMENT

Discipline	Level of Study
Biology	Cellular and anatomical function and change
Psychology	Individual function
	Social interaction
Sociology	Social roles
Anthropology	Cultural patterns
History	Social roles and cultural patterns across time

Human development can be studied at various levels, each leading to a different way of understanding the process. For a complete understanding of development, all levels must be taken into consideration.

ally agreed that these four levels interact in their influence and that no one of them can by itself explain development (Table 2.1). Most also agree that individuals are not passive victims of biological and social forces; instead, each person is seen as an active force in his or her own development.

THE BIOLOGICAL PERSPECTIVE

Biologists focus on development at the cellular and anatomical level, studying biochemical and physiological changes across the life span of organisms. Development is viewed as an expression of a genetic program that interacts with the environment. Each of us has a general genetic program that reflects the evolution of the species and causes us to develop into human beings instead of chimpanzees, horses, or goats. We also have a specific program that reflects the characteristics of our own family; it determines such things as eye color and height range, and it may carry predispositions to a particular disease or temperament. Although the specific program can affect the length of an individual life, the upper limit of the human life span is believed to be set by the general program (Shock, 1977a).

When looking at its biological bases, researchers tend to study development either early or late in the life span. Some are primarily interested in fetal development; some, in development until maturity; and others, in the aging process. Because developmental biologists tend to distinguish between development and aging in the traditional sense of the words, they have developed two relatively independent bodies of knowledge. This separation of research at the biological level has impeded the creation of biological theories of development that apply to the entire life span (Baltes, Reese, and Lipsitt, 1980).

When studying adult development, biologists often focus on the effects of aging on body function or appearance. Because of the nature of the research, most biological studies are done with animals. Animals' genetic makeup can be controlled through breeding, their environment can be manipulated in a way that is neither possible nor desirable with human beings, and short life spans allow researchers to trace development and aging in months instead of decades. The results of such studies cannot be directly applied to human development, but physiological functioning in people and in rats—a favorite experimental species—is often similar enough to produce insight into human development. Studies of pancreatic function in aging rats, for example, could give us clues to the development of diabetes in aging men and women.

Not all research is done on animals. For example, the skin is one of the first places where we notice the signs of aging, and research with human beings indicates that a change in the speed at which surface skin cells are replaced might help to explain why this is so. Investigators (Grove and Kligman, 1983) have found that, among adults ranging in age from 18 to 50, the rate of cell replacement is steady—in about 20 days, old cells have been shed and new ones are in place. After the age of 50, the replacement rate begins to drop, slowing to about 25 days among people in their fifties, to about 31 days among those in their sixties, and to about 37 days among those in their seventies. Interindividual differences in replacement rate tend to be slight among people in their twenties and quite large among those in their seventies. However, one of the oldest individuals studied had a replacement rate as rapid as young adults, and an adult in the early twenties had a replacement rate typical of a person well into the fifties. Such interindividual differences help to explain why some people appear comparatively youthful at 60 whereas others resemble 80-year-olds.

Other researchers have examined changes in sleep patterns, in sexual response, in skeletal structure, in the body's ability to regulate its internal temperature, in brain structure or electrical activity, and so on. Some investigators study diseases that are prevalent during later adulthood, such as cardiovascular disease, diabetes, or cancer, hoping to find ways to postpone them or to prevent their occurrence.

Biologists study the aging process itself in the hope of discovering why people age at all, conducting research at the genetic, the cellular, or the physiological level. If these investigators are successful, they may be able to extend the human life span, devising methods that slow the natural aging process—or postpone it for several decades. Many biologists believe that the ultimate cause of aging will be found at the cellular or molecular level, but that an understanding of the physiological level—the relationship among cells, tissues, and organs—is most likely to enable us to extend the life span (Shock, 1977a).

THE PSYCHOLOGICAL PERSPECTIVE

Psychologists study development at two levels: individual function and social interaction. They are interested in emotional, cognitive, and behavioral changes across the individual life span and in the way these changes affect a person's individual functioning and social interactions.

Looking at development this way leads to the study of intraindividual changes and interindividual differences. As mentioned earlier, interindividual differences become progressively larger as the effects of nonnormative events pile up and age-normative influences decline. Because chronological age becomes an increasingly poorer guide to development, most psychological theories of adult development make little attempt to link changes to specific chronological age. Instead, they look at predictable sequences of development that may occur at somewhat different ages but that progress in the same order (Baltes and Willis, 1977).

In their search for theories to explain the processes of development and aging, psychologists have relied on a variety of models that grow out of assumptions about human nature and behavioral processes. Each model takes a different world view and uses a different analogy to represent development (Table 2.2). The dominant models are mechanistic, organismic, and dialectical. None of them is "true" or "false," but each can be useful as a guide to understanding development (Baltes, Reese, and Nesselroade, 1977).

In **mechanistic models,** the analogy is the machine. This view does not mean that people *are* machines, but that we can understand development better if we assume that it is the result of laws as regular as those that govern the functioning of machines. Because behavior is lawful, the mechanical model assumes it can be studied in isolation. Combining knowledge of all types of behavior would allow us to understand development. Thus, in the mechanistic view, the whole equals the sum of its parts.

External forces are the dominant influence on development; the individual's behavior is shaped by past experiences and present situations. The feelings, thoughts, and actions of human beings change, but not their structure. For example, the cognitive structures of a 30-year-old are no different from those of a 7-year-old, but the 30-year-old has developed more efficient strategies for dealing with information. In mechanistic models, the computer is a favorite metaphor for human beings. In terms of this metaphor, the 30-year-old's hardware is the same, but the software (or computer program) is more sophisticated than the 7-year-old's.

TABLE 2.2   DEVELOPMENTAL WORLD VIEWS

	Mechanistic	Organismic	Dialectical
Analogy	Machine	Organism	Orchestral music
Individual	Generally passive	Active	Interactive
Focus	Observable changes in behavior	Internal changes in structure	Relationship between individual and society
Type of change	Quantitative	Qualitative	Quantitative and qualitative

In the mechanistic model, the computer serves as an analogy of human development. New behavioral or intellectual capabilities appear when the developmental program reaches the proper sequence.

Because structure does not change, any new capabilities that develop have been built into the machine. They appear when the program reaches the proper sequence, just as information appears on the terminal only when the computer reaches a statement in the program telling it to display data.

In the mechanistic model, behavior is the result of some sort of stimulation, so that human actions are often explained in terms of stimuli and responses (Overton and Reese, 1973). A person becomes a lawyer, gets married, has children, goes to concerts, or roots for the Dallas Cowboys because of the rewards connected with similar activities in the past. As rewards (or reinforcements) and punishments explain any activity, the environment becomes all-powerful as a way of explaining behavior.

A mechanistic orientation has been used by learning theorists to explain behavior and by some cognitive theorists to explain intellectual functioning. This approach to human development tends to portray human beings as passive. However, in recent modification of **social-learning theory** that grew out of mechanistic models, the individual is seen as somewhat active, using rewards, punishment, and the example of others as information that forms the basis for goals, plans, and future actions (Bandura, 1977).

In **organismic models**, people are seen as living organisms that are active and changing. As they interact with the environment, people change in basic ways. Any advancement in thought is not simply the result of new strategies and experience; instead, it reflects a change in structure so that the cognitive processes of the 30-year-old are different in quality from those of the 7-year-old.

Although experience in the world is necessary if development is to take place, that experience has meaning for the individual only after it has been incorporated into his or her understanding of the world. Identifying the external cause of behavior, then, is not the ultimate concern of investigators with an organismic orientation. They are interested in the goal of developmental change and in the way behavior is organized into systems. Their aim is to identify the rules of intraindividual change and to describe the entire system (Baltes, Reese, and Nesselroade, 1977).

In the organismic model, the individual is spontaneously active, and what gives rise to activity is often intrinsic. Given this view of human beings, the search for laws of environmental effects on behavior is bound to be unsuccessful, and the study of isolated stimulus-response relationships is unlikely to increase our understanding of development. This lack of understanding is inevitable because the whole system is greater than the sum of its parts.

In the **dialectical approach**, people are assumed to interact with a continually changing environment, so that each generation within a society is assumed to reach a new level of functioning. As yet there is no generally accepted dialetical metaphor for development, although Klaus Riegel (1975) compared it to orchestral music. He viewed development as having biological, psychological, social, and physical dimensions that are never in perfect harmony. Development progresses through a series of small leaps as the individual resolves contradictions and conflicts that arise when one of the dimensions is out of step with the rest. In the orchestra model, the conflicts and their resolution are like musical counterpoint that is synchronized through harmonics or like the disharmonies of jazz that are synchronized through rhythm and beat.

The dialectical approach focuses on the relationship between the individual and society, who are engaged in a continuing "dialectic" in which both undergo change as a result of their interactions. The development of one depends on the development of the other (Buss, 1979). In this view, individual development is heavily influenced by history-normative events, and much knowledge is regarded as social. Because of this social influence, the development of people born in 1890 is likely to be different in many ways from development of people born in 1960.

Some developmentalists (Lerner, 1978) have suggested that the dialectical view is capable of integrating concepts from the mechanistic and organismic views. That is, development at the level of the organism is a synthesis of the sorts of development studied in the mechanistic approach, with the addition of organismic view that the whole system is greater than the sum of its parts.

No matter what model of development psychologists use, the basic concern is the same: individual function. Even when the object of study is social interaction or social roles, the focus is on the individual, not on the wider society. In approaching the study of development this way, however, psychologists need to take into account both biological and social influences on behavior (Featherman, 1981).

Psychologists may study any aspect of adult development. For example, one aspect of aging that has received a good deal of attention is memory. When adults are brought into the laboratory and asked to memorize material, such as a list of words, older adults generally remember less of the memorized material than do younger adults (Craik, 1977).

When we are faced with such research, our first impulse is to say that during the aging process whatever mechanisms are involved in memory deteriorate. However, a recent study (Cavanaugh, 1983) indicates that at least some deterioration is not caused by aging itself. Adults in their early twenties or their late sixties came into the laboratory and watched television programs. Afterward they were asked about the content of the programs they had seen. But this experiment looked at the results in a new way. Before they saw the television programs, the adults took a vocabulary test. Older adults with high verbal ability, as measured by the test, did just as well at recalling programs as did young adults with high verbal ability. There was no apparent decline in memory with age. The customary decline did appear among people with low verbal ability: 20-year-olds recalled much more of the program content than did 65-year-olds. But these 20-year-olds did much worse than the 65-year-olds with high verbal ability. The researcher suggests that people with high verbal ability use much more efficient methods when storing information in memory and that this difference explains the lack of decline in the first group of older adults.

Memory is only one form of cognition studied by psychologists. Cognitive psychologists also study age-related changes in sensation, perception, problem solving, learning, intelligence, and creativity. Other psychologists investigate personality, motivation, self-concept, and the effect of various social roles, such as marriage, parenthood, divorce, or retirement, on the individual. Another way psychologists may approach adult development is by examining the relationship between a person's commitment and attitudes and his or her actual behavior (Lowenthal, 1977). Or they may explore the effect of various situations, such as stress or disease, on mental health. Much of the information gathered by psychologists can be seen in broader context by looking at the work of sociologists.

THE SOCIOLOGICAL PERSPECTIVE

Sociologists study age-related changes in social roles within the social institutions of a culture. Many of the topics studied by sociologists overlap with those studied by psychologists, but the sociological focus shifts from the individual to the group. Although sociologists are aware of the biological aspects of adult development and aging, these are more or less taken for granted. Both biological and psychological aspects of aging are considered, but only as they influence the social institutions in which people function.

The developmental perspective has led many sociologists to adopt an **age-stratification** model in which people are viewed as living through a sequence of age-related positions or roles. Each position carries its own rules that prescribe a person's behavior (Riley et al., 1972). The influence of these roles shows most clearly in social interaction across generations. For example, when a 25-year-old talks with a 70-year-old, each will adjust his or her side of the interaction to take the other's age into account. This adjustment affects language, topic of conversation, whether one person defers to the other, and so on. Because age-related roles

In the age-stratification model, people live through a sequence of age-related roles that prescribe their behavior. These roles show most clearly when people from different generations interact.

may change under the influence of history-normative events, society will change as new cohorts replace older ones (Featherman, 1981).

Another way that sociologists approach adult development and aging is through the concept of **socialization,** or the way in which people absorb the attitudes, values, and beliefs of their society. By studying transitions from one social role to another, sociologists hope to discover just how roles influence behavior and personality.

A third way that sociologists study adult development is by looking at institutions as they respond to changing social conditions. For example, sociologists might consider the effect of retirement communities on family structure by studying family contacts, divorce and remarriage, and relationships between middle-aged adults and their aging parents. The influence of history-normative events may be explored by studying various cohorts in an attempt to discover how social or economic changes affect family size, mobility, or family roles (Featherman, 1981).

In a typical sociological study, Kenneth Ferraro (1983) examined the effect of moving on older adults. Approximately 3500 lower- and middle-class older adults who lived in detached houses or apartments were asked about various physical disabilities, daily activities connected with self-care, illness, and hospitalization. Fourteen months later, the same adults again answered these questions. During that period more than 200 had moved to another house or apartment in the same community.

Ferraro found that although the health of the adults who moved had been similar to that of other adults at the time of the first interview, both illness and hospitalization increased significantly more among the movers whether they had moved out of choice or necessity. What is more, neither the type of new housing nor a person's level of satisfaction with it had any effect on the level of illness or hospitalization.

Moving is apparently stressful, but whether the stress comes from the move itself, from the rupture of old social bonds, or from the unfamiliarity of the new environment is not clear. Results of other studies indicate that health may improve when older people move into retirement communities or senior housing projects (Carp, 1976). Ferraro suggests two factors that could account for such improvement. First, needed services are clustered in or near such communities, making it easy to become familiar with new surroundings. Second, social contacts with other older adults may provide support that is lacking in the wider community. If this is the case, it may be possible to discover the sort of social support that would lessen the stress among older people.

Sociologists are not the only researchers who study the effects of society on adult development. Anthropologists are also interested in society, but they look at a variety of cultures.

THE ANTHROPOLOGICAL PERSPECTIVE

Anthropologists examine differences in developmental patterns across cultures. By studying patterns of development in various societies, they show us the potential range of human behavior and why development may procede differently from one culture to the next (Spencer, 1957). Without this comparison, investigators might assume that the developmental patterns they have found in their own culture are universal and reflect human nature (LeVine, 1982).

Anthropologists have shown us that the way most older adults behave reflects the expectations of the culture and is not the inevitable result of the aging process (Featherman, 1981). For example, some sociologists (Cumming and Henry, 1961) once believed that **disengagement**, or a gradual withdrawal from social roles and a decreased involvement with others, was typical of older adults. But anthropological research in other cultures showed that in a number of societies older people did not withdraw; their level of psychological and social involvement remained relatively high.

Few aspects of life, from personality traits and social roles to attitudes, values, and beliefs, escape the influence of culture. Age-normative influences that are social in nature vary from culture to culture as do history-normative influences. As noted earlier, cultures even divide the life span in different ways.

In addition to studying the way a culture is organized and functions, anthropologists study many aspects of adult development and aging. They may investigate stages of the life cycle, the role and treatment of old people, individual differences in developmental patterns within a single culture, and the way a culture uses age as a basis of social organization.

For example, Thomas Rohlen (1978) has found that Japanese society is ordered around differences in age. The form of the Japanese language reflects the age of the parties in a conversation as does the traditional dress of women. In business, seniority is the basis of rank, responsibility, status, and salary. Authority and career progress are age-graded, and the progress of a Japanese worker (typically male) is judged in comparison with his own cohort. Age is also linked with creativity and wisdom, and older people remain publicly active much longer than they do in the United States.

Some anthropologists study changes in culture and their effect on the course of adult development. Such an approach requires them to use historical as well as contemporary material. A number of historians have also begun to look at adult development and aging.

THE HISTORICAL PERSPECTIVE

Historians study differences in developmental patterns across time. In studying these patterns, they rely on birth, marriage, and death records; government population records, such as census documents; literature written during the period under study; and paintings and sculpture of the time.

A major focus of the historical approach has been the family and its changing role through the centuries. As historians have studied the family, they have discovered that, contrary to popular belief, the small nuclear family has characterized society in Europe and North America for centuries (Laslett, 1972). The large extended family that supposedly was common in an agriculturally based society turns out to be a rarity. Other historians have looked at changes in the family in terms of the interaction among the social and psychological development of its members, the pace of the entire household's development, historical events, and changes in the culture (Featherman, 1981).

Historians also study other aspects of adult development. They may look at changes in the marital relationship, in views of old age, or in attitudes toward death. For example, historian Winthrop Jordan (1978) has traced the development of the concept of ''adulthood'' in the United States. He found that the word did not even exist in English until 1870. The concept of adulthood was late in developing because men and women were believed to have little in common. People talked instead of ''manhood'' and ''womanhood,'' as if men and women belonged to two completely different species. The concept of adulthood appears to have developed as society underwent change, with the term developing the meaning we give it now as women began to vote and their entry into the labor market began to erode the linkage between masculinity and the idea of a career.

Historians, anthropologists, sociologists, psychologists, and biologists have increased our understanding of adult development and aging. But none of these approaches can by itself give an adequate portrayal of the process because each describes development at a different level. Changes at any one of these levels occurs in the context and under the influence of the other levels, so that development and aging involve an interaction among levels.

The awareness of this interaction has led many investigators to use findings from other levels as a way of gaining insight into their own approach. In the study of some areas, such as the family, an interdisciplinary approach is emerging. Such an approach draws on the resources of several disciplines to define research problems, choose the factors to be studied, and analyze the accumulated data (Featherman, 1981).

DEVELOPMENTAL DESIGNS

Researchers investigating developmental questions are faced with the problem of distinguishing the effects of age-normative influences from history-normative influences. No matter what the topic, the influences of age, cohort, and historical time are virtually impossible to separate. Yet the researcher's task is to determine how each contributes to the observed differences. Unless cohort influences can be ruled out, there is no way of being certain that a developmental effect has been found.

Three major research designs are used to study development: cross-sectional, longitudinal, and time-lag. Each looks at development in a different way; none can, by itself, tease apart all three influences (See Fig. 2.1.)

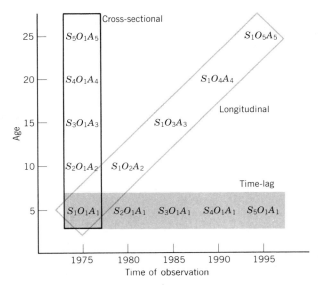

FIGURE 2.1 Experimental designs. In this comparison of developmental studies, the cross-sectional design uses five different samples (S_1–S_5), each a different age (A_1–A_5), observed on only one occasion (O_1). The longitudinal design uses one sample (S_1), observed on five different occasions (O_1–O_5) at five different ages (A_1–A_5). The time-lag design uses five different samples (S_1–S_5), each the same age (A_1), observed on only one occasion (O_1) but at different historical times. Each method looks at development in a different way.

Source: P. B. Baltes, H. W. Reese, and J. R. Nesselroade, 1977, p. 122.

CROSS-SECTIONAL DESIGN

In **cross-sectional designs,** two or more age groups, each from a different cohort, are studied at one time. The study of memory for television programs described earlier is a typical cross-sectional study, in which the performance of 20-year-olds and 65-year-olds on the same task was compared during the same year. Because this design is quick and relatively inexpensive to carry out, it is often chosen by researchers. A decade ago, it was estimated that 90 percent of all developmental research consisted of cross-sectional studies (Wohlwill, 1973).

The cross-sectional method reveals interindividual differences, but because each person is observed only once, it does not show intraindividual change. Even if we assume that the differences we find are age-related, we are left with group averages instead of information about changes in individuals (Baltes, Reese, and Nesselroade, 1977).

A basic problem with cross-sectional studies is that they confound age-related and cohort influences. Given a typical cross-sectional study, there is no way to tell whether age differences are primarily age-related and hence the result of developmental change or primarily the result of membership in a different cohort. Suppose we wonder whether young first-time mothers tend to use different child-rearing methods from mothers who have their first child at a relatively late age. In a cross-sectional study, we observe a group of 20-year-old mothers and another group of 40-year-old mothers in the same year. If we find differences in their styles of child rearing, we know they are not the result of a historical shift because both groups were observed in the same year and each was exposed to the same ''expert'' advice from pediatricians and popular books.

But we cannot be certain whether age or cohort difference is primarily responsible for the different styles of mothering. If women in the first group were born in 1964 and those in the second group in 1944, they grew up under different circumstances. Women in the first group were toddlers during the turbulent 1960s; women in the second group were adolescents. Women in the first group were born into homes with televisions; women in the second group were probably 9 or 10 years old before a TV set came into their homes.

Despite the problem of distinguishing between age and cohort effects, there are times when a cross-sectional design is appropriate (Nunnally, 1973). If we want to know how different age groups perform today on certain tasks or how they feel about certain issues, then a cross-sectional study can tell us. It will tell us only about age differences in 1985, however, and it cannot be used to draw conclusions about developmental changes. If we are trying to find out about developmental change, a cross-sectional design can give us hints about possible age-related change. The differences that appear indicate what topics could be studied, using some other design, to discover whether the observed changes are actually age-related.

One researcher feels so strongly about the influence of cohort effects on cross-sectional studies that he recommends a new way of discussing them. Warner Schaie (1973) has suggested that all such studies be relabeled, substituting the sub-

The mothering styles of these two women contrast sharply, but whether the effect is due to age or cohort differences is uncertain.

jects' date of birth for their ages. In his view, many cross-sectional studies are primarily studies of intergenerational, not interindividual differences.

Going that far may not be necessary, but this sort of recommendation helps keep us aware of the possible pitfalls of cross-sectional research. Consider the following situation. When 20-year-olds, 30-year-olds, 40-year-olds, 50-year-olds, and 60-year-olds take the same intelligence test, the average scores will be lower, beginning with the 40-year-olds. It would seem that intelligence, at least as measured on IQ tests, begins to deteriorate as we enter middle age. But each of these age groups belongs to a different cohort. Is it possible that cohort differences, and not some inexorable developmental influence, is causing the scores to drop? Perhaps a look at a different developmental design will help answer that question.

LONGITUDINAL DESIGN

In **longitudinal designs**, a group from a single cohort is studied at several ages. Because all the subjects are from the same cohort, we know that any observed changes are not due to cohort effects. If, instead of giving an intelligence test to people from five different cohorts, we had tested a group of 20-year-olds in 1940, then again every decade until they were 60, we would have used a longitudinal design. The results from such a study might have surprised us. We would have found that instead of beginning to decline at age 40, the average IQ score kept rising.

How can we reconcile the results of the cross-sectional and the longitudinal study? A good part of it is probably due to changes in society. Those 60-year-olds tested in the cross-sectional study almost certainly had much less education than the 20-year-olds. Because the 60-year-olds in the longitudinal study were compared with themselves at 20, the effects of education remained constant, and all their experiences over 40 years increased their scores.

Another study (Woodruff and Birren, 1972) has turned up similar effects for personality. In 1969 college students and 45-year-old adults took the same personality test. Scores indicated that the middle-aged adults felt themselves to be more competent and better-adjusted than did the college students. It would appear that people's competence and adjustment tend to increase as they become older and settled in the community. But conclusions based on this cross-sectional comparison would be wrong. Twenty-five years earlier, the 45-year-olds had taken the same test as college students—and obtained scores quite similar to their own middle-aged scores. Apparently, people who were in college during World War II had more confidence in themselves than people who were in college during the 1960s.

At first glance, longitudinal studies would seem to solve all the problems of researchers. They eliminate cohort differences and allow us to get at intraindividual change. But longitudinal studies can also be misleading. Longitudinal studies confuse age-related change with historical time. People in the study are tested several times over a period of years, and any changes in society would affect their performance. For example, if we were studying political attitudes, societal shifts during the course of the study could lead us to conclude—inappropriately—that political attitudes change with age. If the study had been carried out from 1945 to 1965, we might have concluded that adults become more liberal with age; but if the study had been carried out from 1965 to 1985, we might have concluded that adults get more conservative as they get older.

There are other problems as well. Testing the same people again and again makes them so familiar with the test that their scores may reflect a "practice" effect. Also, as subjects age, some of the people in poorest health will have begun to die. Because survivors in lengthy longitudinal studies tend to be brighter than those who die (Schaie, 1977), a study that runs for 40 years will eventually be testing a group that lacks some of the people with the lowest scores, thereby raising the average score at older ages and causing the researcher to underestimate the effects of aging.

As if these problems were not enough, the mechanics of a lengthy longitudinal study can be formidable. Such studies are expensive. They are slow. A researcher must remain committed to the project for years. People move or die, so that it is sometimes difficult to contact the same subjects for repeated testing. And records must be stored for years.

THE PIG IN A PYTHON

Cohort differences stand out sharply when the path of a cohort is traced through society. Between 1946 and 1964, there was a sharp—and unexpected—upturn in American birth rates that created what has been called the "baby-boom generation." Because of its size, the bulging path of this cohort over the decades, says Landon Jones (1980), has been like the course of a pig that has been swallowed by a python. As the cohort reaches each new stage of life, its effect on society takes a different form.

After World War II, Americans began marrying earlier, having more children, and having them younger than their parents did. During the years of the baby boom, approximately 4 million children were born each year. These babies began their lives by changing American business. Production of baby food, diapers, baby clothes, station wagons, and three- and four-bedroom houses in the suburbs mushroomed. As the boom grew up, businesses that catered to infants and toddlers shrank, and businesses that catered to school-age children expanded. As the baby boom began entering schools, the educational system had to expand in the

same way—building frantically for 14 years to keep up with the demand, then watching classrooms empty and teachers lose their jobs as the shock of the boom moved on.

This sort of expansion and contraction will follow the baby boom throughout their lives, affecting the sort of products that are available; the approach of advertising; the nature of housing, and the content of television, motion pictures, and other media. Just by being there, the baby boom had an enormous economic impact.

After beginning their existence in the placid 1950s, members of the baby boom found their belief in the stability and safety of American life shattered by a series of events, including assassinations, the Vietnam War, and the draft. These historical events helped shape the baby boom's political and social views.

This cohort's level of education is higher than that of any generation of Americans. For example, more than 20 percent of the baby boom generation born between 1951 and 1957 have completed college as compared with about 6 percent of the cohort born between 1911 and 1915 and 11

Attacking the problem in another way might help us understand age, cohort, and time influences. A third type of design eliminates all age-related differences, allowing us to look at the influence of cohort and time.

TIME-LAG DESIGN

In **time-lag designs**, groups from several different cohorts are studied, but the studies are spaced so that each group is assessed at the same age. Using such a time-lag design, we might test IQ performance in 60-year-olds. We would test in-percent of the cohort born between 1931 and 1935 (U.S. Bureau of the Census, 1982). As they left college, they discovered that their sheer numbers had damaged the value of their education. Competition for jobs was high and, because of the size of the cohort, would always remain so.

Whether it was disillusion with society, the competition they faced in the job market, or some other cause, members of the baby-boom generation developed an attitude toward life and work that is very different from that of previous cohorts. Self-fulfillment seems to be at the heart of their outlook. National surveys (Yankelovich, 1981) have found that people born after 1946 are much more likely than the rest of the population to believe that satisfaction comes from shaping oneself rather than from home and family life, that people should be free to dress and live in the way they want, that travel is a better place for money than possessions, that a creative life is more important than financial well-being, and that although they want to be outstanding in their chosen profession, they need some meaningful goal.

Because attitudes affect life-style, perhaps recent changes in American society are in part the result of the baby boom's quest for self-fulfillment. An increase in the proportion of single adults, a delay in the age of marriage, a rising divorce rate, declining family size, and a shift in priorities among many working women from family to career fit comfortably with the goal of self-fulfillment.

Politically, the baby-boom generation is less conservative than their parents and grandparents. They more strongly support federal spending for social programs, the legalization of marijuana, busing for integration, ethnic and religious intermarriage, the Equal Rights Amendment, and the right of abortion (Glenn, 1980). Because middle-aged and older adults are more likely to vote than young adults, the political force of the baby-boom generation will probably increase in the next few decades.

As the baby-boom generation ages, its effect on society will continue. Its size will change the old-age dependency ratio, affecting government budgets and taxes. Its level of education will change the life-style and buying habits of the elderly, affecting the fortunes of business. The form of that influence may be impossible to predict, but its existence is certain.

dividuals belonging to the 1890 cohort in 1950, those belonging to the 1900 cohort in 1960, those in the 1910 cohort in 1970, and those in the 1920 cohort in 1980.

This design will not show developmental differences because we are studying each group only once, and all subjects are the same age. But by eliminating age-related change, we are able to chart the effect of history-normative influences. However, we cannot separate cohort effects from the effects of historical time. We have no way of knowing whether differences are due to being born in a particular year or to the general social climate at the time the test was given.

Time-lag designs are as time-consuming and expensive as longitudinal designs and require the same sort of commitment on the part of the investigator. However, other problems that sometimes mar longitudinal studies do not affect time-lag designs: Because each person is tested only once, there is no "practice" effect, and there is no worry that the subjects will move or die between tests.

COMBINING DESIGNS

The best way to discover developmental change and to find out how changes in society affect development would be to use all three designs to study the same phenomenon. This would enable us to estimate the effects of age, cohort, and historical time on the differences we find.

Such designs, known as **sequential designs**, have been developed, and they use either a cross-sectional or a longitudinal sequence (Baltes, Reese, and Nesselroade, 1977). In the cross-sectional sequence, a measure, such as an IQ test, may be given to 20-, 30-, 40-, 50-, and 60-year-olds. Ten years later, different groups of 30-, 40-, 50-, 60-, and 70-year-olds are given the same test. Using new groups for the second test avoids the practice effect and makes it simpler to carry out the study. It also gives us an opportunity to compare age-related differences in different cohorts at different historical times.

In the longitudinal sequence, a group of 20-year-olds may be tested every ten years until they are 60. When the 20-year-olds are 30 and are given their first re-test, another group of 20-year-olds is selected. This second group is tested every 10 years until they are 50. This sequence allows us to assess the pattern of age-change in two cohorts at two different times.

These approaches are so time-consuming and expensive that they are rarely possible to carry out in studies of adult development. Although it is often impossible to apply sequential designs, there are ways to diminish the disadvantages of the simple designs. By being sensitive to the particular factors that affect the results obtained with each type of design, investigators can avoid misinterpreting their findings.

Selecting an appropriate design is only the beginning of developmental studies. Other issues can also affect research results and the conclusions drawn from them. Among important issues are the nature of the group studied and the measures used to assess their behavior.

RESEARCH ISSUES

When investigating any aspect of development, researchers want to be able to generalize their results from the individuals they have studied to other people. Two issues that affect the applicability of research are the choice of samples and the measures of assessment.

SELECTING A SAMPLE

The nature of the **sample**, or the people selected to represent the larger group, is important. In studies of adult development and aging, the nature of the sample differs, depending on the goal of the research. For example, if we want to study social interaction among older adults in general, a nursing home would not be a good place to do the study because only a very small percentage of older adults live in nursing homes and those who do are not typical older adults. But if we want to study the effects of life in a nursing home on social interaction, then the nursing home would be an ideal location. Research in adult development and aging attempts to describe, predict, or explain age differences.

When the aim is *description,* a study is meant to describe differences that exist at this moment. In this case the sample must be **random**: every member of each age group that will be studied must have an equal chance of being selected. Otherwise, the results are likely to be based on individuals who differ in important ways from the age groups under study. Many studies of adults use primarily middle-class samples, which means that the results may not apply to working- or lower-class adults who generally have less education and less money than adults in the middle class. Other studies, especially those examining the ''midlife crisis'' or occupational identity and development, use all-male samples, which may indicate very little about the existence or form of a ''midlife crisis'' in women or about their occupational development.

It is easy to see how a nonrandom sample could affect the applicability of research results. Suppose you wanted to find out about the economic status of older people. Are the elderly truly needy? To answer the question, you need a random sample of all older adults. A sample limited to residents of a retirement community would indicate that almost all older adults have above-average incomes, but a sample drawn from the inner city would indicate that few have incomes above the poverty level.

When the aim of research is *prediction,* a study is meant to estimate differences that are likely to exist in the future. In this case, the sample should be selective. Because the characteristics of the population are continually changing, the groups studied should reflect the probable makeup of the population at the future time to be predicted. Before the sample is drawn, a hypothesis about the characteristics of the population in the future is needed to guide selection of the sample.

Suppose you want to know what the economic status of older adults will be in 2020. Studying a random sample of today's older adults would produce an erroneous picture of economic status in 2020. The United States is undergoing a shift from a predominantly industrial to a service-based economy. As the shift takes place, it is accompanied by cohort changes in occupation. This means that few older adults in 2020 will have been factory workers; instead, the majority will be drawn from occupations that provide service, such as insurance, merchandising, health care, communications, food preparation, and banking. Pension policies and salaries as well as the tastes and needs of employees in service occupations may differ radically from those in manufacturing. In this case, the sample should be drawn selectively from today's older adults, so that their occupational backgrounds reflect the occupations of the cohort that will begin retiring about 2010. Because an increasing proportion of older women in 2020 will have had a history of employment, the sample should anticipate this situation and include an appropriate proportion of older women who are retired employees as opposed to older women whose work was confined to the home.

When the aim of research is *explanation*, the study is meant to enhance understanding concerning the causes of observed age differences. Again, the sample should be selective, so that relevant cohort differences or other extraneous age-correlated factors will be controlled and thus can be ruled out as contributing to observed age differences. If education, health, or socioeconomic status were known to be related to the aspect of development under study, you would not want to use a random sample of adults. Because cohort differences are known to exist (on the average, 20-year-olds have more education, better health, and higher socioeconomic status than 65-year-olds), these differences alone could account for age differences. If you are trying to explain age-related differences in memory, for example, you would want to eliminate the possibility that they were simply the result of cohort differences in education. Therefore, you might want to compare 20-year-olds in college with 60-year-olds who had comparable educational background. Such older adults would not be typical of their cohort, but their performance would shed light on the basis of age differences that are not related to education. Similarly, if you are trying to explain the influences of normal aging on memory, you would want to eliminate factors related to depression, because depression is known to be related to poor memory and is also more common among the old. It would be important to select the sample to control for depression.

Depending on the aim of the study and the phenomenon involved, sample characteristics that may be important include sex, education, socioeconomic level, ethnic group, and health. However, simply choosing an appropriate sample is not enough. The procedures used to assess the individuals studied must also be considered carefully.

CHOOSING A MEASURE

Just as important as the nature of the sample is the choice of measures that are used to assess the characteristics or behavior of the individuals in the sample. Unless the measures are relevant to the task and appropriate to the age ranges being studied, little will be learned from the investigation.

Using relevant measures helps to ensure the **external validity** of the research, which has to do with how widely the information produced can be applied in other situations. If measures have external validity, the results can be generalized outside the context of the study. Suppose you are studying memory and ask a cross-sectional sample of adults to come into the laboratory, memorize lists of unrelated words, and then later recall them. Younger adults are likely to do fairly well at the task; and older adults, to do poorly. But poor performance in this situation may have little relevance to the functioning of memory in daily life. Two thousand years ago, the Roman statesman Cicero wrote, "I have never heard of any old man forgetting where he had hidden his money."

Another factor that should be considered is that measures developed for use with children or younger adults may not test similar behavior in older adults (Schaie, 1977). For example, intelligence tests were originally developed for their ability to predict success in school. Test developers made no pretense of measuring all kinds of intelligence, only those skills that are used in an academic setting. Because most older adults are unaccustomed to formal testing situations and few attend school, their scores on a typical IQ test may not be an adequate measure of their intelligence and may have little bearing on their ability to solve problems in daily life.

Cohort differences can also limit the validity of tests for some age groups. For example, even though some IQ tests have special forms for adults, a test may become invalid with the passage of time. In order to restore their validity, tests are revised to reflect cultural changes. It has been suggested, however, that earlier versions of adult intelligence tests, standardized on groups from the cohort now in old age, might be more appropriate for use with today's older adults (Schaie, 1977).

Changes in the language can also limit the validity of measures. This factor can affect most tests of verbal intelligence, attitudes, personality, and questionnaires of any sort. Among a group of adults in Syracuse, New York, 20- and 30-year-olds performed best when tested with items using words that entered the language after 1960, but 40- to 60-year olds did best when the items used words that entered the language in the late 1920s (Schaie, 1973). Similarly, when researchers made tasks attractive and meaningful to older adults, these individuals performed better than younger adults (Labouvie-Vief and Chandler, 1978). Such age differences in performance highlight the importance of considering the appropriateness of a measure for all ages studied.

With care, problems of external validity can be minimized. Moreover, their recognition of the problems makes investigators wary of overgeneralizing their results. As we explore the various aspects of adult development and aging, we will note from time to time when inadequate tests have produced research findings that may not reflect people's functioning or abilities. Our exploration begins with an attempt to understand the biological bases of development.

SUMMARY

Biologists, psychologists, sociologists, anthropologists, and historians who study development are all interested in age-related changes in behavior, but the level of analysis varies from one discipline to the next. The levels interact and development cannot be explained by any one of them. Biologists focus on development at the cellular and anatomical level, studying biochemical and physiological changes across the life span of organisms. Because biologists tend to distinguish between development and aging, there has been little progress toward biological theories of development across the life span. Psychologists study development as it affects individual function and social interaction. Most explain development by using a mechanistic, an organismic, or a dialectical world view. In the **mechanistic model**, the metaphor is the machine, the individual generally is seen as passive, the focus is on observable changes in behavior, and the type of change is quantitative. In the mechanistically based **social-learning theory**, however, the individual is seen as somewhat active. In the **organismic model**, the model is the organism, the individual is seen as active, the focus is on internal changes in structure, and the type of change is qualitative. In the **dialectical approach**, the analogy is with orchestral music, the individual is seen as interactive, the focus is on the relationship between the individual and society, and change may be either quantitative or qualitative.

Sociologists study age-related changes in social roles within the social institutions of a culture, with the focus shifting from the individual to the group. Many sociologists have adopted an **age-stratification** model, in which people are seen as living through a sequence of age-related positions or roles. Also heavily stressed is **socialization**, the process by which people absorb the attitudes, values, and beliefs of their society. Sociologists are also interested in the way social institutions, such as the family, respond to changing social conditions. Anthropologists study patterns of development in various cultures, thereby showing the potential range of human behavior. Such research has shown that **disengagement** is not typical of older adults in all cultures; in many societies, the level of psychological and social involvement remains relatively high. Historians study differences in developmental patterns across time, showing the way social institutions and behavior change within a society over time.

Three major research designs are used to study development: cross-sectional, longitudinal, and time-lag. In the **cross-sectional design**, two or more age groups, each from a different cohort, are studied on one occasion. This design reveals interindividual differences, but does not show intraindividual change. In addition, it confounds age-related and cohort influences. In **longitudinal designs**, a group from a single cohort is studied at several ages. This design eliminates cohort influences and sheds light on intraindividual change. However, a longitudinal design confounds age-related change with the effects of historical time, is subject to the ''practice'' effect, ends up studying only healthy survivors, and is both expensive and slow. In the **time-lag design**, groups from several cohorts are studied, but the studies are spaced so that each group is assessed at the same age. This design eliminates age-related change, practice effects, and any problems with survivors. It reveals the effect of history-normative influences, but confounds cohort effects with the effects of historical time. The time-lag design is also expensive and time-consuming. By using **sequential designs**, researchers have tried to surmount some of the problems of other designs by combining aspects of more than one design into either a cross-sectional or a longitudinal sequence.

The nature of the **sample**, or the group chosen to represent the larger group, determines whether research findings can be generalized. When the aim of research is description, the sample must be **random**, and every member of each age group studied must have an equal chance of being selected. When the aim of research is prediction, the sample should be selective and reflect the nature of the group for which the prediction is to be made. When the aim of research is explanation, the sample should be selective, and relevant cohort differences or other extraneous age-correlated factors should be controlled. Among the factors to be considered are sex, education, socioeconomic level, ethnic group, and health. If research findings are to be generalized, the measures used must have **external validity**. The situations studied must be relevant and the measures must be appropriate for all age groups studied.

KEY TERMS

age-stratification

cross-sectional design

dialectical approach

disengagement

external validity

longitudinal design

mechanistic model

organismic model

random sample

sample

sequential design

social-learning theory

socialization

time-lag design

PART TWO

BIOLOGICAL ASPECTS OF ADULT DEVELOPMENT AND AGING

3

BIOLOGICAL EXPLANATIONS OF AGING

On October 7, 1979, the old, old, very old Charlie Smith died. According to the Social Security Administration, he was then 137 years old, and his Social Security benefits had been based on work that began in 1955 when, at 113 years old, he picked oranges.

Smith claimed that he was born in Liberia in 1842, named Mitchell Watkins, and brought to the United States as a boy. In 1854, the 12-year-old Smith was sold at a slave auction in New Orleans. Purchased by Texas rancher Charles Smith, he grew up in Galveston, where he looked after the rancher's children. The rancher gave the boy his own name, and when the Emancipation Proclamation freed all slaves in 1863, the 21-year-old "C.H.," as the family called him, decided to remain with the Smiths. But the former slave outlived the Smith family. Among his later jobs, said Smith, had been a stint in silent movies as "the Trigger Kid," and work with a circus in 1932, when he was billed as the oldest living man in the United States.

Charlies Smith was a very old man, but attempts to verify his age showed that he was not the old, old, very old man he claimed to be (Freeman, 1982). His marriage certificate, discovered in Arcadia, Florida, after much searching, showed that at the time of his marriage in January 1910, Smith was a lad of 35, not the venerable 66 of his claims. When Smith was born, the Civil War had been over for ten years. When at last he died, Charlie Smith apparently was "only" 104 years old.

Claims of such extreme longevity are probably exaggerated. As we will see, the number of centenarians is far smaller than myth, story, and propaganda would have it. According to the 1980 *Guinness Book of World Records*, the longest authenticated human life span is 114 years old, an age reached by Shigechijo Izumi of Japan.

In this chapter, we take up the topic of longevity, contrasting the maximum number of years scientists believe people are capable of living with the number of years most people reach. After considering the possible effects of extending the life span, we examine the process of normal biological aging and the factors that tend to accelerate deterioration. Then we explore the various theories that have been advanced to explain biological aging and close by looking at research that has extended the life span in animals.

LONGEVITY

As far back as records extend, human beings have fought against the brevity of life and tried to forestall the aging process by determination, prayer, or magic. Today the quest has moved into the laboratory. Researchers are trying to discover just *why* we age and what, if anything, can be done to slow the process.

Although we age in similar ways, we do not all age at the same rate. Appearances can be deceiving, and older adults may look 10 or 20 years older or younger than their chronological age. Function shows similar interindividual differences. Some people join the ranks of the old-old in their sixties, some are still young-old long past their eightieth birthdays, and a handful live for a century before their bodies begin to fail.

Longevity, which refers to the length or duration of life, can be considered in two ways. Average longevity, or the mean age of survival for members of any species, is known as the **average life span**. It is affected by nutrition, health care, and environmental hazards. The oldest age to which any individuals survive is known as the **maximum life span**. It apparently reflects a unique biological characteristic of a species (Cutler, 1981). Looking at longevity in other species may help put the human life span into perspective.

HUMAN AGING IN PERSPECTIVE

Many different species share some characteristics of aging (Rockstein, Chesky, and Sussman, 1977). Skin, hair, posture, muscle strength and vigor, and the ability to react effectively to environmental stress change in a similar manner. Even roundworms and insects age in ways that correspond to human aging.

As Table 3.1 indicates, mammals and nonhuman primates show vast interspecies differences in maximum life span. Most of these figures have come from zoos or other places, such as thoroughbred farms, where well-fed animals live in protected environments.

A number of factors have been suggested as contributing to species longevity. They include brain and body size, metabolism, body temperature, length of gestation, and age of puberty. Although exceptions have been found in every case, there seems to be some support for each of these proposed factors. Perhaps the most consistent evidence is for the proposal that longevity of mammalian species is correlated with the brain weight and body size (Walford, 1983). But even this rule does not always hold true—human beings are smaller than horses and cows yet they live longer. However, the rule of thumb seems to apply within general orders, such as primates.

Rate of metabolism also appears to be related to longevity. Indeed, some researchers have made strides toward altering longevity in rats by manipulating factors that may affect metabolism (Walford, 1983). For more than three quarters of a century, we have known that most animals consume a fairly constant number of calories per ounce of body weight over their entire life span (Rubner, 1908). Animals with a short life span, such as mice, tend to burn calories faster than longer-lived animals, such as elephants. Animals that seem to break the rule by living long lives even though they burn calories rapidly generally have a very low metabolic rate while resting or sleeping. For example, because of its long rest periods, a bat burns no more calories per ounce during its 20-year life span than a mouse burns during its 4 years of life (Sacher, 1977). The notable exception to the rule of

TABLE 3.1   MAXIMUM LIFE SPAN

Species	Years
Tortoise	150.0
Human being	114.0
Whale	80.0
Indian elephant	70.0
Horse	62.0
Great apes	
Gorilla	50.0
Chimpanzee	50.0
Orangutan	50.0
Old World monkeys	
Baboon	40.0
Macaque	40.0
Gibbon	35.0
Brown bear	36.8
New World monkeys	
Spider monkey	35.0
Squirrel monkey	21.0
Dog	34.0
Cat	30.0
Cattle	30.0
Swine	27.0
Sheep	20.0
Goat	18.0
European rabbit	13.0
Guinea pig	7.5
Golden hamster	4.0
Mouse	3.5

Information from: M. Rockstein, J. A. Chesky, and M. L. Sussman, 1977.
  S. L. Washburn, 1981.
  R. L. Walford, 1983.

caloric consumption is the human being, who burns about four times more calories per pound than most other mammals.

Body temperature is closely tied to the longevity of cold-blooded animals because their metabolic rate is affected by the temperature of the environment. Among some lizards, for example, those who live in warm climates have shorter life spans than those who live in cold climates. Because human beings maintain a constant body temperature and a fairly steady rate of metabolism, changes in environmental temperature probably have no effect on longevity.

The length of gestation and childhood also seem to be related to longevity. Length of gestation alone is a reasonably good predictor of longevity in many species although once again human beings deviate from this rule. Their life span far exceeds the span expected for a 9-month gestation period. The human gestation period is 2 months shorter than that of the shorter-lived horse and equals that of shorter-lived cattle and apes. When length of childhood, or immaturity, is also considered, the comparatively long human life span seems to make better sense (Rockstein, Chesky, and Sussman, 1977). It has been suggested that a long period of immaturity is extremely adaptive, for it permits the young of a species to learn the adult skills that are necessary for survival (Bruner, 1964).

Longevity among our early ancestors was much shorter than it is today (Walford, 1983). *Australopithecus*, who roamed the earth about 4 million years ago, was about the size of a chimpanzee but appears to have had a slightly larger brain. The maximum life span of this species was probably about 42 years. Two million years later, *Australopithecus* had vanished; brain size had doubled and *Homo erectus*, with a brain about two thirds the size of modern men and women, may have had a maximum life span of 72 years. When human beings as we know them finally appeared, more than 100,000 years ago, the present maximum life span probably was already possible.

Yet those early women and men did not live very long (Washburn, 1981). Excavations of a pre-Columbian grave site of a Native American tribe found that few tribal members lived past the age of 45 and that the oldest person buried at the site was about 55. Similar findings were made at a burial site in Labrador, but in the Aleutian Islands, some Aleuts had lived past the age of 80. As we will see, it has taken more than 100,000 years for human survival to approach the maximum life span.

MAXIMUM LIFE SPAN

The maximum life span of a species appears to remain constant through historical time and across cultures. Most researchers believe that maximum longevity of human beings is between 110 and 120 years, but the longest verified survival is 114 years.

From time to time, claims are made for individuals like Charlie Smith who live far past the apparent limit. In seventeenth-century England, a Thomas Parr was said to have reached the age of 152; in eighteenth-century Philadelphia, a Samuel Mecutcheon was said to have lived until 122; and in the early nineteenth century, a Yarrow Mamout of Virginia supposedly lived past the age of 134 (Freeman, 1982). All these people lived at a time when it was virtually impossible to verify a person's age.

When researchers (Fries and Crapo, 1981) investigated the claims of 600 people who claimed to have been at least 120 years old, they found no one who had lived to be more than 114. The runners-up appear to be Fanny Thomas, who died in San Gabriel, California, at the age of 113 years and 215 days (Walford, 1983), and Delina Eckert Filkins of Herkimer County, New York, who died in 1928 at the age of 113 years and 114 days (Freeman, 1982).

Occasionally, we hear of remote communities where the average life span is extremely high and it is common to live past the century mark. Ages of 120, 134, or

The maximum human life span is believed to be between 110 and 120 years old. At 103, this woman has outlived most of her peers and is approaching that maximum.

150 are often reported by the residents. Three such settlements have received a good deal of publicity in recent years: the village of Vilcabamba in Ecuador, the Abkhasian region of the USSR, and the province of Hunza in Pakistan. Scientific investigations have discredited these reports.

In the case of Vilcabamba, the first studies seemed to indicate that many centenarians lived in the village. But further research made it clear that parents had been confused with children; that intermarriage was common, leading to the duplication of many names; and that when children died, parents often gave the same name to a new child. Vilcabambans who were less than 60 or 70 generally gave their correct ages, but among those who had passed 70, ages became increasingly inaccurate. In 1944, when he was 61, one man claimed to be 70; in 1949 he claimed to be 80; in 1970, to be 121; and in 1974, to be 127. In 30 years, his claims had increased by 50 years, until he was overstating his age by 36 years. When records were carefully examined, none of the supposed centenarians had reached 100. The average "100-year-old" turned out to be 84; and the average "130-year-old," to be 95 (Mazess and Forman, 1979).

The claims for Abkhasia also have been discounted (Medvedev, 1974). Official birth registration is nonexistent for these old people, and baptismal records generally disappeared when churches were destroyed after the Russian Revolution. In the case of a man named Vakutia, who claimed to be 130, extreme old age turned out to be a way of escaping service in the armed forces. Vakutia had deserted from the army after World War I simply by using his father's name and documents. He was actually only 78 years old. When a journalist later attempted to verify some of the claims of Abkhasian residents, he was told by a Soviet gerontologist that no one in the area had ever reached the 120-year mark (Georgakas, 1980).

SEARCHING FOR THE FOUNTAIN OF YOUTH

Faced with senescence and death, human beings have searched for a fountain of youth. The European discovery of the land that is now the state of Florida was a by-product of Spanish Explorer Juan Ponce de León's search for that magical fountain. One drink from its miraculous waters was said to bestow eternal youth. More than 400 years later, the search continues. Although we have lost faith in a hidden fountain, we gulp megadoses of vitamins, eat yogurt and wheat germ, and flock to clinics that promise rejuvenation.

During the 1920s, it was believed that men could turn back the clock if only they had young testes. The wealthy trooped to Europe, where a physician transplanted ape testicles into their aging bodies. Others found a physician in Kansas who used goat testicles in the operation (Walford, 1983). Later researchers discovered that instead of prolonging life, male hormones tend to shorten it. Eunuchs who are castrated before puberty tend to live longer than normal males and to be relatively free from degenerative diseases that lead to premature death (Sacher, 1977).

In the 1930s, Paul Niehans, a Swiss surgeon, opened a clinic for "cellular therapy." He believed that the cells of fetal animals could restore health and vitality and extend life. Pregnant ewes were slaughtered, and injections were prepared from the cells of fetal lambs. A person with heart trouble got heart cells; one with anemia or cirrhosis, liver cells; and so on. Gonadal cells were good for everything from insomnia, acne, sterility, and aging to diminished sexual desire and homosexuality. Wealthy men received cells from lamb testicles; wealthy women, from lamb ovaries. Among Niehans' apparently happy patients were Pope Pius XII, Charlie Chaplin, W. Somerset Maugham, Konrad Adenauer, and Bernard Baruch (Longone, 1978). Yet no research has ever established the effectiveness of such cellular therapy.

The most recent attempt to restore youth uses the drug Gerovital, a form of novocaine. Gerovital is used in Rumania by physician Ana Aslan (Aslan et al., 1965), whose patients included Nikita Khrushchev and Mao Tsetung, as well as some who had also been through Niehans' cellular therapy clinic. Although Gerovital has not been adequately tested, it did appear to prolong life in one short-lived strain of rats—but only among males. The drug does not seem to retard disease but rather to improve functioning in the central nervous system (Sacher, 1977), In fact, Gerovital seems to be more effective in lifting depression and relieving the pain of arthritis than in extending the life span (Weg, 1983). The drug is still in use and still controversial. The U.S. Food and Drug Administration has funded research into the antidepressant qualities of Gerovital, but it has been approved for general use only in the state of Nevada.

All three areas of reputed centenarians are remote, located high in the mountains, with residents who live a rigorous rural life. In these areas, to be old is to gain authority and respect. It is easy for the residents to claim an advanced age because illiteracy is high and records are sparse.

We should not, however, completely dismiss these places. Even though few of the inhabitants reach or pass their hundredth birthdays, they do remain vigorous and active in community life to a very advanced age. Their low-calorie, low-fat diet, moderate alcohol and tobacco consumption, and active life-style resemble the recommendations of many researchers in the field of gerontology.

AVERAGE LIFE SPAN

The average human life span varies from one culture to another and has changed over historical time. Our ancestors were killed by wars, accidents, disease, predators, and malnutrition. Although accidents and warfare are still with us and other human beings have replaced bears and tigers as predators, deaths from many other causes have plummeted.

For the past two centuries, average longevity has steadily increased. Increased food supplies and better nutrition probably were responsible for any extension until the middle of the nineteenth century, for they strengthened people's ability to resist infection. Then in the second half of the nineteenth century, advances in sanitation—hygiene, safer food and water—began to have an effect on longevity because they reduced contact with infectious microorganisms. Finally, medical measures, such as immunization, surgery, and antibiotics, began to reduce the death rate even further (McKeown, 1978). It seems possible that another major advance may be on the horizon, created by a rapid deepening of our understanding that life-style has a major impact on health and longevity.

In 1900 the average person born in the United States could expect to live for 47 years; by 1979, expectations had increased to 73 years. The increase in **life expectancy,** or the number of years the average person can expect to live, has come about because of reductions in premature death. More people are reaching old age. But once people reach 65, their life expectancy is not much larger than it was for a 65-year-old in 1900. At that time, a person who was 65 could expect another 13 years of life; by 1979, a 65-year-old could expect to live for another 16.6 years (U.S. Bureau of the Census, 1982).

The increase in average life expectancy is not the same for all groups. Women generally live longer than men. Fewer females die at birth, and at all ages, they tend to survive infection and resist the effects of physical deprivation better than men. Women also appear less susceptible to the present number-one killer in the United States—heart disease. This female advantage has not always existed. In 1900 there were as many men as women among the oldest Americans—those over 75 years of age (Walford, 1983). Several factors combined to change that picture. Smoking, accidents, and a higher degree of alcoholism increased male death rates

Age	White Men	White Women	Black Men	Black Women
Birth	70.6	78.0	64.0	72.7
Age 65	14.2	18.7	13.3	17.2
Age 85	5.5	7.0	6.8	9.2

FIGURE 3.1   Life expectancy in the United States. Although whites generally live longer than blacks, the gap in life expectancy is narrowing, and among black men and women who have passed their eighty-fifth birthday, blacks can expect to live longer than whites.
Source: U.S. Bureau of the Census, 1982.

while large reductions in childbirth deaths increased female life expectancy. Despite these external influences, many researchers believe that females may have a biological buffer that increases their chances of longevity. The finding of more long-lived females than males in most animal species supports this biological view.

Whites generally live longer than blacks, but the difference has declined sharply since 1900, when the life expectancy of a white baby was almost 16 years greater than that of a black baby (Butler and Lewis, 1982). The differences are still fairly large at birth, but by the age of 65 they have almost disappeared (see Fig. 3.1). In fact, among 85-year-olds, blacks have a longer life expectancy than whites. Life expectancy at birth among Hispanics is shorter than among blacks, and Native Americans have the shortest life expectancy of all—only 45.7 years in 1967 (Block, 1979).

Because nutrition, sanitation, and medical care are behind the increase in the average life span, it would be reasonable to assume that socioeconomic differences are responsible for most of the ethnic differences in life expectancy. The differences tend to disappear at the end of life because only the hardy have escaped death at an earlier age.

Variations in average life span across cultures are also related to a society's socioeconomic standards. In more developed nations, the average life span is much longer than in less developed countries. This advantage is evident from the greater percentage of older adults in developed societies. For example, in about 1970, 13.7 percent of the Swedish population was more than 65 years old, but only 1.7 percent of Kuwaitis and 2.2 percent of Zambians were more than 65 (Hauser, 1976). In all societies, however, once old age is reached, life expectancy is about the same (Fries and Crapo, 1981).

Extended longevity is moving the average life span closer to the maximum life span. Between 1980 and 1982, the number of Americans older than 85 increased more than 9 percent. Of the 2.4 million individuals in this group, 32,000 were centenarians—75 percent of them women (U.S. Bureau of the Census, 1983b). Another way to understand how average and maximum life spans are coming together is to look at survival rates. If no one succumbed to disease, those who did not die by accident would tend to succumb at about the same time. Plotted on a graph, the survival curve, which shows the percentage of the population surviving at each age, would be rectangular (see Fig. 3.2). Today's survival curve is moving toward that shape. As the life span laid down in the general genetic program takes

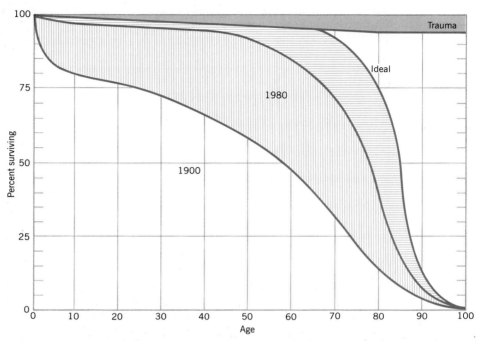

FIGURE 3.2 If premature death from disease were eliminated in the United States, the population would attain the ideal survival curve. By 1980 more than 80 percent of the discrepancy between the 1900 curve and the ideal curve had been eliminated.

Source: J. F. Fries and L. M. Crapo, 1981, p. 73.

increasing control of the death rate and society approaches the ideal survival curve, we can expect to see more and more centenarians. What would life be like in such a society?

QUALITY OF THE LIFE SPAN

Suppose society were free of disease and most people lived at least 85 years. The situation would be very different from today, when the quality of the life span is linked with age and biological deterioration increases as we grow older, becoming prevalent in later adulthood. If most of us reached 85 and the general level of health did not change, a society with a rectangular survival curve would be a society filled with nursing homes and populated by sick old people, unable to care for themselves.

But perhaps for most people, health does not begin to fail until a certain length of time before they die. If that is so, then the condition of extreme biological deterioration is better figured by the number of years until death than by the number of years since birth. Debilitating conditions, such as cancer; diabetes; mental deterioration; and heart, respiratory, and kidney disease, might be postponed.

Heart attacks might strike at 80 instead of at 55; lung cancer might develop at 95 instead of at 60. People would generally be healthier longer.

The development of a group of young-old individuals indicates that something of the sort may be happening. The proportion of vigorous old people is increasing, and some 80-year-olds are as healthy and vital as 60-year-olds were only a decade or so ago. People are still aging, but many seem to be less vulnerable to stress, and their bodies are wearing out later than they once did. Thus, adding years to life will not necessarily add poor-quality years of dependency and lengthy hospitalizations.

Although government economists have warned that increased life expectancy would cause medical costs for older adults to reach staggering heights (Boffey, 1983), some researchers disagree. They suggest that by the middle of the twenty-first century, medical costs may be less than they are today. Debilitating illnesses, such as cancer, heart disease, diabetes, arthritis, and stroke, generally develop when the aging process has led to a decline in resistance and adaptability (Walford, 1983). If the number of vital adult years is increased and the onset of these illnesses delayed until an age near the end of the maximum life span, when the body has little physical reserve and the immune system has lost much of its protective power, then illnesses might be less likely to respond to treatment. In most cases, death would follow quickly (Fries and Crapo, 1981). If this analysis is correct, society will need fewer medical services, the terminally ill will require less intensive care, and people will spend fewer days in the hospital. A look at normal aging may clarify this analysis.

The development of an increasingly larger group of vigorous, active, young-old individuals suggests that as the American survival curve becomes rectangular, people may retain their health for many more years.

NORMAL AGING

Aging generally refers to any age-related deterioration in body and behavior. As aging progresses, the body loses its ability to repair the damage wrought by living. When people enter the final biological stage in life, their ability to adapt to environmental challenge or insult decreases, diminishing their chances of survival (Rockstein and Sussman, 1979). When this process is considered, it is important to distinguish between primary and secondary aging.

PRIMARY AGING

Primary aging happens to all of us. It is universal and thought to be inevitable. It consists of gradual, age-related changes that can be observed in all members of all species. It may be the result of a genetic program.

Primary aging is also known as **normal aging**. It begins early in life although the traces are not apparent for years. When we are still in our twenties, for example, the strength of the heart muscle begins to decrease by about 1 percent per year (deVries, 1983). Some of the signs of primary aging are visible: graying or thinning hair, pigmented patches on the back of the hand, slowed movements, fading vision, or impaired hearing. The invisible aspects of aging diminish the body's adaptability in many ways. Response to temperature change slows. The effectiveness of the immune system to protect the body against infection declines. Recovery from physical exertion takes longer. The ability to handle sugar released into the bloodstream is impaired. Within the cells, the ability of DNA to repair the continual damage it undergoes is gradually reduced. As we will see, this cellular change is important in the general aging process, for DNA is a complex chemical that guides development and functioning.

From cell to organ to system, primary aging goes on at all levels of the body. All body systems age, but not all systems or organs age at the same rate. A person could have a cardiovascular system that was young for his or her years and an excretory system that had aged far beyond his or her years. Because the farther aging advances in a system, the more vulnerable it is, such a person would be likely to develop kidney disease but unlikely to develop heart disease. The effects of aging are most apparent when activity requires the coordination of more than one organ system (deVries, 1983).

That people age at different rates is obvious. It has been suggested that an individual's specific genetic program plays an important part in determining the rate at which he or she ages. This suggestion has led to the adage that the best way to live to a ripe old age is to have long-lived parents and grandparents.

Studies with twins give some support to the adage. Identical twins (who have exactly the same genetic makeup because they develop when a single fertilized egg splits) tend to die within a few years of each other. Whether or not they live in a similar environment seems to have little effect on the time of their death. For example, one identical twin had a large family and lived on a farm; her sister never married and lived in the city. When they were 69, both twins had a cerebral hemorrhage on the same day, and they died within 26 days of each other (Rockman and Sussman, 1979).

This young boy, shown with his great-grandfather, has already taken the first step toward a long life. The longevity of his great-grandparents indicates that his genetic program may be set for delayed aging.

Although such coincidences are rare, the life span of identical twins is closer than that of fraternal twins (who have different genetic makeups because they develop from separate eggs). In one study of longevity (Kallman and Jarvik, 1959), identical twins tended to die within 48 months of each other whereas fraternal twins died about 66 months apart.

There is some indication that the genetic influence on longevity is the result of differences in the susceptibility to disease. A study (Hammond, Garfinkel, and Seidman, 1971) that followed a large group of men and women for six years indicated that family differences in longevity were due to such a difference. People from short-lived families tended to develop heart disease, diabetes, or other chronic diseases at an earlier age. Although an aged organ or system tends to be especially vulnerable to disease, disease is not considered an aspect of primary aging.

SECONDARY AGING

Secondary aging happens to most people, but it is neither universal nor inevitable. Because the changes associated with secondary aging correlate with chronological age, they are often mistaken for the inevitable results of the primary aging process. The confusion of primary and secondary aging often makes it difficult for researchers to follow the course of normal aging. Secondary aging is the result of disease, disuse, or abuse. As more research is done and knowledge accumulates, the distinction between primary and secondary aging changes. For example, at one time wrinkles were thought to be a basic sign of primary aging; today we know that most wrinkles are the result of secondary aging, caused by accumulated radiation from the sun's rays.

The relationship between age and disease is so strong that approximately 85 percent of people over 65 have at least one chronic disease, and about 50 percent say that their normal activity is limited in some way by their condition (Shanas and Maddox, 1976). Besides having some chronic disease that cannot be cured, only controlled, older adults also tend to be troubled by acute illnesses. Most report being ill about once a year, and the disease is usually respiratory.

These various diseases are not caused by aging; 14 percent of older adults are disease-free. Tom Hickey (1980) tells of the 103-year-old woman who complained that her left knee was causing her pain. When the physician said there was nothing he could do and suggested she accept the pain as a result of her advanced age, she retorted: "Well, the other knee doesn't hurt, and it's also 103 years old [p. 4]." Even though normal aging does not cause disease, the reduced resistance of aging bodies makes older adults more susceptible to disease; and because disease becomes more prevalent with age, it contributes to some of the changes commonly associated with aging. Once a chronic disease develops, it can contribute to decay and deterioration in structure and function.

Disuse can also cause secondary aging in all body systems. Lack of exercise can cause muscles to atrophy and joints to stiffen. Many older people do not exercise because they believe they are incapable of it or because they think it is not good for them. Actually, by not using their bodies, they are hastening the effects of secondary aging.

Disease often limits people's activity and leads many to shun even those exercises they could safely undertake. For example, a woman with arthritis who avoids using her hand because of the pain and stiffness involved will soon find the hand unusable because of degenerative changes in the joints. Disease and disuse appear to interact, with disuse compounding the secondary aging effects of disease.

Abuse is the third cause of secondary aging. The obvious sorts of abuse that can lead to decay or deterioration are cigarette smoking, alcoholism, obesity, and malnutrition. Malnutrition is more likely to appear in older people living at or below poverty levels because they cannot afford to buy food for an adequate diet. Studies of these older people have uncovered dietary deficiencies in protein, niacin, thiamin, iron, calcium, vitamin A, and vitamin C (Barrows and Roeder, 1977). Other abuse is not as obvious. For example, some hearing loss generally accompanies primary aging. But exposure to loud noise—whether at work or in listening to rock music—can further limit a person's hearing.

Abuse, disuse, and disease contribute to the changes associated with aging. At present nothing can be done about the effects of primary aging, but the effects of secondary aging can be delayed, slowed, and at times halted or even reversed. Among a group of men and women—all at least 70 years old—both health and work capacity improved after a 26-day program that involved extensive dietary changes and regular exercise (Weber, Barnard, and Roy, 1983). A majority of these adults had cardiovascular disease, hypertension—or both—and some had mild diabetes. They ate a low-fat diet that was high in complex carbohydrates and walked twice each day for up to 40 minutes at a time. In several areas, their functioning improved significantly.

Most people are unwilling to undertake such a strict regimen. Yet the fact that some of these people turned back the clock on some symptoms of secondary aging appears to indicate that not all the symptoms we attribute to aging are an inevitable, irreversible part of growing old.

THEORIES OF AGING

If we set aside stories in which the gods bestow eternal youth or a pact with the devil keeps a person forever young, we are left with the fact that everyone ages. No matter how healthy our environment or our habits, our organ systems gradually deteriorate. Even if we escape degenerative diseases, our bodies become less and less able to adapt to stress and infection. Why should this be so? Just what process causes us to age?

Over the years many theories have been developed to explain aging. Some have been discarded, and others move in and out of favor. Current theories all seem to explain many aspects of the aging process, but none of them can account for all the facts. Most theories of aging can be considered either programmed theories or wear-and-tear theories.

PROGRAMMED THEORIES

Programmed theories of aging are based on the belief that aging is genetically controlled. The information that controls development is coded in genes, which are made up of molecules of DNA. Genetic information guides changes in the body just as a computer program controls the activities of a computer. As soon as the ovum is fertilized, the program is set and begins to run. At various points in development, the program causes particular genes to turn on or off. One theory proposes that aging is a programmed part of development, as natural as puberty, and is regulated by genes. Menopause is seen as an obvious example of this aging program, as are other aspects of normal aging. Several lines of research have indicated a genetic influence on aging.

Premature Aging

A clue to genetic influence on aging might be found by studying people who age in an abnormal fashion. Several conditions, including progeria, Werner's syndrome, and Down's syndrome, cause people to age prematurely.

Progeria is an extremely rare disease that causes young children to resemble wizened old women and men. Its first signs may appear in infancy; and as it progresses, the children's hair becomes sparse and gray; their faces take on an ancient look; their joints become stiff and knobby; and the lack of subcutaneous fat

Meg Casey, who suffers from progeria, began to age while still a young child. At nearly 28 years old, she weighs less than 40 pounds.

makes their muscles, tendons, ligaments, and blood vessels stand out. Their skin becomes dry and mottled. Within their bodies, their cardiovascular system ages, so that the arteries of a nine-year-old resemble those of someone in the seventies. In the laboratory, cells taken from the skin of a child with progeria behave like those of an old person. Some time between the age of 7 and 27, most die from heart attack or stroke (Selmanowitz, Rizer, and Orentreich, 1977).

Until 1983, no person with progeria had lived past 27. The world's longest lived progeriac is Meg Casey, who in mid-1983 was halfway to her twenty-eight birthday. Casey is 4 feet tall and weighs less than 40 pounds. She wears a blond wig over her bald head, her spine is twisted, one arm is shorter than the other, and she walks with a stilted gait. She lives in her own home and heads her town's program for the disabled (Tracy, 1983).

Casey's longevity indicates that progeria is not simply accelerated aging. If, as progeriacs are said to do, she aged at ten times the normal rate, she would now be nearly 280 years old. In addition, some symptoms that are associated with old age do not appear in children with progeria. They do not develop cataracts, their bodies do not respond in the same way to the presence of sugar in the blood, and they show no evidence of mental slowness (Walford, 1983). Although only about 50 cases have been reported, the disease sometimes strikes more than once in the same family, indicating that it may be a genetic disorder (Omenn, 1977).

Werner's syndrome is like progeria in many ways except that it develops later in life. Not until the teens or early twenties does the hair begin to gray. As the disease progresses into the thirties, the individual shows many of the aging symptoms that appear in progeria. However, people with Werner's syndrome develop cataracts and diabetes. Their life span is about 20 to 30 years less than normal.

Werner's syndrome is known to be a genetic disorder, inherited when both parents carry the same recessive gene (Selmanowitz, Rizer, and Orentreich, 1977).

Down's syndrome, also a genetic disorder, usually occurs when an error in cell division in a parent produces a sperm or an ovum with an extra chromosome (No. 21). People with Down's syndrome are short and stocky and have characteristic facial features that led this disorder at one time to be called "mongolism." They generally have some degree of mental retardation and often have congenital heart disease. They, too, age prematurely. Relatively early in life, their hair grays and their nervous system, glands, and immune system show some of the changes characteristic of aging. During their thirties and forties their brains undergo the same structural changes found in older individuals with Alzheimer's disease, which causes severe mental deterioration (Matsuyama and Jarvik, 1980). Death generally occurs by the age of 50.

Researchers are fairly certain that aging is not caused by a single gene, but the genes that produce these extreme and rather rare types of premature aging may have other forms that contribute to the more typical range of aging and to individual differences in its rate. Laboratory study of cells from these patients may uncover the biochemical basis of abnormal aging and eventually lead to an understanding of normal aging (Omenn, 1977). Such study has shown that in most cases these prematurely aged cells display what is known as the Hayflick limit.

The Hayflick Limit

At one time it was believed that human cells, placed in a laboratory dish and given nourishment, would grow and divide indefinitely. Taken away from the control of the body, they were expected to be immortal. Then researcher Leonard Hayflick (1977) showed that human cells seemed to have a built-in life span. He took tissue from a human embryo, exposed it to an enzyme preparation that caused the cells to separate, and placed the separated cells in a laboratory container along with nutrient. The cells attached to the surface of the dish and began to divide. When the surface of the dish was covered with cells, he added enzymes to separate them, divided the total population in half, and cultured them. Again and again he grew the cells and divided the culture until at last, after about 50 doublings, the cells ceased to grow. There were, however, individual differences in the embryonic tissue. Some cells doubled only 40 times; others doubled 60 times.

This approximate boundary to the cell's ability to divide is known as the **Hayflick limit**. Hayflick also found that cells from adults would not divide nearly so often, but that individual differences in the number of cell divisions remained, ranging from 14 to 29 doublings. Age and cell doubling did not seem to correlate. For example, the cells from one 87-year-old divided 29 times before they stopped, and the cells from one 26-year-old divided only 20 times.

When cells from other mammals were cultured, each species seemed to have its own reproductive limit. Mouse cells may double only 15 times, but cells from a long-lived Galapagos turtle may divide as many as 130 times. It appeared that the growth of body cells was linked with the life span of the species.

As Hayflick and others studied this characteristic of cells, they discovered that before cells stopped growing, they began to show numerous changes in function. Some cells do not show the Hayflick limit. For example, cancer cells reproduce indefinitely, cells from a 9-year-old boy with progeria divided only twice, and cells from patients with Werner's syndrome divided from 2 to 10 times.

The Hayflick limit has been supported by many studies that have grown cells in the laboratory. As yet, however, the limit has not been demonstrated with cells in a natural environment. It has been suggested that some aspect of laboratory cell culture may be related to the Hayflick limit on cell reproduction (Daniel, 1977). Attempts to study the Hayflick limit in living animals have included the grafting of skin from one animal to another and the transplantation of mammary glands. In the case of skin, transplants have survived and functioned far longer than the Hayflick limit would permit. When mammary tissue was transplanted in mice, the tissue survived through several generations of transplants and produced milk, but eventually became unable to reproduce itself. Although it appears that the Hayflick limit may be surpassed in life, it also seems clear that there is a natural limit to cells' ability to reproduce.

Other evidence in favor of a programmed theory of aging includes the existence of a maximum life span in each species, the similarity in the life span of identical twins, and the tendency for the children of long-lived parents to outlive the children of short-lived parents. This apparent genetic basis of longevity was demonstrated nearly 30 years ago, when researchers (Jones, 1956) compared the life span of parents and children. They discovered that a person whose four grandparents had lived to be 80 generally lived 4 years longer than a person whose grandparents were all dead by their sixtieth birthdays. A person whose grandparents survived to 90 had a 7-year advantage. Other studies (Abbott et al., 1974) suggest that the longevity of a person's mother may have a more powerful influence on a child's life span than the longevity of the father.

Programmed Destruction

But how does aging begin? One theory is that destruction itself is programmed. Within each cell are one or more genes that, when activated, begin the slow decline of the aging process and eventually lead to death. Another version of this theory suggests there are youthful genes as well as aging ones and that the youthful genes are either turned off or overwhelmed by the aging genes as middle age approaches. Finally, a third version proposes that the same genes have both youthful and aging effects, but that their function changes in midlife. The effect of the female hormone estrogen on women could be an example of this sort of program. Estrogen maintains the reproductive process in women. During the childbearing years, the hormone also protects women from degenerative changes in the arteries that lead to high blood pressure. At menopause, estrogen production drops sharply, and women face an increased risk of high blood pressure (Rockstein and Sussman, 1979).

The program for aging may be located in the hypothalamus, a gland about the size of a marble that is buried deep in the brain. The hypothalamus regulates many body functions, including temperature control, emotional and physiological reactions to stress, hunger, and sexual response. It carries out its job by signaling the pituitary gland to produce various hormones. According to one theory, a biological timer within the hypothalamus is programmed to reduce its signals to the pituitary. When the timer goes off, the amount of neurotransmitters in the hypothalamus decreases markedly. Because signals from one neuron to another are carried by these transmitter chemicals, communication between the hypothalamus and the pituitary is changed. The pituitary may respond with a hormonal imbalance that initiates the aging process (Walford, 1983).

Finally, researcher Roy Walford (Walford et al., 1981) has proposed an **immunological theory** of aging, in which programming is apparently tied to the immune system and set for literal self-destruction. As people age, the immune system begins to attack its own body. The immune system is meant to protect the body by fighting microorganisms, foreign proteins, and cancer cells. It is the immune system that is responsible for the rejection of organ transplants or skin grafts. As Walford (1983) points out, the characteristic signs of aging are similar to those involved in the process of rejecting a transplant: loss of hair, kidney disease, vascular disease, failure to thrive, and a shortened life span.

Programmed self-destruction is not the only problem with the aging immune system. It also begins losing its ability to recognize foreign substances and abnormal cells. This decline in function makes the immune system inefficient at protecting the aging body against diseases and cancer. As we will see, the immunological theory of aging is a combination of programmed theory and wear-and-tear theory.

WEAR-AND-TEAR THEORIES

Wear-and-tear theories of aging are based on the belief that living damages biological systems. As people go through life, damage accumulates, but the damage does not show up as it would in a machine, where parts wear out and break down. Instead the damage is functional; it limits the natural ability of biological systems to repair themselves. Various wear-and-tear theories focus on the importance of particular type of damage.

The **DNA-repair theory**, for example, is based on the fact that DNA undergoes continual damage either in the process of metabolism or from contact with pollutants or radiation. DNA can be damaged in a number of ways, and as soon as it is damaged, it sets about repairing itself. In a common type of damage, one of the strands of a double-helixed molecule breaks. Within each cell are several endonuclei that act as a repair crew. These endonuclei recognize the break, remove the damaged portion, and insert a new segment, using information contained on the complementary strand (Sinex, 1977).

Species with long life spans can repair DNA damage much more rapidly than species with short life spans. For example, ultraviolet light can damage DNA, producing dimers, in which two adjacent organic molecules form a destructive bond. If the organism is to stay healthy, such damage must be repaired. When dimers appear in laboratory cultures of skin cells, repair goes about five times as fast in the cells of long-lived human beings, elephants, and cows as it does in short-lived rats or mice (Sinex, 1977).

According to the DNA-repair theory, repair can never quite keep up with the rate of damage. Studies indicate that the cells of older adults may be more sensitive to radiation damage and less efficient at repairing damage when it does occur (Staiano-Coico et al., 1983). As the cells' ability to repair themselves slows, DNA damage piles up. Because nerve cells and most muscle cells, including those in the heart, cannot divide and replace themselves, the accumulated damage gradually destroys their ability to function. Aging then is the result of the increasing store of unrepaired DNA. Researchers who support this wear-and-tear theory of aging see a programmed aspect to it: The genetic program sets the level of DNA repair (Walford, 1983).

A second wear-and-tear theory of aging is the **cross-linkage theory**, proposed by chemist Johan Bjorksten (1974). Cross-links are stable bonds between molecules or parts of molecules that cannot be repaired. The links change the molecules, making them rigid, so that they can no longer function in the same way. Cross-links are produced during metabolism and can be found in connective tissues and in DNA itself. As cross-links accumulate, tissues lose elasticity and become dry and leathery. In fact, the tanning of leather is an example of the cross-linkage process, for tanning involves the similar binding together of cells. The protein in our bodies is about 30 percent collagen, a supportive tissue that surrounds cells and blood vessels, and collagen is susceptible to cross-linkage. Some researchers (Kohn, 1971) believe that the aging of collagen can have extensive effects on the functioning of many body systems.

A third wear-and-tear theory is the **free-radical theory** proposed by researcher Denham Harman (1968). Free radicals are chemical compounds that have a free electron, usually in an atom of oxygen. Some free radicals are produced during metabolism; others are simply present in the environment. These compounds are so unstable that they bond easily with other molecules. For example, they combine with molecules of unsaturated fats to form lipid peroxides, compounds that can decompose to form aldehydes (Walford, 1983). Because aldehydes are cross-linking agents, the free-radical and cross-linkage theories of aging are related.

Free radicals attack unsaturated fats in the membranes of body cells, damaging the membranes. They can also damage chromosomes. And they are self-propagating, producing more free radicals each time they react with a molecule (Rockstein and Sussman, 1979). The body has a defense against free radicals in the form of scavenger enzymes, but some free radicals escape the scavengers. Over the course of time, the damage builds up, and we begin to age.

As we have seen, aging begins within the cell. In addition to the threats posed by cross-linkage and free radicals, many of our cells accumulate a brown pigment called **lipofuscin**, which contains lipid, protein, and carbohydrate. Although their origin is uncertain, some researchers believe that lipofuscins are by-products of metabolism (Sanadi, 1977). Lipofuscins are inert; they do not react with other body substances. But because they tend to fill up cells, they may interfere with the normal functioning of the cell (Rockstein and Sussman, 1979). Because lipofuscins accumulate throughout life, they are associated with the aging process. However, some older adults have little lipofuscin in their tissues whereas some younger adults have a great deal of it (Sanadi, 1977).

Theories of normal aging will have to explain many aspects of normal aging (Walford, 1983). They must explain the following: Why are cells subject to the Hayflick limit? Why do some people age prematurely? Why is the rate at which any species can repair damage to its own DNA related to its maximum life span? Why does the immune system become less efficient with age? Why do the fibers of connective tissue deteriorate with age? Why do biochemical changes take place in aging bodies? And why do almost all animals have a similar metabolic rate, using in a lifetime about the same amount of energy per pound of body weight?

None of the present theories accounts for all these aspects of aging. With the information we now have, however, researchers have been looking for ways to extend the life span.

EXTENDING THE LIFE SPAN

There are two ways in which the life span can be extended. The average life span can be lengthened if degenerative diseases can be postponed to produce the rectangular survival curve described earlier. The maximum life span might also be lengthened. In that case, there would still be a rectangular survival curve, but the rectangle would be extended so that the future 90-year-old would be as vigorous as today's 50-year-old. The maximum life span might increase from 114 to as much as 140 (Walford, 1983).

Researchers disagree as to whether the maximum human life span can be extended, but two methods have been successful with laboratory animals (Sacher, 1977). The first, undernutrition, consists of feeding animals a diet that is highly nutritious but quite low in calories. The life span of rats has been almost doubled—from 3.5 to 5 years—by reducing their calorie intake by 50 percent. On this restricted diet, some diseases decreased dramatically in frequency, some remained at the same level, and a few forms of cancer increased. There were, however, a few drawbacks. Infant mortality increased, growth was stunted, and behavioral development was impaired. In addition, the rats were more susceptible to bacterial infections and to parasites (Cutler, 1981).

Just why undernutrition prolongs life is uncertain. The best guess is that it lowers the metabolic rate, so that the allotted number of calories per ounce lasts many more months. However, other factors may also be at work, including suppressing the immune system so that it does not go into the self-destruction phase, slowing the developmental rate, and lowering the animals' body temperature (Cutler, 1981).

Another successful method for extending the life span involves manipulating body temperature. The life span of fruit flies has been almost doubled by keeping them in a temperature that is 4°C. colder than normal. A drop in environmental temperature of 9°F. doubled the life span of a South American fish. Fish reared at colder temperatures were not stunted as was the case of the underfed rats. The fish who spent their lives in 59°F. water grew faster and were larger than fish who spent their lives in 68°F. water. Fish who were raised in their customary water and transferred to cold water at maturity did just as well as fish who spent their whole lives in cold water. Because the fish that were in cold water from birth grew so rapidly, the researcher (Walford, 1983) does not believe that a reduction in metabolism was responsible for the extension of life. Yet the rate of aging was slowed. When tissue from these fish was examined, it became clear that they had escaped a good deal of cross-linkage or free-radical effects. The collagen in their bodies did not show the same aging effects found in most old fish (Walford, 1983).

What meaning do these experiments have for human beings? One day it may be practical to develop a variation of undernutrition for human beings although whether many people will be willing to trade the pleasures of the table for a strict dietary regimen is uncertain. It is less clear how temperature reduction can be applied to people, for warm-blooded mammals maintain a constant body temperature. For example, when rats are raised in low temperatures, they increase their metabolic rate. As a result, degenerative disease increases, and their life span is shortened (Cutler, 1981). However, discovering why the fish collagen remained youthful may lead to other human applications.

In some laboratories, researchers are experimenting with ways to increase the body's ability to combat free radicals or to keep the immune system functioning properly. Even if developmental biologists do not succeed in extending the maximum life span, they may well discover ways to slow the rate of aging so that people can retain health and vigor longer.

SUMMARY

Longevity, or the duration of life, can be considered in terms of **average life span** (the mean age of survival) or **maximum life span** (the oldest age to which any individuals survive). Species longevity may be connected with metabolism, body temperature, length of gestation, age of puberty, and brain weight and body size (within general orders). Although the maximum human life span of between 110 and 120 years probably has not changed in the past 100,000 years, only today have survival rates begun to approach that span. Reports of remote communities where most people live past the age of 100 have been discredited although people in these villages do remain vigorous and active to an advanced age.

The increase in average life span over the past two centuries seems largely due to better nutrition and sanitation, with medical measures adding to the increase during the past hundred years. Since 1900, **life expectancy** at birth has increased from 47 to 73 years among Americans, but for 65-year-olds, life expectancy has increased only 3.6 years, from 78 to 81.6. Women generally live longer than men, and whites generally live longer than blacks although once people pass the age of 85, blacks have a longer life expectancy than whites. The population is moving toward a rectangular survival curve in which few people die from disease and most live until near the end of the maximum life span.

Primary aging, also known as **normal aging**, is universal and thought to be inevitable. It begins early in life and affects all body systems. As it progresses, the body's adaptability diminishes. Genetic influences on longevity have been established and appear to be the result of differences in the susceptibility to diseases. **Secondary aging** happens to most people but is neither universal nor inevitable. Secondary aging is the result of disease, disuse, or abuse; and its correlation with age causes it to be mistaken for primary aging.

Programmed theories of aging are based on the belief that aging is genetically controlled, and it is believed that people who age in an abnormal fashion from **progeria, Werner's syndrome,** or **Down's syndrome** could provide clues to the nature of the genetic program. Human cells seem to have a built-in life span, known as the **Hayflick limit**; once that point is reached, the cells cease to divide. Some believe the programming is hormonal, directed by the hypothalamus. According to the **immunological theory** of aging, the programming is in the immune system, which, with age, begins to lose its ability to recognize foreign substances and abnormal cells and instead attacks the body.

Wear-and-tear theories of aging are based on the belief that living damages biological systems and that aging is the result of accumulated damage. Among wear-and-tear theories are the **DNA-repair theory**, which proposed that DNA is damaged faster than it can be repaired; the **cross-linkage theory**, which proposes that the accumulation of cross-links between molecules or parts of molecules damages functioning; and the **free-radical theory**, which proposes that aging develops when free radicals (which become cross-linking agents) are not destroyed. Another aspect of aging is the accumulation of **lipofuscin**, a brown pigment, within cells. Although lipofuscins are inert, they are correlated with aging, and their role in the process is uncertain.

Researchers have succeeded in extending the life span of laboratory animals by undernutrition, which appears to lower the metabolic rate, and by lowering body temperature, which may reduce cross-linkage and free-radical effects. Such experiments may lead to methods of slowing the aging process in human beings.

KEY TERMS

average life span	**longevity**
cross-linkage theory	**maximum life span**
DNA-repair theory	**normal aging**
Down's syndrome	**primary aging**
free-radical theory	**progeria**
Hayflick limit	**programmed theories**
immunological theory	**secondary aging**
life expectancy	**wear-and-tear theories**
lipofuscin	**Werner's syndrome**

4

BIOLOGICAL CHANGES ACROSS ADULTHOOD

Helen Zechmeister is into powerlifting. In competition, her dead lift record is 215 pounds, which is the best in the world for women in her age group. That record may not sound impressive for a healthy young woman, but Helen Zechmeister is a healthy old woman. She is 78 years old. She also holds world records in her age group for the squat lift and bench press. This 5-foot-1-inch woman is working toward new goals: 225 pounds in the dead lift, 125 to 130 pounds in the squat lift, and 100 pounds for the bench press. She jogs 2 miles a day, swims several times each week, and does stretching exercises.

Although she's always been active, Zechmeister began lifting weights only about 3 years ago, when she was 75. She is modest about her skills, carefully pointing out that there's not much competition in her class. And she sees nothing mysterious in her hobby. When asked why she lifts weights, she answers, "I just like to do it. It's as simple as that" (*AARP News Bulletin*, 1983a).

Helen Zechmeister's physical condition is unusual for a 78-year-old woman. But her example shows more clearly than pages of statistics that growing old does not necessarily mean becoming weak and helpless. Her hair may be white, but her muscles are still functioning as efficiently as those of much younger women. Zechmeister is aging slowly but normally, and she seems relatively unaffected by the problems of secondary aging.

Her robust condition may be connected with her lifelong habit of strenuous activity. It may be linked with the fact that she neither smokes nor drinks. Or it may have something to do with her genetic inheritance. Whatever the reason, Helen Zechmeister is not about to spend her eighth decade in a rocking chair on her front porch.

In this chapter, our focus shifts from molecular and cellular aging to the aging system. In considering the biological changes associated with normal human aging, we look at the various processes that are going on in the body of Helen Zechmeister and every other person who has passed maturity. Biological changes are important because of their implications for other aspects of life. For example, aging in the cardiovascular system can be responsible for poorer performance on intelligence tests. Secondary aging in the central nervous system can lead to drastic personality change. Visible signs of aging can affect self-image and self-esteem, and so changes in appearance are the first aspect of biological aging to be examined. Next we explore changes within the body, starting with the cardiovascular system and taking up, in turn, the respiratory, gastrointestinal, excretory, endocrine, reproductive, and nervous systems. This tour of the aging body will help us to separate the ravages of secondary aging from the inescapable, but less debilitating, decline connected with normal aging.

THE AGING SYSTEM

The biological changes associated with normal aging tend to be gradual and cumulative. At first almost imperceptible, the damage to individual cells, organs, and tissues increases as the years pile up. At last, there is a breakdown in the integration of body systems (Shock, 1977b). Advanced aging becomes more than the sum of the changes that take place at lower levels of the body. Tissues become less sensitive to hormones and other substances that regulate the body. As a result, the control mechanisms of the body do not work as well, and adaptation to stress takes much longer.

This means that older people's bodies may function efficiently as long as no extraordinary demands are made on the system. In temperature regulation, for example, the aging body seems to maintain its normal temperature in resting conditions. But faced with large changes in environmental temperature, the older body takes far longer to adapt than it once did. Older people are more susceptible than young people to hypothermia in winter and heatstroke in summer.

Other systems show a similar sluggishness. Adaptation to the stress of exercise is slowed; sensitivity to increases in blood sugar levels diminishes; the ability to regulate the acid content (pH) of the blood decreases; adaptation to high altitudes takes longer; the ability to deal with air pollution is impaired.

A body that can no longer deal efficiently with stress and whose immune system is no longer operating effectively has become vulnerable. It is increasingly susceptible to disease whether the degenerative diseases associated with aging or infectious diseases carried by microorganisms.

It is important to remember that not all a person's systems age at the same rate. One 75-year-old might have a sturdy heart and circulatory system but aging kidneys and excretory system whereas another might have an efficient excretory system but an aged heart. Just as the various systems within the body age at different rates, so does aging progress at different rates among the population. Biological age and chronological age may be widely separated, and people may be younger or older than their actual years. At all ages, people vary in mobility, energy levels, work activity, and health; and the older we get, the greater the differences among us (Weg, 1983). No matter how slowly we age, clear signs of aging appear, and the first ones that we generally notice in ourselves and others are changes in appearance.

CHANGES IN APPEARANCE

Changes in appearance first become visible in a body we still consider young. A few gray hairs appear; wrinkles form at the corners of the eyes; our flesh is not as firm as it once was. The changes are gradual and accumulate so slowly that at first we are not aware of them. One day, however, the evidence in the mirror cannot be ignored.

The recognition is usually unsettling and may damage our ego and diminish our self-confidence. A 30-year-old, in good health, full of energy and functioning efficiently, suddenly realizes that he or she is no longer young. Because American society places a premium on youth, the recognition is difficult in this country. Sterotypes about old age and the attitudes of others toward aging have combined to make growing old seem like a punishment (Weg, 1983).

Once the unsettling recognition of aging is passed, the 30-year-old can brush aside the small signs in the mirror. Aging people rarely "feel" old; one man in his eighties said, "I don't feel like an old man, I feel like a young man who has something the matter with him" (Cowley, 1980, p. 41). The conviction that we are old generally comes from the reactions of others rather than from any inner sense of aging. Being treated like an old man or woman is probably more damaging to a person's self-confidence than the knowledge that the seventieth birthday has been passed. But few people accept old age without a struggle.

Billions of dollars are spent each year in attempts to reverse, slow down, or conceal the unmistakable signs of age. Moisturizing creams, facials, mudpacks, and hair dye are marketed to millions by cosmetic companies. Face-lifting, "full body contours" in which excess fat is removed from hips and thighs, and hair transplants are offered by plastic surgeons. Cosmetic surgery was once primarily sought by women, but during the last decade—just about the time men's cosmetics became big business—the number of men having cosmetic surgery tripled (Kelly, 1977). In most cases, cosmetic surgery does not make a person look younger. Instead, by removing or tightening excessive skin, it erases the tired appearance—but only temporarily. The effects of cosmetic surgery last between 5 to 10 years (Wantz and Gay, 1981).

As with all other aspects of aging, there are wide interindividual differences in appearance. A 35-year-old may look 50; a 50-year-old may look 35. Changes in hair, nails, skin, fat, muscle, skeleton, and teeth all affect the apparent progression of aging.

HAIR

Gray hair has long been used as a sign of the aging process; of more than 50 body measurements, it is considered the most reliable indicator of aging (Damon et al., 1972). Yet genetics play a role in the rate at which gray or white hair replaces the natural color. Some people get their first gray hairs while they are still teenagers; others show only a few streaks at 60. The graying process may be the result of the lack of a particular enzyme (Rossman, 1977) or a reduction or malfunction of pigment producing cells within the hair follicle (Selmanowitz, Rizer, and Orentreich, 1977).

Over the years, hair can change dramatically in character as well (Selmanowitz, Rizer, and Orentreich, 1977). A follicle can produce either a fine, short, colorless hair, called vellus hair, or a coarse, long, colored hair, called terminal hair. Once men are past 30, hair follicles in the ear may gradually switch from vellus to terminal hair production, producing tufts of hair resembling a goat's beard. The tufts are so common that they have given the fleshy projections above the earlobe their names: tragus and antitragus, from the Greek word for goat.

On the scalp, follicles can shift in the other direction, so that terminal hair is replaced by vellus. Because vellus hair is inconspicuous, the scalp appears bald. This transition is called patterned baldness, and it is caused by sex-linked heredity

In patterned baldness, a sex-linked form of hereditary baldness, the coarse terminal hair on the scalp is gradually replaced by fine, downy vellus hair.

factors; men often find it beginning during young adulthood. It appears first at the temples and gradually spreads over the crown of the head. Baldness can also be caused by disease or injury that replaces normal skin with scar tissue.

During aging, some scalp hair is actually lost in both men and women, and the process is well underway by middle age. By the time a person is 50, the density of hair follicles has dropped from 615 per square centimeter to 485 per square centimeter (Rockstein and Sussman, 1979). Some women discover that armpit hair diminishes after menopause and may even disappear. This hair loss is related to hormone levels.

NAILS

Nail growth appears to be influenced by environmental conditions, nutrition, hormones, disease, and changes in circulation. After maturity, the rate of nail growth slows, dropping as much as 38 percent among people in their eighties (Selmanowitz, Rizer, and Orentreich, 1977). As tissue in the nail bed ages and the walls of the blood vessels thicken, nails become ridged and may split into layers. In old age, the nails may take on a dull yellowish, greenish, or gray appearance.

SKIN

Aging of the skin is more likely to disrupt a woman's self-image than aging of the hair. It is easy to color grayed hair, but no matter how many quarts of moisturizer and wrinkle-resistant creams are applied to the skin, nothing can really be done to hide the marks of time that increase after menopause. Men may not be as affected by the aging of their skin, for beard regrowth seems to make changes less noticeable. Despite all the worry about fading youth and fretting about the tiny wrinkles that may begin to appear around the eyes and mouth before we are 30, many of us seem determined to hasten the aging process.

Tanning is one way to induce secondary aging. As the skin tans, production of the dark pigment, **melanin**, is stimulated. But the ultraviolet rays of the sun also interfere with the cells' production of DNA and with protein synthesis in the skin, which keeps the skin from regenerating. As a result, the skin thins and becomes wrinkled (Wantz and Gay, 1981). Yet the quest for a bronzed skin continues, with little apparent concern for the leathery, wrinkled skin and the eventual skin cancers that accompany extensive exposure to the sun.

Sun, wind, and abrasion are responsible for so much of the damage we see that researchers find it difficult to separate normal aging from the cumulative effects of environmental damage (Rockstein and Sussman, 1979). The extent of this damage becomes apparent when the furrowed, weathered facial and neck skin of an 80-year-old is compared with soft, youthful-looking skin on the buttocks.

A person's natural coloring is an important consideration in environmental damage. Fair-skinned blonds or redheads with blue or green eyes run the greatest risk, for their skin is most susceptible to sun damage. The darker the skin, the more resistant it is to solar radiation, so that blacks suffer the least damage from

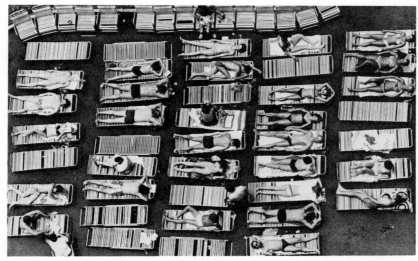

The American quest for a bronzed skin hastens aging, for the tanning process thins and wrinkles the skin and keeps skin cells from regenerating.

exposure to the sun. In addition to complexion, the frequency, intensity, and duration of exposure determines the rate of skin aging (Selmanowitz, Rizer, and Orentreich, 1977). Surface skin cells replace themselves, but as we saw in Chapter 2, the rate of replacement slows markedly after a person is 50. As the ability to replace dead or damaged cells diminishes, aging becomes increasingly apparent.

In the deep skin layers, cross-linkage stiffens elastic fibers and collagen, making the skin less pliable. As aging progresses, the skin becomes thinner and drier, fat deposits directly beneath the skin diminish, and muscles decrease in size. Eventually, the skin sags and wrinkles.

Many wrinkles are use-related; that is, they occur at an angle to the direction of muscle pull on the skin (Rossman, 1977). We recognize this connection when we call small wrinkles around the eyes "laugh lines" or forehead wrinkles "frown lines" or when we say that a person has the face he or she "deserves" at age 50. Habitual facial expressions do accentuate wrinkles, but sunlight also accentuates them as it does other skin damage.

Although pigment-containing cells in the skin, called **melanocytes** decrease with age, those that remain increase in size and sometimes cluster on the hands, forearms, or face. Variously called "age spots," "liver spots," "pigment plaques," or "lentigines," these brown freckles are common in whites with fair skin and are aggravated by exposure to the sun.

Keratoses, warty growths that may be dry and light-colored or greasy and dark-colored, may appear anywhere on the body. Although they become increasingly common with age, they are not necessarily a result of the normal aging process. Keratoses often appear on young adults, but because the growths are permanent and tend to enlarge and because new ones keep forming on susceptible individuals, they have been associated with aging (Selmanowitz, Rizer, and Orentreich, 1977).

Other common skin disorders are also found in the elderly, but they are not part of the normal aging process. Skin cancer, which tends to appear after the age of 50, is primarily the result of exposure to the sun. Older people often complain that, because their skin is dry, it itches or chaps easily. The dryness may be accentuated by vitamin A deficiency, and the itching may be a reaction to the alkalizing effect of soap. Other cases of itching may be due to drug reactions or be symptoms of various degenerative diseases.

BODY COMPOSITION

Unlike skin cells, muscle cells cannot replace themselves. In today's adults, age is related to muscle-cell atrophy and muscle-cell death. Muscle density appears to increase progressively until about the age of 39 (Bulcke et al., 1979); then muscle mass begins to shrink, and muscle fiber decreases in both number and diameter. Because fat tissue tends to increase with aging, a smaller proportion of body weight consists of lean muscle. Through the use of computerized axial tomography, or CAT scans (that provide cross-sectional X rays of living tissue), researchers have found that in men younger than 50, fat is primarily deposited between skin and muscle tissue, but that among healthy men in their sixties and seventies, fat infiltrates in and between muscles (Borkan et al., 1983). Even if weight at 60 is the same as it was at 25, the bodies of most adults will contain more fat than they once did. Most of us gain weight during middle adulthood. Men tend to gain until the mid-fifties; women until the mid-sixties. In old age, both sexes tend to lose weight, with men losing more than women (Rossman, 1977).

Several researchers have questioned how much shrinkage of muscle mass results from normal aging. Because the atrophy of muscle cells is closely related to disuse, at least part of the shrinkage is probably the inevitable result of reduced physical activity associated with aging in our society (Rockstein and Sussman, 1979). In addition, the decrease in muscle mass that appears in cross-sectional studies of adults may reflect the fact that people with smaller, lean body mass live longer (Weg, 1983).

The muscles of older adults show other changes as well: loss of muscle tone, muscle strength, flexibility, and speed of movement. Tests have shown that with the typical life-style of adults in the past generation, muscle strength began to decline at about the age of 30. But the decline may not be part of normal aging. Neither muscle strength nor endurance showed any decline among men who worked in a machine shop; 62-year-olds performed as well as 22-year-olds (deVries, 1983). Some decline in muscular effectiveness seems inevitable, but just how rapidly muscle strength declines in healthy, active people is uncertain.

SKELETON

For many years it was believed that most people shrink several inches in height as they age, a belief that was consistently supported by studies. For example, the average 75-year-old American man was 3.3 inches shorter than the average 35-year-old, and for women there was a difference of 2.7 inches (Stoudt et al., 1965). But such figures come from cross-sectional studies, and Americans have been growing taller over the decades. Over a 40-year period, the average height of army recruits increased 1.2 inches, and among a group of Italian-Americans the increase was 2.1 inches (Rossman, 1977). Although some shrinkage in height does occur, it is probably no more than about 1 inch in men and under 2 inches in women. The loss is due to altered posture, a thinning of the cartilage disks between the spinal vertebra, and a loss of water in the disks.

Changes occur in the composition of bone as well. As people pass the age of 30, calcium is lost from the bones, a process that is generally more pronounced in women than in men. In one study (Garn, 1975), women between the ages of 55 and 85 lost 25 percent of their bone mass whereas men lost only 12 percent. Despite this deterioration, skeletal cells maintain the ability to repair fractures although the repair takes much longer than it once did (Tonna, 1977).

A condition known as **osteoporosis**, which involves fairly pronounced bone degeneration, sometimes develops with age. As a result, the bones become brittle and are likely to break under stress. The condition is four times more common in women than in men and is especially prevalent in postmenopausal women. No one is certain just why it develops. Among the causes that have been proposed for osteoporosis are diminished estrogen levels, lack of exercise, a lactase (the enzyme required to digest milk) deficiency, an inability to adapt to a low-calcium diet, lack of calcium in the diet, and an increase in parathyroid secretion as the calcium level of the blood drops (Tonna, 1977). Various types of therapy have been tried, including estrogen, calcium, vitamin D, fluoride, and vitamin K. None has been able to reverse bone absorption although estrogen can prevent it. Stress and inactivity appear to increase bone loss, and exercise appears to help prevent it (Weg, 1983).

Joints also undergo degenerative change with age, and **osteoarthritis**, a painful inflammation of the joints, sometimes develops. This disease appears to be related to mechanical stress. As the composition of collagen changes, the bone ends rub together. Those joints that bear the greatest weight and receive the greatest shock appear to be particularly susceptible. The condition occasionally appears in young adulthood, but its incidence and severity increase until the age of 80. If the disorder is to develop, it generally appears by that time. Among people who live to be 90, the initial appearance of osteoarthritis decreases sharply (Tonna, 1977). The development of osteoarthritis seems to be related to heredity, to hormonal influences, and to nutritional factors.

TEETH

Although the survival of animals in the wilds appears to depend upon the durability of their teeth, most people's teeth wear down so slowly that human teeth could last for 200 years if they were not lost through decay, root infections, or gum disease (Tonna, 1977). As people age, their teeth become more resistant to decay owing to an accumulation of acid-resistant deposits on the surface and a decreased permeability of tooth enamel. After the age of 17, the majority of people will not develop decay in previously unaffected teeth (Jackson and Burch, 1969).

Within the tooth's central cavity, the fibers, blood vessels, and nerves form the tooth's pulp. With age, the pulp gradually loses cells until about half are gone by the age of 70. At the same time, the number of fibers increase while the blood vessels decrease.

A common cause of tooth loss is **periodontal disease**, an affliction that affects the gums and the surrounding tissue. In periodontal disease, bacteria invade swollen, tender gums, causing the tissue to become more inflamed and to recede from the teeth—a process that is accentuated by the presence of tartar on the teeth. The spreading infection can cause bone loss, loosening the teeth so that they either fall out or must be removed.

The incidence of periodontal disease increases with age, but it is not a part of normal aging and is often found among young people. However, there is some connection between periodontal disease and osteoporosis, and where one condition is diagnosed, the other can often be found (Weg, 1983). Many factors are be-

WHEN YOUNG IS OLD

For professional athletes, old age may come at 30—or even sooner. Small declines in muscle strength or the efficiency of the circulatory or respiratory systems can write an ending to a dazzling sports career.

Few players over 35 can perform well enough to play professional football or baseball. Many players are "too old" by 30, and those who remain past 35 tend to be placekickers in football and relief pitchers or designated hitters in baseball, positions that require less speed, endurance, and strength. Sometimes, by playing only occasionally, a player can prolong a baseball career into his forties, as did Carl Yastrzemski of the Boston

Billie Jean King, who reached the Wimbledon semifinals at the age of 39, may be typical of an increasing number of athletes who retain their speed, endurance, and coordination longer than was once the case.

lieved to be involved in the development of periodontal disease, including genetic influence, nutritional deficiencies, malocclusion, improper care of the teeth, and various diseases. It has been suggested that people who age faster than their chronological age are more likely to develop periodontal disease than those who are biologically younger than their chronological age (Tonna, 1977).

Age changes in appearance are visible, but invisible aging within the body may be progressing faster than changes on the outside.

Red Sox and Bert Campaneris of the New York Yankees. But in 1983, the same team that fielded the aging Campaneris considered 37-year-old Bobby Murcer too old to continue as either a pinch hitter or a designated hitter. By the time Murcer was 35, the Yankees began playing him less and within two years had decided he could no longer make the squad (Murcer, 1983).

Tennis players rarely compete much past 30, yet Billie Jean King continued in professional competition much longer. At 39, this six-time Wimbledon champion tried to win the tournament one more time. When she reached the quarterfinals, King said, "I'm just surviving. . . . I'm playing just good enough to win. I'm so used to being on the edge of the ledge, maybe that will help me" (Vecsey, 1983). Apparently it did help because King reached the semifinals, where she was beaten by 18-year-old Andrea Jaeger.

The fact that Billie Jean King reached the semifinals may be an indication of things to come. Perhaps the generally better level of health that has developed in the United States and increased knowledge of effective training techniques will extend the professional life of more athletes. In the same year that King was beaten

by Jaeger, another athlete showed that aging bodies could be reconditioned. Ed Burke, who won the title of national hammer throw champion of the United States three times in the 1960s, came out of retirement at 39 and started over. When he was 43, he was back at the top, finishing second in three national and international track and field meets (Litsky, 1983). If the trend continues, professional athletes may one day find that old age does not arrive before 50.

In some fields, older athletes already turn in spectacular performances. Although speed and endurance decline among male runners over 40, the effect is less apparent in long-distance running. At distances greater than 40 kilometers, the fastest 40-year-old runs nearly as fast as Olympic competitors. Speeds of older runners decline markedly, but the fastest 70-year-old long-distance runner can still run 70 percent as fast as male Olympic finalists. A researcher (Riegel, 1981) who studied speed and endurance in these athletes points out that the records of older men, who rarely run the hundreds of miles each week covered by Olympic athletes in training, should be regarded as minimum indicators of what the best older men can do rather than the best possible performance.

CHANGES IN THE CARDIOVASCULAR SYSTEM

For centuries, scientists believed that aging of the cardiovascular system—the heart and blood vessels—was the basis of all physical aging. In the fifteenth century, Leonardo da Vinci, after dissecting corpses, wrote that the cause of aging was a slow constriction of blood vessels that cut off the body's nourishment (cited by Belt, 1952). In the seventeenth century, Thomas Syndenham wrote that a man was an old as his arteries. Although the search for the cause of aging is now conducted at the cellular and genetic levels, the health of the cardiovascular system is crucial, and its deterioration is associated with age. Once men pass 45 and women pass 65, cardiovascular disease becomes the leading cause of death in the United States (U.S. Bureau of the Census, 1982).

Because the cells of the heart, arteries, veins, and capillaries cannot divide and reproduce, the cardiovascular system eventually wears out. As cells age, the effectiveness of the entire system is reduced. Some of the changes in function and appearance are the inevitable result of normal aging, but others are connected with age-related disease (Kohn, 1977). We will consider the heart and the arteries separately.

HEART

The heart never rests, pausing only a fraction of a second between beats (Fig. 4.1). It is a muscular organ that pumps blood through the resting body at the rate of about 75 gallons per hour; during strenuous activity, the rate may increase to ten times that amount. In the course of a lifetime, the heart may beat 3 billion times (Rockstein and Sussman, 1979).

Age affects the appearance of this essential organ. Lipofuscin accumulates within the heart, its brown pigment altering the red color of a youthful heart. Although the buildup of pigment is inevitable, its amount has not been related to any disease or cardiac abnormality (Kohn, 1977). Another inevitable change takes place in the consistency of the collagen that surrounds every muscle fiber; it becomes insoluble, stable, and stiff. In some parts of the heart, additional collagen is deposited, thickening valves and muscles and changing the collagen-muscle ratio of the heart. In a study using a cross-sectional design (Davies and Pomerance, 1972), people younger than 50 years old generally had hearts that were 46 percent muscle and 17 percent collagen whereas those who were older than 75 generally had hearts that were 27 percent muscle and 36 percent collagen. Through the years fat is gradually deposited on the heart surface, building up a coating that may cover the entire heart of some people in their forties (Rockstein and Sussman, 1979). It is generally believed that enlargement of the heart found in many older people is not due to normal aging. However, in a longitudinal study of healthy men between the ages of 23 and 76, X rays revealed a slight increase in heart size over a 10-year period, with the largest increase appearing in those who gained weight (Ensor et al., 1983).

Age changes in the heart are reflected in heart function. The rate of the heart at rest seems to decline with age although the decrease has not appeared in all studies. Various studies have shown that **cardiac output,** or the volume of blood pumped by the heart in each minute, decreases about 1 percent per year, beginning at age 20. The decrease is due in part to a drop in the amount of blood pumped by each stroke of the heart and in part to a decrease in heart rate (Kohn, 1977). Thus, the heart muscle appears to lose strength with age.

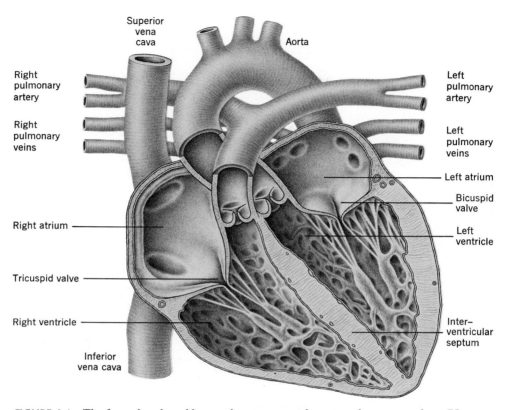

FIGURE 4.1 The four-chambered human heart, a muscular organ that pumps about 75 gallons of blood through the resting body each hour.

Source: G. E. Nelson, *Biological Principles with Human Perspectives*, 2d ed. (New York: Wiley, 1984), p. 111.

Under conditions of stress, the aging heart may be less effective than it once was. During exertion, the heart increases its rate in order to deliver oxygen through arterial blood (Fig. 4.2). When younger men exercise vigorously, their hearts may begin to beat as rapidly as 200 times per minute. By contrast, the hearts of men between 70 and 90 beat no faster than 125 times per minute under the same work load. Although no one is certain just why the maximum heart rate decreases with age and the older heart has trouble meeting the body's demands, research with rats indicates that the older heart takes more time to contract and more time to relax after each contraction. As it cannot start the next beat as soon as it once did, the heart's ability to speed up is limited (Shock, 1977b).

No matter how effectively the heart pumps, if the arteries are constricted, the oxygen-laden blood cannot pass through effectively. Indeed, the arteries age in this characteristic manner.

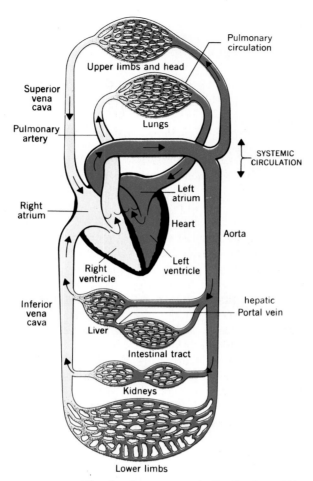

Pulmonary circulation

Upper limbs and head

Superior vena cava

Pulmonary artery

Lungs

SYSTEMIC CIRCULATION

Left atrium

Right atrium

Heart

Aorta

Right ventricle

Left ventricle

Inferior vena cava

hepatic Portal vein

Liver

Intestinal tract

Kidneys

Lower limbs

FIGURE 4.2   The circulatory system's distribution of blood throughout the body. Carbon-dioxide–laden blood flows through the veins into the right ventricle of the heart; from there it goes to the lungs, where carbon dioxide is removed and oxygen is taken up. From the lungs, blood returns to the heart's left ventricle, where it is pumped to various portions of the body.

Source: G. E. Nelson, *Biological Principles with Human Perspectives*, 2d ed. (New York: Wiley, 1984), p. 112.

ARTERIES

As arteries age, the structure of their walls gradually changes. The fibers of **elastin,** the protein that makes up about 30 percent of the arterial wall, are redistributed. They also become thin and fragmented, and some may be destroyed. While this process goes on, calcium is bound to the elastin, making the arterial walls less flexible. As the elastin content of arteries decreases, their collagen content increases. Finally, lipids, or insoluble fat particles, begin to accumulate within the arteries.

Just how much of this change is the result of normal aging is uncertain. Changes in the structure of connective tissue are probably part of the normal aging process, but the accumulation of collagen, calcium salts, and lipids resembles the condition of chronically inflamed tissue, suggesting that the walls of the arteries have been injured (Kohn, 1977). Because arterial disease is fairly common among older adults, it is difficult to separate the deterioration due to disease from the inevitable changes of aging.

These changes affect the functioning of arteries. The stiff arterial walls cannot expand as blood is pumped through them, so blood pressure generally rises somewhat with age. Although changes in the arteries tend to increase blood pressure, the increase is not universal. The blood pressure of some older individuals is no higher than that of young adults. Perhaps the usual increase is linked with factors in modern societies, including patterns of diet, food preparation, and food preservation. Among various tribal societies, the increase in blood pressure is nonexistent, slight, and typically confined to women (Kohn, 1977). These findings, together with the fact that the rise in blood pressure can often be reversed by changes in life-style, indicate that it may not be a universal characteristic of aging.

With age, an increased resistance to blood flow develops in the peripheral blood vessels. This resistance combines with the lessened power of the heart to decrease the rate at which arterial blood flows through body tissues. The decrease is most noticeable in the areas of the kidney, internal organs, fingers, and hands. Least affected are the brain, heart, and skeletal muscles (Kohn, 1977). The progressive decrease in the rate at which blood flows through tissues can explain much of the degeneration connected with aging and supports the observation that we are as old as our arteries.

CARDIOVASCULAR DISEASE

Some degree of the arterial change just described can be found in almost all older people. The thickening and stiffening of arterial walls, or hardening of the arteries, is known as **arteriosclerosis**. When hard, yellow, fatty plaques are also deposited on the arterial wall, the condition is known as **atherosclerosis**. The plaques contain collagen, lipids, and other substances. As the plaques grow, they gradually fill the artery, choking off the flow of blood. Although atherosclerosis is related to aging, plaques may begin to build up in childhood. Some researchers (Rockstein and Sussman, 1979) believe that a slight degree of atherosclerosis is an inevitable part of aging, but severe cases are considered degenerative disease.

Most people with severe atherosclerosis also have high blood pressure, or **hypertension**. The incidence of hypertension increases with age, but it is not part of the normal aging process (Fig. 4.3). A number of factors, including genetic susceptibility, stress, obesity, high salt intake, and kidney abnormalities, have been connected with the condition. Hypertension appears to speed the deposit of plaques in people with atherosclerosis.

Age	Total	White	Black	Female	Male
25 to 34 years	5.5	5.3	7.6	2.6	8.7
35 to 44 years	9.9	8.5	19.6	8.2	11.8
45 to 54 years	17.8	16.5	30.7	14.9	20.9
55 to 64 years	21.7	20.2	37.6	20.0	23.7
65 to 74 years	26.6	25.5	36.5	27.9	24.9

FIGURE 4.3   Hypertension among adults (percent). The rate of hypertension rises steadily with age and is more prevalent among blacks than whites, among men than women. However, the overall rate of hypertension dropped from 16.7 percent in the early 1960s to 14.5 percent in 1980.

Source: U.S. Bureau of the Census, 1982.

In turn, atherosclerosis contributes to the development of **ischemic heart disease**, a condition in which the heart muscle itself is starved for oxygen. Like other cardiovascular diseases, ischemic heart disease is age-related, found in 12 percent of women and 20 percent of men between the ages of 65 and 74 (Rockstein and Sussman, 1979).

Strokes, or cerebrovascular accidents, result when cerebral hemorrhages cut off blood supply to a portion of the brain. Massive strokes can be fatal; they kill more people than any other disorder except heart disease and cancer. When strokes are not fatal, they may be followed by partial paralysis, loss of memory, or aphasia, depending on the area of the brain that is affected. A piling-up of small strokes can cause a degenerative brain disorder, as we will see in Chapter 6, and in Chapter 5 we will also discover how to decrease the chances of developing cardiovascular disease.

CHANGES IN THE RESPIRATORY SYSTEM

Shortness of breath is one characteristic we connect with aging. It is the result of a reduction in the efficiency of the respiratory system. Discerning just what changes in the lungs are inevitable is especially difficult, for air pollution, smoking, and frequent respiratory infections can cause permanent damage that is easily mistaken for the effects of aging. Because the lungs are able to repair themselves, slight traces of damage are often assumed to be caused by normal aging (Klocke, 1977).

As people age, the rib cage becomes increasingly rigid, and muscle fibers become smaller and fewer in number. This tendency is increased by the stooping posture seen in many older adults, in which the spine is curved. As a result, the chest wall does not expand as far with each breath and less air can be taken into the lungs. Studies (Rizzato and Marazzini, 1970) have shown that expansion of the rib cage accounts for 40 percent of the increase in lung volume among young adults but only 30 percent of the increase among 70-year-olds.

The appearance of the lung changes over the years. Its pinkish tissue turns gray, and inhaled carbon particles adhere to it, producing patches of black.

Changes also occur inside the lungs, trachea, and bronchial tubes (Fig. 4.4). Cartilage in the trachea and bronchial tubes calcifies, making them increasingly rigid. The tubes and ducts that lead to the air sacs, or **alveoli**, within the lung enlarge at the expense of the alveoli, so that the air sacs become shallow and narrow. This change begins when people reach their forties and affects more than 80 percent of the alveoli among those in their eighties (Klocke, 1977). Although older adults have just as many air sacs as younger people, the functional respiratory surface of the lungs is gradually reduced.

Changes in the alveoli tissue are the reverse of those in the circulatory system. In the alveoli, collagen decreases and elastin increases. Among young adults, the lungs contain four times as much collagen as elastin; among 70-year-olds, there is only twice as much collagen. Because collagen is believed to be responsible for the lung's elasticity, the change further decreases the ability of the air sacs to expand with each breath (Klocke, 1977).

The blood vessels that bring carbon-dioxide–laden blood into the lung and take out oxygen-rich blood follow the aging process discussed earlier. Arterial and venous walls gradually thicken and become stiff.

As a result of all these changes, the flow of air into the lungs decreases by about 20 to 30 percent between young adulthood and old age. Although total lung capacity seems to be as great as it ever was and the rate of respiration remains about the same, other aspects of lung volume are affected by aging. Vital capacity, or the maximum amount of air that can be drawn into the lungs with a single breath, declines each year, beginning when people are in their twenties. Between the ages of 25 and 85, vital capacity decreases by 40 percent (Norris, Mittman, and Shock, 1964).

Because lung capacity remains steady and vital capacity drops, the residual volume of the lungs (which is the amount of air left in the lungs after a maximum voluntary exhalation) increases with age, rising from 20 percent of lung volume among 20-year-olds to 35 percent among 60-year-olds. Most of this increase takes place after the age of 40 (Klocke, 1977).

The exchange of gases within the lungs also declines in efficiency. The amount of oxygen within the alveoli remains steady, but the amount within the arteries as they leave the lungs drops.

It is no wonder that older people sometimes feel short of breath after exercise. Maximal oxygen uptake, which is the maximum amount of air a person can breathe in and expel during a 12-second period, begins to fall during the early twenties. By the age of 60, the average person has lost 30 percent of the maximal oxygen uptake. There are wide individual differences, however. Studies have shown that regular exercise can increase a person's maximal oxygen uptake, and former athletes have a greater maximal uptake than others (Klocke, 1977). It would appear that the reduction in maximal uptake is probably heightened in most older people by lack of exercise.

Various lung disorders are more common in older people, but they are the results of secondary aging. **Emphysema**, in which the walls separating the alveoli are destroyed, further reducing the already diminished respiratory lung surface,

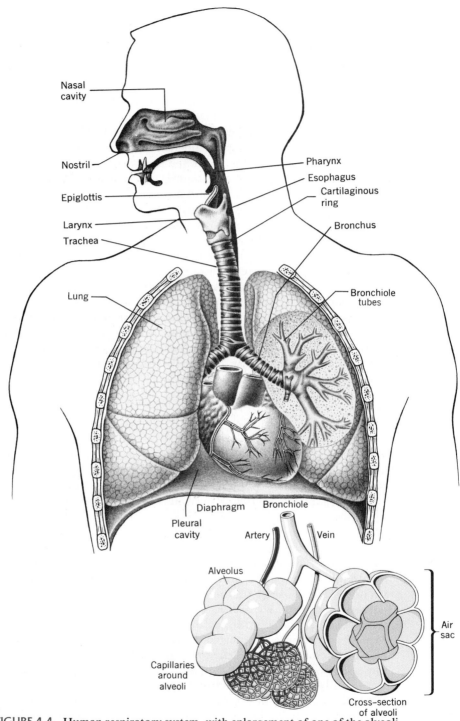

FIGURE 4.4 Human respiratory system, with enlargement of one of the alveoli.

Source: G. E. Nelson, *Biological Principles with Human Perspectives*, 2d ed. (New York: Wiley, 1984), pp. 118–119.

increases with age. People with the disease have large amounts of dead space in their lungs and take in so little air with each breath that they find any exertion difficult. The lung damage results in an ineffective exchange of oxygen and carbon dioxide, and the blood may carry so little oxygen that a person becomes confused, disoriented, or unconscious (Wantz and Gay, 1981).

Although the condition was once believed to be a part of normal aging, studies (Auerbach, Garfinkel, and Hammond, 1974) indicate that emphysema is primarily the result of smoking. The condition is rare among nonsmokers, and the slight increase of this chronic lung disease among people who have never smoked may well be due to other types of environmental damage. Lung cancer, which becomes more common with age, is also primarily the result of smoking or other environmental abuse.

The increased incidence of respiratory diseases, such as bronchitis and pneumonia, among older people may not be due to aging of the lungs. The death rate from pneumonia climbs sharply among those past 65, but such infections are often the result of other disease or may develop when the aging immune system no longer responds to invading microorganisms.

Tuberculosis also becomes more common in people past 65, but when the disease appears, it is almost always a reinfection from a dormant infection that was acquired years before. Again, the aging immune system is probably at fault. Because the incidence of tuberculosis has dropped sharply among all Americans, there will be fewer dormant infections of this disease to flare up among future generations of older people.

CHANGES IN THE GASTROINTESTINAL SYSTEM

Television commercials would lead us to think that most Americans suffer from indigestion and constipation. These complaints appear to increase with age, but the changes that accompany normal aging need not lead to these digestive difficulties (Weg, 1983). Although the esophagus, stomach, and intestinal tract alter in predictable ways (Fig. 4.5), many of the digestive complaints of the elderly are the result of the diseases of secondary aging or their life-style.

Food moves through the esophagus by wavelike contractions that sweep the food into the stomach. With age, these contractions may become less dependable. Among people in their nineties, only 50 percent of swallows are followed by typical contractions. After most of the other swallows, the contractions are sporadic and ringlike, making the esophagus look like a corkscrew, but without moving the food along. In addition, more than 50 percent of the time the muscle that closes the lower part of the esophagus fails to relax after a swallow, retaining food in the passage. Among young adults the wavelike contractions followed swallowing at least 90 percent of the time, with corkscrew contractions apparent after only 10 percent of swallows (Soergel, Zboralske, and Amberg, 1964). Although these changes in the elderly slow the passage of food into the stomach, research suggests that disease, not normal aging, may be responsible for a good deal of the delay. These studies indicate that only one change distinguished

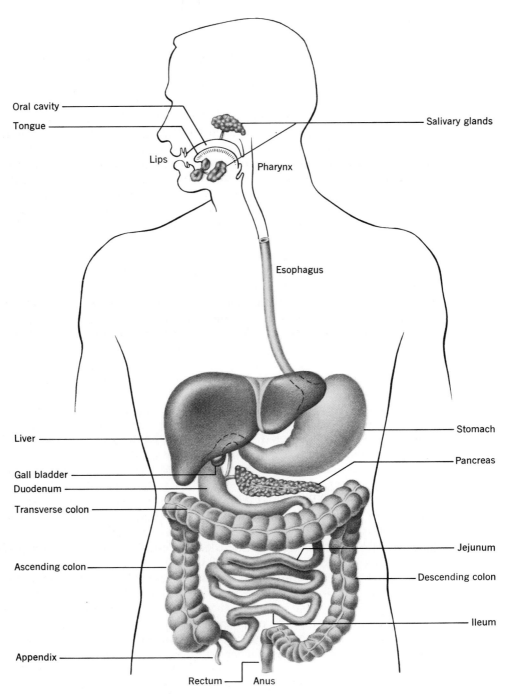

FIGURE 4.5 Major portions of the human digestive tract.

Source: G. E. Nelson, *Biological Principles with Human Perspectives*, 2d ed. (New York: Wiley, 1984), p. 94.

esophageal response in the young and old: weaker contractions from less efficient esophageal muscles (Bhanthumnavin and Schuster, 1977).

Within the stomach, the secretion of hydrochloric acid, which is necessary for protein digestion, decreases steadily from the age of 50, with the drop in production larger in men than in women. Up to the age of 70, a rising proportion of people fail to produce any stomach acid at all, a condition that ultimately affects about 23 percent of the men and 28 percent of women. Such people generally suffer from **atrophic gastritis**, a chronic inflammation of the stomach lining that is characterized by a destruction of both mucous and peptic glands, so that production of the digestive enzyme pepsin is also reduced (Rockstein and Sussman, 1979). Atropic gastritis is not the result of normal aging and may be caused by repeated injury of the stomach lining by such things as aspirin, alcohol, bile salts and acids, and overproduction of gammaglobulin, a substance produced by the immune system in response to foreign material (Bhanthumnavin and Schuster, 1977).

Our knowledge of age-related changes in the intestinal tract is meager because intestinal tissues deteriorate so rapidly after removal from the body. Aging intestines secrete the same enzymes as youthful intestines, but in lesser amounts. The decrease appears to begin before the age of 30 (Rockstein and Sussman, 1979). Although there is marked atrophy of muscle tissue, the mucous layer of the older intestine, and the layers beneath it, most older people absorb nutrients from their food as well as ever. The only exception appears to be the absorption of one of the simple sugars among individuals older than 80 (Bhanthumnavin and Schuster, 1977). The lack of impairment in nutrient absorption is probably due to the enormous reserve capacity of the small intestine.

With age, smooth muscle in the wall of the large intestine is reduced, and the remaining muscle loses some of its tone. However, the prevalence of constipation among older people is probably due to decreased fluid intake, lack of bulk in the diet, and lack of exercise. These same factors, together with laxative abuse and drugs prescribed for other conditions, may lead to the development of **diverticulosis**, a condition in which irregular pouches develop along the walls of the large intestine. These small sacs can become obstructed, infected, and painfully inflamed. The condition is rarely seen in people under the age of 30, but afflicts about 8 percent of adults between 30 and 60. Among adults past 70, 40 percent have diverticulosis. It might be considered a disease of modern society (Bhanthumnavin and Schuster, 1977).

The other gastrointestinal organs also show the effects of age. After a person reaches 50 or 60, the liver may begin to shrink in size, the structure of its cells may change, it may be more sluggish in responding to stimuli that provoke enzyme production, and the enzymes themselves may be less concentrated. However, we have much more liver tissue than we need and can lose 80 percent of the liver without seriously reducing its function (Bhanthumnavin and Schuster, 1977). The primary effect of aging on the liver is to reduce its ability to metabolize some drugs, so that dosages may have to be reduced for older patients.

The walls of the gallbladder tend to shrink and thicken with age, but in most people the organ continues to function efficiently. The primary function of the gallbladder is to store bile produced by the liver. When bile becomes supersaturated with cholesterol, gallstones may develop, a condition that becomes increasingly common with age (Bhanthumnavin and Schuster, 1977). Gallstones may block the bile duct so that the gall bladder cannot discharge its reservoir of bile. The obstruction causes indigestion, nausea, pain, vomiting, an inability to digest fats, and jaundice—a yellowing of the skin and eyes. Surgery is the most common treatment for gallstones, but drugs have now been developed that can dissolve the stones.

Although there is an increasing incidence of gastrointestinal disorders among the elderly, most of the disorders are also found in younger adults. Among older people, however, they are generally more serious. In about 56 percent of the cases, no organic reason can be found for the disorder (Rockstein and Sussman, 1979). Such functional disorders, whose symptoms include heartburn, belching, nausea, and diarrhea, are often the result of emotional or psychological problems.

CHANGES IN THE EXECRETORY SYSTEM

Normal aging of the execretory system can be a minor nuisance. Because the capacity of the bladder gradually diminishes with age, the majority of people past 65 (70 percent of men and 61 percent of women) find themselves getting up in the middle of the night to urinate (Rockstein and Sussman, 1979). Although there are major anatomical changes in the kidney, for most older people, the system continues to work in a reasonably efficient manner.

The kidney's function is to cleanse the bloodstream of waste products; to regulate the salt, glucose, and alkaline (pH) levels of the blood; and to maintain the balance of fluids in the body (Fig. 4.6). Aging of the kidneys begins at about the age of 30, when the organ begins to shrink, until at the age of 90 it has lost 32 percent of its original weight (Goldman, 1977). Within the kidney, glomeruli, tiny coils of arterial capillaries that supply blood to the working kidney units, gradually decrease until the 80-year-old has only half the normal supply. Of the remaining glomeruli, only 63 percent are normal.

The arteries that supply the kidney show the typical changes found in the circulatory system as collagen is deposited and muscle fiber lost. This stiffening process may be mild in people with normal blood pressure, but is often severe in those with hypertension, which accelerates and intensifies the change (Goldman, 1977).

As the kidney ages, the rate at which it filters the blood declines, falling steadily after the age of 21. By the age of 80, the filtration rate has dropped by about 31 percent (Rockstein and Sussman, 1979). The speed with which blood passes through the kidneys and at which glucose is reabsorbed from the tubular fluid that eventually becomes urine also decreases. The urine produced by the older kidney is less concentrated than it once was.

No one is certain just why the capacity of the bladder shrinks during the aging process; there seems to be no structural change in the organ that accounts for it (Goldman, 1977). Signals from the aging bladder also change. During young and

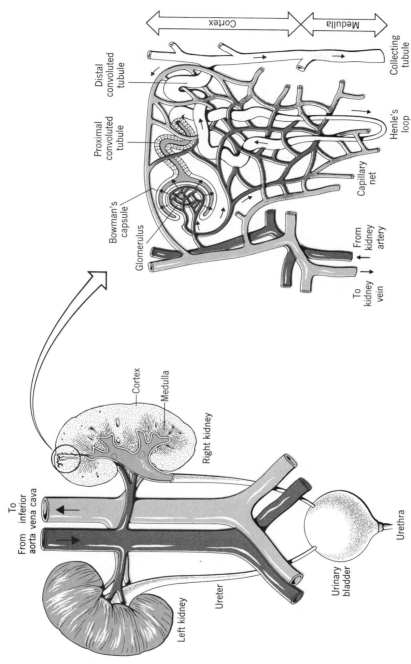

FIGURE 4.6   Excretory system, with enlargement of a nephron, or kidney tubule, which is the functional unit of the kidney.

Source: G. E. Nelson, *Biological Principles with Human Perspectives*, 2d ed. (New York: Wiley, 1984), p. 183.

middle adulthood, the sensation of bladder fullness, which leads us to urinate, is felt when the bladder is about half-full. But among older adults, the urge to urinate is not felt until the bladder is nearly full, and some older people never do receive the sensation. When the signal does come, it reqiires an immediate response. The bladder also fails to empty as fully as it did during youth. Together these changes explain the increased frequency of urination among older adults.

Infections of the urinary tract also increase with age. Among women, the rate of infection jumps from less than 6 percent to more than 20 percent by the age of 65. Among men, the initial rate of infection is lower, but there is a sudden and more severe increase around the age of 70 (Goldman, 1977). This rise may be due to some sort of anatomical change in the execretory system or to a decline in the bladder's ability to maintain sterile urine and defend itself against infection.

CHANGES IN THE ENDOCRINE SYSTEM

Many aspects of development are affected by the endocrine system, including reproduction, metabolism, balance of the body's internal environment, its response to stress and disease, and even the process of aging itself. Although the effects of aging on the endocrine system are crucial, the system is so complex that our understanding of the process is meager. Aging could affect the endocrine system in many ways. It could reduce hormone secretion of the glands. It could produce a loss of responsiveness to hormones in various receptors within body cells. It could lead to changes in the "second messengers" that transmit hormonal signals to the interior of body cells. Or it could alter the level of enzymes that must carry out hormone-regulated activities (Marx, 1979).

Among the glands of the endocrine system are the hypothalamus, pituitary, thyroid, parathyroid, pancreas, adrenals, gonads (ovaries and testes), and thymus (Fig. 4.7). Each of these glands affects body function by releasing hormones directly into the bloodstream. The endocrine system operates through an intricate system of feedback, which is supervised by the pituitary under the control of the brain. Any discussion of the gonads is omitted from this section because we will examine aging of the reproductive system separately.

PITUITARY

Age seems to cause no significant change in the size and weight of the pituitary, which is considered the master gland of the endocrine system. This gland is especially important because some researchers believe that the pituitary sets off the aging process when so instructed by the hypothalamus. In fact, when the pituitary gland is removed from the brain of young rats and three of its ten or more hormones are supplied by injection, the animals do not age. Cross-linking within body cells slows, kidney damage decreases, the heart stays healthy, and the arteries seem to rejuvenate (Walford, 1983).

The pituitary gland itself shows characteristic signs of aging. Beginning with puberty, the supply of blood reaching the gland decreases so that by the age of 60

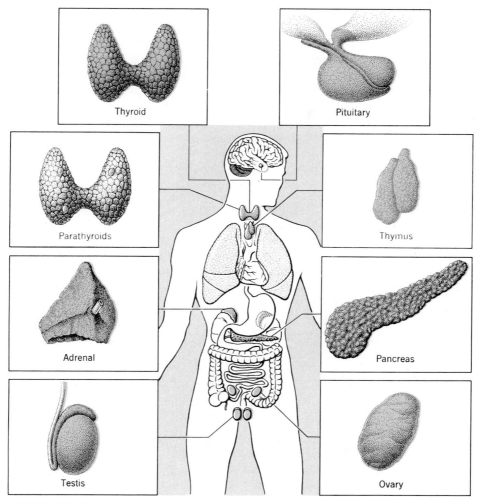

FIGURE 4.7   The endocrine system.

Source: G. E. Nelson, *Biological Principles with Human Perspectives*, 2d ed. (New York: Wiley, 1984), p. 129.

the amount of blood reaching it has been significantly reduced (Rockstein and Sussman, 1979). There is also an increase of connective tissue and a change in the way various cell types are distributed throughout the gland.

Among the hormones produced by the pituitary is growth hormone (GH), which affects metabolism and tissue growth and promotes tissue repair. The amount of GH in the bloodstream is affected by sex and obesity. Women generally have higher levels than men, and the obese have higher levels than the non-obese. Among women of normal weight, GH levels are lower after the age of 40. Although the fasting level of GH appears to decline with age, the pituitary never loses its ability to produce the hormone. In response to a sharp drop in blood sugar, the average increase of GH in the blood of people from 63 to 99 years of age is similar to the response found in younger adults (Andres and Tobin, 1977).

After adolescence, the pituitary's production of thyroid-stimulating hormone (TSH) seems to show no change with age. Although TSH levels are highest in children and adolescents, there appear to be no age-related trends in blood levels among adults. Similarly, the pituitary content of ACTH, the hormone that controls the adrenal glands, seems to remain constant, and the ability to secrete adrenal-stimulating hormones in response to stress is adequate.

PARATHYROID

The parathyroid glands continue to grow after maturity, increasing in weight until the age of 30 in men and 50 in women. Afterward they remain steady, showing no decrease in size among older adults. Nor is there any decrease in the amount of hormones they secrete, which play an important role in the metabolism of calcium and phosphate (Rockstein and Sussman, 1979).

THYROID

Anatomical changes do occur in the thyroid. The individual cells undergo characteristic change with age, and fibers of collagen appear within the gland. The production of thyroid hormones also appears to decrease with age, yet their levels in the blood remain constant. Thyroid hormones play a role in the metabolism of fats and carbohydrates, and they also spur oxygen consumption by body cells. Another thyroid hormone causes the bones to absorb calcium and phosphate. Because elderly people show a marked increase in hormone production during an acute infectious illness, it would seem that the thyroid functions normally despite advanced age (Andres and Tobin, 1977).

PANCREAS

A primary job of the pancreas is to produce insulin, which is essential for the metabolism of carbohydrates. When carbohydrates have been changed to glucose within the body, insulin stimulates its transport into the cells. When this process breaks down, diabetes develops. Although insufficient production of insulin can cause diabetes, most people who develop the disease late in life produce normal or above-normal levels of insulin. "Maturity-onset" diabetes, which shows up during the forties or later, appears to be the result of a reduced sensitivity of body tissues to insulin (Marx, 1979). (See Fig. 4.8.)

Tests show that the ability to dispose of glucose efficiently declines progressively during adulthood. In many older adults, the release of insulin in response to a rise in blood glucose is delayed in comparison with younger adults, and a

	Total Adult	20–44 Years	45–64 Years	Over 64 Years
Male	3.4	0.9	5.0	9.3
Female	4.1	1.4	5.6	9.8
White	3.5	1.1	4.7	9.3
Black	5.8	2.3	10.5	11.8

FIGURE 4.8 Incidence of adult diabetes (percent). The abrupt rise in diabetes among middle-aged and older adults reflects the appearance of "maturity-onset" diabetes in people who produce insulin but whose body tissues have become relatively insensitive to the substance.

Source: U.S. Bureau of the Census, 1982.

smaller amount is released. In addition, more inactive insulin is released by older adults. Because older cells absorb less glucose and leave more in the blood, glucose levels remain high long after a load enters the bloodstream (Weg, 1983). Researchers are uncertain whether this widespread decline in the ability to handle glucose is part of normal aging or a disorder. Although more than half of adults past 65 show reduced glucose tolerance, fewer than 10 percent have any signs of diabetes (Rockstein and Sussman, 1979).

ADRENAL GLANDS

The adrenal glands, which perch just above each kidney, increase in size until the age of 30. After that time the glands remain about the same weight. There are, however, marked structural changes. Lipofuscin accumulates within the glands, collagen proliferates, blood vessels enlarge, and some bleeding occurs (Andres and Tobin, 1977).

Several body systems are affected by the hormones these glands produce. Their production of epinephrine and norepinephrine affects our response to stress. They are involved in the metabolism of fat and carbohydrates, they affect kidney function, and they produce androgens (male hormones) in both men and women.

Androgen production clearly declines with age, as does the level of androgens in the blood. However, when stimulated by injections of ACTH, both young and old people show a similar rise in androgen levels. As the resting level is lower among older individuals, however, their androgen level remains lower than that of young people (Andres and Tobin, 1977). No one knows why androgens decline in old age.

The blood level of hormones that regulate fat and carbohydrate metabolism does not change with age in healthy adults. However, the rate at which these hormones are metabolized slows; it takes 40 percent longer for a 75-year-old man to metabolize them than for a 33-year-old to do so (Andres and Tobin, 1977). Hormones that affect the kidney's absorption of sodium and chloride also show little change, so that the salt and water balance in the elderly remains normal (Rockstein and Sussman, 1979).

THYMUS GLAND

The thymus gland grows until puberty, then begins to shrink, as its cortex slowly atrophies and is replaced with connective tissue and fat. The thymus gland is important because it is an essential part of the immune system, producing T-cells, which reject foreign cell tissue and rid the body of tumor cells. Although B-cells, which are produced in the bone marrow, bear the primary responsibility for the production of antibodies, the thymus plays a role here as well. Most antigen responses of B-cells apparently require the help of T-cells (Mackinodan, 1977).

As the thymus shrinks, its production of hormones decreases, with the decline accelerating between the ages of 25 and 45 (Walford, 1983). In response to the dip in hormone production, the level of antibodies in the blood also declines. The immune functions of T-cells appear to weaken with age—unless people have previously been sensitized to the invading substance. This degeneration of the immune system may predispose people to infections, cancer, and autoimmune diseases such as maturity-onset diabetes and one form of anemia (Mackinodan, 1977). It has been suggested that because of its responsibility for immune system function, the thymus is a primary pacemaker for aging (Walford, 1983).

CHANGES IN THE REPRODUCTIVE SYSTEM

Some older adults have always quietly enjoyed their sexuality in a society that believed sex "didn't matter" in old age and that only abnormal old people were interested in it (Kay and Neelley, 1982). Changing attitudes, backed by research findings, appear to be making active sexuality more common in later years. In fact, sexual expression can continue throughout the life of reasonably healthy adults.

Continued sexuality does not mean that the reproductive system remains youthful. Aging changes the structure and functioning of the reproductive system and alters the experience of sexuality in predictable ways, but none of the changes should prevent the enjoyment of sexuality in reasonably healthy adults. Although we tend to think of reproductive aging as beginning in middle age, some aspects of the process begin during youth. After separate looks at the male and female reproductive systems, we will describe changes in sexuality across adulthood.

MALE REPRODUCTIVE SYSTEM

Because reproductive function is closely tied to the endocrine system, changes in patterns of hormone release should be related to physiological changes with age. In the adult male, two hormones secreted by the pituitary gland, follicle-stimulating hormone (FSH) and luteinizing hormone (LH), control the production of hormones in the testes. FSH is necessary for the maturation of sperm cells, and LH stimulates the production of the male hormone, testosterone, within the testes. As testosterone levels rise in the bloodstream, they signal the pituitary to cut back on its secretion of LH.

There is some uncertainty about the effect of aging on the production of FSH and LH. In some studies, an increase has been found only in LH levels among men past 65 whereas in other studies an increase has been found in both hormones (Talbert, 1977). Testosterone production has long been thought to decrease after the age of 60, but recent research indicates that the drop in testosterone levels found in many studies may be the result of secondary aging. Among a group of 76 healthy older men there was no decline in testosterone levels, and some of the men had slightly higher levels than the average young man (Marx, 1979). It may be that production declines somewhat, but that it takes the aging body longer to metabolize the hormone and clear it from the system. The testes' production of estrogen, a female hormone, rises in old age (Fig. 4.9). (Both sexes produce male *and* female hormones, but in different proportions.) The relationship between hormone levels and sexual activity is not clearly understood.

Sperm production continues throughout life, but as the testes age, fewer sperm are produced. Among men between the ages of 20 and 39, developing sperm cells are present in 90 percent of the sperm-producing tubules. During the forties, tubules gradually lose their function until only about 50 percent are producing sperm, a level that remains fairly constant until men are about 70 years old. Then there is another decline, so that in men past 80, only 10 percent of tubules function. Although sperm production ceases altogether in some men, others are capa-

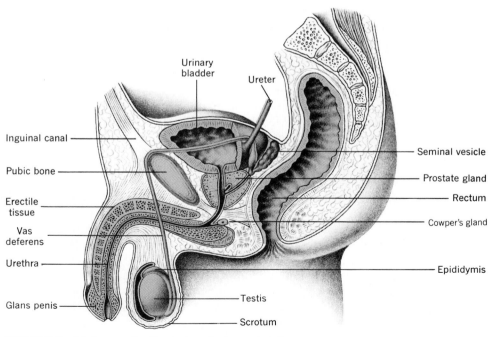

FIGURE 4.9   Male reproductive system and associated structures.

Source: G. E. Nelson, *Biological Principles with Human Perspectives*, 2d ed. (New York: Wiley, 1984), p. 221.

ble of fathering children into their 90s. Among men between the ages of 80 and 90, 48 percent have sperm in their ejaculate (Talbert, 1977).

Cells in the prostate gland, which secretes the sperm-carrying fluid, begin to age in the forties. At the same time, collagen replaces muscle tissue, and blood supply to the gland decreases. In most men the prostate begins to grow, so that it is about 40 percent heavier during the fifties and sixties. By the time men reach their seventies, it may have doubled in size. Often the gland becomes so large that it interferes with bladder function and must be removed (Rockstein and Sussman, 1979).

The penis may begin to show characteristic signs of aging as early as the thirties. Tissues and blood vessels undergo typical hardening and lose elasticity. Because erection depends upon blood supply to the penis, these changes affect the speed and firmness of an erection. Among men in their fifties, it takes about six times as long for an erection to develop as it does among men in their twenties (Solnick and Birren, 1977). By the age of 60, the angle of the erect penis generally has changed from 45° to 90° (Comfort, 1980). Unless some abnormal condition that interferes with penile blood or nerve supply develops, however, no further change will occur.

FEMALE REPRODUCTIVE SYSTEM

Aging in the female reproductive system is also linked to hormone production, and the consequences are clearer. Although men may be able to father children throughout the life span, few women past the age of 50 have given birth. The female pituitary gland produces FSH and LH, just as the male pituitary does. In women, FSH stimulates the growth of ovarian follicles, in which ova mature, whereas LH causes ovulation and the production of the female hormones, estrogen and progesterone. The ovaries also produce male hormones, as do the adrenal glands, and some of these androgens are converted to estrogen within the body (Fig. 4.10).

Although men continue to produce new sperm throughout life, all the ova a woman will ever produce are present in an immature form at birth. If loss of ova is considered a sign of aging, the ovaries begin to age as soon as a woman is born, for these cells decline from 700,000 per ovary at birth to 389,000 at puberty to 162,000 between the ages of 18 and 24. By the time a woman is 40, each ovary probably has no more than about 11,000 immature ova (Rockstein and Sussman, 1979).

Fertility gradually declines during the forties, and menstrual periods become shorter and irregular. The **climacteric**, or "change of life" has begun, and the ovaries gradually cease functioning. At about the age of 50 or so, the menstrual cycle lengthens, becomes increasingly irregular, and finally stops, signaling that the woman has reached **menopause**. With menopause, estrogen and progesterone production drops off sharply, and the amount of these hormones in the blood diminishes. Androgens continue to be secreted, although at lower levels, and an increase in the conversion of androgens to estrogen ensures that some of the hor-

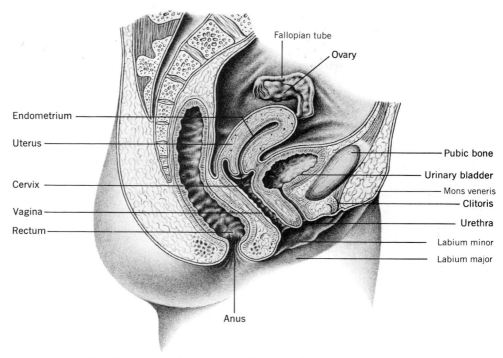

Labels on figure: Fallopian tube, Ovary, Endometrium, Uterus, Cervix, Vagina, Rectum, Anus, Pubic bone, Urinary bladder, Mons veneris, Clitoris, Urethra, Labium minor, Labium major

FIGURE 4.10 Female reproductive system and surrounding structures.

Source: G. E. Nelson, *Biological Principles with Human Perspectives*, 2d ed. (New York: Wiley, 1984), p. 216.

mone will be present in the blood stream (Solnick and Corby, 1983). By two years after menopause, blood levels of FSH are 18 times higher than they were before the climacteric, and LH levels are three times higher (Hammond and Maxon, 1982).

Common symptoms of menopause include headaches, backaches, nervousness, hot flashes, and coldness. Hot flashes coincide with increases of LH, and both the sudden sensation of heat and the surge of hormone appear to be caused by changes in the function of the hypothalamus (Marx, 1979). Other menopausal symptoms may be linked to shifting estrogen level although many women have no symptoms at all. Only 25 percent of the women in a large health-screening program reported any uncomfortable menopausal symptoms (Corby and Solnick, 1980).

As estrogen levels decline, the vagina shortens and narrows because tissues in the vaginal walls have become thinner and less expansive. This vaginal atrophy can be prevented by estrogen therapy, which also controls hot flashes and helps to prevent osteoporosis. However, women must be carefully screened for this treatment, for it may increase the risk of cancer and gallbladder disease (Hammond and Maxon, 1982). Recent research (Leiblum et al., 1983) indicates that continued sexual activity, whether intercourse or masturbation, reduces vaginal atrophy and is accompanied by higher estrogen levels.

AGING AND SEXUALITY

Physiological aging affects the expression of sexuality and generally requires some sort of adjustment (Masters and Johnson, 1966). By the time men are in their sixties, each stage of the sexual response cycle has lengthened. Older men can maintain an erection much longer before ejaculating than younger men; the feeling that ejaculation is inevitable may disappear, the number of orgasmic contractions diminishes, and the refractory period, in which an erection cannot occur, lengthens. In fact, the refractory period is one of the first signs of aging; it begins to lengthen while men are still in their twenties (Rosen and Hall, 1984).

In postmenopausal women, the increase in breast size during sexual stimulation is reduced, vaginal lubrication is slower and scantier, preorgasmic color changes in the external genitals are less common, and the number of orgasmic contractions diminishes.

None of these changes need have a significant impact on the basic ability to enjoy sexual activity. Indeed, the ability of the male to maintain an erection for longer periods may make intercourse more pleasurable for both partners, for some women require extensive stimulation in order to reach orgasm (Solnick and Corby, 1983).

Yet studies consistently have indicated that the rate of sexual activity declines with age, and many older people give up sexual activity altogether. In one study of adults between the ages of 60 and 93, 25 percent of those who had passed their seventy-fifth birthday were still sexually active. In another study, 47 percent of those between the ages of 60 and 71 still had regular, frequent intercourse, as did 15 percent of those past the age of 78 (Comfort, 1980).

One reason for diminished sexual activity is disease. Some diseases, such as diabetes, affect sexual activity directly. About half of diabetic men cannot have erec-

Although physiological aging affects sexual response, it does not eliminate either sexual desire or its expression. Healthy women and men can remain sexually active throughout life.

tions, and diabetic women seem to become less responsive, so that they require long, intense stimulation to reach orgasm (Rosen and Hall, 1984). Any disease that affects male hormone balance, nerve pathways to the pelvic area, or blood supply to the penis can lead to erectile failure as can some medication that is prescribed for other conditions. However, only the most severe diseases make sexual pleasure impossible (Solnick and Corby, 1983).

Another reason for the decline in sexual activity among old people is the lack of a partner. Because women tend marry men older than themselves and to outlive them, the rate of sexual activity tends to be higher in men than in women.

Psychological factors also affect sexuality among older people. One of the best predictors of continued sexual intercourse is early sexual activity and past sexual enjoyment and frequency (Solnick and Corby, 1983). People who have never had much pleasure from sexuality may regard their age as a good excuse for giving up sex.

As we have seen, historical factors can affect the experience of aging, and changed sexual attitudes may affect sexuality among older adults. The change may already have begun. In one study (Starr and Weiner, 1981), 70- and 80-year-olds reported rates of intercourse much like those Kinsey found among 40-year-olds in the 1940s and 1950s. As today's younger adults age, the level of sexual activity among older men and women may rise.

CHANGES IN THE NERVOUS SYSTEM

The myths and misconceptions that surround aging in the nervous system can create unnecessary concern about aging. We fear that growing old means becoming confused, disoriented, and unable to care for ourselves. But this vision of a nervous system in shambles in unwarranted. As we will see in Chapter 6, a relatively small proportion of old people develop any of the conditions commonly referred to as "senility," and they are never the result of normal aging.

Aging in the nervous system is critical because all other body systems are coordinated by this system. The central nervous system, made up of the brain and spinal cord, controls body functioning through nerve fibers in the voluntary muscles, through the autonomic nervous system, or through the brain's signals to the endocrine system. Although we have learned a great deal about the structure and functioning of the nervous system in the past decade or so, we still are not certain about the effect of normal aging on the system's anatomy. Our uncertainty comes from the fact that until recently most of our knowledge of changes in the human brain was limited to evidence present after death. Because nutrition, cardiovascular status, respiratory function, cancer, organic brain disease, and the use of alcohol and drugs can have large effects on brain tissue, it has been difficult to separate such changes from the effects of normal aging and from tissue deterioration after death (Bondareff, 1980).

A good deal of our current knowledge is based on inferences from animal studies, but technological advances promise new information about the aging human brain. CAT scans, which were discussed earlier, show cross-sections of living brain tissue. Position emission tomography (PET) provides a picture of brain function. Short-lived radioactive fluorine is attached to glucose, and the sugar is injected into the body. PET scans produce images of the active brain, allowing researchers to follow its function by tracing the uptake of radioactive glucose. Finally, nuclear magnetic resonance (NMR) scans are made by enclosing the body in a magnetic field and using radio waves to produce images of tissue, biochemical activity, and metabolism. As these new devices are used, our understanding of the central nervous system—as well as all other body functions—soon may take a giant step forward.

CENTRAL NERVOUS SYSTEM

Study of aging in the central nervous system has focused on the brain, which appears to shrink over the years (Fig. 4.11). Studies have shown that with age, the brain loses weight, there is increased space between the brain and the skull, and its ventricles (the spaces deep within the brain) expand. It has been estimated that the adult brain loses 5 percent of its mass by the age of 70, 10 percent by the age of 80, and 20 percent by the age of 90. But when studies are limited to the brains of elderly people who were functioning normally at the time of death, the amount of shrinkage is less (Adams, 1980).

Increases in ventricular size have been studied by using CAT scans. One such study showed a gradual increase in ventricular size from the age of 10, followed by a rapid increase between the ages of 70 and 90 (Barron, Jacobs, and Kinkel, 1976). However, the expected increase has failed to appear in some studies (Brody and Vijayashankar, 1977), and when repeated CAT scans are made of the same individuals, the increases sometimes have reversed themselves (Jernigan et al., 1980).

Changes in Neurons

Like cells in the heart, brain cells cannot replace themselves. Neurons die, perhaps daily, but with little effect on brain function. The loss appears to be limited to particular layers of neurons in certain regions of the brain. Cells in one layer of the cerebellum, a structure at the base of the brain that coordinates voluntary muscle activity and maintains physical balance, begin to decrease noticeably after the age of 60. Cell loss in the cerebral cortex, the gray matter that covers the brain's hemispheres, is selective, with decreases found in a few areas but not in others (Bondareff, 1980).

Over the years neurons may lose some of their dendrites (the fibers that bring nerve impulses into the cell body), and terminal branches of the axon (which conducts nerve impulses away from the cell) may also disappear (Fig. 4.12). Loss of these connecting fibers cuts contact between neurons. However, such atrophy, as well as the growth of new fibers, appears to go on throughout normal life. When researchers (Buell and Coleman, 1979) examined normal brains after autopsy, they discovered more, and longer, dendritic branches in older adults (aged 68 to

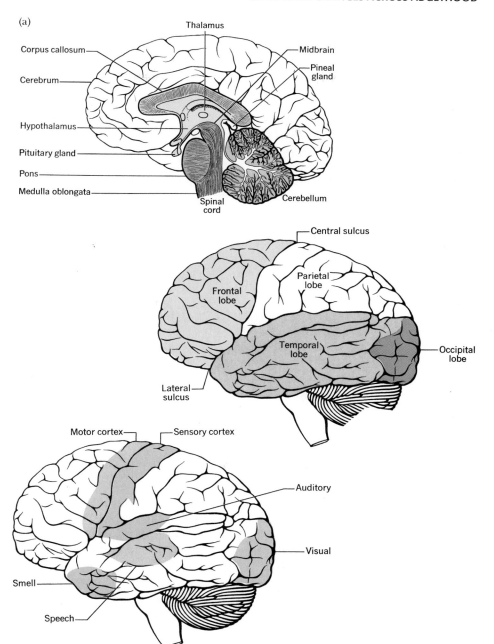

FIGURE 4.11   (*a*) Longitudinal section of the human brain, showing its major parts; (*b*) subdivisions of the cerebrum, showing its left hemisphere; (*c*) functional areas of the cortex, the 2-to-5-millimeter-thick coating of gray matter that covers the cerebrum.

Source: G. E. Nelson, *Biological Principles with Human Perspectives*, 2d ed. (New York: Wiley, 1984), pp. 170–171.

92) than in middle-aged adults (aged 45 to 55). Only neurons in the brains of adults suffering from senile dementia showed gross dendritic atrophy. Serious and permanent loss of neuronal connections is probably the result of organic brain disease, which will be discussed in Chapter 6.

Unconditioned reflexes are often controlled by neurons at the level of the spinal cord, and these reflexes may change with age. After the age of 60, some simple reflexes begin to weaken or disappear in some people. For example, the knee jerk reflex was absent in 15 percent of a group of 70- to 80-year-olds, and the ankle jerk had disappeared in 70 percent of them. By the age of 90, the various jerk reflexes seem to disappear in most people (Rockstein and Sussman, 1979).

Changes are also seen in the cell bodies of the brain. Dense granules surrounded by fluid-filled cavities, called **vacuoles**, may appear after the age of 60. These vacuoles are most prevalent in diseased brains, but some researchers have found them in 75 percent of brain samples from people older than 80. **Senile plaques**, patches composed of debris, are also more likely to appear in diseased than in normal brains, but at least a few seem inevitable once people are more than 90 years old (Adams, 1980). **Neurofibrillary tangles**, bundles of paired helical filaments made up of polypeptides—a type of protein—are often found in aging brains, but their connection with normal aging has not been clearly established (Bondareff, 1980).

Lipofuscin accumulates in the brain as it does in other parts of the body. Its appearance is not always a signal of aging, however, because it has been found in children's brains. Over the life span the pigment accumulates, appearing in different areas of the brain at different ages. There is no clear indication that lipofuscin harms neurons or interferes with their functioning although the accumulation of a related pigment, ceroid, is associated with brain disease (Bondareff, 1980).

As the release of neurotransmitters into the space between neurons either causes a neuron to fire or keeps it from firing, any change in the concentration of these chemicals will affect brain function. With aging, reduced amounts of some important brain transmitters have been found in the brains of rats, as well as an increasing slowness on the part of neurons to take up available transmitters (Bondareff, 1980). Little is known about the effect of age on the production or uptake of neurotransmitters in human beings, but the destruction of pathways that carry one transmitter, dopamine, is connected with Parkinson's disease, a serious condition that becomes more common with age.

Changes in Neuroglia

Neurons are not the only cells in the central nervous system. The tissue that supports the brain and spinal cord is known as neuroglia. At one time, it was believed that these glial cells normally increased in number with age. It is now thought that an increase in the number of glial cells probably does not occur in normal aging, but is a response to the degeneration of neurons or dendrites. One type of glial cell, the **astrocyte**, apparently increases in size during old age. The cell body, and

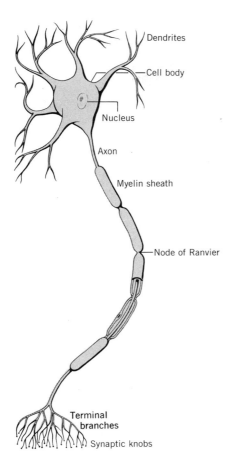

Dendrites

Cell body

Nucleus

Axon

Myelin sheath

Node of Ranvier

Terminal branches

Synaptic knobs

FIGURE 4.12   A brain cell, or neuron, and its major parts.

Source: G. E. Nelson, *Biological Principles with Human Perspectives*, 2d ed. (New York: Wiley, 1984), p. 147.

not its fibers, grows. One of the roles of astrocytes is to keep neurotransmitters from accumulating in the space between neurons, and perhaps the enlargement of these cells is connected with their role in maintaining the neural environment (Bondareff, 1980).

Brain Activity

Although nerve impulses are started and stopped by chemicals, the impulse itself is electrical. This electrical activity can be studied by attaching electrodes to the scalp and recording the impulses on an electroencephalogram (EEG). Several changes in brain activity are associated with aging, and characteristic differences appear between EEGs of healthy older people and those who are suffering from various degenerative diseases.

Brain waves differ in frequency and amplitude and are distinguished by frequency, or cycles per second (Hz). The more rapid the rhythm of the waves, the more alert and mentally active a person is. Delta waves, the slowest (1–3 Hz), predominate in deep sleep. Theta waves are slightly faster (4–7 Hz). Alpha waves, with a frequency of 8–13 Hz, appear when people are awake and relaxed or when they are meditating. Beta waves, the fastest (14–40 Hz), appear during aroused mental activity.

Slow wave activity, a combination of delta and theta waves, appears with increasing frequency as people age and may indicate a decrease of blood flow to the brain, accompanied by a slowing of metabolism. Healthy adults who are less than 75 years old show no more slow wave activity than is found in the EEG of young adults. Once past the age of 75, however, slow wave activity increases in the EEG of about 20 percent of older people. Cardiovascular disease has been proposed as the cause of this slowing of brain waves. When slow wave activity is diffuse, that is, spread over the entire brain, it often is accompanied by impaired mental functioning as measured by IQ tests (Marsh and Thompson, 1977).

Some older people show bursts of high voltage slow waves from small areas of the brain. This activity begins to appear at about the age of 50, and by the age of 65 the bursts are seen in the EEGs of from 30 to 50 percent of healthy older people. There seems to be no connection between such activity and any impairment (Marsh and Thompson, 1977).

Alpha waves seem to decline in amplitude with age. They may also become slower, falling at the low end of the frequency range. Some researchers believe that waves in the 7 Hz range should be considered alpha frequency in older adults. However, not all older adults show this alpha slowing. In fact, nearly a quarter of the 60- to 80-year-olds in one study showed an increase in alpha frequency (Wang and Busse, 1969).

When the amount of alpha activity decreases, it is replaced with slow wave activity. Although slowed alpha is generally connected with decreased blood flow to the brain, especially during stress, it has been found in some healthy adults. In one longitudinal study, decline in alpha frequency over a 12-year period was correlated with drops in IQ test scores, but only among adults in the highly educated, upper socioeconomic group (Wang, Obrist, and Busse, 1970).

Beta activity remains as fast as ever in healthy older adults, and some researchers have reported finding an increase in the amount of beta activity among 60- to 70-year-olds. Among adults who are more than 80 years old, beta activity seems to decrease in amount, and in severely deteriorated hospital patients the amount of beta activity is sharply reduced (Marsh and Thompson, 1977). With age, brain activity also changes during sleep.

CHANGES IN SLEEP PATTERNS

Throughout the life cycle, the amount of time spent sleeping declines from the 16 hours each day of the newborn's sleep to the 7 or 8 hours each adult spends in sleep. Older adults often complain that they sleep very little or that they frequently wake during the night. Their sleep patterns have changed, but most still sleep 7 to 8 hours out of every 24.

With age, sleep no longer comes in one chunk. The aging body rarely remains asleep all night without waking. Most older adults wake during the night, go back to sleep for a second stretch, then supplement their 5 or 6 hours of nightly sleep with a nap during the day. However, there appears to be a sex difference in sleep patterns among people in their fifties. At least during this decade, the sleep patterns of men are more disturbed than those of women (Webb, 1982).

Frequent wakings during the night are sometimes due to the need to urinate, but sleep researchers have found two characteristics of sleep among the elderly that may also contribute to the disturbances (Hubbard, 1982). The first is **sleep apnea,** in which a person stops breathing for at least 10 seconds. As carbon dioxide levels rise, the person is automatically wakened and resumes breathing. The second disturber of sleep is **nocturnal myoclonus,** in which a sleeper's leg muscles twitch or jerk. In most cases, neither condition is serious, but both can interrupt sleep. It has been estimated that between 28 and 63 percent of Americans between the ages of 58 and 86 suffer from one or both of these conditions. When researchers (Okudaira et al., 1983) studied a group of healthy 85- to 94-year olds from Vilcabamba, Ecuador, they found a much lower incidence of both disorders. They suggest the difference could be due to the beneficial effects of the altitude on pulmonary function, to strenuous physical exercise, to the unavailability of sleeping medication, or to some other environmental difference. No matter what the cause, frequent disruptions of sleep can reduce its quality and make a person feel that he or she is not getting an adequate amount.

The changed sleep habits of the elderly are accompanied by changes in nightly EEG patterns. Every 90 minutes or so during the night, sleep cycles through a series of four stages that include a period called rapid-eye-movement (REM) sleep. REM sleep is characterized by rapid movement of the eyes beneath the closed lids and by a pattern of brain waves that resembles stage 1 sleep: a predominance of alpha rhythm, along with a few very slow theta waves and occasional bursts of beta activity. Heartbeat is irregular, breathing quickens, and blood pressure rises. Yet muscles become limp and virtually paralyzed. People are hard to waken from REM sleep, but, when roused, most say they have been dreaming. The length of each REM period declines with age, but among people in their fifties, the drop is much sharper among men than women (Webb, 1982). The proportion of REM to non-REM sleep remains steady until about the age of 80, when it begins to decline.

The stage of deepest sleep, stage 4, is characterized by large, slow delta waves. Heart rate and respiration are slow and regular, and muscles are relaxed. This stage of sleep decreases with age and may be almost absent in some older adults. The decline may not be a part of normal aging, however, because older individuals who are free from depression show the same proportion of stage 4 sleep as younger adults (Marsh and Thompson, 1977).

Depression can affect sleep markedly and is often the cause of insomnia, which is not a normal accompaniment of aging. Insomnia can also be caused by excessive consumption of caffeine or alcohol or by the use of sleeping pills. Sleeping preparations, when used regularly, aggravate insomnia. The person builds up a tolerance for the drug, becomes dependent on it, and develops "drug-dependency insomnia" (Butler and Lewis, 1982).

AGING IN THE AUTONOMIC NERVOUS SYSTEM

The decline in the body's ability to respond to stress is primarily the result of aging in the autonomic nervous system (Fig. 4.13). The autonomic nervous system regulates the body's internal environment. It controls such activities as heart rate, blood pressure, skin temperature, digestion, elimination, respiration, and our reactions to emergencies or stress.

With age, many of the responses controlled by the autonomic nervous system slow or become weaker, so that it takes the body longer to adapt to changed conditions. This slowing may be the result of changes in the metabolism of neurotransmitters, to structural changes in neurons, or to the loss of neurons although there appears to be no marked degeneration of the major branches of the system with age (Everitt and Huang, 1980).

The autonomic nervous system is involved in the regulation of many of the systems already discussed. For example, it regulates blood sugar levels and blood pressure. Age brings only slight changes in such measures, but it is believed that aging in the autonomic nervous system may be involved in the development of hypertension (Everitt and Huang, 1980).

As we saw earlier in the chapter, the aging autonomic nervous system manages to maintain body temperature fairly well when no demands are placed on it but falters when faced with sudden changes in environmental temperature. Similarly, it takes the pulse rate and breathing longer to return to normal after exercise.

In system after system, advanced aging and degenerative diseases come at early ages for some and are postponed or never appear in others. In the next chapter, we will discuss the health aspects of aging, seeing that the way we live can hasten or postpone the arrival of the frailty associated with old-old age.

SUMMARY

Advanced aging eventually leads to a breakdown in the integration of body systems. Because the body can no longer deal efficiently with stress and the immune system has lost much of its effectiveness, the older adult is increasingly susceptible to disease.

Although there are individual differences in the rate at which hair grays, it is considered the most reliable body indicator of aging. By middle age, hair density thins about 20 percent. Cross-linkage, changes in fat and muscle, and habitual muscle use play some role in wrinkles, but the major cause of skin aging is exposure to the sun. The shrinkage of muscles and decline in their strength that accompanies aging may be in part the result of reduced physical acticity. A slight shrinkage in height may result from altered posture, thinning of spinal disks, and

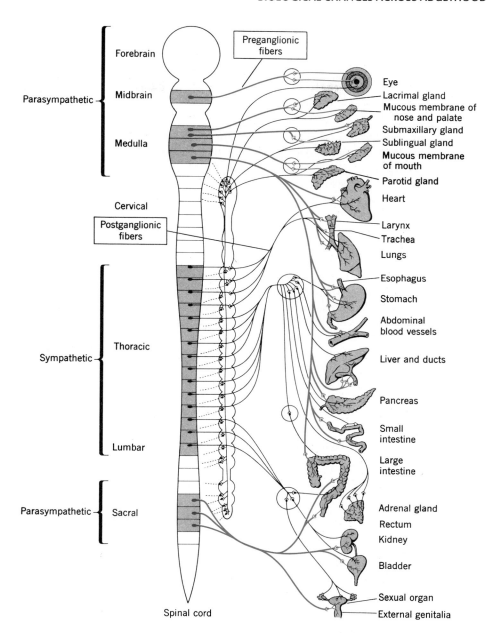

FIGURE 4.13 Autonomic nervous system, which controls the body's internal environment by innervating various organs.

Source: G. E. Nelson, *Biological Principles with Human Perspectives*, 2d ed. (New York: Wiley, 1984), p. 144.

a loss of water in the disks. In the skeletal system, **osteoporosis** and **osteoarthritis** are the major diseases of secondary aging.

As the circulatory system ages, lipofuscin accumulates, collagen stiffens, and additional collagen and fat are deposited in the heart. **Cardiac output** and maximum heart rate decrease. As **elastin** is redistributed, arterial walls become stiff; collagen, calcium, and lipids accumulate; and blood pressure often rises. Although changes in tissue structure and **arteriosclerosis** are inevitable, much of the arterial change may be the result of secondary aging. Secondary aging may lead to **atherosclerosis, hypertension, ischemic heart disease,** or stroke.

Stiffening of the rib cage, shrinkage of muscle fiber, and structural changes in the lung, trachea, bronchial tubes, and **alveoli** result in a 20 to 30 percent decrease in air flow between young adulthood and old age. Residual lung volume increases, and the exchange of gases within the lung declines in efficiency. The drop in maximal oxygen uptake, which leaves people short of breath after exercise, is probably heightened by lack of exercise. Secondary aging may lead to **emphysema**.

Although esophageal muscles contract more weakly in older adults and hydrochloric acid production drops, digestive problems, such as **atrophic gastritis** and **diverticulosis,** in the elderly are the result of secondary aging or life style. Shrinkage of the liver may reduce its ability to metabolize drugs. Changes in kidney structure and function do not prevent it from working efficiently, but bladder shrinkage often forces older adults to get up at night to urinate.

Two of the endocrine glands have been implicated in the aging process. The pituitary, which shows some structural change, may set off the aging process under instructions from the hypothalamus; and the thymus, which is important in the functioning of the immune system, has been considered a primary pacemaker for aging. Changes in the pancreas make the body less effective in handling insulin, but it is uncertain whether this inefficiency is due to normal aging. Some adults older than 40 develop maturity-onset diabetes, a major disease of secondary aging.

The structure and functioning of the reproductive system changes with age in both men and women, but none of the changes should prevent the enjoyment of sexuality. Many men continue to produce sperm into advanced old age; women cease to mature ova by **menopause,** which usually arrives at about the age of 50.

With age, the brain appears to shrink, and neurons are lost in some regions of the brain, especially in the area that coordinates voluntary muscle activity. Some simple reflexes may weaken or disappear. Major changes in the cell bodies of neurons include **vacuoles, senile plaques,** and **neurofibrillary tangles.** Although all these changes may appear in normal brains, they are found in quantity only in diseased brains. Lipofuscin accumulates in the brain, and there may be a reduced amount of some neurotransmitters. **Astrocytes,** which keep neurotransmitters from accumulating in the space between neurons, increase in size during old age. Studies of brain waves indicate that slow wave activity increases with age in some people and is found in healthy adults older than 75. Diffuse slow wave activity is often accompanied by impaired functioning on IQ tests. Alpha activity may slow or be partly replaced by slow wave activity, but beta activity decreases only among adults older than 80 or severely deteriorated hospital patients.

Older adults tend to sleep about as much as they ever did, but not at one stretch. After the age of 80, the proportion of REM sleep begins to decline, and Stage 4 sleep may disappear in older adults, especially those sufering from depression. Sleep disturbances may be caused by **sleep apnea** or **nocturnal myoclonus**. The autonomic nervous system regulates body systems effectively as long as no special environmental demands are placed on the body. But many responses controlled by the system slow or weaken with age, so that the body takes longer to adapt to changed conditions and may not respond effectively to stress.

KEY TERMS

alveoli	**keratoses**
arteriosclerosis	**melanin**
astrocyte	**melanocyte**
atherosclerosis	**menopause**
atrophic gastritis	**neurofibrillary tangle**
cardiac output	**nocturnal myoclonus**
climacteric	**osteoarthritis**
diverticulosis	**osteoporosis**
elastin	**periodontal disease**
emphysema	**senile plaque**
hypertension	**sleep apnea**
ischemic heart disease	**vacuole**

5

PHYSICAL HEALTH ACROSS ADULTHOOD

On June 3, 1983, Harry Lieberman died at the age of 106. Lieberman, who had emigrated from Poland at the age of 29, manufactured candy for a supermarket chain until he retired in good health at the age of 74. Bored with his inactivity, he took up painting and established a successful second career. At 105, he told an interviewer that he felt his life was "paradise" because his paintings would endure long past his own lifetime. "They can put you six feet down," he said, "but the spiritual work you leave lives forever. I don't ask for more" (Barasch, 1983). Lieberman's death was attributed to cardiac arrest: his heart simply stopped.

On November 7, 1980, actor Steve McQueen died in Juárez, Mexico, at the age of 50. McQueen, who projected the screen image of a tough, cool loner, refused a double for many of his dangerous stunt scenes and always drove his own racing car in such films as *Le Mans*. The cause of McQueen's death was mesothelioma, a tumor of the tissue that lines the chest and abdomen, a disease that is believed to be caused by exposure to asbestos dust. No one is certain just how the cancer came to develop, but McQueen may have come into contact with the dust when he worked as a merchant seaman in the early 1950s or from the asbestos suit he wore when driving a racing car (Clark and Henkoff, 1980).

Why do some people live out a long, healthy life when others die prematurely or spend decades struggling with degenerative disease? Although we are not certain why some people remain healthy when others fail, we have discovered a number of factors that seem to have an important influence on health.

In this chapter, we begin by exploring the nature of physical health in adulthood. Next we consider the relationship between our health and the way we live, investigating aspects of life-style that promote good health and those that can speed deterioration. Pushing our exploration past the obvious connections of diet, exercise, and smoking, we try to understand how stress and the manner in which we adapt to it also may affect the quality of our later years.

PHYSICAL HEALTH

We have so thoroughly confused the concepts of aging and illness that we assume to be old is to be ailing, and the absence of illness is often interpreted as the absence of aging (Hickey, 1980). A healthy old person may not feel, or be perceived as, "old." As an 86-year-old Iowan put it, "I just don't think I'm old. I got a lot of zip yet. You got to keep moving to keep young. Keep the old joints greased up" (Donosky, 1982). Although an increasing number of older people are keeping their health for a longer time, their bodies usually are less resilient after temporary illnesses, and many develop degenerative diseases. Acute and chronic illnesses have very different effects on the quality of life, whether we are 25 or 80.

ACUTE ILLNESS

All of us, from the youngest baby to the oldest centenarian, may develop **acute illness**, a physical disorder with a limited duration. Although the illness generally passes and we eventually feel as well as we ever did, some acute illnesses can kill. The once prevalent diphtheria, influenza, and cystitis (a bladder infection) are examples of acute illnesses.

Across adulthood, each individual tends to have fewer acute illnesses each year although each separate incident of illness is likely to be increasingly severe (Fig. 5.1). By the time people are in their thirties and forties, respiratory illnesses are the most common, accounting for 78 out of every 100 episodes of acute illness (Wantz and Gay, 1981).

Acute diseases in older people are complicated by normal aging processes (Hickey, 1980). Temperature may rise only slightly in response to a serious infection. The perception of pain diminishes, so that its source and location are often difficult to determine. The response to treatment is slower and weaker than it once was. Because the older patient has less physical reserve, an illness such as influenza that may be merely a painful nuisance to a younger person can develop into pneumonia in an older person and may lead to death.

An additional factor that complicates acute illness in older adults is the probable presence of some chronic condition, such as cardiovascular disease or diabetes. Some researchers believe that 86 percent of people over 65 have at least one chronic health problem (Satariano and Syme, 1981).

CHRONIC ILLNESS

These long-standing health problems are known as **chronic illnesses**, for they cannot be cured, and they tend to get worse with time. The proportion of any cohort that has some chronic illness increases with age, as does the number of chronic ill-

	Infective and Parasitic	Respiratory Upper	Other	Digestive System	Injuries
Total	24.6	57.0	59.2	11.4	33.4
Male	23.4	50.9	52.9	11.2	39.0
Female	25.7	62.7	65.0	11.6	28.1
By age					
Under 6 years	56.3	127.6	73.5	18.6	35.2
6 to 16 years	42.5	78.0	81.5	13.4	40.4
17 to 44 years	21.3	53.3	60.0	13.0	38.6
45 to 64 years	11.2	31.2	46.0	6.3	23.0
Over 64 years	7.2	27.9	32.4	5.6	19.0

FIGURE 5.1 Incidence of acute illness—1980 (rate per 100 population). The number of acute conditions that either require medical attention or restrict activity for at least one day declines with age although each separate illness is generally more severe.

Source: U.S. Bureau of the Census, 1982.

The majority of older adults enjoy an active social life and have no major health problems until they pass the age of 75.

nesses a person has. In a longitudinal study of Californians, known as the Intergenerational Studies, the shift from acute to chronic complaints occurred when the subjects were in their forties. Instead of reporting sprains or strains, for example, they told of chronic pain, stiffness, and limited movement. By the time these middle-class Americans were 50 years old, chronic bronchitis, emphysema, hypertension, and arthritis had appeared among them. Yet most of them considered themselves in excellent health (Eichorn et al., 1981).

It has been estimated that 20 percent of those over 65 have two chronic illnesses and 33 percent have three or more (Hickey, 1980). As people get older, the degree of disability caused by chronic conditions often increases (Fig. 5.2). In the Duke Longitudinal Studies, in which the health of 300 North Carolina women and men past the age of 60 was followed over a 15-year period, 30 percent showed declines in health. However, decline was not inevitable: the health of 52 percent remained stable, and for 18 percent, health improved (Maddox and Douglass, 1974).

Statistics for illness are usually given for adults past 65, leading to the myth that physical decline begins at 65. According to gerontologist James Birren, most Americans see older adults as "dying a little bit every day" (Langway et al.,

	No Limitation on Activity		Some Limitation		Limitation in Major Activity	
	1970	1980	1970	1980	1970	1980
Under 45 years	94.7	93.2	5.3	6.8	3.3	4.2
45 to 64 years	80.5	76.1	19.5	23.9	15.7	18.8
Over 64 years	57.7	54.8	42.3	45.2	37.0	39.0

FIGURE 5.2   Activity limitation, 1978–1980 (percent). Although conditions that limit physical activity increase with age, the majority of older adults are healthy and have no chronic diseases that limit their daily activities.

Source: U.S. Bureau of the Census, 1982.

1982). When such statistics are analyzed, however, it becomes clear that the majority of people in their sixties are healthy and that significant health-related problems generally do not develop until people pass the age of 75.

Determining the condition of an elderly person's health is often difficult. In order to assess health, one must know the person's actual physical condition, his or her level of functioning—which may be higher or lower than physical examinations and tests indicate—and expectation levels—what the older person expects of himself or herself and what others expect the person to be able to do (Hickey, 1980). Preconceived expectations of old people, health professionals, and family members, based on the stereotype of inevitable decline in the elderly, can interfere with possible improvements in the level of functioning.

Among the older adults in the Duke Longitudinal Study whose health was monitored for 15 years, 60 percent rated their own health at the same level as did the physicians who examined them. Of the rest, more were likely to overestimate (24 percent) than to underestimate (12 percent) their health. These adults were all aware of the physicians' ratings because they received a letter after each examination summarizing the physicians' findings. However, self-ratings at each examination predicted health at the next exam better than did the physicians' ratings (Maddox and Douglass, 1974). Such self-ratings have turned out to be relatively good predictors of mortality—at least when the cause of death is ischemic heart disease. When age, sex, and actual health were held constant, people who rated their health as poor were almost two and one half times as likely to die from heart diseases as those who rated their health as excellent (Siegler and Costa, in press).

Some health professionals (Hickey, 1980) believe that health should be considered primarily in terms of functional adequacy. They note that there is a clear and consistent relationship between a person's level of expectation and actual health status. Physical measures, although important, are often not a reliable guide. When older people accept the negative stereotype, they may function at a level considerably below their actual capacity. This tendency may account for the fact that people with identical symptoms often vary widely in functional age.

The major health problems among older Americans are various forms of cardiovascular disease, cancer, osteoarthritis, and osteoporosis (Wantz and Gay, 1981). Osteoarthritis and osteoporosis can disable an older person; but cardiovascular disease, cancer, respiratory disease, and diabetes are the major causes of death (Fig. 5.3). Cardiovascular disease is by far the most serious. If all cardiovascular disease could be eliminated, life expectancy would increase by more than 11 years, but if cancer were eliminated, life expectancy would increase by less than a year and a half. The elimination of diabetes would add only two months (Grenville, 1976).

The way in which a chronic illness can interact with normal aging to accelerate physical decline is clearest in the case of diabetes. Diabetics have 17 times more kidney disease, 25 times more blindness, 5 times more gangrene, and twice as many heart attacks and strokes as other people (Wantz and Gay, 1981). Most of these disorders can be traced to the effect of diabetes on the circulatory system. The diabetic's blood vessels show accelerated aging, characterized by the forma-

	Heart Disease	Cancer	Stroke	Chronic Pulmonary	Pneumonia, Flu	Diabetes	Liver Disease	Athero-sclerosis
Men	370.4	205.6	65.8	33.0	22.2	12.9	18.1	10.7
15 to 24 years	3.3	7.6	1.0	.3	.9	.4	.3	—
24 to 44 years	36.1	26.2	5.6	1.1	2.9	2.7	10.9	.1
45 to 64 years	516.0	345.6	52.8	33.5	16.0	17.9	50.0	3.7
Over 64 years	2,751.7	1,364.3	571.8	277.0	184.0	91.0	55.2	105.9
Women	297.9	162.1	87.6	12.9	18.8	17.2	9.2	15.4
15 to 24 years	2.1	4.9	.9	.3	.7	.4	.2	—
25 to 44 years	12.4	30.2	5.1	.9	1.6	2.0	4.9	—
45 to 64 years	178.4	266.7	41.8	16.2	7.7	16.8	23.5	1.9
Over 64 years	1,989.5	759.9	598.4	71.7	124.1	101.3	23.4	115.5

Source: U.S. Bureau of the Census, 1982.

FIGURE 5.3 Death rates across adulthood, 1979 (deaths per 100,000 population). As the death rate mounts across adulthood, men are more likely than women to die from every cause except stroke, diabetes, and atherosclerosis. Death rates from accident and suicide are also higher for men.

tion of plaques and the calcification of arterial and venous walls. Plaques cut off circulation in the arms and legs, and changes in the small blood vessels of the eyes can lead to blindness. Changes in kidney blood vessels can decrease the kidney's efficiency in filtering the blood. Through its effect on the nervous system, diabetes can cause complications in many body systems. Infections in feet or legs can cause gangrene, the bladder may be paralyzed, and impotency may develop in men, and women may also find their sexual response impaired.

Diabetes can be controlled through diet, continual monitoring of urine, and, in some cases, the use of insulin or oral hypoglycemic agents. When diabetes develops later in life, it usually takes a milder form than it does in young adults.

As we have seen, the degree of disability from any chronic illness is not determined solely by physiological measures. Attitudes and expectations affect a person's degree of functioning. As we will see in Chapter 6, the development of chronic illness can also affect mental health, perhaps plunging a person into a deep depression. Some of the physical and mental degeneration that characterizes the diseases of secondary aging depend on life-style, which means that the ability to reduce a good deal of secondary aging is within the grasp of most of us.

LIFE-STYLE AND HEALTH

The fewer chronic diseases we take with us into old age, the more rewarding the final phase of life will be. None of us wants to spend the last years confined to a bed or wheelchair, dependent on the care of relatives or paid attendants. Ideally, we would end like the famous "one-hoss shay" in the poem by Oliver Wendell Holmes (1858), which ran smoothly for a hundred years, then simply collapsed when all its parts wore out at the same time.

If such a thing happened, there might be no apparent cause of death. At Case Western University, pathologist Robert Kohn conducted autopsies on 200 adults who died after the age of 85. In 26 percent of the cases, he could find no generally accepted cause of death (Bishop, 1983). There was no indication that atherosclerosis, heart disease, pneumonia, infection, accident, or any of the other customary killers had been responsible. Kohn concluded that the cause of death was "aging itself." It has been suggested that such a "natural" death occurs when the body's ability to respond to any sort of stress has deteriorated so far that it cannot cope with even a slight disruption (Siegler and Costa, in press).

The steady increase in life expectancy means that more and more of us will reach the hundred-year mark and that most of us will live longer than our parents and grandparents did. The evidence we have seen thus far shows that the disabilities of old age are not inevitable and that they are not the result of normal aging.

The importance of lifelong health habits on the quality and length of life has been amply demonstrated. As many as half the deaths in the United States may be due to unhealthy life-styles (U.S. Public Health Service, 1979). Among the aspects of a person's life-style that have strong effects on health are smoking, nutrition, and exercise. The degree of stress that accompanies one's life-style and the quality of the environment also affect health. Some of these relationships have appeared in longitudinal studies.

In the Intergenerational Studies, (Eichorn et al., 1981), seven of the 34-year-old women and six of the men were considered at high risk for cardiovascular disease because of such factors as parental deaths from the disease; overweight; and levels of cholesterol, triglyceride, and other lipids. By the time they were 50, five of the women and five of the men had developed hypertension whereas none of the women and only one of the men in the low-risk category had either increased blood pressure or signs of arteriosclerosis.

Investigators also explored the relationship of personality to health and discovered that members of the study who were calm and not easily aroused or irritated as adolescents tended to have good health in middle age. Apparently, they were less susceptible to stress than other members of the study.

In the Duke Longitudinal Study of normal aging (Palmore, 1974), amount of exercise was the best predictor of health. Older adults who exercised a great deal were less likely to become ill or to die prematurely than those who got little exercise. Smoking was also linked to premature death and weight extremes—either obesity or extreme underweight—with frequent illness. The healthiest members of this study were nonsmokers of normal weight who exercised frequently.

CHANGING LIFE-STYLES

It is beginning to appear that much of the appearance of aging, as health care professionals have encountered it, may be the product of cohort-specific factors. Each cohort grows up and ages in the context of a society, and whatever sanitation, nutrition, medical, and drug practices are common at the time will influence the quality of health.

For example, in the Framingham Heart Study, a longitudinal study that is attempting to discover which aspects of life-style affect the development of cardiovascular disease, parents' health status of 22 years ago was compared with their children's health status today. As a group, the children had lower blood pressure and lower levels of cholesterol in their blood and smoked fewer cigarettes than their parents had at approximately the same age (Riley and Bond, 1981). As these three measures are major risk factors in the development of coronary heart disease, it would seem likely that in the future the children's cohort will show less heart disease than their parents.

Over the past few decades, mortality from cardiovascular disease, which includes heart disease and stroke, has declined by more than 30 percent—with the largest drop taking place during the 1970s (Levy and Moskowitz, 1982). (See Fig. 5.4.) Clearly, some environmental factor—or factors—has affected the development of cardiovascular disease or at least decreased its severity. Because the decline began before antihypertensive medicines were introduced or before many people developed an interest in healthier life-styles, researchers are uncertain as to just what began the decline. They suggest, however, that a combination of factors (improved medical services, the development of coronary care units in the early 1960s, advances in the treatment of heart disease, improved control of high blood pressure, decreased smoking, increased leisure activities, changed eating habits, and modification of life-style) has probably been responsible (Levy and Moskowitz, 1982). The Framingham Study would suggest that the decline is likely to continue—at a time when deaths from heart disease have been rising in West Germany, Rumania, Northern Ireland, and Poland.

However, other statistics indicate a gray cloud behind the silver lining. Between 1966 and 1976, a pattern of increase in major diseases and disability from those diseases began to appear in all age groups. It was especially noticeable among 45- to 64-year-olds. More people were unable to carry out their normal activities, activity was restricted for more days each year, and more chronic diseases were found (Colvez and Blanchet, 1981).

Although we are ignorant about many of the causes of longevity, we do know that secondary aging can be hastened—or perhaps initiated—by health habits. Habits established early in life provide the most benefit, but exchanging bad habits for good ones—even late in life—is likely to increase our chances of emulating the one-hoss shay. If we take the responsibility for our own health and have the knowledge we need to maintain it, we are likely to have many additional disease-free years.

Most people have heard about the factors that have major effects on health, but many do not know that some of these factors are synergistic: The effect of exposure to some combinations can damage health far more than the sum of each factor's probable harm. For example, a person who works with asbestos is 30 times more likely to develop lung cancer than a person who has no extraordinary exposure to the substance. A smoker is 10 times more likely to develop lung cancer than a nonsmoker. But a person who smokes and works with asbestos is 90 times more likely to develop the disease than people who neither smoke nor work with asbestos (U.S. Public Health Service, 1979).

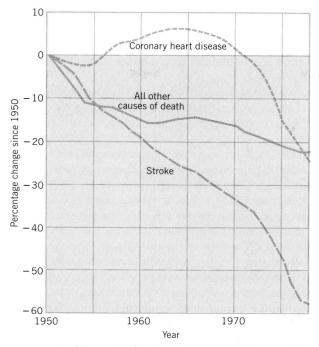

FIGURE 5.4   Changes in death rate, 1950–1958 (percent). During the past few decades, the death rate from heart disease and stroke has dropped sharply among adults between the ages of 35 and 74.

Source: R. I. Levy and J. Moskowitz, 1982, p. 123.

SMOKING

The elimination of cigarette smoking would do more to improve American health than any other single step. Approximately 320,000 deaths each year are associated with tobacco, and another 10 million Americans have chronic diseases that were caused by smoking.

Cigarette smoking has been directly implicated in cancer: Besides having 10 times as much lung cancer as nonsmokers, smokers have from 3 to 5 times as much cancer of the mouth and tongue, more than 3 times as much cancer of the larynx, and more than twice as much bladder cancer (U.S. Public Health Service, 1979). Twenty percent of all cancer deaths are directly caused by smoking, and smoking plays a role in another 33 percent. Nine people out of every 10 who develop lung cancer are dead within 5 years, and smoking is directly responsible for 75 percent of all lung cancer.

It generally takes about 20 years for lung cancer to develop. Although the rate of smoking among men has declined, there has been virtually no drop among women. Twice as many adolescent girls smoke today as did only a few years ago. Since women have begun smoking in greater numbers, their rate of lung cancer has been rising rapidly, and it is expected to overtake the rate of breast cancer, which is now the most prevalent cancer among females.

The presence of tar, a proved carcinogen, in cigarettes is well known. Not as widely known is the fact that cigarettes contain another carcinogen—nitrosamines—as well as radioactive elements. Cigarette smoking can expose the smoker to 40 times the recommended maximum annual exposure to radiation (Brody, 1982).

Cigarette smoking also is directly implicated in heart disease: Twice as many smokers as nonsmokers die of heart disease. The more cigarettes smoked, the greater the risk; when smoking passes a pack a day, the smoker is three, not two, times as likely to have a heart attack (U.S. Public Health Service, 1979). When tobacco smoke is drawn into the lungs, carbon monoxide enters the blood, replacing up to 12 percent of the oxygen in the red blood cells. This concentration cuts down the supply of oxygen to the heart and the brain (Brody, 1982). The concentration of carbon monoxide in the blood may increase the deposit of lipids and the formation of plaques within the arteries. The arteries narrow as atherosclerosis develops. As nicotine in the blood also increases the heart's demand for oxygen, exercise may be followed by the crushing pain of angina, which develops when the heart muscle is oxygen-starved (Wantz and Gay, 1981).

The health toll does not stop there. Smokers are likely to have other problems with their lungs besides cancer. Their lung capacity is reduced, and their lungs are susceptible to various microorganisms and debris. About 70 percent of the cases of emphysema and chronic bronchitis are caused by smoking. Smokers are also likely to develop peptic ulcers, and when they do, they are more likely than nonsmokers to die from them.

Women smokers run additional risks. Those who take contraceptive pills for at least 5 years run an increased risk of heart attack until menopause—even if they stop taking the pill (Layde, Ory, and Schlesselman, 1982). Pregnant women who smoke after the fourth month of pregnancy have more stillbirths than nonsmoking women, and their babies who live are more likely to have a low birth weight and to contract disease or die.

Given this lengthy list of gloomy statistics, it may seem that there is little point in giving up cigarettes. But once a smoker stops, his or her health gradually returns to normal (Figure 5.5). Within 7 years, the risk of bladder cancer has dropped to normal, and within 10 to 15 years, the added risk of other cancers has disappeared. Within 10 years, the added risk of coronary heart disease is also gone (Brody, 1982).

	Increased Risk	Period of Increased Risk After Quitting
Lung cancer	10 times	10–15 years
Larynx cancer	3–18 times	10 years
Mouth cancer	3–10 times	10–15 years
Cancer of esophagus	2–9 times	Uncertain
Bladder cancer	7–10 times	7 years
Cancer of pancreas	2–5 times	Uncertain

FIGURE 5.5 Smoking and cancer.

Information from: Jane Brody, 1982.

NUTRITION

Good nutrition contributes to health and our resistance to disease. Just how much changing our diet would retard secondary aging is uncertain because we are just beginning to understand the subtleties of nutritional influence on health, behavior and well-being. However, a number of studies have suggested that the rate of aging is affected by long-term food habits (Schlenker et al., 1973).

Our food habits are formed early in life, and they reflect the food habits of past generations and of ethnic group, religious practices, and social class (Davis and Randall, 1983). Food habits are also affected by changes in family practices, by advances in technology that affect food processing, and by advertising. In the 1980s, families are less likely to share meals; less likely to eat breakfast; more likely to eat processed foods, fast foods, or restaurants meals; and likely to eat a wider variety of foods than did families before World War II.

The typical American diet has changed greatly from diet patterns prevalent at the beginning of the century. The amount of fat in the average diet has increased by 25 percent, and the sugar-starch balance has also changed. In 1909, Americans got 68 percent of their carbohydrates from complex starches and 32 percent from sugar. By 1976, sugar accounted for 53 percent of our carbohydrates—most of it coming into the diet through food processing and soft drinks (Winikoff, 1978). The character—although not the amount—of protein consumed also had changed, with a larger proportion coming from animal sources.

Reversing this imbalance of nutrients may be another way to combat the effects of secondary aging, and nutritionists have set goals that would do this (see Figure 5.6). Because the current American diet has been linked with heart disease, hypertension, diabetes, and various forms of cancer, dietary shifts might reduce their incidence. Evidence from a longitudinal study of nearly 4000 middle-aged men in-

The typical American diet is higher in fat and sugar than it was at the beginning of the twentieth century, a situation that alarms many nutritionists. Because the effects of diet are generally cumulative, the early establishment of good eating habits may prevent or delay degenerative disease.

dicates that reducing blood cholesterol levels lowers the incidence of heart attack and the risk of death from heart disease (Kolata, 1984). Other connections between food habits and disease come from comparing national diets. In Japan, for example, the diet has less beef and less total fat, more salt, and more pickled food than does the American diet. Japanese have lower rates of breast, colon, and intestinal cancer than Americans, but higher rates of stomach cancer. When Japanese move to the United States, their breast, colon, and intestinal cancer rates climb whereas stomach cancer rates drop (U.S. Public Health Service, 1979). Studies have also indicated that decreased fiber content (especially that found in natural cereals) rather than increased fat content also may be important in the development of many diseases (Burkitt, 1978). However, increasing fiber content generally has the effect of decreasing fat content and vice versa, so it is not certain which effect is more important or whether both factors have an equal role in the cause or prevention of degenerative disease.

As the effects of diet tend to be cumulative, the earlier good food habits are established, the better. Autopsies of preschool children who die from accidents have discovered lipids and plaques in the arteries. About 20 percent of adolescents have significant fat deposits in their arteries, and 45 percent of American servicemen who died in Vietnam had developed atherosclerosis (Brody, 1983a). Reports indicate that Americans have begun to change their diets. The per capita consumption of animal fats, dairy products, and eggs has dropped; and the consumption of vegetable fats has increased (Weg, 1983).

The American taste for salty foods, such as potato chips and salted nuts, combined with the heavy use of salt in processed foods and the prevalent habit of salting food again at the table, worries many physicians. The body requires about 220 milligrams of sodium each day, but most Americans consume 10 to 24 grams of salt (which supplies 4000 to 9600 milligrams of sodium). It has been recommended that salt intake be reduced to less than 2 grams per day. Excess salt consumption is believed to be connected with the development of hypertension, at least among the 15 to 20 percent of Americans who are susceptible to its effects (Brody, 1982).

	Current Diet	Dietary Goals
Saturated fat	16%	10%
Polyunsaturated and unsaturated fat	26%	20%
Protein	12%	12%
Starches	22%	43%
Sugar	24%	19%

Source: U.S. Senate, Select Committee on Nutrition and Human Needs, "Dietary Goals for the United States" (Washington, D.C.: U.S. Government Printing Office, 1977).

FIGURE 5.6 Proposed changes in American diet. Nutritionists believe that reducing the proportion of sugar and fat—especially saturated fat—in the typical American diet and increasing the proportion of starch would reduce the diseases of secondary aging.

Among younger Americans, overnutrition is also a major problem. Many eat too much, taking in more calories than their bodies burn. Ten percent of elementary school children and between 20 and 30 percent of high school students are considered obese: their weight is more than 20 percent above the recommended level (Brody, 1983a). Four out of five fat six-year-olds become fat adults.

Among middle-aged adults, income is associated with obesity, but in a different way for men and women. Thirty-five percent of the women and 5 percent of the men with incomes below the poverty level are obese. As incomes rise, fewer women (29 percent) but more men (13 percent) are obese (U.S. Public Health Service, 1979). Because obesity has been associated with hypertension, heart disease, stroke, diabetes, and gallbladder disease, keeping weight within normal boundaries is one health habit that can have long-term benefits. In addition, people who already have hypertension, diabetes, and high cholesterol levels can improve these conditions by losing weight (Fries and Crapo, 1981).

Older Americans generally need fewer calories per pound of body weight because they tend to be less active than younger people. When the physical activity of 76 older women was monitored, they ranged from sedentary to very sedentary in their life-style, and the average activity level was one third that of college students (LaPorte et al., 1983). However, there are wide differences in individual activity, and older people use more energy than the young in performing the same physical task (Hickey, 1980). Calorie consumption generally decreases with age, and among a group of men who participated in a longitudinal study, the drop in calories was primarily caused by a drop in dietary fat (Elahi et al., 1983).

The actual need of older adults for specific nutrients has not been established, and in some cases, because of a decline in digestive secretions, enzyme activity, or the absorption of nutrients from the intestine, older adults may need more—not less—of the same vitamin or mineral than younger people do (Butler and Lewis, 1982). The most frequent dietary deficiencies found amoung older men and women are calcium, iron, magnesium, and vitamins A, C, and the B vitamins thiamin, niacin, and folic acid. Blood levels of protein also may be low (Weg, 1983). Such dietary deficiencies may lead to false diagnosis of permanent mental deterioration in older adults because they can produce mental confusion, learning difficulties, and depression.

Dietary deficiencies in older men and women are not usually the result of nutritional ignorance. Reduced income, loss of mobility, stress, attitudes, and loneliness can all affect the purchase, preparation, and consumption of food. Those with incomes below the poverty level cannot buy the right foods. Those who have the money but cannot get to a market have no opportunity to buy them. And those who are worried, depressed, lonely, anxious, or low in self-esteem have little appetite. Compared with those who live with other people, older people who live alone have a less adequate diet and a less varied diet, eat fewer foods that require preparation, and are more likely to skip the evening meal (Davis and Randall, 1983). It would appear that older people who retain social ties, whether with spouse, family, or friends, are most likely to maintain an adequate diet throughout life.

CAN DIETARY RESTRICTIONS EXTEND THE LIFE SPAN?

Research with animals has shown that the life span can be extended by radically restricting calories (see Chapter 3). Roy Walford, a gerontological researcher who has successfully extended the lives of rats and fish, has applied his methods to human beings. He is his own guinea pig in an experiment to extend the human life span to 140 years.

Walford (1983) has reduced intake to approximately 1500 calories a day, with a maximum of 15 percent fat and 25 percent protein. He distributes this calorie intake by fasting completely two days each week and adding the calories saved to his meals on the other five days. Walford is now somewhat underweight and hopes to have lost 25 percent of his normal body weight by 1987. When a computer analysis showed that he could not provide a balanced diet with the specified calorie, fat, and protein restrictions, he added B-complex vitamins, vitamins A and C, and zinc to his diet.

But Walford went even farther. Convinced that he needed antioxidants to detoxify the free radicals he believes play a central role in the aging process, Walford added vitamin E, selenium, BHT (a food preservative), cysteine, methionine, ascorbyl palmitate, more vitamin C, and bioflavonoids to his daily vitamin supplements. He also takes calcium pantothenate (to supply pantothenic acid, a part of the B complex that has also been implicated in extended life spans among mice and rats) and DMAE, or Deaner, a brain-reactive drug that inhibits the buildup of lipofuscin in the brain cells.

Although exercise is not a requirement in the undernutrition regime, Walford runs 10 to 15 miles each week, swims two miles, and lifts weights. He believes that such exercise does not extend the life span but helps to maintain health during the normal span.

Because Walford was born in 1925, it will be 2065 before his experiment, if successful, is concluded. He contends that people who followed this life style would have the appearance of today's 50-year-olds at the age of 75. Because rats and mice who are put on similar diets at birth tend to live longer but to have a high rate of infant mortality, Walford suggests that his diet plan works best when started at about the age of 30 or 35. He further points out that some of the supplements he takes can be harmful in large doses.

Will Walford's experiment be successful? Leonard Hayflick, another prominent researcher, says that biologists know the program will work, but that such radical food restrictions take all the joy out of life. "The pain isn't worth the effort," he says. "The quality of life is more important than the quantity to everyone but Roy Walford" (quoted in Krier, 1982, p. 3F).

EXERCISE

When the United States became a technological society, a sedentary life-style crept up on Americans. As technological advances decreased the amount of energy we expended in physical labor, automobiles cut down our opportunities and inclinations to walk. At the same time, the growing popularity of professional sports encouraged us to watch sporting events instead of participating in them.

Yet regular exercise appears to be a major foe of the aging process. As we saw in Chapter 3, the cardiovascular and respiratory systems go through characteristic changes with age. In addition, muscle strength and joint flexibility declines. We assume that these are the result of natural aging, but older Americans lead such a sedentary life that it is extremely difficult to find older people whose activity levels are high enough to make a comparison of their performance with young adults meaningful (deVries, 1983).

It may be that declining activity, not aging, is responsible for a good deal of the "natural" deterioration of body systems. Inactivity causes muscles to shrink and reduces muscular endurance. Researchers (Saltin et al., 1968) have found that putting young, well-conditioned men to bed for three weeks will decrease their cardiac output by 26 percent, their maximum breathing capacity by 30 percent, and their oxygen comsumption by 30 percent. It has been suggested that many of the physical changes of aging are the result of not one, but three processes: aging, hidden disease (such as silent atherosclerosis in young people), and disuse

Inactivity can be responsible for the deterioration of body systems. Regular exercise can improve physical and mental health in both sexes, and it can slow or prevent the development of osteoporosis in older women.

(deVries, 1983). Although there is nothing that can be done about aging, declines from disuse can sometimes be reversed.

Regardless of age, people who have become inactive generally find that exercise improves their mental health. Men and women who exercise regularly say they feel better, have more energy, and require less sleep. Many find their self-esteem improved, their anxiety decreased, and mild depression lifted. They feel more self-reliant (U.S. Public Health Service, 1979). Other psychological effects of exercise include improved memory, faster reaction times, and increased attention (Wiswell, 1980). The degree of improvement shown, of course, depends on a person's initial fitness level.

An immediate psychological benefit of exercise was demonstrated when researchers (deVries and Adams, 1972) tested exercise (walking for 15 minutes at a moderate rate) against tranquilizers (meprobamate) and a harmless sugar pill with 10 elderly men who complained of high levels of anxiety. Walking was more effective than the tranquilizer in relieving anxiety, and the relief was apparent in electrical measures of muscle tension. The effect lasted for about an hour.

The physical benefits of exercise extend to several systems, and people who exercise regularly reduce their risk of developing heart disease. Among 17,000 Harvard alumni, those who exercised regularly had about half the rate of heart disease and significantly fewer heart attacks than those whose exercise was slight and sporadic (U.S. Public Health Service, 1979). The protection appears to be the result of increased respiratory endurance, reduced triglyceride and cholesterol levels, increased red blood cells and blood volume, improvement in the condition of blood vessels in the heart, and better circulation (Wantz and Gay, 1981). Regular exercise can even halt the course of disease. Six months of regular exercise reduced blood pressure significantly in 23 people with hypertension (Boyer and Kasch, 1970). In other cases, exercise has reduced the pain of angina, allowing patients who were recovering from heart attacks to increase their activity (U.S. Public Health Service, 1979).

Exercise also leads to improvement in the respiratory system, reduces obesity, improves joint mobility, and increases bone growth and strength in older women, for whom osteoporosis is often a problem (deVries, 1983). The specific effects of exercise in older adults can be seen in Table 5.1.

In order to produce such effects on an aging body, an older man or woman must engage in a regular exercise program that focuses on the rhythmic activities of large muscle masses, such as walking briskly, jogging, running, or swimming. The exercise must raise the heart rate to a predetermined rate based on the person's age and present heart condition. In practical terms, this means that 70-year-old men of average physical fitness need to raise their heart rate above 95 beats per minute and that well-conditioned men in the same age bracket need to raise their heart rate above 103 (deVries, 1983). Exercises that focus on small muscle masses or isometric muscle exercises that use high levels of muscle contractions without any pauses for relaxation are undesirable and do not have the same beneficial effects.

TABLE 5.1 EXERCISE AND THE AGING PROCESS

Structural Change	Functional Effects	Effects of Exercise
MUSCULO-SKELETAL SYSTEM		
1. Muscular atrophy with decrease in both number and size of muscle fibers. 2. Neuromuscular weakness. 3. Demineralization of bones. 4. Decline in joint function. 5. Degeneration and calcification on articulating surface of joint.	1. Loss of muscle size. 2. Decline of strength. 3. Reduced range of motion. 4. Reduced speed of movement. 5. Joint stiffness. 6. Declining neuromotor performance. 7. Changes in posture. 8. Frequent cramping. 9. Gait characteristics affected. 10. Shrinkage in height. 11. Increased flexion at joints due to connective tissue change.	1. Muscle hypertrophy. 2. Increased muscle strength. 3. Increased muscle capillary density. 4. Increased strength of ligaments and tendons. 5. Increased thickness of articular cartilage. 6. Increased strength of bone.
RESPIRATORY SYSTEM		
1. Hardening of airways and support tissue. 2. Degeneration of bronchi. 3. Reduced elasticity and mobility of intercostal cartilage.	1. Reduced vital capacity with increased residual volume. 2. Oxygen diffusing capacity reduced. 3. Increased rigidity of chest wall. 4. Declining functional reserve capacity.	1. No chronic effect on lung volume but may improve maximal ventilation during exercise and breathing mechanics.
CARDIOVASCULAR SYSTEM		

1. Elastic changes in aorta and heart.
2. Valvular degeneration and calcification.
3. Changes in myocardium:
  (a) Delayed contractility and irritability.
  (b) Decline in oxygen consumption.
  (c) Increased fibrosis.
  (d) Appearance of lipofuscin.
	1. Diminished cardiac reserve.
	2. Increased peripheral resistance.
	3. Reduced exercise capacity.
	4. Decrease in maximum coronary blood flow.
	5. Elevated blood pressure.
	6. Decreased maximal heart rate.
		1. Increased heart volume and weight.
		2. Increased blood volume.
		3. Increase in maximal stroke volume and cardiac output.
		4. Decreased arterial blood pressure.
		5. Increase in maximal oxygen consumption.
		6. Myocardial effects increased:

TABLE 5.1   (*Continued*)

Structural Change	Functional Effects	Effects of Exercise
4. Increase in vagal control		(a) Mitochondrial size.
		(b) Nuclei.
		(c) Protein synthesis.
		(d) Myosin synthesis.
		(e) Capillary density.
		7. Decreased resting heart rate.

From: Robert A. Wiswell, ''Relaxation, Exercise, and Aging,'' in *Handbook of Mental Health and Aging*, edited by Birren/Sloane, © 1980, p. 945. Reprinted by permission of Prentice-Hall, Inc., Englewood Cliffs, N.J.

Given the obvious benefits of regular exercise, why do so many men and women remain sedentary? In 1975, 51 percent of American adults told interviewers for the National Health Survey that they engaged in no physical activity for the sake of exercise (U.S. Bureau of the Census, 1982). When asked why, most of those who made no effort to exercise felt they did not need it.

The amount of exercise people engage in is linked to age, sex, and education. All groups become less active as they grow older. Women become inactive earlier than men, and people with lower levels of education become inactive earlier than college graduates (Ostrow, 1980). Older adults tend to have extremely negative attitudes toward exercise. According to one researcher (Conrad, 1976), they believe that older adults do not need to exercise; they are convinced that exercise is dangerous for old people; they think that slight, sporadic exercise is extremely beneficial; and they think they are physically incapable of vigorous activity.

Their attitudes probably reflect stereotypes formed in childhood about appropriate behavior and levels of activity among the old. As few models of vigorously active old people exist, older men and women are unlikely to have their attitudes changed, and so they conform to the stereotype (Ostrow, 1980). Perhaps we need to hear more about people like the late King Gustav of Sweden, who played tennis regularly at the age of 80, or former Olympic champions among the elderly whose functional capacity is better than the typical 25-year-old with a sedentary job (Wiswell, 1980).

STRESS AND ADAPTATION

Being a nonsmoker who eats carefully and exercises vigorously lays a solid basis for a long and healthy life, but health—either physical or mental—is also affected by other aspects of living. Development takes place within a social context, and aspects of the environment continually affect us. The way we react to events and situations may increase or decrease our chances of avoiding the diseases of secondary aging.

STRESS

Stress can have a detrimental effect on physical and mental health. It can accelerate the aging process, it can lead to the development of physical disease or mental disorder, and it can impair a person's ability to respond to new challenges (Eisdorfer and Wilkie, 1977). **Stress** is an ambiguous term that covers the physiological and psychological responses to unpleasant or threatening stimuli. Such a stimulus, known as a **stressor**, can be located in the outside world or within the person, and it can be either physical or psychological. Stressors can threaten our lives, threaten our status, signal some loss, or attack our belief systems (Renner and Birren, 1980). Stressors can be as specific as the death of a parent or impending surgery, as chronic as an unhappy marriage or competition at work, or as elusive as the piling up of daily hassles—misplacing things, running out of money before payday, being unable to stick to a diet, not finding a taxi on a rainy night, or worrying about the future.

Stress and Health

Whether a potentially stressful situation affects our health depends on how we perceive it and the way we react to it. If we perceive it as threatening and react in nonadaptive ways, the effects can be major. Stressful events have been connected with triggering diabetes in individuals who were predisposed to the disease and to making existing cases of diabetes worse (Renner and Birren, 1980). Stress has been connected with heart attacks, hypertension, respiratory disease, ulcers and other disorders of the gastrointestinal tract, anxiety, paranoia, mental deterioration, and depression.

Research with animals suggests that inescapable and uncontrollable stress may lead to a condition known as **learned helplessness**, in which a person simply stops trying to cope with a stressful situation. When animals develop learned helplessness, they quickly succumb to disease. In one study (Visintainer, Volpicelli, and Seligman, 1982), rats were injected with cancer cells and then given electric shock. Some of the rats could escape the shock by pressing a bar; others could neither stop the shock nor get away from it. Twice as many of the helpless rats developed tumors as did either rats who could turn off the shock or rats in a control group who were injected with cancer cells but received no shock. Later research with animals indicates that inescapable stress weakens the immune system, paving the way for cancer and other diseases to develop (Laudenslager et al., 1983).

Not everyone who encounters intensive stress becomes helpless. Whether learned helplessness develops may depend on how people perceive the stressful situation. If they see their inability to control the situation as permanent, as the result of deficiencies within themselves, and as affecting many areas of their life, they are believed to be in danger of developing learned helplessness (Abrahamson, Seligman, and Teasdale, 1978). Other researchers (Rodin, 1980) propose that when people perceive themselves as having control over their lives, the effects of stress may be reduced, with consequent reduction in the rate of disease, death, and psychological distress. Inmates of World War II concentration camps lived under uncontrollable stress, and survivors of those camps show the effect of the lengthy stress on the aging process. Many of these individuals have aged prematurely, with the degenerative diseases of old age showing up early in life (Renner and Birren, 1980).

Any event is a potential stressor because it causes changes in the course of life. As events mount up, the possibility of destructive stress increases. In order to estimate the effect of such stress, Thomas Holmes and Richard Rahe (1967) devised a Social Readjustment Rating Scale that assigns a specified number of life change units to 43 different events, depending on their intensity and duration. For example, the death of a spouse, the most stressful event, is rated at 100 units; being fired, at 47; an outstanding personal achievement, at 28; and Christmas, at 12. Holmes and Rahe's research indicated that as the total of life change units passes 300, the likelihood of illness—and even accident—increases. However, the scale makes no distinction between pleasant and unpleasant events, nor is there any place on the scale for chronic stress, which many people encounter on the job or within their personal relationships. Persistent marital discord may be more stressful than getting a divorce (House and Robbins, 1983). In addition, many physical and mental disorders have a long, silent onset, so that items on the scale may be the consequence of illness, not the cause of it (Dohrenwend and Dohrenwend, 1978).

The context of life events must also be taken into account. Age, sex, marital status, ethnic background, socioeconomic level, and education all affect the way events are perceived and thus modify the level of stress that is likely to be experienced. Events that are expected, such as marriage or getting a first job for young adults, menopause or children leaving home for middle-aged adults, or retirement for older adults, may not be as stressful as nonnormative events (Neugarten, 1970). When people can anticipate stress, they may be able to work it through beforehand, so that when the event finally arrives—elective surgery, retirement, the death of a spouse after a long illness—coping is far more effective (Fiske, 1980). Unexpected events, such as the loss of a job, or events that happen at the "wrong" time of life, such as the death of a spouse in young adulthood, may be especially stressful.

Events that place a strain on a person's life roles, such as worker, spouse, parent, or child, are also likely to lead to increased stress. Chronic role strains, such as economic deprivation, occupational stress, and persistent marital conflict, are more common among people of all ages than expected life transitions (House and Robbins, 1983). One researcher (Fiske, 1980) has suggested that too little stress may become stressful. Routine, boring jobs may lead to a resignation and lassitude that permeate all areas of life and may result in self-pity.

Stress Across Adulthood
Various stress-producing events and situations, whether normative or nonnormative, tend to be related to age. Most of them are clustered in young and middle adulthood, so that older people face fewer stress-producing events than younger

Many stress-producing events are clustered in young and middle-adulthood. However some of these stresses, such as buying a new house, are challenging and full of promise.

adults do. Research also indicates that a person's age has a powerful effect on the degree of perceived stress that accompanies any event (Chiriboga and Cutler, 1980). When asked to estimate the degree of disruption caused by various life events, older people produce consistently lower ratings. Older people also seem to worry less than younger people, and they report greater satisfaction with their jobs and less job stress and are more likely to say their lives are "free." Younger people tend to describe their lives as "hard" and "tied down" (Campbell, 1979). Studies of natural disasters, such as floods and tornadoes, have also shown that older people were less anxious than younger people and perceived less stress concerning their experience (House and Robbins, 1983).

Do such findings indicate that older adults are under less strain than young and middle-aged adults? Probably not. Older adults are more worried about physical health than young and middle-aged adults. Under some conditions, they perceive community events such as social and economic change as particularly stressful whereas middle-aged adults find the same situation generally reassuring (Miller, 1980). The recent political squabbles over funding of Social Security and medicare, for example, are likely to have been much more stressful for older adults than for young or middle-aged individuals.

The balance of stress is also likely to change in old age. Along with the negative stresses of earlier life go many positive stresses. The birth of a child, a promotion, buying a new house, having children leave home, though stressful, are also challenging and full of promise. During later adulthood, the positive stresses decline sharply, leaving the balance skewed toward pain instead of pleasure (Chiriboga and Cutler, 1980).

Finally, older adults may be more vulnerable to stress than at any other age. The aging process affects the immune system, decreasing the ability to resist stress and making the person more vulnerable to the development of disease as a response to stress (House and Robbins, 1983). In addition, the prior presence of a degenerative disease, which is more likely in old age, may interact with the stress, increasing the strain.

Interindividual Differences in Coping Styles

The way people cope with stress affects the influence various events and situations have on health. Some people seem to thrive on situations that would defeat others. In a longitudinal study that followed four cohorts of middle- and lower-class men and women, about two fifths of the people whose lives were filled by stress were challenged by it (Fiske, 1980). They seemed to pay little attention to the stress that surrounded them, were open to new experience, and generally had close interpersonal relationships. The remaining three fifths who encountered a great deal of stress were overwhelmed by it. Their behavior showed high stress, they dwelt on stressful situations at great length, and they were preoccupied with past stresses, present stress, and stresses that might develop in the future. They were also unlikely to have close interpersonal relationships. General styles of coping with stress tend to remain relatively consistent across adulthood. Experience in coping with stress early in life may provide a source of strength that makes older people able to handle the stress and losses of age. Older people who have had little stress in earlier life seem unprepared to handle the stressors that accompany aging (Fiske, 1980).

Two extreme ways of coping with life have been found to affect the development of coronary disease. These behavior patterns, Type A and Type B, were first detected in a study of 3400 men between the ages of 39 and 59, none of whom had cardiovascular problems at the beginning of the study (Rosenman, 1974). Type A men were highly competitive, aggressive, tense, and restless, and they felt that life was a struggle against time. Such men seemed to have a strong need to be in control of stressful situations. Type B men seemed relaxed, felt no pressure from time, and showed none of the competitive striving that characterized the Type As. Eight and a half years later, Type A men were twice as likely to have developed heart disease as Type B men and twice as likely to have had a fatal heart attack. Among those who survived one attack, the Type As were five times as likely to have a second attack.

These behavior patterns had physiological accompaniments, producing all the biochemical changes that signal probable cardiovascular disease, including high levels of cholesterol and triglycerides. Although little research has been done on women, Type A women appear to show similar biochemical changes (Eisdorfer and Wilkie, 1977). Studies with young men faced with mental arithmetic and reaction-time tasks have led to the suggestion that extreme physiological responsiveness by Type As may help to explain why they tend to develop heart disease (Williams et al., 1982). During these tasks both cardiovascular responsiveness and the production of hormones that may be associated with atherosclerosis were significantly higher in Type As than in Type Bs.

Few people are pure Type As or Type Bs; only about 10 percent of the men in the original study fell neatly into one of the categories. However, the researchers (Friedman and Rosenman, 1974) believe that heart disease is unlikely to develop before the age of 70 unless Type A behavior is present. Among people past 65, however, Type A behavior loses its ability to predict heart disease. In the Framingham study, Type A behavior was a good predictor of heart disease among men and women between the ages of 45 and 64, but was of no value in predicting heart disease in older adults (Haynes et al., 1978). There is as yet no indication that Type A behavior is linked to any other disease (Eisdorfer and Wilkie, 1977), but its strong connection with the development of heart disease in apparently healthy men shows the interrelation of perceived stress and disease.

Stress is intimately connected with another factor that affects life-style: the environment.

ENVIRONMENT

People can never be separated from the environment, for it always surrounds them (Windley and Scheidt, 1980). The physical environment can affect physical and mental health, and it can affect them either directly or indirectly.

Noise, air pollution, and extreme temperatures can have direct effects on health. Prolonged exposure to high-intensity sounds can cause irreversible hearing loss. Noise can also act as a stressor; laboratory tests indicate that people respond to unpleasant or loud noises with the typical physiological reactions to stress, such as the increased electrical skin response that denotes muscle tension, increased blood pressure, and the production of epinephrine (Holahan, 1982). It is not certain whether the stress from noise can damage physical or mental health; however, some studies (Crook and Langdon, 1974) have found a relationship between noise and headaches, nervousness, and insomnia, and others (Cameron, Robertson, and Zaks, 1972) have found a correlation between prolonged noise and the incidence of acute and chronic physical illness.

Polluted city air contains carbon monoxide, sulfur dioxide, nitrogen oxides, photooxidants from automobile engines, asbestos particles, and substances formed when automobile tires pass over the pavement. As the level of pollutants increases, the incidence of respiratory diseases rises. In addition, when air contains high levels of carbon monoxide, heart patients develop symptoms of angina after much less exertion (Anderson et al., 1973). Older adults, especially those who have developed emphysema, are more sensitive than younger people to the effects of air pollutants. During temperature inversions, the heavy accumulation of pollutants near the ground surface can cause serious illness or death.

As we saw in Chapter 4, older adults' ability to regulate body temperature decreases. When summer temperatures soar, they are especially likely to develop heatstroke. During a heat wave in July 1980, 148 heat-related deaths were reported in Kansas City; 72 percent of the deaths occurred among people past 65 (*Time*, 1980). The death rate was concentrated among older people in low-income areas, who tend to be in poorer health than other old people and to lack air conditioners or other means of keeping cool. A similar heat wave in 1983 led St. Louis city officials to provide air-conditioned shelters for such people.

The effect of other environmental factors on health is generally less direct than the action of noise, air pollution, or heat. As people age, their senses pick up less information from the environment, and they process the information they receive more slowly. When information is sharply reduced or distorted, people may tend to become increasingly cautious, move more slowly, require more help, interact less with other people and the environment. They may even become confused, disoriented, or extremely suspicious (Howell, 1980).

Their level of adaptation to the environment changes. Lucille Nahemow and Powell Lawton (1976) have proposed that adaptation results from the interaction of individual **competence** (the ability of the person to respond) and **environmental press** (aspects of the environment that have some motivating force for the individual). Competence encompasses physical vigor and health, sensory functioning, and intellectual skills. People with a high level of competence can adapt to a wider range of press, including stressors. Moderate levels of environmental stress in relation to competence appear to lead to the most efficient adaptive behavior and positive moods (Figure 5.7). When a person is functioning at adaptation level, he or she is minimally aware of the environment, and behavior and emotions are normal.

If environmental press is either extremely high or extremely low, the effects on the individual's health can be negative. For example, if older people's environment is oversimplified by reduced role demands, constraints on economic freedom, dwindling connections with friends and family, and reduced physical surroundings, they may adapt with very low levels of sensory and emotional experience (Nahemow and Lawton, 1976). Ultimately, their competence is reduced, and they lack the resources to adapt to any high environmental press.

Various aspects of the environment may create a level of stress that leads older people to avoid going out into the community. High curbs, fast traffic, signals that do not give them time to cross the street, poorly labeled buildings, and wind-tunnel effects between some high-rise buildings may discourage city-dwelling adults from leaving their apartments (Holahan, 1982). In some neighborhoods, older people may also fear being preyed on by muggers or purse snatchers. They adapt by cutting back on their exposure to stressors and thus reduce environmental press. If various services are available in their building, they may rarely leave the premises. When asked, older adults may report satisfaction with the arrangement, but may become dependent on it, so that their mobility and competence are ultimately reduced (Parr, 1980). Such a reduction of mobility has appeared in studies. One researcher (Lawton, 1977) found that a year after they moved into housing projects, tenants in housing with many services showed small gains in morale but were less likely to engage in activities that took them outside the project than were tenants in housing without services.

A reduction of competence, together with a lack of independence and perceived control over their lives may be responsible for the high levels of mortality among older individuals who are moved into institutions, especially those who already have physical or mental impairments (Lawton, 1977).

None of the factors that affect life-style acts in isolation. Nutrition, exercise levels, stress, and the environment work on all of us all the time. If we also smoke, we have added an additional factor that interacts with all the others. Together these factors play a major role in determining the speed with which we age.

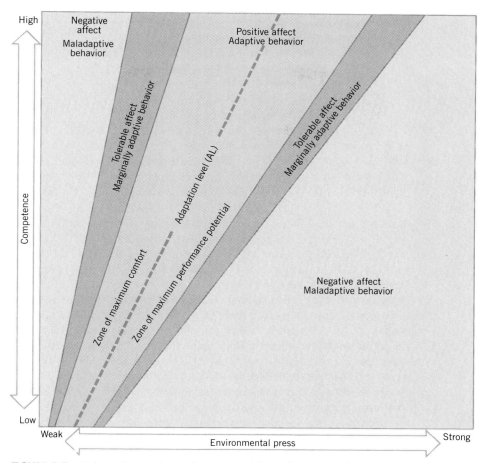

FIGURE 5.7   Adaptation to the environment. Adaptation results from the interaction of environmental press and competence. An individual's adaptation level is the point at which environmental press is average for his or level of competence.

Source: M. P. Lawton and L. Nahemow, "Ecology and the Aging Process," in C. Eisdorfer and M. P. Lawton (eds.), *Psychology of Adult Development and Aging* (Washington, D. C.: American Psychological Association, 1973).

SUMMARY

Acute illness, a physical disorder with a limited duration, becomes less common with age although each incident of illness tends to become increasingly severe. Normal aging processes may complicate acute illness in older adults. The proportion of any cohort with a **chronic illness**, which cannot be cured and tends to get worse, increases with age.

Life-style has an important influence on health; as many as half the deaths in the United States may be due to unhealthy life-styles. Aspects of life-style may be synergistic, so that some combinations can damage the health more than the sum of probable harm from each aspect. Cigarette smoking is the most deleterious life-style factor; smoking has been implicated in various forms of cancer, heart disease, emphysema, chronic bronchitis, and peptic ulcers. The typical American diet (high in fat, low in fiber, high in sugar, high in salt) has been associated with heart disease, hypertension, diabetes, and cancer. Lowering blood cholesterol levels reduces the incidence of heart attack. Older adults need fewer calories per pound of body weight because they tend to be less active than younger adults; however, older adults use more calories when performing the same physical tasks.

Declining activity may be responsible for a good deal of the "natural" deterioration of body systems that is generally assumed to be the result of aging. Exercise sometimes can reverse physical declines that develop from inactivity.

Stress can accelerate the aging process, leading to the development of physical disease or mental disorder and impairing a person's ability to respond to new challenges. **Stressors** can be either physical or psychological, located in the world or within the person. Whether stress affects health depends on how it is perceived and how a person reacts to it. When people face uncontrollable stress and believe that their inability to control it is permanent and the result of inner deficiencies and that it affects many areas of their life, they may develop **learned helplessness**. Some researchers believe that the cumulative stress from life events, whether pleasant or unpleasant, can lead to disease. However, such an approach does not allow for chronic stress, for the fact that some events may be the consequence—not the cause—of illness, or for the context of life events. Expected events are probably much less stressful than those that are unexpected. Events that place a strain on life roles are likely to be especially stressful. Older people face fewer stress-producing events than do the young, but the balance of stress is likely to change in old age so that negative stresses outweigh positive stresses. Older people also may be more vulnerable to stress than the young. There are interindividual differences in the way people cope with stress, with some appearing to thrive on a stressful life and others seeming to be overwhelmed by it. Two coping styles have been found to affect the development of heart disease, with Type A individuals at high risk and Type B individuals at low risk.

Aspects of the environment (noise, air pollution, extreme temperatures) can have direct effects on health. Older adults are especially sensitive to air pollutants and temperature extremes. Adaptation to the environment results from the interaction of individual **competence** and **environmental press**. People function best at moderate levels of stress, and when environmental press becomes extremely high or extremely low, health may suffer. As people age, their level of adaptation to the environment changes. All factors that affect life-style interact, affecting the speed at which an individual ages.

KEY TERMS

acute illness	**learned helplessness**
chronic illness	**stress**
competence	**stressor**
environmental press	

6

MENTAL HEALTH ACROSS ADULTHOOD

I n 1981, Allene Roach, a teacher at a bilingual Montessori school, was diagnosed as having Alzheimer's disease. She was 52 years old. For about two years, it had been apparent that something was wrong. Once she wandered away from home, and when she returned four days later, she had no idea where she had been. She had become increasingly disoriented, never sure of the time or the date. Her memory was failing; she repeatedly asked the same questions and told the same stories again and again. By 1983 she was unable to drive a car, her memory had deteriorated so severely that she could not be left alone, and until she was given sedatives regularly, she hallucinated. Within a few years her autonomic nervous system will "forget" how to function and she will die (Roach, 1983).

Alzheimer's disease is a form of mental deterioration and personality disintegration that is accompanied by physical changes within the brain. Although this disorder has a physiological basis, many mental disorders appear to develop from the individual's interactions with the environment, and some seem to have both physiological and environmental components.

Mental disorders are not limited to any phase of the life span. Children, adolescents, and younger adults also have disorders that seem to come from the interaction of personality and experience and—in most cases—to have no physical cause. When all degrees of emotional disorders are lumped together, no particular increase in prevalence appears with age. Some types of disorders, such as the physiologically based brain disorders, become more prevalent with age, and other varieties are less likely to develop. The best estimate is that about 15 percent of people past 65 have at least moderately severe mental disorders that need some sort of treatment (Pfeiffer, 1977).

In this chapter we begin by exploring the organic brain disorders that were once thought to be an inevitable accompaniment of aging. Then we consider mental disorders with no identifiable physiological basis, first looking at psychotic disorders and then turning to the less severe, but more common, conditions, including depression, hypochondriasis, and alcoholism. The chapter ends with a brief overview of various forms of treatment.

ORGANIC BRAIN DISORDERS

Similar symptoms appear in most **organic brain disorders**. These symptoms are related to physical changes within the brain but may have different causes. When behavioral and emotional changes have no identifiable organic basis and so are not related to known brain deterioration, they are called **functional mental disorders**. The signs of organic brain disorder may be slight or profound, appear slowly or develop with amazing speed. Robert Butler and Myrna Lewis (1982) have described five kinds of mental change that generally accompany organic brain disorders:

1. *Impaired memory.* The person's inability to remember may be caused by a failure to register an event in the mind, a failure to retain a memory that was registered, or the inability to recall a memory voluntarily.
2. *Impaired intellect.* The person has trouble comprehending facts or ideas, handling arithmetical chores, or learning any new behavior.
3. *Impaired judgment.* The person finds it difficult to comprehend personal situations and make plans or decisions.
4. *Impaired orientation.* The person becomes confused about time, place, and people's identity, with confusion concerning time appearing first.
5. *Excessive or shallow emotions.* The person may react excessively to an event, perhaps throwing a temper tantrum, or be apathetic. Emotions may also shift rapidly, for no apparent reason.

A person with organic brain syndrome may not show all five signs at once, and some signs may be more pronounced than others. For some, these symptoms can be reversed; they are suffering from **acute brain dysfunction**. For others, the symptoms are irreversible. They herald a steady decline that will become an inability to handle the simplest self-care and finally end with death; these people are suffering from **chronic brain dysfunction.**

ACUTE BRAIN DYSFUNCTION

From 10 to 20 percent of people with organic brain syndrome have acute brain dysfunction, a disorder called **delirium** by the American Psychiatric Association (1980). Although the condition often develops swiftly, it may also come on slowly, depending on its cause. Whatever the specific cause, metabolism is disturbed throughout the brain. Acute brain dysfunction may result from medications, malnutrition, brain tumors, liver disease, cardiovascular disease, strokes, fever, emphysema, or acute alcoholic intoxication. In most cases, the delirium has more than one cause (Sloane, 1980).

For example, any drug that affects the central nervous system can cause delirium, especially if the patient has cardiovascular disease that reduces the brain's oxygen supply or if dehydration develops. An older person whose memory has been affected may forget that a prescribed medication has already been taken and take multiple doses without realizing it.

The patient may be confused, stuporous, or actively delirious, and the level of awareness may fluctuate (Butler and Lewis, 1982). Some or all of the organic brain syndrome signs are present, and there may be hallucinations or delusions of persecution. Fever, muscular tremors, rapid heartbeat, sweating, flushed face, dilated pupils, and elevated blood pressure are also common. EEGs are always abnormal.

If properly identified, acute brain dysfunction generally lasts less than a week. It is treated by correcting the underlying condition. The patient may need oxygen, transfusions, blood glucose, fluids, or treatment of infection or need to have body temperature controlled. If the underlying condition is not diagnosed, however, the patient may develop a chronic brain dysfunction or even die. Approximately 40 percent of the patients die—either from exhaustion or the underlying condition (Butler and Lewis, 1982). Often, however, complete recovery is possible. Chances seem best when social or environmental factors may have played a part in the development of the dysfunction, as when isolation leads to malnutrition or alcoholism.

CHRONIC BRAIN DYSFUNCTION

About 5 percent of the population who have passed the age of 65 have a chronic brain dysfunction that severely interferes with cognitive functioning. In another 10 percent, there is mild to moderate cognitive impairment (Coyle, Price, and De-Long, 1983). However, the condition is most likely to develop later in adulthood, when people are in their seventies or eighties, so that the proportion of afflicted adults between the ages of 65 and 70 is actually much lower than statistics would indicate.

Occasionally, older men and women who seem to be suffering from one of the common forms of chronic brain dysfunction actually have a treatable brain disorder. For example, in one group of 60 patients, 18 had a disease that could be relieved by treatment, such as chronic drug toxicity, liver failure, or hyperthyroidism (Freemon, 1976). In other cases, the apparent organic deterioration is a functional disorder. Because a misdiagnosis carries with it the assumption of irreversibility, it is important that physicians keep the less common brain disorders in mind when examining patients.

Alzheimer's Disease

The major cause of chronic brain dysfunction in older adults is **Alzheimer's disease**, a disorder that affects approximately half of those with severe intellectual impairment (U.S. Public Health Service, 1980). The terminology for this disorder has been shifting. When it was considered to be the result of aging, it was known as *senile dementia,* with the same condition in younger adults called *presenile dementia,* or Alzheimer's disease, after the German neurologist who first identified the structural brain changes that characterize it (Leroux, 1981). In their latest classification of psychological disorders, the American Psychiatric Association (1980) refers to senile dementia as *primary degenerative dementia, senile onset* and to presenile dementia as *primary degenerative dementia, presenile onset.* Many investigators believe the two conditions are physiologically identical (Bartus et al., 1982; Coyle, Price, and DeLong, 1983) and prefer the term Alzheimer's disease regardless of the patient's age. The condition is more common in women than in men.

Dementia is the result of characteristic changes in the brain that can be identified with certainty only at autopsy. As noted in Chapter 4, the brains of people with Alzheimer's disease show gross dendritic atrophy, as well as many senile plaques and vacuoles. These diseased brains also show an abnormally large number of neurofibrillary tangles. In addition, brain shrinkage is more pronounced than in normal aging.

Diagnosis is generally made by eliminating other causes of brain disorder. A thorough physical, neurological, and psychiatric examination is necessary. CAT scans, EEGs, taps of spinal fluid, and comprehensive blood analyses can rule out some possible causes. Psychological tests can rule out others, such as severe depression, which is a functional disorder. PET scans can help to confirm the diagnosis, for an Alzheimer's brain takes up glucose much more slowly than a normal brain (Roach, 1983).

Alzheimer's disease develops so slowly that family members do not realize for some time that the person is deteriorating. It may first show as an inability to write checks or to make change. Sometimes it progresses even farther before the condition is apparent. For example, one morning at breakfast a 62-year-old salesman asked his wife what time it was. Before half an hour had passed, he asked her again. She stretched out her arm so he could see her watch, but he could not read the dial. She asked him a few simple questions about telling time from a book their children had used as preschoolers. From his answers, she became aware that he was having a real problem understanding time. Until that moment, she had no idea there was anything seriously wrong with her husband (Burnside, 1979).

The mystery of Alzheimer's disease is still being untangled. There seems to be a hereditary component, with close relatives of Alzheimer patients much more likely to develop the condition than other people. In addition, people with Down's syndrome (an inherited chromosomal disorder that was discussed in Chapter 3) are likely to develop Alzheimer's disease if they live past 40, and the disease also appears among their relatives (Heston and Mastri, 1977). In most cases, however, it is difficult to find any hereditary cause (Roach, 1983).

It also has been suggested that a slow-acting virus is the culprit, but whatever the ultimate cause, recent research indicates that Alzheimer's disease affects behavior through its action on the brain's supply of the neurotransmitter, acetylcholine. It has been known for some time that acetylcholine was somehow involved with the disorder. Within the cortex of people who die of Alzheimer's disease, levels of an enzyme that synthesizes acetylcholine are from 60 to 90 percent less than are found in the brains of people without the disorder.

Joseph Coyle, Donald Price, and Mahlon DeLong (1983) followed this trail and have discovered that Alzheimer's patients—whether young or old—have lost a significant proportion of the neurons that supply the critical enzyme. These neurons extend into other parts of the brain, and as they are gradually destroyed, their fibers appear to provide the basis for the plaques that infest the brain of the Alzheimer disease patient. Gradually, the supply of acetylcholine diminishes. Earlier studies had shown that when acetylcholine is blocked from entering neurons, cognitive functioning is disrupted, and temporary amnesia may follow (Longo, 1966) and that when the pathways for acetylcholine are severed, learning and memory are impaired in experimental animals (Olton and Feustle, 1981).

Although the disruption of acetylcholine supply may not be the whole story in the development of Alzheimer's disease, it has given researchers an insight into the condition and one day may lead to a method of treatment (Bartus et al., 1982). One difference has already been found that may distinguish presenile from senile dementia. In the brains of younger patients with Alzheimer's disease, an area of the brain that provides the neurotransmitter noradrenaline to the cortex often degenerates. In patients with senile dementia, this area of the brain is relatively intact (Coyle, Price, and DeLong, 1983).

At present little can be done for people with Alzheimer's disease except to make them comfortable and to provide a situation in which it is easier for them to function. As memory fails, recall (the ability to remember voluntarily in the absence of the sought-for information) is destroyed before recognition (the ability to remember in the presence of the information). Substituting recognition for recall in daily situations may help patients manage their lives in earlier stages of the disease (Zarit et al., 1982). Labels on drawers and appliances ("turn off the burner"), an automatic telephone dialer, calendars, clocks, and notes left in conspicuous places can increase their functioning and prolong their independence. As the disease progresses, people become progressively less able to care for themselves. Finally, they cannot even feed themselves and require continual nursing attendance. The disease is believed to halve life expectancy, with some patients living for more than 10 years after the disease appears (Zarit, 1980). Once the condition has been diagnosed, however, the average life expectancy is five years.

Alzheimer's disease is the most prevalent form of organic brain dysfunction. Among older patients, 48 percent of all deaths attributed to organic brain dysfunction are due to Alzheimer's disease, and it plays a contributing role in another 12 percent, in which multiinfarct dementia is also present (Butler and Lewis, 1982).

Multiinfarct Dementia

Multiinfarct dementia is the second major form of chronic brain dysfunction. It is a disorder apparently caused when blood clots repeatedly cut off the supply of blood to the brain. The patient often has hypertension, and although atherosclerosis may be present, it seems to be important in only a minority of cases (Sloane, 1980). Multiinfarct dementia appears to cause about 20 percent of the deaths from chronic organic brain dysfunction, in addition to its presence in the 12 percent who also have Alzheimer's disease (Butler and Lewis, 1982).

The first symptoms of multiinfarct dementia may appear at about the age of 50 although the average age of onset is 66. It is more common in men than in women, apparently because estrogen provides women with some protection against cardiovascular disease until menopause.

The brains of patients with multiinfarct dementia show cerebrovascular lesions, with areas of softened and deteriorated tissue. The first symptoms may be dizziness or headaches although about half the cases begin with a sudden, acute attack of confusion (Butler and Lewis, 1982). Sometimes the patient hallucinates or shows signs of delirium. Memory loss may be spotty, and the patient may retain a large measure of insight until relatively late in the course of the disease. Often a patient will have periods of seeming remission in that memory will suddenly clear and lucidity return to the extent that only careful testing will show the cognitive impairment (Sloane, 1980).

Treating the underlying hypertension and cardiovascular disease can slow the progress of this form of dementia. Patients may live for 15 years or more, and death is usually the result of stroke, heart disease, or pneumonia.

Because patients with multiinfarct dementia may hallucinate, a substantial minority of the people believed to be suffering from this organic condition may, in fact, be afflicted by a functional brain disorder. In one state hospital, investigators discovered that 30 percent of the patients referred to them as having multiinfarct dementia actually had paranoia, a functional mental disorder (Butler and Lewis, 1980).

Parkinson's Disease

A third chronic brain disorder, **Parkinson's disease**, may appear as early as the thirties although it usually shows up when people are in their sixties. The disease develops slowly, beginning with a slowing of movement, a stooped posture with the head forward and elbows flexed, and a much shortened step. The face lacks emotional expression, and the voice becomes a monotone. A tremor appears about four to eight times per second, which is most noticeable in the fingers, forearm, eyelids, and tongue. At times the patient can temporarily control the tremors so completely that he or she may be able to do some task that requires fine muscular coordination, but the characteristic shaking soon returns (Bootzin and Acocella, 1980)

A patient with Parkinson's disease may have difficulty concentrating, and memory may begin to fail. Mental impairment occurs in about 25 to 80 percent of the patients (Drachman, 1980), and many develop a severe depression. If left untreated, Parkinson's disease causes disability within five years. The disorder is twice as common in men as in women.

No one is certain just what causes Parkinson's disease. Encephalitis, viruses, and various other causes have been suggested. However, a deficiency of the neurotransmitter dopamine is apparently involved. Researchers have found that patients with Parkinson's disease have lost brain cells in the substantia nigra, a small area on each side of the brain that produces dopamine (Wyatt and Young, 1983). Some drugs that treat psychosis by reducing dopamine activity can cause a Parkinsonian tremor as a side effect. Increasing the availability of dopamine through the drug Levadopa (l-dopa), a substance the body uses to make dopamine, has been successful with some patients. Although it does not cure the disorder, it reduces or eliminates symptoms, allowing individuals to function in a relatively normal fashion.

PSYCHOTIC DISORDERS

Normal mental activity is severely impaired in **psychosis,** and the patient's perception of reality is drastically distorted. Hallucinations and delusions are common; impulses are poorly controlled. Because they have lost the ability to deal adaptively with the world, people with psychoses often cannot handle the details of daily life. If the psychosis is in an acute stage, they are usually unable to hold a job or even to carry on a coherent conversation.

It is often said that psychoses increase with age. Statistics indicate that people past 75 are twice as likely to be psychotic as 24- to 34-year-olds (Jaco, 1960). But this figure is misleading: It includes organic brain disorders as well as functional disorders. In addition, many older psychotics developed their disorder in youth or middle age and have simply survived. The major psychotic disorders are schizophrenia and paranoia.

SCHIZOPHRENIA

Schizophrenia is the most common psychosis. Although a good deal less than 1 percent of the population has ever had a schizophrenic episode, approximately half the patients in mental hospitals are diagnosed schizophrenics (Bootzin and Acocella, 1980). The disorder is characterized by disturbed thought, disturbed perception, and disturbed emotions. Delusions and hallucinations are common, and the patient's behavior is often bizarre. A schizophrenic might be highly active (running around and knocking things about), engage in moderately active but highly repetitive behavior (tearing paper, counting cornflakes, rubbing his or her head), or be completely immobile (not moving or speaking for days).

In most cases, schizophrenia first shows itself in adolescence or early adulthood. It can appear suddenly—in what seems like a few days—or develop gradually over a period of years. After an acute phase, recovery may be rapid or gradual. In some patients, recovery is complete; others never completely recover and go on to have further acute phases, with their level of functioning deteriorating further after each acute attack. It has been estimated that 25 percent of schizophrenics recover completely, up to 65 percent will continue to have acute episodes, and about 10 percent will never recover from the acute phase of the disorder (Bleuler, 1978).

Young adult schizophrenics are more likely to be males than females. After the age of 35, however, women are more likely than men to develop the disorder (Post, 1980). Schizophrenia rarely appears for the first time in old age. Most older schizophrenics developed the disorder early in life and were committed to hospitals, where they often received little or no treatment. Some of these "chronic schizophrenics" have been hospitalized as long as 60 years (Butler and Lewis, 1982).

When schizophrenia does make its initial appearance in older adults, it is called **paraphrenia.** These patients seem to have a milder form of the disorder than patients with an early onset. Although they generally have a good work history, their intimate relationships are either unstable or nonexistent. They tend to be unmarried, to live in isolation, to have few surviving relatives, and to belong to lower socioeconomic classes (Post, 1980).

The causes of schizophrenia are complex and not completely understood. Part of the difficulty lies in the fact that schizophrenia is actually a collection of disorders, not a single psychosis. A complicated interaction of biology, personality, and society appears to be involved in its development. Some kinds of schizophrenia appear to have a genetic component. For example, children of schizophrenic mothers have an increased likelihood of developing the disorder whether they are reared by their mothers or in a family with no history of mental disorders (Higgins, 1976).

Physiology is also important. Schizophrenics appear to have an excess of dopamine activity within the brain. When schizophrenics are given drugs that block neurons' ability to take up dopamine, a neurotransmitter, many of their symptoms disappear. When they are given drugs that increase dopamine activity, their symptoms become pronounced and dramatic.

Finally, environment is certainly implicated. Psychoanalysts have suggested that an anxious and hostile parent–child relationship causes the child to withdraw to fantasy. Behaviorists have suggested that a consistent failure to reinforce a person's social responses together with consistent reinforcement of their bizarre behavior teaches schizophrenia (Ullmann and Krasner, 1975). Psychiatrists have blamed patterns of family interaction. In younger schizophrenics, the disorder often appears after some stressful event, such as a love affair or the birth of a child. No matter what combination of causes is responsible for schizophrenia, most patients respond to antipsychotic drugs, which eliminate symptoms and make it possible for them to return to society.

PARANOID DISORDERS

Although delusions are a frequent symptom of schizophrenia, they are the central symptom of **paranoid disorders**. The basic abnormality is either a grandiose delusion, as in the man who thinks he is God, or delusions of persecution, as in the woman who believes that someone from another planet is torturing her with invisible rays. The person's intellectual processes are intact, but mood, behavior, and thought are all distorted by the basic delusion. If the basic delusion were true, the thoughts, attitudes, and behavior would seem logical.

Paranoid delusions in young people are generally fleeting and are part of schizophrenia. Once people are past 35 or 40, chronic paranoia may develop, but it is extremely rare (Post, 1980). Brief paranoid disorders may develop when people are placed in severely adverse conditions, such as a prison. Perhaps the most common causes of paranoid disorders are isolation from human contact and severe hearing loss (Butler and Lewis, 1982). Women are more likely than men to develop paranoid reactions.

It may be that paranoid reactions develop in older people as part of an attempt to fill in the "blank spaces" in the environment that result when hearing, vision, or memory fail (Pfeiffer, 1977). In fact, deafness is often involved. Older people with severe paranoid disorders tend to have long standing hearing loss in both ears that makes them socially deaf (Post, 1980). An older man who is deaf may believe that people are deliberately speaking softly, so that he cannot hear what they are saying about him. One who cannot remember where he put his billfold, glasses, or keys may accuse others of stealing them. An older woman who has been having arguments with her daughter and whose taste perceptions have changed may accuse her daughter of trying to poison her.

Because paranoid reactions explain bewildering events in the world, they are in a sense adaptive. Perhaps this adaptive function explains why paranoid reactions are sometimes seen in the early stages of an organic brain syndrome. In fact, researchers (Allen and Clow, 1950) have described one type of paranoid reaction as "consistent," for it can be regarded as an exaggeration of the understandable annoyance caused by the physical and environmental limitations that begin to curb older people's activities and capabilities.

Paranoid reactions in old age may even escape the notice of others. In one case (Post, 1980), it was only after an older man died that his family discovered in his diary that he believed people followed him in the street whenever he went out. Many of those who develop paranoid reactions have been eccentric for years. The disorder does not affect their ability to care for themselves, and so others see no dramatic change in their conduct or appearance.

Often simple paranoid disorders can be dealt with, at least temporarily, by changing the social situation. A stable, friendly environment that is not connected with the delusions may end the fears although not the person's belief in the delusion. Correcting any contributing sensory loss is helpful. Small doses of antipsychotic drugs are sometimes used although paranoid patients are generally suspicious of medical treatment (Pfeiffer, 1977).

NEUROTIC DISORDERS

Functional disorders commonly called **neuroses** are less severe than psychotic disorders. Although the person may find it difficult, or even impossible, to carry out normal functions, he or she remains in touch with reality. It has often been said that the neurotic builds castles in the air but the psychotic lives in them. Thinking and judgment may be impaired in neurotic disorders, but personality does not disintegrate. Psychosis and neurosis generally differ in another way as well. The psychotic believes that he or she is well; the neurotic knows that something is wrong and wants relief.

The American Psychiatric Assocation (1980) no longer classifies the less severe neurotic disorders as neuroses. The term "neurosis" comes from psychoanalysis and assumes that such disorders develop when people try to protect themselves against unconscious anxiety in maladaptive ways. By reclassifying neurotic disorders into several categories, psychiatrists have avoided making assumptions about their cause.

The disorders included in this section are only a few of those formerly classified as neuroses. Like the psychotic disorders, some may develop in adolescence or young adulthood. Neurotic disorders rarely arise for the first time in old age, but many disturbances do become apparent for the first time when a person has to deal with the tasks of later adulthood (Simon, 1980).

DEPRESSION

Depression, which is classified as an *affective disorder* by the American Psychiatric Association (1980), can occur at any time of life, including childhood. From 18 to 23 percent of women and from 8 to 11 percent of men have a major depressive episode at some time in their lives. About 50 percent of these people will have at least one recurrence of depression (Skodol and Spitzer, 1983). It is the most common functional mental disorder of later adulthood, with as many as 30 percent of older adults going through a period of at least mild depression. However, the results from two longitudinal studies indicate that increased age itself is not associated with depression (Lieberman, 1983). Increased age, when controlled for social class, showed no association with depression. In fact, several studies have shown a correlation between low socioeconomic status and depression (Stenback, 1980).

Depression is more than the fleeting sadness, despondency, or grief we all feel at some time or another. It cannot be chased away by a fine meal, a new suit, a vacation in St. Thomas, or expressions of affection from a loved one. In a major

Although depression is the most common functional disorder of later adulthood, studies indicate that life events—not aging—are usually responsible.

depression, the despondent mood persists and may be accompanied by pessimism, low self-esteem, and feelings of foreboding. The depressed person's posture and facial expression often change to reflect mood. Although some patients are agitated and jittery, others show slowed speech and movement and stare into space, and most have trouble making decisions, perhaps because they find it difficult to concentrate on any activity or problem. They may begin to contemplate suicide. Among the physical symptoms of depression are insomnia, anxiety, loss of appetite, weight loss, fatigue, and bodily aches and pains (Klerman, 1983).

The causes of depression are often difficult to discover. There may be some clear-cut, precipitating event, or the disorder may seem to develop out of the blue, with no noticeable life event to explain it (Skodol and Spitzer, 1983). Often the loss of some important person, thing, or activity precedes the depression. Bitter disappointments, criticisms, and real or imagined threats may be in the background (Butler and Lewis, 1982). At times, guilt appears to be implicated, a guilt produced by the conviction that the person has failed in carrying out life tasks (Stenback, 1980).

At one time it was thought that menopause could lead to a form of depression called involutional melancholia. The physiological adjustments to a new hormonal balance, together with the psychological adjustments to the loss of youth and the ability to bear children, were supposed to plunge middle-aged women into depression. The condition could be distinguished from other types of depression because these women had never had a previous depressive episode. Once researchers began to study the situation, it became apparent that there was no rise in depression at menopause. In fact, the rate of depression was about the same whether women were under 45 (premenopausal), between 45 and 55 (menopausal), or older than 55 (postmenopausal) (Weissman, 1979). And when depression did develop in middle-aged women, it was no different from depression in anybody else. As a result, involutional melancholia is no longer recognized as a separate mental disorder (American Psychiatric Association, 1980; Skodol and Spitzer, 1983).

Longitudinal studies (Lieberman, 1983) have found that some life events can lead to depression, but only when they change the circumstances of a person's life. For example, demotion, losing a job, and poor health are associated with depression, but the association appears to come from the way these events place a strain on marriage, parenthood, and economic and occupational situations. Such strains were most apparent among middle-aged men, who showed the highest rate of depression. Divorce was also associated with depression, but only when divorced people faced changes in their economic situation and when they had no supportive personal relationships to take the place of the marital partner.

As people age, they go through a number of life events that could lead to depression, such as poor health, retirement, and the loss of a spouse. Whether depression actually develops depends in part on how these events affect a person's roles in everyday life (Lieberman, 1983). Some investigators (Jarvik, 1983) have pointed out that other losses, such as the loss of work, status, prestige, financial security, friends, and relatives, can be handled fairly successfully as long as older people maintain their health. Disabling disease often means becoming dependent on children or caregivers, accepting their decisions as well as their help. This reversal of roles may be harder to bear than most losses.

Not all people with disabling disease become depressed. Life situations interact with personality, genetics, and biochemistry. Some types of severe depression appear to have a genetic component (Davis, Segal, and Spring, 1983). For example, if an identical twin develops an affective disorder, the other twin is four times as likely to develop the disorder as a fraternal twin.

Several brain chemicals have been implicated in severe depression. Norepinephrine was the first neurotransmitter discovered to be involved, but later studies have added serotonin and perhaps acetylcholine to the list. Low levels of norepinephrine are associated with depression whereas high levels of the transmitter are associated with manic episodes, which are the mirror image of depression. (In a manic episode, there is elation, optimism, hyperactivity, and a feeling of power.) Drugs that lift depression either block the reabsorption of norepinephrine, prevent its destruction, or increase its production. Low levels of serotonin have also been associated with depression, and the same dugs that increase the availability of norepinephrine also increase serotonin levels.

More recently, acetylcholine has been implicated in depression, with researchers (Davis, Segal, and Spring, 1983) pointing out that many body functions involve a balance between acetylcholine and norepinephrine. They have found that when acetylcholine destruction is blocked, raising its level in the brain, a manic patient becomes depressed within minutes. These researchers have suggested that it is the balance of transmitters in the brain and not the deficiency or excess of a single transmitter that can trigger depression. High levels of acetylcholine and low levels of norepinephrine—and perhaps low levels of serotonin as well—may be the contributing combination.

Sometimes depression is caused by drugs, which can either aggravate a depression that already exists, cause a depression to arise, or produce symptoms that resemble the disorder but are not a true depression (Klerman, 1983). Because the symptoms may not appear until as long as 14 months after the person begins taking a drug, it is often difficult to discover the connection. Antihypertensive drugs are the most likely offenders, with true depression developing in 20 percent of older adults who take them. Other drugs that may be involved include female hormones, corticosteroids, and drugs used to treat Parkinson's disease, tuberculosis, and cancer. Sometimes a mixture of drugs, prescribed and over-the-counter, can lead to a depressed state.

When a depressed person talks about suicide, he or she should be taken seriously; between 30 and 50 percent of all suicides are among depressed individuals (Murphy and Robins, 1968).

SUICIDE

The older the person, the more urgent any message of suicidal intent becomes. Suicide attempts by people younger than 35 fail more often than they succeed, but after people pass 50 their attempts are likely to be successful. And once they are past 65, the attempt rarely fails (Butler and Lewis, 1982). The high success rate among older adults may be traced to the fact that suicide attempts among the young are often meant to affect other people; attempts among the elderly are unlikely to be aimed at affecting others (Zarit, 1980).

White men are more likely to commit suicide than any other group, and their self-inflicted deaths reach a peak between the ages of 80 and 84, when the suicide rate is 51.4 per 100,000 (Zarit, 1980). Among adults past 85, twelve times as many men as women kill themselves (Levy et al., 1980). Suicide rates for black males and females peak between the ages of 25 and 34, and for white females between the ages of 45 and 54 (U.S. Bureau of the Census, 1982. (See Fig. 6.1.)

The typical person who attempts suicide and survives is a native-born white woman in her twenties or thirties who does not work outside the home. She swallows sleeping pills, and the reason she gives for her attempt is either marital problems or depression. The typical person who succeeds in a suicide attempt is a native-born white man who is older than 40. He shoots or hangs himself or else uses carbon monoxide. The reason for his suicide is either poor health, marital problems, or depression (Shneidman and Farberow, 1970).

These statistics encompass only those deaths officially ruled as suicides. Older adults often use methods that are not as direct as firearms, ropes, or pills. They may starve themselves, refuse to take prescribed medication, engage in hazardous activities, or delay medical or surgical treatment (Miller, 1978).

Social isolation appears to play a role in the suicide of older depressed people.

| | Men | | | | | | Women | | | | | |
| | White | | | Black | | | White | | | Black | | |
	1970	1975	1979	1970	1975	1979	1970	1975	1979	1970	1975	1979
All ages	18.0	20.1	20.0	8.0	10.0	11.6	7.1	7.4	6.6	2.6	2.7	2.8
5 to 14 years	0.5	0.8	0.6	0.1	0.1	0.2	0.1	0.2	0.3	0.2	0.1	0.1
15 to 24 years	13.9	19.6	21.0	10.5	12.9	14.4	4.2	4.9	5.1	3.8	3.3	3.4
25 to 34 years	19.9	24.4	26.2	19.2	24.3	26.3	9.0	8.9	8.0	5.7	5.6	5.7
35 to 44 years	23.3	24.5	22.5	12.6	16.0	16.9	13.0	12.6	10.1	3.7	3.9	4.1
45 to 54 years	29.5	29.7	23.9	13.8	12.1	13.0	13.5	13.8	11.7	3.7	4.0	2.9
55 to 64 years	35.0	32.1	26.6	10.6	10.8	12.9	12.3	11.7	10.2	2.0	3.5	4.0
> 64 years	41.1	39.4	39.2	8.7	11.3	12.9	8.5	8.5	7.3	2.6	2.3	2.5

FIGURE 6.1   Suicide, 1970–1979 (rate per 100,000). The rate of suicide is highest among older white men and lowest among older black women; rates decline with age for all except white men.

Source: U.S. Bureau of the Census, 1982.

Among white males over 60 who committed suicide in Arizona over a 5-year period, most had recently lost a confidant. They also were less likely to pay social visits than men who died from natural causes (Miller, 1978).

When a depressed person commits suicide, it is rarely while he or she is in a deep depression. Instead, the step is taken as the depression seems to lift (Butler and Lewis, 1982). Whether a person appears to come out of a depression because the decision to commit suicide has been taken or whether it is only as the depression lifts that a person has enough energy to commit suicide is not clear.

HYPOCHONDRIASIS

Hypochondriasis, an exaggerated fear of disease, is another common functional disorder among older adults, ranking third, behind depression and paranoid reactions. It appears to increase with age and is more prevalent among women than men (Pfeiffer, 1977). Hypochondriasis is classified as a *somatoform disorder* by the American Psychiatric Association (1980) because it involves symptoms of physical illness without an organic basis.

Hypochondriac patients are preoccupied with their bodily functioning, and this preoccupation interferes with family, friends, social organizations, or occupation. They may report a list of symptoms that include every organ and system in the body. Or they may shift from system to system. This week they have a slipped disk, next week emphysema, and the week after they are certain they have a malfunctioning kidney. Often they are in good physical health although they cannot be convinced of it. The worst news a physician can give a hypochondriac patient is, "There is nothing wrong with you" (Pfeiffer, 1977).

Hypochondriasis serves an important function because it allows people to avoid their problems by escaping into the role of invalid. It can make a person's

Hypochondriasis, or a fear of disease that is so exaggerated that it interferes with a person's family, social, and occupational life, appears to increase with age.

sense of deterioration concrete; it gives such people a valid reason for interacting with medical personnel and other caregivers; it displaces anxiety from other problems; it allows them to identify with a deceased loved one who had a similar disease; it punishes them for whatever they feel guilty about; it allows them to escape unwanted duties or social interactions; it punishes those around them; it regulates intimacy with others (Butler and Lewis, 1982).

In addition to serving all these psychic functions, hypochondriasis allows a person to ask for help in an acceptable way. Often there is an underlying psychological stress that the individual cannot acknowledge. Because emotional disorders are unacceptable to the hypochondriac patient, he or she rejects any attempt to explain the emotional basis of the physical symptoms (Pfeiffer, 1977). When hypochondriasis develops for the first time in old age, it may be an indication of depression or a signal that the patient has some underlying degenerative disease that he or she knows nothing about (Simon, 1980).

ALCOHOLISM

Alcohol is the most widely used drug in the United States. Nearly 70 percent of the population take a drink some time during the year, and 58 percent drink at least once a month (Abelson et al., 1977). Millions of Americans—at least 18 million—are considered heavy drinkers: a minimum of five or six drinks a day. People begin to abuse alcohol at a very early age, and in the past few years the existence of child and adolescent alcoholics has come to the attention of the country.

Alcoholism is considered a *substance abuse disorder* by the American Psychiatric Association (1980). It results when a person becomes so dependent on alcohol that it interferes with health, personal relationships, occupation, and social functioning (Simon, 1980). Judging from admissions to psychiatric hospitals and outpatient clinics, the peak years for alcoholism are from 35 to 50. But in a New York City survey, there were two peaks of alcoholism, one between the ages of 45 and 54 and the other between the ages of 65 and 74 (Bailey, Haberman, and Alksne, 1965).

Men are also more likely to become alcoholics than women. However, because women who do not work outside the home and retired individuals can more easily conceal their drinking, the sex and age differences may be smaller than statistics indicate. In addition, as many alcoholics are also depressed, men may be diagnosed as ''alcoholic'' whereas a woman with the same symptoms may be diagnosed as ''depressed'' (Kaplan, 1983).

Although alcoholism appears to decline with age, alcohol is clearly a problem for many older adults. Testimony before the United States Senate indicated that at least 10 percent of older adults had a ''drinking problem,'' that up to 56 percent of all hospital admissions of older adults were attributable to alcohol, and that widowers past 75 had the highest alcoholism rate in the country (Gaiter, 1983). Older alcoholics fall into two groups: Those with a lengthy history of alcoholism, dating back to early or middle adulthood; and late-onset alcoholics, who

As people age, their tolerance for alcohol decreases, and at least 10 percent of older men and women are believed to have a drinking problem.

have turned to alcohol in old age because of grief, depression, loneliness, boredom, or pain (Butler and Lewis, 1982). In a study of 100 consecutive admissions to a geriatric treatment unit (Gaitz and Baer, 1971), 44 patients had problems with alcohol, but only 5 had recently turned to the drug.

Alcohol is a central-nervous sytem depressant that slows the rate of neuronal firing. Small amounts of the drug make people feel euphoric, but the euphoria is accompanied by slowed reaction time, decreased alertness, and impaired motor coordination. As levels of alcohol in the blood increase, people's speech begins to slur, they become unsteady, and they finally lapse into unconsciousness. As people age, their tolerance for alcohol is reduced. Older adults appear to metabolize alcohol more slowly, and the drug may cause greater changes in brain chemistry and be more toxic than when they were younger (Zarit, 1980). Its effects on their behavior thus seem intensified, and it takes them longer to recover from a drinking spree.

Because alcohol affects the central nervous system, it temporarily impairs memory processes, interfering with the formation of new memories (Loftus, 1980). The long-term consequences of social drinking appeared when investigators (Parker and Noble, 1977) studied a group of California men. Among men who customarily drank heavily at a single sitting, cognitive processes and memory were impaired, but among those who had consumed the same amount of alcohol, but spread it out so that they were having only a drink or two at a time, there was no sign of impairment. Apparently, getting smashed every Saturday night takes a greater toll of memory processes than having a drink or two each evening.

IS MENTAL HEALTH IMPROVING?

If one community survey is used as a yardstick, American mental health appears to be improving. Among the nearly 700 men and women who took part in a longitudinal study of Midtown Manhattan residents, the general level of mental health improved over a 20-year period (Srole and Fisher, 1980). In 1954 and again in 1974, residents of the same middle-class and upper-middle-class area of New York City were asked about their mental health. The results resembled the trend of IQ scores discussed in Chapter 2.

When the replies were analyzed on a cross-sectional basis, it appeared that mental disorders are connected with aging; in both surveys the incidence of impaired mental health was greater at older ages. But when the replies were analyzed longitudinally, most groups showed improved functioning over the years. Asked in 1954 about their mental condition, 22 percent of the 50-year-olds (the 1900 cohort) said that it was impaired, but as 70 year olds, only 18 percent of the same cohort complained of impaired mental health. The same trend appeared in the 1910 and 1920 cohorts. Only the 1930 cohort, who aged from 20 to 40 over the course of the study, failed to show a decline in mental disorder. Although none of these declines is statistically significant by itself and may reflect the fact that mentally healthy individuals are more likely to survive than those with mental disorders, the trend is consistent and hopeful.

Because four cohorts were studied,

	Cohort			
	1900	**1910**	**1920**	**1930**
Age in 1954	50–59	40–49	30–39	20–29
Impaired mental health	22%	16%	14%	7%
Age in 1974	70–79	60–69	50–59	40–49
Impaired mental health	18%	12%	10%	8%
20–year difference	−4%	−4%	−4%	+1%

FIGURE 6.2 Mental health in Mid-Manhattan.

Source: L. Srole and A. K. Fischer, 1980, pp. 209–221.

Chronic alcoholics may develop organic disorders. Extreme alcoholic intoxication can cause acute organic brain disorder at any age. In some cases, the organic disorder is not directly caused by alcohol, but by dietary deficiencies. Alcoholics generally eat very little because alcohol provides energy (calories) without nutrients. Alcohol-related protein deficiency can lead to cirrhosis of the liver, a potentially fatal disease. Long-term deficiencies of vitamin B can lead to **Korsakoff's syndrome**, a chronic organic brain disorder.

there are two cross-sectional comparisons that could provoke a good deal of speculation. When they were in their forties, members of the 1910 cohort showed an impairment rate of 16 percent, but members of the 1930 cohort showed a rate of only 8 percent at the same age. When they were in their fifties, 22 percent of the 1900 cohort complained of mental impairment, but only 10 percent of the 1920 cohort had similar complaints.

Individuals of different cohorts seemed mentally healthier in 1974 than in 1954. This 20-year period covered the relatively tranquil and prosperous period after World War II as well as the turbulent Vietnam era. Historical events appeared to have affected individuals in the entire group similarly. All cohorts (except the 1930 group) showed the same improvement in mental health over the 20-year period (4 percent), and in the two cases where the comparison could be made, the prevalence of mental impairment had dropped by at least one half. (See Fig. 6.2.)

The study also covered a period in which sex roles were changing in the United States. The change appeared to be good for Mid-Manhattan women. When various cohorts are compared at the same age, women's mental health shows a significant increase over the two decades. During the 1950s, the rate of impaired mental health in 40- and 50-year-old women was much greater than in men of the same age. But by the 1970s, there was almost no difference between the sexes. (See Fig. 6.3.) In both cases, the improvement in women's mental health was significant.

Srole and Fisher studied a small area of a large American city, so their results cannot be applied to the United States as a whole. In fact the results cannot be applied to the entire island of Manhattan. But their news is good and should send researchers looking for signs of similar improvement in other areas.

	Men	Women
50-year olds (1900 cohort)	15%	26%
50-year-olds (1920 cohort)	9%	11%
40-year-olds (1910 cohort)	9%	21%
40-year-olds (1930 cohort)	9%	8%

FIGURE 6.3   Mental health impairment (by gender).
Source: L. Srole and A. K. Fischer, 1980, pp. 209–221.

A patient with Korsakoff's syndrome looks very much like a patient with Alzheimer's disease. However, differences between the two disorders exist. When researchers (Weingartner et al., 1983) tested the memory of patients with the two disorders, they discovered that both groups had severely impaired episodic memory. They could not remember specific events. But unlike patients with Alzheimer's disease, those with Korsakoff's syndrome still had access to semantic memory. They could recall general knowledge (meanings, relationships, and rules for manipulating information). As a result, the patients with Korsakoff's syndrome could assemble complex perceptual figures, identify words from fragments, and read inverted text. Patients with Alzheimer's disease simply could not handle these tasks.

Patients with Korsakoff's syndrome have both *anterograde amnesia,* the inability to form new memories, and *retrograde amnesia,* the inability to recall events that occurred before the disease developed (Sloane, 1980). They seem otherwise alert, and their social behavior is normal. Reasoning and judgment may be unimpaired. However, some tend to fill in their memory gaps by inventing facts, a process known as *confabulation,* so that in conversation the amnesia may go undetected for a time.

TRENDS IN THERAPY

At one time little effort was made to treat functional mental disorders in older adults. Sigmund Freud (1924), the father of psychoanalysis, had felt there was little purpose in using individual psychotherapy with people who were more than 45 years old. They were, he thought, so inflexible that even when they gained insight into their problems, they could not make the necessary personality changes. In addition, if their memory was failing, essential childhood memories might no longer be recalled from the unconscious.

Although some therapists disagreed, many tended to believe that the disorders they saw were in large part organic, that organic brain disorders were an inevitable part of aging, and that "you can't cure aging" (Eisdorfer and Stotsky, 1977). As more has been learned about normal aging, as the biochemical involvement in some disorders has become apparent, and as new therapeutic techniques have been developed, therapy with older adults has become more prevalent.

As yet no studies have demonstrated that age differences affect the therapy process, and it seems apparent that a good many older adults can benefit from present forms of therapy (Levy et al., 1980). Older adults are not a uniform group, and their vast interindividual differences place generalizations about the effectiveness of therapy on shaky ground. It would appear, however, that individual psychotherapy, behavior therapy, group therapy, and family therapy are probably most suitable for older adults with problems of personal or family adjustment. Some therapists have also incorporated a form of "life review," in which reminiscence is used to reorganize and integrate the person's life, into the therapeutic process. Through leading individuals to recall occasions when they were in control of their lives, this approach may help to alleviate the feelings of powerlessness that may underlie depression in some older adults (Sloane, 1983).

Other older adults have mental disorders that have developed as a result of physical illness or their social circumstances. For these individuals, suggests Steven Zarit (1980), the most helpful course might be to arrange for economic supports, coordinate various aspects of medical care, find home services for those with physical impairment, or develop an informal support network that ensures regular visitation by neighbors or friends. (Such social services will be explored in Chapter 14.)

For example, in a case described by Zarit, a 64-year-old woman who sought therapy for depression had recently been fired and had little income. Her counselor put her in touch with an employment agency that specialized in placing older adults, and she soon had a job. Within two months, her depression had lifted, she left therapy, and continued to function well on her own.

As research has shown that older adults are more capable and less alike than psychotherapeutic stereotypes once indicated, therapists have become more optimistic, and the approach to the treatment of mental disorders in later life has changed.

SUMMARY

Some mental disorders have a physiological basis, others appear to develop from the individual's interactions with the environment, and some seem to have both physiological and environmental components. About 15 percent of people past 65 have at least moderately severe mental disorders that need treatment.

Five kinds of mental change accompany most **organic brain disorders:** impaired memory, impaired intellect, impaired judgment, impaired orientation, and excessive or shallow emotions. In **acute brain dysfunction**, also known as **delirium,** the symptoms are reversible. There are many causes of delirium, but metabolism always is disturbed throughout the brain. When the causes are identified and treated, recovery occurs in about a week; when these are not identified, the patient may either develop a **chronic brain dysfunction** or die.

Chronic brain dysfunction is most likely to develop in late adulthood. The major cause is **Alzheimer's disease**, a slowly developing condition that is responsible for about half of the cases. The disorder can also develop in middle-aged adults and is more common in women than men. Alzheimer's disease affects behavior through its action on the brain's supply of acetylcholine, a neurotransmitter. **Multiinfarct dementia**, the second major chronic brain dysfunction, is caused when blood clots repeatedly cut off the supply of blood to the brain. It may appear as early as 50 and is more common in men than in women. **Parkinson's disease**, a third chronic brain dysfunction, may appear during the thirties and is apparently related to a deficiency of dopamine, a brain transmitter.

Mental disorders with no identifiable organic basis are known as **functional mental disorders**. In **psychosis**, a person's perception of reality is drastically distorted, and normal mental activity is severely impaired. **Schizophrenia**, the most common psychosis, is characterized by disturbances of thought, perception, and emotions. The disorder usually appears early in life, and when it makes its initial appearance in older adults, it generally takes a milder form, known as **paraphrenia**. The causes of schizophrenia are not understood, but patients usually respond to antipsychotic drugs.

Delusions are central to **paranoid disorders**, a condition in which behavior would be logical if the central delusion were true. Isolation from human contact and severe hearing loss are the most common causes, and the appearance of paranoid disorders in older adults may be part of an attempt to compensate for sensory or memory loss. Changing the social situation is often an effective treatment.

Neuroses are less severe than psychotic disorders, and personality does not disintegrate. **Depression** can appear at any time of life; although it is the most common functional disorder of later adulthood, it is not caused by aging. Life events may lead to depression, but only when they change the circumstances of a person's life and place a strain on social roles. Several neurotransmitters have been implicated in severe depression, but it can also be caused by drugs. Between 20 and 30 percent of all suicides are among depressed individuals, and the rate of suicide increases with age among white men, with deaths reaching a peak in the early eighties. Social isolation has been implicated in suicide, which is most likely to occur as a depression lifts.

Hypochondriasis, an exaggerated fear of disease, is the third most common functional disorder among older adults. The condition allows people to avoid their problems by escaping into the role of invalid and to ask for help in an acceptable way. Although **alcoholism** is believed to decline with age, it affects at least 10 percent of older adults and is especially prevalent among widowers older than 75. As people age, their tolerance for alcohol is reduced. Through long-term vitamin B deficiency, chronic alcoholics may develop **Korsakoff's syndrome**, a chronic brain disorder that resembles Alzheimer's disease.

It was once believed that older adults with mental disorders would not respond to therapy, but this belief has been rejected by most gerontologists. Today therapists are optimistic about the benefits of therapy with the elderly. Older adults with problems of personal or family adjustment can probably be helped by individual psychotherapy, behavior therapy, group therapy, or family therapy. Older adults whose disorders have developed because of physical illness or social circumstances can probably be helped by providing needed services.

KEY TERMS

acute brain dysfunction

alcoholism

Alzheimer's disease

chronic brain dysfunction

delirium

depression

functional mental disorder

hypochondriasis

Korsakoff's syndrome

multiinfarct dementia

neurosis

organic brain disorder

paranoid disorders

paraphrenia

Parkinson's disease

psychosis

schizophrenia

PART THREE

PSYCHOLOGICAL ASPECTS OF ADULT DEVELOPMENT AND AGING

7

SENSATION AND PERCEPTION ACROSS ADULTHOOD

Harry Porter runs an aviation service out of the Chattanooga, Tennessee, airport. His favorite plane is a twin-engine Beechcraft, which he feels is considerably safer than a single-engine plane. Other than mechanical malfunctions, Porter believes that bad weather is the greatest danger he can face in the sky. Heavy fog or wind shear can bring down the best of pilots. Porter's occupation would not seem unusual except for the fact that he is 89 years old. By mid-1983, he had logged more than 17,000 hours of flying time since he learned to fly half a century earlier (*AARP News Bulletin*, 1983c). Although he is still an active pilot, Porter no longer teaches others to fly.

The achievement of Harry Porter seems especially impressive when we consider that sensory ability generally declines with age and that most people's vision and hearing—two senses that are essential for pilots—undergo pronounced impairment long before their eighty-ninth birthday. Most of us accept the idea that glasses are inevitable and that we will begin to have trouble distinguishing some sounds as we get older. We are less aware that our sense of smell, taste, and touch, as well as our experience of pain, may also change.

The accomplishments of some individuals raise the question of whether our expected sensory impairment is entirely caused by the aging process. For example, 101-year-old John Henry Smart, a retired Utah farmer, has no serious visual problems. He says, "My eyesight's awfully good—I take the paper every day" (Barasch, 1983, p. 34). In fact, about 10 percent of 80-year-olds still have "perfect" 20-20 vision.

In this chapter, we investigate the sensory changes associated with normal aging. After considering some of the factors that may lead to sensory impairment, we take up the senses, one at a time, exploring vision, hearing, smell, taste, touch, and pain. In the process, we will discover how changes in sensation and perception affect the experiences of daily life.

SENSORY AGING

With age, the sensory systems slowly become less sensitive to stimulation from the environment. Despite the existence of a few Harry Porters, virtually all of us experience some loss of sensitivity. When light and sound waves stimulate our eyes and ears, gaseous molecules stimulate our noses, soluble molecules stimulate our taste buds, and temperature or pressure stimulates our skin, the perceptual experience that follows may be different in quality and quantity from our youthful perceptions.

As we get increasingly older, sensory problems generally become more intense, so that there is an age-related increase in the percentage of individuals with severe sensory limitations. For example, between the ages of 45 and 64, less than one person in 200 is legally blind. But among centenarians, five in 100 are legally blind. More than half of all cases of blindness develop after the age of 65 (Rockstein and Sussman, 1979).

Sensory loss in some older adults my be severe enough to make an ordeal out of a trip to the supermarket, where glare, noise, and precariously stacked cans can create a disorienting situation.

Sensory information comes to us as energy changes in the environment. The changes are picked up by specialized receptors, converted into electrical nerve impulses, and processed by structures in the nervous system. The sensory loss that accompanies aging may be caused by deterioration of the receptors, degeneration in the peripheral nervous system (the nerve fibers that connect muscles, glands, and sense organs with the central nervous system), or changes in the central nervous system itself. The decline may reflect normal developmental changes, but it may also be caused or speeded up by environmental abuse or disuse of the sensory system.

Without some kind of sensory information, we could not deal with the environment at all. Any limitations that accompany aging curtail access to knowledge of the world and may interfere with the ability to communicate effectively with others. A decided impairment in vision or hearing can isolate a person, producing serious psychological or social effects (Wantz and Gay, 1981). For example, a person with a severe hearing loss may find it so tiring to try to follow conversation that he or she simply stops listening, a habit that can lead to withdrawal from social interaction.

In an attempt to simulate the sensory loss encountered by many older adults, research assistants wore specially treated lenses over their eyes and put plugs in their ears (Pastalan, Mautz, and Merrill, 1973). Then the assistants went into the sort of situations commonly encountered by older adults, such as supermarkets. The distorted visual and auditory information that came through the sensory barriers threw them into a state of disorientation. They became cautious and moved very slowly. Sudden perceptual changes are, of course, likely to create a more intense disorientation than gradual impairment, which enables an individual to make a series of small adjustments to sensory decline.

However, Diana Woodruff (1983) has suggested that, compared with the young, older adults are in a state of sensory deprivation. As the brain seems to need a certain level of stimulation in order to function efficiently, severe sensory loss could affect cognition, explaining some of the disorientation and confusion that sometimes appear in older people without organic brain disorders. Although no research has demonstrated that age-related sensory restriction has this effect, Woodruff reports that the staff at one hospital has found that talking to patients in comas, thus increasing the level of stimulation, seems to speed recovery.

Few buildings are designed with the sensory capabilities of the elderly in mind. Because the proportion of older adults is rising rapidly, designing environments that consider such limitations might make it easier for people to adapt to old age and increase their satisfaction and enjoyment (Fozard and Popkin, 1978). The goal is not simply to increase physical comfort and safety, but to promote independence. One way to compensate for any sensory loss is to improve the amount or quality of sensory information that is available. Information can be presented through more than one sense. For example, some institutions are designed so that smells from the kitchen penetrate the living quarters, providing an aroma that acts as a cue supplementing the bell or buzzer that announces each meal (Windley and Scheidt, 1980).

Glasses and hearing aids are obvious ways to increase the amount and quality of available information, but changing the environment can also be effective. Increasing the amount of light can sometimes compensate for an older person's visual problems (Fozard and Popkin, 1978). For example, older people frequently fall on stairs, and the accident tends to occur at the top of the landing. Windows often make a corridor much brighter than the staircase, so that when people turn away from the light to go down stairs they must adapt to lower levels of illumination. Older people adapt so slowly to changes in light levels that they misjudge the first step. Simply placing a light above the top stair can sharply reduce these accidents. As we will see, slowed adaptation to changes in light is not the only problem with the aging visual system.

VISION

The ability to see was important in human evolution, for without sight our early ancestors could neither locate prey nor escape predators. Today vision remains central to a society that is heavily dependent on the automobile, the airplane, television, computers, and the printed word (Walsh, 1982). Severe visual impairment can sharply curtail an older person's independence. Many of the changes in vision that occur with age can be explained in terms of normal physiological aging in the structure of the eye, others are due to secondary aging, and still others as yet cannot be readily explained.

STRUCTURAL CHANGES AND VISION

Age brings changes in many parts of the eye, and structural changes in two areas—the pupil and the lens—have a decided effect on the ability to receive visual stimulation (see Fig. 7.1). With age, the pupil, the small opening in the center of the iris that allows light to enter the eye, gets smaller. This decrease in size, called senile miosis, begins in young adulthood, but its progression is slow. Eventually, older adults need a good deal more light in order to see as clearly as they once did. The pupil's responsiveness to changes in light also is modified. Although it continues to alter size in response to variations in light-level (widening as light is reduced and constricting as light is increased), with age the difference in size between the light-adapted and the dark-adapted pupil diminishes. Both of these changes are believed to be due to muscle weakness, with the muscles controlling dilation weakening more rapidly than those controlling contraction (Fozard et al., 1977).

Once adults are past 70, the pupil responds more slowly to changes in light levels so that it takes older eyes longer to adjust to sudden changes in illumination, as when older people enter or leave a dark movie theater. This change is believed to be due to altered sugar metabolism that affects the delivery of oxygen to the retina. The impairment becomes pronounced as people switch between rod and cone vision. Rods are receptor cells that pick up information about brightness, but not color, and they function in dim light. Cones pick up information about color and detail, and they function in increased light. Driving in the dark, a situation in which headlights of oncoming cars and lighted intersections cause the level of illumination to change rapidly, can be especially difficult for older adults be-

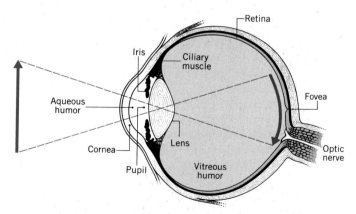

FIGURE 7.1   Structure of the eye. For clear perception, an image must be sharply focused on the fovea, a small indentation in the retina that is primarily responsible for color vision. The cones (color receptors), which respond in bright light, are densely packed within the fovea; and rods (black, white, and gray receptors), which respond in dim light, dominate the rest of the retina.

Source: G. A. Kimble, N. Garmezy, and E. Zigler, *Principles of Psychology*, 6th ed. New York: Wiley, 1984), p. 106.

cause there is a longer period of "blindness" when one set of receptors has switched off and the other set has not yet begun its full function (Fozard et al., 1977).

A second structural change with major effects on vision takes place in the lens of the eye. Cells in the lens grow throughout life, but none are shed, so that the lens gradually thickens, becoming densely packed with shrunken cells that have lost much of the water they once contained. In the lens, this change reduces transparency, decreasing the intensity of entering light that reaches the retina.

The lens also becomes yellow, causing it to absorb some of the shorter wavelengths of light and reducing sensitivity to color in the blue end of the spectrum (Pollack and Atkeson, 1978). Studies (Dalderup and Fredericks, 1969) indicate that severe loss in color sensitivity begins at about the age of 70, and by the time people are in their nineties, they can identify the color of less than half the objects they are shown. This lack of sensitivity to blues, greens, and violets means that older people are more successful at distinguishing colors in the longer wavelengths—yellows, oranges, and reds. This appears to be an area where prevalent environmental design poses fewer hazards for older people: Stop and caution lights are still easy for them to interpret.

As the lens becomes less transparent, the eye becomes sensitive to glare. Increased sensitivity to glare begins during adolescence, but is slight until about the age of 40. Between 40 and 70, sensitivity increases markedly. People in their seventies may require almost a hundred times as much illumination as people in their twenties to detect a target in the presence of glare (Fozard and Popkin, 1978). Because of the effect of glare on the aging eye, the use of diffused light in public places would make navigation easier and safer for older adults.

As the lens thickens, it becomes less flexible, so that it has difficulty changing its shape in order to focus properly at short distances. This ability of the eye to change its focal length is called **accommodation**. The lens's inability to accommodate to short focal lengths becomes noticeable around the age of 40 and keeps worsening until about 55. People may first notice their inability to focus at short range, called **presbyopia**, or farsightedness, when they realize that they must hold a book or newspaper at arm's length in order to read it. Presbyopia is easily corrected with reading glasses, and people who already require glasses for distant vision may need bifocals when they reach their forties. Not only the ability to accommodate but also the speed with which the process takes place appear to slow with age (Fozard et al., 1977). Perhaps as a result of the lens's greater rigidity, the muscles that control its accommodation tend to atrophy, with collagen replacing some of the muscle tissue. The process begins as we approach our forties.

Other structural changes also occur with age, but none have such decisive consequences for visual processing (Fozard et al., 1977). The cornea, which covers and protects the iris and pupil, becomes thicker and less sensitive to mechanical stimulation and appears to lose its sparkle. This dimming of the eye's appearance may be due to changes in its ability to refract light and to a decrease in the amount of fluid that bathes its surface.

The iris may shed surface cells, which are deposited across the iris, the lens, and the inside of the cornea. These cells tend to break up the entering light, scattering it and perhaps contributing to the increased illumination required by older people.

Not all impairments in vision can be easily traced to structural change. At present, no one is certain just why visual acuity, or the clarity of vision, declines so much with age. Acuity seems to begin a slight decline in the mid-twenties and speeds up after the age of 50. For people of all ages, increasing contrast improves acuity as does increasing the amount of illumination. But no matter how much the light level is raised, 60-year-olds cannot see as clearly as 20-year-olds, perhaps because as light increases past a certain point, glare begins to interfere with vision (Fozard et al., 1977). Yet the decrease in acuity after the age of 50 is much larger than would be expected from either the yellowing of the lens or the reduction of pupil size (Pollack and Atkeson, 1978).

Structural aspects of aging can indirectly affect depth perception. Decreased acuity and increased susceptibility to glare can impair depth perception because they reduce the value of monocular cues that reveal the distance of objects. Monocular cues consist of information that can be picked up by one eye, such as relative changes in retinal images when a person moves, the way one object blocks the view of another, linear perspective, and the apparent differences in texture that depend on an object's distance from the eye. Any decrease in the amount of light that strikes the retina can interfere with depth perception because it interferes with binocular cues that require the cooperative use of both eyes. Brightness and contrast are essential for binocular vision (Fozard et al., 1977).

Depth perception appears to decline slightly during the thirties, and some time between the ages of 40 and 50 the ability to perceive depth becomes noticeably impaired in most people. The decline continues until the age of 70, the oldest group that has been studied (Bell, Wolf, and Bernholtz, 1972).

VISUAL DISORDERS

The aging visual system has been associated with two disorders, but neither is the result of normal aging. **Glaucoma**, a steady increase in pressure within the eye, may develop when fluid is unable to leave the eye by its normal channel. As pressure constricts the blood vessels, nerve cells and fibers are starved for oxygen and die. Vision is gradually destroyed at the periphery of the visual field, so that untreated glaucoma leads first to tunnel vision and eventually to blindness. Among people past the age of 40, 1 in 200 develops the disorder (Rockstein and Sussman, 1979). It is more common among people in their sixties, and although there is no cure, the progress of glaucoma can be stopped with medical treatment. Drugs that either improve drainage or reduce the formation of fluid halt further destruction of nerve cells.

A second common visual disorder is **cataracts**, a condition in which the lens becomes opaque so that light cannot penetrate it. Cataracts also become increasingly common with age, but strike even fewer people than does glaucoma. Of those with cataracts, three out of four are past 65, and one in five is between the ages of 45 and 65 (Brody, 1982). When a cataract impairs vision, surgical removal of the lens and its replacement with an artificial lens generally restore partial vision.

AGE-RELATED CHANGES IN VISUAL PROCESSING

As people age, they seem to process visual information more slowly than they once did. For example, even when their visual acuity is as sharp as a young adult's, people past 60 take longer to extract information from a display that is flashed briefly on a screen before them (Kline and Szafran, 1975). Some older adults may learn to compensate for this slowing in daily life by using cues from their surroundings or taking advantage of advance information.

An aspect of vision that has been extensively investigated is the ability to detect when a light that flashes rapidly is not a steady source of illumination. The point at which a flickering light can be detected as such is called the "critical flicker frequency" (CFF). Most older adults find that the flickering light fuses into a steady beam at a level at which younger adults are still reporting a decided flicker. It has been suggested that this difference in performance can be explained by the fact that the older nervous system takes longer to recover from stimulation, a condition known as **stimulus persistence** (Botwinick, 1973).

In one study of critical flicker frequency that focused on color vision, alternate flashes of red and green light, which produced yellow when fused by the eye, were used in a cross-sectional study of adults in their twenties and sixties (Kline, Ikeda, and Schieber, 1982). All subjects were healthy and highly educated, the younger adults were college students, and the older adults were retired faculty members and older alumni. In line with the stimulus-persistence proposal, older adults reported seeing a yellow light significantly more often than did younger adults. The effect could not be attributed to the decreased amount of light reaching the retina because it remained even when young adults were tested in dim light and older adults were tested with more illumination. It appears that aging within the nervous system is partly responsible for this age difference in visual processing.

Another aspect of vision, sensitivity to contrast, has also been found to change with age. When given brief glimpses of stationary patterns, made up of light and dark bars of the same width, older adults find the patterns more difficult to detect when the bars are very narrow or of medium width. When the bars are wide, little age difference appears (Kline et al., 1983). Older adults also reacted more slowly to the appearance of the patterns, and the difference in reaction time was not fully explained by diminished contrast sensitivity. The investigators suggest that the slowing of visual processing in the nervous system is responsible.

This experiment in contrast sensitivity underscores the wide range of interindividual difference in aging. One of the older subjects was a man in his late sixties, who had had 50 years of experience in shooting at targets. This marksman's response time and sensitivity to contrast was matched by only two of the college students, and no one surpassed his performance. It would appear that practice and experience affect even aspects of aging that are considered inevitable.

The response to some visual illusions also seems to change with age (Fozard et al., 1977). For example, children are quite susceptible to the Mueller-Lyon illusion, but young adults often see both lines as the same length (Fig. 7.2). In most studies, older adults again become susceptible to the illusion, and in some studies the susceptibility begins to reappear during the fifties. The evidence on other illusions is contradictory. With the Titchener circles, it is generally agreed that children younger than five see both center circles as the same size and that young adults are very susceptible to the illusion. But some investigators have found that susceptibility begins to decline at about the age of 50 and that it does not increase among older adults whereas other investigators have found that susceptibility increases with age.

It seems clear, however, that perceptual flexibility declines with age. For example, the Necker cube, which appears to reverse in perspective as a younger person looks at it, tends to reverse less often or not at all when older adults view it (Fig. 7.2c). Various explanations have been advanced for the responses to illusion and the Necker cube. J. L. Fozard and J. C. Thomas (1975) have suggested that older adults are more susceptible than younger people to unusual variations in a complicated visual stimulus. This tendency may reflect some developmental change in perceptual processing, or it may be no more than a cohort difference. Younger adults are more familiar with visual illusions and ambiguous figures, and experience plays a major role in guiding perceptions.

From what we can tell, aging in the visual system appears to take place at two levels (Fozard et al., 1977). The first level of change becomes noticeable between

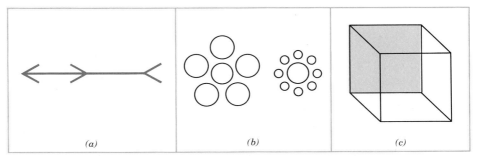

FIGURE 7.2   In the Mueller-Lyon illusion (*a*), although one line segment may appear longer, the two segments are actually the same length; in the Titchener circles (*b*), although one of the two central circles may appear larger, both are the same size; and in the Necker cube (*c*), the cube seems to reverse in depth spontaneously, so that the tinted side can appear as either the outer or inner surface of a box.

the ages of 35 and 45, and it affects the transmission of light to the retina and the ability of the eye to accommodate. These changes are reflected in presbyopia, sensitivity to glare, sensitivity to color, and depth perception. The second level of change becomes noticeable between the ages of 55 and 65, and it affects the retina and the nervous system. These changes are reflected in reduced visual field, sensitivity to dim lighting, and sensitivity to flicker. Some of the changes in the visual system are paralleled by changes in the auditory system.

HEARING

Much of the information from the environment comes to us through our ears. Sound waves, caused by pressure changes in the atmosphere, travel through the air and strike the ear drum, causing it to vibrate and transmit an amplified sound wave through the bones of the middle ear, then deep into the inner ear, where the sound receptors are located in the cochlea (Fig. 7.3). These sound receptors, called hair cells, produce a signal that passes along the auditory nerve to the brain. Sounds have both intensity, which determines the loudness of a sound, and frequency, which determines its pitch. The higher a sound's frequency, the higher the pitch.

HEARING LOSS

As we get older, our ability to receive and interpret sounds declines, and some researchers have found that a small, but gradual, hearing loss over all sound frequencies begins by the age of 25 (Rockstein and Sussman, 1979). By the time men

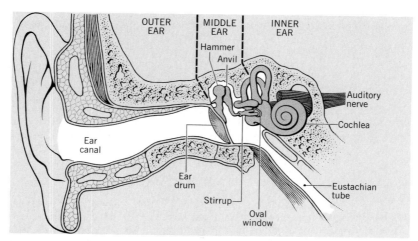

FIGURE 7.3   Major structures of the ear.

Source: G. E. Nelson, *Biological Principles with Human Perspectives*, 2d ed. (New York: Wiley, 1984), p. 163.

are older than 32 and women older than 37, nearly all show some degree of impairment. Pitch discrimination deteriorates steadily until about the age of 55, then falls off rapidly in the higher frequencies. Interindividual differences are great in this range and increase with age, so that the spread of ability at 8000 Hz is 3½ times as great among 65-year-olds as it is among 25-year-olds (Corso, 1977). (The human voice has a customary range of about 120 to 600 Hz although a soprano can soar well above 1000 Hz. The highest note on a piano is 4100 Hz, and the highest frequency that can be detected by human beings is about 20,000 Hz.)

Although not everyone suffers a large loss of hearing, a sizable minority have such impaired hearing that they find it interfering with their daily activities. Significant hearing loss is more common in men than in women. It has been estimated that the incidence of total deafness rises from 0.5 percent among people between the ages of 25 and 34 to 2.8 percent by the age of 55. By the age of 75, 15 percent of the population is deaf. A much larger proportion has easily detectable hearing difficulties: 1.6 percent among the 25- to 34-year-olds and more than 27 percent of those who have reached the age of 75 (Rockstein and Sussman, 1979).

Some of this hearing damage is caused by aging in the auditory system, and the result may affect the ability to detect frequency or intensity. The progressive, age-related loss of the ability to hear high-frequency sounds is known as **presbycusis**. The disorder can be caused by aging or by damage to the cochlea, the fluid-filled chamber in the inner ear. John Corso (1977) has described four kinds of presbycusis: (1) sensory presbycusis, caused by atrophy and degeneration of the hair cells; it produces a loss of high-frequency sounds but does not interfere with sounds in the range of speech; (2) neural presbycusis, caused by the loss of auditory neurons; it affects the ability to distinguish the sounds of speech but does not affect the ability to hear pure tones; (3) metabolic presbycusis, caused by vascular changes within the cochlea; it affects all sound frequencies, so that sounds must be louder before they are heard; and (4) mechanical presbycusis, caused by atrophy of the membranes that divide the cochlea; it increases hearing loss at all sound frequencies, but especially in the higher frequencies.

Other sources of hearing loss include accumulations of wax in the outer ear, which lessen the conduction of sound through the ear; an obstructed Eustachian tube that causes fluid to accumulate in the middle ear; and the formation of new bone in the middle ear, which also decreases sound conduction (Corso, 1977). Although obstructed Eustachian tubes can also affect hearing in younger people, the other kinds of damage are concentrated among the elderly. Hearing loss from these sources can be mistaken for presbycusis; it can also cause an additional source of impairment in people with presbycusis.

In the region between the cochlea and the auditory cortex of the brain, a loss of cells and a shrinkage or change in shape of other cells can damage the ability to tell which direction a sound is coming from and impair the discrimination of speech sounds although the ability to detect pure tones is not affected (Corso, 1977).

Another age-related hearing difficulty is **tinnitus**, which is a persistent ringing, roaring, or buzzing in the ears. Its incidence rises from 3 percent among young

Steady exposure to loud noise can so damage hearing that many industries must provide noise protectors for their employees.

adults and 9 percent among the middle-aged to 11 percent among those betwen 65 and 74 (Rockstein and Sussman, 1979). Tinnitus can be caused by wax, tumors, middle-ear infections, bone growth in the middle ear, drugs, or allergies. The majority of cases of tinnitus cannot be cured, but they are often successfully treated by providing the patient with a mild noise-producing device that masks the internal sounds (Brody, 1982).

It is difficult to distinguish age-related presbycusis from that caused by damage to the inner ear. Despite improved general health, the rate of damage-related presbycusis may be increasing. Most Americans live in a noisy environment, and excessive exposure to noise can permanently impair hearing by destroying hair cells or damaging other cochlear structures. For example, the vibration of extremely loud sounds can literally tear apart the hair cells, eliminating the ability to hear sounds in that frequency range. If exposure is infrequent, the muscles around the stirrup (the delicate, stirrup-shaped bone in the middle ear that transmits amplified sound to the cochlea) restrain its movements, but they cannot protect the hair cells from excessive noise that continues for long periods. The louder the noise, the less time it takes to inflict its damage.

The loudness of a noise is measured in decibels; as the intensity of a sound increases by 20 decibels, it is experienced as being ten times louder. Among familiar sounds, a whisper is about 30 decibels; normal conversation, about 60 decibels; traffic noise at a city intersection, 75 decibels; a vacuum cleaner, 85 decibels; the roar of a subway train, 90 decibels; a power lawn mower, 96 decibels; a rock band or a discotheque, 115 decibels; a sonic boom, 128 decibels.

Steady exposure to noises of 75 decibels begins to damage hair cells so that working at such noise levels for 40 years would cause hearing loss even in people without degenerative presbycusis. Work environments are allowed to reach 90 decibels, a level that can cause hearing damage within a few years (Brody, 1982).

As people begin to develop presbycusis, they find themselves missing certain high-frequency sounds: the song of birds, the ring of a telephone, the ticking of a clock. High-frequency consonants, such as *s, z, t, f,* and *g,* become inaudible, and a person must strain to follow a conversation. It becomes difficult to distinguish one-syllable words, so that "sit" sounds just like "fit." Older individuals may also find some women's speech harder to distinguish than the speech of men, for men's voices tend to be louder and lower in pitch. By the age of 80, a person may miss 25 percent of the words in a conversation (Feldman and Reger, 1967). As a result, older people sometimes are forced to guess at the words they have just heard.

The experience may have psychological consequences. As Blasa Aparicio, a 101-year-old woman explained it:

It's also difficult when you can't hear well, because they ask you one thing and you answer another. You have no control of your hearing. It's embarrassing.

(Barasch, 1983, p. 20).

Such embarrassment can make an older person feel inferior and without any control in a social situation. If the older person with presbycusis withdraws and stops trying to distinguish what people are saying or if continued difficulty in making themselves understood causes others to reduce their conversation, social isolation can follow. As a consequence, older people may find themselves unable to express their feelings with words. Some investigators have found that people whose hearing loss exceeds 50 decibels tend to have severe emotional disturbances, becoming compulsive, anxious, or hypochondriacal (Corso, 1977).

The hearing difficulties of older people can be eased if their conversational partners lower their voices, speak slowly and distinctly, and look directly at them while talking. Although hearing aids can sometimes help, they rarely return hearing to preimpairment levels. Until recently, hearing aids magnified all sounds equally. If hearing loss is primarily in the higher frequencies, increasing the intensity enough to make higher frequencies audible may make lower frequencies far

The public use of a hearing aid by the president of the United States may encourage some adults with impaired hearing to overcome their reluctance to use such a device.

too loud. Now, however, a hearing aid that amplifies sounds selectively has been developed. In 1983, the 72-year-old president of the United States began to wear such a hearing aid in public. President Reagan's hearing aid was a miniaturized device that was molded to fit his ear canal and was barely visible (Weisman, 1983). His example might encourage other adults with impaired hearing to overcome their hesitation and investigate the use of a hearing aid.

For some people, hearing aids are of little value. For example, adults with neural presbycusis are not helped by an increase in sound intensity. Many older adults buy hearing aids without an adequate medical evaluation of their impairment. As a result, they are often disappointed, and some may react as did the sharp-eyed centenarian John Henry Smart, who said:

Hearing aids are a joke. I bought two of 'em and throwed both of 'em against the wall. They're no good!

(Barasch, 1983, p. 34)

Despite the possibility that older people with presbycusis can become withdrawn, insecure, depressed, confused, or isolated, if hearing loss is their only problem, older adults seem to adjust to it. In a group of 259 healthy, middle-class individuals between the ages of 60 and 89, 45 percent tested as hearing impaired. Among those who had an uncorrected hearing loss, their presbycusis had no effect on anxiety, depression, hostility, or complaints about their health. Those with hearing loss were no different from the others in their social integration. In fact, many were angry over the fact that people—including those who provided services to the elderly—tended to assume that older individuals with hearing problems automatically functioned less efficiently than others. The investigators (Thomas et al., 1983) suggest that when people have good health and economic security, they find it possible to adapt to a gradual hearing loss.

Nor did the hearing loss affect these adults' intelligence test performance exactly as expected. In several studies (Granick, Kleban, and Weiss, 1976; Ohta, Carlin, and Harmon, 1981), hearing loss has been closely related to losses in intellectual functioning. Among the adults in this study (Thomas et al., 1983), those with impaired hearing had lower scores on a verbal test of cognition but did just as well on a nonverbal test. It may be that the usual questionnaires used to screen older adults for impaired cognitive functioning sometimes underrate the abilities of adults whose hearing loss keeps them from accurately perceiving words.

AGE-RELATED CHANGES IN AUDITORY PROCESSING

Whether or not people have presbycusis, the problem of speech discrimination seems to worsen with age. For example, speaking more loudly generally increases the intelligibility of speech, but the effect diminishes with age and the degree of hearing loss. With young adults of normal hearing, increasing the intensity of spoken words from 30 to 40 decibels improves understanding to 90 percent. Among people in their seventies without severe hearing loss, understanding reaches only 65.5 percent at the same intensity level (Punch and McConnell, 1969). This sort of difference appears even when young and old make similar scores on the ability to hear pure tones.

Under conditions of stress, the ability of older people to understand the sounds of speech decreases even further. Sentences that can be heard under test conditions become unintelligible when words overlap or are interrupted. This effect begins to appear as early as the thirties and becomes pronounced by the sixties (Corso, 1977). Because of this effect, older adults who can follow a conversation under ideal circumstances may have trouble when several people are talking together or in such situations as a cocktail party.

The decreasing ability to discriminate speech among older adults without severe hearing loss is believed to be the result of a slowness in processing sounds. For example, increasing the intensity of speech at normal rates of speed (140 words per minute) brings the older individual's comprehension to almost 100 percent. But when speech is speeded up to 350 words per minute, older adults cannot understand more than 45 percent of the words, no matter how loudly they are spoken. Yet younger adults can understand the rapid, but louder talk (Calearo and Lazzaroni, 1957).

Not only speech is affected. Older adults also seem to process pure tones more slowly (Corso, 1977). Among men, reaction time to a tone increased from .2 seconds in 20-year-olds to .37 seconds in 60-year-olds and .53 seconds in 70-year-olds. When asked to make a decision about sounds, such as indicating when they detected a sound in the presence of noise, older adults took much longer than younger adults to make their decision although both groups had the same ability to detect the tones (Rees and Botwinick, 1971). It seemed that the older adults were more cautious, making "certain" they heard the tone before they indicated its presence. For this reason, an apparent impairment in hearing may sometimes have little to do with whether the sounds have actually been detected.

SMELL AND TASTE

Although we get much less information through the nose and mouth than we do through our eyes and ears, smell and taste are important human senses. Both can save our lives—our olfactory sense can detect dangerous odors in the air, and our gustatory sense can detect the bitter taste that often signals the presence of poison. The final flavor we assign to food is a combination of smell and taste, and when smell is temporarily impaired, as occurs with a cold, food may taste flat.

SMELL

Sensitivity to odors may decline with age. Olfactory bulbs in the nasal lining appear to atrophy, beginning in early childhood. By the age of 15, 8 percent of the olfactory nerve fibers are gone, and the loss continues at a slow but fairly steady rate so that it reaches 73 percent among 76 to 91-year-olds (Rockstein and Suss-

CAN DEAFNESS MAKE YOU PARANOID?

As we saw in Chapter 5, deafness seems to be connected with paranoid reactions (Post, 1980). Among older adults in mental hospitals, those who have been diagnosed as paranoid are much more likely to be deaf than those who have been diagnosed as depressed.

Why should the two disorders be linked? When deafness develops gradually, older people are at first not aware that their hearing is becoming increasingly impaired (Maher, 1974). They may attribute their inability to follow conversations to the fact that people are whispering. Yet when they accuse others of speaking too softly, their charges are denied. It has been suggested that continued denials of what seems an obvious fact lead the deaf person to assume that others are lying and trying to keep information from him or her. As suspicion and hostility grow, the deaf person's friends and acquaintances regard such reactions as bizarre and may begin to avoid the person. What was once a simple search to explain why speech cannot be heard becomes paranoia (Beck, 1974).

Psychologists Philip Zimbardo, Susan Andersen, and Loren Kabat (1981) were familiar with this explanation and attempted to test it. They decided that if the explanation were valid, college students who were suddenly unable to hear and could not explain their deafness would develop symptoms of paranoia.

Three groups of college men were told that they were to participate in a study of the effects of hypnotism on creative problem solving. Instead, men in two of the groups were told that when they came out of their hypnotic state they would have difficulty hearing. Men in one of the "deaf" groups were told that they would not remember the instruction to become deaf; men in the other "deaf" group were told that they would remember the instructions. In order to make certain that induced amnesia for the hypnotic instruction was not responsible for any symptoms shown by the first group, the researchers had the men in the third group hypnotized and told that they would feel a compulsion to scratch their ears but would not remember the instruction. All students were hypnotized and then received their instructions by

man, 1979). The effect of this loss on the detection of odors does not seem to be profound. When the odor of menthol was used, the average healthy older adult (aged 66 to 93) needed twice as much menthol in a quantity of air in order to detect the substance as did the average younger adult (aged 18 to 26) (Murphy, 1983). (Menthol is a common ingredient of sweets, cigarettes, and toiletries.) Interindividual differences were great, and there was some overlap between the two coded tape; neither the researchers nor the hypnotist knew which students received which instructions.

When the "problem-solving" part of the experiment began, the students, one at a time, began solving anagrams in the company of two confederates of the experimenters. The confederates carried on a rehearsed conversation, in which they talked about a party they had attended, laughed at an incident, made a funny face, and then decided to work together on the problem. Finally, they asked the student who had been hypnotized if he would like to work with them.

The three men were asked to create stories about pairs of people shown in ambiguous relationships. Afterward, the student who had been hypnotized filled out personality tests. His reactions during interactions with the confederates were rated by judges, and the student rated his own feelings during the experiment. Each student was then debriefed, rehypnotized, and told to recall everything that had happened during the entire session.

The proposal that paranoia and unexplained deafness go together was supported by this experiment. Students who did not know why they were deaf were more irritated, agitated, hostile, tense, and unfriendly than students in the other two groups. Only one of them agreed to work with the pair of confederates on the creation of stories, and although the students with unexplained deafness said they were not suspicious, their stories about the pictures showed the same judgmental attitude toward others that is a hallmark of paranoia.

Does this experiment explain the development of paranoia in some older people? As we have seen, when older adults have no health or economic problems, presbycusis does not seem to have emotional effects. In addition, a sudden plunge into unexplained deafness is undoubtedly much more stressful than the gradual loss of hearing over the period of months or years. Although the results of this experiment do not duplicate the experience of older adults, they may give us some clues. As Zimbardo and his colleagues point out, older people may not realize they are becoming deaf, and they may also believe that admitting deafness is admitting that they are old. The search for a rational explanation for their inability to hear might lead some middle-aged and older adults who are predisposed to be suspicious into developing paranoid reactions.

groups. In fact, one 70-year-old man had the same threshold for the odor as the average young adult.

In other studies (Chalke, Dewhurst, and Ward, 1958), adults' ability to detect the odor of natural gas in the air dropped sharply after the age of 65, with 30 percent unable to recognize the smell. Because many homes use gas for heating and cooking, this finding could cause concern, but further analysis showed that illness

Older adults may be somewhat less sensitive to odors than younger people, but for most the loss is slight. Severe loss of the ability to detect odors is probably connected with illness.

appeared to be responsible for most of the difference between the two groups. Healthy adults past 65 could recognize gas when only 10 parts per million were in the air. In a test of retired university staff members, those between the ages of 60 and 90 were *more* sensitive to some odors than adults between the ages of 20 and 50 (Rovee, Cohen, and Shlapack, 1975).

Unless an odor is dangerous, as when it comes from leaking gasoline or gas from an unlighted stove, the pleasantness or unpleasantness of an odor may be more important than simple detection (Engen, 1977). People's preference for odors seems to be related to age. Children between the ages of 7 and 12 prefer fruity odors, such as strawberry, but adults prefer the smell of flowers, such as lavender. In this study, there was no change in odor preferences after the age of 30 (Moncrieff, 1966). Familiarity appears to have a good deal to do with odor preference. When people are asked to rate odors, they generally dislike any that are unfamiliar (Engen, 1974). Thus, our past experiences play a large role in determining whether a particular odor will evoke appreciation or disgust.

It might be expected that the intensity of an odor would affect a person's reaction to it. Age appears to reduce sensitivity to concentrated smells. In the study that compared adults' reaction to menthol, older adults required a much larger concentration of the scent before indicating that the intensity had increased (Murphy, 1983). With the younger group, increasing the amount of menthol ten times led them to rate the odor as four times as intense. Among the older group, a tenfold increase brought a rating only twice as intense. As the menthol concentration rose, younger adults said that the smell became more pleasant, but older adults tended to rate most concentrations about the same.

Another difference appeared between the two groups: After repeated exposure to the odor, younger adults began to find the same concentration of menthol less pleasant, but older adults rated it the same throughout the session no matter how many times they smelled it. Again, however, interindividual differences were large. The same 70-year-old whose threshold for odor matched that of people in their twenties reacted just as the younger group did to increase in intensity. If odors do seem less intense to older adults, the results of another study fall into place (Springer and Dietzmann, 1970). When asked to rate their reactions to diesel exhaust fumes, people past 65 found them much less objectionable than did younger people. Smell and taste are so closely related that it is difficult to consider either in isolation.

TASTE

The number of taste buds appears to decrease slightly during young and middle adulthood, but no large destruction has been noted before the age of 75. In fact, taste buds are continually replaced during adulthood, and one researcher has found no change in the number of tastebuds in each of the tongue's papillae (surface projections) whether an individual was 2 days or 90 years old (Arvidson, 1979). The results of some studies indicate that, for people who have reached 60, a flavor must be more concentrated for it to be tasted, but no decline with age has appeared in others. In one study, adults between the age of 80 and 85 could discriminate among various flavors as well as people in their forties (Kare, 1975).

The result may depend on which taste—sweet, salty, sour, or bitter—is tested and the manner in which the testing is done. Some researchers ask the people they are testing to sip a flavored solution, some fail to have their subjects rinse their mouths after each taste, some drop the substance on the tongue, some use a weak electric current that simulates the concentration of various solutions, and some blindfold their subjects. Although any of these methods may rate the sensitivity of taste buds, only sipping the solution and then rinsing the mouth would seem to duplicate normal taste methods and keep one sample from interfering with the taste of another.

Recently, researchers have been using this latter method to test sensitivity to salty and sweet tastes. Among a group of 23- to 92-year-olds, sensitivity to salty tastes declined with age, but the difference in the ability to taste salt was much smaller than had been found in earlier studies (Grzegorczyk, Jones, and Mistretta, 1979). One of the same researchers (Moore, Nielsen, and Mistretta, 1982) took part in an investigation of the ability to detect sweet flavors among 20- to 88-year-olds. In this study, there was again a slight loss of sensitivity with age, with most people over 60 requiring about twice as much sugar in a solution before they could detect it. But the decline was small, and the difference in taste thresholds was large. The oldest person tested was as sensitive to the taste of sugar as some of the subjects in their twenties.

EFFECTS ON NUTRITION

What does all this mean for older adults? It is widely believed that as people grow older, food no longer tastes as good and that this decline in the enjoyment of food is responsible for loss of appetite and consequent malnutrition in the el-

Older adults who have a diminished sensitivity to the intensity of aromas and tastes may not be motivated to vary their diet, a situation that could lead to malnutrition.

derly. Yet research findings indicate that whatever loss of appetite develops is not primarily due to the loss of receptors for taste and smell. Investigators have advanced various explanations for declines in taste sensitivity.

Loretta Moore, Christine Nielsen, and Charlotte Mistretta (1982) suggest that it is not the threshold for a taste but a diminished sensitivity to intensities of flavor that is responsible for a decline in the enjoyment of food. As we saw, some odors seem much less intense to older people than to younger adults. The case of a woman whose taste threshold rose sharply after radiation therapy for cancer of the neck also supports this proposal. Even after the woman's taste threshold returned to preradiation levels, she complained that various tastes remained ''weak'' (Marks and Stevens, 1980). And when foods are blended so that their origin is impossible to detect, older adults have more difficulty than younger people in identifying the flavors (Schiffman, 1977; Schiffman and Pasternak, 1979). In this view, the magnitude of tastes and odors decreases with age, diminishing the older person's enjoyment of food.

Trygg Engen (1977) has suggested that sensitivity to tastes and smells is more affected by smoking than by any aging process. Although there is little research to support the suggestion, anecdotal evidence is plentiful. One healthy 75-year-old man who abruptly quit his two-pack-a-day habit reported with some surprise that the flavor of food suddenly became intense and his meals tasted better than they had for years.

Finally, Claire Murphy (1983) has suggested that older people's failure to find an odor less pleasant after extended exposure to it may go a long way toward explaining some cases of malnutrition. The sense of smell is often crucial in the identification of flavor. With the nose blocked, it is almost impossible to tell the difference between raw apple and raw potato. It is also possible that the pleasantness of taste follows the same pattern after exposure. Murphy proposes that because the same food continues to taste good, the older adult is not motivated to seek a varied diet. If a few foods are cheap and taste reasonably good, they may make up the entire diet, eventually leading to malnutrition.

TOUCH AND PAIN

Touch and pain are considered somasthetic senses because their receptors are located throughout the body (soma), primarily in the skin but also in the viscera. Receptors within the skin or nerve endings in the cornea and deep within the body send signals through neurons to the brain, carrying the message that some object has come into contact with the body or that real or possible injury threatens. Other somasthetic senses inform us of temperature, the position of body parts, or body posture and movement.

TOUCH

It generally has been accepted that sensitivity to touch begins to decline when people are in their fifties and that the loss of sensitivity is due to a decrease in the number of receptors and their individual sensitivity. It has also been proposed that this loss of sensitivity then reverses itself during the sixties and seventies, becoming more sensitive as the skin thins with age (Rockstein and Sussman, 1979).

Yet this picture is clouded by conflicting evidence. It is by no means clear that sensitivity to all types of touch declines, that sensitivity declines in everyone, or even that the skin thins with age.

The effect of aging on skin receptors has been confirmed. Beginning in childhood, the Meissner corpuscles, a type of sensory receptor believed to respond to light touch and perhaps to vibration, grow in size, change in shape, and decrease in number. They are concentrated on the soles of the feet, the palms of the hand, and the hairless side of fingers and toes. Free nerve endings, found in the skin, in the cornea, and deep within the body, show no changes with age (Kenshalo, 1977). Pacinian corpuscles, sensory receptors in the skin that may respond to deep pressure and to vibration, appear to grow in size with age but to decrease in number (Verillo, 1980).

Adults in their sixties and seventies seem to be less sensitive to slight pressure on the palms and fingers than are adults in their twenties and thirties (Kenshalo, 1977). The loss of sensitivity to vibration appears in a sizable minority of older adults, beginning at about the age of 50. The loss appears first in the feet. In one study of 64- to 73-year-olds (Skre, 1972), sensitivity to vibration was impaired in the feet of 40 percent of the group but in the hands of only 5 percent. In another study of children and adults ranging in age from 8 to 74 (Verillo, 1980), age brought no decline in sensitivity to vibration at low frequencies, but was related to a definite decline in sensitivity at high frequencies. Although some people with reduced vibratory sensitivity seem to be healthy, degenerative diseases such as diabetes and anemia, as well as thiamin deficiency, are known to impair sensitivity (Kenshalo, 1977).

PAIN

Pain can be caused by pressure, heat, cold, twists, scratches, punctures—any sort of stimuli that warn the body of possible damage. If we were unable to feel pain, we would not realize when we had been injured. Cuts, burns, sprains, broken bones, and appendicitis would go unnoticed. But evoking the perception of pain is not a mechanical matter like flipping a light switch. Whether a stimulus will be perceived as painful, the degree of pain, and whether it can be borne are affected by such factors as ethnic background, socioeconomic status, motivation, attitudes, emotions, beliefs, and suggestion. Reports of pain in a laboratory situation may not be related to reports of pain in daily life (Kenshalo, 1977).

Pain is usually studied in two ways: the threshold level, which is the amount of stimulation required to create a perception of pain; and the tolerance level, which is the amount of pain a person can stand. In laboratory experiments, the tolerance level is especially sensitive to the relationship between the subject and the experimenter, the actions of the experimenter, and the instructions received by the subject (Gelfand, 1964). For example, when people are told an experimental technique will be painful, they report pain at lower levels of stimulation than when they have no reason to expect pain.

Perhaps because of all the factors that influence the perception of pain, researchers have been unable to demonstrate conclusively whether sensitivity to painful stimuli decreases, increases, or remains the same as people age (Kenshalo, 1977). Research with animals, where many of the confounding factors do not apply, indicates that the pain threshold rises with age, so that it takes more stimulation to evoke a reaction (Nicak, 1971).

In a study of sensitivity to painful heat, investigators (Clark and Mehl, 1971) attempted to control for confounding factors by using the signal detection method. People were asked to rate the intensity of pain from radiant heat, but the light was hot on only half the trials, forcing them to decide whether they could detect the stimulus (the activation of sensory receptors) as well as determining the degree of pain (affected by cognition and emotion). Under these circumstances, there was no difference in the pain experienced by men, no matter what their age, and young women. But women around the age of 60 seemed to experience less pain at the same levels of stimulation. As we saw in the discussion of visual processing, older adults seem to be more cautious in making judgments. Such was the case in this experiment. Older men and women reported pain only when they were certain the pain was present, but younger men and women tended to report the stimulus as painful before they were sure it actually hurt (Kenshalo, 1977).

Pain signals do not travel through specialized nerve fibers, but are carried by the pattern of firing neurons. According to the gate-control theory of pain, sensations travel from receptors and free nerve endings up the spinal cord to the brain. A gatelike mechanism in the system may be open, closed, or partially open. Unless signals can get through the gate, the person will feel no pain (Melzack, 1973). The gate can be controlled by several means, including signals from the brain. For example, during anxiety or fear, the brain opens the gate, allowing messages from pain receptors to flood through to the brain and increase a person's perception of pain.

The body appears to manufacture its own painkiller. Endorphins, a type of neurotransmitter manufactured by the brain, act like opiates. Beta endorphins provide long-lasting pain relief, such as would come from an injection of morphine whereas enkephalins provide a brief but powerful relief from pain. Both kinds of endorphins send messages to the spinal cord that close the gate, blocking the transmission of pain signals to the brain. By using endorphins as a pattern, researchers hope to develop a nonaddictive natural painkiller that can provide safe and effective relief (Gurin, 1979). Some investigators (Brunner and Suddarth, 1975) report that older people may have little or no pain from normally painful conditions such as appendicitis, peritonitis, pneumonia, or heart attack. They attribute this to diminished sensitivity to pain, but it is also possible that endorphin production explains at least part of their relief.

Despite the existence of people whose sensory apparatus seems to show little evidence of failure, a substantial number of older people develop sensory impairment. Indeed, reduced sensory functioning is probably the most nearly universal loss of ability associated with aging. The effects of failing senses can spread to all aspects of life, and the ability to learn and remember depends in good measure upon what we perceive.

SUMMARY

With age, sensory systems slowly become less sensitive to stimulation from the environment, curtailing access to knowledge of the world and sometimes interfering with the ability to communicate with others. Compared with the young, older adults may be in a state of sensory deprivation that could be responsible for disorientation and confusion in the absence of organic brain disorder.

Several factors lead to changes in vision with age. The pupil decreases in size, the difference in size between the light-adapted and dark-adapted pupil diminishes, and it responds more slowly to changes in light levels. The lens thickens, yellows, becomes less transparent, and more sensitive to glare. As the lens loses flexibility, **accommodation** becomes less efficient and **presbyopia** may develop. Adults become less sensitive to color. Although visual acuity declines with age, structural changes in the eye cannot fully explain the change. Because the eye's ability to pick up monocular and binocular cues declines, depth perception is generally impaired in older adults. The major eye disorders of later adulthood, **glaucoma** and **cataracts**, are not the result of normal aging. With age, the processing of visual information slows, and **stimulus persistence** appears, revealed by changes in sensitivity to flicker. Sensitivity to contrast changes, as do perceptual flexibility and response to illusions.

During young adulthood, a small, but gradual, hearing loss develops that increases with age. The progressive loss of ability to hear high-frequency sounds can take four forms: sensory **presbycusis**, neural presbycusis, metabolic presbycusis, and mechanical presbycusis. Neural changes can impair the discrimination of speech, and **tinnitus** may add to the older adult's hearing problems. As hearing difficulties increase, paranoid symptoms may develop, or an adult may become socially isolated although adults in good health seem to adjust to their hearing loss. Because slowed auditory processing seems to be a major factor in the inability to discriminate speech sounds, increasing the intensity of speech may not solve a hearing problem, and stress may further reduce the ability to distinguish speech.

Sensitivity to odors may decline with age, with olfactory bulbs beginning to atrophy in childhood. Older adults may need an increased concentration of an odor before they can detect it, and they seem less sensitive to concentrated smells. Studies of taste have produced conflicting results, with findings varying according to the kind of taste tested and the methods used. Sensitivity to sweet and salty tastes appears to decline slightly with age, but interindividual differences are wide. Any decline in the enjoyment of food tastes with age may be due to a diminished sensitivity to flavor intensities or to smoking. Some cases of malnutrition may develop because older adults may not tire of a single food and so fail to eat a varied diet.

The effect of aging on the sensitivity to touch is inconsistent; however, some skin receptors change in size, shape, and number with age. Older adults may be less sensitive to slight pressure and vibration than younger adults. Many factors affect the perception of pain, including ethnic background, socioeconomic status, motivation, attitudes, emotions, beliefs, and suggestion. The effect of aging on sensitivity to pain has not been established although the pain threshold appears to rise in aging animals. Reports that some older people have little pain from normally painful conditions may be explained by diminished sensitivity to pain or by the body's manufacture of endorphins.

Reduced sensory function is probably the most nearly universal loss of ability connected with aging. However, some people show little sensory impairment even at advanced ages.

KEY TERMS

accommodation	presbyopia
cataracts	stimulus persistence
glaucoma	tinnitus
presbycusis	

8

LEARNING AND MEMORY ACROSS ADULTHOOD

In 1983, Ilse Kaim received a degree in urban studies from New York University, and Patricia Abramson received a degree in art history from Columbia University. Degrees are awarded every May by these universities, but the graduates are usually younger. Kaim, who was 70, had always wanted to get into urban studies, but was prevented from pursuing her youthful wishes in Germany by Hitler's rise to power. Like an increasing number of middle-aged women, Abramson returned to school to do something *she* wanted to do for a change. It took a long time, and, at age 63, she reaped the reward of 15 years of work. Not all the new college students are women. Charles Wanker, 62, returned to New York University after 42 years in naval architecture. Today he is working for a degree in art history (Ferretti, 1983). And at the age of 81, Frederick F. Block received a Ph.D. in history from New York University, the culmination of studies he began 15 years earlier when he retired from business (Johnston and Anderson, 1983). What is more, his dissertation on the social aspects of the British army in the Victorian era is being considered for publication by a university press.

Most older students go after degrees as full- or part-time students in the regular university programs. But some colleges are trying innovative programs. At the University of California in Santa Cruz, for example, a program called Elders in Residence was begun. During the program's first year, six women in their sixties were brought onto the Santa Cruz campus to take classes, live in student housing, and participate in college social life.

The program seems to be successful. Some of the women already had degrees, some had previously attended college, and some (like Mary Franc [Frankie] Merrifield) had always worked at blue-collar jobs. Merrifield, 69, built ships during World War II, worked in a steel mill after the war, and spent time as the driver of a San Francisco streetcar. The women took classes in writing, psychology, computer programming, religion, sociology, law, and sexuality. And they were also involved in extracurricular activities, joining student committees, helping in the student garden, and attending club meetings (Stix, 1981).

This return to the classroom makes it apparent that older adults are capable of learning. Now that many college classes have at least one middle-aged or older adult in them, such a statement seems obvious. But at one time researchers wondered about the ability of older adults to profit from formal education—about their ability to learn much of anything.

As we will see in this chapter, cognitive processes do not become radically different in older adults. Some of the observed changes in learning and memory may be smaller and less important than was once believed. After a brief discussion of information processing, we will explore the way learning skills change with age. Because learning, in a sense, means remembering, we will also investigate memory skills, discovering which aspects of memory seem to change with age and which appear to remain the same. The chapter closes with a look at the way older adults demonstrate their learning and memory skills in daily life.

INFORMATION PROCESSING

Whether we are looking at a sunset, chatting with a friend, balancing a checkbook, reading a book, fantasizing about our next vacation, or trying to fix a squeaking floorboard, we are processing information. All aspects of cognitive functioning, from recalling whether the front door is locked to writing a poem, may be considered in terms of the way information is processed.

The terminology used in the **information-processing** view of cognition comes from an analogy between the human mind and the computer. As the computer accepts information that is fed into it, human beings take information from the environment. The information is manipulated, stored, classified, and retrieved; its patterns are recognized. The human mind becomes the "system," and psychologists attempt to trace the flow of information through it (Neisser, 1976b). In the last chapter, we explored the reception of information by the system; in this chapter we examine the processing of information that leads to learning and memory.

Learning and memory depend on time-based processes that transfer information within the cognitive system (Perlmutter, 1983). Learning has to do with the acquisition of information or skill as a result of experience. Memory has to do with the retention and retrieval of information or skill that has been learned. But it is very difficult to separate the two processes because people cannot demonstrate learning without using memory and memory cannot be demonstrated unless something has been learned.

Whether we look at learning or memory, the cognitive system can be seen as using several kinds of operations or several levels of processes to handle information. And whether the topic is learning or memory, the information must be acquired, stored, and retrieved. This sequence assumes that people are not passive recipients of information. They participate actively in the processing, and the way they deploy their cognitive resources will affect what and how much is learned or remembered, as will their expectations, emotions, and attitudes.

Changes in learning and memory skills with age show the same sort of pattern we have seen in other areas of functioning. By itself, age is not a very good predictor of performance. As a group, younger adults do better than older adults in most experimental tasks. But the differences are often small, and the spread of individual ability is generally large. In almost every case, some adults in the older group perform better than some adults in the younger group.

When age changes are examined, two things become apparent. First, cohort differences may play an important role in the observed changes. As we have seen, most older adults today have less formal education than younger adults. In fact, the young subjects in learning and memory experiments are generally college students. Unless researchers control for the level of education, the older group is likely to be at a disadvantage. More important than the amount of education may be the fact that the younger group routinely face situations similar to learning experiments in the course of their daily lives. Among members of the older group, half a century may have passed since they last sat in a classroom. For this reason, the time since completing formal education may have an important effect on age differences in learning and memory skills.

If this man took laboratory tests on learning and memory, he might show impaired performance relative to younger adults. Yet in daily life, he learns new tasks and works comfortably with computers.

In addition, education in the second half of the twentieth century may have different cognitive effects from schooling in the pre-World War II era. On the one hand, television viewing from the cradle may produce a level of information that could have been attained in the past only with many more years of education. On the other hand, older people learned in a more disciplined atmosphere that might have produced a greater breadth of scholarship (Perlmutter, 1983). Finally, as we will see in Chapter 9, the substantial decline in intellectual performance that occurs a few years before death may be responsible for a good deal of the observed age differences in learning and memory (Siegler, 1975). So age until death may be as important as time since the completion of formal education in assessing cognitive function in later life.

A second striking effect on observed age changes may be the way they are studied. Most of the research on learning and memory has been done in the laboratory, where skills are taken out of the context of everyday life. When skills are broken down and the effect of various factors on the stages of information processing are studied, an important aspect of cognitive functioning may be overlooked. There is as yet no way to determine the importance of these factors in life situations, so at present we do not know if—and how—the interaction of the factors affects performance (Perlmutter, 1983). Discovering whether older adults can repeat the same number of digits as college students or whether it takes older adults more than the allotted 3 minutes to learn a new task may tell us little about how people in their sixties and seventies learn to use a microwave oven, adapt to changed bus schedules, or adjust to the way information is presented on computerized bank statements.

Other factors may also affect information processing in older adults. Their expectation that memory will fail and that cognitive tasks will become too difficult for them may become a self-fulfilling prophecy. Convinced that they cannot function as they once did, they may cease to try. Disuse may also help to explain declines in cognitive skills. Just as physical skills decline from disuse, the failure to use cognitive strategies may make them less available when they are needed. Depression may also affect cognition. As we saw in Chapter 6, severe depression can be mistaken for organic brain syndrome. If memory and learning studies include depressed individuals among the older group, age differences in cognitive functioning may appear to be larger than they actually are.

However, the possibility of a biological contribution to these age differences in information processing cannot be discounted (Albert and Kaplan, 1980; Butters, 1980). Changes within the central nervous system, whether due to wear and tear, to age-related changes in biochemistry or cellular structure, or to degenerative disease, may affect the older person's ability to learn and to remember.

A vital aspect of cognitive functioning in daily life is the way learning and memory are affected by a person's familiarity with the material to be learned and his or her expertise with related material (Perlmutter, 1983). Outside the laboratory, information is not encountered in isolation. It is acquired and stored within the context of previous knowledge. Given new information, a person who has related knowledge can organize, assess, and acquire it more easily. A person who is used to electric typewriters will probably adapt with ease to a computerized word-processing system whereas a person who has never seen a typewriter will find all elements of the task strange.

In an attempt to relate laboratory studies of memory to the demands of everyday life, researchers (Waddell and Rogoff, 1981) showed arrays of objects to middle-aged (31 to 59) and older (65 to 85) women. The small objects (cars, animals, furniture, people, household items) were arranged either in a landscape or in a box containing cubicles of various sizes. Both the landscape and the cubicle display contained similar props: mountains, houses, church, parking lot, and street. The women watched the researcher place the objects in either the landscape or the cubicles and were later asked to reconstruct the display. When the cubicles were used, the older women did much worse at the task than the middle-aged women, but when the landscape was used, both groups replaced the same proportion of the display. Stripping objects of context may be similar to the procedures used in many studies of memory and learning. It forces people to process information in a void, so that the only aids they have are those they supply themselves. Daily life may be similar to replacing objects in the landscape: The context is always provided. Because older adults have many years of experience, they may discover that their greater store of knowledge will allow them to function as well as—or even better than—younger adults in daily situations where they must use their learning and memory skills.

LEARNING ACROSS ADULTHOOD

Our knowledge of learning across adulthood is complicated by the fact that learning is an invisible process. We cannot observe it; we can only infer its presence by observing some change in a person's behavior. If a person learns something and no occasion arises for its use, we have no way of knowing that learning has taken place. When behavior does change, unless we can eliminate other factors that can affect performance, such as drugs, fatigue, or motivation, we cannot be certain that the change is the result of learning. Similarly, if a person appears to forget something, it is possible that he or she has not really forgotten, but is simply tired or lacks the motivation to do whatever has been learned.

Researchers have used various methods to get around these problems. Using techniques that come from the mechanistic approach to development, investigators attempt to discover what characteristics of a task affect learning, whether these influences change with age, and how this may affect learning in daily life.

AGE CHANGES IN LEARNING SKILLS

Although some basic learning skills probably decline a bit in later adulthood, the rate of decline and the age at which it begins have not been established. One of the reasons for this lack of information is that most studies are cross-sectional, comparing adults in their sixties with college students. In such research, age differences have been found in studies of conditioning, verbal learning, and the learning of cognitive skills.

Conditioning

Conditioning is considered the simplest form of learning, and the pattern of age changes depends on whether classical or operant conditioning is examined. In **classical conditioning**, some normally involuntary response, such as the blink of an eye, is conditioned to a new stimulus. For examples, researchers (Kimble and Pennypacker, 1963) asked adults to press a key on the right when a light appeared on the right-hand side of a board and a key on the left when a light appeared on the left-hand side of the board. Each time the light appeared, a puff of air blew into their eyes. When they blinked at the sight of the light, even though there was no blast of air, the adults were conditioned. It took older adults longer than younger adults to develop the conditioned eye-blink, and the blink was weaker among the older group.

Although there are few studies of classical conditioning among middle-aged adults, one study that included subjects as old as 55 found no significant difference with age (Gendreau and Suboski, 1971). The decline apparently begins sometime during the sixties, and it has been suggested that changes in the central nervous system are responsible for weakening the involuntary response (Schonfield, 1980). As we saw in Chapter 7, there is some sensory decline with age, so it may be that the stimulus (the puff of air) is perceived as less unpleasant by older adults. Finally, the length of time allowed for the appearance of the response, which may be as little as 300 milliseconds, may affect results, for it takes older people longer to register stimuli and respond to them than it does younger people (Perlmutter and List, 1982).

In classical conditioning, people are generally unaware of the response that is being conditioned. A person may transfer an emotion or some involuntary muscular response to a new stimulus, but he or she is not trying to do anything. There is no voluntary action the person can take toward a goal.

In **operant conditioning**, what the person chooses to do either brings some reward or removes some unpleasant situation. The consequences of the action produce reinforcement, and as a result of reinforcement, behavior changes. Little research has been directed toward discovering whether people become less responsive to operant conditioning as they age, but it seems clear that older individuals can be conditioned.

For example, an 82-year-old heart patient who was staying in bed all morning, rarely exercising, not taking his medication, and failing to drink his orange juice was placed on token reinforcement. Each time he walked around the block without being reminded, drank a small glass of orange juice, or took his medication, he earned tokens, which could be exchanged for such privileges as a weekend dinner at a restaurant of his choice. Within a few weeks his walks had increased from once every seven days to three times a day, he was drinking three glasses of orange juice each day, instead of one—or none—and he was taking each of his three medications regularly. During the same period, his angina pain disappeared (Dapcich-Miura and Hovell, 1979).

Conditioning has been successful even with older patients who have organic brain syndrome. Through the use of prompts and reinforcement, patients up to 90 years old who had been bathed by an attendant at a nursing home began bathing themselves (Rinke et al., 1978). Conditioning techniques have been used among older mental patients to increase social interaction, food consumption at meals, and exercise, as well as to reduce incontinence (Schonfield, 1980). However, attempts to use operant conditioning with older adults are not always successful, perhaps because the rewards that work best with young adults are not always the most effective for changing the behavior of older adults (Perlmutter and List, 1982). Considerably more complicated than conditioning are studies of verbal learning.

Verbal Learning

When investigators study verbal learning, they are looking at the processes involved in rote learning. The goal is to repeat specific information presented by the researcher. The experiment generally takes the form of either a serial-learning task or a paired-associate task. The serial-learning task is the simplest. As the person watches a screen, a list of words appears, one at a time, and the person tries to memorize them. Learning is demonstrated by repeating the list. In a paired-associate task, a person learns pairs of words, such as moon-zebra. Then, when given one member of the pair, the person produces the other.

Although the performance of older adults on cross-sectional studies of verbal learning is invariably worse than that of younger adults, the two groups almost always overlap. Some older adults perform as well on learning tasks as younger adults. Yet there is no way to be certain whether the observed differences are due to aging or to cohort effects.

Because the results of cross-sectional studies are probably magnified by cohort effects, a look at the few longitudinal studies may be helpful. One investigator (Gilbert, 1973) retested fourteen 60- to 74-year-olds who had taken part in a study of cognitive function nearly 40 years before. As a group, their scores for learning and retention of what they had learned had declined significantly since the original testing, but their vocabulary remained high. No information is available on the individual scores of these adults, nor do we know how typical they were of the original group.

In the Baltimore Longitudinal Study, well-educated men of high socioeconomic status were retested after 8 years (Arenberg and Robertson-Tchabo, 1977). The men, born between 1885 and 1932, were from 32 to 75 years old at the time of the first testing and represented six cohorts. At that time, there was little difference in learning among those who were less than 60 years old, but large age differences among the older men.

At both tests, the men were given a paired-associate and a serial learning task. Results on the two tasks were similar. In the paired-associate task, the youngest cohort, who had been in their thirties at the time of the first testing, showed a small improvement over the eight years. Middle-aged men, who had been in their forties and early fifties at the time of the first testing, showed a small decline. But older men, beginning with those who had been 55 at the first testing, showed a large decline, which became quite steep among those who had been between 69 and 76 eight years before. Interindividual differences were smallest within the youngest cohort and increased with age. At least in the area of verbal learning, there seems to be a decline after the age of 60.

Learning Cognitive Skills

As older adults are beginning to enroll in college courses in increasing numbers, the question of whether declines in learning abilities will severely handicap them in advanced education arises. Obviously, some older adults are as capable of learning as are typical college students. But as we will see in Chapter 9, studies have demonstrated changes with age in problem solving, reasoning, and other advanced cognitive skills.

Learning extends to complex cognitive activities, and a few researchers have attempted to teach problem-solving and reasoning skills to older adults. Their success has been mixed. In some cases, reasoning and problem-solving skills improve, but are not transferred to other situations. Other researchers are more successful. For example, after receiving training in inductive reasoning, in which they had to generalize rules from bits of information in order to solve a problem, some older adults were able to transfer their improved ability to another inductive reasoning task (Labouvie-Vief and Gonda, 1976).

Training in concept identification has also been successful. Concept identification requries a person to look at several objects that may differ in a number of ways—shape, color, size—and classify them according to a rule set by the experimenter. The experimenter does not say what the rule is, but merely tells the person whether the answer is right or wrong. Older adults who were given training in simple concept identification were much better at identifying more complicated concepts a year later than adults who had not had the training (Sterns and Sanders, 1980).

Finally, older adults who were given a 6-week training program in discussion and role-playing of problems showed improved functioning in social cognition (Zaks and Labouvie-Vief, 1980). When compared with a control group and a group that had participated only in discussions, they were better at taking the perspective of another person. They did a better job at understanding the way a scene would look to a person standing from another vantage point. They also showed superior skills in referential communication, in which they had to describe an object (usually a geometric figure) clearly enough so that an unseen listener could pick the object out of an array of similar figures.

It would seem that even if cognitive skills have deteriorated somewhat from disuse or lack of motivation, it is possible to regain at least some of the former skills. And when we look at the factors that affect an older adult's performance on learning tasks, it would seem that changing the learning situation might make learning much easier.

INFLUENCES ON LEARNING

It has been extremely difficult to discover just how much of the decline in learning ability is due to the effects of aging and even whether aging itself actually affects the ability to learn (Perlmutter and List, 1982). Although older groups do worse than younger groups in laboratory experiments, changing the conditions of the experiment can increase or narrow differences, depending on the technique used. Among the factors that may contribute to age differences in verbal learning are pacing, motivation, caution, distractibility, and interference.

Pacing

A major influence on older people's ability to learn in the laboratory is their slowness. As we saw in Chapter 7, the elderly need more time than younger people to extract visual information. It would seem that all stages of processing are slowed (Salthouse and Somberg, 1982), so that the pace at which experiments are conducted has a major effect on the performance of older adults.

In paired-associate tasks, the experiment is paced in two ways: by the length of time the pair of words appears together (a study period) and by the length of time between the presentation of the first word in each pair and the presentation of the two words together (the testing period). Lengthening either period improves the performance of older adults. They seem to take more time to learn and more time to produce an answer after they have learned it. Younger adults also do better with more time, but older adults narrow the performance gap noticeably when the testing period for both is lengthened. When searching for an answer, a person must first register the word, then search the memory for its partner and come up with it before the pair appear on the screen together. When the testing interval is only 1.5 seconds long, older adults do much worse than younger adults; when the interval is increased to 3 seconds, older adults improve much more than the young (Canestrari, 1963). When both periods are lengthened, older adults do their best.

An operant-conditioning experiment that required men to learn complicated light patterns showed that older men can adapt to all but the very fastest pace. In this study (Perone and Baron, 1982), men earned money by duplicating a 10-light sequence produced by pressing four keys in the proper order. When a light sequence was thoroughly learned, 67- to 75-year-old men did as well as 18- to 20-year-olds as long as they had a second or more to produce the sequence. But when they were given only half a second, the performance of older, but not younger men, suffered. In the learning of new light sequences, the gap between the performance of young and old men widened considerably. By the fifth presentation of the sequence, however, the older men did as well as the younger men except at the half-second interval.

Pacing problems are not confined to the elderly. Once people reach the age of 40, rapid pacing begins to cause poorer performance on paired-associate tasks (Monge and Hultsch, 1971), and adults in their thirties begin to leave fast-paced industrial jobs where work is done under a constant, externally imposed time pressure (Welford, 1958).

The extra time older adults require to learn new material may not be entirely due to slowness in information processing. When attempting to learn new information, older people often fail to use any of the techniques customarily employed by younger people to ease learning. As we will see in the discussion of memory, providing specific learning instructions can reduce the age gap.

Motivation
Motivation invariably affects performance. Just as a full rat is unlikely to work at bar pressing to get food pellets, so a person who has no interest in the outcome of an experiment is unlikely to strive for peak performance. Some researchers have assumed that older adults see laboratory experiments as meaningless and have no motive to learn a list of words or word pairs. However, others believe that older adults who participate in research tend to be especially interested, involved, and motivated.

The response of **arousal** is often closely related to motivation. When people encounter some new situation, sensory information travels to the brain, activating (or arousing) both the cortex and the reticular formation, a portion of the lower brain that regulates consciousness and attention. The reticular formation further arouses the cortex, and the person undertakes some action that is aimed at reaching a goal. But there is an optimum level of arousal. Too little arousal and a person will not act; too much arousal and the person will be unable to act effectively because the aim of the body will be to reduce stimulation (Hebb, 1955).

In classical conditioning experiments, sensory declines may lead older adults to be underaroused and hence undermotivated, but researchers have questioned this explanation when intentional learning is involved (Botwinick, 1978). It has been suggested that older adults may be more motivated than younger people and may become so involved in the experimental situation that they are overaroused, anxious, and unable to perform at their best.

Using physiological measures, researchers have found higher arousal during learning experiments in older subjects as compared with subjects younger than 50, whether the measure of arousal is free fatty acids in the blood (Eisdorfer, 1968) or heart rate and skin conductance (Furchgott and Busemeyer, 1976). In a test of the overarousal hypothesis, researchers (Eisdorfer, Nowlin, and Wilkie, 1970) divided older adults into two groups, giving half of them an inactive injection and the other half an injection of propranolol, a drug that blocks receptor sites for the autonomic nervous system. Those who received the drug had lower levels of free fatty acids and performed better on the learning task, indicating that at least some older adults are too aroused during experiments to do their best.

These findings have implications that go beyond the laboratory. If older people are placed in situations that make them feel anxious or likely to fail, their performance may deteriorate far below their capabilities (Schonfield, 1980). In an experiment involving detailed pencil-and-paper work (Bellucci and Hoyer, 1975), female college students and female college graduates between the ages of 60 and 74 either worked in the presence of a silent experimenter or worked with one who told them that they were doing better than most people of their age—no matter how they performed. Whether young or old, those who heard their performance was superior made higher scores than the women who worked in silence. An age difference appeared in the way the women judged their own work. After completing a task, each was allowed to take S&H green stamps as a reward, and the number of stamps was to reflect their own evaluation of their performance. Told they were doing well, both young and old took the same number of stamps, but when they worked in silence, the older women took fewer stamps than did the younger women. Apparently, older women who lacked outside approval had less confidence in their performance.

Caution

If people do not respond, there is no way to discover whether they have learned anything. When the errors of older adults are analyzed, they turn out to be primarily errors of omission (Arenberg and Robertson-Tchabo, 1977). Instead of giving wrong answers on paired-associate or serial learning tasks, older adults tend to stop answering. As we saw in Chapter 7, older adults take longer to decide whether they have heard sounds, making certain they hear them before reacting. This caution not only makes older adults slower to respond, but it also makes them seem to have learned less then they have—expecially in experiments that give them only a second or so to answer and do not penalize them for incorrect answers.

In one experiment (Leech and Witte, 1971), researchers were able to reduce errors of omission by paying older adults for their answers even when they were wrong. When this technique was used, the adults were less cautious. Their rate of responding increased, and they needed fewer trials to learn the material than did adults who were paid only for correct answers.

Distractibility

If people cannot keep their attention focused on a learning task, they are unlikely to learn much. Some researchers (Rabbitt, 1965) have suggested that older adults are so distracted by irrelevant information that they have trouble concentrating. The irrelevant information can be stimuli that distract a person from the learning task or ideas that intrude into consciousness (Schonfield, 1980). Whether information is distracting depends on the intensity and movement of the stimulus and the extent of the person's previous experience with it. The suggestion that older individuals are troubled by distraction fits the notion of stimulus persistence that has been used to explain age differences in critical flicker frequency (Chapter 7). If all information becomes a bit more persistent in the older information-processing system, irrelevant information may become bothersome.

In a recent experiment testing the distractibility proposal (Madden, 1983), male and female college students and older men and women between the ages of 63 and 77 were asked to search for particular letters in a visual display. As a group, older adults made more errors than the younger adults. After using the same target letters for four days, the investigators substituted different letters on the fifth day, but continued to use letters from the previous days' tasks as distracting items. The presence of the familiar letter increased reaction time, but by about the same amount for young and old. The researcher suggests that problems with attention in older adults are more likely to be caused by a difficulty in focusing on relevant information than from being distracted by irrelevant information.

Interference

Another possible aspect of the learning situation that can affect the result of laboratory experiments is interference. One sort of disruption is called **proactive interference**, in which old material interferes with new material to be learned. If the task requires paired-associate learning, for example, old associations interfere with the new ones. Given a list of common associations (blossom/flower; hot/cold), older adults have more trouble than young adults in forming new associations (blossom/cold; hot/flower) (Lair, Moon, and Kausler, 1969). That is, previously established habits are believed to become so strong in older people, that they have difficulty in establishing new ones. Others have agreed that interference affects learning, but not interference from old information. They point to retroactive interference as the culprit. In **retroactive interference**, learning new material interferes with previously learned material. For example, if a person learns a list of words, then learns a second list, the information from the second list will make it more difficult to recall the first.

Retroactive interference may be strong in older adults; however, younger adults are known to be subject to both proactive and retroactive interference. Whether such interference is stronger in older adults seems impossible to discover because so many other factors are also at work in these experiments (Arenberg and Robertson-Tchabo, 1977). Before the presence of interference can be compared, equal learning of the original material must be established, but when individuals learn at different rates, there seems no way to equate the two groups. However, in one study (Schonfield, Davidson, and Jones, 1983) that began with almost perfect performance in both young (18 to 30) and older (63 to 77) adults, proactive interference seemed stronger in the elderly. Among the young adults, only recall (the ability to remember in the absence of the sought-for information) was disrupted by proactive interference, but both recognition (the ability to remember in the presence of the information) and recall suffered among older adults. As we examine changes in the memory system, the distinction between recall and recognition will become clear.

MEMORY ACROSS ADULTHOOD

If information processing resembles the operations of a computer, then we can consider the nervous system and sensory receptors as the basic computer—the hardware—and the methods people use to process information as programs—the software. No one has yet established which aspect is responsible for the generally poorer performance of older adults on memory tasks as compared with the young. Whether the basic system slows and becomes less effective with age or whether older people are less likely to use programs that process information efficiently is uncertain. Perhaps both elements are involved.

At the shallowest level of the memory system is **sensory memory**, which holds environmental information (sights, sounds, touches, smells, or tastes) for a second or so. The information then decays, so if it is to be used, it must be processed at a deeper level. Once past the sensory store, memory may be seen as divided into two basic systems: short-term memory and long-term memory. Aging appears to affect each system differently.

SHORT-TERM MEMORY

Short-term memory is a limited capacity system that keeps information in consciousness. It can hold a telephone number long enough to dial it, but because short-term memory is not permanent storage, unless the material is maintained—as when you repeat a phone number over and over to yourself as you walk to the phone—it is generally lost within about 15 seconds. If you have ever been interrupted as you picked up the telephone and found that you had to look up the number again, you have experienced the unintentional loss of information from short-term memory.

Because short-term memory holds information that is being consciously processed, it utilizes a control system (Atkinson and Shiffrin, 1971). It is here that we apply whatever strategies we have developed, organizing material to make certain it is permanently recorded, or **encoded**, so that we can retrieve it later.

The capacity of short-term memory is usually studied by the digit span test. A person hears or sees a string of digits or letters and repeats back as many of them as he or she remembers. Short-term memory apparently holds about seven (± 2) items and anything over that amount must be retrieved from long-term memory (Miller, 1956). There appears to be only a slight decline in short-term memory when span is tested although there are some differences depending on whether digits, letters, or words are used. When decreases are observed, they seem to begin around the age of 60 (Craik, 1977).

If material must be manipulated in short-term memory, age differences consistently appear. For example, if people are asked to repeat a string of digits backwards, a feat that requires them to reorganize the information, fairly large declines in memory span are seen among older adults. This apparent contraction may be due to a lack of flexibility in information processing, to a loss of information during reorganization, and to the drained capacity required to carry the reorganization (Walsh, 1983).

Age differences also appear when attention must be divided between two tasks. Perhaps the capacity of short-term memory does not change with age, but its contents become more fragile and are easily disrupted (Arenberg, 1980). For example, when uninterrupted, an older person may have no trouble holding a phone number in short-term memory until it is dialed, but a minor distraction that would not bother a younger person may wipe out the number so that it must be looked up again.

Finally, short-term memory seems to slow with age. Although the system may be able to store as much information, it takes longer to retrieve it. When given a list of digits and then asked whether a test digit was part of the original list, the time required to decide increases with age (Anders, Fozard, and Lillyquist, 1972). People between the ages of 58 and 85 needed more time to make up their minds even when the original list contained only one digit, and as the number of digits on the list approached the limits of short-term memory, people in their thirties needed more time than 20-year-olds. Time in such experiments is measured in milliseconds, so that it may take a 35-year-old 100 milliseconds longer than a 20-year-old to run through five digits in short-term memory and a 75-year-old an extra 300 milliseconds. Whether such a difference reduced the effectiveness of memory would depend upon the task.

LONG-TERM MEMORY

Long-term memory is assumed to be a system with unlimited capacity. It is the storehouse of our past experience, holding memories of childhood, our knowledge about the world, and all information that exceeds the span of short-term memory. As information is encoded, it is transferred to long-term store, where it is held until needed. At retrieval, the information is transferred back into short-term memory, where it can be consciously manipulated (Fig. 8.1).

Age does not seem to affect the storage of information; once material has been placed in long-term storage it is kept as efficiently by 80-year-olds as by 20-year-olds (Walsh, 1983). Even if a person is unable to retrieve the information, it is believed to be in storage but inaccessible. Presumably, given the right cue in the right situation, the memory could be retrieved.

Stored information also seems to be organized similarly in young and old (Salthouse, 1982). Regardless of age, adults have available both episodic and semantic memories (Tulving, 1972). **Episodic memories** include everything that happens to us, so that each memory is linked with a time and place. Recalling a childhood birthday party, last week's football game, or the name of a person you met at a dance retrieves an episodic memory. **Semantic memories** are organized factual knowledge such as the fact that basenjis are dogs and dogs are mammals, that the United States is made up of 50 states, and that the past tense of "break" is "broke." It is believed that episodic memories may be vulnerable to the effects of aging, but that semantic memories are generally unimpaired (Craik and Simon, 1980).

Although the retention of information in storage may not be affected by aging, older adults seem to be less proficient both at encoding material and transferring it into long-term memory and at getting it back out again. In exploring encoding and retrieval problems, researchers have studied two types of memory retrieval: recall and recognition.

Recall of episodic memory, in which stored material must be remembered spontaneously or in response to some cue, is generally worse in older adults. Some researchers have found that when people are asked to learn a word list and recall it spontaneously, the number of words recalled begins to decline as people enter their thirties and becomes smaller with each passing decade. However, given a retrieval cue (the name of a category, such as "animals"), people can remember more words from the list and age differences generally diminish (Craik, 1977).

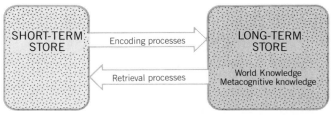

FIGURE 8.1   This model of the memory system represents two aspects of memory: capacities and contents. The basic memory capacities include short-term memory, a limited capacity store that keeps information in consciousness; long-term memory, a store that is assumed to have unlimited capacity; and the encoding and retrieval processes that transfer information back and forth between the two stores. The contents of memory consist of our knowledge about the world (semantic and episodic) and metacognitive knowledge (our understanding of the way the memory system works).

Because the cue makes more words accessible, it appears that older people have trouble retrieving words from storage.

This decline in episodic memory does not appear to be the result of less formal education because older individuals with Ph.D.s show the same decline when compared with doctoral students in their twenties that older individuals with high school educations show in comparison with high school graduates in their twenties (Perlmutter, 1978). Yet education has some effect: Both younger and older adults with more education recalled a greater number of words than did their age peers with less education. Despite worsening episodic memory, the recall of facts is good in older adults; whether they had Ph.D.s or high school educations, both older groups were better at answering factual questions about history than were young people with similar educational backgrounds (Fig. 8.2).

A person's memory for pictures appears to be stronger than the memory for words. Both older and younger adults seem to have less trouble recalling objects they have seen in line drawings than those they have seen in word lists (Winograd, Smith, and Simon, 1982). Because both groups improve by about the same amount when recalling pictures, older adults still show poorer retrieval than the young.

The notion of retrieval difficulty is supported by the fact that recognition shows much less decline with age than does recall. In recognition experiments, a person might be shown a group of pictures or a long list of words, then later shown a second group and asked whether these pictures or words are new or were included in the first group. In such an experiment, the items themselves serve as a cue to the original list, making it is easier to retrieve the information (Perlmutter, 1979). We might say that the sight of items from the first group jogs the person's memory. Some researchers have found little or no age difference in recognition memory, but consistent differences in recall, which is more difficult because it must be accomplished without the aid of the cue provided by the original information.

Through the use of memory cues, such as these snapshots, older adults can gain access to long-stored material they may believe has been forgotten.

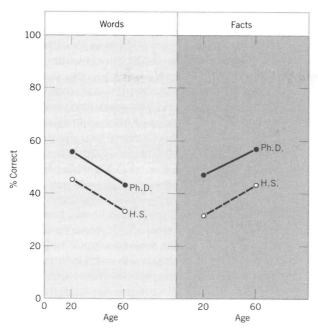

FIGURE 8.2 Age, education, and recall. When asked to recall a word list, older adults with Ph.D.'s did worse than young graduate students, and older adults with high school educations did worse than young adults with the same level of education. But highly educated older adults remembered more words than young adults with high school educations. When given a test of historical facts, older adults did better than younger adults, no matter what their educational level.

Source: M. Perlmutter, 1978, pp. 330–345.

Whether age differences appear in recognition experiments seems to depend on the conditions in which information is encoded and retrieved and on the characteristics of the individuals studied. In one experiment (Bowles and Poon, 1982), the IQ scores of older adults were closely linked with recognition memory. Among a group of subjects in their seventies, those with high scores on the verbal part of the IQ test recognized just as many words on a recognition test as did college students with high verbal IQ scores. Among those with low verbal IQ scores, the picture was very different. Although all recognized significantly fewer words than the old and young individuals in the high IQ groups, the subjects in their seventies did much worse than the college students with low IQ scores.

Retrieval is not the only memory problem faced by older adults. Encoding seems to present as large a problem. Even when given cues, older adults do not recall as many words as do the young, indicating that less material may have been placed in storage. Another indication of encoding difficulty is the finding that when older and younger adults can be induced to reach the same level of learning on the tested material, age differences are reduced (Perlmutter, 1983).

It has been suggested that older people simply need more time to encode information. Their visual system seems to take longer to register information, they seem to integrate information more slowly, and they may encode only general features, neglecting details that will help them to distinguish one event from another. This slowing can affect recognition as well as recall. In one study (Waugh and Barr, 1982), people looked at pictures or words, which were presented at varying rates of speed. Given half a second to view a picture or a word, older adults later could not recognize many of the targets; but given an entire second to view the display, they narrowed the gap between themselves and the young adults considerably. As we saw earlier, pacing has a major influence on information processing.

MEMORY STRATEGIES

Retrieval and encoding failure often seem to be the result of **production deficiencies**. That is, older adults often fail to use memory strategies spontaneously that they are capable of using if reminded to do so (Perlmutter, 1983). Memory strategies are believed to elaborate on information or to process it at a deeper level, making it more likely that material will be encoded in the first place and increasing the ease of later retrieval.

Material that is handled at the sensory level receives only shallow processing; when material is handled at the semantic level, so that meaning is attached to it, it receives deeper processing. Thus, noting that a green hillside is covered with black objects is an example of shallow processing. Realizing that the black objects are animals processes the material at a slightly deeper level. Noting that the animals are black cattle processes the material at an even deeper level, but noting that they are Angus cattle and, therefore, destined to become beef elaborates on the memory as well as deepens the processing. And as processing deepens, the duration and retrievability of the memory is likely to increase (Walsh, 1983).

Material also can be processed without moving to a deeper level. Repeating the words in a list again and again maintains the memory as long as the repetition lasts. However, the memory trace then begins to decay at the same rate as any other material that has been processed at this shallow level.

Any encoding strategy that increases the depth of processing is believed to increase learning. One strategy that moves information to a deeper level is to organize it by category, for example, grouping together all the animals on a list to be remembered. A second strategy is to use some sort of verbal aid to memory, such as making a word out of the first letters of each item to be remembered. A third strategy is to construct a vivid image of items to be remembered, such as visualizing a dog at the helm of a sailboat to remember the paired associate words dog/boat. And a fourth strategy is to devise a systematic plan for rehearsing the material. No matter which strategy is used, the amount of material remembered should increase. Researchers frequently find that college students use such strategies spontaneously in memory tests, but that older adults do not. It has been suggested that the failure to apply deep processing to information is responsible for inferior recall and recognition found in older adults.

In one experiment (Zacks, 1982), researchers asked college students and adults in their seventies to memorize a list of common words drawn from several categories. As expected, the students were much better at the task than the older adults. But when the researcher kept students from using strategies by requiring them to repeat each word in the list out loud until the next one appeared, their performance plummeted, and they did only slightly better than the older adults. Other studies (Perlmutter and Mitchell, 1982) have indicated that when the conditions of the experiment direct the way the information is to be processed, perhaps by suggesting that word lists be organized by category, older and younger adults encode material in a similar manner.

This finding is supported by a study that compared recall of word lists in young, middle-aged, and older women (Zivian and Darjes, 1983). The major difference in this experiment was the fact that half of the middle-aged women were also university students. The students, whether young or middle-aged, performed similarly, with the middle-aged students recalling as many words as the 20-year-olds. But the middle-aged women who were not in school performed much worse than the two students groups although better than the older women, who were between 60 and 86 years old. Apparently, when our everyday situation requires us to process material so that it can be produced on demand, we maintain memory strategies that we might otherwise cease to use.

METAMEMORY

Several reasons have been suggested for older adults' failure to use spontaneous encoding or retrieval strategies. One suggestion is that older adults are unaware of possible memory strategies. They do not use them because they do not know as much as younger adults about **metamemory**, which is an understanding of the way the memory system works. Some studies (Murphy et al., 1981) have indicated, for example, that older adults spend less time studying word lists than younger adults and increase their study time less as the task becomes more difficult, as if they were unaware of the demands of the task. But in other studies (Perlmutter, 1978), younger and older adults spent about the same amount of time studying, and their responses on a questionnaire indicated that they understood memory strategies and used them about as much as younger adults did in their daily activities. Some researchers (Zivian and Darjes, 1983) have found that students, whether young or middle-aged, have a clearer understanding of metamemory and the effectiveness of various strategies than middle-aged and older adults who are not in school. Students also seem to use the strategies in an appropriate manner.

Not all memory strategies are spontaneously used by the young. When instructed to use imagery, both younger and older adults improved their recall by a similar amount. In this case, participants in the study were instructed to form an interactive image for each pair of words in a paired-associate learning task. For example, given the words "tree" and "telephone," the person might form an im-

OUTWITTING AN AGING MEMORY

When psychologist B. F. Skinner (1983) reached the age of 79, he shared some of the means he had discovered for getting around the problems of an aging memory. It is Skinner's contention that shortcomings in the environment are responsible for many of the intellectual lapses encountered by older adults. An environment that produces an abundance of cues and reinforcements for a younger person will lack the appropriate stimuli for a person whose senses have dulled and whose processing of information has slowed.

Most of the difficulties Skinner encountered with memory were problems of retrieval, and he developed the systematic use of cues to ease recall. At one time he found himself responding to weather reports predicting rain by resolving to take an umbrella. But too often he found himself forgetting his resolution and leaving the house without the um-

brella, only to be caught in a shower. Now when he hears predictions of rain, he immediately hangs an umbrella on the doorknob or puts it through the handle of his briefcase. As he leaves the house, the sight of the umbrella reminds him to carry it along—and perhaps to take his raincoat.

When he forgets names, he uses such cues as going through the alphabet and testing each letter to see if it began the person's name. Given half an hour, he can usually recall a name. Because forgetting a person's name when trying to make an introduction is embarrassing, the situation is aversive and becomes one that most of us may try to avoid. In addition, having forgotten names in similar situations in the past may set up enough anxiety to cause us to forget names in similar future situations. Skinner's solution is to eliminate the aversive aspects of the situation by appealing to his age,

age of a telephone hanging from a tree. The fact that recall of younger adults also improved indicates that they are no more likely than older adults to make spontaneous use of imagery as an encoding strategy (Rabinowitz et al., 1982). Young and old seemed equally ignorant of the effect the use of imagery would have on their recall, and both consistently underpredicted the number of word pairs they would remember when using imagery just as both made accurate predictions of their recall when allowed to learn the words in any way they wished.

Older adults seem just as proficient as the young when it comes to a type of metamemory process that is part of daily life—the "feeling of knowing" (Lachman and Lachman, 1980). Asked a series of general knowledge questions, such as, "What was the former name of Muhammad Ali?" older adults were as accurate as the young in assessing whether they definitely knew the answers, definitely did not know, or "could recognize if told." (A multiple-choice test later confirmed the ability to recognize the correct answers).

If ignorance about the memory system is no greater among older adults, what is responsible for their failure to use memory strategies? Some researchers have by flattering his listener, or by recalling instances in which he has forgotten his own name.

Lapses of memory in the midst of a conversation are also unpleasant. Skinner found that when he digressed, he sometimes forgot why he began the digression and what he was talking about when he began it. His solution was to rearrange the situation. He no longer "interrupts himself," and he tries to use only simple sentence construction to keep himself on the track. When someone else is talking and he is trying to keep a point in mind that he wishes to make, he may pull out a pad and make a note or else rehearse the point to himself, keeping it in short-term memory.

Notes, whether written or taped, are other cues that Skinner has found valuable. After repeatedly forgetting to make important changes in articles that occurred to him in the middle of the night or while he was doing other things, Skinner began carrying a notepad and pencil or keeping a tape

recorder beside his bed. As he put it: "The problem in old age is not so much how to have ideas as how to have them when you can use them" (Skinner, 1983, p. 240). By recording his thoughts, he made them available when he sat down at his desk to write.

As Skinner's work is intellectual, he finds that providing an abundance of cues helps compensate for retrieval problems. Reference books, rereading relevant material, and the use of a thesaurus increase his responses to a problem he is writing or thinking about. Good files; a tape recorder; a word processor; an abundant supply of pens, pencils, and paper; and an increasing reliance on detailed outlines have enabled him to continue the production of scholarly and popular papers.

Skinner has made the problems of an aging memory less aversive by recognizing that retrieval has become more difficult and by changing the conditions under which he must retrieve information.

suggested that the amount of energy available for information processing at any one time declines with age (Craik and Byrd, 1982). Because the use of memory strategies requires conscious effort, older adults are either unable or reluctant to carry out the demanding strategies involved in deep processing.

For example, when older adults are unaware that they will be tested on words they are shown, they generally remember more of the words than when they understand that they are memorizing the words for a test. And when distractor words are presented along with the target words, the performance of older individuals suffers more than the performance of the young. Evaluating such research, Marion Perlmutter and David Mitchell (1982) have suggested that instead of regarding older adults as having an impaired processing capacity, it might be more helpful to regard younger adults as having a processing surplus, a surplus that they can call upon when learning conditions are less than optimum.

Finally, it may be that even if strategies are used at encoding, older adults still may encounter retrieval problems. In one study, researchers (Simon et al., 1982) arranged the situation so that deeper processing was "forced." But it was the young and not the old who profited by being compelled to process material at a deeper level. Adults read a 500-word text about a family with financial problems. The story was read under several conditions. In the first, spelling and grammatical errors were circled, presumably leading to extensive but not very meaningful processing. In the second condition, the text was rated for interest, organization, readability, and closeness to life, presumably leading to processing at a somewhat deeper level. In the third condition, the reader was to supply advice to the family after reading the text, presumably calling forth the deepest processing. In each case, the young adults (18 to 32) recalled far more of the main ideas in the story than did middle-aged (39 to 51) or older (59 to 76) adults. But in an unusual switch, when told simply to read and remember the story, middle-aged and older adults recalled at least as many of the main ideas as did the young.

The researchers suggest that although the two older groups may have processed the material as deeply as the younger group under the three earlier conditions, their recall suffered because at the time of retrieval, they were unable to reinstate the mental operations they used during encoding. When they engage in deep processing, older adults may encode material in a less specific and distinctive manner than that used by young people. If so, they would require different or more general retrieval cues for successful recall (Craik and Simon, 1980).

In a situation that encourages memory, older adults seem capable of using various strategies. Offered a method of learning to connect names and faces, a group of retired middle managers used the strategy effectively, doubling the number of names they could recall (Yesavage, Rose, and Bower, 1983). In this study, the retired adults were told to identify a prominent facial feature (a large mouth), produce a concrete image from the person's name ("Whalen" became "whale"), and to produce a second image associating the feature with the transformed name (a whale in a person's mouth). The retired adults remembered the most names when they were also told to judge the pleasantness or unpleasantness of the associative image they had formed. Presumably, this judgment forced them to process the image at a deeper level. Because this memory technique has obvious practical applications, the older adults may have had more incentive to focus their available energy on the encoding strategy.

Despite the problems older adults seem to have with memory on laboratory tasks, in daily life we see older adults learning and remembering everywhere.

LEARNING IN NATURAL SITUATIONS

Although some age-related decline in learning and memory skills does exist, adults continue to learn and remember new things as long as they live. The learning that goes on in daily life is much more complicated than the sort of learning that is studied in the laboratory—so much more complicated that it seems likely that some important factors that affect learning and memory are missing from present theories (Perlmutter and List, 1982).

Natural learning gets very little scrutiny by psychologists, primarily because it is untidy and affected by so many different variables. It may even be that some of the factors that deter learning in the laboratory increase the ease with which material is learned in daily life. For example, the existence of proactive interference may mean that well-established habits can sometimes make related learning easier for older adults (Arenberg and Robertson-Tchabo, 1977). The elderly are often aware of this. When interviewed by Robert Coles (1975), an 83-year-old New Mexican woman told him:

Habits are not crutches; habits are roads we have paved for ourselves. When we are old, and if we have done a good job, the roads last and make the remaining time useful: we get where we want to go, and without the delays we used to have when we were young [p. 39].

As people age, they adapt to changes in physical, sensory, and cognitive functioning; and this adaptation itself is a form of learning. They learn to compensate for a loss in one area by substituting in another. For example, when a person begins to suffer a hearing loss, he or she begins to watch people's faces more closely during conversation and soon becomes fairly proficient in lipreading and at deciphering meaning from context. And we have seen how Skinner (1983) learned to compensate for his memory failures. Because of such compensations, functioning is not nearly so curtailed as laboratory studies of memory and learning would indicate.

Physical training programs regularly produce significant improvement in physiological and intellectual performance (Perlmutter and List, 1982). As we saw in Chapter 5, regular exercise improves the condition and function of the muscles, bones, respiratory system, and cardiovascular system of the elderly. When older adults who are out of condition undertake a physical training program, their reaction time often becomes faster.

The ability to learn may also improve. In one study (Ohlsson, 1976), physical conditioning increased the attention span of the elderly and led to improved performance on simple cognitive tasks. Others (Elsayed, Ismail, and Young, 1980) have found that the ability to grasp complex relationships in nonverbal material also increases after physical training. It seems clear that the ability to learn physical skills remains good in old age and that using that ability may improve learning in other areas.

Older adults continue to show their cognitive fitness. We hear of retired adults starting second careers in new fields, a switch that is impossible without learning and memory. People who read regularly keep on reading into old age, and the extent of their reading is linked with their educational level. In fact, educational level is a better predictor of reading than is age. When it comes to electronic media, older adults are likely to increase their reliance on radio and television as an informational source, a trend found even among cohorts who were not introduced to television until middle age (Parker and Paisley, 1966).

Although enrollment in formal education declines with age, nearly a decade ago 10 percent of 60-year-olds and 4 percent of 70-year-olds were engaged in some continuing education classes (Knox, 1978), and the newer Elderhostel programs seem to have captured the enthusiasm of many older adults. If part of the

In natural situations, people generally adapt to new demands. The introduction of television posed no problem for older adults, who quickly learned to use the new technology and to depend on it as a source of information.

difference in learning ability between the young and the old stems from the recency of formal education, an increase in adult enrollment could go a long way toward reducing the differences that appear in tests of verbal learning. Continued enrollment in education is correlated with previous educational level, and as the educational level of older adults rises, their participation in formal education is likely to increase. It has been suggested that the use of formal education by middle-aged and older adults is a "wave of the future" and that it will have a powerful influence on patterns of life (Neugarten and Hall, 1980).

Each time adults face new social demands, they must learn new social skills or adapt to new roles. Although this sort of learning is informal and primarily a matter of trial and error, it is a form of learning. The loss of a spouse and retirement are two obvious major life events that require people to learn new social skills.

As adults approach retirement, they begin to plan for it either formally or informally. Informal preparation consists of talking to people who have already retired and to fellow workers and relying on information from the media. But formal retirement planning programs, provided by companies or Social Security personnel, are increasing. Most workers are much less interested in counseling programs that aim at reducing anxiety and changing attitudes than they are in programs that give them concrete information about pension benefits, financial and legal planning, medical benefits and health care, nutrition, exercise, and activity planning (Perlmutter and List, 1982). The continued ability of adults in their sixties to apply cognitive skills to such matters has been demonstrated by a study indicating that older adults learn just as much as younger adults from a formal retirement planning program that used self-paced programmed instruction (Sieman, 1976).

Life requires more of us than learning; It also requires us to solve problems and adapt to the world. Building on the information in this chapter, we turn to changes in problem solving and intelligence during adulthood.

SUMMARY

All cognitive functioning can be considered in terms of **information processing**, in which people take information from the environment, then manipulate, store, classify, and retrieve it. Learning and memory are two processes by which information is transferred within the system, and it is difficult to separate them. Although biological aging may be involved in apparent age changes in learning and memory, other factors may also be important, including cohort differences, the study of cognitive functioning removed from life situations, expectations that cognitive skills will decline, and depression.

The rate of decline in learning skills and the age at which it begins has not been established. **Classical conditioning** seems to take longer to establish, and the response may be weaker in adults past the age of 60. **Operant conditioning** appears to be effective with adults of any age. Scores on tests of verbal learning seem to decline after the age of 60 although there are wide interindividual differences. Older adults can learn cognitive skills even if their skills have somewhat deteriorated from disuse or lack of motivation. Among the factors that may contribute to age differences in learning studies are pacing, motivation, caution of older adults, distractibility, and **retroactive** or **proactive interference**. **Arousal** may affect motivation, with underarousal slowing the rate at which older adults are classically conditioned and overarousal leading to poor performance in other learning situations.

The memory system includes **sensory memory**, where environmental information is fleetingly registered; **short-term memory**, where information is kept in consciousness; and **long-term memory**, where memory, knowledge, and past experience are stored. In short-term memory, where information is organized for **encoding** in long-term memory, speed and flexibility appear to decline with age. In long-term memory, information is stored in the form of **episodic** or **semantic** memories, and this storage is not affected by aging. With age, retrieval difficulty may appear for episodic memories, but neither recall of semantic memories nor recognition shows much decline. Encoding also presents a problem for older adults, often because of **production deficiencies**, with the elderly failing to use memory strategies spontaneously even though they have as good a grasp of **metamemory** as the young. The failure to use memory strategies may be due to a decline in the amount of energy available among the old or to a processing surplus among the young. In addition, older adults may encode information in a less specific and distinctive manner than the young, making retrieval more difficult.

Although they have problems in laboratory tests of learning and memory, older adults learn and remember in daily situations that are more complicated than laboratory tasks. Some factors that impede learning in the laboratory, such as **proactive interference**, may make it easier to learn in daily life.

KEY TERMS

arousal

classical conditioning

encode

episodic memory

information processing

long-term memory

metamemory

operant conditioning

proactive interference

production deficiency

retroactive interference

semantic memory

sensory memory

short-term memory

9

INTELLIGENCE AND CREATIVITY ACROSS ADULTHOOD

Age changes in cognition vary widely from person to person. They are hastened or slowed by genetic differences, physical health, emotional factors, and life situation. In 1978, when he was 74 years old, neuropsychologist Donald O. Hebb described to his fellow psychologists the course of the "slow, inevitable loss of cognitive capacity" he had been observing in himself. As Hebb pointed out, his own account is "personal, idiosyncratic, and self-centered," but it provides one view of cognitive aging, and as Hebb's area of expertise is brain function, it is the report of a highly skilled observer.

Hebb found that as he grew older, his vocabulary seemed to shrink. When he was lecturing to students, he would sometimes find himself unable to recall a common psychological term. The tendency became so annoying that he began to write out his lectures in advance and worked to slow his vocabulary loss by relearning terms that once easily came to mind. But the technical terms apparently had not been wiped from his memory, for Hebb still could master the London *Observer* crossword puzzle, a task that demands verbal recall but lacks the stress that accompanies the delivery of a lecture.

A second manifestation of cognitive aging was a change in motivation. Hebb lost his drive to do research and the need to manipulate ideas. He retained an interest in psychology, but it became almost casual—the urgency was gone. Because he also lost interest in solving the puzzles in Martin Gardner's *Scientific American* column, Hebb concluded that his change in motivation was actually the result of a diminished ability to hold and manipulate several ideas at one time.

Finally, the third and perhaps most annoying manifestation of cognitive change was a persistent repetition of thought patterns, in which a saying, a song, or a few lines of poetry would run through his head for as long as half an hour at a time. One day when he made himself a cup of tea, for example, the nursery song "I'm a little teapot" began repeating itself. He could banish the refrain by reciting William Blakes's "Tyger, tyger, burning bright . . . ," but as soon as he stopped, the little teapot again began to dance through his head.

Yet Hebb's cognitive problems did not include rigidity of thought, an aspect of cognition many people assume is an inevitable part of aging. He retained his creativity and flexibility and, building on his recent experiences, revised his own theory of brain function. Hebb's theory views brain function as based on assemblies of neurons. Because of the persistence of his thought patterns, Hebb decided that neurons were continuing to fire in his brain, holding the same material in his short-term memory. In his original theory, he had proposed that closed neural circuits kept cell assemblies firing (Hebb, 1949). The role of closed neural circuits, he now proposes, is to *inhibit* cells as soon as they have fired, eliminating extraneous thought. With age, the inhibitory neurons begin to degenerate, and teapots are allowed to tumble through the brain. (Hebb has, in effect, provided a possible explanation for stimulus persistence.)

It is doubtful that any two brains produce exactly the same experiences as a result of aging, but Hebb's reports were so familiar as to provoke a young psychologist in the audience to observe that at some time he had experienced all of Hebb's problems. Hebb replied that it was a matter of degree; what was once an occasional, annoying event had become a common experience that altered his normal cognitive processes.

We have already looked at the cognitive processes of perception and memory. In this chapter, we examine changes in intelligence and creativity across adulthood. After considering age changes in problem solving, we will attempt to define the nature of intelligence, looking at the ways in which researchers measure intelligence and how current tests were developed. Building on this background, we can explore how test performance changes with age and the significance of that change. Widening our view of intelligence, we examine cognitive styles and creativity and conclude the chapter with a look at the most elusive aspect of cognition: wisdom.

AGE CHANGES IN PROBLEM SOLVING

As we go about our daily lives, we encounter a wide range of problems that must be solved if we are to function effectively. Figuring out why the car refuses to start when the key is turned in the ignition; adapting a recipe that serves six to provide two portions; and deciding which air conditioner is the best buy, whether to invest savings in stocks, bonds, or money market accounts, whom to support for president, or whether to take an umbrella on a cloudy morning are typical problems encountered by adults. Solving such problems generally requires the use of higher mental processes that might be considered intelligence.

On a variety of problem-solving tasks, there appear to be age differences in the way adults approach and handle the tasks, with older adults performing somewhat worse than younger adults. The source of this disparity is not known because most research with adults does not allow us to separate the effects of various cognitive processes on the ability to reach a solution (Rabbitt, 1977). Among the possible explanations are differences in memory, processing speed, ability to organize information, and factors related to performance. It is unlikely that any one of these influences can explain all the changes in problem solving that have been observed.

Although laboratory studies consistently show a breakdown in cognitive control with age, older people often may learn to compensate for their lessened efficiency. Motor control deteriorates, for example, so that older people begin to walk clumsily, relying on reaction to sensory feedback, such as heel contact with the ground or pressure on the soles of their feet, instead of anticipating motor changes as young adults do. Theoretically, very old people should be unable to play golf, type, drive a car, or play the piano with any skill at all because their motor control presumably lags behind events (Rabbitt, 1982). Yet typing speed is not affected by age (Salthouse, 1983), and Vladimir Horowitz was giving scintillating concerts well into his eighties. It would appear that experience and practice can compensate for some deterioration in cognitive control.

In most cases, healthy older adults perform much better in daily life than their responses to laboratory experiments would lead us to predict. As we examine the research on problem solving, it will become apparent that performance on problem-solving tasks does not always indicate a person's competence, that is, what he or she is capable of doing under favorable circumstances. Older adults may have retained abilities that do not appear in their behavior, and some abilities that seem to be lost are often relearned quickly in training situations (Denney, 1979).

Most research on problem solving is done from a mechanistic viewpoint, focusing on specific aspects of information processing, or from an organismic view, which assumes that performance reflects the structure of thought. Studies in the first group investigate concept formation, classification, and the solution of puzzles. Studies in the second group explore the use of logical concepts.

THINKING ABOUT PROBLEMS

Thought about a problem draws on our general knowledge of the world, which is organized by concepts. A concept is a symbol with many examples, such as "tree," "automobile," "music," "software," or "democracy." We use these concepts to organize the world, classifying the objects and people we encounter into various categories. And when we solve a problem, we organize aspects of the problem in terms of these concepts. An efficient problem solver will organize them into a pattern that can produce a simple, rapid solution. A lack of organization or an inefficient organization makes the problem difficult, if not impossible, to solve (Kausler, 1982).

Concept Formation
The way in which adults form concepts can be studied by asking them to discover the rule that the experimenter has used to divide a universe of geometric objects. Shown a series of objects (for example, circles and squares that are large or small, red or blue), a person must decide which concept has been used to partition the objects into two categories. As each object is shown, the person guesses whether it is an example of the concept, and the experimenter tells the person whether the guess has been right or wrong. If "roundness" is the governing concept, then a circle will be "right," whether it is large or small, red or blue. (In a more complicated version, the concept could involve more than one dimension, so that the circle may be "right" only when it is also red.)

In one study in which the "correct" concept had two dimensions, middle-aged adults (35 to 51 years old) took longer to identify the concepts and made more wrong guesses in the process than did young adults (Wiersma and Klausmeier, 1965). When children (10 to 14 years old), young adults (18 to 22 years old), and older adults (60 to 78 years old) tried a similar problem, young adults were faster and made fewer errors than either the children or the older adults, whose performance was about the same (West, Odom, and Aschkenasy, 1978).

When trying to discover which concept the experimenter has in mind, people generally form hypotheses, changing them according to the feedback that follows each of their guesses. A standard rule governing hypothesis formation is to stick with your choice if you are right and to switch to a new hypothesis if you are wrong. In a study comparing schoolchildren, college students, and older adults, the older adults performed the worst and tended to break the standard rule more often than those in the other groups (Offenbach, 1974). Older adults often discarded a hypothesis that was right or clung to a hypothesis that was clearly wrong. It was as if they did not remember the results of earlier trials. Yet memory aids do not always help. In one study (Brinley, Jovick, and McLaughlin, 1974), when the results of previous trials were kept before them, the performance of older adults did not improve.

Older adults clearly are able to form new concepts, but it takes them longer to do so. When given direct instruction in a systematic strategy for testing hypotheses, their skill at forming concepts improves significantly, and the improvement lasts for at least a year (Sterns and Sanders, 1980). Some older adults also seem to differ from the young in the way they classify objects.

Classification Skills

When asked to sort objects, older adults are being asked to discover similarities among them. Various bases of similarity may be used: shape, color, size, substance, abstract category, or function. Studies of American adults indicate that men and women past the age of 60 are more likely to sort by functional groups (Cicirelli, 1976). When given 50 pictures of common objects and asked to sort them, adults who were less than 60 tended to use such categories as kitchen utensils or appliances, but older adults were increasingly likely to sort by function, placing the frying pan with the stove because it was used there or a match with a pipe because the match was needed to light the pipe. Among adults in their sixties, about 80 percent of the sortings took the form of abstract categories, but among those in their eighties, fewer than 60 percent of the groupings were abstract. At the same time, the proportion of functional groupings was less than 15 percent among the 60-year-olds but more than 30 percent among the 80-year-olds. Note that although abstract groupings are less common among older adults, a majority of those in their eighties were still using them at least some of the time. The researcher suggested that the environment of most older people does not require the use of abstract groupings, so that functional grouping probably makes more sense to them.

Although educational level did not account for differences in classification in this study, when other researchers (Laurence and Arrowood, 1982) compared college students with 75-year-old alumni, both groups classified objects in the same style. But older residents of a veteran's hospital were far less likely to use abstract categories than the other two groups, a finding that the researchers attributed to a decline in neurological, intellectual, and social competence.

People who have never attended school tend to group objects by function instead of into abstract categories, a tendency whose reappearance among older literate adults is probably adaptive.

However, research in other societies has shown that school attendance and the use of abstract categories are closely connected. During the 1920s, when Soviet society was in the midst of great change, psychologist Alexander Luria (1976) traveled to a remote area where few people had been to school and asked them to sort common objects. Luria found that 80 percent of the illiterate peasants grouped objects by function. They would group a wooden log with a saw because the saw was used on the log or a pail with a camel and a horse because the pail was needed to water the livestock. Such groupings made sense to them because that was the way they used the objects. But young people with a few years of school all grouped objects by abstract category, using such terms as tools, animals, and so forth, taking them out of their functional context.

The increased use of functional classification by older adults probably has little to do with cognitive decline. In daily life, the function of objects, not their category, is vital, and some researchers (Kogan, 1982) have suggested that grouping objects in a similar manner is adaptive for older adults (and thus a demonstration of intelligence).

Solving Puzzles

The sort of puzzles presented to adults in laboratory studies are often similar to popular games. A version of the game called Twenty Questions, for example, has been used by several researchers to investigate the way older adults solve problems. In one version of the game, adults look at colored pictures of 42 common objects and try to figure out which picture the experimenter is thinking of. They may ask any question they like, but the experimenter can answer only yes or no, and they are to reach their solution in as few questions as possible. Presumably, their strategies for solving the problem are revealed by the sort of question they ask.

In 20 questions, the efficient strategy uses constraining questions, that is, questions that refer to an entire class of items and thereby eliminate a number of incorrect objects. For example, the question, "Is it alive?" divides all 42 objects into two classes—animate or inanimate—and eliminates all the objects in one class at once. But the question, "Is it the hammer?" tests the hypothesis that the examiner is thinking of a hammer, but, if the question is wrong, it eliminates only one object.

In one experiment (Denny and Denny, 1982), adults between the ages of 30 and 90 were given the Twenty Questions task. With age, the proportion of constraint-seeking questions dropped, and the number of questions required to reach a solution increased (Fig. 9.1). Two thirds of the questions asked by men and women in their thirties referred to a class of objects ("Is it a tool?" or "Is it an animal?" or "Can you ride in it?"), but only half of the questions among people in their fifties were of this type, as were less than a quarter among those in their eighties.

In this cross-sectional study, the disparity in performance was not solely a matter of age. Educational level also predicted the type of question that would be asked, indicating that cohort differences probably played some part in performance. However, the number of questions required to reach a solution was not connected with education; age alone accounted for the increase.

This failure to use constraint-seeking questions does not denote cognitive decline because training is effective in changing performance. Older adults quickly learn to ask constraint-seeking questions when someone models the use of the strategy. In fact, they learn so rapidly that researchers decided the technique is already in the problem-solving repertoire of most older adults and the training merely leads them to rediscover it (Denney, 1979).

In a longitudinal study of problem solving (Arenberg, 1982), the task was to discover the poisoned food. From a pool of food choices (two beverages, two

	Age Group					
	30–39	**40–49**	**50–59**	**60–69**	**70–79**	**80–89**
Constraint-seeking questions (percent)	66.36	60.93	49.24	38.71	28.93	22.83
Hypothesis-testing questions (percent)	32.95	36.64	41.60	59.46	62.20	66.70
Number of questions asked	14.88	15.25	18.54	20.93	24.59	23.03

FIGURE 9.1 Twenty Questions. When playing the Twenty Questions game, adults show consistent age differences in the use of strategies. The proportion of constraint-seeking questions drops with age, and the proportion of hypothesis-testing questions increases.
Source: N. W. Denny and D. R. Denny, 1982, p. 192.

meats, two vegetables, two desserts), a person selects one item of each type for a meal. If the poisoned food is included, the experimenter says, "Died." If it was omitted, the experimenter says, "Lived." Once the person is certain of the solution, he or she tells the experimenter which food is poisoned. (In more complicated versions, two foods are poisoned, but the meal is safe to eat unless *both* poisoned foods are included; or else two foods are poisoned, and either by itself is fatal.)

The adults who took part in this study were white males between the ages of 24 and 87, and they were either employed or retired managers, professionals, or scientists. When their solutions were analyzed on a cross-sectional basis, the average number of correct solutions was found to differ with age, beginning as early as the thirties. Men in their twenties had the most correct solutions (10.4); and men in their eighties, the least (5.4), with the sharpest difference between men in their sixties (8.0) and men in their seventies (6.6). On a longitudinal basis, the performance of the youngest men improved over a 7-year period whereas only among men in the oldest cohort (in their seventies when the study began) did it decline. Among these highly selected older men, the decline in problem-solving ability was correlated with age.

David Arenberg (1982), who conducted this study, believes that older adults suffer from information overload when trying to solve complex problems. They seem to have difficulty reviewing their possible choices and planning and carrying out their next choice. Memory does not seem to be a factor because the men kept a record of all their previous choices and the results were in front of them. Apparently as adults age, they become less efficient at organizing the elements of a problem, a factor that might be related to Donald Hebb's (1978) complaint that once he reached his seventies, he found it difficult to hold and manipulate several ideas at one time.

STRUCTURE OF THOUGHT

Another way to understand problem solving across adulthood is by applying theories of cognitive development. The theory proposed by Swiss psychologist Jean Piaget (1983) dominates the study of children's intellectual development. According to this organismic theory, intelligence develops through four invariant stages, and in each stage the structure of thought is qualitatively different. In the sensorimotor stage (birth to about 2 years), perceptions and actions are intertwined, and there is no symbolic thought. In the preoperational period (2 years to about 7 years), thought is symbolic but intuitive. In the concrete operational period (7 years to about 11 years), thought is logical but limited to concrete situations. Cognitive development is believed to culminate at about adolescence, with the attainment of **formal operational thought**. At this time, thought is logical and abstract and can be applied to hypothetical situations.

Piaget did not extend his theory across the life span except to say that the development of formal thought continued "throughout adolescence and all of later life'' (Piaget and Inhelder, 1969, pp. 152–153). As research has continued, it has become apparent that formal thought is not as prevalent as Piaget once supposed and that its presence is closely related to formal education (Keating and Clark, 1980).

Research with older adults indicates that in most cases performance on Piagetian tasks of cognitive development declines with age, leading some investigators (Storck, Looft, and Hooper, 1972) to suppose that cognitive development eventually reverses itself, with the more advanced cognitive skills disappearing first. In one of the few experiments involving formal thought (Overton and Clayton, 1976), college women performed significantly better than older women, and women in their sixties and seventies were progressively less able to solve tasks involving formal reasoning, such as discovering the factors that determine the speed of a pendulum as it travels through its arc. However, measures of intelligence were positively related to formal thought in the entire group. Other researchers (Hawley and Kelley, 1973) have found that intelligence and educational level are a better predictor of formal thought than age. In one study (Sabatini and Labouvie-Vief, 1979), older scientists were better than young scientists at formal thought. Only among older nonscientists did the use of formal thought decline.

A number of researchers have investigated the performance of older adults on tasks of concrete operational thought, especially on conservation (the understanding that irrelevant changes in the appearance of objects do not affect their quantity, mass, weight, or volume). The results have been mixed, with some researchers (Eisner, 1973) reporting no difference in conservation ability and others (Papalia, 1972) finding older adults less able to solve more difficult conservation tasks but having no problem with simpler tasks, such as the conservation of number. Classification into abstract categories is one of Piaget's concrete mental operations, and as we have seen, some older adults tend to return to functional classification.

Although age differences have been found on most Piagetian tasks, the proposal of cognitive regression in old age has not been clearly supported. As Frank Hooper and Nancy Sheehan (1977) have pointed out, most studies lack any information on logical functioning in normal adults; the nature of the elderly samples generally confounds age with chronic disease, brain damage, or institutionalization; the studies are cross-sectional in nature; and performance on the tasks is more highly correlated with intelligence than with age. Thus, cohort effects may well be implicated in the findings. An additional problem is the nature of the tasks. Designed to be used with children, the tasks involve repetitive questioning that may seem tiresome or ludicrous to adults and thus lead older people to give childlike responses.

As with problem solving, performance on Piagetian tasks comes down to a question of competence (the person's underlying knowledge) versus performance (what the person does in the test situation). Attempts to train older adults in logical thought have generally been successful in that such adults seem to transfer the ability to closely related situations. For example, the behavioral technique of feedback (in which people are given immediate responses as to the correctness of their answers) has been effective in teaching conservation (Hornblum and Overton, 1976), and the social-learning technique of modeling (in which another person demonstrates a skill) has been effective in teaching classification (Denney, 1974). Hooper and Sheehan (1977) have suggested an explanation of adult performance on Piagetian tasks that requires a dialectical model of development. In this view, the individual's interaction with historical conditions affects cognitive function. Such a perspective assumes that the social situation of older adults in contemporary society may be at the base of poor performance among those whose nervous system has not been affected by secondary aging. When adults are stripped of their social roles, as many are in a technological society, their roleless existence may well affect cognitive functioning. An investigation of the nature of intelligence may make its connection with problem-solving skills clearer.

NATURE OF INTELLIGENCE

Everybody seems to know what intelligence is, but no psychologist has been able to produce a formal, useful definition that satisfies everyone (Resnick, 1976; Botwinick, 1977; Salthouse, 1982). All of the many definitions that have been suggested seem limited. At various times, psychologists have defined intelligence as the "effective use of stored information" or the ability to "learn to adjust to the environment," to "carry on abstract thinking," or to "benefit from experience." Like learning, intelligence is invisible and must be inferred from behavior. However, it is possible to develop a broad, general statement describing intelligence that most researchers can agree on, no matter what their theoretical background. In these broad terms, **intelligence** involves mental operations that enhance the ability to function effectively in the environment. As we have just seen, problem solving is essential to effective functioning.

The problem arises when we attempt to become specific. When we talk about intelligence, are we referring to a single general attribute or to a group of processes, and, if so, how many are there? Most attempts to pin down intelligence in this way rely on **factor analysis**, a complicated statistical technique by which researchers examine people's performance on a variety of intellectual tasks, looking for relationships among them. It is believed that highly correlated tasks measure some common mental ability and perhaps that the ability reflects an aspect of intelligence.

This type of research has convinced some investigators that intelligence is a general ability. For example, Charles Spearman (1927) noted that performance on all sorts of intellectual tasks showed a moderately high positive correlation. This correlation led him to argue that a general factor of intelligence, which he called *g,* pervaded all cognitive function. He saw *g* as the ability to grasp relationships quickly and to use them effectively. Spearman admitted that specific abilities existed; in fact, he regarded each task as requiring a different ability, but maintained that *g* was common to all intellectual tasks and affected the level of performance on them. A person with a low level of *g* would be poor at any intellectual task, and individual patterns of ability would be determined by the levels of the various specific abilities a person possessed.

Using similar techniques, others found it difficult to conceive of intelligence as a "common central factor" and denied that *g* existed. For example, Lewis Thurstone (1935) proposed that intelligence was based on seven factors, which he called primary mental abilities: verbal comprehension, number, space, perceptual speed, memory, reasoning, and word fluency. Because these factors are specific to different areas of functioning, each person would develop a particular pattern of abilities.

J. P. Guilford (1973) maintained that intelligence could not be confined to seven primary abilities. Instead, he believed that the kind of mental operation used on a particular task was as important as whether, for example, the task had to do with numbers, symbols, words, or behavior (which he called the "contents" of intellect). He saw human intellect as structured by the action of five different mental processes on the four contents, to produce six forms of information. Guilford's five mental operations were evaluation, which refers to judging the accuracy or appropriateness of information; convergent thinking, which refers to the production of logically necessary solutions; divergent thinking, which refers to the production of alternative solutions; cognition; and memory. The forms that information can take are units, classes, relations, systems, transformations, and implications.

When all the possible interactions are considered ($5 \times 4 \times 6$), 120 factors emerge. Guilford's concept of intelligence was broader than that put forth by other theorists because he included divergent thinking, a cognitive process generally related to creativity.

More recently, Howard Gardner (1983) has proposed a theory of "multiple intelligences," which he suggests can be identified by their susceptibility to brain damage, the existence of prodigies who excel in a specific intelligence, an identifiable set of mental operations, a distinctive developmental history, a plausible evolutionary history, its encoding in a symbol system, and support from laboratory experiments and standard tests. Gardner believes he has identified six broad forms of intelligence: linguistic intelligence, musical intelligence, logical-mathematical intelligence, spatial intelligence, bodily-kinesthetic intelligence, and personal intelligences (knowledge of self and others). These forms of intelligence interact with and build on one another. What is generally known as "common sense" is, he suggests, a highly developed skill in either spatial and bodily-kinesthetic intelligences or personal intelligences.

No matter how many individual factors are involved, many researchers assume that the quality we refer to as "intelligence" is the product of two fundamental types of skills: fluid intelligence and crystallized intelligence. In this view of intelligence, which was proposed by Raymond Cattell (1971), **fluid intelligence** corresponds to the basic cognitive processes and is similar to Spearman's *g*. Fluid intelligence is required to identify and understand relationships and to draw inferences on the basis of that understanding (Horn, 1982). **Crystallized intelligence** corresponds to acquired knowledge and developed intellectual skills; it may be regarded as reflecting the application of fluid intelligence to cultural content. Crystallized intelligence is shown in a person's breadth of knowledge and experience, quantitative thinking, judgment, and wisdom (Horn, 1982). This way of looking at intelligence is useful in the study of adult development because the two types follow different developmental paths, which diverge widely during the last few decades of life.

No less persistent than the attempt to define the nature of intelligence is the quest to measure it.

MEASUREMENT OF INTELLIGENCE

Intelligence cannot be measured without some kind of yardstick, and the traditional measuring tool has been the standardized test, in which test norms are developed by giving the test to large groups of people. Once the distribution of normal scores is established, the score of any individual easily can be compared and evaluated in terms of its relationship to the performance of the standardization group. If the test is a valid measure of intelligence, a person's score can be used to predict his or her performance in other situations assumed to require intelligence. As we saw in Chapter 2, the problem of external validity is central to intelligence testing.

The field of mental testing is known as **psychometry**, and psychometric tests of intelligence were first developed to predict the academic success of school children. Alfred Binet, a French psychologist, believed that children who were failing in school should not be dismissed without being examined to see if they could learn in special classes. But no efficient way existed to pick out students who could profit from special instruction. With psychiatrist Theodor Simon (Binet and Simon, 1905), Binet developed a set of 30 problems that emphasized judgment, comprehension, and reasoning. The problems, which were arranged by difficulty, were given to normal children, mentally retarded children, and mentally retarded adults. Behind the construction of the scale was the belief that the test performance of a less intelligent child would resemble the performance of a younger child with average intelligence.

The scale went through several revisions and was soon used on normal children as well as on those believed to be mentally slow. It produced a measure of a child's mental level, and in 1911 the scale was extended to cover adults (Anastasi, 1976). Binet's test drew the attention of psychologists in other countries, who adapted it to their own societies. In the United States, a revision of the Binet scale known as the Stanford-Binet was the first to use the concept of IQ, or intelligence quotient, which refers to the ratio between a person's mental and chronological ages. Although the intelligence quotient is no longer used by psychometrists, the term ''IQ'' has become firmly attached to the intelligence test and now refers to an individual's score on a scale that has been normalized so that the average score made by people in his or her age group is 100. All versions of the Binet test are individual intelligence tests that require a highly trained examiner; thus they are time-consuming and expensive.

The first group intelligence tests were developed for the United States Army, where they were used to screen a million and a half recruits in World War I. This screening marked the first widespread use of intelligence tests with adults. Two timed tests on various aspects of cognitive function were developed: the Army Alpha test, used routinely with the majority of recruits, and the Army Beta test, designed to be used by illiterates or immigrants who did not know English. Each test produced a single score based on a group of subtests. These army tests became the model for later group IQ tests (Anastasi, 1976).

Intelligence tests now are widely used in research with adults and have been the basis of many studies of the effect of aging on cognition. Two of the major tests are the Wechsler Adult Intelligence Scale (WAIS), which is influenced by Spearman's view of intelligence, and the Primary Mental Abilities Test (PMA), which is based on Thurstone's concept of intelligence (Morrow and Morrow, 1973). The PMA uses five separate scales, which test number, word fluency, verbal comprehension, reasoning, and spatial ability, for these five abilities seem more or less independent. Perceptual speed and memory, Thurstone's other primary mental abilities, are not evaluated by the PMA.

Despite the widespread use of these tests, it is still unclear how performance on them relates to an individual's everyday functioning in the world. The tests grew out of the school situation, where their purpose was to predict the future academic performance of children. Thus, they compare the performance of older and younger people on youth-oriented tasks (Willis and Baltes, 1980). The tests were constructed as a measure of "academic intelligence," and Ulric Neisser (1976a) has pointed out that they require the rapid solution of uninteresting arbitrary problems that have been stripped of any connection with ordinary experience. As Neisser has noted, many academically intelligent people seem no better than unintelligent people at managing their own lives. Yet because no satisfactory test exists that predicts the application of intelligence to problems in daily life, adult intelligence is still measured with the sort of test developed to assess children (Salthouse, 1982).

This reliance on IQ tests in the assessment of adult intelligence has been developed primarily by psychometrists (Willis and Baltes, 1980). Researchers who study intelligence by examining various cognitive processes have not produced broad measures of cognitive functioning.

Intelligence tests can measure only the sort of cognitive skills that are assessed by the various subtests. Any aspect of intelligence that is not part of the academic situation is omitted from consideration. If intelligence is reflected in the ability to function effectively in the environment, the mental operations involved are displayed in the solution of problems, where we combine our general and specific knowledge to surmount obstacles, reach goals, or render life's complexities a little more manageable. Yet such problem-solving skills are probably not tapped by most intelligence tests. Other global stylistic qualities like creativity, flexibility, and wisdom also escape the measuring net thrown out by standard intelligence tests. The narrow focus of intelligence tests may have some bearing on the pattern of age changes in test scores that appears in many studies.

AGE CHANGES IN INTELLIGENCE TEST SCORES

The picture of intelligence across adulthood seems quite different, depending on one's perspective. When adults of various ages take IQ tests, their scores seem to indicate that performance remains steady throughout middle age and then begins to decline. But when we look at the various subtests, the pattern changes. Taking a single figure as a measure of IQ is in accord with Spearman's view of intelligence, but it does not give us an accurate picture of cognitive function. If scores on some subtests rise and scores on others fall, both increases and declines in various mental abilities could be masked. In other words, the same IQ score may have different meanings at different ages (Salthouse, 1982). What is more important, as we saw in Chapter 2, cross-sectional and longitudinal studies are likely to present radically different pictures of aging.

CROSS-SECTIONAL AND LONGITUDINAL STUDIES

Most cross-sectional studies present a pessimistic picture. The earliest studies were the most depressing. When soldiers took the first Army Alpha and Beta tests, their performance was inversely related to age, with each cohort scoring lower than the cohorts born after it. This systematic pattern was evident from about the age of 25 (Yerkes, 1921). Community studies a few years later confirmed the army findings although they indicated substantially lower scores with age on some subtests and little difference on others. As new intelligence tests were standardized, the difference did not appear until about the age of 40, but the disparity was still present (Schaie, 1979).

The classic picture of aging that has developed from cross-sectional studies is one of little or no change in verbal functions, but of declines in nonverbal and psychomotor functions, especially when speed is involved. Although age differences begin to appear during middle age, the slope is gentle until about the age of 70, when scores of younger and older adults differ sharply. This pattern is seen in both sexes, in both whites and blacks, in various socioeconomic levels, and in institutionalized adults as well as in community residents (Botwinick, 1977).

Most longitudinal studies paint a rosier picture of intellectual performance; they show rising test scores during middle age with no declines apparent until after the age of 60. For example, scores on the verbal portion of the Army Alpha test increased between the ages of 19 and 50 whereas scores on the performance section, which involves the manipulation of objects, failed to show significant declines. Among individuals in their sixties, scores were still higher on many of the verbal substests than they had been at 19 although there was a significant decline in the ability to solve arithmetic problems (Owens, 1966).

In the California Intergenerational Studies (Eichorn, Hunt, and Honzik, 1981), middle-aged adults (36 to 48 years) tended to show a modest increase in IQ levels over their scores at the age of 17 or 18. However, an analysis indicated that many had undergone a modest decline in performance IQ after the mid-thirties. Interindividual difference was great, and a number of people showed extreme changes in IQ over the period. Although losses occurred, the scores of some men and women showed large gains. Generally, those whose IQs rose sharply had traveled extensively outside the United States and had married a spouse whose IQ was at least 10 points higher than their own had been at adolescence. Those whose IQs showed large drops tended to drink heavily and to have severe health problems.

Older adults who were followed for 10 years in the Duke Longitudinal Study (Eisdorfer and Wilkie, 1974) showed only a slight decline among those who were in their sixties at the time of the first testing, and most of the drop was in performance IQ. Adults who were in their seventies at the time of the first testing showed clear declines in both verbal and performance IQs.

The apparently late onset of decline in longitudinal studies may be due in part to selective dropout. As the study continues, the people who die or fail to return for later testing tend to be those who obtain low scores. Over the years, the study becomes heavily weighted in favor of superior subjects (Botwinick, 1977).

Much of the discrepancy between cross-sectional and longitudinal studies, however, seems to be explained by cohort differences. As the general educational level rose, as sophisticated technology increasingly pervaded society, and as radio and then television brought the world into the home, succeeding generations grew up in quite different worlds and consequently performed better on intelligence tests. This view receives some support from the fact that over the years, as IQ tests have been standardized, each new test finds IQ peaking at a higher point and at a slightly later chronological age (Schaie, 1983). In 1916 the Stanford-Binet assumed a peak in adult intelligence at age 16. By 1930 the peak had moved to age 20; by 1939 it was 20 to 24 years; by 1939 peak age had moved to between 25 and 30; and by the mid-1950s the average peak came between the ages of 25 and 35.

The most extensive study of intelligence across adulthood was carried out between 1956 and 1977 by Warner Schaie (1979; 1983; Schaie and Hertzog, 1983). Its sequential design combines cross-sectional and longitudinal elements as described in Chapter 2 and uses the Primary Mental Abilities (PMA) test whereas many of the other longitudinal studies have relied on the WAIS. A look at Schaie's results may help to clarify the role of cohort differences (Fig. 9.2).

When examining scores on subtests, Schaie (Schaie and Hertzog, 1983) found that, at the same age, different generations perform at different levels of ability. On most of the PMA tests, such as inductive reasoning, verbal comprehension, and spatial ability, younger cohorts did best; but on the word fluency test, the advantage was with the older cohorts. Schaie (1983) has suggested that in many respects older adults continue to function at a level they reached in their younger days, but that the level may not be most appropriate for success in modern society. In some areas of cognitive functioning, older adults are not deficient, but simply have become obsolete.

Cohort effects have caused an overestimation of cognitive decline. However, as both longitudinal studies and this lengthy sequential survey indicate, small, statistically significant declines in some tested mental abilities appear during the decade of the fifties. Although declines become noticeable after the age of 60, the co-

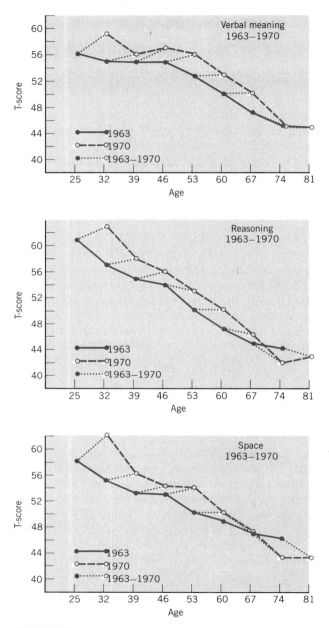

FIGURE 9.2 IQ scores across adulthood. In this comparison of cross-sectional and longitudinal scores on the verbal meaning, reasoning, and space subtests of the PMA, dotted lines indicate longitudinal results, and solid lines indicate cross-sectional results on tests given in 1963 and 1970. Until late in the life span, retests generally show improvements or stability, yet the cross-sectional comparisons show declines.

Source: K. W. Schaie and G. Labouvie-Vief, 1974, pp. 305–320.

hort effect is also present and magnifies the decline (Schaie and Hertzog, 1983). It is important to remember that the declines described may have little effect on daily life. If at the age of 30, a person could produce 40 words beginning with "s" in three minutes, but at 70 he or she can produce only 36 words (a test of word fluency), the practical difference may well be nonexistent (Schaie, 1983). Perhaps looking at the data from another perspective will help to clarify these age differences.

FLUID AND CRYSTALLIZED INTELLIGENCE

When test performance is analyzed in terms of fluid and crystallized intelligence, a pattern similar to that shown by performance and verbal IQ scores appears. Fluid intelligence appears to remain stable through middle adulthood and to decline in later adulthood, but crystallized intelligence continues to increase until the mid-sixties.

In cross-sectional studies with all male samples, John Horn (1982) has attempted to discover just what changes in cognitive functioning are responsible for declines in fluid intelligence. It has been suggested that perceptual slowing accounts for many of the changes in test performance that appear with age (Birren, 1974), but Horn believes that declines in perceptual speed are a consequence of another decline: a lessening of the ability or inclination to concentrate on simple intellectual tasks. He points out that giving older people extra time decreases but does not eliminate age differences and that older people who can solve fluid intelligence problems solve them just as rapidly as the young do.

A second factor that leads to lowered performance on tests of fluid intelligence appears to be an increasing obliviousness to incidental environmental features. That is, older adults seem to pay little attention to things about them that are not obviously relevant to the task in hand whereas younger adults note these features and remember them a few minutes or hours later when their relevancy becomes apparent. It may be that older adults have limited cognitive capacity that can be concentrated on a task, as well as less extra capacity to pick up possibly useful extraneous information surrounding it.

When attempting to link these factors to specific cognitive processes, Horn suggests that older adults have trouble organizing information at the encoding stage, in keeping their attention focused, and in forming expectations about a task. These three processes, he says, account for about half of the age decline that appears in tests of fluid intelligence.

But until the age of 65, this loss in fluid intelligence is balanced by a rise in crystallized intelligence of about the same amount. Older adults do better than the young on vocabulary tests, on tests that require them to understand analogies, and on tests of divergent thinking, in which they must come up with multiple uses for some common object, such as a brick or a paper clip. Horn believes that older people have more knowledge available than the young and that older adults have organized their store of knowledge so that it is more cohesive, more correct, and more accessible (Fig. 9.3).

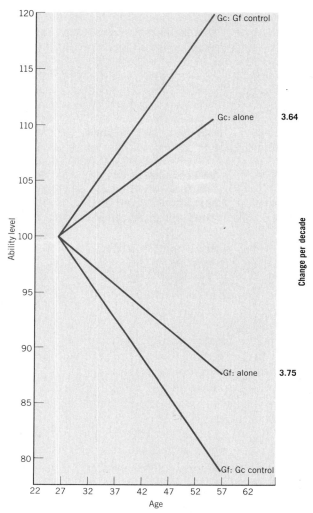

FIGURE 9.3   Aging of fluid and crystallized intelligence. This comparison of age differences in IQ scores shows a steady decline in fluid intelligence that is matched by an increase in crystallized intelligence.

Source: J. L. Horn, 1982, p. 267.

Indeed, some older adults continue to perform as well as the average young person on IQ tests. Interindividual differences in intelligence are wide, and even where IQ declines are "significant," they are often only a few points. For example, the average age difference for fluid intelligence increases by about 3.75 points each decade in old age (Horn, 1982). But intelligence does not always decline with age. Lissy Jarvik (1973) describes an 82-year-old woman in a New York State longitudinal study, whose scores on nonspeeded intellectual tasks were higher than they had been 20 years earlier. And on speeded psychomotor tests, her scores had declined less than 1 percent per decade.

TERMINAL DROP

Among older adults, average test scores may be pulled down by a phenomenon called **terminal drop**, in which people who are only a few years from death show a distinct drop in IQ scores, no matter what their age. This tendency was discovered in a longitudinal study of older men. Those who died during the 12-year study showed much steeper declines at their last testing than did those who survived (Kleemeier, 1962).

In another longitudinal study (Blum, Clark, and Jarvik, 1973), age was not a good predictor of mortality, but critical declines on scores of cognitive functioning were a good predictor of death within 5 years. In this study, declines on speeded psychomotor tests had no connection with mortality. Because declines in speed seem to be a part of normal aging, but declines in verbal skills appear to distinguish survivors from nonsurvivors, it has been suggested that the presence of cardiovascular disease may be responsible for the terminal drop (Birren, 1968).

The connection between physical health and IQ appears to be somewhat more complicated. Among older adults in the Duke Longitudinal Study, high blood pressure was connected with significant intellectual decline over a 10-year period (Wilkie and Eisdorfer, 1974a), but its relationship to terminal drop was different. Although terminal drop was sometimes connected with cardiovascular disease, a larger terminal drop appeared in adults who were free from cardiovascular disease. Among these adults, largest drops were found in individuals who had both acute illness (such as urinary tract infection) and chronic disease (such as diabetes or emphysema) (Wilkie and Eisdorfer, 1974b). The connection suggests that although cardiovascular disease has a destructive effect on cognitive functioning, any degenerative disease may be responsible for a terminal drop in IQ test score. However, among residents of a Veterans Administration home, IQ scores showed terminal drop no longer than 10 months before death (Berkowitz, 1965). Although the nature of terminal drop is controversial, findings seem to indicate that natural aging does not necessarily mean cognitive decline and that older people who retain their health can expect little substantial change in intellectual function (Jarvik, 1973).

REVERSING THE DECLINE

Our first impulse is to assume that IQ test scores reflect the intellectual competence of older adults, but we would probably be wrong. Such an assumption, which is fairly common, generalizes from the artificial test situation to daily life and attributes an external validity to the tests that has not been established (Willis and Baltes, 1980). Test scores reflect performance, the average performance of individuals on a single occasion. Whether these scores also reflect the competence of older adults is unknown.

Think about the activities of most retired people you know. Are they more likely to be interested in computer programming or gardening? Reading *Scientific American* or *Reader's Digest*? Few older adults encounter any environmental press (see Chapter 5) that would lead them to engage in abstract academic tasks.

SEX DIFFERENCES IN TEST PERFORMANCE

Most studies of American children indicate that girls have an advantage in verbal abilities whether we look at complex written material, logical relations, or remote associations. Boys appear to be better at mathematical reasoning and problem solving and at spatial ability (Hall, Lamb, and Perlmutter, 1982). The differences are not large, and there is a wide overlap between the scores of boys and girls, but some researchers believe that biology is implicated in this development (Benbow and Stanley, 1980).

When IQ test performance across adulthood is analyzed, the traditional differences in performance appear. In Schaie's cross-sequential study, women consistently performed better on tests of word fluency and men on tests of space and number (Schaie and Hertzog, 1983). The pattern was consistent across cohorts and across the life span. In the California Intergenerational Studies, women tended to show greater increases in verbal IQ than in performance IQ whereas men showed just the opposite pattern (Eichorn, Hunt, and Honzik, 1981).

The possible cultural roots of sex differences in IQ was explored by researchers in Israel (Shanan and Sagiv, 1982). Middle-aged men (from 46 to 65 years old) generally scored higher than middle-aged women on all subtests, whether verbal or performance; but when age, education, and cultural origins were considered, the pattern was different.

As we saw in Chapter 2, educational level affects IQ scores and is

The daily decisions concerning farm management made by this North Carolina farming couple probably reflect a shrewdness and intellectual competence that would not appear in their IQ test scores.

probably implicated in cohort effects. In this study, educational level also affected sex differences in IQ. Among adults with less than 10 years of education, the men did significantly better on all subtests; among adults with at least 10 years of education, the men did better on only one subtest. In this educated group, the women did as well as the men in block design, a test of spatial ability. Age was also important, but only among those with more education. There were no significant differences on any test between younger (from 46 to 55 years old), highly educated women and men.

The cultural origin of these Israelis marked the performance of the older (from 56 to 65 years old) men and women. There were no significant sex differences between older men and women with European backgrounds, but significant differences appeared between older men and women with Middle-Eastern backgrounds. In an earlier study of Israeli college students (Shanan and Sharon, 1971), sex differences in IQ were small among students from the United States and Western Europe, but sharp among students from the Middle East.

Among these middle-aged adults, the highest scores went to younger, better-educated Western adults; and the lowest, to older, poorly educated Eastern adults. The researchers (Shanan and Sagiv, 1982) propose that social position is a major determinant of intellectual functioning and that lower socioeconomic levels, less education, and a subordinate position in the culture combine to produce the sex differences they found.

If the majority of older adults live in an environment that de-emphasizes academic and cognitive achievement, then traditional IQ tests are unlikely to be measuring their competence (Labouvie, Hoyer, Baltes, and Baltes, 1974). When tests are constructed around topics that have relevance to an adult's life, older adults do better on them than younger adults (Gardner and Monge, 1977). Asked about transportation, financial matters, disease, and death, older adults perform competently, and in some areas adults in their sixties tend to score highest.

Convinced that changing the environment of many older persons would reveal unsuspected intellectual potential, Paul Baltes and Sherry Willis (1982) have begun a research program at Pennsylvania State University meant to explore intellectual competence in old age. Because fluid intelligence consistently declines with age, Baltes and Willis have been providing 60- to 80-year-olds with training and practice in three fluid-intelligence skills: figural relations, inductive reasoning, and attention and memory (perceptual discrimination, selective attention, attention switching, and concentration). Their preliminary results indicate that training is followed by improved performance on these aspects of fluid intelligence. All skills transferred to tasks that are closely related to the training task, with figural relations training also transferring to tasks that are less similar. On measures

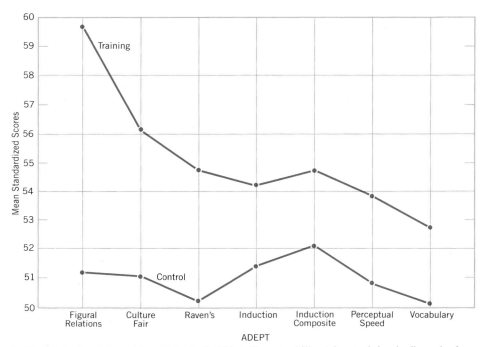

FIGURE 9.4   Training older adults in fluid intelligence skills. After training in figural relations, an aspect of fluid intelligence, older adults showed a transfer of skill on measures that were closely related to the training situation. The gains were still apparent 6 months after the training sessions.

Source: P. B. Baltes and S. L. Willis, 1982, p. 372.

of close transfer, test-score increases approximately equaled the decline with age in fluid intelligence that appears in most studies (Fig. 9.4). It would appear that many older adults can become more competent than IQ scores suggest.

AGE CHANGES IN COGNITIVE STYLE AND CREATIVITY

The disparity between declining test performance in older adults and the obvious capability of many older adults in the community indicates that intelligence tests and laboratory studies of problem solving apparently do not accurately reflect the ability of many older adults to function effectively in the environment. Long after the age at which experimental evidence indicates they should be visibly failing, judges, legislators, corporation executives, business people, teachers, lawyers, physicians, scientists, writers, and artists demonstrate their ability to think clearly and handle problems. When chemist Joel Hildebrand was 102 years old, he wrote the lead article in the *Annual Review of Physical Chemistry,* in which he discussed for his fellow chemists the history of the Hildebrand theory of solutions (a formula for predicting the solubility of various gases in different liquids) (Barasch, 1983).

Perhaps a view of intelligence that goes beyond test performance and experimental situations would be more useful. It may be that other aspects of cognitive

Despite the decline in problem solving shown by the average older adult in laboratory studies, many elderly men and women continue to serve efficiently in professions that require clear thought and the solution of intricate problems.

functioning are a better guide to adult intelligence and that we should take a broader perspective, looking at cognitive style, creativity, and wisdom.

BEYOND FORMAL REASONING

Piaget's theory assumes that biological maturity and cognitive maturity go hand-in-hand, so that cognitive development reaches its peak in adolescence with the development of formal reasoning. Once the peak is reached, there is a period of stability and then an inevitable decline. Some investigators (Arlin, 1980) have suggested that dealing with total abstraction—the hallmark of formal thought—may not be the way in which adults use formal thought. Instead of liberating thought from concrete reality, as Piaget (1967) described its adolescent function, formal thought in adulthood may be used to advance the understanding of daily life. Edith Neimark (1982) suggests that during the adult years cognitive growth can be seen in the application of experience, knowledge, and wisdom to the affairs of daily life. In other words, cognitive development in adulthood is the development of common sense.

Most problems in life have uncertain outcomes. Without certain knowledge of the results, an entrepreneur must decide whether to start a business; a farmer must decide whether to expand a cattle herd; a physician must decide whether to recommend surgery; a senator must decide whether to support a new weapons system.

Although college students tend to make high scores on IQ tests and do well in problem-solving experiments and at Piagetian tasks, they do not seem to carry their rational abilities into the sort of situations that they may face in later life. When graduate students are asked to make decisions about situations that involve lives or money, they rarely apply their ability to reason logically. Instead, their decision is generally determined by the way the problem is phrased. Given exactly the same information, when the problem is presented in terms of possible losses, they make a risky decision; when it is presented in terms of possible gains, their decision is cautious (Tversky and Kahneman, 1981). When they judge other situations, their formal reasoning ability is generally cast aside in favor of simple guidelines that lead them to ignore pertinent information, biasing their decisions. As a result, they often make clearly erroneous or unwise choices (Tversky and Kahneman, 1974). Studies indicate that these judgment errors are not limited to college students; even experts can be influenced by the way a decision is framed or rely on rules that lead them into bad decisions. The point is that college students' excellence at abstract reasoning does not seem to help when certainty is lacking.

If we know little about the application of adult cognition to the tasks of daily life (Neimark, 1982), we are learning more about the effect of context on intellectual competence. Convinced that health status, terminal drop, educational level, cultural and technological change, and cultural and subcultural differences are responsible for much of the decrement older adults show in laboratory situations, Gisela Labouvie-Vief and Michael Chandler (1978) have suggested that intellectual competence may have little relationship with age. For example, they propose that changes in a person's social, economic, and intellectual situation that accompany retirement may be responsible for the sharp decline in measures of intelligence that often appears between the age of 60 and 70. Furthermore, any cognitive ability develops in the context of a culture's material surroundings and symbols, and as Labouvie-Vief (1982) points out, the content of present tests of formal reasoning reflect a scientific academic education. In this view, current findings about the course of cognitive development are more likely to reflect a temporary historical situation than the biologically guided course of cognition over the life span.

If we take a broader view of intelligence, what appear to be declines in adult cognition may actually indicate the emergence of a new organization of thought (Labouvie-Vief, 1982). As adults begin to relate logic to action, emotions, social responsibility, and interpersonal relations, thought becomes more global and directed toward new goals. The older adult may be less interested in following a narrow chain of reasoning to its logical end than in pursuing broader moral and practical concerns.

Discussing thought in general may obscure the fact that different people approach cognitive problems in different ways. A factor that can heavily influence an individual's response to any situation requiring judgment is his or her cognitive style.

COGNITIVE STYLE

Cognitive style is an aspect of intelligence that is related to personality. It refers to consistencies in an individual's *way* of attending to information, perceiving it, remembering it, and thinking about it (Kogan, 1982). A person's cognitive style, then, emphasizes the manner and form of cognition whereas narrow views of intelligence emphasize the *level* of ability. Among the cognitive styles that have been studied are field dependence–field independence, reflection–impulsivity, and flexibility–rigidity.

Field Dependence–Field Independence

Field dependence is a cognitive style related to a person's sensitivity to context. People who are **field-dependent** find it difficult to separate a part from an organized whole and rely on surrounding stimuli when making perceptual judgments. People who are **field-independent** easily separate a part from the whole and are able to ignore surrounding stimuli when making a perceptual judgment. As a result, field-dependent individuals appear to perform poorly on tests that assess formal reasoning (Neimark, 1981), and field-independent individuals seem to do well on tests of fluid intelligence, such as Raven's Progressive Matrices, a test that is made up of 60 designs, each of which is missing a part (Tramer and Schulderman, 1974). The correct part must be selected from a group of six or eight possible solutions. This difference in test scores has led some researchers to suggest that field-independent individuals approach problems in a thoughtful, logical manner and enjoy using their intellectual skills whereas field-dependent individuals are sensitive to social interaction and tend to be drawn into social situations (Neimark, 1982).

Wide interindividual differences exist in this cognitive style, and the differences are especially large among the elderly. There is, however, some evidence of typical changes in field dependence across adulthood. Young children are generally field-dependent, with field independence increasing throughout childhood and adolescence. During middle age, a shift back toward field dependence appears, and it accelerates in old age. Older adults thus appear to revert to "childlike" styles of perception (Kausler, 1982).

As tidy as this description seems, the same problems that flaw studies of intelligence make it difficult to assess just how closely—or whether—field dependence and field independence follow this course of development. Most studies of this cognitive style rely on two tests: the Embedded Figures Test, in which a person must locate a simple figure hidden within a geometrically complex design; and the Rod-and-Frame Test, in which a person seated in a dark room must adjust a glowing rod to a horizontal or vertical plane while ignoring a tilted frame that surrounds the rod. Both tests generally support the developmental picture described.

However, all studies of field dependence have used a cross-sectional design, so that cohort effects may be at least partly responsible for the trend. When we look at separate experiments, it becomes clear that educational level has a strong influence on the results. For example, among women on the nursing staff of a pediatric hospital, those in their twenties performed better on the Rod-and-Frame Test than those in their sixties. But when researchers controlled for education, the difference became insignificant (Gruenfeld and MacEachron, 1975). In studies that match women for education level and visual acuity, conflicting trends have been found. In one study (Lee and Pollack, 1978), no differences in performance on the Rod-and-Frame Test appeared before the age of 40. Fifty-year-olds performed worse than younger adults, but no subsequent age differences were found. In a second study, no significant differences appeared at any age on the Embedded Figures Test (Lee and Pollack, 1980). A third study (Panek et al., 1978) indicated small but significant differences in performance on both tests, with each group from young adulthood to old age obtaining lower scores.

Further problems arise when we look at sex differences. Among children younger than 8, there are no sex differences on tests of field dependence. Then boys begin to show greater field independence than girls, with the differences sharp throughout high school. During adulthood, the differences begin to narrow, disappearing by the age of 60 (Kogan, 1973). Because society's emphasis on sex roles is strongest in adolescence and weakest in old age, cultural factors may influence this aspect of cognitive style.

Health and environmental situation also appear to affect field dependence. Among older adults, retired individuals have a more difficult time with the Embedded Figures Test than do employed people, and institutionalized individuals do worse than residents of homes for the aged. On the Rod-and-Frame Test, healthy, highly active, tennis players in their seventies perform much better than community volunteers of the same age (Kogan, 1982).

The Embedded Figures Test and the Rod-and-Frame Test may seem like purely academic exercises, but a person's perceptual style may have important consequences in the world. No matter what their age, people who are field-dependent have higher rates of automobile accidents than people who are field-independent (Mihal and Barrett, 1976). As we saw in Chapter 7, many older adults have perceptual problems that affect night driving. If they also are unable to ignore irrelevant stimuli, their driving skills may be seriously affected.

Reflection–Impulsivity

A second cognitive style has to do with the way a person approaches an uncertain situation. Called reflection–impulsivity, this aspect of cognitive style is connected with whether a person carefully considers all possibilities, takes a long time to reach a decision, and makes few errors (**reflection**) or scans possibilities hastily, decides quickly, and makes many errors (**impulsivity**). People who are impulsive appear to be little troubled by the prospect of being wrong, but reflective people apparently work slowly because they wish to avoid mistakes. Reflection is considered adaptive, for it leads to better performance in school and on most cognitive tasks (Kogan, 1973).

Again, at all ages there are wide individual differences in this cognitive style. Most research has been done with children, who show a strong trend from impulsivity toward reflection with age. Because, as we saw in Chapter 7, older adults tend to make errors of omission, it has been assumed that some of the slowness in their performance is due to their wish to avoid error. In fact, Nathan Kogan (1973) once predicted that tests would show older adults to be highly reflective.

In the only studies of reflection–impulsivity with adults, Kogan's prediction was not supported. When men and women between the ages of 30 and 80 were compared, decision time was slower for older adults, but errors were also greater, indicating that these older adults were neither impulsive nor reflective—merely

Adults whose cognitive style is reflective rather than impulsive consider all possibilities before acting and make few errors.

slow and inaccurate (Denney and List, 1979). Sex, education, occupation, and retirement had no effect on this trend.

When individuals in their twenties were compared with individuals in their sixties, seventies, and eighties, younger adults were generally reflective whereas older adults tended to be impulsive (Coyne, Whitbourne, and Glenwick, 1978). Level of education had no effect on these results. Although both studies disconfirm the prediction of greater reflectiveness with age, their results are contradictory. At present we can reach no conclusion on the course of reflection and impulsivity over the life span.

Flexibility–Rigidity

A third cognitive style reflects a person's tendency to change methods or opinions to conform to new information. Someone who is **flexible** will shift from one activity or method to another when it becomes apparent that the previous approach no longer is useful. Someone who is **rigid** is unlikely to change even though the change is likely to be beneficial.

Most studies indicate that older people are much more rigid than the young. Adults past 50 were much less flexible than younger adults when solving the water-jar problem, in which a complicated method that works well on a series of problems must be abandoned to solve a new problem that at first appears to be similar. In this study (Heglin, 1956), adults were told to imagine that they had three jars of varying capacities and that they must use the jars to come up with a specific amount of water. For example, in one task they were to use a 22-pint jar, a 9-pint jar, and a 3-pint jar to produce 7 pints of water. The correct strategy is to fill the 22-pint jar and from it fill the 9-pint jar once and the 3-pint jar twice $(A - B - 2C)$. The water remaining in the 22-pint jar will measure 7 pints.

After being given a series of problems that could be solved with this method, the adults were asked to produce 4 pints of water, given three jars that held 17, 7, and 3 pints respectively. The correct strategy is to discard the large jar and simply fill the 7-pint jar and from it pour water into the 3-pint jar $(B - C)$. Adults between the ages of 50 and 85 found it much more difficult to switch their strategy than did adults between the ages of 20 and 49, even when the experimenter warned them that one method would not solve all the problems.

Older adults also appear to be less flexible at shifting their strategies on other problems, such as the concept formation studies described earlier. In order to test cognitive flexibility at concept formation, the researcher waits until a person figures out the governing rule, then switches the rule and begins a new "game." Now a different concept must be discovered. Instead of "round," the concept may be "blue" or "square." About half of older adults find such shifts extremely difficult to make whether they must reverse the concept (from "round" to "square") or form an unrelated concept ("blue"), yet most young adults can handle either sort of shift although they find reversal shifts easier than shifts to entirely new concepts (Kausler, 1982).

As Donald Kausler (1982) points out, performance on such tests can be viewed in two ways: We can say that older adults do worse than the young at learning concepts or solving problems because they are rigid, or we can say that older adults appear to be more rigid because they do worse at learning concepts or solving problems. When we consider the fact that IQ scores and flexibility–rigidity are related, the latter suggestion at first appears attractive. People with high IQs turn out to be more flexible than people with low IQs (Schaie, 1958).

Yet out of three studies (Schaie, 1958; Shields, 1958; Chown, 1961), two continued to show age differences in rigidity when adjustments were made for IQ. So older adults do appear to be more rigid than the young, but the increase may have little to do with age. Studies (Schaie and Labouvie-Vief, 1974) indicate that cohort effects account for most of the age differences in rigidity. Younger cohorts appear to be more flexible than older cohorts, and, over a 14-year period, each cohort shows little sign of increased rigidity with age.

CREATIVITY

Creativity is another aspect of intelligence that has been investigated, but for several reasons its study is complicated. Valuable as creativity is, little agreement exists about what it is, how to measure it, or the way it is affected by age. **Creativity** involves novel responses; in a creative act, previously unconnected elements are brought together in a new and unusual way. For this reason, creativity has been connected with divergent thinking, a cognitive operation related to intelligence in Guilford's structure of intellect.

Many highly intelligent people show few signs of creativity, but a certain level of intelligence appears necessary for creativity to flourish. In studies of successful writers, artists, and architects, performance on intelligence tests is consistently above the norm, but outstanding creators score no higher than the moderately successful (Barron, 1968). However, the consistent correlation of general IQ test performance with tests of divergent thinking has led researchers (Wallach and Kogan, 1965) to develop measures of divergent thinking that do away with time limits and place the tests in a relaxed, gamelike situation that does not have an evaluative context. Such measures have successfully separated divergent thinking from IQ test performance in children, adolescents, and college students (Kogan, 1973). As yet, however, such tests have not been applied to young adults outside the academic community, or middle-aged and elderly adults.

In attempting to study the course of creativity across adulthood, researchers have used three approaches: product-centered, personality-centered, and process-centered (Kogan, 1973). The product-centered approach focuses on the output of creative individuals of the past who have made enduring contributions to the arts, humanities, and sciences. The personality-centered approach studies the thought, motivation, and personality of notable creative individuals who are now working. The process-centered approach uses tests to explore cognition, looking at the way originality, fluency, spontaneous flexibility, and unusual responses change over the life span.

The results of product-centered research point to peak creativity in early middle age, followed by a decline. The precise pattern differs from one area of specialization to the next. In a study of scientific contributions (Lehman, 1968), the quality and quantity of creative achievement peaked at about the same point: the years between 35 and 39. This research focused on "notable" contributions; when total productivity is considered, the creative decline virtually disappears in some fields.

In a study of individuals who lived to be at least 80 years old, Wayne Dennis (1968) found that productivity held up through middle age for most creative professions and extended into old age for some. Composers of chamber music peaked early, reaching the height of productivity during their thirties. Architects, dramatists, poets, composers of opera, and the majority of scientists were most prolific during their forties. For novelists, the most productive decade was the fifties; and historians, philosophers, and inventors were most productive during their sixties. Mathematicians continued to be highly productive between the ages of 30 and 69. As these creators reached their seventies, scholars continued to produce at a high rate, but most scientists showed a considerable decline in productivity, and, among those in the arts, the drop was sharpest.

Many factors may influence the differences in productivity across disciplines. On various occasions, lengthy educational preparation, the time required to produce a single work, or the amount of effort expended have been advanced to explain the disparity. According to Dennis (1968), however, the custom of relying on assistants in collecting, arranging, and assessing basic materials helps to extend the productivity of scholars and some scientists. Such plodding, but necessary, spadework is not part of the creativity of poets, dramatists, composers, and novelists.

Declining productivity in later years is not universal. At 89, Sophocles wrote his tragedy of old age, *Oedipus at Colonus*. Francisco de Goya produced his famous lithographs and "black paintings" while in his seventies. Pablo Picasso and

Georgia O'Keeffe were painting magnificently at 90. Tolstoy wrote *Resurrection* at 71, and P. G. Wodehouse was writing comic novels during his nineties. At the age of 62, Scott O'Dell, a successful author of novels for adults, switched to the field of children's literature and wrote *Island of the Blue Dolphins,* a book that won national and international literary honors. When he was 85, O'Dell completed his twenty-first book for young people and immediately began work on his twenty-second.

Listing the creative achievements of older adults tells us little about the process of creativity. Process-centered studies generally disclose a decline in divergent thinking with age even when the adults studied have similar educational and IQ levels. For example, in a study of Southern California teachers between the ages of 20 and 83, divergent-thinking scores differed markedly with age, with adults beginning to make lower scores during the thirties. Among these same teachers, scores on the Barron-Walsh Art Scale, a measure of the preference for complexity, showed age differences from about the age of 25 although the disparity was less marked. P. K. Alpaugh and James Birren (1977), who conducted the study, believe that some of this decline may be due to cohort differences, but see a connection between a lessened preference for complexity and divergent thinking among older adults and the decline with age generally found in creative production.

In most process-centered research, no attempt is made to study people with demonstrated creative ability. Recently, however, researchers (Crosson and Robertson-Tchabo, 1983) compared highly educated, active women (ages 25 to 74) who had never shown evidence of high creativity with women (ages 22 to 87) who were professional artists and writers. The customary age difference in preference for complexity appeared among the noncreative women, with younger women preferring more complex designs than older women. Their scores showed approximately the same pattern found by Alpaugh and Birren. Among creative women, however, no significant difference appeared at any age. Nor were any cohort effects apparent among the creative group. In an attempt to understand this discrepancy, the researchers propose two possible explanations. Perhaps traits, preferences, and abilities that are important to an individual tend to be retained into old age. Or perhaps when highly established skills are continuously exercised, they are unlikely to decline with age.

WISDOM

Wisdom is an aspect of cognition that is traditionally supposed to ripen with age, yet its investigation has been neglected by most developmental psychologists, who tend to study forms of thought that emerge in childhood. Each society seems to regard wisdom as a positive characteristic and to link it with maturity, but as Vivian Clayton and James Birren (1980) have pointed out, the qualities that make up wisdom and the path that leads to it differ from one culture to the next.

Western societies tend to see wisdom as composed of cognition, emotion, and intuition. In the Judeo-Christian tradition, it requires time to become wise, but

In the Eastern tradition, wisdom seekers follow a wise teacher whose understanding of life has developed through many years of experience, intuition, and compassion.

the old do not necessarily possess wisdom. The path to wisdom is seen as three-fold: through formal education, learning from one's parents, or as a divine gift. The Greek tradition embodied two types of wisdom: an understanding of the ultimate nature of things and an understanding of the good. For the Greeks, wisdom went beyond formal knowledge and included moral behavior.

In Eastern societies, rational intellect was seen as a possible impediment to wisdom, which consisted of the direct experience of life's meaning. Such an experiential understanding required intuition and compassion. As in the West, time was needed to attain wisdom, but age did not always make a person wise. Wisdom could be reached by meditation and through observing and interacting with a wise teacher.

Although the emphasis is different, the major traditions seem to agree that wisdom involves an understanding of life's purpose, that wisdom is reflected in behavior, that wisdom is not attained without study, and that it takes time for wisdom to develop. Disagreement arises as to which human abilities are required for wisdom and what sort of education effectively imparts it.

Psychological approaches to wisdom are based on elements common to East and West. The relationship between age and wisdom is reflected in the theory of personality development put forth by Erik Erikson (1982). He sees wisdom as an "informed and detached concern with life itself in the face of death itself" (p. 61) and proposes that wisdom develops in the old when they find meaning in life and accept the imminence of their own death, successfully resolving the struggle between integrity and despair. Yet his theory allows for earlier forms of wisdom at other stages of life (Erikson, 1980b). Although Erikson's view of wisdom has strong philosophical aspects, his theory's focus on the social and emotional aspects of development gives us no way to study the cognitive elements of wisdom.

In Lawrence Kohlberg's (1973) cognitive-developmental approach, the sort of wisdom Erikson refers to is not possible for many people. To attain it, an individual must first develop formal reasoning. Equipped with formal thought, a person may then develop principled morality, which is distinguished by a commitment to moral principles that are seen as universal. Now wisdom is possible, but it cannot emerge without lengthy experience in living according to these advanced moral principles.

Cultural variations in the meaning of wisdom led Clayton and Birren (1980) to try to establish just how contemporary Americans perceive this quality. They asked well-educated men and women of various ages to rate a number of qualities that might be connected with wisdom. All age groups (college students, middle-aged university faculty, and elderly community volunteers) agreed that wisdom consisted of reflective, affective, and cognitive qualities and that wisdom was age-related or developmental. But the young and middle-aged groups saw old age and wisdom as more closely related than did the elderly group, and the older adults saw themselves as no wiser than any other group.

The old appeared to be the most aware that age does not necessarily bring wisdom and to perceive understanding and empathy as more important than experience or age in its development. This view also was expressed by an 84-year-old retired British schoolmaster, who was interviewed by Ronald Blythe (1979): "I don't think you grow in wisdom when you're old, but I do think that, in some respects, you do grow in understanding. The very old are often as tolerant as the young. The young haven't yet adopted certain formal codes, and the very old have seen through them or no longer need them" (p. 186).

Clayton and Birren (1980) suggest that technological society downgrades wisdom by focusing on productivity and problem-solving abilities instead of on reflection and the search for life's meaning. Formal education may not be an effective method of transmitting the sort of knowledge that is required for wisdom. Wisdom may instead depend on the type of experiences a person has, their number, their timing, and the way in which they are processed. If we could learn more about the acquisition of wisdom, we might develop an increasing pool of wise adults who could play a valuable role in society.

SUMMARY

Older adults generally perform somewhat worse than younger adults on problem-solving tasks, but the reason for the difference is not known. It takes older adults longer to form new concepts, they show an increased tendency to classify objects by function instead of by category, and they use less efficient strategies when solving puzzles. However, with instruction, older adults learn to form concepts more quickly and to use more efficient problem-solving strategies. In addition, functional classification may be more adaptive than abstract groupings in daily life. The performance of older adults on Piagetian tasks of cognitive development is also generally worse than that of younger adults. Again, instruction brings about improved performance. Because intelligence and educational level seem related to **formal operational thought,** cohort differences may be an important factor in this apparent decline. The roleless existence of older adults in a technological society may also play a part in age differences.

Intelligence involves mental operations that enhance the ability to function effectively in the environment. Attempts to discover whether intelligence is a single general attribute or a group of processes have relied on **factor analysis,** and no consensus has been reached. Some researchers propose that intelligence can be divided into **fluid intelligence,** which corresponds to basic cognitive processes, and **crystallized intelligence,** which corresponds to acquired knowledge and developed intellectual skills.

The effect of aging on cognition has been studied by using intelligence tests, which were developed by **psychometrists** to predict future academic performance. Thus, they measure the ability to solve arbitrary, context-free problems and do not consider any aspect of intelligence that is not part of the academic situation. Two major tests in use are the Wechsler Adult Intelligence Scale (WAIS) and the Primary Mental Abilities Test (PMA).

Cross-sectional studies of intelligence show an apparent decline in IQ, with slight differences appearing in middle age and a sharply increased gap after about the age 70. On subtests, there is little or no change in verbal function, but there are declines in nonverbal and psychomotor functions. Longitudinal studies show rising test scores during middle age, with no significant declines until after the age of 60. The disparity between results from the two types of studies may be due largely to cohort differences although selective dropout may also play a part. About half of the decline in fluid intelligence with age may develop because older adults seem to have trouble organizing information, keeping their attention focused, and forming expectations about a task; but until about the age of 65, any decline is usually matched by a rise in crystallized intelligence. Average tests scores of older adults may be pulled down by **terminal drop.** Some of the decline in tasks requiring fluid intelligence has been narrowed by training programs.

Sex differences in IQ scores appear across cohorts and across the life span, with women performing better on tests of word fluency and men on tests of space and number. It has been suggested that cultural differences may be responsible for a large share of these consistent differences.

What appear to be declines in some aspects of adult cognition may indicate the emergence of a new organization of thought. The way an individual responds to a situation is influenced by **cognitive style.** Although interindividual differences are wide, young adults tend to be **field-independent; field dependence** tends to be reappear during middle age and to become prevalent during old age. This cognitive style is heavily influenced by education, sex roles, health, and environmental situation, so cohort differences may influence the trend. There is no clear-cut trend in **impulsiveness–reflectivity** over the life span. Younger adults tend to be **flexible,** with **rigidity** common among older adults, but cohort effects seem to account for a good part of the difference.

Although there are many exceptions, **creativity** seems to decline during late middle age. However, the decline in divergent thinking that has been found in cross-sectional studies failed to appear in a study of professional artists and writers. Wisdom has been linked with age in most traditions. Erik Erikson has proposed that wisdom develops in the old when they find meaning in life and accept the imminence of their own death. Lawrence Kohlberg believes that wisdom develops when formal reasoning leads to a principled morality. A cultural focus on productivity and problem solving may downgrade the acquisition of wisdom.

KEY TERMS

cognitive style

creativity

crystallized intelligence

factor analysis

field dependence

field independence

flexibility

fluid intelligence

formal operational thought

impulsivity

intelligence

psychometry

reflection

rigidity

terminal drop

10

PERSONALITY AND MOTIVATION ACROSS ADULTHOOD

Changes in the American view of old age became apparent when *Taking My Turn*, a musical revue about aging, opened at New York's Entermedia Theater in mid-1983. Seven years earlier, Robert H. Livingston had put together the revue, based on his collection of more than 3000 accounts of what it is like to grow old. Much of the material came from 88-year-old Gertrude Weil Klein, a professional writer who had been a union activist during the 1930s. But no one was interested in a musical about growing old, Livingston discovered. The view of old people as not useful and certainly not interesting was so engrained in society that the material had to be put aside (Blau, 1983).

As attitudes changed, it became possible to stage the revue. Critics applauded and audiences of all ages flocked to see it. The musical has no plot; instead the songs and sketches allow eight aging characters to reflect on their past, to consider their present, and to grow and change through their interactions with one another. The musical's message is that old people have been unnecessarily—and unwisely—cast aside by society. Its view of personality in old age is summed up in singer Margaret Whiting's line, "Age doesn't make you boring; boring makes you boring." Whiting, who is 57, says that it is wrong to call *Taking My Turn* a show about old people. She sees it as a musical comedy about living (Lawson, 1983). And one of the other performers, Marni Nixon, discovered that her role in the musical had changed her own ideas about aging. "It's OK to be 'older,'" she told a reporter. "It's a meaningless term. . . . The fun side of me is 12 years old" (Blau, 1983).

If "older" can be meaningless to older people and if they often feel as if they were 12 years old, some of the assumptions about personality across adulthood may have to be changed. In this chapter, we will discover that many researchers now question the idea that personality undergoes a predictable pattern of change with age. After discussing the concept of personality, we investigate what happens to personality across adulthood, whether there are any typical changes, and how the personalities of men and women differ. Our exploration of emotional development centers on various theories that have been put forth to describe its progression in adults, and we close the chapter by considering similarities and differences in the motivation and emotional development of women and men.

PERSONALITY

Each of us is unique. Our ways of thinking, feeling, and reacting to the environment are not exactly like anyone else's. But we do not respond at random. Within each individual is a thread of consistency that accounts for similarities in his or her behavior in various situations and explains why, placed in the same situation, two people behave differently. That consistency is called **personality**, and, without it, we would have no individuality. From infancy, socialization tends to push people into prescribed paths, making them more and more alike. But personality ensures that we will react differently to society's push, which distinguishes us from our relatives, our friends, and the rest of our fellow citizens.

As a result, people differ on all personality characteristics, whether loyalty, shyness, or honesty. These characteristics, or **traits**, are enduring dispositions to thoughts, feelings, and behavior. Traits tend to be stable over time. Thus, the concept of personality indicates a certain predictability of behavior. A person who is generally sociable and outgoing is unlikely to be withdrawn and shy at a party.

But behavior is not entirely predictable, and traits are unlikely, by themselves, to determine specific behavior in a specific situation. A sociable, outgoing person is more likely to run for political office than a person who is habitually withdrawn and shy. However, some sociable people run for office, and others do not. Knowing a person's traits tells us about the range of reponses he or she is likely to make, but it does not allow us to predict what she or he will do in a given situation, such as receiving an extra $10 in change at the supermarket, being fired from a job, or being tempted to have an extramarital affair. Yet if behavior over a long period of time is considered, the influence of traits can be seen (Epstein, 1979).

Traits interact with situations. As Paul Costa and Robert McCrae (1980) point out, an anxious person tends to become apprehensive when threatened, and a sociable person tends to be friendly when other people are present. Finally, enduring traits can express themselves differently at different times of life. A fearful person may fear losing a job at midlife and fear dying in later adulthood.

Personality is reflected in behavior, attitudes, values, feelings, and motivations. It is seen in cognitive style. It is central to the way we perceive ourselves. It affects the way we meet people and solve problems of living. Clearly, personality is a basic part of being human. Yet psychologists are still trying to explain just what personality is, how it develops, and why—or whether—it changes. Some take an organismic view and see personality as global; others take a mechanistic approach and break personality down into small units of behavior. Finally, some take a cognitive view of personality, which focuses on a person's *perception* of himself or herself instead of on the person's behavior (Neugarten, 1977).

A number of psychologists believe that using traits to study personality is misleading, and they have criticized trait approaches to personality. They point out that calling someone "shy" does not explain the behavior, but merely labels it; that using traits to describe behavior may obscure intraindividual differences; and that, from one situation to another, a person's behavior is much less consistent than we suppose. However, using traits to study personality has been helpful in understanding many aspects of personality.

When studying personality, researchers have taken various approaches. Most assessments of personality use standardized tests that are considered objective, for each person is scored on exactly the same questions, administered in the same way, and the results can be quantified. The resulting scores make it possible to compare the dimensions of a person's personality with norms established for the test. Most standardized tests take the form of the self-report inventory, in which a person responds to statements (such as "When I get bored, I like to stir up some excitement") in terms of his or her own personality. The 16 Personality Factor Questionnaire (16PF), a self-report inventory developed through factor analysis, is frequently used in studies of aging and personality.

A second way of assessing personality is to have a trained investigator interview the person, observing him or her closely, then rate the person on a standard scale. This method has been used in some longitudinal studies of development (Livson, 1973). A popular rating scale, the Q sort, involves sorting 100 personality statements (such as "gets anxious easily") into a 9-point distribution that describes the person. The results of observer ratings often correspond closely with a person's self-report, and both types of ratings tend to be consistent over time (Mischel, 1981).

Sometimes personality is rated subjectively by asking a person to reflect on his or her own personality and then to rate it directly. Instead of answering questions or responding to statements, the person looks at pairs of opposing adjectives (such as hostile/friendly or impulsive/controlled) and indicates which position on a 10-point scale between the adjectives best describes his or her own personality.

Other studies of personality use projective tests, which require a person to respond to ink blots with whatever comes to mind or to respond to ambiguous pictures by describing what is going on in them. The responses are scored by a trained person. Projective tests are subjective because the situation is ambiguous, the answers are not standard, and their meaning must be interpreted. A projective test that is frequently used in studies of aging is the Thematic Apperception Test (TAT), which consists of 19 ambiguous black-and-white pictures and one blank white card. The task is to describe what happened before the pictured scene, what is going on in the picture, and what will happen next. For the blank card, the person imagines a scene and responds to it as to the other cards (Anastasi, 1976). The TAT measures thoughts and fantasies, so any connection with the dimensions of personality is indirect.

Using these tests, researchers have investigated the stability and predictability of personality across adulthood. One kind of predictability is the consistency of personality dimensions over time. Another kind of predictability involves change. Do people change in predictable ways as they grow older?

STABILITY AND CHANGE IN PERSONALITY

Many people, whether professionals or average citizens, are certain that aging affects personality in predictable ways, and they have developed stereotypical ideas about the nature of these changes. Hans Thomae (1980) has collected the stereotypes and reports that American graduate students see old people as stubborn, touchy, bossy, and apt to complain excessively. Germans see them as inactive and withdrawn and textbooks in German elementary schools portray them as incompetent, dependent, and passive. Psychiatrists describe old people as rigid, irritable, and extreme, and French writer Simone de Beauvoir (1972) believes they are bored, lazy, resigned, and suspicious.

Thomae explains the existence of these stereotypes as overgeneralizations from specific, isolated cases. Until recently, he points out, most studies of the elderly took place in institutions, so that the old people seen by researchers were not typical of older adults. De Beauvoir was undoubtedly influenced by the handful of eminent French politicians, scientists, and writers, whose reaction to a suddenly roleless existence she reports. The lack of social role that isolates older adults from society may affect the average person's picture of aging, which is heavily influenced by stereotypes in the media.

The stereotype itself, however, creates a role for the aged, and they may feel forced into playing the "old role" by society. Florida Scott-Maxwell, a Jungian analyst, made this point forcefully when, well into her eighties, she wrote: "My kitchen linoleum is so black and shiny that I waltz while I wait for the kettle to boil. This pleasure is for the old who live alone. The others must vanish into their expected role" (1979, p. 28).

Only a minority of older individuals fit the stereotypical picture of the aging individual. Studies indicate that most personality characteristics do not change from young adulthood to old age among healthy adults who live in the community (Thomae, 1980). No matter which theoretical approach is used, personality remains stable (McCrae and Costa, 1982). An imaginative young person becomes an imaginative old person, a sociable young person becomes a sociable old person, and so forth. In the few instances of age-related change that seem to occur, the changes are slight, and the differences among individuals of the same age are greater than the differences between age groups.

When they reflect on their past, individuals may believe they have changed more with age than they actually have. As we saw in Chapter 1, a middle-aged person's recollection of his or her adolescent personality tends to be faulty. Middle-aged individuals generally believed that they had changed greatly in 15 years, but their self-report scales in 1969 showed little change since they had taken the same test in 1944 as adolescents. When asked to retake the test, answering it as they believed they had done as adolescents, there was a great disparity in the scores, with the retrospective test portraying a much more negative image than shown in their actual adolescent self-report (Woodruff and Birren, 1972).

The search for influences of aging on personality has used cross-sectional, longitudinal, and cross-sequential designs. Some studies look only at single traits; and others, at personality structure, which is the relationship of traits within an individual. No matter which approach is taken, care must be used in generalizing the findings. Most studies of adult personality are studies of white middle-class men, and they may tell us little about white working-class men or men from ethnic minorities—and even less about women.

PERSONALITY TRAITS

A host of cross-sectional studies have tested various personality characteristics in an attempt to discover whether they increase or decrease with age. Among the traits investigated have been egocentrism, dependency, introversion, dogmatism, cautiousness, conformity, imaginativeness, risk taking, sociability, happiness, activity, need for achievement, life satisfaction, social responsibility, creativity, and hope. In most cases, for every study that finds an age-related change, another study finds stability in that characteristic. In only one trait—introversion—were consistent changes found with age. Most of the studies found that as people grow older, they shift from outer to inner concerns. This inward shift tends to be accompanied by increased cautiousness and conformity (Reedy, 1983).

Evidence for increased interiority was seen as reflecting older adults' disengagement from society. According to disengagement theory, which was introduced in Chapter 2, the disengagement was mutual (Cumming and Henry, 1961). Limited physical and psychic energy supposedly led older adults to withdraw from active participation in a society that was simultaneously withdrawing from the old, taking from them active social roles. Disengagement was regarded as "natural" and as the most satisfactory way to adjust to aging. But for most adults, interiority did not seem to translate into disengagement, and, among adults in the Duke Longitudinal Studies, disengagement appeared to be a pattern found primarily among people who had always been relatively uninvolved in society (Maddox, 1970). Today most researchers regard disengagement as merely one pattern of adult personality development.

The inconsistent results of cross-sectional studies seem to result from a number of causes. According to Bernice Neugarten (1977), researchers often use the same words in different ways; they compare groups with different educational, socioeconomic, and IQ levels; and they use tests that were devised for younger groups and thus may not be meaningful for older adults. If personality traits, such as sociability, take different forms in young and old adults, then a test constructed to tap the trait in young people may not pick it up in the elderly. Finally, most investigators looked at personality traits without considering the possible effect of major life events such as marriage, parenthood, career changes, retirement, or illness. Instead, they have assumed that any change found was age-related. The cross-sectional nature of these studies means that generational changes could also be clouding the results. Wars, depressions, technological change, and the tightening or relaxation of social codes all could affect personality.

Most longitudinal studies have shown that personality tends to be stable. In a study that followed boys and girls from birth to their thirties, personality seemed to stabilize by middle childhood and show little change after that time (Moss and Susman, 1980). When individuals are followed from youth to middle age or from middle age to late adulthood, similar patterns of stability are found. Nor is change the general rule among the elderly. In a longitudinal study of older West Germans (ages 60 to 79) (Thomae, 1980), there was no decrease in the level of activity, no tendency for rigidity to increase with age, nor any change in attitudes toward life. Other life factors, such as finances, health, sex, and education, seemed as important as age in accounting for personality change.

Another longitudinal study of older men and women living in a rural community indicated that, for most people, personality remains stable. Seventy-eight percent of the men and 62 percent of the women showed no real change in personality or adjustment over three years. The rest showed negative changes. The researchers (Britton and Britton, 1972) could find no life factors that distinguished those who declined from those who remained stable, but they believe that environmental changes may have affected both personality and social characteristics in those who declined.

In a cross-sequential study that covered a 7-year period, investigators (Schaie and Parham, 1976) found that most personality traits remain stable over the years. The only age-related changes they could identify were increases in excitability and humanitarian concern. This sort of change appeared in Scott-Maxwell, who wrote: "Age puzzles me. I thought it was a quiet time. My seventies were interesting, and fairly serene, but my eighties are passionate. I grow more intense as I age. To my own surprise I burst out with hot conviction. Only a few years ago I enjoyed my tranquillity; now I am so disturbed by the outer world and by human quality in general that I want to put things right, as though I still owed a debt to life. I must calm down. I am far too frail to indulge in moral fervour'' (1979, pp. 13–14).

DIMENSIONS OF PERSONALITY

Instead of looking at single traits, Paul Costa and Robert McCrae (1980) have looked at **personality dimensions**, made up of a number of related traits. They have identified three dimensions of personality: *neuroticism*, made up of anxiety, depression, self-consciousness, vulnerability, impulsiveness, and hostility; *extraversion*, made up of attachment, assertiveness, gregariousness, excitement seeking, positive emotions, and activity; and *openness*, made up of ideas, feelings, fantasy, esthetics, actions, and values. These dimensions, say Costa and McCrae, can predict and explain attitudes, behavior, and feelings. This view of personality structure developed out of a study of 2000 men, ranging in age from the twenties to the nineties, so its applicability to women is unknown.

Compared with men who are low on neuroticism, men who are high on this dimension tend to complain about their health, smoke heavily, may have drinking problems, report sexual and financial problems, and may be unhappy and dissatisfied with life. Over a 10-year period, no change appeared in the level of neuroticism among the men studied by Costa and McCrae. When the results of longitudinal studies were examined, neither a group of more than 900 men (Douglas and Arenberg, 1978) nor a group of more than 300 women and men (Siegler, George, and Okun, 1979) showed any change in the average level of traits connected with neuroticism.

Compared with introverted men, those who are high in extraversion seem to value power and humanitarian concerns more highly, are happier, and show higher levels of well-being. This personality dimension influences occupation, with introverts tending to seek out jobs that are task-oriented and extraverts seeking out jobs that involve dealing with people. Cross-sectional studies generally indicate increased introversion with age, but over a 10-year period the men studied by Costa and McCrae showed only one change in the traits associated with extraversion: They tended to become slightly less independent. Other longitudinal studies have produced mixed results. In one study (Siegler, George, and Okun, 1979), no change in related traits appeared in either men or women; in a second study (Douglas and Arenberg, 1978) a slight decline in general activity was found in men; and in a 30-year study that spanned the period from middle to old age (Leon et al., in press), there was a small, but significant increase in introversion among men.

Compared with men who are low in openness, men who are high on this dimension tend to score high on theoretical and aesthetic values and low on religious and economic values. Openness is connected with above-average IQ scores; and highly open men are more likely to change jobs, quit, or be demoted; and they are often involved in lawsuits. Their lives tend to be eventful, and their experience of both good and bad events is more intense. This dimension also affects occupation, with open men tending to become psychologists, psychiatrists, or ministers and shunning the occupations of banker, veterinarian, and mortician. Over an 11-year period, Costa and McCrae (1980) found no longitudinal differences but some cross-sectional differences in openness. Among other longitudinal studies, one (Siegler, George, and Okun, 1979) indicated no change in related traits among men or women, and another (Angleitner, 1976) showed very small, but significant, increases in personal rigidity but decreases in dogmatism among both men and women.

Looking at increases or decreases in the level of personality factors is only one way of examining age-related change. Another measure of stability is based on personality structure. In this view of personality, the levels of particular traits may not change, but their relationship may be altered with age. If that should happen, the structure of personality would be different.

Research on this aspect of personality has been contradictory, with some studies showing no change in personality structure with age and others showing dramatic age differences in the way various aspects of personality are related. For example, one early study (Craik, 1964) indicated that emotional adjustment and sociability are related in different ways in men and women and that the relationship changes with age. However, these studies have been cross-sectional (Neugarten, 1977). In the case of neuroticism and extraversion, Costa and McCrae (1980) found no change over time in the men they studied. The same interrelation of traits that originally formed these personality dimensions was present a decade later. In the case of openness, although most of the related factors were similar, some changes appeared in the strength of the relationships. In addition, among younger men (ages 36 to 51), an openness to feelings was not strongly related to other forms of openness, as it was in the two older groups of men.

The determinants of happiness, an essential part of satisfaction with life, do not appear to change with age.

Finally, stability can be considered in regard to an individual's rank among other members of his or her cohort, a type of constancy known as **normative stability**. In normative stability, personality characteristics may change in relation to the population as a whole but remain at the same point in relation to other members of one's own cohort. For example, a 30-year-old woman who scores higher in extraversion than most of her peers will continue to score higher than most peers at the age of 75, although in relation to a 25-year-old, she may have an average score. Normative stability is revealed by longitudinal studies, which indicate high levels of correlation across the years on many aspects of personality (Mortimer, Finch, and Kumka, 1982). In Costa and McCrae's (1980) study of personality dimensions, neuroticism and extraversion both showed high correlations over 10 years, with openness showing lower, but still strong (.44 to .63) correlations. As correlations across age, though impressive, are far from perfect, it is clear that individual personality can—and often does—change. However, the changes apparently are not related to age but to life events.

It has been suggested that personality tends to remain stable as long as there is continuity in life situations (Moss and Susman, 1980). A sudden crisis, such as the unexpected death of a spouse, could affect personality, altering some aspects more than others. In this view, neither stability nor personality change are developmental in nature, but probably reflect the psychosocial situation. A life that continues in the same pattern makes any change in self-concept—and therefore in personality—unlikely.

LIFE SATISFACTION

Another way of considering the question of stability is by examining the relationship between aging and life satisfaction. Following this line of thought, a number of researchers have studied the effect of age on feelings of well-being, happiness, and satisfaction. Some believe that environmental conditions are the major influence on well-being, some believe that personality is the major factor, and others point to age as a powerful force. As we saw in Chapter 6, depression becomes more common with age, suggesting that older people are less likely to be happy than the young.

Interested in the effect of age on satisfaction, Paul Cameron (1975) studied this state in more than 6000 people ranging in age from 4 years old to 99. After assessing people at home, school, work, and play, he concluded that satisfaction, expressed as happiness, sadness, or neutral moods, was the same among the young, the middle-aged, and the old. Mood seemed to be primarily determined by social class, sex, and the immediate situation.

In most studies of life satisfaction and well-being among the elderly, mood plays an important role in the ratings. Older adults are asked to respond to such statements as "I am just as happy now as when I was younger" or "I sometimes feel that life isn't worth living." After looking at the results of 30 years of such research, one investigator (Larson, 1978) concluded that age had little influence on feelings of well-being. Health seemed to be the most important determinant, although money, social class, social interaction, marital status, housing, and transportation also affected a person's satisfaction with life.

If age affects happiness, its influence is not immediately apparent. In a longitudinal study of mood among the elderly, researchers (Kozma and Stones, 1983) found no influence of increasing age on happiness over an 18-month-period. Among these older men and women, the degree of happiness remained stable, with such environmental factors as satisfaction with housing, health, activity, life events, and marriage emerging as the predictors of happiness. For urban elderly, satisfaction with their housing arrangements was the most important influence on general happiness; and for rural elderly, health was most important.

Among gifted men and women in their sixties, who had been followed since childhood by Lewis Terman, the deepest life satisfaction came from their families (Fig. 10.1). A simple joy in living also was a major source of life satisfaction for both sexes. Friends and culture weighed heavily on life satisfaction for women whereas men derived much of their satisfaction from their occupations (R. Sears, 1977; P. Sears and Barbee, 1978). Income had no relationship to life satisfaction among these highly advantaged adults; those with the highest incomes in the group were no happier than those with the lowest incomes.

When disengagement theory was prominent, it was assumed that the disengaged elderly would be more satisfied with life than older adults who remained

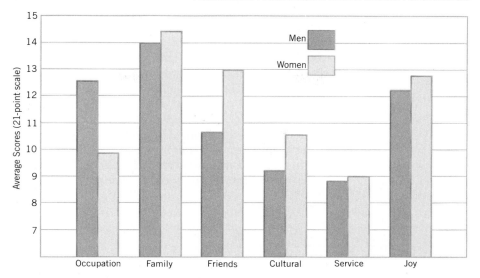

FIGURE 10.1   Life satisfactions of the gifted. In 1972, older men and women in the Terman study of the gifted reported on the relative importance of six sources of life satisfaction. "Joy" refers to overall pleasure in living.

Source: D. Goleman, "1,528 Little Geniuses and How They Grew," *Psychology Today*, 13 (February 1980), p. 40.

active and engaged. Among adults in the Duke Longitudinal Study, however, high activity and life satisfaction went hand in hand. Forty-three percent of the highly active adults, but only 14 percent of the disengaged adults, reported higher than average life satisfaction (Maddox, 1970).

The effect of personality on well-being and happiness cannot be discounted. In a study of 35- to 85-year-old men, the personality dimensions of neuroticism and extraversion were related to happiness (McCrae and Costa, 1983). Men who were high in neuroticism were more likely than others to feel dissatisfied or unhappy, and men who were high in extraversion were more likely to feel happy or satisfied. The relationship held regardless of the psychological maturity of the men. And as we saw earlier, these personality dimensions seem to remain stable over the life span.

When a 75-year-old says she or he is "happy," does it mean the same thing as the 25-year-old's report of happiness? In other words, does the nature of life satisfaction change with age? After reviewing the evidence, Richard Schulz (1982) summed up the apparent effects of aging on these attitudes. He believes that older people's feelings about life are just as intense as those of the young although their quality may change. A person's attitude toward life may not be as "pure" as it once was because years of living have tinged positive emotions with negative overtones and negative emotions with positive overtones. As Schulz puts it, love may be less euphoric and more bittersweet the fourth time around. Because the body's regulatory systems change with age, as we saw in Chapter 4, once an older person becomes aroused, it takes longer for the feeling to subside than it does in the young. For the same reason, within any one day, an older person is likely to show fewer changes in mood than a young adult.

Schulz believes that negative feelings and attitudes are not necessarily more prominent among the old. Although age often brings such negative events as loss of spouse, poor health, or decreasing income, these may not evoke the expected negative mood. As people age, their expectations may change, and these changing expectations may well offset negative life experiences. For example, it is often assumed that retirement lowers a person's morale because he or she suddenly has lost social roles. But a study of men (Thompson, 1973), both working and retired, indicated that health, age, and income were the primary influences on mood. It is possible that any effect of aging on personality and mood is related to self-concept.

SELF-CONCEPT AND PERSONALITY CHANGE

In the cognitive view of personality, a person's self-perceptions are central to personality, and an individual's perceptions of himself or herself have major effects on personality patterns. Changed self-perceptions are seen as leading to changes in behavior, and perceptions will change if a person's beliefs, concerns, or expectations change. **Self-concept**, which is the organized, coherent, and integrated pattern of perceptions related to the self (Thomae, 1980), includes self-esteem and self-image.

In a longitudinal study of college men, Jaylan Mortimer, Michael Finch, and Donald Kumka (1982) found self-image, an important part of self-concept, to have four dimensions: well-being, interpersonal qualities, activity, and unconventionality. Well-being was made up of self-perceptions concerning happiness, lack of tension, and confidence. The interpersonal dimensions consisted of self-perceptions concerning sociability, interest in others, openness, and warmth. The dimension of activity indicated self-perceptions of activity, strength, competence, and success. The unconventional dimension was made up of perceptions of the self as impulsive, unconventional, and a dreamer. The closeness of three of these aspects of self-image to Costa and McCrae's (1980) dimensions of personality suggests that self-concept and personality are also closely related. Because the study was limited to men, caution should be used in applying the findings to women.

The men in this study were followed for 14 years, beginning with their freshman year. Throughout their transition from adolescence to adulthood, the structure of self-concept remained stable, as did normative stability. There were, however, some changes in the levels of various aspects of self-image. Well-being and competence both declined during the college years and then rose after graduation. Perceptions of the self as unconventional declined when these men left college and established themselves in the business world. Sociability declined steadily throughout the 14 years of the study.

In addition to examining self-concept at the group level, Mortimer, Finch and Kumka also examined intraindividual changes in the perception of competence in

Feelings of competence appear to be related to all areas of life. In one study, middle-aged men whose feelings of competence were above average generally had close relationships with their parents.

order to discover the factors that accounted for divergence from group trends. A man's perception of his competence was related to events in his life. The actual course of his career, as well as his satisfaction with it, his relationship with his parents, marital satisfaction, and satisfaction with life in general tended to follow patterns that could be predicted by changes—or the lack of them—in the dimension of competence. For example, men whose sense of competence had declined since college tended at some time to have been unemployed, to have worked at jobs beneath their abilities and skills, or to have been forced into part-time employment. Men whose competence scores were above the group average throughout the study were much less likely to have encountered such occupational problems. They also had much closer relationships with their parents than did men whose competence scores declined after they left college. These family relationships were positively correlated with marital satisfaction as 30-year-olds and with general life satisfaction.

Yet these men were not simply buffeted about by fortune. Analysis showed that a man's degree of confidence as a college senior had an important influence on his later evaluation of life events and may even have served as a self-fulfilling prophecy. The researchers suggest that there may be a strong interaction at work, with the individual actively creating experiences that eventually affect personality. In the Terman longitudinal study of the gifted, women who were high in self-confidence during their early years tended to be high in life satisfaction during their sixties (P. Sears and Barbee, 1978).

Few researchers have traced self-concept in longitudinal studies. Among middle-aged women, self-esteem is higher in working women than in those who do not work outside the home (Coleman and Antonucci, 1983). There is no research, however, to tell whether women who already have high self-esteem are more likely to seek employment.

In a study of older West Germans (Bergler, 1968), the self-concept of men and women in their late sixties remained positive. The older adults in this study perceived themselves as active, self-controlled, and competent. Such positive self-concepts are likely to affect aging. As Thomae (1980) points out, a person who already has a positive self-concept is likely to incorporate positive elements of the aging stereotype, but a person who already has a negative self-concept is likely to incorporate the negative elements, with all the limitations on life that implies.

Self-concepts do not necessarily reflect reality. If aspects of self-concept help to protect a person's psychological well-being, any change—such as a perception of the self as "old"—will be resisted. An older person may completely exclude the notion of old age from his or her self-concept, and many do, seeing themselves as "middle-aged" long past their seventieth birthdays. According to one researcher (Turner, 1979), older adults who have a middle-aged self-concept tend to be better adjusted and have higher morale than those who see themselves as old. Along with a middle-aged, self-concept go better health, employment, high levels of activity, and the absence of major illness or the loss of a spouse. Again, life events apparently play a role in self-concept.

Perhaps because so many different influences can affect it, there seems to be no general effect of aging on self-concept (Thomae, 1980). Health, socioeconomic status, educational level, marital status, sex, housing conditions, and community involvement may have more influence on self-concept than age. The self-concept of a 75-year-old retired bookeeper with an inadequate pension who suffers from emphysema and whose opinions are no longer sought out by others is more likely to change than the self-concept of a healthy, financially secure 75-year-old professor emeritus at a prestigious university who is regarded as a major contributor in his field.

It is generally assumed that men are more self-confident than women. This assumption is related to the perception of male and female personality as being radically different.

SEX DIFFERENCES IN PERSONALITY

Considering the personality of men and women together can be misleading. If men score low on a dimension and women score high, lumping their scores together results in a score midway between the two that reflects neither group. Should there be a great disparity between the sexes on any trait or dimension, the result would be as illuminating as learning that a person with one foot in a bucket of hot water and the other in a bucket of ice water was standing in water that was, on the average, tepid.

Most of the longitudinal studies we have encountered reflect the effect of aging on male personality. Yet it is generally assumed that men and women differ in self-concept, aggression, dependence, emotional expressiveness, and social orientation (Frieze et al., 1978). These differences are believed to be strengthened or created by traditional patterns of socialization. From childhood, girls are taught to be passive, dependent, warm, and emotionally expressive, and boys are taught to be assertive and independent. By adulthood, the differences are believed to be firmly established. Personality differences do exist, but variations among each sex are generally wider than the average differences between the sexes, and some researchers believe that as men and women age they get more alike.

Sex-Related Traits

Men are believed to have higher self-concepts, including self-esteem and self-confidence, than women. This personality difference is supposed to develop because stereotypical masculine traits are valued more highly by society than stereotypical feminine traits. Studies indicate that such beliefs are not entirely accurate. During young adulthood, men and women have similar levels of self-esteem and both sexes value themselves more highly than they did as adolescents (Frieze et al., 1978).

However, when young adults rated themselves on various personality traits, the highest self-esteem in both sexes was found among those whose personalities did not fit the stereotype for either gender (Spence, 1979). These individuals were high in both personality traits considered masculine (such as self-reliance, independence, assertiveness) and those considered feminine (such as affectionate nature, sympathy, understanding). Such people are considered **androgynous**, a term that comes from the Greek words for male (*andro*) and female (*gyne*), and 32 percent of the men and 27 percent of the women in this study fit that description.

Individuals next highest in self-esteem were men and women who were high only in traditional masculine traits (34 percent of the men and 14 percent of the women). Lower in self-esteem were those men and women who were high only in traditional feminine traits (32 percent of the women and 8 percent of the men). The lowest self-esteem was found among men and women whose personality was undifferentiated. They were low in both masculine and feminine traits (being neither assertive nor sympathetic), a category that included 25 percent of the men and 28 percent of the women. So it would appear that, among college students in the late 1970s, only about one out of three men and women fitted the stereotype for his or her sex and that traditionally feminine women who saw themselves as lacking self-reliance, independence, or assertiveness did tend to be lower in self-esteem than traditionally masculine men.

The belief that men are more self-confident than women appears to have some basis in fact. Women do tend to have less self-confidence than men, seeing themselves as not nearly so competent. When young adults are asked to predict their performance on a task or to evaluate their own abilities, women consistently rate themselves lower than men do (Tavris and Offir, 1977).

Aggressiveness is another aspect of personality that is considered to be stronger among men. This is one stereotype that research has supported again and again. No matter what type of measure is used—behavior, self-report, observation— men score higher on aggression than women. The difference between the sexes is much higher when aggression is expressed physically than when it is expressed verbally, and some researchers (Frieze et al., 1978) have suggested that because the culture defines aggression as unfeminine, women feel guilty and anxious about being aggressive and tend to inhibit such impulses.

Women see themselves as more sensitive, submissive, helpful, gentle, and kind than men see themselves, and other people rate women as higher on these traits (Hoyenga and Hoyenga, 1979). Men see themselves as more ambitious, assertive, competitive, and independent than women see themselves, and other people view them in the same manner. However, the difference is a matter of degree and often depends on the situation. A traditional woman may be independent and assertive when it comes to making decisions at work or managing her household, and a traditional man may be gentle and sensitive with his family.

The Move Toward Androgyny

As men and women age, these sex differences in personality appear to diminish, and both sexes may move toward androgyny. During middle age, as children leave home, each sex may feel freer about expressing traits that are traditionally linked with the other gender, a trend that will be examined in Chapter 12. Some researchers (Hyde and Phillis, 1979) believe that older men may find it easier to express feminine traits than women find it to express masculine traits. In their study, no trend toward androgyny appeared among the women. Among the men, those between 21 and 40 showed little androgyny, with only 4 percent rating themselves high on both masculine and feminine qualities. After the age of 40, however, an increasing tendency for men to see themselves as androgynous appeared, with 31 percent of the middle-aged men and 40 percent of the men past 60 showing androgyny. They had incorporated such traits as "gentleness" and "loves children" into their self-concepts.

The problem with this study is that the measure of masculinity and femininity that was used was developed with college students, and some of its masculine tratis, such as "athletic," may not be pertinent to older women. In another study (Chiriboga and Thurnher, 1976), older women saw themselves as becoming more assertive, less dependent, and more capable of solving problems and as exerting more authority at home than they did when younger. Among middle-aged, blue-collar workers, women became more self-assertive, autonomous, and competent whereas those qualities decreased in men (Fiske, 1980).

Not all studies have found androgyny appearing so early in the life cycle. For example, one group of middle-aged parents showed traditional sex differences although their children were no longer at home (Feldman, Biringen, and Nash, 1981). It was not until men and women became grandparents that the androgynous trend appeared, with women showing increased autonomy and men showing increased compassion and tenderness.

How strongly do these findings depend on cohort effects? We do not know, but in almost every case the studies have been cross-sectional in nature, and even those results vary from study to study. Changing cultural standards, especially the tendency for young men to take more responsibility for child care and for

As men grow older, many move toward androgyny, incorporating such concepts as "gentleness" and "loves children" into their self-concept.

young women to see their occupations as more than just a way to mark time until they have children, could lead to sharp shifts in future decades. As we will see in the next section, the course of emotional development also may be different for men and women.

EMOTIONAL DEVELOPMENT

Adults seem to progress through a series of stages in which their motivations and emotional energies are focused on different issues. The timing of this progression is not specific, but seems related to the life circumstances of the individual. For example, establishing a career or becoming a parent leads to similar motivational and emotional changes in people regardless of their age. In a society with rigid age-related roles, nearly all people of the same age would be occupied with the same issues, but in an age-irrelevant society, which the United States may be moving closer to, the stages of emotional development would be less closely related to age. Somewhat different, but related, theories of adult emotional development have been put forward by Erik Erikson, Daniel Levinson, and Roger Gould.

ERIKSON'S PSYCHOSOCIAL THEORY OF DEVELOPMENT

The most comprehensive theory of emotional development was set forth by Erik Erikson (1980a; 1982). It is the only theory that covers the entire life span and the only one that considers late adulthood in any depth. Erikson's theory grew out of Freudian psychoanalysis, but shifts the spotlight from the child within the family to the individual within a changing, evolving society. Erikson's theory is organismic, but his focus on the interaction of individual, society, and history has led some developmentalists (Buss, 1979; Riegel, 1977) to regard it as also being dialectical. The importance of social and historical factors shows clearly in Erikson's biographies of Gandhi (1969) and Martin Luther (1962), in which their accomplishments are seen to depend not only on their talents but also on the fact that their personal conflicts were exactly what were needed for them to be able to resolve the problems of a particular historical situation (Erikson and Hall, 1983).

Erikson refers to his theory as a theory of "ego development," meaning that he is tracing the development of the conscious self throughout life. In devising his theory, Erikson drew on his clinical experience as a psychoanalyst and on his studies of healthy adolescents and of the Sioux and Yurok Native American tribes. The theory is meant to apply to both sexes and, because of its cross-cultural background, to people in all societies. Whether emotions and motivation develop similarly in men and women will be discussed in a later section.

Erikson divides the life span into eight stages, from infancy to old age, and in each developmental stage there is a characteristic emotional crisis that arises out of the conflict between two opposing trends (Fig. 10.2). The life task of each period is to resolve its conflict so that the self is strengthened, "laying another cornerstone" for the mature personality (Erikson, 1962). Erikson's use of the word "crisis" is not meant to indicate impending disaster, but to stress the fact that the resolution of the conflict can send development in either direction, either fostering or impairing it. In each stage of development, the social world widens, so that the infant, whose society began with a dim image of the first caretaker—generally the mother, at last becomes an elder whose view of the world encompasses all humanity.

The Stages of Childhood

In infancy, the first stage of development, the individual faces the conflict between *trust* and *distrust*. The task of this first year of life is to develop a basic trust, an attitude toward the world and the self, in which the baby feels certain that caregivers will be present when needed and comes to regard himself or herself as basically trustworthy. Out of basic trust develops hope, which is the ego strength of infancy.

After the successful resolution of this—or any—developmental crisis, the defeated quality (in this case, mistrust) does not disappear from a person's personality. Instead, the balance between the opposing trends shifts, so that trust dominates mistrust, but a certain degree of mistrust continues (and is needed) throughout life. A person without a trace of mistrust would be gullible and constantly

	1	2	3	4	5	6	7	8
Old Age VIII								Integrity vs. Despair **WISDOM**
Adulthood VII							Generativity vs. Stagnation **CARE**	
Young Adulthood VI						Intimacy vs. Isolation **LOVE**		
Adolescence V					Identity vs. Identity Confusion **FIDELITY**			
School Age IV				Industry vs. Inferiority **COMPETENCE**				
Play Age III			Initiative vs. Guilt **PURPOSE**					
Early Childhood II		Autonomy vs. Shame, Doubt **WILL**						
Infancy I	Basic Trust vs. Basic Mistrust **HOPE**							

FIGURE 10.2   Erikson's stages of development. From the major conflict in each life stage, a different strength may develop. Erikson places the stages in a steplike arrangement in order to stress the fact that each step grows out of the previous one and that the strengths and weaknesses of each period are present in some form all during life.

taken advantage of. A person without any trust would be suspicious of others and withdraw from society.

In the second stage, which lasts until about the age of 3, children first feel the impact of socialization. At the same time that they are beginning to adapt their wishes and needs to the forms of society, they are learning to divide the world into "I" and "you," "me" and "mine." The developmental crisis is the struggle of *autonomy* (or self-determination) against *doubt* and *shame*. As children learn to do things "for themselves" within the context of the family, they need to be protected against experiences that make them feel ashamed. Shame leads to self-doubt and the loss of self-esteem, and autonomy requires self-control without any loss of self-esteem. If autonomy predominates over shame, the basic strength of early childhood, a rudimentary will, develops.

Erikson sees several consequences of the failure to develop autonomy. If doubt and shame prevail, the child may develop into a compulsive adult who is overcontrolled in matters of time, money, and affection. Or the result may be an adult whose abiding wish to "get away with things" is accompanied by an apologetic, ashamed manner. Yet successful development does not eliminate shame or doubt from life, and a certain amount is present in healthy personalities.

During the later preschool years, children are in the third developmental stage, which Erikson calls the "play age." In the years from 3 to about 6, the child's physical, cognitive, and linguistic skills are developing rapidly. Building on their budding sense of autonomy, they are now ready to develop initiative, taking the responsibility for planning and executing various tasks purely for the joy of being active.

The play age corresponds to Freud's Oedipal stage, when a child is attracted to the parent of the opposite sex and wishes to push the parent of the same sex out of the way. In resolving this illicit attraction, the child identifies with the parent of the same sex and, during the process, develops a conscience. Until this time, a child whose misdeeds were discovered felt only shame. Now the child anticipates the discovery and fears being "found out"; guilt has developed.

And so the developmental crisis of the play age is the struggle between *initiative* and *guilt*. When initiative predominates, a sense of direction or purpose, which is the basic strength of the play age, flourishes. When guilt dominates initiative, the child becomes convinced that he or she is basically "bad." The adult filled with guilt may become excessively inhibited or develop a self-righteous moralism. Instead of seeing the possibilities of life, he or she is concerned with what cannot or should not be done.

As children begin school, they enter the next developmental stage, and their social world widens beyond the family. Children learn to gain recognition by producing things, and a sense of industry begins to develop. As they learn to make things, they discover that completing a task brings pleasure. They gain experience in the tools of the culture, learn its technology, and begin acquiring the skills they will need as adult workers. The crisis of the school age is the struggle between this new sense of *industry* and *inferiority*. If industry predominates, the child will develop the basic strength of the school age, a sense of competence. If instead the child feels inadequate and becomes convinced that his or her skills are not up to the requirements of the new world of school, a sense of inferiority develops.

Adolescence and Identity

Adolesence, the fifth of Erikson's stages, is important because identity is a central concept in Erikson's theory, and it is during adolesence that a sense of identity develops. By **identity**, Erikson means that an individual possesses a stable sense of self that is confirmed by experience, so that the individual's self-perception matches the perceptions others have of him or her. This new identity is not simply an extension of the self-concept of childhood. As adolescents go through a period of rapid physical growth and attain genital maturity, develop new cognitive abilities, and face choices that will determine adult roles, they begin to question their resolution of the crises of preceding developmental stages. Each aspect of self-concept is reevaluated, and the adolescent begins to form a new ego-identity that will enable him or her to fit within the wider social world.

The developmental struggle of adolescence is between *identity* and *identity confusion*. The development of a firm ego identity is a major task, and society appears to recognize this by allowing adolescents a **psychosocial moratorium**—a time between childhood and adulthood when choices can be worked on but commitment is not yet made. Young people are free to experiment with various role choices. During this moratorium, the group fads and clannishness of adolescence can serve as a temporary defense against identity confusion.

Occupational identity is one obvious concern of adolescence, but not the only one. There is the matter of gender identity, of just how the adolescent will incorporate masculinity or femininity into the self-concept. Ideals suddenly become important. The adolescent can think about religion, ethics, morality, and politics in a new way; and choices made in these areas will affect choices of other kinds. The task of forming an identity faces both boys and girls at this age, but the content of the task may differ, for it is heavily influenced by culture (Erikson and Hall, 1983).

Once ego identity is established, fidelity, which is the basic strength of this stage, can emerge. The individual is able to commit his or her loyalty to some cause or goal. When the young person makes no occupational or ideological commitment, identity confusion predominates. As Erikson (1980a) describes identity confusion, deep inside, you do not know whether you are a man (or woman), whether you will ever be attractive, whether you will be able to master your drives, who you really are, who you want to be, what you look like to others, or how to make the right decisions without committing yourself to the wrong friend, sexual partner, leader, or career.

Stages of Adult Development

Once past adolescence, we are into the realm of adult development. It was necessary to trace the earlier stages because the way each crisis is resolved affects the nature of the developmental conflict in all subsequent stages. In addition, the strengths (or weaknesses) of each period are present in some form throughout life. For example, hope, the strength that grows out of the infant's struggle between trust and mistrust, in old age becomes faith; and autonomy affects adult independence in matters relating to occupation and politics. Adulthood encompasses three stages of emotional development that roughly correspond to young adulthood, middle adulthood, and older adulthood.

In young adulthood, the task is to develop *intimacy*, a development that requires the prior establishment of some sense of identity. In intimacy, young adults are able to fuse their identities and commit themselves to relationships that demand sacrifice and compromise. In the developmental crisis of young adulthood, intimacy struggles with *isolation*. Out of successful resolution of the struggle, emerges the basic strength of young adulthood: love. When the struggle is not resolved successfully, isolation predominates, and a person's relationships with others lack spontaneity, warmth, or any deep emotional exchange. There may be a fear of intimacy, in which fusion with another is seen as a loss of personal iden-

The major task of middle adulthood is to develop generativity, a quality this public school teacher expresses through his work.

tity. The establishment of sexual relationships does not necessarily signify the development of intimacy. In fact, a person whose sexual activity is purely recreational may feel extremely isolated because he or she never perceives the partner as a person (Erikson and Hall, 1983).

In middle adulthood, the struggle is between **generativity** and the forces of *self-absorption and stagnation.* Generativity concerns the establishment of the next generation. It can be expressed in the bearing and rearing of children, in guiding other people's children or younger adults, and in contributing to society through productivity or creativity. Generative acts are infused with the strength of middle adulthood, which is care. And for care to develop, a person must possess the strengths of previous developmental stages: hope, will, purpose, competence, fidelity, and love. Some people express generativity through their occupations: the teacher, the artist, the writer, the nurse, the physician. Some express generativity by working to maintain or improve society. In fact, Erikson sees generativity as a driving power in human organization.

When generativity fails to predominate, stagnation pervades a person's life. Such people may develop a need for "pseudo-intimacy." They are generally bored and tend to treat themselves as if they were their own spoiled only children, indulging their every whim. Erikson believes that generativity is an expression of a human drive to procreate and that people who decide not to have children need to direct their generativity into a socially fruitful channel in order to avoid an eventual sense of frustration and loss (Erikson and Hall, 1983).

The eighth and final stage of the life cycle is later adulthood, when the task is to develop *ego integrity*, a sense of coherence and wholeness to one's life. A person accepts that life, sees meaning in it, and believes that he or she did the best that could be done under the circumstances. The struggle in late adulthood is between integrity and *despair,* and when despair predominates, a person fears death and wishes desperately for another chance. A degree of despair is healthy. A person with integrity might still despair over certain things in his or her own life or about the existence of exploited people (Erikson and Hall, 1983). When integrity predominates, wisdom, which is the strength of old age, can emerge. Along with wisdom goes a shift in identity. Out of the psychosocial identity that first came together in adolescence emerges an existential identity, which comes from facing the border of life and realizing the utter relativity of your own psychosocial identity (Erikson and Erikson, 1981).

As life expectancy has increased, Erikson has indicated that later adulthood may be changing in this society. He has suggested that the stage of generativity may stretch farther into the life span, lasting much longer than it generally has in the past (Erikson and Hall, 1983). This may mean a lengthening of the period of middle adulthood. Productivity and creativity are still open to people for decades after they can no longer bear and care for young children. Older adults have traditionally expressed generativity as grandparents, but Erikson foresees longer working careers and a larger proportion of older artists, writers, and musicians in society.

Testing the Theory

The intricate meshing of individual, society, and history that is the core of Erikson's theory harmonizes with the developmental view of the human life span, but its complexity makes the theory difficult to test. Clear definitions of terms are not given nor are the concepts clearly defined. This vagueness means that different researchers may use different objective standards when setting up a study.

Most tests of the theory have focused on the development of identity among college students. The bulk of such studies support the theory. Young people—both men and women—appear to consider alternative identities during this period and form personally meaningful commitments (Waterman, 1982). In one study (LaVoie, 1976), both male and female adolescents who had established identities were confident of their sexual identity, had a sense of basic trust and industry and good self-concepts, and seemed generally well adjusted. Adolescents who had not yet established firm identities seemed generally maladjusted and lacked personality integration. Other researchers (Marcia, 1976) have found a connection between identity status in the college years and the development of intimacy 6 years after graduation.

A sequential study has also provided some support for Erikson's theory (Whitbourne and Waterman, 1979). When college students were given a self-report scale that tapped the opposing qualities in Erikson's first six stages and were retested 10 years later, the general trend was toward growth in trust, autonomy, initiative, industry, identity, and intimacy over the decade, with the largest increases appearing in industry, identity, and intimacy—the qualities developed between childhood and young adulthood. At the same time, a second group of college students filled out the self-report scale, providing a cohort comparison. A sex difference appeared between college women in 1966 and those in 1976, with the younger cohort scoring much higher on industry as opposed to inferiority. Whether this difference was due to changes in the university's recruiting procedure or changes in sex roles could not be established. However, the researchers believe that their results indicate predictable change, as opposed to stability, in adult personality.

Some longitudinal studies of personality seem to support Erikson's theory. The life patterns of a group of Harvard men generally followed the adult stages of the theory through middle adulthood, when the study ended (Valliant, 1977). At the age of 47, men in the Harvard Growth Study who seemed most successful, in terms of maturation, adaptive style, and adjustment to the world, tended to have negotiated the first seven stages of the cycle gracefully. Those who seemed least successful tended to mistrust themselves and the world, to have problems with autonomy and initiative, to have insecure identities, and to have failed at mastering the task of intimacy; and they were less willing to assume the responsibility for other adults. Other theories of adult development are related to Erikson's view.

LEVINSON'S MALE SEASONS

Psychologist Daniel J. Levinson (Levinson et al., 1978) speaks of his theory of adult development as portraying the "seasons of a man's life." It is an accurate description, for Levinson's theory begins with the close of adolescence, and the primary source was a series of in-depth interviews with 40 men. The theory may also describe the course of women's emotional and social development, but Levinson interviewed no women and made no attempt to apply his findings to them.

The men (10 executives, 10 biologists, 10 factory workers, and 10 novelists) whose lives provided the framework for this empirically based theory were born between 1923 and 1934, and they were from 35 to 45 years old when first interviewed. Their socioeconomic backgrounds ranged from working- to upper-class, their religions were diverse (Catholic, Jewish, Protestant), their educational levels extended from high school dropout to doctoral degree, and five of the sample were black. In addition to the extensive interviews (from 10 to 20 hours with each man), Levinson's information included a shortened version of the TAT, an interview with most of the wives, and a follow-up interview with the men two years after the first series of interviews. Added to these descriptive studies was information on the lives of other men—both real and fictional—made by analyzing biographies, fiction, poetry, and drama. The interviews took place during the latter part of young adulthood and early middle age. As each man's interviews were concentrated into a 3-month span, much of the early material is retrospective and necessarily colored by the men's status at the time of the interview, but the material for the midlife period is abundant.

Like Erikson's view, Levinson's conception of the life cycle grows out of psychoanalytic ground. Freud, Jung, and Erikson are the primary influences on Levinson's theory, which is both organismic and dialectical. Levinson acknowledges a kinship between his periods and Erikson's developmental stages, but sees a difference in emphasis. Erikson's focus is within the person whereas Levinson's focus is on the boundary between self and society. He finds no conflict between the two theories and regards his own as building on and expanding the base established by Erikson.

Levinson focuses on **life structure**—the underlying pattern of each man's life. In developing this idea, he tried to consider the nature of the person and the nature of society, regarding each as equal in importance. When external events seemed to affect the pattern, he tried to see how the man's personality might have helped to cause the event and how it buffered the event's effects. When some inner conflict erupted to change the pattern, he tried to see what external events might have touched off the conflict or affected the way it was resolved. This perspective led him to look at the life structure in terms of each man's sociocultural world, aspects of the self, and the man's participation in the world.

When analyzed, nearly all the men's lives fell into a similar pattern. The men progressed through a relatively orderly sequence of periods that alternated between stable phases (when developmental tasks are solved and goals are pursued within the existing life structure) and transitional phases (when the structure is questioned, new possibilities are explored, and crucial choices are made). (See Fig. 10.3.) These choices could change the life structure, perhaps drastically.

The major periods of adulthood in Levinson's theory are these, following a transition from adolescence (17 to 22 years): early adulthood (ages 17 to 45), middle adulthood (ages 40 to 65), and late adulthood (ages 60 to ?). Also projected is a possible new period, late-late adulthood (after 80), which may develop to accommodate the increase in life expectancy. The periods overlap because each is bridged by a 5-year transition that is part of both periods. These transitions between major developmental periods are generally crucial turning points in a man's life. The timing and length of each period and the development that takes place within it vary from man to man depending on the biological, psychological, and social conditions of his life. However, individual differences are usually no greater than 2 or 3 years.

Early Adulthood (ages 17 to 45)
Early adulthood begins during the transition from adolescence, when the developmental task is to move out of the adolescent world. Autonomy, which first occupied a man in early childhood, again becomes a concern. Now he needs to become psychologically independent from his parents. By about the age of 22, the move is complete, and a stable phase of approximately 6 years begins. During this

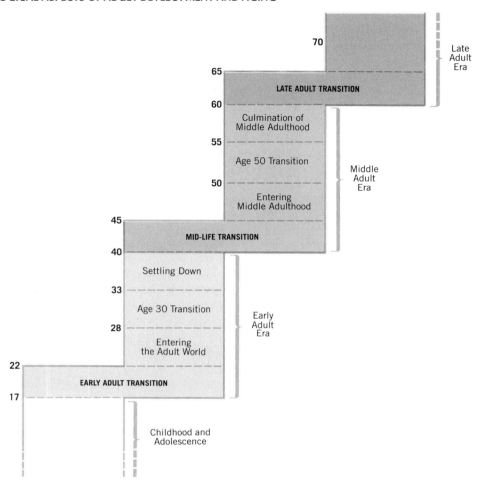

FIGURE 10.3   Levinson's seasons of male development. In Levinson's view of adult development, each adult era is bridged by a transitional period when the life structure is questioned, new possibilities are explored, and crucial choices are made.

Source: D. J. Levinson et al., 1978.

"entering the adult world" phase, a man works to establish himself in the adult world, where he is considered a novice. He attempts to create a stable life structure while keeping open as many options as possible. His life aspirations take shape, and he establishes a "dream." He forms an occupational identity, and he learns to relate to women as friends, collaborators, and intimate companions. These tasks are quite similar to Erikson's developmental tasks of establishing an identity and intimacy. During this period most of the men married and established a home and family. Despite this stress on intimacy, few of Levinson's men had an intimate male friend, and most had never had a close, nonsexual relationship with a woman.

At about 28, the age 30 transition begins, a 5-year span that is often a time of crisis, when flaws in the life structure become apparent and new choices must be made. By 33 the transitional phase has ended, and the second stable phase of early adulthood, the "settling down" period, begins. No longer a novice, a man now works at furthering his career and gaining prestige. He tries to establish a place in society and build a good life. Toward the end of this period, he is busy at "becoming one's own man," when he once again is engaged in the process of establishing his autonomy, this time trying to reduce his dependence on individuals and institutions. If he has had a mentor, an older adult whose advice and counsel has helped him get on with his career, the relationship may be broken off or at least become more distant.

Midlife Transition (ages 40 to 45)

At 40, the midlife transition begins, and a man begins to cross the bridge into middle adulthood. During this period, which usually lasts about 5 years, a man appraises his life thus far, usually discovering that he has failed to match his early aspirations and his dream is out of reach. He loses many of his illusions, reevaluates his job, his marriage, his assumptions and beliefs. He works at making a better balance between self and society. His life structure changes as he makes new choices. Sometimes the choices are drastic: He may divorce, remarry, change jobs, move to another city.

For 80 percent of the men in this study, the midlife transition was a time of major crisis. The process of reappraisal awakened old conflicts, and the men were in emotional turmoil. Slight declines in strength and energy, coupled with the first visible traces of age, became apparent. Men were forced to deal with this evidence and with the recognition that they would one day die. As a man resolved the problems of this transition, he sometimes began to act as a mentor to younger adults, providing them with guidance and counsel. This process is similar to Erikson's idea of attaining a generativity that extends beyond the family by taking responsibility for the next generation.

Middle Adulthood (ages 40–65)

Like early adulthood, middle adulthood consists of two stable phases divided by a transitional phase. During the years from about 45 to 50, a man is "entering middle adulthood." With the conflicts of the midlife transition resolved, life may be more satisfying and productive than at any other time. Active questioning seems to be over. The task of building a new life structure based on the choices made during the transition occupies a man for the next 5 years. During this period, qualities like wisdom, judiciousness, and compassion may flourish. Although for many men these years are filled with growth and continued generativity, for others they are a period of stagnation and decline.

As men enter their fifties, they must deal with the age 50 transition. The period is similar to the age 30 transition, when modifications may be made in the life structure. The period may be a time of crisis, especially if a man went through the mid-life transition with little change. Levinson believes that it is impossible to get through middle adulthood without at least one crisis. Once past the transition, another stable phase, the "culmination of middle adulthood," begins. This part of the life span may be one of great fulfillment and is much like the settling down phase of early adulthood. It lasts until the late adult transition, which starts at about the age of 60 and forms the basis for late adulthood.

As none of the men studied by Levinson was older than 47 at the last contact, the theory necessarily becomes sketchy after the midlife transition. Although Levinson believes that the general sequence of development he depicts is universal, he points out that his findings may apply only to men in this culture during this historical period. And as all the men in the study came from the Northeastern section of the United States, the applicability of its findings to men in other areas of the country has not been tested. We don't know, for example, whether a Midwestern farmer or a West Virginian coal miner experiences these sequences in the same way as men in the industrialized Northeast. Perhaps a look at another view of adult development would be helpful.

GOULD'S TRANSFORMATIONS

Psychiatrist Roger Gould (1975, 1978) sees adult development as progressing through a series of transformations, in which self-concepts are reformulated as childhood illusions are faced and conflicts are resolved. His view of development grew out of a cross-sectional study he designed after noting that outpatients who came to the university psychiatric clinic tended to have similar problems at similar ages. After observing men and women from adolescence through middle adulthood in group therapy sessions, he studied 524 white, middle-class American men and women between the ages of 16 and 60. From their responses to a questionnaire, in which they responded to such statements as "My personality is pretty well set" and "Life doesn't change much from year to year," he discerned a pattern to life made up of predictable transitions, in which concerns were similar to those expressed by the patients he had observed. Like Levinson, Gould found adulthood to be a time of change, with seven distinguishable phases—not a time of stable emotions and motivation.

Late adolescence, the years from 16 to 22, was a time of ambivalence. The major concern was forming an identity and leaving the parental world. Among young adults, aged 22 to 28, autonomy seemed established, and their energies were devoted to attaining their goals.

The next group of adults, between the ages of 28 and 34, seemed to be going through something that resembled Levinson's age 30 transition. They were questioning some of the goals they had set in their early twenties, and many were re-evaluating their marriages. Fewer agreed that "For me, marriage has been a good thing," and many more indicated that they wished "my mate would accept me for what I am as a person." Economic problems became sharper, and there was an increase in the number agreeing that they did not have enough money to do what they wished.

Adults approaching the midlife decade, between the ages of 35 and 43, were still questioning values, but a new element had entered the picture. Time had begun to press sharply, and with it came the realization that any major life changes that were to be made must be made soon. An awareness of mortality developed, and the meaning of work began to change. This phase of life, like Levinson's midlife transition, was an unstable period, full of turmoil and personal discomfort.

Once into middle age, the years from 43 to 50 became stable. Marital satisfaction rose, friends became more important, and money seemed less important. There was a positive acceptance of life. This acceptance increased during the fifties among the oldest age group in the study. An awareness of time running out sharpened, and more people said that there was not enough time left to do all the things they wanted to do. Concerns about health also rose, but personal relationships became even more important, and marital satisfaction was even higher than it was during the forties. Many indicated a flowering of generativity—a desire to contribute in some way to society.

The results of Gould's study agree in good part with Levinson's findings. At the approximate time Gould's cross-sectional data were collected in Southern California, about 1970 or 1971, the Northeastern men in Levinson's study were being interviewed, and many were in the midlife transition. It is possible that the widespread midlife crisis that appeared in both studies is in part a reflection of cohort effects. One of the questions that faces developmentalists is whether the midlife crisis exists.

SEX DIFFERENCES IN EMOTIONAL DEVELOPMENT

From time to time, we have noted that male and female emotional development is probably not identical. There is good reason for this belief. In addition to whatever basic biological differences separate the sexes, from birth men and women have been pushed into separate sex roles. As we saw in the discussion of personality, they have been socialized to behave in different ways, to value different things, to have different attitudes toward life, and to fill different roles in society.

The Different Worlds of Men and Women

Because of their socialization, women and men may experience the world in different ways. After studying the way in which people respond to moral dilemmas, Carol Gilligan (1982) has concluded that theories of adult development omit women and so present a lopsided picture. Throughout childhood, separation and autonomy are seen as basic to masculinity whereas attachment and empathy are seen as basic to femininity. By adolescence, each sex has a different interpersonal orientation and a different range of social experiences.

IS THERE A MIDLIFE CRISIS?

Both Levinson and Gould discovered the presence of a midlife crisis in the adults they studied. The concept has become widely popular, in large part owing to journalist Gail Sheehy's *Passages* (1976). This book, which relied on Levinson's and Gould's theories, used interviews with men and women to locate a ''predictable crisis'' at about the age of 35 in women and at 40 in men. *Passages* was selected by three book clubs and became a national best-seller. Portions of the book appeared in eight magazines, ranging from *Family Circle* and *McCall's* to *New York*. It was syndicated in newspapers throughout the country. As a result, Americans who do any reading at all are familiar with the midlife crisis that awaits each one of us. Or does it?

When developmentalists talk about a **midlife crisis**, they are generally referring to a state of physical and psychological distress that arises when developmental tasks threaten to overwhelm a person's internal resources and systems of social support (Cytrynbaum et al., 1980). This situation appears to be more ominous than the developmental crisis in each of Erikson's stages and goes beyond the concept of a midlife transition.

A number of researchers believe that the midlife crisis is neither widespread nor inevitable, and some even object to the term. George Valliant (1977), who reported the results of a 40-year longitudinal study of 95 Harvard men, complains that midlife crisis brings to mind ''the renegade minister who leaves behind four children and the congregation that loved him in order to drive off in a magenta Porsche with a twenty-five-year-old striptease artist'' (p. 222). Valliant agrees that some inner exploration and reevaluation take place during the forties, but he fails to see high drama or major crisis in the process.

Many of the men in his study divorced, changed jobs, or became depressed between 35 and 50; but Valliant notes that divorce, job disenchantment, and depression occur at about the same frequency throughout adult life and that crisis is the exception, not the rule, at midlife. Some of the men in his study said that the years between 35 and 49 were the happiest in their lives. Of course, these men were not typical: they were white, upper-socioeconomic level, well-educated Harvard men, and the intent of the study was to show development under the most favorable circumstances. And perhaps cohort influence spared these men; they were born between 1920 and 1922, making them from 6 to 12 years older than the men in Levinson's study, who had reached or passed the midlife transition. Their experiences in the Great Depression of the 1930s and World War II would have been very different and could have affected subsequent development.

Investigators (Baruch, Barnett, and River, 1982) who conducted a 3-year study of American women suggest that if the study of middle age had begun with women, the midlife crisis might never have become part of our vocabulary. They focused on women between the ages of 35 and 55 and found that it was during their twenties and not at midlife that uncertainties and dissatisfactions tended to surface. These women rarely mentioned anticipated developmental events (such as marriage, childbirth, or menopause) as marking major turning points in their lives. Instead, they reported that unexpected events (such as divorce, automobile accidents, or job transfers) or normative events that occurred off-schedule (such as the early death of a parent) were likely to cause life crises.

The midlife crisis also failed to show up in the lives of men and women who took part in the California Intergenerational Studies. These adults, though mostly middle-class, are less privileged than the men in the Harvard Growth Study. Some were born between 1920 and 1922; the rest, in 1928 and 1929, so that they span the age range in the two studies. Even among the men, the crisis was not typical. At midlife, most men found their jobs satisfying and their careers rewarding (Clausen, 1981). Both men and women appeared to have developed cognitive breadth and become more self-confident, insightful, introspective, and more open to others. They seemed better equipped to handle stress, deliberately processing new information, integrating it with their knowledge, and then using their understanding to reach their goals (Haan, 1981).

A direct attempt to locate the male midlife crisis found that it occurred in only a few men and that it could come at any time from 30 to 60 (McCrae and Costa, 1982). In another study,

more than 300 of the men who took part in McCrae and Costa's earlier study of personality structure responded to a series of statements reflecting the presence of a life crisis. The statements ranged from "I find myself becoming more emotional than I used to be" to "I feel the years I have spent at my job were meaningless and unfulfilling" (Costa and McCrae, 1978, p. 136). Again, a crisis was as likely to appear before 40 or after 45 as during the years of the midlife transition. The men who did have a crisis tended to be men who were high on the neurotic dimension of personality. These researchers feel that most men never have a midlife crisis, that a crisis can occur at any age, and that when it does erupt, it is usually due to a long-standing emotional instability or neuroticism.

Finally, among the men and women studied over the years at the University of Chicago, no evidence could be found for the midlife crisis (Neugarten, 1973). As adults made the transition to middle age, new developmental issues arose, having to do with family roles, generativity, and occupational life. Men and women seemed to have less energy and power and became more introspective and reflective, but the drama of a major life crisis was missing.

Some researchers have suggested that the midlife crisis is a white, middle-class phenomenon that has developed because of increased leisure, high technology, and the acceptance of self-fulfillment. Freed from the toil of past centuries, a large segment of the population is now free to engage in introspection and self-expres-

IS THERE A MIDLIFE CRISIS? (*Continued*)

sion (Cytrynbaum et al., 1980). Other researchers (Haan, 1981) believe that the midlife crisis may have been exaggerated by taking the self-descriptions of participants at face value or by using the concerns of people in therapy as a framework for studying the average person. A man or woman in therapy is more likely to dwell on personal problems than on personal strengths.

Bernice Neugarten (1979b) has suggested that the normal turning points in life, such as marriage, parenthood,

occupational achievement, or retirement, lead to changes in self-concept and identity. But when they are expected and occur "on time," a crisis is unlikely to develop. When we anticipate an event, whether it be graduation or widowhood, we tend to rehearse it mentally beforehand. When the event finally arrives, much of the anguish has been worked through. Our strategies for handling it are adequate, and our sense of the life cycle's continuity remains whole.

Erikson has indicated that the various developmental tasks do not differ for men and women, but that the content of the tasks may vary from one society to another and at different times in the same society (Erikson and Hall, 1983). However, Gilligan sees the disparity between the sexes as so great as to place them on the opposite sides of a great gulf.

In Gilligan's analysis of emotional development, relationships are at the center of women's experience of life. The key to female development is women's recognition of the continuing importance of attachment throughout the life span. As a result, they place autonomy and identity in the context of relationships and view morality as a problem of care and responsibility. Underlying the ethic of care is a psychologic of relationships. Because relationships are central, moral problems can be considered only in a context that takes into account the consequences of a decision.

In male development, autonomy is ripped from the web of relationships. Separation defines the self, and this self-definition affects later intimacy and generativity. For example, in Levinson's theory, which stresses autonomy, relationships with others are subordinate to the male dream. All his men seem distant from others, and few of them have close friends. Morality is seen as a problem of rights and justice. Underlying the ethic of justice is the formal logic of fairness. Because relationships do not enter into rights, moral problems can be abstracted from context and considered in isolation.

Although Erikson attempts to integrate the female ethic of care into his tasks of intimacy and generativity, the path that leads to them makes the integration difficult. Between trust and intimacy, he places only autonomous tasks: autonomy, initiative, industry, and identity. When men confront the task of intimacy, their primary experience has been one of separation, for society endorses these values as masculine. For men, intimacy changes their adolescent identity and prepares them for the struggle between generativity and stagnation that can lead to the ethic of care.

As women have worked on these tasks, society has pulled them the other way, teaching them to be dependent, gentle, and compassionate. Indeed, adolescent women may be working on identity and intimacy simultaneously, for they tend to define themselves in terms of relationships. From childhood they are pointed toward generativity and its ethic of care, and for many the postponement of its development until middle adulthood, when their children may be grown, seems strange.

The consequences of this socialization are seen by Gilligan as being responsible for much of the misunderstanding between men and women in all areas of life. Both use the same moral vocabulary, but for men and women the words describe radically differing experiences of self and social relationships. Communication becomes garbled, and cooperation and care become the casualties. One way to consider Giligan's perspective is to look at a longitudinal study in which sex differences were analyzed.

Paths to Emotional Maturity

Among the men and women in the California Intergenerational Studies, the relationship between a person's adolescent personality and the culture's sex roles was important in determining the course of adult emotional development. Looking only at men and women who were above the mean in psychological health at age 50, Florine Livson (1981) found that those who adhered to traditional sex roles had a relatively smooth course, being above the mean all through adulthood. Those who adopted nontraditional sex roles traveled a bumpier road; they tended to be in relatively poor psychological health at age 40, then improved dramatically during the decade, becoming just as successful at age 50 as the traditional men and women. By adolescence, each group had developed a central personality style that evolved and became more complex over the years. In all groups, intelligence scores and socioeconomic level were similar.

Women' Paths   All the traditional women were married, although about one third had been divorced. Almost one third of the nontraditional women were divorced, but fewer had remarried, and about one third worked full time. They were less family- and home-oriented than the traditional women, but their relationships with children did not differ.

In high school, traditional women were sociable and popular, conventional, and clearly feminine. They were establishing firm identities. At 40, traditional women showed no sign of a midlife crisis. They were trusting, sympathetic, and cooperative, if not submissive. Still gregarious, they had developed intimacy. They continued to grow emotionally, and by 50, their gregariouness had taken on a giving quality, and their sociability had become nurturing. They had developed generativity. They were well-functioning, conforming, extroverted women with high interpersonal skills whose personality structure harmonized with the traditional wife-mother roles. Their main satisfaction came from affiliation with others.

As adolescents, nontraditional women were more ambitious, more intellectual, and more unconventional in their thinking than traditional women. They, too, were forming firm identities. At 40, the picture changed. Nontraditional women were unpredictable, irritable, and their intellectual skills were no longer apparent. Their achievement needs unmet, their "unfeminine" characteristics suppressed, they seemed to be in a midlife crisis. Their identities were no longer stable. By 50, their crisis was solved, and their nontraditional identities were reestablished. Their intellectual skills were flourishing, along with insight and skepticism. They were more ambitious than traditional women, more autonomous, and more spontaneous, finding it easy to express their feelings. Their main satisfaction came from developing themselves.

Men's Paths Both groups of psychologically healthy men were successful in their careers, with strong family ties and conventional life-styles. They viewed their health as satisfactory. All had married, and two in each group had divorced and remarried.

As adolescents, traditional men were concerned with controlling their impulses and lacked emotional spontaneity. They were skeptical, objective, and unconventional in their thinking. Their main focus was on achievement. At 40, they were productive and dependable. Competence, rationality, achievement, and self-control were important to them. However, they were beginning to express their feelings and appeared to have developed intimacy. At 50, they continued to be productive. They were highly ambitious, had realistic perceptions of themselves, and valued self-discipline and rationality.

In adolescence, nontraditional men were emotionally expressive, somewhat impulsive, and humorous. They failed to choose between their expressive and assertive styles, leaving the establishment of identity open. At 40, they had adopted an assertive style that was power-oriented and exploitative. They were angry, defensive, anxious, and distrustful. They no longer expressed their emotions, but had adopted an artificial identity, which was an exaggerated stereotype of masculine behavior. Like nontraditional women, they had an identity conflict. By 50, the conflict was resolved. They had cast off their exaggerated masculinity and were moving into the stage of intimacy. Once again, they were emotionally expressive, gregarious, and outgoing.

The development of men and women in this study gave some support to Erikson's theory. The traditional men and women tended to pass through the stages at the appropriate times, but the nontraditionals seemed unable to adhere to the timetable. At 40, they seemed in a midlife crisis. According to Livson (1981), the developmental paths of nontraditional women and men were parallel because both had personalities that did not fit conventional sex roles. During young adulthood, both groups accepted traditional sex roles, leading them to suppress their cross-sex traits. The suppression caused them to pause, if not regress, on the path of emotional development. As they moved toward middle age, their social roles changed, and they felt free to express this "hidden" side of their personalities. Their psychological health improved, and they were ready to resume their developmental tasks. These men and women were born between 1920 and 1922, when sex roles were more rigid than they are today. Because of the loosening of sex roles, the same bumpy path may not face future generations of adults.

SUMMARY

Personality assures each person of individuality, and the stability of **traits** indicates a degree of predictability in behavior. Personality may be assessed by standardized, objective tests (self-report inventories or rating scales), by subjective self-assessment, or by projective tests.

Only a minority of old people fit the stereotypical picture of aging; most personality characteristics do not change after young adulthood. Consistent changes with age have been found for only one personality trait—introversion—and disengagement appears to characterize only a minority of older adults. Researchers who have looked at **personality dimensions** have identified three dimensions (neuroticism, extraversion, and openness), which show no longitudinal changes in level but some change in the relative strength of the traits that make up the dimension of openness. Longitudinal studies indicate that **normative stability** in personality is the rule but that changes can occur when life situations are disrupted. Because most studies of personality have focused on white, middle-class men, caution must be used in generalizing the results.

There appear to be no age-related changes in happiness or life satisfaction. Housing arrangements, health, high activity, personality, and expectations appear to be related to life satisfaction. No general effect of aging on **self-concept** has been found.

Men and women differ in personality, but variations among each sex are generally wider than the average differences between the sexes. During young adulthood, men and women have similar levels of self-esteem, with the highest levels found in those who are **androgynous**. On the average, women are less self-confident and less aggressive than men. Some researchers believe that age tends to increase androgyny in both sexes.

Erik Erikson has proposed the most comprehensive theory of emotional development, in which each person passes through eight stages from infancy to old age. At each stage, there is an emotional crisis that arises out of the conflict between two opposing trends, and in each stage, the individual's social world widens. **Identity**, which is central to the theory, develops during adolescence, when society allows a **psychosocial moratorium** that permits the individual to work on the development of ego identity. In young adulthood, the task is to develop intimacy; in middle adulthood, to develop **generativity**; and in old age, to develop integrity.

In Daniel Levinson's theory of adult development, each man's **life structure** goes through an orderly sequence of periods that alternate between stable phases and transitional phases, which are crucial turning points. In Roger Gould's view of adult development, each person progresses through a series of transformations, in which self-concept is reformulated. Both Levinson and Gould found the

midlife crisis to be prevalent although other research has not indicated that crises increase in frequency at midlife. The midlife crisis may be a white, middle-class phenomenon of the late twentieth century, or the concept may have developed when individual self-reports exaggerated the nature of developmental issues.

Socialization appears to widen emotional differences between men and women. Women are socialized to place autonomy and identity in the context of relationships and to view morality as a problem of care and responsibility. Men are socialized to remove autonomy from any relational context, to subordinate relationships to personal goals, and to view morality as a problem of rights and justice. Among psychologically healthy middle-aged men and women, those who adhered to traditional sex roles followed a smooth course of emotional development and adhered to Erikson's timetable of stages, but those who adopted nontraditional sex roles had a period just before middle age when their emotional development either stalled or regressed. However, by the end of their forties, they were as psychologically healthy as the traditional men and women.

KEY TERMS

androgynous	**personality**
generativity	**personality dimension**
identity	**psychosocial moratorium**
life structure	**self-concept**
midlife crisis	**trait**
normative stability	

PART FOUR

SOCIOLOGICAL ASPECTS OF ADULT DEVELOPMENT AND AGING

11

RELATIONSHIPS WITHIN GENERATIONS

I n Boston, 16 adults, whose ages range from 23 to 84, have formed a "family." Members of the Shared Living House, a commune that was established in 1978 by the Back Bay Aging Concerns Committee, reside in a former boardinghouse. Each contributes to the rent, and each shares in household tasks. Nathan Saperstein, the oldest member of the commune, is responsible for polishing the furniture and stair railings, for making purchases at the local hardware store, and for seeing that the premises are secure—he checks all the doors at eleven o'clock each night and puts out the lights. Saperstein, a bachelor who used to live in an apartment by himself, explains, "Other places you don't even know your neighbor. Here, you're part of a family" (Zabarsky, 1982).

A commune of unrelated adults does not fit the traditional picture of important adult relationships, in which a woman and man marry and establish a family. Indeed, the nuclear family is alive and well although its structure is often complicated by the pattern of divorce and remarriage. But the rising tide of single adults, made up of the never-married, divorced, and widowed men and women in our society, has not eliminated the need for relationships. Not all unattached people want to live by themselves, and some have formed unconventional units to avoid social isolation. Arrangements like the Shared Living House provide social contacts without restricting privacy or independence.

The path these men and women have chosen is not a common one, but it reminds us that interindividual differences need to be recognized no matter what aspect of adulthood we consider. In this chapter, we will investigate the nature of adult relationships that are usually, but not always, between members of the same generation. First, we look briefly at the importance of social contexts for individual behavior and development. In exploring specific types of relationships, we begin with mates, considering the way we select a marital partner, the roles within marriage, and the progression of the relationship across adulthood. The effect of divorce, remarriage, and widowhood are examined, as well as ways of handling intimate relationships outside the traditional marriage. Whether or not a person marries, relationships with siblings continue and can have powerful effects on life. After exploring the relationship between adult siblings, we close with a consideration of the course of friendship across adulthood.

THE IMPORTANCE OF RELATIONSHIPS

"No man is an island, entire of itself," wrote poet John Donne in the seventeenth century. Donne was referring to all of us when he wrote those words, and they evoke general agreement. The importance of social relationships and the serious consequences of social isolation are usually taken for granted. Individual development occurs in a human context, and the person who grows up without social interaction or affection has little chance of being normal. Even in adulthood, the absence of other people can be devastating. It is no accident that prisoners are punished by being thrust into "solitary."

Perhaps the best-known example of an isolated person is Genie, a young woman who spent her first 13½ years in almost total isolation. She was confined to a small bedroom, where no one played with her or talked to her. Her only contact with other human beings occurred when her nearly blind mother entered the room to feed her or her father came in and abused her. When Genie finally was discovered, she was, in the words of a researcher who studied her, "unsocialized, primitive, hardly human" (Curtiss, 1977, p. 9). Placed in a foster home, Genie responded to other people. Gradually, she was socialized, and her eagerness to join in group interactions soon became apparent to all. Genie's experience supports the contention of philosopher and social psychologist George Herbert Mead (1934) that we could not become human if we were not social. Socialization, the basis for the way we experience life, can take place only in the context of human relationships.

Human relationships are obviously important to early development, and they continue to be central in adulthood as well. Mead went on to say that without social contact we would not remain human. As we saw in Chapter 10, Erik Erikson (1980a) sees our very identity as dependent on social roles and on our meaning in the eyes of other people whereas intimacy and generativity, the developmental tasks of young and middle adulthood, are both social tasks. Other personality theorists (Maslow, 1954) believe that our psychological needs are closely bound up with social relationships and propose that the needs to affiliate with others, to be accepted, and to belong are outweighed only by such basic demands as hunger, thirst, and safety. Some of us require more human contact than others, but few of us are without either mate, kin, or friend.

Among members of the same generation, the closest relationships are generally with sexual partners.

MATES

There appears to be a universal human need for emotional relationships with other people, and the relative strength of this need is linked to sex and age (Huyck, 1982). It seems stronger in women than in men, stronger in younger women than in older women, and stronger in older men than in younger men. As we have seen, women traditionally have been socialized to define themselves in terms of relationships whereas men have been socialized to subordinate relationships to other goals. In American society, a primary means of satisfying the need for human connections is through an intimate relationship with a mate. Studies indicate that married people are healthier than single adults and have a lower rate of mental illness (Traupmann, Eckels, and Hatfield, 1982). Whether being married is good for physical and mental health or people who are healthy are more likely to marry is uncertain, but the relationship consistently turns up.

CHOOSING A MATE

The connection between love and marriage seems natural to us, but we are not always certain just what we mean by the terms "love" and "intimacy." Researchers (Rubin, 1973) often divide love into two kinds: loving and liking. Loving is passionate love; it is a compelling, intense emotion, made up of intimacy (the partners feel they can confide in each other), caring (they would do almost anything for each other), and attachment (they are miserable when separated). Liking is a companionate love; it is a steadier, more tranquil state made up of favorable evaluation (each partner thinks the other is unusually well-adjusted), respect and confidence (each has great confidence in the other's judgment), and perceived similarity (they believe that they are similar and almost always share the same moods). Some relationships are predominately passionate; and some, predominately companionate. Passionate love appears to have a natural life span of about 2 years (Tennov, 1979), but it often settles down into a companionate love marked by moments of passion.

Passionate love may, however, continue to remain important. Among a group of middle-aged women, most of whom had been married for 30 years, passionate love played a significant role in their marital relationship and was strongly correlated with marital and sexual satisfaction (Traupmann, Eckels, and Hatfield, 1982). Continued romance also characterized some of the happy couples in the California Intergenerational Studies. One man, who had been married for nearly 30 years, said, "I still have stars in my eyes" (Skolnick, 1981).

Loving relationships are not always intimate, even when they involve marriage and sexuality. **Intimacy** is an emotional state that is characterized by acceptance, self-disclosure, and feelings of trust and closeness (Rosen and Hall, 1984). It can be expressed in different ways, but it always involves caring and commitment. Although intimacy is generally connected with mates, it can be a part of nonsexual relationships.

In the United States, the ideal marriage is based on an intense romantic relationship. This has not always been true, and in many societies romance is not expected to precede marriage. Marriage may be regarded by the culture as a means of preserving the ancestral line, of transmitting property, and of cementing alliances between families. In traditional India, for example, the parents had a religious and social duty to marry off their children early, and girls were to be wed before their first menstruation (Gagon and Greenblatt, 1978). However, as countries become industrialized, the old patterns slowly give way, and freedom of choice in marital partners tends to develop (Murstein, 1980). The decline of arranged marriages has probably been accelerated by employment among women, which enables them to postpone marriage and to choose a romantic partner.

According to John Money (1977), the American mating system developed from a combination of the Scandinavian and the Mediterranean systems, a mixture of incompatible elements. The tradition of romantic mating is believed to have come from Scandinavia, where young people selected their own mates in an atmosphere of sexual equality. Betrothal and pregnancy were expected to precede marriage, and—as the family was the foundation of the fishing and farming culture—unless

When choosing a mate, people generally select someone of the same religion, race, ethnic background, economic status, intelligence level, and social class.

the woman became pregnant, the marriage was unlikely to take place. In the Mediterranean tradition, family approval was required (although a young man might select his own bride), and the marriage transaction, which involved a dowry from the bride's family, took place in an atmosphere of sexual inequality. The bride was required to be a virgin, and the groom was expected to be sexually experienced. American society combined romantic mate selection with virgin brides and the double sexual standard, a practice that prevailed until the development of cheap, effective contraceptives was followed by a relaxation of the double standard.

Despite the ideal of romantic mate selection, various social factors influence the choice. Most mates tend to be similar in many ways. They are generally of the same religion, race, and ethnic group and have a similar economic status and educational background. This is not accidental. Some sort of contact is required in order to select a mate, and neighborhoods tend to be populated by people of similar backgrounds who send their children to the same schools. Such neighborhood and school segregation limits the chances for young people to meet members of other groups. And although marital choice primarily rests with the individual, many parents still retain a veto power over their children's choice of mate—especially during adolescence and early adulthood (Gagnon and Greenblatt, 1978). As society has become more fluid, marriage across racial, ethnic, and religious groups occurs more often, but the tendency to stay within one's own group remains strong (Murstein, 1980).

The similarity between mates goes further than social background. Marital partners are generally similar in physical attractiveness although the reason for this similarity is not clear. Perhaps we tend to seek out someone who is as attractive as possible, but not so attractive that he or she is likely to reject us. Or perhaps we look for physical attractiveness but are rejected by people who have similar goals and believe they can find better-looking partners.

There is hardly an area of life in which mates are not likely to be similar. Married couples generally have similar attitudes, similar intelligence, similar sex drives, and similar levels of interest in sex. They also tend to have similar personalities, but this trend is much weaker than any of the others (Murstein, 1980). Similarity between mates is lower among couples who marry during pregnancy. In such cases, for example, the likelihood of both partners having the same socioeconomic background drops sharply (Coomb et al., 1970).

In attempting to account for the choice of a marital partner, Bernard Murstein (1980) has proposed an equity theory, in which each person brings certain assets and liabilities to the relationship, and the choice to marry depends on their exchange value. After a stage of initial attraction, people assess the compatibility of their values and attitudes and, if a prospective partner passes this hurdle, they decide whether the pair can function in compatible roles. Because lovers are generally on their best behavior before marriage, neither partner may have enough evidence to make a wise decision. Murstein's research indicates that people with many assets and few liabilities *choose* each other, and that people with fewer assets and more liabilities *settle* for each other. He also found that despite some changes in male and female roles, men continue to have higher status than women, which gives them more power during courtship.

The decision to marry is influenced by the social and economic context, which may vary according to social class and ethnic group. The timing is often a compromise between society's standards (the "proper" age for marriage), economic demands (economic resources, career stage, income), and the urges of the partners (Ankarloo, 1978). Indeed, these external influences may either keep people from thinking about marriage so that no one seems "right" or lead them to perceive members of the other sex as possible marital partners, making a choice imminent.

MARRIAGE

More than nine out of every ten Americans marry at some time. Among middle-aged adults, 94.9 percent of the men and 95.3 percent of the women have been married, but the age at first marriage varies over the years. In 1890, the average woman was 22.0 years old at the time of her first marriage. During the first half of the twentieth century, average marital age dropped, until in 1956 the average age at first marriage was 20.1 years. For the past two decades, marital age has been rising, and by 1980, a woman's age at first marriage was 22.1 (U.S. Bureau of the Census, 1983a). The longest delay occurs among young women who postpone marriage in order to establish careers. Men's age at first marriage also has been increasing over the past 20 years but to a lesser degree, with the average age rising from 22.8 in 1950 to 23.4 in 1979 (U.S. Bureau of the Census, 1982). (See Fig. 11.1.)

| | | | | Who is married? | | | | | |
| | | | | Age | | | | | |
	18–19 Years	20–24 Years	25–29 Years	30–34 Years	35–44 Years	45–54 Years	55–64 Years	65–74 Years	>74 Years
Men	4.2%	28.6%	60.7%	74.7%	82.1%	86.2%	84.7%	83.0%	72.0%
Women	14.7%	44.2%	68.9%	77.1%	80.7%	78.6%	70.3%	50.1%	23.3%

FIGURE 11.1

Source: U.S. Bureau of the Census, *Statistical Abstract of the United States, 1982–1983*, 103d ed., 1982.

Marital Roles

Once married, mates have to learn to live together. During the first year of marriage they generally fall into complementary roles that affect the way decisions are made and tasks divided. For example, one partner may become dominant and the other submissive; or one partner may become nurturant and the other receptive. In any marriage, the division of power between the partners is central to marital roles, with one partner (usually the man) having the upper hand. This is, of course, the traditional marital arrangement, but it does not describe all marriages. One team of researchers (Scanzioni and Scanzioni, 1976) found that most marriages fit one of three categories: husband as the head and wife as complement; husband as senior partner and wife as junior partner; and husband and wife as equal partners. Studies have shown that men and women use different methods of exerting power in intimate relationships (Falbo and Peplau, 1980). When wives have no recognized power in the relationship, they generally fall back on indirect methods. These techniques include such tactics as the expression of feelings (pouting or threatening to cry, smiling or being affectionate), hinting, withdrawal (becoming silent, cold, and distant), and simply doing things on their own. When women use direct methods, they tend to limit themselves to such tactics as making a simple request and saying how important it is to them. Men, who generally expect compliance, tend to use direct methods.

Men and women marrying for the first time in the 1980s tend to be older than their counterparts of the 1950s.

SEXUAL SATISFACTION

What happens when a husband or wife feels unfairly treated by the marital arrangement? Among a group of more than a hundred Wisconsin couples, those who felt that their partners were getting a better deal out of the marriage were generally dissatisfied with their sexual relationships and felt angry and distant after sex. In contrast, men and women who felt either that marriage was a better deal for them than for their partner or that both husband and wife had an equally good (or bad) deal tended to be more satisfied with their relationships and to feel loving and close after sex (Hatfield et al., 1982).

For many married couples, sex appears to be more pleasurable than it was for their parents. When Alfred Kinsey (Kinsey et al., 1953) interviewed American women at midcentury, 45 percent of the wives who had been married for 15 years almost always experienced orgasm and another 27 percent experienced orgasm at least one third of the time. Twenty years later, when Morton Hunt (1974) interviewed American women, the rate of consistent orgasm had risen to 53 percent among wives who had been married for 15 years, and another 32 percent experienced orgasm at least one half of the time.

The marriages of most of the middle-aged women studied by Lillian Rubin (1979) also followed this trend. Describing her marriage of 33 years to an electrician, a 52-year-old homemaker said:

Marriage is probably too complex to fall neatly into a three-category division. When other researchers (Miller and Olson, 1978) followed a thousand young couples for several years, they discovered nine different types of marriages, and in three of the types the wife was clearly in charge. About 26 percent of the marriages fell into these categories. In a "wife-led disengaged" marriage, the wife took the initiative, there was little conflict, but there was also little love expressed between partners. In a "wife-led congenial" marriage, the wife took the initiative, the partners were compatible, and an average amount of love was shown. In a "wife-led confrontive" marriage, the rarest of the three types, the wife took the initiative, conflict between partners was high, but the partners expressed an average amount of love toward each other. The most common types of marriage, each accounting for about 18 percent of the couples, were both husband led. In one type, both affection and conflict were low, and in the other, levels of affection and conflict were average.

When asked, most young couples say that the marriage of equal partners is their ideal, yet few actually have that sort of marriage. In the study of a thousand couples, 80 percent said that they had a cooperative marriage in which leadership was shared, yet the researchers rated only 12 percent as being equal partners. In a study of three generations (Hill et al., 1970), most of the younger couples said

Sex? It's gotten better and better. For the first years of our marriage— maybe nine or ten—it was a very big problem. But it's changed and improved in a lot of ways. Right now, I'm enjoying sex more than I ever did in my life before—maybe more than I ever thought I could [p. 75].

Among the women in this study who were married, almost 90 percent reached orgasm at least some of the time, and more than half did so more than 50 percent of the time. More than half of these women had sexual intercourse once or twice a week, and another fifth did so three or four times each week. A review of research concerning marital sexuality indicated that although the frequency of intercourse declines with age (see Chapter 4), American couples are

having sex more effectively and use a greater variety of techniques than did couples at midcentury (Rosen and Hall, 1984).

However, sexual problems do not necessarily destroy marital happiness if the experience of 100 Pennsylvania couples is typical of most Americans. Although 83 percent of these couples said that their marriages were "happy" or "very happy" and 90 percent would remarry the same person, more than a third of the men complained of premature ejaculation and nearly half the women were slow to reach orgasm (Frank, Anderson, and Rubenstein, 1978). Apparently, a couple's perception of their sexual relationship and the emotional tone of the relationship are more powerful than behavior in determining satisfaction.

that their marriages were equal partnerships and not at all like the marriages of their parents and grandparents. But once again, perception and reality seemed separate. As the researchers observed the younger couples interacting, they could see little difference between their marriages and those of the older generations.

Marital Satisfaction
In general, marital satisfaction is high in the early years, then drops after the first child is born. Satisfaction seems lowest when the children are adolescents and living at home, then rises when the children leave and the couple are again alone. The problem with these findings, which are relatively consistent from one study to the next, is that they are all cross-sectional. It is possible that satisfaction rises in the later years because the unhappiest marriages have been ended by divorce or that people who remain married for 30 years cannot bring themselves to say that they invested all that time and energy in an unhappy, unsatisfying enterprise (Huyck, 1982). It is also possible that cohort effects or age-related factors outside the marriage influence reports of satisfaction, for most of these studies are cross-sectional, and at least one study of middle-class couples failed to find the traditional pattern (Spanier and Lewis, 1980). The pattern was also absent in the California Intergenerational Study, in which marital satisfaction was as high after 16

to 18 years of marriage (when many had adolescent children living at home) as it had been ten years previously (Skolnick, 1981). Among these couples, neither length of marriage nor stage of the family cycle was associated with marital satisfaction.

So many factors can affect marital satisfaction that lumping together all people at a particular phase of marriage may confuse the issue. For example, among a group of more than 200 women between the ages of 35 and 55, those who got the most pleasure (a measure of happiness, satisfaction, and optimism) out of their marriages had children, and those who got the least pleasure had no children and did not work outside the home (Baruch, Barnett, and Rivers, 1983). Whether a woman with children was employed had no influence on the level of pleasure in her marriage, but it did affect the pleasure of childless wives. Those who were employed fell midway on the pleasure scale between the childless women who did not work outside the home and women with children. In Chapter 13, we will see how occupational and marital roles interact.

Social and economic factors appear to have little influence on marital satisfaction. Age does not affect marital satisfaction, nor does income. Couples in upper socioeconomic brackets are no happier than couples who barely scrape by (Spanier and Lewis, 1980). Among older adults, income affects happiness only when it is very low. If their income is below the poverty level, they are no happier married than single. But once income is enough for basic needs, married adults are happier than the unmarried (Hutchinson, 1975).

Older couples often seem to be more satisfied with their marriages than any except honeymoon couples. It has been suggested that the rise in satisfaction is due to the absence of responsibility for children, but childless older couples express the same feelings of peacefulness, lack of stress, and marital satisfaction (Troll, Miller, and Atchley, 1979). Although it is generally assumed that companionship replaces romance and passion among older couples (Huyck, 1982), this assumption may not be true for those whose marriages are happy. Among the elderly couples in the Duke Longitudinal Study, happily married couples reported engaging in sexual activity more than once a week (Busse and Eisdorfer, 1970). These happily married couples shared two other characteristics that distinguished them from less happily married couples. In most of the happy couples, the husband was older than the wife and the spouses had similar IQ levels. When older couples do have a happy marriage, it becomes the center of their lives, providing comfort, support, and increasing intimacy over the years. Such couples tend to have a more egalitarian relationship than do unhappy couples, so that traditional sex roles and perhaps power relationships are blurred (Troll, Miller, and Atchley, 1979).

"Happy families are all alike," wrote Tolstoy (1875); "every unhappy family is unhappy in its own way." Researchers have tried to find out what characteristics typify a good marriage. In the California Intergenerational Studies (Skolnick, 1981), the happily married husband and wife liked, admired, and respected each other; and each enjoyed the other's company. Their marriage improved over time, and, given a second chance, they would marry the same person again. These middle-aged couples had a close personal relationship, and their marriage was not simply a utilitarian living arrangement. In addition, their personalities were very much alike. It has been estimated that these companionate marriages are found among only about 20 percent of American couples. Such marriages resemble the ideal that most young couples hold as they begin married life.

The other 80 percent of American marriages are believed to be institutional marriages, in which material concerns, not emotional bonds, hold the marriage together. The marriages of unhappy couples in the California Intergenerational Studies were most likely to be of this type. They were utilitarian living arrangements, but, in addition, the personalities of wife and husband tended to be discordant.

The individual personality traits that predicted marital satisfaction among these California couples were linked with traditional sex roles: self-confidence in the men and nurturance in the women. It would seem that aspects of their personalities harmonized with the marital roles they grew up expecting to assume. In addition, both husbands and wives scored high on social maturity and achievement.

The results of this study are in line with other research on personality and marital satisfaction. Such characteristics as emotional maturity, the ability to demonstrate affection, consideration, self-esteem, and adaptability have been found to predict marital satisfaction in cross-sectional studies. It would appear that well-adjusted people are more likely to find satisfaction in marriage than are poorly adjusted people. But then well-adjusted people are more likely to be successful at most of life's tasks.

Although couples with satisfactory marriages may share some characteristics, Tolstoy appears to have been wrong. Not all happy marriages are alike. In a study of more than 400 upper-middle-class marriages (Cuber and Harroff, 1965), stable, satisfactory marriages came in five different varieties. Two kinds of satisfactory marriage were companionate: vital and total. Couples with *vital* marriages shared most aspects of family life and found their marriages exciting. Couples with *total* marriages, the rarest form of all, were immersed in every detail of each other's lives. They shared their moods, hopes, and dreams, as well as all aspects of family life. Three types of institutional marriage turned out to be satisfactory. Couples with a *conflict-habituated* marriage argued continually. Although tension and bickering were habitual, the couples found their battles acceptable. Couples with a *devitalized* marriage had lives that seemed boring but without tension. There was little closeness in their relationship. Couples with a *passive-congenial* marriage lived comfortable, uninteresting, conflict-free lives. They were content with their arrangement. It may be that satisfaction with marriage depends on the expectations each partner holds at the outset. If expectations are too high, marital satisfaction is likely to be low. But if couples do not expect a "total marriage," they may be perfectly content with some variety of an institutional bond.

Sex Differences in Marital Satisfaction

Most studies of marital satisfaction are based on self-reports by the marital partners, but in the California Intergenerational Survey, marital satisfaction was also rated by two trained observers. The outside ratings correlated highly with separate self-ratings by wife and husband, and the correlations were considerably higher than that between the husband's and wife's self-ratings. Apparently, sociologist Jessie Bernard (1973) was correct when she suggested that every marriage is actually two marriages: his and hers.

Bernard suggested that marriage benefited husbands but not wives; it might be more accurate to say that husbands seem to benefit more than wives from the marital state. In a national survey (Douvan and Kulka, 1979), 75 percent of the men said that marriage was as important as their occupation or their children in contributing to the gratification of the important values in life. But whereas 85 percent of the women said that their children contributed a great deal as sources of gratification, only 65 percent of the women ranked marriage and occupation that high.

At any rate, men seem to be more satisfied with their marriages than women. Asked what they did not like about their marriages, 45 percent of the men in one study could think of nothing to complain about, but only 25 percent of the women were as fortunate (Veroff and Feld, 1970). Middle age seems to be the period when a woman's dissatisfaction with her spouse is highest. In a study of San Francisco couples (Lowenthal, Thurnher, and Chiriboga, 1975), 80 percent of the men (at all ages) had favorable views of their wives, and 80 percent of the young and older wives had positive views of their husbands, but among middle-aged wives, only 40 percent viewed their husbands favorably. The husbands of the other 60 percent appeared to be aware of their wives' feelings, for they admitted that they tended to be inconsiderate and failed to give their wives much attention or companionship. Among a group of older couples, marriage was successful at filling more of the husbands' emotional needs than those of their wives (Stinnett, Collins, and Montgomery, 1970). The specific needs investigated were for love, personality fulfillment, respect, communication, finding meaning in life, and integration of past life experiences. The husbands' major complaint was that they did not get enough respect; the wives, like the middle-aged wives in San Francisco, complained about a lack of communication.

The complaints of women in both studies are understandable when we consider the findings from a survey of happily married couples (Reedy, Birren, and Schaie, 1981). No matter what their age, women said that emotional security and intimacy were most important in determining their marital satisfaction. But intimacy did not seem to have much effect on men's happiness. No matter what their age, men said that loyalty and a commitment to the future of the relationship were most important in determining marital satisfaction.

Some marriages have always been satisfying. When Roland Blythe (1979) interviewed Owen and Megan Roberts, retired political activists in their late nineties, the quality of this Welsh couple's 73-year-long marriage came through. Owen said:

She was a student teacher when I first saw her—and what do you think I fancied about her first? Her legs. We went for a walk, and we've walked hand in hand ever since [p. 164].

Megan's pleasure in the marriage was tempered by recollections of all the necessary adjustments, and she said:

I ought to have a medal for living with him. I think sometimes it's very wonderful to have had him all these years and not to get tired of him. It's wonderful, it is really. It is seventy-three years. And longer than that, even, because we actually met eight years before we courted [p. 164].

Marriages may be getting better. National surveys indicate a strong trend toward increased happiness in marriage over the past 20 years. In 1976 married men and women reported greater satisfaction with their marriages than did men and women in 1957 (Veroff, Douvan, and Kulka, 1981). The reason for the rise in happiness is not established, but at least two possibilities come to mind. Easier divorces have made unhappy couples less likely to stay together, and women's increased participation in the work force may have given them more power at home.

ALTERNATIVE ARRANGEMENTS

Marriage is not the only way to form close relationships. Although younger adults are more likely than members of older cohorts to look for another path, some people have always found alternative ways to fulfill the need for intimacy. The most common alternative solutions are cohabitation, homosexuality, and singlehood.

Cohabitation

The path to intimacy closest to marriage is **cohabitation**, in which two unmarried, heterosexual people live together. Cohabitation differs from common-law marriage, which is recognized in some—but not all—states. In **common-law marriage**, a cohabiting couple declare themselves to be married and are so regarded by the state. Their assets are mingled, and they file joint tax returns. Like traditional marriages, common-law marriages can be dissolved only by death or divorce (Hirsch, 1976).

Cohabitation first came to public attention when it became popular with college students toward the close of the 1960s. By 1978 it appeared that approximately 25 percent of American college students had cohabited at some time. The practice spread among adults of all socioeconomic levels and ages. A random survey of selective service registrants indicated that 18 percent of them had cohabited for a period of at least six months, and the majority were not college students (Macklin, 1978). In 1981, 1,808,000 couples were reported to be cohabiting; in 150,000 of these couples, either the man or the woman was older than 65 (U.S. Bureau of the Census, 1982). Many of these older couples, who grew up when society's standards were much stricter, were pushed by economics into what they may regard as an "immoral" arrangement. They find it difficult to go against the rules they learned half a century ago, but if they marry, the wife will lose her widow's pension and family income will be sharply reduced.

Relationships between cohabitants can take at least six different forms, distinguished by the degree of commitment the partners feel toward the relationship (*Cohabitation Research Newsletter,* 1974). At the least committed stage are couples who see cohabitation as a temporary convenience; at the second stage are affectionate relationships, in which each partner is free to have other intimate relationships; third are affectionate, monogamous relationships, much like "going steady"; fourth is the trial marriage, in which the partners are testing their relationship with the idea of legal marriage in mind; fifth is the temporary alternative to marriage while one or both of the partners is waiting for graduation or a divorce; and sixth is the alternative to marriage in which the partners regard their commitment as permanent although the bond is not legal. Few college students who cohabit regard their arrangement as a permanent alternative to marriage; this stage of cohabitation is largely reserved for later in the life span.

A number of researchers regard college cohabitators as simply adding a step to the courtship process, so that living with a member of the other sex is not seen as putting students on a path that leads away from marriage. This seems to be true of most younger cohabitors, and because most of the research on cohabiting couples has taken place on college campuses, we have little information about the experience as an alternative to marriage.

After reviewing a series of studies, Eleanor Macklin (1978) concluded that married couples and cohabiting couples derived about the same amount of satisfaction from their relationship and that when the data were controlled for age and length of relationship, the two types of couples were very similar. When married couples who cohabited before marriage were compared with married couples who had never cohabited, there was no difference in degree of emotional closeness, satisfaction, conflict, or egalitarianism in the marital relationship. The only difference between the two groups seemed to be in age at marriage: the cohabitors married about a year later than the noncohabitors.

It seems unlikely that cohabitation as a permanent alternative to marriage will reduce the formation of families in the United States. Among college cohabitors, 96 percent say they plan to marry some day (Bower and Christopherson, 1977). Men and women who have cohabited generally have only favorable things to say about the experience. It may continue to flourish as a courtship stage for the young and as a satisfying alternative to marriage among adults past the childbearing years.

Homosexual Relationships
Some individuals reserve their intimate relationships for members of their own sex. As yet only one detailed study has investigated the life-styles of homosexuals (Bell and Weinberg, 1978). Among a group of San Francisco homosexuals (Bell and Weinberg, 1978), relationships fell into five general types. *Close-coupled* homosexuals had a relationship much like a marriage. They lived together, had a close emotional bond with the partner, and were monogamous. This sort of relationship was most prevalent among lesbians, and 28 percent of them, as well as

Many gay men seek warmth and tenderness in their relationships, although they are less likely than lesbians to establish long-term emotional commitments.

about 10 percent of the gay men, were in close-coupled relationships. *Open-coupled* homosexuals also lived together, but the relationship was more like an open marriage or the stage 2 cohabitors. Each partner was free to seek outside sexual relationships. Open-coupled relationships were found among 17 percent of the women and 18 percent of the men. *Functional* homosexuals were more like swinging singles. They lived alone, had sexually active lives, and seemed self-reliant and comfortable with their homosexuality. Ten percent of the women and 10 percent of the men fell into this group. *Dysfunctional* homosexuals lived alone and sometimes had active sex lives, but they were unhappy and troubled about their situation. About 5 percent of the women and 12 percent of the men were dysfunctional. Finally, *asexual* homosexuals lived alone and had little sexual activity. They lived quiet, withdrawn lives and had little contact with others. They were not, however, troubled about their sexual orientation. Eleven percent of the women and 16 percent of the men were asexual. Altogether, these categories account for 71 percent of the men and women in the study; the other 29 percent did not fit easily into any category.

This study may not reflect the actual life of most homosexuals, for all the subjects volunteered to take part and all were drawn from a single area of the country. In addition, for most homosexuals, these categories are unlikely to be permanent (Gagnon, 1979). For example, only 28 percent of the men studied were living with a partner, but most of the men had had at least one long-term relationship some time in the past. Although legal marriages are not now possible for homosexual couples, the prevalence of marriagelike arrangements appears to be growing within the homosexual community (Macklin, 1980).

Many gay men seek warmth and tenderness in their relationships, but lesbians are believed to be more likely than gay men to live in a long-term, committed relationship. In a survey of *Psychology Today* readers, 60 percent of the lesbians but only 33 percent of the gay men who responded were living with a partner (Athanasiou, Shaver, and Tavris, 1970). Considering the difference in male and female socialization and the importance women learn to place on relationships, the difference is not surprising. When researchers (Peplau, 1981) compared gay men, lesbians, and heterosexual men and women, they found that whether a person was male or female had more to do with their attitudes toward intimacy than whether they were homosexual or heterosexual. Some researchers (Nichols and Lieblum, 1983) have found that lesbian relationships, formed with *two* people who have been socialized in ways that stress long-term emotional commitments, are generally warm, tender, and caring and that the partners often become over-involved emotionally.

Little research has been done on aging homosexuals, so we are left primarily with speculations about the course of their relationships over the life span. Research on aging lesbians is virtually nonexistent. What research has been done with men indicates that the stereotype of the lonely, frustrated, depressed, aging gay male does not fit those who have been studied (Kimmel, 1978). This same researcher found that the life course of a group of middle-class gay males between the ages of 55 and 81 tended to correspond to that set forth by Daniel Levinson (1978) for adult male development. For example, all long-term relationships among men in the study either flourished or began during the so-called Settling Down period.

Some researchers (Francher and Henkin, 1973) have suggested that the homosexual community functions almost like an extended family for most gay men and that their friendship networks may be as supportive in time of need as children or other relatives would be. Given the large changes in society's attitude toward homosexuality over the past 20 years, different cohorts of homosexuals are likely to experience various aspects of development in radically different ways.

Singlehood

Only a quarter of a century ago, anyone who remained single was regarded with suspicion by most people. The judgment of single women was extremely harsh: in 1957, 80 percent of Americans believed that they were either "sick," "neurotic," or "immoral." Today the judgment has been reversed: 75 percent believe that single women are simply women who have chosen a different way of living (Yankelovich, 1981).

The change in public attitudes reflects a change in society. In 1960, 17 percent of the men and 12 percent of the women past the age of 18 were unmarried; in 1981, 24 percent of the men and 17 percent of the women were single (Fig. 11.2). Almost 19 million adults were living alone (U.S. Bureau of the Census, 1982). Some of these adults will eventually marry, but an increasing number are likely to remain single throughout life. It has been estimated that the proportion of adults who never marry will rise from the present 5 percent among those in their fifties to about 8 or 9 percent among those now in the twenties (Glick, 1979).

The rising popularity of the single life may seem like a new development, but a large single population is not a new factor in American life. If we assume that most people who marry will do so by the age of 40, the figures from Essex

County, Massachusetts, for the years 1875–1885 may prove startling. During those years, the proportion of unmarried men between the ages of 35 and 39 ranged from 14 to 29 percent in various areas of the county. And the proportion of unmarried women of that age ranged from 23 to 31 percent (Ankarloo, 1978). In 1981, 8.6 percent of American men and 6.2 percent of American women were unwed at that age (U.S. Bureau of the Census, 1982).

Why were so many Massachusetts women unmarried? There is no way to be certain, but historical events apparently played some part in the development. Industrial areas of Massachusetts were attracting immigrants—both from the Massachusetts countryside and from other nations. The highest rate of unmarried women (and the lowest rate of unmarried men) was found in industrial areas, where women worked in the labor force, and the lowest rate of unmarried women (and the highest rate of unmarried men) was found in rural areas. The family's need for earnings of adult children may have prevented some from marrying. And, finally, possible husbands for some of the women may have been killed during the Civil War.

When today's single adults are asked why they have not married, most say that the personal freedom, career opportunities, and availability of sexual partners outweigh the economic, emotional, and sexual security of marriage (Stein, 1975). However, there are two kinds of single adults: self-selected, who prefer the single life, and socially selected, whose real or imagined handicaps have left them unable to attract a mate (Corby and Zarit, 1983).

Whether people are single by choice or by chance, social conditions play some role in their fate. The increased tolerance of alternative life-styles and the active social and sexual life now available to singles make the unmarried life more attractive to self-selected men and women. Technology has made their lot comfortable: Frozen foods, Laundromats, permanent press and drip-dry clothing, improved transportation, and other services that cater to single adults have simplified life. Among self-selected women, more education and expanded opportunities for employment have made them financially independent. They no longer *have* to marry. And the relative shortage of marriageable men has increased the pool of socially selected single women.

How does the single life affect intimate relationships? Among single adults who live alone, some "swing," and others have long-term sexual relationships. Some are celibate. Although the majority of single adults say they are satisfied

Who is single?

	18–19 Years	20–24 Years	25–29 Years	30–34 Years	35–44 Years	45–54 Years	55–64 Years	65–74 Years	>74 Years
					Age				
Men	95.7%	69.5%	33.8%	16.4%	8.5%	5.1%	5.1%	4.9%	3.5%
Women	84.7%	51.9%	21.8%	10.4%	5.4%	4.7%	4.2%	5.4%	6.2%

FIGURE 11.2

Source: U.S. Bureau of the Census, *Statistical Abstract of the United States, 1982–1983*, 103d ed., 1982.

Less restrictive social attitudes, together with a technology that has made the single life easier, have contributed to the growing number of adults who choose not to marry.

with their sex lives, they seem less satisfied than the married. Among several hundred Dayton, Ohio, adults, 80 percent of the married reported sexual satisfaction as compared with 51 percent of the singles. And although single adults had a greater variety of partners, married adults had sex more often (Cargan and Melko, 1982).

Nonsexual relationships do not appear to be a problem for single adults. They have friends and family, and some studies have found that their physical and mental health is no different from that of people who live with others (Rubenstein, Shaver, and Peplau, 1979). Some singles may be lonely. When the young, middle-class readers of *Psychology Today* were surveyed, 56 percent of the married and 72 percent of the unmarried readers said that they felt lonely "sometimes" or "often" (Parlee, 1979). Young singles in the Dayton, Ohio, sample were just as physically healthy as married adults, but they seemed under more stress. Single women were more likely than married women to be lonely, have nightmares, crying spells, and irrational fears. Single men were more likely than married men to be lonely and despondent and to feel guilty and worthless (Cargan and Melko, 1982).

Such studies do not distinguish between self-selected and socially selected singles. By old age, single adults are not especially lonely. They appear to be autonomous and self-reliant, and most do not feel isolated (Troll, Miller, and Atchley, 1979). Their contact with relatives appears to depend on social class, with middle-class older women reporting more frequent contacts than married women, but working-class older women reporting fewer contacts (Atchley, Pignatiello, and Shaw, 1975).

Older single adults' satisfaction with life is much like that of older married adults, and they seem better off than the widowed and divorced (Corby and Zarit, 1983). They escape the pain of divorce and the grief of being widowed.

Most adults who have chosen the single life are independent people who prefer solitary pursuits and do not appear to miss the family involvement they might have had as spouses or parents.

DIVORCE AND REMARRIAGE

If Americans never truly believed that all marriages were made in heaven, they once did believe that marriages were "forever." In cases of desertion or adultery, divorce was possible, but even the injured party was stained with the brush of public disapproval. Divorce just did not happen to "nice" people. Most people who were clearly in a bad marriage struggled along, often "for the sake of the children." Today 6.7 percent of the population past the age of 18 have been divorced, up from 1.4 percent in 1940 (U.S. Bureau of the Census, 1982). The situation has changed so radically that 60 percent of Americans believe that people who get married do not expect their marriage to last for the rest of their lives (Yankelovich, 1981). Today cultural standards seem almost to require a rupture of the marriage if the couple do not share a deep emotional involvement (Furstenberg, 1982). As we will see, however, marriage is still popular. Most people who divorce soon find another marriage partner.

Divorce

At the time of the Civil War, about 4 marriages out of every 100 ended in divorce; by 1970, divorce ended 44 out of every 100 marriages. Yet approximately the same percentage of marriages remained intact during the 1970s as during the 1870s. In the last quarter of the nineteenth century, about as many marriages were dissolved by the death of the husband or wife as are now dissolved by divorce. What has happened over the past hundred years or so is that the rise in divorce rate and the decline in death rate nearly balanced each other. It was not until 1974 that the number of divorces (977,000) was greater than the number of deaths among married people (947,000) (Glick, 1980). The difference is that in the past many happy marriages were ended by death, and today it is the unhappy marriages that wind up in the divorce courts (Fig. 11.3).

The average divorce occurs after six or seven years of marriage, when the man is 31 and the woman almost 29 years old. Age is no insurance against divorce, however; nearly 10,000 divorces take place each year among adults who have passed their sixty-fifth birthday (Troll, Miller, and Atchley, 1979).

We would expect that the stability of a marriage can be predicted by its level of satisfaction, but that is not always the case. Some marriages that seem to be of high quality end in separation or divorce whereas other marriages that seem dismal survive. According to Graham Spanier and Robert Lewis (1980), the quality of a marriage is determined by a balance of its rewards and tensions, including each partner's social and personal resources, satisfaction with established lifestyle, and rewards from interacting with the spouse. But the stability of that marriage is strongly affected by forces outside the marriage—alternative attractions (another possible mate, a crucial career decision) and external pressures. The combination of costs and rewards, pushes and pulls, of all these forces will determine whether the marriage breaks up.

A number of factors appear to predict the likelihood of divorce. If the woman is pregnant at the time of marriage or if the man is younger than 21 or the woman younger than 19, the marriage's chances of survival are lessened. If the couple is black, divorce becomes more likely, for 9.4 percent of blacks are divorced. If the couple is Hispanic, divorce becomes less likely; 5.9 percent of Hispanics are divorced (U.S. Bureau of the Census, 1982). Economic factors also play some part, with low income increasing the probability of divorce.

But divorce has increased in all groups, not just among the young, the pregnant, blacks, and the poor. Wider changes in society have contributed their share to the increased divorce rate. Women are more deeply involved in the labor force, and child rearing has declined in significance as woman's central role. The availability of welfare reduces women's dependence on continuation of a marriage. There has been a reduction of both legal barriers to divorce and social disapproval afterward. Finally, there is a new emphasis in society on personal fulfillment.

Even these factors, suggests Frank Furstenberg (1982), do not entirely explain the rise of divorce and remarriage. He contends that the cultural meaning of marriage has changed, and it no longer is seen as the central event in the passage to adulthood. This has come about for a number of reasons. Most people today have sexual relationships before marriage. They feel free to cohabit. They establish their own households before marriage so that marriage no longer marks the transition to householder. They no longer feel obligated to have children. As a result, marriage is a more voluntary and less permanent arrangement, and the standards for a satisfying marriage have risen. Today divorce acts as a recycling mechanism that allows people another chance at establishing a rewarding relationship.

Although divorce is easier today, it is still a painful process. The divorced partners find that they have lost one of their social roles (wife or husband) and that they have taken on a role for which society has not yet established any expectations. Both partners, but especially the wife, may find that their income and standard of living drop. Friends may disappear as they ''choose'' husband or wife or as they find that the presence of an unattached person does not fit into their social scheme.

The period after the divorce is rarely a happy one. Although the cutting of the marriage tie generally makes divorced people feel free, they are more likely to feel anxious, guilty, incompetent, or depressed than either married or remarried people; they have lower self-esteem, are lonelier, drink more alcohol, and smoke more marijuana (Cargan and Melko, 1982). They may be pervaded by a sense of personal failure over the breakup of the marriage. Compared with all other groups in society (married, single, widowed, remarried), divorced people have the highest rate of emotional disturbance, accidental death, and death from heart disease, cancer, pneumonia, high blood pressure, and cirrhosis of the liver (Brody, 1983b). If children are involved, the first year or so after divorce is especially trying, and in Chapter 12 we will examine some of the special problems faced by a divorced parent.

					Who is divorced?				
					Age				
	18–19 Years	20–24 Years	25–29 Years	30–34 Years	35–44 Years	45–54 Years	55–64 Years	65–74 Years	>74 Years
Men	0.1%	1.8%	5.4%	8.8%	8.9%	7.3%	6.1%	3.9%	2.5%
Women	0.7%	3.8%	8.8%	11.6%	11.6%	9.9%	7.1%	4.4%	2.3%

FIGURE 11.3

Source: U.S. Bureau of the Census, *Statistical Abstract of the United States, 1982–1983*, 103d ed., 1982.

Remarriage

About a third of all marriages are remarriages, and the average remarriage follows divorce by about three years. The majority of divorced people remarry, and the younger a person is at the time of divorce, the more likely he or she is to remarry. In a study of more than 200 divorced adults in Pennsylvania (Furstenberg, 1982), two thirds said that they were reluctant to consider another marriage, but in less than three years 28 percent of the disenchanted had remarried. Among adults in early middle age who have been divorced, five out of every six men and three out of every four women are remarried (Glick, 1980). Marriages among older adults are remarriages in 95 percent of the cases, but three out of every four remarriages by older Americans unite people whose marriages were ended by death, not divorce (Troll, Miller, and Atchley, 1979).

A second (or third or subsequent) marriage seems different in several ways from a first marriage. The factors that complicate remarriages have been spelled out by Furstenberg (1982). First, the expectations and habits formed during the first marriage influence a partner's behavior in a subsequent marriage. Most remarried couples use the first marriage as a baseline by which they judge the new marriage and generally take care to develop a different style for the new union. Second, contact with the previous spouse is often unavoidable. Partners at remarriage are likely to be parents, and the children are usually young. Their presence often makes contact with the previous spouse necessary, and, whether the new spouse likes it or not, present and former mates become linked. When both partners in the remarriage have children from a former marriage, relationships can become complicated.

Third, people remarry under changed personal circumstances. They are older: The average man is 35 when he marries for the second time, and the average woman is 32. Their social status, level of maturity, and wealth of experience are different. In addition, the difference in age between husband and wife is likely to be larger than in most first marriages—on the average the husband is six years older instead of two. Two factors are believed responsible for the increased age gap: Men who remarry tend to look for younger women and women who remarry tend to look for an older man with a relatively high income (Glick, 1980). When adults older than 65 are wed, 20 percent of the grooms marry women younger than 55, but only 3 percent of the brides marry men that young (Treas and VanHilst, 1976). These tendencies combine with the longer female life span to produce an increasingly larger pool of unmarried middle-aged and elderly women (Fig. 11.4).

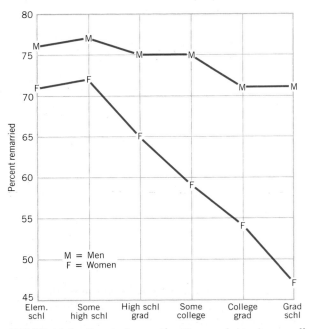

FIGURE 11.4 Remarriage, education, and sex. Among divorced women between the ages of 35 and 44, remarriage is closely related to educational level, perhaps because more education makes a woman more employable and self-reliant and because women tend to look for men with higher incomes.

Source: U.S. Bureau of the Census, *1970 Census of Population*, Vol. II, 4C, *Marital Status*, Table 4.

A final factor that makes remarriages different from first marriages is that a second marriage puts a person into a different marriage cohort, so that the relationship is played out under the influence of different cultural standards and historical events (Furstenberg, 1982).

Marriage tends to be just as good the second time around. When people remarry, they are likely to do so with fewer romantic illusions and lowered expectations. In a study of a hundred couples who married in later life (McKain, 1969), the most frequent reasons given for a second marriage were companionship, lasting affection, and regard. Most of the remarried adults in the Pennsylvania study (Furstenberg, 1982) said that, compared with their first marriage, they had better communication with their mate, felt more trust and goodwill even during disagreements, were more likely to make decisions jointly, and shared domestic chores in a fairer manner. In most second marriages, the level of marital satisfaction, personal happiness, and worry seems to be about the same as in first marriages. Women in second marriages often say they are very happy, and men are unlikely to find a middle ground; either they are very happy or very unhappy (Huyck, 1982).

Whether the second marriage is more stable than the first is uncertain. Some (Glick, 1980) have predicted a higher divorce rate in second than first marriages, and others (McCarthy, 1978) find that, at least among blacks, second marriages are more likely than first marriages to endure. When couples do not divorce, sooner or later either the wife or husband is widowed.

WIDOWHOOD

The death of one of the partners ends the cycle of a family and casts the surviving spouse into a different role, one that requires painful readjustments. In most marriages, it is the wife who is left to make a new life for herself. In the United States, there are nearly 11 million widows but only about 2 million widowers. Between the ages of 65 and 74 there are more than six widows for every widower, and past the age of 75 there are more than five widows for every widower (U.S. Bureau of the Census, 1982) (Fig. 11.5). Among older adults, men are more likely to remarry than women. If they are younger than 70 when widowed, most men remarry, but only 5 percent of the women who are widowed after the age of 50 ever marry again (Troll, Miller, and Atchley, 1979).

Immediately after the death of a spouse there is a period of bereavement, in which the surviving spouse slowly adjusts to his or her new status, a process that will be investigated in Chapter 16. Several factors determine how disruptive the death is for the widowed partners (Lopata, 1975). They include the survivor's degree of dependence on the deceased partner; the way in which the couple had been immersed as a team in family, community, and occupation; the social and economic resources of the surviving partner as well as any limitations on the partner's future actions; and the steps taken by the survivor either to assume the role of a widowed person or to move into another social unit or life-style.

Another factor that affects immediate adjustment is whether the death is seen as being "on time." The accidental death of a young husband presents a much

Loneliness may be a major problem for the middle-class widow in a traditional marriage, who often finds that her husband's death has made her an unattached person in a world of couples.

Who is widowed?

	Age				
	35–44 Years	45–54 Years	55–64 Years	65–74 Years	>75 Years
Men	0.5%	1.4%	4.1%	8.2%	22.1%
Women	2.2%	6.8%	18.4%	40.1%	68.2%

FIGURE 11.5

Source: U.S. Bureau of the Census, *Statistical Abstract of the United States*, 103d ed., 1982.

more difficult adjustment than the death of an older husband, especially one who has been suffering from a chronic disease. In the case of the young widow, the unanticipated nature of the death plunges her into an existence for which she has no economic or social plans. The older widow has usually made such plans and has also gone through a period of psychological preparation for widowhood. Faced by the deaths of her friends' husbands, her own husband's declining health, or his terminal illness, she is likely to have gone through mental rehearsals that prepare her to meet the event when it actually happens (Treas, 1983).

The status of widowhood varies from one society to another. Some cultures have a specific role for the widow; she may be in charge of organizing social rituals, of acting as arbitrator, or serving as matchmaker (Lopata, 1980). In Chicago, the Greek and Puerto Rican communities have developed definite roles for the widowed woman. Among high-caste Hindus, who forbade remarriage, she was expected to cast herself on her husband's funeral pyre. Although this regulation was more honored in the breach than the observance, it acted as an ideal and helped enforce other behavior on widows who did not join their husbands in death (Lopata, 1975).

The special role of widow seems linked to the subordinate status of women in most societies. Only for women does the death of a spouse require social roles and rituals. Searches of anthropological studies have found no society that reports a special role for widowers; the only references are to remarriages by the surviving husband (Lopata, 1980).

American behavioral scientists have also largely ignored the widower. Most studies have focused on widows, in part because there are so many of them and in part because a man's primary identity comes from his occupation and the death of a wife has little or no effect on that part of his life. Yet, among older individuals, men seem to find the adjustment to the death of a spouse much harder than do women (Bernardo, 1970).

The widower's greater difficulty may be due more to his subsequent isolation and loneliness than to the loss of his wife (Lopata, 1980). Older men tend to have depended on their wives to maintain kin and social ties, so that the widower's social contacts and supports may be sharply reduced. Widowers are also less likely than widows to have a close friend other than their spouse. Other problems come from the structure of the traditional marriage. The widower suddenly faces a struggle for survival—he must cook, clean, and take care of the domestic chores most men in present older cohorts have never tackled. However, most widowers are much better off financially than widows and more accustomed to managing money. It is no wonder that widowers tend to remarry rapidly.

When they do not remarry, they tend to die. Among the middle-aged, the death rate for widowers is 32.5 per thousand compared with 13.2 per thousand for widows. Among older adults, widowers die at the rate of 113.5 per thousand and widows at the rate of 66.9 per thousand. The disparity is not entirely due to the longer female life span, for the death rate among married individuals in middle age is 13.1 for men and 6.7 for women, and among older adults it is 57.4 for married men and 32.9 for married women (Lopata, 1980). The death of a spouse clearly has profound effects on the survivor, but the toll it takes seems greater on men.

Like widowers, widows face loneliness and problems in child rearing and daily living without a partner. They also are more likely than widowers to face financial problems. Adjustment often differs according to socioeconomic level. Helene Lopata (1973; 1979; 1980), who has studied widows extensively, has found that a working-class wife generally suffers less disruption in her life than does a middle-class wife. The world of working-class couples is segregated by sex: The husband's social life is lived with male friends outside the home; the wife's social life is limited to relatives, neighbors, and church activities. The world of middle-class couples is integrated: They establish friendships with other couples and their social activities tend to be joint undertakings. As a result, the middle-class couples develop a greater mutual dependency, and the death of the husband not only robs the wife of her social partner and companion but also makes her an unattached person in a social world of couples. Thus, if the marriage were a traditional one, a widow may be uneasy about going out in public alone and may also have been socialized to look on social activities with a female companion as "second-rate."

However, her higher level of education, greater income, and job skills make the middle-class woman better equipped to break through the isolation and loneliness of widowhood. She generally becomes much more socially active than a working-class widow. When a working-class widow does venture out, she generally restricts her companions to her children.

Most widows live alone. Younger widows who live with others generally are the heads of households composed of themselves and their children. Among older widows, 78 percent are heads of their own households, and most of the rest live in households headed by a relative. It is the poor, the less educated, and the very old widows who tend to live with someone else. The reason so many widows choose a solitary life appears to be a desire for independence and the wish to be in charge of their own households. When asked about remarriage, more than 75 percent of older widows in Chicago (Lopata, 1973) said they were not interested in having a husband. Some said they wanted to be independent, some said they had no wish to play the wife role, some said they did not want to have to care for another sick man, and others regarded the idea of remarriage as impossible. Although the scarcity of possible partners may have entered into this last reason, it is also true that many widows sanctify the memories of their husbands, idealizing them to the point where the widows cannot find any man who could possibly live up to the image they have created.

The failure to marry does not mean that widows give up sexual activity. Among widows between the ages of 26 and 30, 55 percent are sexually active (Gebhard, 1970). Frequency declines once widows pass the age of 30, but throughout life their rate of sexual activity exceeds their rate of remarriage. Among older widows, 20 percent agree that men continually make them sexual propositions and that some of them come from friends of their husbands. As we have come to understand the importance of sexuality across the life span, some researchers (Corby and Zarit, 1983) have proposed that society seek alternative solutions to the sexual needs of older widows. Among their suggestions are cohabitation with younger men, polygamous marriage, and homosexual relationships.

Although we know a great deal about widows, what we know applies to older women today, most of whom have had traditional marriages. Many traditional widows devote themselves to their children and grandchildren, and their system of social support is often limited to relatives. As today's young women are widowed, their adjustment and social roles may be very different. Compared with women who entered their sixties in 1975, women who will become sixty around the year 2000 are more likely to be native born (94 percent compared with 46 percent), to have a high school diploma (84 percent compared with 53 percent), to have graduated from college (20 percent compared with 8 percent), and to have a professional or technical background (25 percent compared with 12 percent) (Neugarten and Brown-Rezanka, 1978). Accustomed to working and handling money, mothers of fewer children, and possessing occupational identities in addition to their role as wife, they may be better equipped to handle a decade or more of widowhood. Indeed, Lopata (1975) has found a group among today's widows who, once past the period of mourning, become independent, taking on roles and developing life-styles that they never would have considered as girls or wives.

SIBLINGS

Most of us have at least one sibling. Among American families with children, 64 percent have at least two offspring in the home, and many of the one-child families are young families that later will expand (U.S. Bureau of the Census, 1982). In the population as a whole, only about 10 percent are only children (Cicirelli, 1982). Today's older Americans are about as likely to have a living sibling (79 percent) as to have a child (81 percent), and older women are more likely to have a sibling available (86 percent) than a husband (50 percent) (Troll, Miller, and Atchley, 1979).

The sibling relationship is unique in several ways (Cicirelli, 1982). It is the most enduring of all relationships, beginning with birth and ending with the death of the sibling, generally outlasting the parental relationship by several decades. Siblings have more in common with each other than with anyone else: They share a genetic heritage, cultural surroundings, and early experiences. The relationship is one of approximately equal power and freedom. Finally, no sibling has to ''earn'' the relationship; it is awarded by circumstances of birth. Our brothers and sisters certainly affect development during childhood, and if they are older, they are present within the family from the day we are born.

As children grow up and leave home, sibling relationships generally diminish in importance, but most people maintain contact with brothers or sisters, and in some cases the bonds are intense. For example, a group of four brothers were as close as the three musketeers, whose motto, "All for one, and one for all," reflected their relationship (Bank and Kahn, 1982). These college-educated brothers, whose ages ranged from 36 to 45, lived within a 100-mile radius; their contacts were frequent; and they shared common values, resolved their conflicts openly and rapidly, relied on one another, and defended one another against outsiders. The youngest brother summed up their relationship, saying:

I know as I sit right here, if I ever got in any trouble—the first ones I go to is my brothers. I don't call my father. I don't call my in-laws. I don't call my wife. I call my brother [p. 255].

Such intense sibling loyalty appears to develop when children either lose a parent (by death, desertion, or divorce) or else perceive their parents as weak or hostile. Their social support system is either missing or unpredictable, and they cling together for support (Bank and Kahn, 1982).

Sibling loyalty rarely runs so deep, and researchers (Circirelli, 1982) have discerned three types of relationships among adults. Some siblings feel a mutual apathy, getting together only at ritual family events. In such cases, they are likely to see little of each other after the death of their parents although it is extremely unusual for them to lose touch completely. Some siblings are close, and others maintain an enduring rivalry. Sisters seem more likely than brothers to develop extremely close relationships, and cross-sex relationships are generally closer than the relationships between brothers (Adams, 1968). Sibling rivalry may be common in childhood, for 71 percent of adults say they have experienced such feelings at some time in their lives (Ross and Milgram, 1982), but the rivalry rarely seems to outlast childhood. Only 2 percent of middle-aged adults report any feeling that they are in competition with their brothers or sisters (Cicirelli, 1981).

Throughout life most people express feelings of closeness to their siblings whether or not they often see or hear from them. A large majority of middle-aged adults say they get along well with their siblings, find their relationships satisfying, and feel that their brothers or sisters are interested in them. Yet less than half say they discuss intimate topics with siblings, and only a handful talk over important life decisions with them (Cicirelli, 1982).

As people get older, their relationships with their brothers and sisters seem to deepen. Studies consistently indicate that feelings of closeness intensify with age although visits, telephone calls, and letters may decrease in frequency. Siblings appear to be especially close to adults who never marry, and after the death of a spouse, widows and widowers tend to renew contacts and reestablish associations with brothers and sisters (Troll, Miller, and Atchley, 1979).

For many elderly people, siblings are a reliable source of help. There seems to be a clear pattern of mutual aid in sibling relationships, with assistance infrequent among young adults, being extended in times of crisis among middle-aged adults, and often expanding to encompass the role of substitute parent or spouse during old age (Cicirelli, 1982).

Whether the patterns of sibling relationships that have been detected in cross-sectional studies will reflect relationships in future generations is unknown. No longitudinal studies have traced sibling feelings and interactions across the life span, and various changes in society could alter the pattern. The encouragement of emotional openness, the loosening of strong family ties as ethnic groups move from first and second to third generation, increased geographic mobility, and the increased frequency of divorce could change the course of this family bond.

FRIENDS

Our need for emotional relationships is also filled by friends. Friendship differs from other close relationships because its ties do not depend on kinship or the law; it is a purely volitional relationship (Hess, 1972). Because neither custom nor law forces us to maintain a friendship, the bond is fragile and can be broken by a single defection by either party.

THE NATURE OF FRIENDSHIP

Like lovers, friends tend to be similar in many ways: age, sex, race, ethnic or religious group, social background, proximity, interests, and attitudes. Yet many friendships break the rule of similarity. Although age is considered such an important factor in friendship that most people feel it necessary to explain these bonds between people of widely different ages, such relationships are common. Among 4000 urban men and women, less than half said that most of their friends were the same age as themselves (Riley and Foner, 1968). Shifts in cultural attitudes may be making exterior similarities less important than they once were. A survey of 40,000 young, well-educated readers of *Psychology Today* indicated that 38 percent had close friends of a different racial group and 47 percent had close friends from a different ethnic or religious background (Parlee, 1979). Even in this very special group, however, similarity of attitudes and interests remained important: A common reason for the rupture of the friendship was the discovery that the pair had very different views on issues that were of great importance to one of them.

The reason for similarity's importance in the maintenance of friendship lies in its function. Friendships appear to provide self-affirmation and ego support, with the friend validating our identity, and our acceptance by friends contributing to our self-acceptance (Tesch, 1983; Hess, 1972). Friendship also has other functions: Friends provide intellectual stimulation and interesting activities and are useful in many practical situations. For example, friends provide information in learning new roles, such as spouse or parent, mutual opportunities for role rehearsal, and control on one another's behavior (Hess, 1972).

Many friendships endure for decades whereas others are fleeting. An original attraction between friends based on age and a common life stage (such as enrollment in graduate school or new parenthood) may cool as continuing communication reveals differences in values, attitudes, and interests. Among the young *Psy-*

chology Today readers (Parlee, 1979), 13 situations led to the cooling or rupture of friendships: moving, betrayal, different views on important issues, marriage, the friend's involvement with a disliked person, borrowing money, taking a vacation together, childbirth, sudden discrepancy in wealth or occupational levels, and divorce. These situations can be encompassed by proximity, roles, interests, and values. For example, the interests and activities of a person who becomes a parent suddenly shift, and he or she may no longer have much in common with a single friend.

Although the moving of a friend is a common reason for the ending of a friendship, many friendships endure transcontinental separation. Friendship across miles can be maintained by letters, phone calls, and sporadic visits, made easier by jet travel. When middle-class couples who had moved within the past 5 years were studied (Babchuk and Bates, 1963), both wife and husband tended to name someone from their previous areas as "best friend." Sustained, intense interaction over a period of years, as in childhood, college, or military service, may establish so strong a bond that any new contact quickly reestablishes the original intimacy (Hess, 1972).

In fact, "friendship" is such a subjective classification that is is not a reliable guide to interaction, as several studies have shown (Huyck, 1982). For example, older adults who lived in Manhattan hotels listed their friends and indicated their daily contacts with others (Cohen, Cook, and Rajkowski, 1980). But the people labeled as "friends" were often seen infrequently and considered neither intimate nor important whereas "nonfriends" were often a source of regular interaction. In addition, a significant minority of "nonfriends" were considered both intimate and important.

Friendships are often linked to a person's other life roles (Hess, 1972). Being married makes other married people available as friends, for many adult friendships are between couples, not individuals. Becoming parents makes other parents available; friendships may develop out of children's activities, with such activities as scouting, music lessons, Little League, or car pools bringing parents with shared interests together. When their children's interests are the only basis for friendships, the bond tends to dissolve as the children drift into differing paths. Often friendships develop between co-workers, and when a person retires, such friendships may also dwindle. As is true of friendships between parents, some other basis for shared experiences is required to maintain the bond.

Among older adults, sex and social class tend to be similar among friends, but roles continue to influence friendships (Riley and Foner, 1968). Older married people have more interaction with friends than either the single or widowed elderly. Childless older people have more contact with friends and acquaintances than older people with children. Retired older adults are less likely than employed adults to make new friends. A 92-year-old widow noted this tendency with some distaste:

Friendship is one's own responsibility. Old age shouldn't make one less friendly or interested in making new friends. All my old friends are in the graveyard, and if I hadn't made some new ones, where would I be? I think a lot of old people just aren't very sensible. They only have old friends, and then they live to be ninety or something, like me, and then they start moaning because their friends have gone before, as they say. My advice to the aged woman is find some young people. Don't go to these dreadful old folks' clubs, but find some young people [Blythe, 1979, p. 266].

MEN'S AND WOMEN'S FRIENDSHIPS

It is generally assumed that friendships are very different among men and women. Some (Tiger, 1969) believe that true friendship flourishes among men and that women lack the capacity for deep and lasting friendships whereas others (Booth and Hess, 1974) believe that women's friendships are emotionally richer than those of men. Bonds between male friends seem to be based on shared activities and shared experiences, in contrast to the mutual assistance, emotional support, and intimacy that seem to characterize bonds between female friends (Weiss and Lowenthal, 1975). When queried, a majority of women say that women's friendships are superior, but a sizable minority say that they are inferior and always of less value than a woman's friendship with a man (Wright, 1982). Most men say they have never thought much about the subject.

Several studies have explored the quality of friendship and have discovered a complexity that supports some of the assumptions and shatters others, but not to an overwhelming degree. For example, research has confirmed the tendency for women's friendships to be person-oriented and to involve all aspects of life and for men's friendships to be more activity-oriented and segmented (Wright, 1982). In this same study, a difference appeared in the way the sexes handled strains in the relationship. Both men and women were equally likely to terminate a strained friendship, but women were more likely than men to confront the source of strain, discussing it with their friend in the hope of eliminating it. Men who did not end the relationship simply tolerated the strain.

One common belief, based on sex-role socialization, is that men are likely to hide their feelings and private thoughts from friends, but that women are likely to express them. In a study of young, single, Catholic, middle-class adults (Hacker, 1981), men seemed to confide in their male friends about as much as women confided in their female friends. Married women were more likely than single women to disclose themselves to friends—a trend that was also present, but weaker, among men. Between cross-sex friends, men were likely to hide their weaknesses from female friends and women to conceal their strengths from male friends, indicating a tendency to fulfill sex-role expectations (Fig. 11.6).

Robert Bell (1981) believes that conflicting findings about the effect of gender on friendship may be resolved by looking at what he calls the "conventionality" of the people involved. Nonconventional women and men want to influence change, to seek pleasure or greater happiness, to exert more control over lives; they are fairly satisfied with their lives but are willing to take gambles to improve them. Conventional women and men have opposite tendencies.

Among upper-middle-class Australian and American adults in their mid-thirties, the nonconventional had similar attitudes toward friendship (Bell, 1981).

	Same-Sex Pairs		Cross-Sex Pairs	
	Women	Men	Women	Men
Reveal strengths and weaknesses	77%	86%	50%	62%
Reveal only weaknesses	18%	0	33%	0%
Reveal only strengths	0	9%	0	31%
Reveal neither	5%	5%	17%	7%

FIGURE 11.6   Sex differences in self-disclosure.

When it was a matter of revealing both strengths and weaknesses, men and women reported high rates of self-disclosure to a friend of the same sex. But in this young, educated, mostly single group, men concealed their weaknesses from female friends and women concealed their strengths from male friends. The pattern follows the culture's sex-role standards.

Source: H. M. Hacker, ''Blabbermouths and Clams: Sex Differences in Self-Disclosure in Same-Sex and Cross-Sex Friendship Dyads,'' *Psychology of Women Quarterly*, 5 (1981), p. 393.

They valued both being alone and being with friends; they stressed the emotional aspects of friendship and tended to reveal themselves to friends. They were also more likely to have friendships with members of the other sex and were not bothered if the friendships took on a sexual quality. Conventional women had more personal, intimate, and emotionally based friendships than conventional men, whose bonds were characterized by shared activities and who were unlikely to reveal themselves to friends. Conventional men and women disliked being alone. They were unlikely to have friends of the other sex and felt that a sexual involvement was likely to destroy such friendships. Bell sees nonconventional women and men as having more in common than conventional and nonconventional women (or men). Although he did not ask the adults he interviewed to rate themselves on masculine and feminine personality traits, we might speculate that the nonconventional adults would have seen themselves as more androgynous than either traditionally male or female.

Relationships with mates, siblings, and friends are important influences on the shape and quality of our lives. In the next chapter, we will investigate relationships across the generations and the nature of the family.

SUMMARY

Individual development occurs in a human context, and the person who grows up without social interaction or affection has little chance of being normal. The need for human relationships is also central in adulthood, but the degree of human contact that seems to be required varies from one person to the next.

In American society, a primary means of satisfying the need for human connection is through an intimate relationship with a mate, but some marriages lack **intimacy**. Although Americans hold to the ideal of romantic mate selection, in practice social factors influence the decision. The division of power between the partners is central to marital roles, and in the traditional marriage the man has the upper hand. In a sizable minority of marriages, however, the wife appears to be in charge. Cross-sectional studies indicate that marital satisfaction is generally high in the early years, drops after the first child is born, reaches its lowest point when the children are adolescents, and rises again when the couple are finally alone. Most American marriages are institutional marriages, held together by material concerns; only about one in five is a companionate marriage, based on emotional bonds. Men seem to get more benefits out of marriage than women do, and men seem to be more satisfied with their marriage. Sexual and marital satisfaction have both increased in recent decades.

Cohabitation, which first became popular on college campuses, has spread to all age groups and socioeconomic levels. It differs from **common-law marriage** in that cohabiting partners can dissolve their arrangement without going through the courts. The degree of commitment felt by the partners determines the form cohabitation takes. Satisfaction among cohabitating and married couples is very similar.

Homosexual relationships seem to fall into types that are similar to various heterosexual relationships, but homosexual relationships are less likely to be permanent. Lesbians are thought to be more likely than gay men to live in a long-term, committed relationship. Cohort differences may have radically changed the experience of homosexual relationships.

Although most Americans marry, an increasing number are remaining single throughout life. Historical events and social conditions appear to affect the size of the single population. Singles may be either self-selected or socially selected. Although single adults seem to be under more stress than the married, by old age they appear to be as satisfied as married adults and better off than the widowed and divorced.

The high divorce rate may be an indication that the cultural meaning of marriage has changed. Divorce tends to occur after six or seven years of marriage. Divorced people lose one of their social roles and often find that their income drops and their friends disappear. The divorced have higher rates of serious illness, emotional disturbance, and accidental death than any other group in society. A high percentage of divorced people remarry, and the remarriage may be quite different, as it is influenced by efforts to avoid the style of the previous marriage, contact with the previous spouse, changed personal circumstances, and different cohort effects. The stability of second marriages is uncertain.

The death of marital partner forces the survivor, usually the wife, into a new social role. Among the factors that determine the disruption caused by widowhood are how much the survivor depended on the deceased partner, what the survivor's social and economic resources are, and whether the death is seen as being "on time." Men seem to find adjustment to the death of a spouse much more difficult than women do, and most widowers tend to remarry rapidly or to die. The widow's adjustment varies according to socioeconomic level, with the middle-class woman better equipped to cope with the situation. Much of what we know about adjustment to widowhood is based on older women with traditional marriages and less education than today's women, who may be better prepared to handle life without a spouse.

Siblings have much in common: their genetic heritage, their cultural surroundings, and their early experience. Although sibling relationships generally diminish in importance during adulthood, most siblings maintain contact. Siblings tend to be apathetic about the relationships, to be extremely close, or to be rivals. Bonds between siblings tend to deepen during later adulthood, and mutual aid is common.

Friendships are voluntary associations and can be broken by either party. Friends tend to be similar in many ways, and the relationship provides self-affirmation and ego support, as well as intellectual stimulation, pleasure, and practical benefits. Friendships are often linked to other life roles, and shifts in roles may affect the bond. Male friendships are typically based on shared activities and shared experiences whereas female friendships are characterized by mutual assistance, intimacy, and emotional support. However, the quality of friendship is affected by a person's degree of conventionality, with standard gender differences found among conventional men and women, but not among the nonconventional.

KEY TERMS

cohabitation

common-law marriage

intimacy

12

RELATIONSHIPS BETWEEN GENERATIONS

Katherine Rose Pruzan, who is 1 year old, has been growing up in a non-traditional household. Since she was born, her 34-year-old father, Mark, has been at home with her on unpaid paternity leave as her primary caregiver. Katherine's mother, Jo Ann, also spent time at home on maternity leave, but only for the first three months after Katherine's birth. Thirty-two-year-old Jo Ann's job as field director for a marketing and research company pays substantially more than Mark's job as a county welfare frauds investigator, so it seemed sensible for her to return to work instead of Mark.

"Someone has to watch the baby," explained Mark. "I don't want a surrogate parent from eight to six. Why have a child in the first place?" (Melvin, 1983, p. WC6).

Jo Ann and Mark's marriage has never followed the traditional family script. From the beginning, all household responsibilities have been divided down the middle, and there is no "woman's work" or "man's work" in their arrangement. Once Mark returns to his job, Jo Ann plans to work part time, meshing her hours with Mark's so that Katherine's care will be managed smoothly.

Although few families have adopted the sort of arrangement that seems to be working well for this couple, paternity leave—which would have been un-

Some businesses have begun to offer paternity leave, a development that could lead to major changes in the lives of many young couples.

thinkable only a few years ago—has made its first appearance in the work situation. In many respects, choices for today's families are wider than they once were, and alternative family forms have become more popular.

In this chapter, which investigates relationships between generations, we begin with a look at the family, where we learn the rules of relationships and what to expect from them. After exploring the family as a system, we move to the parent-child relationship, considering traditional as well as nontraditional ways of relating to children. Next we examine another bond that crosses generations, the relationship between grandparent and grandchild. Returning to the parent-child relationship, we investigate its changing nature across adulthood as child becomes parent and parent enters old age. We close the chapter with a look at the ways in which influences pass up and down the ladder of generations.

THE FAMILY AS A SYSTEM

Our most important relationships occur within the context of the family. Our first relationships are with our parents, and—unless we are abandoned or orphaned—we grow up and are socialized within the family unit. Siblings, grandparents, and perhaps stepparents become important; and in some families aunts, uncles, and cousins also play important roles. Our relationships with our first family endure even as we find mates, establish new families of our own, and continue the cycle of generations. And should we choose to remain single, we still have a role to play in our family of birth.

One way to look at the family is to see it as a social system whose structure is affected by the addition, development, and departure of individual members and sometimes by the demands of the culture and changes in the environment (Hill and Mattessich, 1979). The system is established with the marriage of mates and lasts until that bond is dissolved by divorce or death. Within the system, each member has a series of roles that at any time are determined by age and gender and by relatedness. Each family goes through stages of development that occur whenever new members are added by birth or adoption, present members leave to take jobs or establish their own families, or any family member moves into a new role, as when a child becomes an adolescent.

Because the family is a system, a change in any of its parts changes all the other parts. When the first child is born, wife and husband acquire the new roles of mother and father. The addition of a second child shifts the relationships of mother, father, and firstborn to one another and creates new relationships with the infant. Although many of the changes in family roles, such as school entry, puberty, and retirement are age-related, others, such as divorce, are not. Family roles and structure are also affected by changes in type of residence (as from renter to homeowner, from apartment to house), changes in status (parenthood, grandparenthood, widowhood), changes in job (through promotion or switching occupations), and historical events (depressions, wars, sweeping technological change) (Hill and Mattessich, 1979).

Although the family responds to the needs of its members and actively manipulates the environment so as to fill those needs, the location of the family in historical time will affect the way the family views needs and the range of possible responses. As Glenn Elder (1978) has pointed out, the social meanings of age and the basic facts of birth, sexual maturity, and death change in meaning across cultures and at different times in the same culture. Social expectations tell us when "the time is right" for school entry, completion of education, economic independence, leaving home, marriage, childbirth, and retirement—and the timetable in rural areas may be different from the accepted timetable in small towns or in cities in the same society. If society changes its expectations or the roles it assigns people at various ages, the structure and function of the family may change (Hill and Mattessich, 1979).

Another factor that affects family roles is the age of husband and wife at each step of family life (Elder, 1978). A marriage begun at the age of 23 is a different experience from a marriage begun at the age of 35. Age also affects the experience of parenthood. When children come early in life, neither husband nor wife is likely to have become established in a career, the couple will have few assets, and economic constraints on the young family are likely to be sharp. When childbearing is postponed, the family's situation is likely to be more secure, lessening economic pressures.

Cohort differences affect family life just as they affect cognition and emotional development. A historical event affects each cohort at a different stage in the members' careers. The experience of World War II, for example, had very different effects on the lives of the cohort that was in high school during the early 1940s, the cohort whose members fought in the war or worked in the factories, and the cohort whose sons were on the battlefields. Historical events can make it easier or more difficult to attain life goals, so that even if social expectations remain the same, the opportunities for reaching those goals change (Hill and Mattessich, 1979). Recently, for example, it has become very difficult for a young couple to buy a first house. If fewer people are able to own homes and those who do buy them make the purchase later in the life span, family structure will adjust to new social reality, perhaps by a postponement of childbirth.

In the past few decades, social and economic influences seem to have stretched out the family cycle. Today's families tend to be characterized by later marriage, postponement of childbearing, compressed period of childbearing, smaller families, and a longer period without children at both ends of the family cycle (Glick, 1977).

Despite alterations in the cycle, the family continues to fulfill its primary functions. In addition to meeting its members' needs, the family serves a social purpose. It socializes children, preparing them to take on adult roles and transferring the culture from one generation to the next. Anthropologist Margaret Mead (1978) saw the transmission of culture as occuring in one of three styles: postfigurative, cofigurative, and prefigurative. In the *postfigurative culture,* at least three generations take the culture for granted. As the culture is unquestioned, the child also takes it for granted. Most aspects of the culture are not labeled or put into words for the child; they are simply *there* and remain below the level of consciousness. Authority comes from the past. Tribal societies and small religious and ideological groups within larger societies are primarily postfigurative. Such cultures are stable, and the course of family life remains the same from one generation to the next.

In the *cofigurative culture,* not the past but the present is the standard. The parental generation assumes that each generation's behavior will differ from that of the previous generation, and each child accepts the behavior of his or her peers as a model. In such societies, elder peers establish standards for the young and set boundaries to their behavior. Cofigurative cultures include groups within a postfigurative culture, as when the children of immigrant groups are socialized in the new society. Most complex societies, which have had to develop a way to incorporate change, combine cofigurative with postfigurative styles.

Finally, in the *prefigurative culture,* neither the past nor the present is seen as a trustworthy guide. Changes within society are so rapid that the lessons of parents and elder peers are unreliable, and the future is unknown. In a prefigurative culture, said Mead, ''elders have to learn from children about experiences they [the adults] have never had'' (1978, p. 13). Mead believed that atomic energy had thrust the world into a prefigurative state and that generations who grew up after World War II could not rely on the culture of the past. As a result, society was extremely unstable and, until members of the post-World War II generation became grandparents, there would be no reliable tradition to pass on.

Whether or not Mead's analysis is correct, American society has been changing rapidly since World War II. Under the influence of such factors as lengthening periods of education, divorce and remarriage, early retirement, and second careers, the American life cycle has become fluid, with many role transitions (Neugarten and Brown-Rezanka, 1978). Expectations are not as rigid and timetables are not as strict, making chronological age a less reliable guide to family events. Changes are especially apparent in our expectations concerning parenthood.

CHILDREN

The majority of couples eventually have children, but the course of parenthood in this country has been changing in several ways. Today's parents have fewer children. By their thirty-fifth birthday, today's women expect to have given birth at the rate of 2048 children for each 1000 women—down from an expected 2160 births in 1976 (*The New York Times,* 1983a)—and from 3288 births per 1000 in 1967 (U.S. Bureau of the Census, 1982). Since 1870 the overall birthrate has been declining in the United States, with the large, steady drop interrupted only during the decade between 1947 and 1957, when there was the post-World War II flurry of fertility that produced the baby boom (Uhlenberg, 1978).

Thanks to cheap, reliable contraceptives, these births are more likely to be planned than they were in previous generations. And births are coming somewhat later than was once customary as an increasing number of women are choosing to establish themselves in their careers before they pause to have a child. In 1980, 40.4 percent of the married women between the ages of 20 and 24 and 26.3 percent of the married women between the ages of 25 and 29 were childless. Twenty years earlier, only 24.2 percent of the 20- to 24-year-old married women and 12.6 of the 25- to 29-year-olds had never given birth (U.S. Bureau of the Census, 1982). As a result of this trend, births have risen among women in their thirties. Between 1980 and 1983, the birth rate for women in the 30- to 35-year-old group increased 15 percent (*The New York Times,* 1984b).

One consequence of reduced family size is a decrease in the proportion of the life span that parents devote to child rearing. Although many women are postponing the first birth, most of the increase in child-free years is coming during middle age, when children have become independent (Alpert and Richardson, 1980). When a woman has only two children, her childbearing period is generally compressed, so that she is younger when her last child leaves home.

The proportion of mothers employed outside the home has increased, especially among women with preschool children. In 1981, 47.8 percent of all married mothers with children younger than 6 years old were in the labor force, compared with only 18.6 percent in 1960 (U.S. Bureau of the Census, 1982). The rate of outside employment was even higher among separated (51 percent) or divorced (65.4 percent) mothers of young children.

Finally, the rising divorce rate has increased the number of one-parent families. In 1980, about 20 percent of American children younger than 18 years lived with one parent, usually the mother. One million children lived with their fathers; and 11 million, with their mothers. (Children's Defense Fund, 1982).

Because of these trends, talking about the traditional nuclear household, in which the mother stays at home and the father is the sole breadwinner, means talking about a minority of American families. Life in today's family cannot be understood without considering employed mothers, stepparents, and single-parent households.

Not much on pregnancy in Bee

PREGNANCY AND CHILDBIRTH

The experience of parenthood begins before the birth of a child. From the first awareness of conception, relationships within the family begin to shift, as psychological and practical provisions are made to accommodate a new member into the family system. Most studies of pregnancy concentrate on the mother and pay little attention to the father except to assess his role in providing emotional and financial support.

Both partners participated in a longitudinal study of pregnancy among just under a hundred middle-class married couples, half of whom were expecting their first child (Grossman, Eichler, and Winickoff, 1980). During early pregnancy,

The marital relationship begins to change during pregnancy, as couples make psychological and practical provisions for their expected child.

the mother's general psychological health appeared to be the strongest predictor of adaptation although whether the pregnancy was planned also had some effect. Women who were anxious about the process tended to have husbands who showed a high degree of anxiety. For women having their first child, the pregnancy seemed central to their lives: "they are the pregnancy and the pregnancy is them" (Grossman, Eichler, and Winickof, 1980, p. 24).

The marital relationship had clear effects on the course of pregnancy. Women with high marital satisfaction had fewer physical and emotional symptoms, and among first-time mothers, the more egalitarian their marriage, the fewer symptoms they developed. Among women who had already borne children, couples with egalitarian relationships tended to feel closer than couples with traditional relationships. But the existence of marital problems late in pregnancy tended to be linked to socioeconomic level, with women in lower level occupations being more likely than others to report difficulties with their marriage.

The researchers stress the finding that psychological and environmental variables unrelated to the biological aspects of pregnancy influence the experience. For example, women who said during early pregnancy that they had wanted to become pregnant were less likely to have complications during pregnancy or delivery than women who said they had not wanted to conceive. However, the strongest predictor of a complicated delivery was a high level of anxiety during pregnancy.

Other research (Chester, 1979) indicates that men may be more concerned than women about the role changes involved in becoming a parent, perhaps because women are preoccupied by the physical aspects of pregnancy. A woman's absorption with the coming birth and her feelings of closeness with her prospective baby may make her husband feel shut out.

Discrepancies in sexual desires and curtailment of sexual activity may add to the problem. Some men say there is no change in their sexual desire during their wives' pregnancies, some say their desire increases, and others say their desire wanes or disappears entirely. According to Susan White and Kenneth Reamy (1982), in large studies of pregnancy, most—but not all—women report a progressive decline in sexual interest, sexual activity, and orgasm during pregnancy. However, most women also say that they want to be cuddled and held more by their husbands. When the sexual reaction to pregnancy of wife and husband is greatly discrepant, the result may be sexual frustration and a strained marital relationship. Wives in the longitudinal study (Grossman, Eichler, and Winickoff, 1980) who seemed to adapt best to labor and delivery had husbands who were satisfied with their marriages as a whole and who were content with a low level of sexual contact.

A working woman's feelings about her job may also affect the course of her pregnancy. Among 120 pregnant employed women, those who enjoyed their work adapted well to being pregnant and were less anxious, depressed, tired, and guilty during their pregnancies than women who disliked their jobs. Rather than finding it difficult to adapt to the idea of motherhood, women who enjoy their occupations may also enjoy their pregnancies—perhaps because they have a generally positive attitude toward life (Newton and Modahl, 1978).

In a traditional hospital birth, the father is generally ignored during labor and delivery. When natural childbirth methods are used, the father becomes an active participant and coach. This sort of involvement in the birth process may make it easier for a man to adjust to his new role as parent. Fathers who have such a part in childbirth afterward say that they felt as if their role was important (Romalis, 1981).

Once their infant is born and the joy and exhilaration that often accompany the birth are past, adjustments to the physical presence of the new family member must be made. These adjustments generally require the expenditure of much time, emotion, and energy. During this period, some women develop **postpartum depression**, which includes crying jags, nightmares, and fears or worries about the baby. Although it usually lasts only a short time, some women find themselves depressed for several months (Rosen and Hall, 1984).

Shifting hormone levels may play a role in this emotional reaction, but the most reasonable explanation for postpartum depression seems to be the strain of adapting to the new role of mother (Laws and Schwartz, 1977). If a woman has the sole responsibility for child care, she may feel socially isolated, if not trapped. And because society has traditionally frowned on mothers with small children who work outside the home, a woman who is deeply committed to her career may be especially vulnerable to a bout of depression. However, most postpartum depression may have a simple cause: lack of sleep. Few new mothers escape a period of weeks or months in which their sleep is interrupted several times each night.

The father's adjustment to his new role has received little notice. Various studies (Alpert and Richardson, 1980) have indicated that fathers are under many of the same stresses that mothers encounter, that they feel they have lost a good share of their wives' attention, and that they tend to have trouble developing their changed role in regard to their wife and infant. The adjustment to parenthood has been seen as serving an adaptive purpose.

THE PARENTAL IMPERATIVE

The human species can continue only if it reproduces itself, and psychologist David Gutmann (1975) has proposed that in the course of evolution, parenthood has come to play a pivotal and controlling role over the entire life span. He calls this development the **parental imperative**, and believes that basic personality differences between the sexes have evolved with the requirements of young children in mind. These differences, which function to protect vulnerable infants and children, are sharpest among young parents and diminish markedly in later life.

In Gutmann's view, parenthood is a state of chronic emergency, in which the sort of maternal and paternal behavior that is encouraged by traditional female and male traits supplies the infant's needs for physical and emotional security. The usefulness of these traits, he says, becomes apparent when we look at subsistence societies, which may be closer to the conditions of scarcity and danger in which the species evolved. In such societies, traditional male characteristics (such as aggression, autonomy, competence, and control) provide the child with physical security, for they send the father out to hunt large game and to guard the child against predators. Traditional female characteristics (such as nurturance, sympathy, gentleness, and understanding) provide the child with emotional security, for they keep the mother near the child and home.

According to Gutmann, evolution provides only the *potentials* for sex roles. Society channels these potentials through socialization, so that men and women come to enjoy exercising the traits that characterize their own gender. A cultural consensus gives meaning to traditional sex roles and surrounds them with moral incentives.

When a child is born, the young father's behavior changes; he directs his masculine potentials toward creating and controlling security for his family, ignoring any longing for pleasure, passivity, or dependence that might interfere with his child's safety. (A passive, dependent, sympathetic father might not be tough enough to provide adequate economic or physical security.) The young mother directs her feminine potentials toward her child, muffling any aggressive or assertive qualities. (An aggressive, insensitive mother might harm her child or drive off her husband, leaving her child unprotected.)

Gutmann does not claim that each sex lacks the qualities of the other, but that each suppresses those qualities in carrying out parental roles. Once the child is grown and has left home, both parents are free to indulge the qualities that have been suppressed all during the child-rearing period. Fathers become more interested in love than in power; they tend to become dependent, to defer to their wives, to take greater pleasure in diffuse sensuality, enjoying food, aesthetic pleasures, and human associations. Mothers tend to become more aggressive, assertive, and domineering, preferring autonomy to nurturance and understanding. As each sex takes on some of the qualities of the other, men and women become androgynous.

Is Gutmann's theory supported by research? Socialization does not have equal effects on everyone. Differences in these traits among women and men are as large as, if not larger than, the differences between the average woman and the average man. However, as we saw in Chapter 10, there is some indication that people do tend to become androgynous in later adulthood. Gutmann's own research in the United States and several other cultures is based primarily on the results of TAT tests (see Chapter 10), and it has been largely cross-sectional, although a five-year longitudinal study among Navajo and Druse men indicated age shifts toward dependency. Looking at the other end of the scale, researchers (Abrahams, Feldman, and Nash, 1978) have found that young fathers rate themselves higher on masculine traits and young mothers rate themselves higher on feminine traits than do men and women among cohabiting couples, childless married couples, and married couples expecting their first child. And in another cross-sectional study (Feldman, Biringen, and Nash, 1981), expectant mothers were least autonomous, and grandmothers showed the most autonomy. Among men in this study, compassion increased steadily from single adulthood to grandfatherhood. These shifts were related to the stage in the family life cycle, not to the age, and so seemed to depend on specific situations.

In an accounting for these role changes, there seems little chance of untangling the influences of genetics and society, and Gutmann does stress the role of socialization in developing them. However, rigid parental roles that were adaptive for our early ancestors are not necessarily the most adaptive roles in a highly technological society of relative abundance. Mothers no longer must spin yarn, weave cloth, make all the clothing, grind grain to obtain flour, bake bread, tend the vegetable garden, and scrub clothes in the nearby stream. Fathers no longer must guard against predators, go after big game, or assume total financial support of the family. When child care is no longer so labor intensive, the parental imperative becomes less important and perhaps less adaptive.

Changes in personality and role required by parenthood may be much briefer and less intense among future cohorts (Self, 1975). It is even possible that the changes may differ from those proposed by Gutmann. In a recent study of well-educated, middle-class parents, parenthood had an unexpected effect on the fathers (Feldman and Aschenbrenner, 1983). Longitudinal measures, taken a month or two before the baby's birth and again when the child was 6 months old, indicated that fathers showed increased nurturance, responsiveness to babies, warmth, sensitivity, emotional expressiveness, and tolerance for others' short-comings. The fathers had become more *feminine,* and 77 percent of them shared in the housecleaning, shopping, and cooking. But there was no decline in their masculine identity or in their dominance scores, and their scores on autonomy increased. Among these adults, the care of a small infant made both women and men more feminine, indicating the influence of life situations on behavior and personality. As more parents share the responsibility for their children's physical and emotional security, mothers may become more autonomous and fathers more nurturant than was customary in earlier generations.

BEING A PARENT

Parenthood is generally a stressful, but rewarding, experience. When parents were asked whether, if they could live their lives over, they would have children, 90 percent said they would (Yanekelovich, 1981). The rewards they found in parenthood included joy, fun, self-fulfillment, maturity, and pride. Women may derive a sense of personal worth from their ability to bear and rear children, and fathers may find their self-esteem enhanced (Bell and Harper, 1977). Among the stresses of parenthood are restrictions on personal and economic freedom and the disruption of the relationship between the spouses. Life in a household with children is very different from life in a childless home. There is usually less conversation between the parents, and some of the spontaneity that characterizes a couple's emotional and sexual life may disappear. Depending on the situation, the care of children can either raise or lower the parents' perception of well-being.

Although babies become attached to both parents at about the same time, when they are between 6 and 8 months old, the relationship to each parent is different. Society has set standards for the maternal role and assigned the major responsibility for infant care to the mother. The mother tends to focus on caregiving; when she picks up the baby, it is generally to feed, diaper, or comfort her child, and together they play traditional games, such as peekaboo. Mothers who value the maternal role find their effectiveness as a caregiver closely linked with their self-esteem.

Social expectations for the paternal role are few, and even when the father helps care for the child, he is rarely the primary caregiver. The father tends to focus on social interaction; when he picks up the baby, it is generally to play, and the games are generally rough-and-tumble. A traditional father's contact with a baby is often limited because he is likely to avoid caretaking routines. As a result, his clumsy performance at occasional diapering or feeding is unlikely to affect his self-esteem (Lamb and Easterbrooks, 1981).

These differences in responsibility may be at the heart of dissatisfaction among mothers with young children. Researchers (Brown and Harris, 1978) have estimated that one fourth of mothers whose children are younger than five at some time take tranquilizers for depression or related disorders. It may be that the younger the new mother, the lower her satisfaction (Fig. 12.1). Among first-time mothers between the ages of 16 and 38 who were not employed outside the home, younger mothers were the least satisfied although they generally had fewer care-taking responsibilities and more social time away from the baby than older mothers. Satisfaction increased steadily with age, and the effect was especially pronounced among mothers of babies born prematurely (Ragozin et al., 1982).

Another factor in maternal satisfaction may be the division of household tasks. With the birth of the first child, chores tend to be divided along more traditional lines, no matter what arrangement the couple had previously established (Cowan et al., 1978). If a couple has been sharing household tasks and the new mother suddenly finds herself with more work as well as the burden of childcare, conflict may develop, and marital satisfaction may plummet.

A third aspect of motherhood that can reduce satisfaction arises from the mother's responsibility for organizing family life and seeing that necessary tasks are carried out. As mothers work to make the system run smoothly, they are

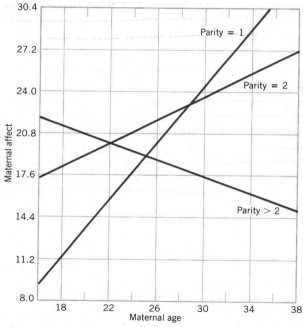

FIGURE 12.1   Maternal feelings and age. Among first-time mothers of young babies, the older the woman, the more pleasure she derived from the maternal role. Only among women with three or more children did younger mothers find motherhood more satisfying. In this study, maternal affect was a combination of the mother's gratification from interactions with her baby, the general emotional tone of their relationship, and her sensitivity to her baby's needs.

Source: A. S. Ragozin, R. B. Basham, K. A. Crnic, M. T. Greenberg, and N. M. Robinson, 1982, p. 631

likely to run into anger and resistance from their children and to receive little support in their attempts to reduce chaos. Researchers (Maccoby, 1980) have suggested that the situation reduces self-esteem and contributes to the depression found among mothers of young children.

At 44, one mother recalled her situation when the children were young:

They want what they want when they want it! There is no sense of fairness—no sense that you have to have a little peace and quiet. You're there to dispense what they want and sometimes you feel like a nothing because you're just there for everyone. I think in these darker periods you start wondering if there's any point to it. But fortunately, these feelings are more prevalent when the children are small, and looking back, I think other mothers took steps to prevent that overburdened feeling—which I didn't do [Baruch, Barnett, and Rivers, 1983, p. 89].

When the second child comes along, new adjustments in family relationships are required. A new balance must be struck between the parental and marital roles, and fitting the demands of a fourth family member to various housekeeping and child-care tasks creates added stress. In a study that followed 16 families for two years after the birth of their second child, researchers (Kreppner, Paulsen, and Schuetze, 1982) discerned several ways in which parents handled these problems. Some parents played interchangeable roles, "doubling" for each other so that the same responsibility was passed back and forth, depending on the situation. In some families, the father assumed increased responsibility for the other child, leaving the mother free to establish an intimate relationship with the new baby. In other families, the father took on more household tasks while the mother took most of the responsibility for child care. As the baby began to grow out of babyhood, the situation changed again. Instead of being parents of a child and a baby, the mother and father began to see themselves as parents of "children" and reacted on the basis of each child's personality as opposed to his or her developmental stage. Now family priorities changed, and the parents' own needs and wishes began to receive attention.

Among a group of midlife women, two kinds of relationships with children, "autonomous" and "coupled" mothering, were found (Baruch, Barnett, and Rivers, 1983). In *autonomous mothering,* rewards came from seeing children as individuals instead of as extensions of the mother. Mothers felt proud of their children, enjoyed doing things with them and watching them mature, and liked the kind of people they were. An autonomous mother, a 37-year-old college administrator, described some of the rewards she got from her maternal role:

Children teach you a tremendous amount. The older they get, the more important are the questions that arise, and you have to think and rethink the issues you've grappled with before in childhood or adolescence. I look on it as a tremendous opportunity because it means I'm always growing. They're really just lovely people, each very different, and it's kind of neat for me to see how different three people can be who came out of the same gene pool'' [Baruch, Barnett, and Rivers, 1983, p. 84].

In *coupled mothering,* rewards came from children's importance to the mother's sense of identity. These mothers felt that children gave meaning to their own lives and provided them with a sense of being needed; as mothers, they felt special and irreplaceable. A coupled mother described her relationship with her children:

It's the kids that keep me going, really. This is how I feel. I don't see how people can be married and not have kids. The kids are my life, that's it in a nutshell, and I live for my kids and I do things for my kids. I'm in the car running here and there. I'm always running for everybody. I can't say no'' [Baruch, Barnett, and Rivers, 1983, p. 84].

Both kinds of mothers tended to derive much pleasure from their offspring, but compared with coupled mothers, autonomous mothers were higher in self-esteem, felt that they were in control of their lives, and were less likely to complain of anxiety or depression.

Youngsters have such a powerful influence on family life that researchers (Rollins and Galligan, 1978) have suggested marital satisfaction is determined by the presence, number, and age of a couple's children. These factors are believed to affect the way each parent perceives the quality of the spouse's performance as husband or wife, the sacrifices each makes in carrying out family roles, and the quality of each parent's own performance as wife or husband.

The family continues to be a center of attention for mothers of adolescents, even when the women are employed. Asked about the ''best'' and the ''worst'' things that had happened to them in the past year, two thirds of a group of Massachusetts mothers' replies concerned family members (Rossi, 1980). Younger women, in their late thirties and early forties, mentioned children twice as often as they mentioned their husbands; and older women, in their late forties, mentioned children three times as often as they mentioned their husbands. In fact, older women indicated greater satisfaction from their children than from their marriage or their own accomplishments. Among the younger women, the pleasures of children, marriage, and their own accomplishments contributed about equally to their satisfaction with life. Whether younger or older, general marital satisfaction was related to satisfaction with their homes, their neighborhood, and their social life, but their satisfaction with their children was related only to time for themselves. Whether a mother is employed outside the home can also affect her general level of satisfaction.

EMPLOYED MOTHERS

From time to time, voices are raised in criticism of the working mother, especially the mother whose children are young. Yet the proportion of families in which the mother has no outside employment continues to shrink, dropping from just over 50 percent among mothers with babies and preschoolers to 38 percent among married mothers of schoolage children (U.S. Bureau of the Census, 1982) (Fig. 12.2).

	1960	1970	1980	1981
Children between 6 and 17 years	39.0%	49.2%	61.7%	62.5%
Children younger than 6 years	18.6%	30.3%	45.1%	47.8%

FIGURE 12.2   Employed married mothers (percent).

Source: U.S. Bureau of the Census, *Statistical Abstract of the United States, 1982–1983*, 103d ed., 1982.

The major objection to maternal employment comes from those who believe a small child requires the presence of a full-time mother although some object to any mother working outside the home. Most of the evidence appears to indicate that maternal employment is not detrimental to young children. In one study (Gold and Andres, 1978b), 4-year-old children of mothers who had worked since the child's birth showed better social adjustment than 4-year-olds whose mothers were always home. However, IQ scores among sons tended to be lower when their mothers worked. Lois Hoffman (1979) has suggested that the issue is not whether mothers work, but what happens to the child while the mother is working.

Some parents have handled this problem by working different shifts. More than a million American families have adopted the split shift approach to child care, and in most cases the husband works nights and the wife works days (Dullea, 1983). For example, Patricia Craemer, who works as a reservation agent for Delta Air Lines, arrives home each day 20 minutes before her husband, Richard, leaves for his shift as a mechanic for the same airline. Richard says, "We don't want anybody else taking care of Erika. Nobody can do that better than her parents" (p. B12).

The advantages to shift work are that children always have one parent's care and attention, that children of shift workers tend to take responsibilities early, and that couples sometimes find their relationship improves because they value

Although few women are able to take their children along with them to work, the employed mother has become the norm in American families.

their time together. The disadvantages of shift work are that an older child may find him- or herself acting as surrogate parent, that children of shift workers rarely see their parents interacting, and that a couple's sex life may suffer (Dullea, 1983).

But shift workers encompass a minority of families with employed mothers. Among nonshift-working parents of 3- to 6-year-olds, the mother's employment did not affect the type of relationship between children and their mothers and fathers (Stuckey, McGhee, and Bell, 1982). Each parent tended to adhere to the gender-typical parental role described earlier, with the mother spending more time on caregiving and quiet play and the father spending more time on active play. However, when the mother's role did not match parental attitudes toward maternal employment, both parents tended to be dissatisfied. Other studies have produced similar patterns and indicate that satisfied mothers have more positive interaction with their children than dissatisfied mothers (Houser and Beckman, 1980) and that the nonemployed mother who prefers to work is the most dissatisfied (Yarrow et al., 1962).

The effect of outside employment on mothers is sometimes very positive. Midlife women who scored highest on all measures of well-being had high prestige jobs, were married, and had children (Baruch, Bennett, and Rivers, 1983). Juggling three roles, they were happier than women who faced only the strains of a single role (either nonemployed wife or single employed woman). Such women apparently learn to balance their roles by dropping off unwanted aspects of some roles, perhaps cooking less elaborate meals or withdrawing from some community responsibilities.

Although some studies have found that the division of household tasks is less traditional when mothers work outside the home (Gold and Andres, 1978a), others have found that housekeeping and child-care tasks are just as heavy for the employed as for the nonemployed mother (Stuckey, McGhee, and Bell, 1982). As outside employment has become the rule rather than the exception, husbands have begun to assume some of the household tasks, but rarely is the work shared equally.

The division of labor within the household appears to be closely related to marital power (Ericksen, Yancey, and Ericksen, 1979). The higher the wife's status (in terms of her education) in relation to her husband's status (in terms of his income), the greater her power in the home and the more likely it is that her husband will do part of the household chores. Despite the effect of the wife's education on the power balance, even highly educated wives who work full time outside the home and have unsuccessful husbands tend to do the greater part of the housework. This consistent finding may be changing. According to psychologist Joseph Pleck (cited in Baruch, Barnett, and Rivers, 1983), role overload among employed women has recently begun to drop—not because husbands are doing more at home, but because wives are doing less. Working wives and mothers appear to be discovering that a number of "necessary" tasks are not as necessary as they once thought.

As Hoffman (1979) points out, maternal employment is a part of modern family life. Because it diminishes rigid sex-role stereotypes, it may equip children to meet their adult roles more effectively. And because employment gives women added sources of identity and self-esteem, it may make it easier for them to allow their growing children to develop autonomy.

THE LONE PARENT

The number of parents without partners continues to rise, so that an increasing number of adults can expect to spend some time rearing their children by themselves. Although in most cases, the single parent is a divorced mother with custody of her children, sometimes the mother has never married, the divorced father has custody, the absent parent has died, or the single parent (mother or father) has adopted a child. In 1981, more than 9 million women and about 650,000 men were heads of households composed of their own children younger than 18 years (U.S. Bureau of the Census, 1982). Most of what we know about relationships in the one-parent home comes from studies of divorced, middle-class mothers and their children. But no matter what the structure of the one-parent family, many of its problems have nothing to do with the gender or marital status of the parent.

In all one-parent families, a single person is responsible for dealing with all tasks and demands that are ordinarily shared by two parents. Having to take full responsibility for meal preparation, cleaning, home and car maintenance, financial management, child care, and meeting children's emotional needs produces more problems for the lone mother or father than any other aspect of the single-parent role. After interviewing more than 200 separated, divorced, widowed, and married parents—as well as their children, Robert Weiss (1979) found that children are more likely to help out in single-parent families. They take care of some household tasks, shoulder extra responsibilities, and often participate in major household decisions.

Some of the problems that beset lone parents cannot be handled by turning to the children. The single parent may be lonely, lack a sexual partner, have no source of emotional support, nowhere to turn in emergencies, and find his or her social life sharply curtailed. Many single parents work at bulding up support networks to help with social and emotional problems, turning to family members, the other parent, friends, lovers, counselors, and such groups as Parents Without Partners.

Despite the problems that accompany the single-parent role, parents find rewards for both their children and themselves (Weiss, 1979). Children tend to grow up faster than youngsters in intact homes, apparently because of the added responsibilities most assume. Children often find a great improvement in home atmosphere, because the bickering, anger, tears, and obvious emotional upset that characterize partners in an unhappy marriage are absent from the one-parent

BECOMING A STEPPARENT

When divorced women and men remarry, stepparents are often created. More than 6 million children live in homes with a stepparent, making this family variation extremely common (Santrock et al., 1982). Because society has not developed expectations for the role of stepparent and because few studies have investigated the relationships between stepparents and stepchildren, men and women who find themselves suddenly cast into this role have few guidelines.

In most cases, children live with their mothers, so that the role of the stepfather has received the greater share of attention. In one study, John Santrock and his co-workers (1982) compared interactions in stepparent families and intact families. They found that family atmosphere differed, depending on the gender of the stepchild. In families with sons, stepfathers appeared to be more competent in the father role than did the biological fathers, and marital conflict was less intense. Perhaps as a result, stepsons were more socially competent than sons in intact families.

Indeed, most studies indicate that a stepfather may have a comparatively easy adjustment if his new child is a young boy. Although the child may resent having to share his mother, the advantages of having a male role model in the house seems to help the new relationship flourish. Research (Wallerstein and Kelly, 1980) indicates that many young boys become excited at the prospect of a new father and quickly develop an attachment to him. In most cases, the stepson's cognitive and emotional development is affected favorably.

When the child is a girl, the presence of a stepfather can disrupt the relationship between daughter and mother, and feelings of rivalry and competition may develop between them. Among the families studied by Santrock and his colleagues (1982), girls with stepfathers showed more anxiety than girls in intact families and tended to show more anger toward their mothers and less warmth toward their stepfathers than did boys. With stepdaughters, stepfathers were no more competent in the parental role than were biological fathers.

Little research has been done into home. Single parents are often closer to their children than are parents in intact homes, and child-parent interactions are more open and cover a broader range of situations. Single parents may have additional responsibilites, but they also tend to feel proud and happy about their accomplishments. Parents may also develop new aspects of their personality as women are forced to become more self-reliant and men are forced to become more nurturant. The increased self-reliance that Weiss found in the women he studied mirrors the sense of mastery that appeared in another study (Baruch, Barnett, and Rivers, 1983) among midlife divorced the relationship of stepmothers and their stepchildren, but it would appear that the situation might be the mirror image of the stepfather relationship. A stepmother may be accepted more readily by a young stepdaughter than by a stepson. It seems that relationships in the family founded on remarriage run more smoothly when the custodial parent and child are of the opposite sex, allowing a stepparent of the same gender as the child to be more easily accommodated.

Relationships between stepparents and stepchildren are sometimes complicated by the fact that each parent has children from a former marriage. Adjustment in such cases calls for multiple shifts in roles and relationships. Family structure becomes most intricate when the children can be divided into "his, hers, and ours." When both partners have children from a former marriage, marital quality (as measured by both self-report and observations of interaction between the spouses) is lower than when only the wife has children from her former marriage (Clingempeel, 1981). Conflicting loyalties on the part of the stepfather, who has to divide his time and attention between his biological children (who live with his former wife) and his stepchildren, may be responsible for the lowered marital quality found in this study.

In both groups of families (Clingempeel, 1981), marriages in which former spouses were seen a few times each month were happiest. When former spouses were seen too often (at least once a week), the frequent contact, together with the lack of any social guidelines for such roles as stepfather, noncustodial parent, and former spouse, may have placed the new marriage under so much strain that it never became solid. When former spouses were seen infrequently (less than once a month), marital quality also suffered. The reason for this effect is uncertain, but the researcher suggests that when there is very little contact with a former spouse, children may become resentful at being denied membership in their other biological family. That resentment may erode their relations with their stepfathers, ultimately affecting the relationship between husband and wife. It is clear that we have much to learn about family dynamics in the new complex American family.

mothers who were employed. These women showed high self-esteem, a feeling that they controlled their own lives, and few symptoms of anxiety or depression.

Such findings from cross-sectional studies tell us little about development of functioning single-parent households. Newly divorced parents, suddenly faced with the sole responsibility for their households, often feel that they will never be able to cope. A longitudinal study of households made up of middle-class children and their divorced mothers provided reassuring evidence that the disorganization and problems that often accompany the sudden transition tend to ease by the second year after divorce. Mavis Hetherington, Martha Cox, and Roger Cox (1979) followed for two years the families of 48 divorced couples in which the mother received custody of the children, comparing them with intact families that resembled them. At first many of the women felt overwhelmed by the tasks that confronted them and were convinced that they lacked the time and energy to deal competently with the demands of child care, home management, occupation, and social contacts. Economic stress was generally severe as available money had to be stretched over two households, and many women felt helpless owing to economic scarcity, financial discrimination, and lack of experience in dealing with financial matters.

Two years later, these women's ability to handle their myriad responsibilities had improved sharply, but the single-family households were still more disorganized than those of intact families. Maternal employment had positive effects on most women and did not seem to bother their children unless the mother first began working around the time of the divorce. Within two years, economic stress had lessened as the combined income of the divorced parents rose about that of the intact families, but a majority of the women still felt inadequate. This inadequacy came from their lack of knowledge concerning insurance, mortages, taxes, wills, and judging the appropriateness of charges by service personnel (such as auto mechanics or plumbers).

Problems in parent-child relationships were prevalent during the first year after divorce, with mothers of sons having more difficulty than mothers of daughters. Although stresses had not disappeared at the end of two years, they had lessened, and at least half of the mothers said that their relationships with their children were better than they had been before the divorce.

Hetherington and her co-workers concluded that divorce is often a positive solution to destructive family functioning. They noted that conditions may well keep improving in the one-parent households they studied and that adjustment would probably have been easier for both mothers and children had they been realistically prepared for the problems associated with divorce.

THE EMPTY NEST

Eventually, children grow up and leave home, taking at least partial responsibility for their own support. When the last child has departed, parents are left with an "empty nest," a situation that once was believed to be especially difficult for parents. Textbooks sometimes discussed the "empty nest syndrome" as if it were an expected part of adult development and as if all parents grieved when their children left home. Men were supposed to find the situation less traumatic because their occupations provided a major source of meaning in their lives. (Yet there has been no systematic research on how fathers are affected by the departure of their children [Troll, Miller, and Atchley, 1979].) After two decades of a life centered around children, women were thought to be ripe for a bout with depression. And when menopause and the empty nest coincided, as they often do, a crisis was seen as virtually inevitable.

Then Bernice Neugarten (1970) and her co-workers studied midlife women, comparing those with all their children home, those who were in the transitional stage—having launched some of their offspring—and those with empty nests. Their study indicated that instead of causing a stressful period, the empty nest was a time of life when satisfaction was greater than in earlier stages of parent-hood. Coping with the problems of children at home appeared to be more taxing than the emptiness that followed their departure. The notion that women who were not employed outside the home would be especially vulnerable to the empty nest syndrome also failed to hold up. Home- and community-oriented women displayed even greater satisfaction than work-oriented women. The absence of the empty-nest syndrome in this study is not an isolated finding. In a national sur-vey (Glenn, 1975), morale tended to be higher among women whose children had left home than among those who still had a full nest. Other researchers (Lowen-thal and Chiriboga, 1972) have reported that the minority of women who are un-happy when their children leave home generally have a history of emotional prob-lems.

It is not difficult to discover why parents fail to be devastated by the departure of their offspring. Unless they are footing the bill for one or more college educa-tions, disposable income suddenly rises. Time expands as parents no longer have to supervise children and as laundry, cleaning, marketing, and cooking chores shrink. Wife and husband once again have the privacy they enjoyed as newly-weds, so that intimacy can flourish and sexuality can be spontaneous. Travel no longer must be scheduled around school vacations. Among a group of midlife women, almost every one described the departure of her children with a sense of relief. A nonemployed, middle-class 50-year-old mother of three said:

When the youngest one was ready to move out of the house, I was right there helping him pack. We love having the children live in the area, and we love seeing them and the grandchildren, but I don't need for any of them to live in this house ever again. I've had as much as I ever need or want of being tied down with chil-dren [Rubin, 1979, p. 16].

The effect of children's departure does not, of course, depend solely on the re-lationship between parent and child. The marital relationship is likely to have a powerful effect on satisfaction in the empty nest. When husband and wife have stayed together only for the "sake of the children," the empty nest may be torn apart by divorce. When husband and wife care deeply for each other, their new privacy may lead to a second honeymoon. Yet other couples may develop sepa-rate lives, living together amicably but without great affection while each follows his or her own interests. It has been suggested that the diversity of marital style during the empty nest period is greater than at any other time (Troll, Miller, and Atchley, 1979).

Perhaps our view of the devastating impact of the empty home has grown from our perception of the typical family as one in which the mother is a homemaker with no outside employment, a person whose identity depends on the roles of wife and mother. But even among married women who were between 45 and 64 in 1960, 36 percent had a job outside the home; and among women of the same age

Most parents find that the departure of their grown children brings them new freedom and an increased satisfaction with their marriage.

in 1981, 47 percent were employed outside the home (U.S. Bureau of the Census, 1982). As the identity and interests of more and more women have a broader base than home, children, and spouse, it would seem increasingly unlikely that the departure of children would lead to an emotional crisis.

The final launching of children is no surprise to parents. The empty nest is an expected state of family life, and parents begin to prepare for it long before the day their last child departs. As with other life transitions, timing is important in determining the effects of the empty nest. When children leave at what parents perceive as the "right time," the transition is likely to be smoother than when the departure is too early or too late. Parent-child relationships continue, and bonds of affection and support are maintained. According to one woman (Troll, Miller, and Atchley, 1979), the empty nest is surrounded by telephone wires.

GRANDCHILDREN

When adult children become parents themselves, family relationships change once again. Parents become grandparents, and children, who have begun their own families, become parents, continuing the cycle of generations. Few specifications exist for the grandparent-grandchild relationship, making it especially vulnerable to social changes.

THE CHANGING GRANDPARENT

The stereotypical view of white-haired grandparents, with grandmother dispensing comfort and cookies and grandfather rocking on the front porch as he whittles toys for grandchildren, is probably further out-of-date than other stereotypes of aging. Today's grandparents are likely to be middle-aged and in the prime of their careers; the chances are good that grandmother goes off to work each morning. Early childbearing for successive generations, together with close spacing of fewer children, has made many of today's Americans grandparents while they are still in their forties or fifties.

The current crop of grandparents differs from some of the older cohorts in other ways. For one thing, most have no children at home. When large families were common and women bore children as long as they were fertile, the first children to leave the nest frequently produced offspring that were about the same age as their young aunts and uncles. Smaller families, born at an earlier age, mean that today's grandparents are unlikely to be dividing their identity and attention between two generations of young children (Troll, Miller, and Atchley, 1979).

Increased life expectancy has created four—or even five—living generations, so that grandparents may not be the family elders, but an intermediate generation. Approximately 40 percent of today's older adults are great-grandparents. (Troll, Miller, and Atchley, 1979). When Jimmy Carter was president of the United States, his mother, Lillian Carter, was seen as the prototypical American grandmother. She *was* Amy Carter's grandmother, but people tended to forget that she was also a great-grandmother and that President and Mrs. Carter were grandparents who, in age and life stage, resembled today's grandparents more closely than did Lillian Carter. (People also forgot that Amy was an aunt.)

The existence of grandparents in their forties creates great-grandparents in their sixties and raises the prospect of living great-great-grandparents. How long this trend will last is impossible to ascertain because alterations in childbearing practices change the relationship between generations. The rise in births among women in their thirties has already postponed grandparenthood for many in today's parental generation.

Increased life expectancy has had another effect. More children have living grandparents because there are more older people, creating a larger pool of prospective grandparents. In addition, the prevalence of divorce may be changing the experience of grandparenthood. In one study of divorce (Matthews and Sprey, 1984), grandparents tended to see even more of their grandchildren when their own child was the custodial parent and to have less contact when custody was given to the former in-law child. Events often complicate relations with grandchildren. Most young divorced adults remarry, and they are likely to do so within three years of divorce. Their children now may have four sets of grandparents. Besides their two sets of biological grandparents, they have acquired the parents of their stepfather and the parents of their biological father's second wife. All these grandparents are likely to enter children's lives in some way, and no one knows just how this abundance will affect relations between grandparents and grandchildren (Cherlin, 1983).

PATTERNS FOR GRANDPARENTS

The age span of grandparents—and grandchildren—is so large, the grandparent-grandchild relationship so varied, and the research so scanty that sweeping generalizations about these relationships are impossible. Ethnic group, religion, socioeconomic level, and personality also affect the relationship. Grandparents have

A special bond often develops between grandparent and grandchild, a bond that lacks the friction characteristic of many parent-child relationships.

no prescribed function, and so they can relate to a grandchild in any way they please. The same grandparent may have a different kind of relationship with each grandchild. As Lillian Troll (1980a) has suggested, the most practical course is to talk about the diversity of grandparental patterns.

In one of the first studies of grandparents, Bernice Neugarten and Karol Weinstein (1964) discerned five different styles among middle-class grandparents. Grandparents who adopted the *formal style* carefully separated themselves from the child-rearing role and offered no advice. They were interested in their grandchildren, providing special treats and indulging them, but never played surrogate parent. Grandparents who adopted the *fun-seeking style* played with their grandchildren, enjoying them as a source of leisure activity, and cultivated an informal relationship. *Distant* grandparents were benevolent but remote. They had only fleeting contact with their grandchildren, emerging at such occasions as Christmas and birthdays and then disappearing. An occasional grandmother became a *surrogate parent,* a style that developed when the mother worked and the grandmother became the primary caregiver. Finally, a few authoritarian grandfathers acted as *reservoir of family wisdom,* with the grandfather dispensing skills or resources and the parents playing a subordinate role.

Age had a powerful effect on a grandparent's style. Grandparents in their fifties or sixties might adopt any of the major styles, but those in their late sixties and seventies tended to be formal grandparents. Whether this difference is the result of cohort influences or whether people who become grandparents during middle age are more relaxed and less concerned about respect than older grandparents is uncertain. In either case, it would seem likely that during the 1980s fun-seeking grandparents have been more prevalent than formal grandparents.

Although about a third of the grandparents studied by Neugarten and Weinstein expressed some discomfort or disappointment in the role of grandparent, the majority of adults adjust easily and find a great deal of pleasure in the relationship. Once again, age appears to make a difference. Grandparents between the ages of 50 and 79 generally have positive feelings about the experience, but very young grandparents (those in their forties) and very old grandparents (those older than 80) tend to give neutral replies when asked how they feel about their role (Troll, 1980a). Perhaps this is another instance of people's perceptions of the "right time" for life events. A 40-year-old grandparent may feel too young to be cast in a role that carries an aged stereotype, and an 80-year-old grandparent may feel too old to have to bother with the noise and disorder that are a feature of children's play.

Being a grandparent has various meanings, and after studying nearly three hundred grandparents, Helen Kivnick (1982) found five major dimensions in the role: centrality, valued elder, immortality through clan, reinvolvement with personal past, and spoil. All grandparents seemed to be aware of all five dimensions, but the emphasis shifted from person to person, and the same grandparent might emphasize a different dimension at various times in the relationship. The dimension of *centrality* included the belief that activities with grandchildren were of central importance, the sense that being a grandparent gave meaning to life, and the incorporation of the role into a person's identity. The dimension of *valued elder* included the role of resource person for grandchildren and the concern with the way grandchildren regarded them and would remember them when grown.

The dimension of *immortality through clan* described the grandparent's sense of personal immortality through descendants. The dimension of *reinvolvement with personal past* included the grandparent's reliving earlier experiences through relationships with grandchildren and reminiscences about the grandparent's own grandparents. Finally, the dimension of *spoil* included the lenient attitudes grandparents display toward their grandchildren and the tendency they have to indulge grandchildren. Which dimension of the grandparent role a particular individual emphasizes appears to be influenced by the grandparent's socioeconomic level, health, personality, and family-related circumstances.

Most grandchildren seem to enjoy their grandparents. A special bond may develop, in which positive relations can develop without any of the friction that is often present between parents and children. Grandparents can enjoy and indulge their grandchildren without feeling the degree of responsibility that may burden a parent. The added perspective on life that grandparents have, now that they have survived the parental role, may also contribute to the special quality of the relationship. The bonds appear to be closest until grandchildren are about 10 years old, with preschoolers enjoying the treats, presents, and special indulgences they receive and schoolage children enjoying the way grandparents enter into their play (Kahana and Kahana, 1970). Among a group of young adult grandchildren, nearly all had warm feelings toward their grandparents, enjoyed being with them, and said they would help them in any way they could. The grandchildren expected little from their grandparents except the emotional relationship (Robertson, 1976).

The presence of young grandchildren has added benefits for grandparents (Hagestad, 1981). Interactions with grandchildren give older adults opportunities to break norms regarding age-appropriate behavior. They can be "foolish," giggling and playing games that their age and dignity would normally forbid. The hugs and cuddles that children expect (or endure) from their grandparents also give the older adults opportunities for touching in a culture that restricts most expressions of physical intimacy. Although grandparents derive a great deal of pleasure from their children, a grandparent's level of satisfaction with life does not appear to be related to the degree of involvement with their grandchildren (Wood and Robertson, 1976). What is more, few grandmothers are eager to baby-sit, and many resent being asked (Cohler and Grunebaum, 1981).

The relationship a grandchild develops with a grandparent stretches far into the future, for it appears that the way the child experiences this relationship affects the way he or she relates to grandchildren half a century later (Kivnick, 1982). Yet the grandparent-grandchild relationship is largely controlled by the intermediate parent generation. In some cases, the relationship is ruptured after a divorce, when the parent with custody refuses to allow the parents of the former partner access to the grandchild. According to Helen Kivnick, this deprivation could affect children two generations later when the deprived grandchild has difficulty establishing a rewarding relationship with his or her own grandchild.

PARENTS

Contrary to popular belief, the elderly are not isolated from their adult children. Most old people have frequent contact with their grown children, and the family provides them with consistent emotional and social support as well as with aid in times of crisis. Yet even old people who are not isolated tend to accept the myth that the family has become alienated from its older members. According to Ethel Shanas (1979), after describing their deep involvement with their children and grandchildren, many older adults say, "But, of course, my family is different." And old people who agree with the statement "Children don't care anything about their parents except for what they can get out of them" are generally men and women who have never been parents. Shanas sees the alienation myth as a Hydra, like the many-headed mythological monster that grew two new heads each time one was cut off. As we will see, the relationship between adult children and their parents may be closer than it has ever been. However, when we reach the twenty-first century, the family may face new challenges created by current population trends.

TODAY'S FAMILY IN PERSPECTIVE

Myth has it that our forebears lived in three-generation families, that grandparents were venerated, and that, by comparison, today's family is a cold, isolated place—no longer a haven in a heartless world (Lasch, 1977). A review of historical research indicates that the three-generation family has always been rare, primarily because few adults lived long enough to see their grandchildren born, and many of those who did lived only a few years. Older adults did seem to be venerated, but there were few of them, and those who survived usually held the family pursestrings. In Colonial America, fathers held onto the land so tightly that many sons had to postpone their own marriages for years, and parental control extended to the choice of children's marital partners. For example, before the American Revolution, daughters nearly always married in the order of their birth—a practice that declined in the nineteenth century, and sons whose fathers died before they were 60 years old married at an earlier age than sons whose fathers lived to be 60. According to Andrew Cherlin (1983), relationships between parent and child in Colonial America seem to have been relatively cold and distant, with the authoritarian position of the fathers creating considerable tension between generations.

The tension appears to have lasted into the nineteenth century, when fathers who relinquished control of the land or family business generally retained the title or else set up elaborate legal provisions for the support of themselves and their wives. Three-generation families were indeed more common in the nineteenth century than they are today, but they usually involved grandparents who could contribute to the household economy. In nineteenth-century England, for example, grandmothers who could act as primary caregivers or handle housework were generally welcome, and farming families might take in grandparents during the spring and summer when crops had to be planted, tended, and harvested, only to return them to the poorhouse when winter arrived (Bengston and Treas, 1980). Cherlin (1983) believes that relationships between adult children and their parents tend to be closer, warmer, more loving, and more affectionate when neither generation has to depend on the economic support of the other. It is only during the past few decades that such conditions have been prevalent in the United States.

Fewer than eight American households in every hundred contain three generations (Troll, Miller, and Atchley, 1979). This situation represents a clear decline from the nineteenth century, but earlier three-generational households were created by necessity, not choice. The wealthier a family, the less likely it was that grandparents lived with their adult children. Each generation preferred to live alone, and older adults often took in boarders or rented out rooms in order to maintain their independence (Bengston and Treas, 1980).

In contemporary families, the elderly move into a child's home only when they are poor, so sick that they cannot care for themselves, or—in a few cases—when a spouse has died. The parent who moves in is usually a mother (81 percent), and the child who provides the home is more likely to be a daughter. In most cases, the grandchildren have already left the nest (Troll, Miller, and Atchley, 1979). The majority of parent-adult child households, however, are established in the

home of the aging parent, when an unmarried adult child (a daughter in 65 percent of the cases) moves into the parent's home.

INTERGENERATIONAL SOLIDARITY

Despite each generation's fondness for independence and the establishment of
their own homes, the contact between parents and adult children is generally frequent and relatively close. American society is concentrated in nuclear households, but the bonds with the elder generation are so strong that the American
family is considered a **modified extended family**, in which the generations live
apart but are linked by mutual aid and affection (Litwack, 1960).

Solidarity between the generations can be demonstrated by interaction, by affection, or by supplying assistance. Elderly parents see or hear from their adult
children frequently (Bengston and Treas, 1980). In study after study, more than
half of the older adults say they have seen a child within the past 24 hours. Gender, marital status, and social class seem to influence the amount of contact.
Married daughters are more likely to be in contact with their elderly parents than
are married sons. Widows are generally in closer contact than married parents;
unmarried children see their parents more often than do married children. Finally, working-class men, especially those who are upwardly mobile, are more
likely to be in contact with their parents than middle-class men.

Although middle-class families are more mobile and thus are more likely than
working-class families to be separated by geography, they keep in touch by phone
or letter and pay frequent visits. The separation appears to be temporary (Troll,
Miller, and Atchley, 1979). A middle-class child may move to establish a career,
but in later years either the child moves back near the parental home or the parent
moves to the vicinity of the middle-aged child.

Most parents and children report a feeling of closeness. Among a group of Boston adults, good health and financial independence on the part of the aging parents tended to increase feelings of warmth between the generations, as did positive attitudes toward aging in the parents (Johnson and Bursk, 1977). Positive
feeling generally prevailed, with parents and adult children tending to report
about the same degree of warmth. When there was a discrepancy, the parents saw
the relationship as closer than did the child. This tendency has appeared in other
studies. For example, when middle-aged children and elderly parents rated each
other on understanding, trust, fairness, respect, and affection, both generations
expressed high levels of positive sentiment, but elderly parents consistently rated
the relationship somewhat more positively than did the middle-aged child (Bengston and Treas, 1980).

Such a discrepancy is believed to reflect the **generational stake** of parent and
child (Bengston and Cutler, 1976). Each person's stake in the relationship reflects
the way in which the bond enables the person to attain personal goals. Parents,
who often see their children as perpetuating parental ideals and valued institutions, have a stake in a close relationship, and so they tend to deny differences.

Children, who need to see themselves as distinct from their parents, have a stake in autonomy, and so they tend to magnify existing differences.

Children do not have to feel close to aging parents to remain involved with them. Among middle-aged adults in the California Intergenerational Studies (Clausen, Mussen, and Kuypers, 1981), there was no connection between warmth and involvement. It may be that obligation, guilt, or the desire to set an example for the middle-aged parent's own children led adults who felt distant and cool toward their aging parents to remain in close contact with them. When adults felt warmly toward their parents but had little contact with them, the situation may have been the result of preoccupation with other activities, wide differences in life-style, a belief in independence, or a feeling that the parents were being taken care of by others.

Nor is warmth required for one generation to assist another. However, old people prize their children's affection and respect, valuing them more than they value assistance (Treas, 1983). Although most older adults seem unwilling to intrude on their children's lives, adult children often aid their parents. The situation is not one-sided, for the aid flows in both directions, taking the form of services or financial assistance. Housecleaning, baby-sitting, meal preparation, and transportation are forms of services that can be exchanged. It appears that the proportion of old people who assist their children exceeds the proportion who get some kind of assistance (Riley and Foner, 1968). Aid is especially likely to flow from parent to adult child during the early years of the child's marriage, and, among the middle class, aid may continue for many years. Among the working class, aid is more likely to flow in the other direction, with middle-class parents receiving moral support from their children and working-class parents receiving material aid (Bengston and Treas, 1980).

Assistance in dealing with bureaucracies is another sort of aid provided elderly family members by their children (Sussman, 1976). Kin serve as a buffer between the elderly and government agencies, providing information about housing, pensions, medical care, and other benefits; helping to fill out endless forms; and giving advice when problems arise.

In time of need, family members turn to kin. Among 100 primarily working-class, three-generational Minneapolis families (Hill et al., 1970), family aid flowed in all directions, with elderly grandparents receiving more aid than they gave but continuing to dispense all sorts of assistance. It would seem that as long as elderly parents are able to provide financial or personal assistance to their children and grandchildren, they will do so. However, as grandparents become quite elderly and their income is inadequate or their health deteriorates, it is the middle generation of parents who are likely to be caught in a *life-cycle squeeze*. Such squeezes are produced by the interaction of basic life-cycle patterns associated with work and family (Oppenheimer, 1981).

Thus, as children reach middle age, they often find themselves having to assume considerable responsibility for aging parents—or even grandparents. The burden may fall on them before their maturing children are completely self-supporting, placing these middle-aged adults under heavy emotional and economic

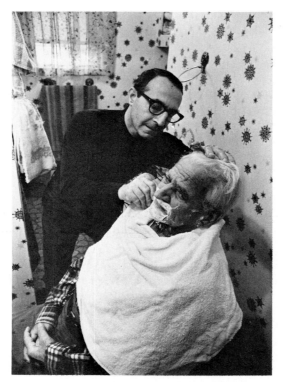

Grown children and parents continue to aid one another, with money, services, and emotional support flowing up and down the generational ladder.

stress. When middle-aged women report a sense of "overload" in caring for their parents, they generally have young adult children whose own development is not "on time" or has run "off the track" (Hagestad, 1982). For example, they may have an unemployed son in his late twenties or a divorced daughter who has moved back home. Middle-aged men are more likely to encounter the overload in terms of financial pressure. The burden may even continue into early old age. Among men between the ages of 60 and 65 who were still members of the "middle generation," about 6 percent were supporting both their elderly parents and their children. At this age, 10 percent were supporting only their parents, and 26 percent were continuing to support their children (Morgan, 1983).

The life-cycle squeeze becomes especially constrictive when middle-aged adults must care for elderly relatives who live in another city. Among the middle class, the phenomenon of long-distance care has appeared, apparently the result of today's mobility combined with increased longevity. The trend is so new that no one knows how many people are involved, but it seems clear that many who are responsible for making long-distance arrangements and who spend their weekends traveling hundreds—or even thousands of miles—are under extremely severe stress. A 42-year-old management consultant in Manhattan who travels to Chicago each week to care for her 91-year-old father and 87-year-old mother, says: "To take on parenting of your parents is the true mark of being an adult, but sometimes I feel that my whole life is on hold" (Collins, 1983b, p. C10).

Some of the consequences of long-distance care have been broken marriages, financial crisis, and lost jobs (Collins, 1983b). A network of services is developing to assist people caught in this squeeze, with at least 22 "case-management" services in seven states. Whether present patterns of family relationship will continue into the next century is a question that has recently received a good deal of attention.

FAMILY TRENDS

As today's middle-aged parents become elderly, they are likely to have children to call on for assistance. But these baby boom children are having small families, and more of them are remaining single. As a result, future generations of old people may not have the family resources that are now available.

More and more people are surviving into old age, but they are likely to have fewer descendents to call on for services or financial aid. The burden of one or two generations of elderly that falls on the middle-aged is likely to become even heavier because there will be fewer siblings to share the responsibility (Bengston and Treas, 1980).

Changes in women's roles may also affect available resources of the elderly. Women provide most of the family services for older adults. When middle-aged women are employed outside the home, they are not available to clean, cook, or provide transportation and care for elderly parents. When a parent becomes unable to care for himself or herself, the middle-aged daughter must either hire someone to care for the parent, quit her job, or place the parent in an institution. None of the options is desirable, and whichever is selected, guilt or resentment may follow.

Curious as to how changes in their roles were affecting women's attitudes toward helping elderly parents, a group of researchers (Brody et al., 1983) studied three generations of women: elderly women, their daughters, and their young-adult granddaughters. The grandmothers were most receptive to government programs and private services for the aged, and the granddaughters were the least receptive. All generations believed that elderly parents should be able to call on their grown children for help, but agreed that a working daughter need not quit her job to provide that help. Sixty-one percent of the middle-aged daughters were employed outside the home, and their consistent endorsement of filial responsibility indicated that they may one day be caught in the life-cycle squeeze. The willingness of these daughters and granddaughters to assist older family members indicates that values concerning family care of the aged remain strong.

According to Vern Bengston and Judith Treas (1980), a third situation could also interfere with the family assistance now available to the elderly. As society becomes increasingly age-irrelevant, more and more middle-aged adults are going back to college or starting new careers. Just as they have their children launched and can at last gratify some of their long-postponed desires or when they retire themselves and plan to embark on a life of travel, study, or leisure, a parent suddenly requires major assistance. Again, the choice must be made between their own lives and their parent's needs.

Taken together, say Bengston and Treas, these changes may lead to a kin network that is overburdened by cross-generational demands. However, they point out that studies have consistently shown that close family interaction is not essential to the morale or mental health of the elderly. Furthermore, future generations of elderly are more likely to be financially secure than aged adults in the past, lessening the economic—if not the psychological—burden of caring for frail elderly.

INFLUENCE ACROSS GENERATIONS

Throughout their lives, parents, children, and grandchildren influence one another. Great writers often anticipate the discoveries of psychologists, and the French novelist Victor Hugo indicated his awareness of cross-generational influence when he wrote, "If you want to reform a man, start with his grandmother" (Plath, 1980). Although parents and grandparents often consciously try to shape the ideas, attitudes, values, and behavior of their young, the influence runs up the generational lines as well as down (Hagestad, 1982). When we find similarities between generations, we cannot be certain which way the likenesses were transmitted or whether some historical event has influenced more than one generation in a similar manner.

Various researchers have looked for resemblances between parents and children. For example, parents and adolescent children tend to share similar attitudes toward authoritarianism (Scarr and Weinberg, 1978). Similarities in personality may be even broader. Adolescent daughters of the women in the California Intergenerational Studies and adolescent sons of the men in the study tended to resemble their parents significantly more than unrelated adolescents and adults of the same age (Clausen, Mussen and Kuypers, 1981). The resemblances were closest in aspects of information processing (such as insightful, values intellectual matters, or self-defensive) and appropriate social behavior (such as productive, fastidious, or withdraws when frustrated). Least resemblance was found in aspects of personality having to do with the way adolescents presented themselves or reacted to other people.

These teenages also resembled their parents in their personal values. Both parents and adolescents believed that honesty, dependability, and considerateness were the most important values—ranking them above such values as self-control, obedience, ambition, independence, and being a good student. Yet adolescents perceived their parents as valuing scholastic achievement over all other values but honesty. In this case, the researchers suggest that values may be coming as much from community consensus on valued personal qualities as from the parent.

In general, closeness with parents fostered children's identification with their parents and led to greater resemblances. When an adolescent reported that the parent of the same sex had a strong influence and that parent and child tended to agree on issues related to values, the adolescent generally regarded the parent as a happy, competent person who was easier to talk with than the parent of the other sex.

Family resemblances do not always remain stable after the adolescent reaches adulthood. Once adult children establish their own homes, parents and children have less opportunity to exert influence on each other. When the personalities of middle-aged children and their parents were compared, the same parents whose adolescent children resembled them in many ways were no more like their own aging parents than strangers picked at random.

When adult children first establish their own homes, resemblances may still be strong, as they were between grandmothers and mothers in three-generation Italian-American families studied by Bertram Cohler and Henry Grunebaum (1981). Instead of developing their independence, the mothers tended to be dependent on their own middle-aged mothers, both for information and affection. The mothers' degree of comfort with this close relationship varied, but in every case the grandmother felt some discomfort and was outspoken about her frustration, wanting more privacy and freedom and displaying some annoyance at demands for assistance, emotional support, and baby-sitting services.

Cohler and Grunebaum believe that such dependency is not uncommon between generations and that it results from childhood socialization practices. Across the first half of their lives, most women are taught to be dependent, and this dependency is further encouraged as the daughters become mothers themselves, increasing the similarity of interests and concern between generations. In this study, the dependency was apparent even between a pair in which the grandmother had deliberately sought to develop autonomy in her daughter at an early age.

Other studies have found consistent attempts of parents (whether aging or middle-aged) and children (whether middle-aged or young adult) to influence one another in almost every sphere of life, from diet and health practices to political attitudes and views on parenthood (Hagestad, 1982). Sometimes the influence is welcome. The same researcher (Hagestad, 1981) describes how middle-aged parents interviewed in the early 1970s said that events in the turbulent 1960s would have been incomprehensible and frightening without the interpretations they received from their children. Young-adult children had influenced these parents on matters of work, life-style, and social issues. Grandparents were influenced by both children and grandchildren, but the grandparents also influenced the two younger generations (Hagestad, 1978). In another study (Angres, 1975), 60 percent of middle-aged mothers who were interviewed said that they had been influenced toward a more liberal sexual attitude by their daughters' behavior.

Yet the influence of parents on children endures throughout life. When Lillian Troll (1980b) studied three generations in Detroit, she asked adults of all ages to describe a man and woman they knew. More than half of them—including those in their eighties—described their parents. Personalities may differ, but influence remains so strong that parents serve as our source of reference for decades after their deaths.

SUMMARY

The family can be regarded as a social system whose structure is affected by the addition, development, and departure of its members; by the demands of the culture; and by changes in the environment. The family system is established with the marriage of mates and lasts until the marriage is dissolved by divorce or death. Each member of the system has a series of roles that are determined by age, gender, and relatedness. The purposes of the family are meeting its members' needs and socializing children. Cultures may be postfigurative, in which authority comes from the past; cofigurative, in which the present is the standard; or prefigurative, in which neither the past nor the present is regarded as reliable.

Although most people still have children, reduced family size has decreased the proportion of the life span that is devoted to child rearing. The increase in maternal employment outside the home, together with the rising divorce rate, has reduced the traditional nuclear household to a minority of American families. Family roles begin to shift early in pregnancy, with the male partner apparently more concerned than the female partner about the role changes involved in becoming a parent. Pregnancy is affected by psychological and environmental variables, including the marital relationship, a woman's feelings about her job, and attitudes toward the pregnancy. Afterward, both partners may face stresses as they adjust to their new roles, and some women undergo **postpartum depression.**

It has been proposed that parenthood plays a controlling role over the life span, an influence known as the **parental imperative.** Among the stresses of parenthood are restrictions on personal and economic freedom and the disruption of the relationship between the spouses. The major responsibility for infant care, the return to a traditional division of household tasks, and the responsibility for keeping the family system functioning may be at the base of the dissatisfaction or depression found in many mothers of young children. Children have such a powerful influence on the family that marital satisfaction may be determined by the presence, number, and age of a couple's children. Although some parents handle the child-care problem by working different shifts, maternal employment does not appear to be detrimental to young children, and its effects on the mother are often positive. When a stepparent enters the family system, relationships appear to run more smoothly when the stepparent and the child are of the same sex. It seems to take about two years for a custodial parent to work through the problems that accompany divorce. Despite the heavy financial and psychological burdens of filling both parental roles, the parent may develop new aspects of personality. Parents generally react to the empty nest with relief, and the marital relationship often improves. However, both the marital relationship and the timing of the children's departure help to determine the effects of the empty nest.

The relationship between grandparent and grandchild is affected by ethnic group, religion, socioeconomic level, and personality. Age has a powerful effect on a grandparent's style, and many of today's grandparents are younger than those of earlier generations. A younger grandparent is more likely to be "fun-seeking" and less likely to be formal in relating to grandchildren. A special bond often develops with grandchildren, and the relationship allows grandparents to break norms regarding age-appropriate behavior and gives them opportunities for affectionate physical contact.

Most older adults have frequent contact with their grown children, receiving consistent emotional and social support as well as aid in crises. The generational bonds are so strong that the American family is considered a **modified extended family.** Fewer than 8 percent of American households contain three generations, and most older adults who live with their children do so from necessity, not by choice. Discrepancies in parents' and adult children's view of their relationship have been attributed to the **generational stake** each has in the relationship. When parents enter the old-old group, the adult children may be caught in a "life-cycle squeeze," in which they are responsible for two generations besides themselves. Because of smaller families, future generations of older adults may not have the family resources available to today's elderly. In addition, changing female roles and the trend toward age-irrelevancy may limit the ability of grown children to provide family services. Influence between generations runs both up and down generational lines, and, no matter what their age, parents and children consistently attempt to influence one another.

KEY TERMS

generational stake	**parental imperative**
modified extended family	**postpartum depression**

13

WORK AND LEISURE ACROSS ADULTHOOD

What makes an occupation rewarding? What turns off an employee? The first impulse is to say that salary and social status determine the way we feel about our work. They are important, but the answer is not so simple. Asked to talk about her job, Babe Secoli, who has been a checker in a supermarket for 30 years, says:

I love my job. I've got very nice bosses. I got a black manager and he's just beautiful. They don't bother you as long as you do your work. And the pay is terrific. . . . I'm a couple of days away, I'm very lonesome for this place. When I'm on a vacation, I can't wait to go, but two or three days away, I start to get fidgety. I can't stand around and do nothin'. I have to be busy at all times. I look forward to comin' to work. It's a great feelin'. I enjoy it somethin' terrible [Terkel, 1974, pp. 377, 380].

Secoli stands eight hours a day at her register, and her feet hurt. By middle-class standards, her pay is low. She has no authority. Yet she is not alienated, and she likes her job.

It is not whether a person has a career or a job that makes an occupation fulfilling but whether it provides satisfying activity, an opportunity to be creative, and social stimulation. Some supermarket checkers are happier at their jobs than some stockbrokers.

At the other extreme is Ray Wax, an upper-middle-class stockbroker about the same age as Secoli, a man whose commissions put him in a privileged group. Wax commutes each day from the New York suburbs to Wall Street. Asked about his work, he says:

People like me start out with a feeling that there's a place for them in society, that they really have a useful function. They see it destroyed by the cynicism of the market. . . . I can't say what I'm doing has any value. This doesn't make me too happy. . . . I'll continue with my personal disillusionment. (Laughs). Oh, I'd like one morning to wake up and go to some work that gave me joy [Terkel, 1974, pp. 446-447].

Despite high financial returns and social status, the stockbroker is clearly alienated. He says he feels that he is no more important than a ribbon clerk, who takes orders but makes few decisions.

Neither Secoli nor Wax may reflect the views of the majority of people who hold similar jobs. It would be fairly easy to find an alienated supermarket checker and dedicated stockbroker. A variety of factors help determine whether a person's occupation is disillusioning or fulfilling, and in this chapter we investigate some of them. We begin with an exploration of the role of work in our lives and how we come to be in one job rather than another. Next we look at the way careers tend to develop, noting typical differences between men's and women's careers. As fewer people die in midcareer, retirement becomes more important to all of us, and so we examine influences on the decision to retire and the ways in which people adjust to retirement. We trace the pattern of leisure activities across adulthood and close by exploring the recent return to formal education by many adults.

CHOOSING AN OCCUPATION

Most of us would work even if we did not have to take a job in order to support ourselves. Having a job indicates that we have grown up, and it serves as a measure of maturity and responsibility. A young man who could not find work put this feeling into words:

Who wants to have that kind of time on his hands? I hate myself; then I hate everyone else. . . . It's a rotten deal when you can't find a job and don't earn your own money. Who wants to draw unemployment money, then borrow from the parents? I feel myself getting younger by the day—becoming a kid, feeling sorry for myself, and getting lazier by the minute. No good. After a while you're ready to return to elementary school! [Coles, 1978, p. 226].

Occupation is also entwined with the sense of identity, so that it is rare to hear people talk about themselves without including some reference to their work. The link is so close that sudden unemployment can threaten identity and self-esteem.

THE WORKING POPULATION

Most of us seem reluctant to contemplate a life without some job. When middle-aged and older adults were asked whether they would keep on working if they did not need the income, 90 percent of the men and 82 percent of the women said they would continue at their jobs (Pfeiffer and Davis, 1974). When the younger readers of *Psychology Today* were surveyed, only 9 percent said they would stop working entirely under such circumstances, and almost 75 percent said they could keep on at their present jobs. Women were as likely as men to want to continue working (Renwick and Lawler, 1978).

Work can give meaning to our lives, defining our position in society as well as providing satisfying activity, an outlet for creativity, and a source of social stimulation. In the case of Babe Secoli, the supermarket checker, it served such purposes. If work does not do these things, we feel that something is wrong, and we may become alienated like Ray Wax, the stockbroker. Studs Terkel (1974), who listened to Americans talk about their jobs, sees work as a "search . . . for daily meaning as well as daily bread, for recognition as well as cash, for astonishment rather than torpor; in short, for a sort of life rather than a Monday through Friday sort of dying. Perhaps immortality, too, is part of the quest" (p. xiii). Work is so vital to our sense of self that when asked what a healthy person should be able to do, Freud replied with three short words: *Lieben und arbeiten* (to love and work). According to Erik Erikson (1968), this simple rule meant that people needed to become productive without becoming so immersed in their work that they lost the ability to be sexual, loving persons. In his view of the life span, the sense of industry, on which work is based, develops during middle childhood.

Most of us who are able to work are part of the labor force: 77 percent of the men and 53 percent of the women are either employed or looking for work (U.S. Bureau of the Census, 1982) (Fig. 13.1). Not counted in the labor force are women whose occupation is homemaker (33 percent); people who are retired, in school, in prison, ill or disabled; and those who do not wish to work. About 75 percent of the labor force work at **jobs.** Jobs are occupations in which upward advancement is limited and movement is primarily horizontal. A carpenter may move from one employer to another, accumulating experience and developing skills, but the job remains more or less the same.

The rest of the labor force work at **careers.** Careers are occupations that are characterized by interrelated training and work experiences, in which a person moves upward through a series of positions that require greater mastery and responsibility and that provide increasing financial return. An executive, a banker, a college professor, or an officer in the armed forces has a career. If the carpenter should develop the knowledge and experience to become a contractor, he or she would move onto the career ladder, advancing in position with advances in age.

THE PROCESS OF SECTION

Ideally, each person would work at the job or career that best suits his or her interest, abilities, and personality. However, life does not seem to work in that way, and occupational choice is often accidental and guided by what may seem to be

	1960	1970	1981
BY RACE AND SEX:			
White men	83.4%	80.0%	77.9%
White women	36.5	42.6	51.9
Black and other men	83.0	76.5	70.6
Black and other women	48.2	49.5	53.6
BY AGE AND SEX:			
Men, 18–19	69.3%	66.7%	70.4%
20–24	88.1	83.3	85.5
25–34	97.5	96.4	94.9
35–44	97.7	96.9	95.4
45–54	95.7	94.3	91.4
55–64	86.8	83.0	70.6
Older than 64	33.1	26.8	18.4
Women, 18–19	50.9%	53.5%	60.9%
20–24	46.1	57.7	69.6
25–34	36.0	45.0	66.7
35–44	43.4	51.1	66.8
45–54	49.8	54.4	61.1
55–64	37.2	43.0	41.4
Older than 64	10.8	9.7	8.0

FIGURE 13.1 Civilian labor force, 1968 to 1981 (percent).

Over a period of two decades, the proportion of men in the labor force dropped, in part because of the trend toward earlier retirement. At the same time, the proportion of women in the labor force increased among all except the oldest.

Source: U.S. Bureau of the Census, *Statistical Abstract of the United States*, 103d ed., 1982.

irrelevant factors. Sex, social class, proximity, apparently unrelated decisions, and luck can play at least as great a role in career choice as factors that match individual with the best-suited occupation. In a survey of *Psychology Today* readers (Renwick and Lawler, 1978), almost 40 percent said that chance had determined their present occupations. Only 23 percent of these well-educated adults (43.4 percent were professionals and another 15.9 percent were executives or managers) were working in the occupation of their choice.

Among the factors that restrict job access is sex. Although women are now hired as fire fighters, few apply, and those who do face an uphill battle to win consideration for the job. Because many women are too small or have paid too little attention to developing muscle power to be able to handle the physical demands of fire fighting, all women are seen as incapable of its demands, no matter how strong they are. Until recently, a girl was encouraged to consider a job as no more than a way station until she entered her ''true'' occupation—wife and mother. As we will see, such socialization practices may also affect women who do not choose to marry or have children or who wish to embark on a dual-occupational identity, combining the roles of home and workplace. Sex can also restrict job access for men. Few men decide to become kindergarten teachers, although they may be nurturant and enjoy working with young children.

Social class affects occupational choice, with adolescents in the upper socioeconomic brackets steered toward careers and those in the lower brackets steered toward jobs. The cost of lengthy professional training may put careers out of the reach of some young people who have as much aptitude for the career of physician, research scientist, or lawyer as those who have the required financial resources.

Proximity can be a powerful force in occupational choice. A young person who grows up in the Pacific Northwest is more likely to go into some kind of work connected with forestry than one who grows up in Manhattan. And someone who lives near Detroit is more likely to work in auto production than someone who grows up on a Midwestern farm. Childhood experiences are important because the availability of role models is likely to increase the chances that a child will aim his or her sights on a particular occupation.

Luck is also important. Classified ads, job listings with employment agencies, and campus interviews do fill some jobs, but informal connections are more likely to lead to employment. Knowing someone in an organization—or knowing someone who knows someone—is a common path to jobs and careers. Between 50 and 90 percent of blue-collar workers are believed to have found their jobs through informal channels (Reid, 1972). Openings in business and academic occupations are often filled by contact with the ''old-boy network,'' in which a member (male or female) of the network, comprised of friends, acquaintances, and former co-workers in a particular field, relies on other members to fill openings or to provide new career slots.

A person must be aware that a job exists before he or she can begin training for it—or even consider it, and few children have any idea of the variety of occupations that are available. Nor do they understand the barriers that may stand between them and what they think they would like to do. A 10-year-old boy might, for example, dream of becoming an astronaut without realizing that an eye defect, one that does not interfere at all with his school or play activities, has put his dream forever out of reach.

Although children do not have to choose an occupation, the educational choices they make as young adolescents may—without their awareness—shut off some careers, narrowing their future selection. The decision not to take third and fourth year math courses in high school, for example, puts a student so far behind others of the same initial ability that by the twelfth grade a wide range of math-related careers have been eliminated (Abeles, Steel, and Wise, 1980). When adolescent pregnancy leads to marriage or the adoption of the parental role or both, college education—and with it, most careers—is shut out for most youngsters. In a study that matched young people for aptitudes, aspirations, and socioeconomic background, fewer than 2 percent of the adolescent mothers and 10 percent of the adolescent fathers had completed college by the age of 29, compared with 22 percent of the women and 27 percent of the men who postponed parenthood until they were at least 24 years old (Card and Wise, 1978).

An individual is most likely to find an occupation that matches interests and abilities if he or she knows what those interests and abilities are and what occupations require those talents. At a time when young people are making occupational decisions, however, most may not realize what day-to-day work in a particular field entails. They are likely to go by stereotypes they have picked up from the media and casual contacts and may either pass over fields that would be rewarding or else embark on lengthy preparation in a field that is nothing like their stereotypical ideas (Anastasi, 1976).

Vocational tests have been developed to assist people in making wise occupational choices. For example, the Strong-Campbell Interest Inventory (Campbell, 1974) uses the answers to several hundred specific items (Do you ''like'' or ''dislike.'' or are you ''indifferent'' to, making a speech?) to determine a person's interests and the sort of work environment he or she would find congenial. The pattern of scores is compared with the pattern of choices made by people who have been successful in various occupations.

The Strong-Campbell Interest Inventory groups answers into general occupational themes that are derived from the research of J. L. Holland (1976). Holland proposed that people in a particular occupation tend to show certain correlations in the strength of six themes: realistic, investigative, artistic, social, enterprising, conventional. For example, a farmer is likely to score high on realistic and conventional themes and low on their opposites, social and artistic themes. Holland believes that these themes reflect a person's major personality characteristics and that when the themes of a chosen occupation match a person's personality, his or her job satisfaction, job stability, and occupational achievement are likely to be high. In this view, choosing a particular occupation is choosing a way of life. From the initial choice of occupation until retirement, most careers appear to follow a predictable pattern.

DEVELOPMENT WITHIN A CAREER

Although the developmental course of many careers is orderly and its outlines can be charted, this has not always been true. In the nineteenth century, more people worked on jobs related to physical strength, and the kind of job a person held was related to age. According to Tamara Hareven (1978), workers younger than 20 or older than 45 were employed in agriculture or at unskilled labor. A permanent job was rare, and most careers were ''disorderly.'' Progression was not necessarily upward, and no principle of seniority protected the older worker. After working hard for 20 or 30 years, a skilled employee in the forties or fifties was suddenly moved to a semiskilled or unskilled position, there to work until he or she died. A factory worker might move up from sweeper to skilled textile operator to supervisor, only to be made sweeper again after the age of 50.

The great change that has taken place in the world of work becomes clear when we contrast the ''average'' male worker in 1870 with his counterpart in 1970 (Miernyk, 1975). In 1870, a man entered the work force when he was 14 years old and worked an average of 3120 hours per year (a 60-hour work week with no vacation) until he died, still at work, at the age of 61. In 1970, a man entered the work force at the age of 20 and worked an average of 2000 hours per year (a 40-hour work week with a 2-week vacation) until he retired at the age of 65. Over his lifetime, the 1870 worker would have earned $90,000 (in 1970 dollars) for 146,640 hours of toil. The 1970 worker would have earned $360,000 for 90,000 hours of labor—four times the real income for two thirds as much work. (A 1970 college graduate would have entered the work force several years later but would have earned more than $500,000 by retirement.)

THE DEVELOPMENTAL COURSE OF CAREERS

We not only work less and get paid more today; our work careers have changed as well. In the twentieth century, seniority, tenure, health insurance, pensions, and other forms of occupational protection have made orderly job histories and careers possible. This orderly course of development begins in adolescence when a person's ideas about work crystallize and tentative occupational decisions are made (Super, 1957). In this **crystallization stage,** the adolescent explores various fields and matches—as closely as possible—personal needs, interests, capacities, and values with the opportunities that present themselves. The selection may be vague or unrealistic, but the usually irrevocable choice between broad areas, such as humanities or science, is made, and a vocational self-concept is developed. The adolescent may see himself or herself as an engineer, an accountant, a restaurant owner, or an architect, although usually without much knowledge of what the occupation entails.

From the crystallization stage, a person moves into the **specification stage,** when more is discovered about specific careers, and reality shapes career decisions. This is a transitional phase and is occupied by job training. The specification stage roughly corresponds to the undergraduate years in college.

With the **implementation stage,** at about 21 or 22, a person has made an initial commitment to a vocation and takes an entry-level position. Additional training, either on-the-job or graduate work, may occupy a good part of this period. There is often some job shifting as the person searches for the "right" position with prospects for advancement.

In trades, business, and most professions, the new employee may find a mentor, an established, often powerful, sponsor who takes a personal interest in the young man or woman. The mentor generally provides guidance, advice, and additional contacts and smooths the way for promotion and advancement within the field. In some careers, a mentor is almost a requirement if the entering employee is to move ahead. Among the men in the Harvard Study (see Chapter 10), those with relatively unsuccessful careers had no mentor during their twenties or thirties (Vaillant, 1977). Women corporate executives who have made it into the top ranks almost always emphasize the influence of a mentor on their success (Hennig, 1970). However, not all young workers find a mentor; among the men in Daniel Levinson's (1978) study (see Chapter 10), the mentor was more the exception than the rule.

By about the age of 25, the **stabilization stage** begins. For the next decade, a person settles down and becomes established in a chosen field. Finally, at 35, the **consolidation stage** begins, when a person, now regarded as experienced and knowledgeable, advances as far as possible and consolidates his or her gains. The consolidation stage lasts until retirement.

Not all careers follow such an orderly progression. Men are more likely than women to have orderly careers, and each sex tends to approach occupations differently.

HOW IMPORTANT IS AN ORDERLY LIFE?

How important is it that careers follow an orderly sequence? As society tends toward age irrelevance, an increasing number of people have formed life patterns that scramble the normative order of events, which is the completion of school, the first full-time job, marriage, and parenthood. Information from Project TALENT, a project that followed 400,000 American men and women over a 15-year period that began during their high school years, gives some indication of the effect of nonnormative patterns during early adulthood (Abeles, Steel, and Wise, 1980).

In the normative sequence, individuals go from high school directly into college, and among individuals in Project TALENT, between 20 and 23 percent had earned a degree within five years of high school graduation. Delay in completing college appeared to be less harmful for men than for women, for another 13 percent of the men but only 2.5 percent of the women received a degree later in their occupational careers. Other studies have shown that delaying college costs people about a year's advanced schooling and more than $1000 each year in annual earnings (Featherman and Carter, 1976).

A large proportion of the men and women in this study had lives that interspersed education, work, military service, or homemaking. Many returned to school after time spent working, in military service, or rearing children. Although Ronald Abeles, Lauri Steel, and Lauress Wise (1980) expected to find that scrambling the life structure had a major detrimental impact on careers, they found that the relationships were weak. The pattern of school, marriage, job, and parenthood was not a major determinant of either job prestige or annual income.

Men and women whose work careers were interrupted tended to have lower income and prestige than those whose careers were not interrupted. Such relationships generally are assumed to be the result of falling behind as knowledge and skills become obsolete through lack of practice or lack of exposure to new knowledge and skills. The negative effects of an interrupted career tended to be stronger among women, a relationship that was attributed to the fact that such interruptions usually reflect time out for marriage or child rearing.

In explaining the weakness of the relationships they found among life patterns, job prestige, and income, Abeles and his colleagues suggest that norms and social sanctions may not have as pronounced an effect on careers as they do in other areas of life or that different subgroups adhere to different norms. They also speculate that some of the effects on careers may be cumulative and that the relationship may strengthen as these young adults move into middle age. Another researcher (Hogan, 1979) has found that when men's lives scramble the order of school, job, and marriage, they tend to earn less money than men who follow the normative pattern and also that the relationship between money and a scrambled life pattern becomes stronger with increasing age. It may also be that some careers are more susceptible to the negative effects of a disorderly sequence than others.

MEN AT WORK

Men have been socialized toward the role of worker. They grow up expecting to work for the rest of their lives, to find meaning in that work, and to take the responsibility of providing for others. Although 66 percent of husbands have financial assistance from employed wives or other family members (U.S. Bureau of the Census, 1982), at least until very recently socialization has proceeded as if men were the sole breadwinners. During childhood, boys learned the social skills that enabled them to get along in the world of work. Team sports can be seen as management training (Hennig and Jardim, 1977). Boys learned to follow the rules while competing, understood that various talents were important to joint success (blockers are as important as runners or passers), got practice in following a leader, learned how to lose as well as win, and came to see a team victory as more important than individual success.

The Male Career

Prepared from childhood to be autonomous, competitive, and task-oriented, men set out on their careers. In the study of Harvard graduates (Vaillant, 1977), men seemed to devote their thirties to their occupations, focusing so intently on mastering their work and climbing the career ladder that they paid little attention to other aspects of life. For most men, it was a period of narrowness and materialism. Pointing out that the decade of the thirties is an uncharted period between the intimacy of the twenties and the generativity of the forties, George Vaillant (1977) has suggested inserting a stage of *career consolidation* into Erikson's developmental sequence. Indeed, in most major studies of adult development, a pattern of concentration on intimacy, then on career consolidation, and only afterward on generativity has been detected.

As we saw in Chapter 10, Levinson (1978) views the male life structure as evolving through a relatively orderly seqeunce, in which the stages of early adulthood roughly parallel the developmental course of careers (Fig. 13.2). In Levinson's theory, career development plays an important part in the formation of a life structure. During the early adult transition, the first serious career choice is made, but the work of forming an occupation does not end there. Whether a man makes an early, intense commitment to an occupation (as did some of the biologists in the study), remains undecided, or makes a major occupational shift during his twenties, the formative process extends throughout the novice period, which lasts through the age thirty transition. Among the men Levinson studied,

Experience in team sports can be regarded as management training, and the social skills learned on the playing field can help an employee climb the career ladder in the corporate business world.

even orderly careers were marked by this lengthy procedure, which was as true of working-class men as it was of executives.

Throughout the settling down period, in which career consolidation takes place, the men in Levinson's study were working at advancing their careers, and most had set rough timetables for reaching various occupational levels. Their sense of well-being seemed to depend on how fast they reached these goals. Five different career patterns developed during this period. For some men, life went according to their timetables, and they advanced within a stable life structure. A second group of men stayed within the life structure they had established, but

Levinson's Stages of Life Structure	Super's Career Stages
Midlife Transition (40–45)	
	Consolidation (35–65)
Settling Down (33–40)	
Age 30 Transition (28–33)	Stabilization (25–35)
Entering the Adult World (22–28)	Implementation (21–24)
Early Adult Transition (17–22)	Specification (18–21)
	Crystallization (14–18)

FIGURE 13.2   Life structure and careers.

Sources: D. Levinson et al., 1978; D. Super, 1957.

failed to advance as they had hoped—or even slipped back. For a third group of men, the life structure they had formed early in the settling down period became intolerable, and toward the end of the period, they broke out and tried to establish a different life structure. A fourth group of men advanced so swiftly and did so well that their old life structure could no longer accommodate their new status and income. They, too, had to establish a new life structure. Finally, a fifth group of men did not conform to the orderly sequence. Their life structure remained unstable throughout the settling down period, and no clear occupational direction appeared. One man, for example, led a nomadic existence, moving around the country and working variously at careers in radio, art, sales, and counseling. As men entered the midlife transition, they faced the task of making a place for themselves in the middle-adult generation and, depending on how they had met their timetables, the task of modifying and consolidating their occupational goals.

Job consolidation and the settling down process seem to indicate a tendency to stay with a job once the implementation period is over. Most job turnover is concentrated in the first five years or so of a worker's employment history, but about 20 percent of all workers change their jobs each year. Nearly seven out of every ten job shifts are voluntary. Men in the California Intergenerational Studies (Clausen, 1981) reported a number of job changes during their thirties and forties, with top executives and professionals and those who were moving up in the middle-class being more likely to have changed jobs than others. Such men in their early forties reported an average of two job changes within the past decade, and those in their late forties and early fifties reported an average of 1.4 job changes. Blue-collar workers in the study reported no job changes in the previous decade.

As men in the California study passed 45, all but the most successful began to cut back on their working time, by about four hours each week. Top executives and professionals showed the opposite trend; they increased their investment of time, working a 51-hour week at the age of 50, as compared with a 48-hour week among top executives and professionals in their early forties.

Personality and Careers

Although socioeconomic background affects careers, personality also influenced the occupational success of men in the California Intergenerational Studies. In early adolescence, those who had made it to the top could be distinguished from other men by their intellectual capacities and interests and their adherence to the "work ethic"—they were ambitious, productive, dependable, and not self-indulgent. During the middle years, work-ethic attributes tended to narrow among the groups, but the men's cognitive skills and intellectual interests could be ranked by occupational level, with the blue-collar workers scoring lowest, and scores progressing steadily to the professional and top executive level, with upwardly mobile middle-class men scoring especially high.

A reverse progression appeared in several personality attributes that tend to impair personal effectiveness. Men in the top levels scored lowest on anxiety, fearfulness, punitiveness, and the tendency to withdraw when frustrated, to feel victimized, and to complicate simple situations. As adolescents, working-class men who moved up to the middle-class tended to be more dependable, considerate, likable, sympathetic, and warm than middle-class adolescents. As middle-aged men, these upwardly mobile men remained warm and sympathetic, developed intellectual skills and interests, tended to be conventional, and were unlikely to push limits.

Influence between career and personality runs both ways, and sociologist Melvin Kohn (1980) has investigated the effect of a man's work on his personality. He believes that the complexity of a job, how closely it is supervised, and the sort of pressure it places on the worker—not the status of a job—influences personality. A job's complexity, that is, the degree to which it requires thought and independent judgment, appears to affect many facets of personality. When a job is complex, it challenges a person, and in meeting the challenge, a person is likely to develop increased intellectual flexibility. In a 10-year longitudinal study. Kohn discovered that although intellectual flexibility and job complexity interact, the complexity of work continues to affect intellectual flexibility even when social background and original levels of flexibility are taken into account. As Kohn puts it, if two men with equivalent levels of intellectual flexibility were to start their careers in jobs that differed in complexity, the man in the more complex job would eventually outstrip the other in intellectual growth. Because intellectual flexbility is related to values, self-concept, and social orientation, Kohn believes that job complexity may alter such characteristics as self-esteem, anxiety, receptiveness to change, standards of morality, authoritarian conservatism, intellectuality of leisure-time interests, and alienation.

The discovery that work affects personality should come as no surprise because the work environment can be considered as a stimulus that is present over a long period of time (Garfinkel, 1982). This prolonged exposure could well have a cumulative effect on personality. Looking at the other end of the scale, researchers (Geyer, 1972) have found that fast-paced, repetitive, sedentary, and mindless work can be deadening, alienating, and lead to health disorders.

WOMEN AT WORK

Women have always worked, whether within the home or in the labor force. A major change in the occupation of women is the movement of mothers into the working world over the past 20 years. Mothers of young children, who were once least likely to be employed, now are more likely to be working outside the home (47.8 percent) than are married women who have no children (46.3 percent) (U.S. Bureau of the Census, 1982).

This shift has attracted so much attention that little notice has been paid to a change in the character of many women's work. Since 1961, for example, women have moved from a minority share of jobs to a majority of the positions in six large categories: insurance adjusters (up from 9 percent); examiners and investigators, bill collectors (up from 22 percent); real estate agents and brokers; photographic process workers; checkers, examiners, and inspectors; and production-line assemblers. In two other categories, they hold almost half the jobs: bar-

Over the past 25 years, there has been a shift in the character of women's work. Although many women still work in traditional women's jobs, they now hold a majority of positions in a number of occupations, from insurance adjuster to photographic process worker.

tenders and bus drivers. Although women still hold only a handful of positions in some of the more prestigious fields, their numbers are growing. In 1971, 4 percent of judges and lawyers were women; in 1981, women accounted for 14 percent of the positions. During the same period, women physicians increased from 9 percent to 22 percent, and the proportion of women engineers quadrupled—from an almost invisible 1 percent to 4 percent (Prial, 1982).

The Female Career

For the most part, women's childhood preparation aims them at motherhood. As we have seen, women are socialized to be nurturant, dependent, gentle, and compassionate. Until recently, women who chose to work were expected to go into nursing, teaching, librarianship, or office work, all occupations in which they could use their nurturant skills or act as "office wives," helping executives wield power but never thinking of such achievement for themselves.

One factor in women's acceptance of "helping" jobs may have been the influence of feminine stereotypes, which portray women as incompetent (Huston-Stein and Higgins-Trenk, 1978). Compared with men, they have lower levels of aspiration, are less likely to think they will succeed at a task, are more anxious about failure, and when they do fail, are more likely to feel personally responsible. Such attitudes make it difficult for them to move into top positions in business.

Even their childhood games serve them poorly when they try to climb the corporate ladder, say management experts Margaret Hennig and Anne Jardim (1977). Taught to excel in tennis, swimming, and gymnastics, girls are good at individual performance but often have no chance to learn the lessons that can be derived from team sports. And as we have seen, team play has been critical to job performance in management situations, where workers must operate in a network that depends on friendship, persuasion, favors, promises, and connections.

Hennig and Jardim believe that female socialization has also led women to be more cautious in corporate strategy, thereby slowing their rise to the executive suite. Corporate women they have studied tend to see risks primarily in terms of losses, as situations that threaten their present positions, and so they try to avoid risks whenever possible. Male executives tend to see risks in terms of possible gains or losses, often worth a gamble in the hope of advancing their careers.

Yet an increasing number of women are succeeding in traditionally male fields—including corporate management. Women who remain single tend to have orderly careers, and their working lives may resemble those of men in many ways. However, many married women do not follow the "typical" career plan, either delaying entry into the labor force until their children begin school—or even until they leave home—or else starting their careers "on time" but interrupting them to bear and rear children. As noted earlier, such interruptions have been connected with lower income and lower job prestige (Fig. 13.3). Women's failure to progress as far and as fast as men on the climb up the management ladders also has been attributed to their practice of taking time out for child rearing. Economist Lester Thurow (1980) has pointed out that successful careers are generally established between the ages of 25 and 35–the stabilization period—and that when women leave their jobs to care for children during those years, they may find it impossible to catch up.

No matter what their occupation, women generally earn less than men, and economist Victor Fuchs (1983) believes that career interruptions are only one of the factors responsible. He sees male and female sex roles as the strongest factor and points out that early socialization practices affect women's choice of subjects in school, occupation, location of employment, and hours of work. Because traditional socialization emphasizes the maternal role, it weakens women's commitment to work outside the home, making them likely to refuse job transfers or to drop out of the labor force at any time. Fuchs believes that women who are committed to continuous, full-time employment are often discriminated against because employers form expectations based on the "average" behavior of women.

In a study that traced the working careers of retired women, Norah Keating and Barbara Jeffrey (1983) discovered five different patterns among women who had recently retired from work. Only one of these resembled the typical male pattern. No married women—but 55 percent of the single women—had had the continuous, orderly career pattern found in most men, and 30 percent of the married women had unstable careers, interrupted as many as five times. No single women had so many interruptions; 23 percent of the single women had dropped out of the labor force once, and another 22 percent had dropped out twice during their careers. These women had been born between 1910 and 1920 and were subject to a particular set of social influences and historical events.

An additional problem faced by many women is the disparity in pay between typically male and typically female jobs of equal worth. That is, when a blue-collar occupation that is primarily filled by men requires approximately the same level of skills and responsibility as a pink-collar occupation that is primarily filled by women, the male job consistently pays more money. Court decisions and union negotiations are beginning to chip away at this disparity. For example, after a job evaluation study was completed, a federal judge recently ordered Washington State to pay its female workers nearly a billion dollars in back pay and wage increases (Lewin, 1984)—a decision that has been appealed. It has been estimated that equalizing pay on jobs of comparable worth could increase American women's wages by as much as $150 billion each year.

Education	Ages 25–29		Ages 40–44	
	Men	Women	Men	Women
9–11 years	$13,868	$ 8,174	$16,279	$ 8,956
12 years	15,685	10,143	19,934	10,685
13–15 years	16,104	11,857	21,032	13,326
16 years	19,398	14,581	33,718	18,076

FIGURE 13.3   Sex differences in earnings, 1979 (in dollars).

Sources: U.S. Bureau of the Census, "Money Income of Families and Persons in the United States, 1979," *Current Population Reports*, series P-60, No. 129, Table 53.

The Effects of Employment

Home and family obligations influence employed wives and mothers, forcing most of them to work at two full-time jobs. This double demand can lead to stress, role overload, and role conflict, although as we saw in Chapter 12, many working mothers are developing ways to deal with the demand. The stress is especially hard on working women who work only because their income is necessary for family survival. These women tend to be unhappier than either homemakers or women who choose outside employment. Among one group of midlife women, role strain appeared in working mothers but not in working childless wives and in nonemployed mothers as opposed to childless wives, indicating that it is the responsibility for children that creates strain and overload (Baruch, Barnett, and Rivers, 1983). Among these women, the extent to which husbands were involved in chores and child care had a powerful influence on role strain.

The effect of employment appears to vary, perhaps depending on whether a woman has a career or a job. Among highly educated women in a large national sample, working women were more satisfied with their lives and marriages than women who did not work outside the home (Campbell et al., 1976). In some studies, no difference has appeared between the self-esteem and satisfaction of homemakers and employed married women, and, in others, middle-aged career women have displayed much higher self-esteem than other women, whether they are single, married, mothers, or childless. Other studies have indicated that working-class women and women with more than three children tend to be less satisfied when they work (Huston-Stein and Higgins-Trenk, 1978).

Although some homemakers are happy and satisfied and some working women are dissatisfied, as they move into the midlife period, women who work outside the home tend to have higher self-esteem, better health, and higher levels of marital satisfaction and to be less anxious than homemakers. Having a job was the *only* significant predictor of high self-esteem, which was unrelated to income, education, marital status, or stage in the family life cycle in a group of 40- to 59-year-old women drawn from a representative sample of Americans. In explaining these findings, which indicate that the benefits of working are not strongly related to salary or job prestige, the researchers (Coleman and Antonucci, 1983) suggest that employment during the midlife period may have a stabilizing influence, speculating that it takes a woman's attention away from any problems or tension that might be connected with marriage or the launching of children.

A question that remains is whether working women are employed outside the home because they are happy and confident or whether working outside the home increase happiness and self-confidence. The California Intergenerational Studies provide an opportunity for a longitudinal look at the working careers and personalities of a group of midlife women. Among these women, psychologist Janice Stroud (1981) found that commitment to a career was predicted by failure to conform to the feminine sex role during adolescence. This lack of conformity appeared to affect values and preferences, leading adolescents to seek higher education, to pursue ''masculine'' intellectual interests (such as science), or to become intensely involved in acceptable ''female'' intellectual interests (such as creative writing). At the age of 40, these women were ambitious, insightful, warm, and rational, showing a mixture of traditional male and female personality characteristics. (Some of them were among the nontraditional women discussed in Chapter 10). Work-committed women were highly involved in their careers, identified with their work, and derived major satisfaction from it. Despite their emotional investment in their careers, these women's lives did not center on their work to the extent that a highly involved man's life did. Few had had orderly careers, and, for most, their commitment to work had developed during the past 10 years.

Women in the California study who were employed outside the home but saw it primarily as a source of income or a way of keeping busy were different from work-commited women and homemakers. Those who had been to college had been assertive adolescents and were still the most assertive women in the group. They were independent, but lacked warmth. Their self-esteem and morale was low, and they seemed to have the worst of both worlds—employment and family. Their counterparts who had not been to college and were not committed to their jobs tended to have shallow intellectual interests, to be rebellious, power-oriented, and less warm than other women.

Homemakers who had either dropped out of the labor force when their first child was born or had never worked since their marriage had conformed to traditional feminine sex roles during adolescence. (Some of them were among the traditional women discussed in Chapter 10). Among the college educated, morale and self-esteem were the highest of any group. These women were oriented toward pleasing others, submissive, happy, and highly nurturant. They tended to be married to men with high job status. Homemakers who had not been to college had also been traditionally sex-typed during adolescence. However, they were ambitious and self-critical as well as being warm, nurturant, and insightful. They seemed to have channeled their youthful ambition into their roles as wives and mothers and regarded themselves as successful because economic necessity had not forced them into routine jobs.

College-educated homemakers who had worked at some time while they were rearing children, but had dropped out of the labor force, tended to be the most depressed women in the California study. They were hostile and angry, dissatisfied with the work world and with their family roles, and tended to be critical of their children.

Stroud's finding that both the happiest and unhappiest women were homemakers has been supported by other studies (Baruch, Barnett, and Rivers, 1983). Whether occupational attitudes of women in the future will resemble those of women in past studies is questionable. As Stroud points out, the women she studied had attended high school during World War II and were subjected to intense socialization pressures toward family roles. It was a time when women learned that their fulfillment lay in being good wives and mothers. Except for the work-committed women, they tended to have large families, and, at the age of 40, most still had children in elementary school.

Among these women, personality seemed to play a role in determining their occupational careers and interests. But, like men, their careers influenced their personalities. In another cross-sectional study (Miller et al., 1979), job complexity was shown to have the same effect on women's intellectual flexibility as has appeared in longitudinal studies of men. Women whose jobs required thought and independent judgment were much more flexible than women whose jobs were repetitive and thoughtless.

A career's influence on personality does not always follow expected lines. When a group of women physicians were followed for 10 to 12 years after they left medical school, researchers (Cartwright, 1977) found that they had become more emotionally expressive and nurturant. This pattern is somewhat like that of men, for these women were developing expressiveness after a stage of career consolidation, becoming nurturant at a time when women who had reared children before entering the labor force might be showing greater autonomy, drive, and leadership (Garfinkel, 1982). For both women and men, job satisfaction and job success are affected by similar forces.

JOB SATISFACTION

Given the enormous changes in the character of working conditions since 1870, we would expect to find today's workers happy and contented. Yet there is no sign that job alienation is less today than it was a century ago (Miernyk, 1975). Workers may not have been satisfied in the nineteenth century, but they were probably too busy and too exhausted to contemplate their situation. Greater freedom, the democratization of the workplace, as well as a newfound affluence, appear to have developed hand in hand with anxiety, discontent, and alienation.

What makes a job or career satisfying? According to Mark Twain, the satisfaction is not in the job itself but in the worker's view of the job. When Tom Sawyer was faced with the drudgery of whitewashing a fence, he pretended the job was a rare privilege that required great skill. His act was so convincing that the neighborhood boys paid him for the privilege of doing his work. As Twain pointed out, Tom had discovered "that Work consists of whatever a body is *obliged* to do, and that Play consists of whatever a body is not obliged to do. And this would help him to understand why constructing artificial flowers or performing on a treadmill is work, while rolling tenpins or climbing Mont Blanc is only amusement" (1876, p. 29).

Following Twain's line of reasoning, Renee Garfinkel (1982) decided that unless work includes the element of creating, producing, or achieving, it can be extremely destructive. The contented supermarket checker who began this chapter took pride in her knowledge of thousands of item prices, her speed and accuracy, and her ability to detect shoplifters. Her job included the element of achievement, and she liked it so much that she came to work 45 minutes early every morning. The alienated stockbroker felt that his job was superfluous, that his middle-income customers had no hope of making much money in the market, and that he had no opportunity to make decisions; for him there was no sense of personal achievement in his career.

This chef works hard, fast, and spends long hours at his job, but its complexity keeps him from being alienated by his occupation.

Drawing on a national survey of working conditions, researchers (Seashore and Barnowe, 1972) discovered that job satisfaction was related to the challenge presented by a job, by its financial and security rewards, by the availability of resources that allow the worker to do the job well, and by the comfort or convenience of the job. Salary turned out to be an important factor among low-income workers, but not among blue-collar or white-collar workers with high income. Particularly alienating were having skills a person would like to use on the job but couldn't, no chance to learn new things, no opportunity to be creative, and no freedom to decide how the work should be done. These factors seem related to job complexity, which has been found to affect workers at all levels. Being required to work hard, fast, or long hours had little relationship to job satisfaction.

The finding that low-income employees are strongly affected by wages fits with other research indicating that satisfaction among workers who have jobs is most affected by salary whereas, among those who have careers, it is most affected by opportunities to advance in the future. Sociologist Rosabeth Kanter (1976) has found that people in dead-end careers tend to give up hope, lose ambition, suffer a drop in self-esteem, and watch their commitment to work evaporate.

Working conditions may not be the major influence on job satisfaction, but they do count. The move toward flextime in business, industry, and government has increased worker satisfaction by giving employees control over their working hours, allowing clerical and blue-collar employees some of the flexibility traditionally enjoyed by managers and professionals (Stein, Cohen, and Gadon, 1976). By 1980, about 12 percent of American workers were on flexible schedules (U.S. Bureau of the Census, 1982).

In most organizations that use flextime, employees must be on the job by 10:00 A.M. and are not allowed to leave before 3:00 P.M., but the remainder of their working day can be scheduled at their convenience, with some coming in at 7 A.M. and leaving early and others arriving at 10 A.M. and staying until 7 P.M. Such flexibility allows parents to juggle child-care responsibilities and to adapt work schedules to their own biological rhythms and outside interests. The result has generally been a rise in satisfaction, increased work commitment (as shown in decreased absenteeism, sick leave, and tardiness), and increased productivity (Stein, Cohen, and Gadon, 1976).

When workers are dissatisfied and have no sense of achievement, they may spend the last decade or so on the job marking time, counting off the years and months until retirement. Highly satisfied workers may have mixed feelings about the approach of retirement.

RETIREMENT

The concept of retirement, of withdrawing from the labor force yet continuing to be paid, is a relatively new development, one that appears to be connected with industrialization. As we discovered earlier, during the nineteenth century only a minority of the population lived long enough to reach today's retirement age, and the average worker was still employed at the time of death. Those who survived continued to work as long as they were physically able, and in predominantly agricultural areas there was always work for them to do.

Several forces associated with industrialization made the practice of retirement possible (McConnell, 1983). First, beginning about 1870, as productivity mounted and fewer people were needed to provide the country's goods and services, there was a decline in the demand for labor. The change was most striking in the field of agriculture, where jobs shrank from 50 percent of the workforce in 1870 to 38 percent in 1900 and 4 percent in 1975 (Foner and Schwab, 1981). Second, as technology radically transformed many occupations, older workers' skills and knowledge quickly became obsolete. Third, as large business and governmental bureaucracies developed, careers began to be governed by impersonal rules and regulations that were devised to make the organization run smoothly but made no allowance for interindividual differences. Finally, private pensions and the establishment of the Social Security system in 1935 provided an economic base that made the retirement of older workers possible and established the age of 65 as the normative time of departure from the labor force.

The choice of 65 as the retirement age was purely arbitrary and had nothing to do with the aging process. But its use by the government to determine eligibility for full retirement benefits caused it to be gradually accepted as the time of entry into old age (Neugarten and Hall, 1980). The first official retirement age, set in 1891 to determine eligibility for the German old age pension, was 70 (McConnell,

1983). Recent changes in Social Security regulations will push retirement age to 66 by the year 2009 and to 67 by 2027. If the age of retirement bore the same relationship to later life expectancy as it did in 1935, when the system was established, people would now be expected to work until they reached the age of 80 (Swensen, 1983).

The notion of paid retirement was slow to be accepted. When older steelworkers were asked about retirement in 1950, more than half said that it should be limited to physically impaired workers. By 1960, fewer than 25 percent of older workers in the same company held that belief (Ash, 1966). In the second half of the twentieth century, workers have come to accept the idea of retirement as a reward or a well-earned rest.

The pool of retired workers has been growing rapidly since the early 1950s because people are retiring earlier and living longer. In 1900, 68.3 percent of men older than 65 and 9.1 percent of older women were still in the work force (Riley and Foner, 1968); by 1981, only 18.4 percent of older men and 8 percent of older women were still employed. Investigators have been especially interested in how retirement affects people psychologically and physiologically, what factors contribute to the retirement decisions, and whether the aging process diminishes the value of workers.

THE PROBLEMS OF THE AGING WORKER

One factor that may push an older worker into retirement is job discrimination. Most people, including a good many individuals older than 65, believe that the aging worker is less efficient, less adaptable, slower, and weaker on the job than younger adults. When people across the country were surveyed by a national polling organization, the young displayed perceptions of older adults that could affect their access to jobs (Harris, 1975) (see Fig. 13.4). Younger people tended to see the old as wiser than themselves and as extremely warm and friendly, so some attitudes toward the elderly were favorable. But in those qualities that determine job performance—efficiency, flexibility, alertness, and physical capability—older people were seen as failing badly. Older people did not agree. Except for physical activity, older people's view of their own job qualities was fairly high and differed little from the self-image of younger people. However, the old did not believe they were either as wise or as warm as the young thought them to be.

The general public does not hire, fire, or promote workers, but the views of people who exercise that responsibility closely resemble the views of the general public. Approximately one fifth of the younger adults polled were in positions that required them to make personnel decisions, and more than half believed that older workers were not as capable as they once had been.

Stereotypical beliefs about older workers can be translated into discriminatory employment practices. When more than 1500 *Harvard Business Review* subscribers were asked to make personnel decisions in fictitious cases, discrimination was rampant (Rosen, 1978). All subscribers got the same cases, but the age of the

	Older Adults as Seen by People 18–64	Older Adults as Seen by People >64	People 18–64 as Seen by Themselves
Very good at getting things done	35%	55%	60%
Very open-minded and adaptable	19	63	67
Very bright and alert	29	68	73
Very physically active	41	48	65
Very wise from experience	66	69	54
Very friendly and warm	82	72	63

FIGURE 13.4   Perceptions of older people (percent).

Adapted from   L. Harris and Associates, 1975.

employee was varied. The decisions reflected the same view of older employees picked up by the national survey and resulted in such actions as firing an older computer programmer whose skills had become obsolete but retraining a younger employee in the same situation. Various studies have indicated that older workers are laid off first and rehired last; that when they do find another job, it generally carries less prestige and less pay than their old position; that they are passed over for promotion; and that they are less likely than a younger worker to get education and retraining that would upgrade their skills (Wanner and McDonald, 1983).

The Age Discrimination in Employment Act, passed in 1967, attempted to protect workers younger than 65 from being retired, fired, or passed over for hiring simply because of their age. In 1978, the law was amended to cover workers up to the age of 70. No one knows how much age discrimination still goes on, but one researcher (Quinn, 1979) found that, after correcting for education, vocational training, job experience, and health, older workers received lower wages than younger workers. In a recent study, Richard Wanner and Lynn McDonald (1983) looked at the earnings records of men who were part of a longitudinal study of labor market experience. Workers between the ages of 55 and 64 who had been in the study for 10 years showed a decline in real earnings over the period—at a time when the average full-time worker showed a 12.4 percent gain. Yet nearly a third of these men had had some sort of recent occupational training.

Is there any basis for age discrimination? If older workers are less productive than younger workers, then their employment at similar salary levels could be costly. No one has yet demonstrated that there is much difference between the job performance of the old and the young. In most studies, productivity—whether measured in output or sales—either remains about the same or shows a very slight decline in older workers (Foner and Schwab, 1981). Some studies have found that older workers are more productive than the young, but when output is corrected for job experience, any significant difference in productivity disappears (Schwab and Heneman, 1977). However, such research is cross-sectional, and until longitudinal research is available, there is no way to be certain that differences in attitude and education are not affecting the results. At present, we can say that in the industries studied (clerical work, factory production), older and younger workers seem to perform at about equal levels and to maintain the same quality of work.

Older workers seem to excel in some aspects of work. They work at a steadier pace, week in and week out, they are more committed to the work they do, and they show less absenteeism (Foner and Schwab, 1981). Again, whether this is a cohort difference or the result of job survival, in which employees who do not measure up have left, is uncertain.

The widespread belief that young employees are innovative and that older employees are inflexible and conservative is probably wrong. Young employees are intent on learning company politics, advancing their careers, and avoiding risks. Older employees, being near retirement, risk little by proposing radical innovations. It has been suggested that instead of a roster of young Turks and old fogies, most companies are staffed by young fogies and old Turks (Schrank and Waring, 1983).

Because older workers tend to be concentrated in dying industries, their skills often become obsolete. When this happens to a younger worker, employers frequently provide retraining. But when they consider the number of productive years remaining to the older worker against the cost of retraining, it may be more economical to train a new worker. In addition, the older worker's experience often has pushed his or her wages to the high end of the salary scale, further increasing the annual cost. Skill obsolescence and higher salaries, together with beliefs that aging is associated with rigidity and low productivity, tilt the scales against the older worker. Following this line of reasoning, employers are reluctant to hire older workers and often encourage early retirement among long-time employees. However, because age is a rough index of knowledge and experience, this practice deprives companies of employees with long employment histories and the benefit of their experience and wisdom (Schrank and Waring, 1983).

Many older unemployed workers either cannot find jobs or feel they have been dismissed or demoted purely because of their age. Although the unemployment figures for older workers are lower than rates among younger workers (see Fig. 13.5), many believe that most older unemployment is hidden. When older workers lose their jobs, they often become discouraged and drop out of the job market—either because they have encountered discrimination or because they believe their age makes employment unlikely—and so they fail to show up in the statistics (Schram and Osten, 1978). If they are eligible for retirement benefits, older workers may decide to take them as soon as their unemployment checks run out, making them "reluctant retirees."

When asked, the overwhelming majority of workers past the age of 55 say they intend to work until they are 65—or even longer. Eight out of ten say they would like to work part-time after they have retired and three out of four retirees would also like to work (Harris, 1981). Given the prevailing beliefs about older workers, it is often difficult for them to find such work.

	Male	Female
All workers	7.4%	7.9%
18–19 years	20.1	19.0
20–24 years	13.2	11.2
25–34 years	6.9	7.7
35–44 years	4.5	5.7
45–54 years	4.0	4.6
55–64 years	3.6	3.8
65 and over	2.9	3.6

FIGURE 13.5   Unemployment rates—1981 (percent of labor force).

Although unemployment rates for older employees are low, the statistics reflect only those workers who are looking for jobs. Older workers who have become so discouraged that they have dropped out of the job market or taken "early retirement" are not included.

Source: U.S. Bureau of the Census. *Statistical Abstract of the United States, 1982–1983*, 103d ed., 1982.

THE RETIREMENT DECISION

Many people retire at the age of 65, when they are entitled to full retirement benefits. At one time, all workers could be required to retire at this age, but today—except for occupations that clearly require abilities that decline with age—no one can be forced to retire before the age of 70. Some people continue working long past the accepted retirement age of 65. But an increasing number of people have been choosing early retirement, in which they may leave work any time after their sixty-second birthday and accept a reduced pension. The factors behind the decision to retire differ, depending on whether a person chooses early or "on time" retirement.

Workers who retire "very early," that is, before the age of 62, tend to be either wealthy and in good health or strapped financially and in poor health. The vast majority fall into the distressed category, and many die within a few years (McConnell, 1983). In some occupations, where physical condition and reaction time are critical, full retirement comes earlier. For example, police officers tend to retire before they are 50.

Early retirement, between the ages of 62 and 64, has become increasingly popular. In 1979, more than two thirds of eligible workers accepted early retirement and began to draw Social Security payments (Social Security Administration, 1980). Some may retire because they have been unable to find new employment after being laid off, but other factors influence the majority of early retirement decisions.

Health, financial situation, the nature of a person's occupation, job satisfaction, and attitudes toward retirement all affect the decision to retire early. Among workers in the automobile industry, poor health, adequate finances, job dissatisfaction, and favorable attitudes toward retirement were factors that led to early retirement (Barfield and Morgan, 1975). Finances appeared to be the most important influence, with workers who could expect an income that would permit them to live comfortably being the most likely to retire early.

Among workers in several national longitudinal studies, poor health and positive attitudes toward retirement were associated with early retirement (Palmore,

JOINING THE JOB CLUB

The results of a recent experiment indicate that when older people are shown how to go about finding jobs and encouraged in their search, their chances of being employed rise dramatically. Based on a method devised by psychologist Nathan Azrin (1978), a "job club" was established in an industrial city with unemployment rates above the national average. Fifty-two percent of the job seekers chosen for the study were older than 62, 56 percent were women, 85 percent were white, 39 percent considered themselves retired, and 68 percent preferred part-time work. In terms of their former jobs, 31.3 percent had held manual or unskilled jobs, 33.3 percent had held skilled or clerical jobs, and 35.4 percent had held managerial or professional jobs.

Half the adults were assigned to a control group. They were given information on the state-run job service, additional assistance by a state specialist in older worker placement, and referrals to community agencies that offered employment assistance to older adults with income below the poverty level. Their experience resembled prevailing practices in the area. The rest of the adults, each one matched to a member of the control group, formed the job club. Club members took part in a workshop that provided orientation, education, and skill training; they learned how to locate job leads and how to set concrete goals for their job search. Twice each week they met to practice job-seeking techniques, share information and job leads, set public goals for their search, and provide mutual support.

The effects of the job search were assessed at 4, 8, and 12 weeks after the beginning of the program. Compared with the control group, club members were spectacularly successful at finding jobs, with three out of

George, and Fillenbaum, 1982). Poor working conditions, including noise, odors, and extreme temperatures; the lack of any chance to make decisions; and physical or mental job stress have also been connected with early retirement (Quinn, 1978), but the importance of job conditions was more likely to be connected with "on time" than with early retirement among workers in the longitudinal studies. Job dissatisfaction appears to lead to early retirement only when a worker's occupation is central to his or her life (McConnell, 1983).

Among male workers in the longitudinal surveys who retired "on time" or later, education, occupation, and financial considerations were of major importance (Palmore, George, and Fillenbaum, 1982). Those with high levels of education and high-status occupations tended to work longer and often worked past retirement age. People in high socioeconomic brackets appeared to have more opportunities to work and more incentive to continue working. Similarly, self-employment also predicted continued work whereas working for others, pension

| | At 4 weeks | | At 8 weeks | | At 12 weeks | |
	Job Club	Control Group	Job Club	Control Group	Job Club	Control Group
Jobs found	39%	4%	62%	22%	74%	22%
Income (cumulative)	$92.04	$4.17	$203.78	$19.73	NA	NA
Hours (cumulative)	19.43	1.35	45.95	6.04	NA	NA

FIGURE 13.6 Employment success.

Most older adults who were part of a job club were able to find work even in an area with high unemployment. The club provided instruction and encouragement, as well as an opportunity to share job leads.

Source: D. Gray, 1983, p. 367. Reprinted by permission of the *Journal of Gerontology.*

four members working within 12 weeks (see Fig. 13.6). Both groups found similar kinds of employment: jobs that were generally low status and low paying. The marginal level of work secured was due in part to the low sights generally set by the adults and in part to the fact that so many wanted part-time employment—which is generally low-status, low-pay work.

This preliminary program, says researcher Denis Gray (1983), indicates that the job club is an effective employment service for older job seekers. He believes that among the secrets of its success are the emphasis placed on mutual support among club members (a factor that prevents discouragement in the job search) and the sharing of job leads. The program does nothing to attack the problems of job discrimination or the obsolescence of job skills, but it seems effective at finding available jobs that might otherwise be overlooked by older workers in search of employment.

plan coverage, and mandatory retirement rules predicted retirement at age 65. These considerations appeared to have little effect on women's decision to retire. Only age predicted retirement among women in these longitudinal studies (George, Fillenbaum, and Palmore, 1984). (Most retired workers in these surveys stopped working before mandatory retirement was pushed to age 70.)

Attitudes toward work and retirement appeared to be of little importance, but they may have influenced retirement decisions indirectly (Palmore, George, and Fillenbaum, 1982). Work attitudes influenced the likelihood of continued full-time employment or part-time employment after retirement. Workers who had said earlier that they preferred work to leisure or that they would work if they did not have to generally stuck by their words. By the end of the studies, they were working more hours each year than other workers.

The condition of a worker's health had little connection with the decision to retire at 65 or later. This finding contradicts the conclusions of many cross-sectional studies, but the researchers suggest that poor health is a socially acceptable reason for retirement and that, in retrospect, it may take on exaggerated importance to the retired worker.

ADJUSTING TO RETIREMENT

If work gives meaning to our lives and promotes a sense of well-being, how do we adjust to a life of leisure? Most of today's retirees grew up believing strongly in the work ethic, and, as we have seen, as late as 1950 the majority of steelworkers believed that people should work as long as they were physically able. Retirement has been variously described as an affliction, a crisis, traumatic, or a stressful transition (Foner and Schwab, 1981). Yet more people opt for early retirement each year, and studies consistently indicate that most retired people are satisfied, continue to feel useful, and maintain their sense of identity. Retirement is unlikely to be followed by depression, decline, or death.

In fact, some researchers (Atchley, 1976) believe that retirement either has no effect on health or that it tends to improve general health levels. Such beliefs are supported by surveys in which from 22 to 40 percent of retired people say that stopping work has made their health better. Less than 6 percent say that retirement has led to worsened health (Streib and Schneider, 1971). Such studies rely on retrospective data, which is notoriously unreliable. In Chapter 10, we saw that adults' recollections of their adolescent personality could not be trusted.

Curious as to the accuracy of retirees' claims about improved health, researchers (Ekerdt, Bossee, and LoCastro, 1983) examined information obtained in a longitudinal study begun by the Veterans Administration in 1963. They compared retired workers' reports of their health made just before retirement and during the first three years after retirement with the same men's responses to the question, "Do you think that retiring has had any effect on your health?" Replies were similar to those of other studies: 50 percent of the men said that retirement had had no effect on their health, 38 percent claimed it had had a good effect, 1 percent said it had harmed their health, and 12 percent were uncertain. Claims of improved health were not accompanied by increases in health levels. However, men who claimed to be healthier since their retirement were more likely than other men to have been dissatisfied with their working conditions. They also were likely to have worked at stressful jobs, reported serious health problems while working, rated their health during that time as poor or fair, and retired for health-related reasons. The researchers suggest that the men's perception of improved health was due at least in part to the lifting of job strains and demands of the job role. It may be that claims of improved health simply reflect their enthusiasm for the retired life.

When we examine studies of retirees closely, it becomes apparent that retirement is good for many people, has no influence on others, and is bad for the rest (McConnell, 1983). Prior attitudes, personality characteristics, economics, and health all affect the way a person adjusts to a life of retirement. For some people, the abrupt loss of the work role, with its associated sense of power and the belief that their work contributes to society, can lead to a troubled transition. Such people are likely to have made work a central part of their lives and to have held high-status professions. High-occupational status does not foretell an unhappy retirement, however. Among high-status retired employees from seven large corporations, 55 percent said that retirement had given them "the best years of my life" (Kimmel, Price, and Walker, 1978).

It has been suggested that retirement is likely to be pleasant for people who have a comfortable income, are relatively healthy, retire voluntarily, are not wedded to their work, and who have made some sort of plans for their retirement (McConnell, 1983). Economics seems particularly important. Between 1974 and 1978, the proportion of retired people who said they would prefer to be working rose from 31 percent to 46 percent, a change that has been attributed to increased inflation during that period (Foner and Schwab, 1981).

Until recently, only a minority of women spent their lives in the labor force. As the majority of people who have retired from a life of paid employment are men, most of the information on adjustment to retirement comes from studies of retired men. One such longitudinal study followed a large group of men from 1966, when they were between the ages of 45 and 59, until 1977, when they were between 55 and 69. Almost 30 percent of the men were black, but race had no effect on replies. Among these men, retirees were twice as likely as workers to be unhappy, with 11.2 percent of the retirees but only 5.6 percent of the workers expressing general unhappiness. However, when Scott Beck (1982) analyzed the replies, he discovered that when health conditions were controlled, workers were only slightly happier than retirees, and that when income was considered, the difference virtually disappeared. Loss of the work role appeared to have no negative impact on happiness, but marital status did. Divorced, widowed, or separated men were more likely than married men to say they were unhappy. In addition, men who retired five or more years before they had expected to leave the labor force tended to be unhappy compared with men who retired at the expected age.

The finding that health and income are the most powerful predictors of satisfaction among retired men was supported by a controlled study of retired, urban, working-class men and women who sought part-time employment (Soumerai and Avorn, 1983). These adults worked halftime for the Park Maintenance Corp., gardening and removing litter in parks and playgrounds. They were also encouraged to develop ways to improve park landscaping. After 10 weeks on the job, their levels of life satisfaction rose, and they reported increased health. The researchers believe that the improvement was caused by a combination of increased income, the opportunity to exert control over their environment, and the feeling that they were engaged in useful, valued activity. Considering the deleterious effects of inactivity on health, we might speculate that 20 hours each week of outdoor activity may have played some part in reports of improved health.

When adjusting to retirement is traumatic, the stress may be due to the abrupt change connected with the shift from worker to retiree. The sudden removal of a useful social role may make a worker feel bereft, useless, and unhappy. As the part-time employment study indicates, limited employment might help older adults make a smoother transition. Few people do much conscious planning for retirement, and not many companies provide formal counseling programs for their workers who are about to retire (Foner and Schwab, 1981).

What may be a new trend could make adjusting to retirement much easier. Polaroid Corporation has initiated a program that promises to cushion the shock of retirement—as yet the only major American company to do so. Their program has two routes to gradual retirement (Clendinen, 1983). In one, employees may take a three-month leave of absence with all their benefits intact. If they find that retirement does not agree with them, they may come back to work. Thus far, about half the people who have tested retirement this way have come back to work.

The other route to retirement consists of tapering off the employee's working hours. A worker may cut back to a four-day work, taking a salary that is reduced by 20 percent. The extra time can be accumulated and taken in chunks. For example, one 67-year-old employee, Robert Woodward, says that he has 76 days off each year, which he spreads out by taking several vacations, including 3 weeks in Florida during the spring, a 3-week summer vacation, a 10-day cruise on the *Queen Elizabeth II*, and long weekends with his grandchildren. More men than women have taken advantage of this program, and company officials believe that this is due to women's tendency to fit their own retirement to their husbands' retirement plans. One Polaroid employee who retired happily after his 3-month leave advised his fellow workers not to follow his example unless they had a hobby. This man spends several hours each day repairing jewelry and cutting and polishing stones. As we will see, most retirees manage to keep busy.

LEISURE

With retirement, the amount of free time expands enormously. But by historical standards, the average adult has an incredible amount of leisure even when fully employed. As we have seen, the average work week has dropped from 60 to 40 hours within the past century, and vacations—unheard of as late as the nineteenth century—are a standard benefit of employment. In response to the growth of free time and discretionary income, a large leisure industry has developed. This booming multibillion dollar industry produces goods and services of every description, from tennis rackets and televisions to Caribbean cruises, computers, and cookbooks.

The importance Americans place on leisure activities seems to have increased in recent years, and this increase is probably related to the emphasis most of us place on self-fulfillment. National studies indicate that about 80 percent of the population now believe that life should be more than a matter of economic survival and duty and say that choice, flexibility, and freedom are important in their lives (Yankelovich, 1981).

Of course, not all the time away from work is spent in **leisure** activities—doing those things we are not obligated to do. Family or other obligations may consume a great deal of nonworking time. The view of leisure as freely chosen means that a specific activity may be obligatory in one situation and freely chosen leisure in another. For example, a half hour spent preparing a family meal is probably an obligation, but several hours devoted to preparing an elaborate meal by a person whose hobby is gourmet cooking could be leisure. It would seem that the classification of any activity as leisure depends on our attitude toward it rather than the characteristics of the activity.

OBJECTIVES OF LEISURE

According to Chad Gordon, Charles Gaitz, and Judith Scott (1976), leisure has five major objectives: relaxation, diversion, development, creativity, and the pursuit of sensual pleasure. Each required a different intensity of cognitive, emotional, and physical involvement, and as intensity increases, so does the expenditure of energy, the need for focused attention, and the level of sensory stimulation. **Relaxation,** the least intense form of leisure, includes resting, daydreaming, and sleeping. **Diversion,** a medium-low form of involvement, gives us a change of pace and some relief from our routine activities of work and chores. It includes watching television or movies, light reading, most hobbies, conversation with friends, parties, games and toys, and watching athletic events.

Developmental pleasures require involvement of medium intensity, and their pursuit, though intrinsically enjoyable, often increases our physical or cognitive skills. They include exercise, individual sports, serious reading, education not aimed at furthering career goals, going to museums and art galleries, clubs and interest groups, learning to play a musical instrument, travel, ''educational'' games and toys.

In **creative pleasures**, we are involved at medium-high intensity, and such activities might be considered ''useful play.'' They include obvious creative activities in artistic, literary, and music fields, altruistic activities, serious discussion, and the blending of art and play with work.

At the most intense level of involvement is the pursuit of **sensual pleasures,** which go beyond sexual activity to include any form of leisure in which the activation of the senses provides intense pleasure, gratification, excitement, rapture, or joy. An ecstatic religious experience, intense and rhythmic dancing, or highly competitive games and sports can all be forms of sensual pleasure. These high-intensity forms of leisure are sometimes addictive (as in the use of psychoactive drugs and perhaps running) or dangerous (as in skydiving or mountain climbing).

Sometimes these objectives may blur. For example, the computer hacker who majors in computer science, gets a job programming or maintaining computers, sits in front of a terminal 16 hours a day, and sees no one except other hackers is probably functioning at the addictive level rather than blending work with play (Zimbardo, 1980). However, in our leisure activities most of us move from one level of involvement to another. The activities we find most rewarding seem to change over the life span and are influenced by our age, sex, education, personality, and socioeconomic level.

Leisure takes many forms and serves a number of purposes, depending on the cognitive, emotional, and physical involvement required. Visiting a museum is a developmental pleasure that increases cognitive skills, whereas shooting the rapids is a sensual pleasure that excites and gratifies the senses.

LEISURE ACROSS ADULTHOOD

Many leisure activities are popular among all age groups, but others are found primarily among young, middle-aged, or older adults. Sometimes this pattern can be traced to cohort differences. For example, when the oldest adults were youngsters, horseshoes were common items. In a society with little extra money, simply driving two stakes into the ground produced an hour's activity on a leisurely Sunday afternoon for all ages. Today the game's popularity has faded as a profusion of more exciting activities has mushroomed. A survey might turn up pockets of horseshoe players in areas with large elderly populations and almost no players among young or middle-aged adults. At the other end of the age scale, video games and computer programming are probably most prevalent among the young, with a few adherents among the middle-aged and almost none among the elderly. However, in general, as we get older, our free time is spent in less active and less social kinds of leisure.

Among nearly 1500 adults in the Houston area, some activities were found to be more popular with age, some were equally popular across the life span, and others were less popular with older people (Gordon, Gaitz, and Scott, 1976). At older ages, both men and women spent more time in relaxation and solitary activities than the young, and men spent more time cooking, beginning at about the age of 45. Activities that were equally popular with all age groups included television viewing, discussion, spectator sports, looking at paintings, listening to music, entertaining, participating in clubs and organizations, and such home-centered activities as sewing, decorating, building, and gardening. Activities that were less popular with the old tended to be those that take place outside the home and involve excitement, escape, physical exertion, or sensorimotor skill. They included going out dancing and drinking, attending movies, physical exercise, active sports, hunting or target shooting, outdoor activities, traveling, reading books, playing musical instruments, singing, drawing, and painting.

When these activities were charted according to the five objectives discussed earlier, only the lowest level—relaxation—showed an upward trend across the life span. The downward trend in developmental and creative pleasures was not steep, with women reporting higher levels of creative activity in every age group. Diversion and sensual pleasure showed precipitous declines from youth to old age. Such activities were primarily engaged in by the young and by men.

According to Rhona and Robert Rapoport (1975), the choice of leisure activities is best understood in terms of the family life cycle, with changes in leisure interests and activities paralleling changes in roles and values. They see young adulthood as a time of identification with job and family. Taking on the role of husband or wife leads to a modification in leisure choices, and in today's companionate marriage, many activities are shared. The birth of children affects leisure, for child care poses both an economic and logistic problem. Going out dancing or to see a movie requires finding and paying for a baby-sitter, so it is not surprising that such activities begin to decline.

Sensual pleasure, in the form of sexuality, is most popular among young adults. However, a study of married couples indicated that men and women appear to regard recreational sex differently (Mancini and Orthner, 1978). Among couples who have been married less than five years, a strong majority of husbands but less than half the wives view sexual activity as a highly desired form of recreation. Across the years of married life, the popularity of recreational sex declines, with men generally substituting some other form of joint activity—although not necessarily with their wives—for sex, but women substituting something they can do independently. The researchers suggest that men may regard their free time as an opportunity to interact with others, but women—who spend more time catering to the demands of others—look for recuperative activities that require less personal involvement.

Another way to look at younger adults' feelings about leisure is to examine their attitudes and practices concerning vacations. Among 10,000 *Psychology Today* readers, about half thought they got as much vacation time as they deserved (Rubenstein, 1980). However, about a quarter said they would like more time for developing special skills, and another fifth said they would like more time to develop their intellectual abilities. These young, well-educated adults gave six reasons for taking vacations: to rest and relieve tensions (37 percent), to seek intellectual enrichments (18 percent), to be with their families (13 percent), to seek some sort of exotic adventure (12 percent), to be alone (11 percent), and to escape daily routines (8 percent). Most enjoyed their vacations—except for a small group of workaholics. This group, about equally divided between men and women, consisted of 13 percent of the sample, who worked more than 65 hours a week. Workaholics were just as happy as the rest of the people in the survey, but they regarded vacations as a waste of time, and 42 percent of them took less vacation time than they were entitled to.

Between the ages of 30 and 44, most leisure activities are centered around home and family. Watching television, visiting, gardening, working in a home workshop, hobbies, reading, walking, and such physical activities as fishing, hunting, camping, or swimming are popular (Gordon, Gaitz, and Scott, 1976). At this stage, working mothers may find themselves with no free time at all, especially if they are divorced or have a traditional marriage. Socioeconomic levels appear to influence the precise choice of activity, with people at lower levels engaging in relaxation, diversion, and sensual pleasure, and people at upper levels engaging in developmental, creative, and sensual pleasures. In a study of Kansas City adults (Havighurst, 1961), middle-class individuals tended to try new activities and to select activities they truly enjoyed, that developed their skills, and that had some bearing on their personal lives. Working-class adults tended to repeat activities, to do something to "kill time," and to select an activity because it was near their homes.

Part of this class difference is undoubtedly due to income differences. Studies have indicated, for example, that differences in activities between older black and white adults are due to socioeconomic level, not race (Heyman and Jeffers, 1970). Part of the class difference can be traced to education, which widens leisure possibilities. Critic George Steiner (Steiner and Hall, 1973), pointing out that a four or a three-and-a-half day week might become standard by the twenty-first century, once said:

In the last analysis, high literacy means that you are less vulnerable to boredom. You carry inside you resources that make you less and less dependent upon stimuli around you. What will happen to people who do not have that luggage inside them and do not want it? [p. 69].

Another explanation for this class difference in recreational choice has been advanced by Harold Wilensky (1962), who believes that two seemingly contradictory factors guide our selection: compensation and "spillover." When influenced by compensation, we may choose activities that give us satisfactions lacking in our jobs, perhaps leading to sensual pleasures, such as drunkenness, extramarital sexuality, and violence. When influenced by "spillover," we generalize the qualities of our occupations to our leisure, so that people with dull, repetitive jobs that take all decision-making power away from a worker may become alienated and choose leisure activities characterized by isolation, apathy, and inertia. However, other factors such as general life-style, personality, previous experiences, the meanings attached to leisure, the availability of various types of leisure, and the interests of friends are probably involved in recreational choices (Gordon, Gaitz, and Scott, 1976).

After the age of 45, as children grow older and parents are less tied to the home, the focus of leisure activities may broaden. When children leave the nest there are fewer constraints on recreational choices and many child-related obligations (such as PTA) disappear. Increased disposable income, freedom from responsibility, and additional time may lead to more evenings out, to travel, and to new interests in creative activities.

After adults retire, education and income continue to influence their leisure activities, and health may also begin to affect their choices. Some years ago, more than 5000 retired adults were asked what they had done on the preceding day (Riley and Foner, 1968). The most popular activities were television, visiting, reading, and such solitary activities as napping or daydreaming. In another study, 68 percent of men older than 65 were satisfied with the amount of leisure time they had available, but 16 percent said they had too much free time (Pfeiffer and Davis, 1974). Among men in the group who were still employed, 68 percent found work more satisfying than leisure, and only 10 percent found leisure more satisfying. Their continued employment was apparently based on interest as well as financial necessity: 97 percent said they would continue to work even if they did not need the money.

About 25 years ago, it was suggested that during the normal course of aging, adults tend to disengage from society (Cumming and Henry, 1961). However, most research has shown that life satisfaction among older adults depends on continued contact with the social environment. Among men and women in the Duke Longitudinal Study, life satisfaction was strongly related to high levels of activity. Over a period of several years, most maintained the same general level of activity, curtailing their actions only when faced with declining health. A few of these adults were disengaged and satisfied, but in most cases the "disengaged" life style had been established early (Maddox, 1970).

At the last interview, men and women in the Duke Study were between the ages of 70 and 93. During the 10 years of the study, men showed no general reduction in their total activities, but women showed a small drop—less than 7 percent. The researcher (Palmore, 1970) points out that the men had retired before the study began and may already have changed their activity patterns. Although there was a decline in some areas (belonging to organizations, attending meetings), it may have been compensated for by increases in such areas as visiting family or friends and reading.

Among today's elderly adults, women generally have less leisure time than men. Most men are married, and in a traditional relationship the wife handles the cooking and housework. So whether single, divorced, widowed, or married, women have household responsibilities that do not diminish after the age of 65. When today's young adults retire and wives are also drawing pensions and worker's Social Security, free time may be more equally distributed.

Future retirees will also have higher educational levels and perhaps more disposable income than today's elderly. They are also likely to be in better health. Although their leisure activities are likely to continue to be more sedentary than those of younger adults, many changes may occur in recreational patterns. They may still enjoy listening to records of the Bee Gees, but the frequency and intensity of their dancing is likely to diminish. Reading by today's retirees tends to be focused on newspapers; tomorrow's retirees may read more books and attend more cultural activities. One form of leisure that is becoming more popular with older adults is education.

EDUCATION

Just as development was once believed to stop at maturity, education was reserved for childhood and adolescence. Our attitude seemed to be that education worked like a vaccine—a large dose early in life immunized us against the need for further formal learning (Birren and Woodruff, 1973). Today, however, formal education appears to be spreading across the life span, with middle-aged and elderly adults enrolling in traditional college programs, in special college programs devised for "mature students," and in community adult education courses (Fig. 13.7). Classes have been held at colleges and universities, at elementary and secondary schools, in churches, and at recreation centers. Some older adults take correspondence courses or enroll in courses given on educational television.

THE RETURN TO SCHOOL

This return of adults to educational settings, which many expect to accelerate, has been brought about by a combination of social and historical changes. James Birren and Diane Woodruff (1973) have detected half a dozen such shifts in society that have contributed to the rise. First, the age structure of society has changed. The proportion of older adults has grown enormously, and many of them are retiring at an early age. Before too many years, college graduates who retire at the age of 62, after 40 years of employment, will have spent less than half their life in the labor force. The increased leisure of retired individuals gives them ample opportunity to go back to school. Second, with the last of the baby-boom generation moving into the "over-25" bracket, college enrollment has begun to drop. The resulting empty classrooms and unemployed academics mean that school facilities for older adults are already available.

Age	Total	Male	Female	White	Black	Hispanic
17–34 years	16.2%	14.6%	17.7%	17.8%	9.3%	9.9%
35–54 years	15.1	14.1	16.0	16.4	8.2	8.9
>54 years	5.3	5.0	5.5	5.7	2.5	2.9

FIGURE 13.7   Enrollment in adult education—1981 (percent).

Source: U.S. Bureau of the Census, *Statistical Abstract of the United States, 1982-1983*, 103d ed, 1982.

Third, the educational level of older adults is rising. In 1960, 67 percent of the adults past 65 had no high school training at all; they were functioning with an elementary school education obtained before World War I (Eklund, 1969). In 1970, about 29 percent of adults past 65 had *graduated* from high school; by 1981, the proportion was up to nearly 42 percent. Among adults between the ages of 25 and 29, more than 86 percent have graduated from high school; by 2021 this cohort will have passed the 65-year marker (U.S. Bureau of the Census, 1982). As a general rule of thumb, the more education people have, the more likely they are to be involved in some sort of continuing education course. For example, in 1965, 57 percent of adults in their thirties had taken at least one adult education course, compared with 30 percent of adults past the age of 60 (Johnstone and Rivera, 1965). Rising educational levels portend steady increases in the return to formal schooling among older adults.

Fourth, the rate of change appears to have accelerated in virtually every area of life. When change was perceived as gradual, a person noted little social change during his or her lifetime, and the inoculation approach to education worked fine. Today, however, much of our knowledge seems to become obsolete every year. If we continue to depend on what we learned in the first 25 years of our life, we will eventually be as out of touch as if a time machine had suddenly whisked us back to the nineteenth century. For this reason, lifelong education is becoming common in many professions. For example, most states will not renew a license to practice medicine unless a physician has taken a prescribed number of continuing education courses. Periodic returns to school are fast becoming a necessity in today's society.

Fifth, new occupational patterns are developing. Technological change is making some jobs obsolete, forcing workers to choose between additional training and dropping out of the labor force. Other workers are starting second careers during middle age, requiring a return to school. For example, a retired military officer (who may be as young as 42) may enroll in business school in order to begin a new career in management, or a middle-aged executive may enroll in a seminary in order to begin a new career as a priest or minister.

Finally, many middle-aged women are reentering the labor force as their child-rearing responsibilities slacken or end. Often they return to school for job training, to complete their college education, or to get an advanced degree. Taken together, these trends may foretell the development of a society that mixes work and study throughout life.

EDUCATION IN LATER ADULTHOOD

Although many older adults are returning to school spontaneously, the proportion that is enrolled at any time is probably no more than about half a million, roughly 2.5 percent of the elderly (National Center for Educational Statistics, 1978). Yet many gerontologists feel that continuing education could greatly improve the quality of old age. Older men and women can reap many benefits from continued education that go beyond keeping up with social change. Education provides knowledge, but it also is stimulating and acts as a socializing agent, affecting attitudes, beliefs, and behavior.

According to Harold Johnson (1982), education can provide the knowledge and skills that will help older adults to maintain and improve their health. It can help them qualify for part-time employment and show them how to manage their money more efficiently. It can give them factual information that can dispel some of the negative stereotypes of aging most have absorbed. It can broaden their view of life and help them to establish appropriate new goals. It can give them opportunities to explore new social relationships and discuss their feelings with others like themselves. It can give them a renewed interests and excitement about life and provide them with the wish to contribute to society—as well as the knowledge to implement the wish.

It has taken society some time to open the college doors to older adults, in part because of our attitudes toward old age. Not too many years ago, the elderly were simply rejected. Retirement was mandatory; aging was seen as synonymous with decline, decay, and death; and no provision was made for formal schooling experiences. Absorbed with the inoculation model of education, in which schooling is aimed at preparation for future, we regarded educating the elderly as a waste of time and money. And most people believed the elderly were incapable of much learning.

As older adults began to live past retirement—many of them in good health—gerontological research got underway, and our beliefs about education in old age changed. Today, according to Harvey Sterns and Raymond Sanders (1980), three attitudes about its value can be found. In a prevalent view, education is seen as a way to fill leisure time, entertaining older adults and keeping them busy. Although the general cultural attitude still embodies this view of education for the elderly, some gerontologists see its primary value as enabling older adults to participate fully in society. They believe that education improves the functioning of the elderly, teaching them how to compensate for minor physiological and cognitive problems and helping them to live a normal life, perhaps starting second careers or becoming involved in volunteer organizations. Other gerontologists believe that education in old age is important because it encourages personal growth and satisfaction. This view is closely related to Erikson's (1980) theory of the life span, in which old age is a period with its own developmental tasks. Education enables the elderly to achieve integrity and to enrich the meaning of their lives.

How well do older adults perform in school? In Chapter 8, we met middle-aged and elderly adults who had earned degrees or were enrolled in special college classes. The research reported in the chapters on cognition indicated that high levels of intelligence, learning, and thinking are possible far into old age—as long as secondary aging is held at bay. Few studies have been done in classroom settings, but those that are available indicate that most older college students do as well as—if not better than—younger students (Kasworm, 1980). Interindividual differences are, of course, wide, with some older students outperforming most of the young and others just barely getting by.

When older adults return to class, they do face problems, especially if they enroll in regular college classes. Stereotypes of the aging as incompetent, dependent, and nonproductive may weaken their self-confidence and threaten their school performance. If techniques can be used that convince older adults of their capability, most are likely to do much better. Several ways of producing a perception of their own effectiveness in older adults have been suggested (Rebok and Offermann, 1983). Arranging courses so that older adults experience early success, perhaps by using recognition instead of recall on initial tests, is important. Success helps to create a sense of effectiveness, for we judge our future performance partly on the basis of what we have done in the past.

A second way to bolster self-perception may be through observing other older students succeed (and thereby demolishing the stereotype of the incapable old person). Verbal encouragement from instructors, family members, and other students may also help although such social influence is probably less effective than the first two methods. Finally, perceptions of the self as ineffective or incapable in a stressful situation can lead to overarousal, which may be followed by poor performance. If older adults learn ways to reduce overarousal (for example, through relaxation techniques), this destructive condition may be minimized.

Many older adults manage quite well in classes. Among new developments in adult education is Elderhostel, a network of colleges and universities that provide inexpensive, short-term courses for retired individuals. Founded in New Hampshire in 1975, the program spread from 220 students in five colleges within the state to 30,000 students in all 50 states by 1981 (Romaniuk and Romaniuk, 1982). In one type of Elderhostel program, students live for three weeks in dormitories and eat in college dining halls while they take courses taught by members of the regular faculty. The courses are aimed at challenging the students and exposing them to new ideas. People must be at least 60 years old to enroll in this program (*AARP News Bulletin*, 1983d).

When Michael Brady studied 900 students in Elderhostel programs at New England colleges and universities, he discovered that the typical student was 68 years old, was retired, and had an advanced degree or a professional background and a comfortable income (*AARP News Bulletin*, 1983d). Two out of every three students were women. Only 10 percent of the students had never been to college before their enrollment in the Elderhostel program, and the greatest intellectual growth took place among these women and men. Students between the ages of 71 and 86 seemed to benefit more than the "younger" students in their sixties.

The success of Elderhostel can be seen in the repeat enrollments. Among students in 14 Virginia colleges and universities, 58 percent had participated in other Elderhostel programs (Romaniuk and Romaniuk, 1982). Most of these older students were motivated to return to college by the desire to learn something new and to become involved in new experiences.

Such programs, though well received and beneficial, tend to segregate the older students from the rest. Perhaps their favorable experiences in Elderhostel will motivate increasing numbers of elder students to enter the regular educational program. Because the cognitive differences that develop with age are generally unimportant, classes that integrate students of all ages might benefit young and old alike (Birren and Woodruff, 1973). The experience of older students could help make the often abstract material presented in the classroom meaningful to the young, and contact with the young might help the old understand the rapidly changing culture. In addition to its other benefits, such integrated education might help break down age segregation in society.

SUMMARY

Work serves many purposes: It is a measure of maturity and responsibility, a reflection of identity, a source of meaning, a definition of social position, a satisfying activity, an outlet for creativity, and a source of social stimulation. About 75 percent of workers have **jobs,** the rest have **careers.** Occupational choice is often accidental, guided by such seemingly irrelevant factors as sex, social class, proximity, apparently unrelated decisions, and luck. Vocational tests, which match a person's interests and abilities with occupations, can assist in the selection of an occupation.

An orderly career moves through a predictable pattern of stages: **crystallization, specification, implementation, stabilization,** and **consolidation.** During the implementation stage, a mentor is almost a requirement for a successful career. An increasing number of careers are not following the normative life sequence. Although this pattern does not seem to be a major determinant of job prestige or annual income during young adulthood, it may have a cumulative effect in later life. The interruption of a work career generally has negative effects, especially on women.

Men have been socialized into the role of worker, and the stages of their careers tend to parallel the stages of Levinson's theory of emotional development. Personality influences men's occupational success, but occupation—in the form of job complexity—also affects personality. Women's socialization for motherhood may be an important factor in their acceptance of low-paying, "helping" jobs. Single women tend to have orderly careers that follow the male pattern, but married women rarely follow the typical career plan. Women's lower earnings may be the result of career interruptions and sex-role socialization. Although the responsibility for child care can create stress, employed women tend to be satisfied and have high self-esteem, with career women being the most satisfied. Job satisfaction is generally related to a job's challenge (which is related to its complexity) and its financial rewards, but salary is an important issue only among blue-collar workers. Among those with careers, the opportunity to advance is more important.

Some adults may be pushed into retirement by job discrimination, which is the result of stereotypical beliefs about the capabilities of older workers. Since 1978, it has been illegal to retire, fire, or refuse to hire a person younger than 70 on the basis of age. Older workers appear to be as productive as younger workers, but they may not be retrained when their jobs become obsolete because their salaries tend to be high and their probable future work life too short to make retraining economical. The choice of 65 as the retirement age is arbitrary, and an increasing number of workers have been choosing early retirement. Workers who retire early are generally in poor health and have positive attitudes toward retirement. Among men who retire "on time" or later, education, occupation, and financial considerations are major factors in the decision; among women, only age is a predictor of retirement. Health and income are the major predictors of satisfaction in retirement. Workers who find it difficult to adjust to retirement may be mourning the loss of a useful social role.

Leisure has five major objectives: **relaxation, diversion, developmental pleasure, creative pleasure,** and **sensual pleasure.** In cross-sectional studies, only relaxation shows an increase with age, with slight downward trends in developmental and creative pleasures, and precipitous declines in diversion and sensual pleasures. Socioeconomic levels appear to affect the choice of leisure activity, perhaps because of differences in income and education. However, it has been suggested that the differences are due to compensation (seeking satisfactions that are lacking in an occupation) or spillover (generalizing the quality of an occupation to leisure).

Adults of all ages are enrolling in formal education courses. It has been suggested that this surge of enrollment is the result of a change in the age structure of society, the existence of empty classrooms as the baby-boom generation completed college, rising educational levels among older adults, accelerated rates of change in all areas of life, the development of new occupational patterns, and the reentry of middle-aged women into the work force.

KEY TERMS

career	**job**
consolidation stage	**leisure**
creative pleasure	**relaxation**
crystalization stage	**sensual pleasure**
developmental pleasure	**specification stage**
diversion	**stabilization stage**
implementation stage	

14

COMMUNITY INVOLVEMENT AND SOCIAL SUPPORTS

A t 78, Maggie Kuhn is proud of her age. "My wrinkles are a badge of distinction," she says. "I earned them. Don't flush away my life by denying them" (*The New York Times*, 1984a, D15). Kuhn is leader of the Gray Panthers, an activist group of 60,000 Americans generally considered to be the most militant of the organizations that lobby on behalf of older adults. She has led the Gray Panthers ever since she helped found it in 1970 after she was forced to retire because of her age. But Kuhn feels that the Gray Panthers are misperceived by the media and the rest of society. The group, she explained to a reporter from *The New York Times*, is an intergenerational organization that aims at change throughout society, and one of its goals is the abolition of age segregation. Complaining that society categorizes people by age and puts them into boxes, she says she want to "take people out of boxes and get them together."

Kuhn realizes that categorizing people on the basis of age can lead to the exclusion of the aging from society and that the community is vital to each of us. Most developmentalists would agree. Researchers, pointing out that social living has been the key to human evolutionary progress, maintain that personal survival depends on supporting one's social context (Lerner and Busch-Rossnagel, 1981). Although American society stresses individual achievement, that achievement takes place within the context of the social order. We are workers, taxpayers, and voters. Some of us are directly involved with the community institutions that create a social fabric: schools, churches, government, hospitals, charitable organizations, and other social agencies. As long as we—and our family members—are healthy, employed, and functioning efficiently, we tend to pay little attention to social service agencies. But need, in the form of unemployment, serious illness, or emotional disturbance, can quickly teach us the importance of community services we generally take for granted.

In this chapter we consider various forms of community involvement and social supports, beginning with adults' involvement in the church and their feelings about religion. Next we explore political activity in adulthood, paying attention to the effects of education and gender, and then examine age discrimination—against young and old. After looking at the economic aspects of the life course, we investigate housing, paying special attention to the housing of older adults. Finally, we consider various social supports and how they enable older adults to remain independent.

RELIGIOUS INVOLVEMENT

Although there have been many studies of religiosity in adulthood, our knowledge of developmental trends is sparse. Age differences have been found in various areas of religious involvement, such as church attendance, personal ad-

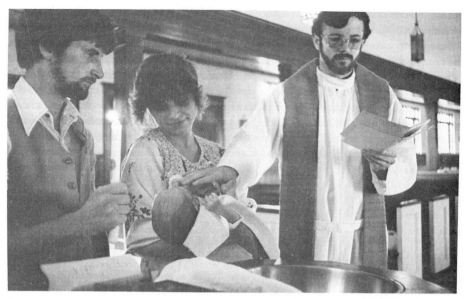

At every age, more Americans participate in the church than in all other voluntary community organizations combined.

herence to religious practices, and the importance of religious beliefs in an individual's life. Whether these trends are developmental or reflect cohort or historic time differences is not known. Most studies are cross-sectional, and the few longitudinal studies that exist, in addition to being contaminated by the effects of historical time, cover too narrow a slice of the life span to be very informative.

At every age, participation in the church is higher than in other voluntary community organizations combined (Moberg, 1968). Attendance, whether at services or other church functions, tends to be higher for children than for young adults, but in general, attendance tends to be fairly stable across adulthood (Hammond, 1969). However, various factors affect attendance, including denomination, sex, income, education, and length of residence in the community. For example, church attendance is more prevalent among adults with high income, high education, and longtime community residence.

In a national survey conducted about 20 years ago (Riley and Foner, 1968), a majority of Protestants and Catholics attended church regularly or often, no matter what their age. Regular attendance was lowest among young Protestant adults (ages 21 to 24) but then increased, remaining stable after the age of 30. Catholics showed steady, high attendance across adulthood, and few Jews younger than 50 were found to participate regularly. At every age, women were more likely to attend church than men, and in a sample of Detroit adults (Orbach, 1961), attendance by both sexes seemed stable until the age of 75.

A good many studies have indicated that health influences church attendance among older adults. Once adults pass the age of 65, a strong tendency appears for attendance to decline with age. Poor health, transportation problems, or finances are the major reasons the elderly give for nonattendance, with health apparently the most important (Moberg, 1968). When a group of healthy older Catholics in Chicago was studied, those who were older than 75 had the highest rates of church attendance and the reception of communion (Riley and Foner, 1968).

Among older adults, cohort differences that affect church attendance include a preponderance of women (which tends to inflate attendance figures) and a smaller proportion of Catholics (which tends to deflate them). The historical timing of a study also affects attendance figures. During the 1950s, for example, there was an upsurge in church attendance across all cohorts, followed by a general decline after 1965 (Wingrove and Alston, 1974).

Declines in church attendance among older adults are not necessarily paralleled by a waning of interest in religion. Among a national sample of Mennonites, for example, church attendance declined with age, but private religious activities tended to increase (Ainlay and Smith, 1984). Many older adults say they watch services on television or listen to religious broadcasts, which allows them to attend church without leaving their homes. Studies indicate that older adults are more likely than younger or middle-aged adults to read the Bible, pray in private, believe in immortality, believe the world needs religion more than it needs economic security, and say that religion has great personal meaning for them (Hammond, 1969). However, aspects of religious belief appear to change little across adulthood. National surveys show virtually no change in belief in God, hell, or the devil with age and show increases of only about 4 percent in belief in heaven or immortality. But when it comes to applying religious faith to national and world problems, younger adults are much less likely than middle-aged or older adults to believe that religion can provide a solution (Glenn, 1980).

Older adults generally say that religion means more to them as the years go by (Moberg, 1968). Cross-sectional studies indicate a steady increase in those who rate religion as "very important"—from 64 percent among adults younger than 24 to 84 percent among those past the age of 65 (Riley and Foner, 1968). Among a group of poor, black, inner-city elderly, one third said that religion had become more important to them over the years although their religious attitudes and practices had remained stable (Heisel and Faulkner, 1982). Results from longitudinal studies have been mixed. Gifted adults who were studied from childhood showed a greater interest in religion during their mid-fifties than they had either 10 or 20 years earlier (Marshall and Oden, 1962). When groups of older Anglo and Mexican-Americans in Texas were studied for four years, ratings of their own religious feelings showed a small but significant increase in Mexican women and men and in Anglo women, but not in Anglo men (Markides, 1983). Church attendance declined slightly in both groups. On another occasion, an elderly Mexican-American woman told Robert Coles of her faith:

After all, even if there has been trouble, there has been God's grace: He has helped us; He has healed us; He has enabled us to try to be worthwhile and decent people . . . God has given each of us a soul, and it is the soul that really counts.

. . . The soul finally tires of the body; it is a prison and the soul wants to leave. Words struggle to leave us, but, once spoken, they are dead. The soul leaves and lives forever. I believe it does. I hope it does [Coles, 1973, pp. 17–18].

An increase in the personal meaning of religion among the elderly is in accord with Erik Erikson's (1982) view of development. The hope that is the basic strength of infancy ripens to faith in old age, and during Erikson's final stage of development, integrity can overcome despair only if a person finds meaning in life. Erikson is careful to point out that faith and meaning need not be embodied in a traditional religion, but for most adults meaning is found within the traditional framework. This relationship appeared among a group of elderly, white, rural residents of upstate New York. In this study (Telis-Nayak, 1982), which combined religious attitudes, beliefs, and practices into a single measure of religiosity, religiosity bore no relationship to health, marital status, or happiness. Its strongest correlation was with an individual's sense of meaning and purpose in life.

Although religious faith or a belief in an after life does not appear to be closely related to good adjustment in older adults, there does seem to be a connection among adjustment, life satisfaction, and religious activities. In several studies, a relationship has appeared between good personal adjustment and religious activities (Moberg, 1968). However, whether engaging in religious activities promotes adjustment or whether the well-adjusted elderly tend to engage in religious activities is not clear. In the longitudinal study of Anglos and Mexican-Americans, self-rated religious attitudes and private prayer predicted life satisfaction among Anglos but not among Mexicans at the beginning of the study whereas church attendance was a predictor of life satisfaction for both groups at both periods. Noting a similar connection between religious activities and life satisfaction in the Duke Longitudinal Study (Blazer and Palmore, 1976), the researcher suggests that church attendance has some positive effect on satisfaction, but that much of the relationship can be traced to the fact that attendance also reflects an older person's ability to get to church and hence may be related to health or income. Age appears to affect community religious involvement more than it affects involvement in the area of politics.

POLITICAL INVOLVEMENT

Politics is a sphere of life where personal involvement can have an impact on the lives of others. When a person works actively for a candidate, a political party, or an issue, his or her influence can go far beyond the weight of a single vote. If age affects political attitudes and behavior in predictable ways, changes in the proportion of various age groups could alter the political course of the country. One way to understand the connection between age and political involvement is to consider its relationship to the assumption of various social roles (such as student, worker, spouse, parent, retiree). In this approach, change is stimulated by the individual's movement through the life cycle. Another way is to interpret age differences as cohort differences, looking at the exposure of various cohorts to social trends and historical events (Foner, 1972). Both approaches have been used to explain the differences that appear with age in political attitudes and behavior.

AGE AND POLITICAL ATTITUDES

According to the common wisdom, we become more conservative with age. As young people, we are likely to be liberal, trying to bring society into line with our humanitarian ideals. But as we pass through adulthood, we supposedly begin to resist change, becoming conservative, either because our experience and wisdom have led to more accurate perceptions of human nature (say conservatives) or because we have been successful in life and now have an economic investment in the status quo (say liberals). Looking at attitudes in connection with social roles, we could also say that the young adult's devotion to humanitarian ideals is weakened by the assumption of family responsibilities. Concern for the poor and oppressed is overshadowed by worry about the immediate family (Glenn, 1980). For the advantaged adult, the needs of others give way to the demands of mortgage payments, orthodontists' bills, and tuition. In support of the general belief in a trend toward conservatism with age, we can point to older adults' tendency to be against school busing, legalization of marijuana, women's rights, abortion, and protest politics; to oppose federal aid to education or federal activity in civil rights; to be hawks in matters of foreign policy; or to be members of the Republican party (Cutler, 1983).

A careful analysis of this age trend is likely to shake our confidence in the common wisdom. Part of the conservative trend among older people is apparently the result of lower levels of education. Well-educated people tend to be more liberal than people with less education. For example, in 1972, 18 percent of those younger than 30 believed that premarital intercourse was always wrong compared with 41 percent of these between the ages of 30 and 49, and 52 percent of those 50 and older. When these findings are corrected for education, the gap between young and old shrinks from 34 to 30 points. Now 20 percent of the youngest group are unalterably opposed to premarital intercourse, compared with 39 percent of those between the ages of 30 and 49, and 50 percent of those 50 and older (Glenn, 1980).

Accounting for education does not eliminate the gap, but the rest of the difference may be due to the circumstances in which each cohort grew up. Members of a cohort are exposed at the same time and the same age to common patterns of schooling, family life, economic cycles, wars, and political events, so that the relative conservatism or liberalism of any cohort may be largely a reflection of shared experiences and perceptions (Hudson and Binstock, 1976). Some researchers believe that the social climate at the time people become voters has a powerful influence on political outlook. Those who vote for the first time when the country is in the midst of a conservative swing are likely always to be more conservative in their outlook than those who vote for the first time when the country is swinging to the liberal position.

Most adults do not become more conservative with age; instead shifts in their political views reflect general trends in society.

Although people tend to retain the political orientations they develop early in life, their outlooks are not set in concrete. They respond to general trends in society (Foner, 1972). Whether society moves in a conservative or liberal direction, each cohort is affected by the trend and, as it ages, shifts in the same direction. It seems that older adults have not become *more* conservative; instead, as society became less conservative, new generations of young people developed more liberal attitudes and perhaps greater openness to change. For example, over a 20-year period, national surveys indicated an increasing tolerance for nonconformity at all ages, but smaller changes in older cohorts. The changes remained even when researchers controlled for education, race, and sex (Cutler and Kaufman, 1975). The conservative trend that reasserted itself in the early 1980s is likely to affect all cohorts, and when today's middle-aged adults retire, they may become a generation of older Americans who are more liberal than some of the younger cohorts.

Although cohorts respond to historical influence, the response is not necessarily equal. The position of a cohort in the life cycle may interact with social influences to produce an age-period effect. When an issue is connected with the perceived self-interest of a cohort, its members may be more or less susceptible to change, depending on the way the issue affects them. For example, older adults are generally more favorably disposed to government-supported medical care (a liberal position) than are younger adults. And we might expect adults in their late twenties and early thirties to be more favorably disposed to government-supported day care than are older adults.

When we examine the observation that Republicans outnumber Democrats among older adults, we find no general switch to the Republican party with age. Between 1946 and 1958, a series of national polls consistently indicated a steady increase with age in the proportion of adults identifying themselves as Republicans. However, a reanalysis of the data showed that cohort differences were responsible for much of the effect (Cutler, 1983).

Nor did the Republicanism of any cohort remain stable. When individual cohorts were followed across the 12-year period, each showed fluctuations in its proportion of Republicans, apparently swayed by historical events. In 1946, for example, 58 percent of the 49- to 52-year-olds were Republicans; in 1950, 60 percent were Republicans; in 1954, 58 percent; and in 1958, when they were in their early sixties, 55 percent said they were Republicans. The "maturational" trend toward Republicanism disappeared, and the preponderance of Republicans in older cohorts was seen as the result of socialization in the years before the Great Depression of the 1930s (Glenn, 1980).

Social climate does not affect all members of a cohort in the same way. There are a good many liberals among older adults although they are a minority. Nor do cohort effects act in isolation. Among the factors that shape political orientation are personality characteristics. A relationship between personality and politics appeared in the California Intergenerational Study, which followed individuals who were socialized during the Great Depression (see Chapter 10). Specific personality characteristics were related to the development of a liberal or conservative political philosophy, and major differences between future liberals and conservatives were apparent during adolescence and remained stable into middle age. Among this group of adults, three quarters could be classified as either liberal or conservative. Their political attitudes clearly differed from the rest of the group, who were "middle-of-the-road"—and their personalities were also distinctive.

By analyzing Q-sort personality ratings made in early and late adolescence, young adulthood, and middle age, Paul Mussen and Norma Haan (1981) discovered that, since early adolescence, middle-aged liberals had been independent, unconventional, rebellious, objective, and interested in philosophical matters. They had accepted their own motivations and desires and taken responsibility for their own actions. In contrast, from early adolescence, middle-aged conservatives had lacked independence and had tended to be submissive, in need of reassurance, and moralistic. They had spent little time in introspection and were uncomfortable with uncertainty. Mussen and Haan concluded that the child-rearing practices of their parents may have encouraged these adults to develop broad general qualities that predisposed them toward a particular political orientation. This predisposition operated within the context of each individual's social and economic fortunes and wider social, historical, and economic events, so that personality—though influential—can account for only part of the individual differences in political behavior. The rest can be traced to the interaction of life cycle, cohort differences, and social climate.

AGE AND POLITICAL ACTIVITY

As people grow older, they appear to become more interested in political activity. The highest levels of political interest are found in adults past the age of 60, and the difference is apparent at all educational levels (Hudson and Binstock, 1976).

Political activity, such as working actively in community organizations, helping in political campaigns, and contributing money, appears to peak during the fifties and then fall off. But the drop in political activity melts away when corrections are made for education, sex, residency, and socioeconomic level. Older adults who become politically active tend to maintain their activity well into their sixties and beyond (Verba and Nie, 1972).

Older adults who have assumed positions of political leadership do not retire from the scene when they reach the age of 65. Political leaders tend to be in their fifties or older, and 50- to 70-year-olds fill many of the decision-making positions in government. The majority of legislators, judges, diplomats, governors, local public officials, and community decision makers are drawn from adults (mostly male) in this age group. In most cases, the more important the office, the older the officeholder. The membership of voluntary political associations is also skewed toward people older than 55 (Riley and Foner, 1968).

Older adults not only dominate command positions in society, but they also vote out of proportion to their numbers as well. Election figures indicate that young adults are the least likely of any group to vote and that voting is heaviest between the ages of 45 and 70. In the congressional elections of 1982, 49 percent of adults voted, but late middle-aged and older voters were influential in determining the results. Only 25 percent of the 18- to 24-year-olds voted and 45 percent of the 25- to 44-year-olds. Among older adults, 64 percent of the 55- to 64-year-olds and 65 percent of the 65- to 74-year-olds cast ballots (Pear, 1983).

When we look more closely at voter turnout, however, it becomes clear that age alone does not determine whether an individual will vote. Only in interaction with other personal characteristics, such as education, sex, income, marital status, occupation, and mobility does age determine who votes in any election (see Fig. 14.1). A careful analysis of the 1972 and 1976 presidential elections by Raymond Wolfinger and Steven Rosenstone (1980) indicated that education is the most powerful influence on voter participation. At every level of income, an increase in education is matched by an increase in the probability of voting. Wolfinger and Rosenstone believe that education affects voter participation in three ways. It gives people the skills that enable them to process political information and make political decisions. It generally increases the sense of citizen duty, giving people more gratification from voting. And it provides experience with such bureaucratic relationships as learning requirements for participation, filling out forms, waiting in line, and meeting deadlines so that educated people find it easier to register and then vote. This last factor may be more important than it seems at first glance. For example, it has been speculated that farmers' experience with endless Department of Agriculture forms may be one of the factors that puts them among the occupational groups with the highest voter participation.

Sex was once a potent predictor of voting, and it still is powerful among older adults. Even when education is held constant, older men are more likely to vote than older women. Employment among younger women does not explain the female voting pattern because employed women are no more likely to vote than women who do not work outside the home. The major factor that depresses voter turnout among older women appears to be socialization practices. Although we take women's right to vote for granted, it was not until 1920 that the Nineteenth

	Adult Population (percent)	Voters (percent)
Education		
0 to 11 Years	36.4%	29.0%
12 Years	37.6	38.7
> 12 Years	26.0	32.3
Family Income		
< $10,000	55.2	48.0
$10,000 to $14,999	25.6	28.1
$15,000 to $24,999	14.5	17.6
> $24,999	4.8	6.2
Age		
18 to 24	17.9	14.2
25 to 31	14.6	13.7
32 to 36	8.2	8.3
37 to 69	49.7	54.8
70 to 78	6.5	6.6
> 78	3.1	2.4
Women	53.2	52.7
Unmarried or separated	30.2	26.4
Students, 18 to 24	2.7	2.8
Unemployed	2.7	2.2
Blacks	9.8	8.2
Puerto Ricans[a]	0.6	0.3
Chicanos[a]	1.9	1.3
Length of residence[a]		
< 3 years	33.4	20.8
3 to 5 years	16.1	16.3
6 to 9 years	13.5	15.8
10 or more years	37.1	46.6

FIGURE 14.1 Voters compared with adult population (1972 election).

[a]From 1976 election data.

A comparison of each group's representation in the adult population with its participation in voting shows how education, income, age, gender, marital status, unemployment, ethnicity, and mobility affect the tendency to vote.

Source: R. E. Wolfinger and S. J. Rosenstone, 1980, pp. 106–107.

Amendment to the Constitution was ratified and women could vote in every state. Some of today's older women grew up believing that they were not entitled to vote at all—and all of them grew up at a time when society agreed that men should have a predominant influence in political affairs.

If cohort differences are responsible for much of the gender disparity in voting among older Americans, we would expect the gender gap to begin narrowing. It appears to be doing just that. Demographers at the Bureau of the Census have announced that the gap is closing and predict that women will outvote men in 1984 (Pear, 1983). In 1982, a decade after the research reported in Figure 14.1, voter participation among women younger than 45 was higher than among men of the same age, and the difference between voter turnout in older men and women had diminished.

Another factor that depresses voter participation among older women is marital status. At every age and at every educational level, married people are more likely to vote than those who are single, separated, divorced, or widowed (Wolfinger and Rosenstone, 1980). Since most older men are married and the majority of older women are single, widowed, or divorced, the gender gap at the polls is widened.

The effect of marriage on voter participation increases steadily with age. Among 18- to 24-year-olds, a married person is only 3 percent more likely to vote than a single person. In this group, students vote at a much higher rate than nonstudents. Assumption of the spouse role seems to have only a slight effect on voter participation among the young, and there is even a slight dip in voting among young adults after they leave college. It has been suggested that it is not the role of spouse, but the role of parent that increases voter participation (Adelson and Hall, 1980). Voter turnout among high school graduates jumps from 44 percent among 18- to 24-year-olds to 63 percent among 32- to 36-year-olds, and it may be that by the time their children start school, parents become concerned about the next generation and develop a real sense of commitment to the political process.

Voter participation begins to decline as adults pass through their seventies, with the rate dropping faster and earlier for women than for men. This decline is generally attributed to physical infirmities (Milbrath and Goel, 1977), but when education, marital status, and sex are held constant, aging does not produce a decline in turnout. Instead, it produces an increase—even in the oldest adults (Wolfinger and Rosenstone, 1980). The effect of age shrinks as education increases, so that, over the life span, occupational and general life experience appear to be a partial substitute for schooling.

THE POLITICS OF AGING

The combination of higher levels of education, longer life expectancy, and changes in the socialization of women might be expected to increase the political influence of a group that already has a higher rate of political participation than younger adults. These demographic changes immediately raise the question of whether older people will be politically active as citizens or as "old people," combining their political clout to form a pressure group that sees all issues in terms of the effect on the elderly.

The young-old among today's elderly are relatively healthy and have plenty of free time. As Bernice Neugarten (1974) has pointed out, should they channel their interests and energies into "age politics," they could have an enormous influence on society. In order to become active in a pressure group, a person must first identify with the group, and, as we have seen, many older adults do not think of themselves as old. In fact, 55 percent of those past the age of 60 say they are middle-aged. However, Neal Cutler (1983) believes that people are becoming more conscious of their age and found an increase between 1972 and 1976 in the proportion of people aged 50 to 74 that identified themselves as old. He also has found that subjective age makes a difference in political attitudes, with the subjectively old being more pessimistic about their financial future, more liberal on some traditional issues (such as government controls on inflation or the provision of medical care by the federal government), and more conservative on some contemporary issues (such as abortion under certain conditions or government action against environmental pollution).

Age-consciousness need not lead to a politics of age, but the possibility is present. Our new awareness of racial, ethnic, and sexual status was followed by the formation of groups for the purpose of overcoming discriminatory laws and practices. However, some gerontologists (Hudson and Binstock, 1976) have taken the position that any marked increase in the political power of old adults is unlikely. Others (Neugarten and Hall, 1980) believe that a politics of age has not yet developed in the United States and that except for specific issues that affect them directly, such as property-tax relief or Social Security, older people are more likely to vote by income level than by age. Yet others (Campbell, 1971) have noted that the political differences among older adults are at least as large as the political differences among age groups.

A number of organizations have begun to lobby on behalf of old people, and some of them have large memberships. But as late as the early 1970s, their influence was sporadic at best. According to Henry Pratt (1982), during the 1960s groups such as the National Council of Senior Citizens, the Gray Panthers, and the American Association of Retired Persons were so concerned with recruiting members and establishing their own turf that they often worked at cross-purposes. Toward the end of the 1970s, these groups began to work together to pass such bills as the Age Discrimination in Employment Act, which outlawed mandatory retirement at age 65, and 26 organizations banded together to form the Leadership Council of Aging Organizations, a group that has been credited with blocking proposals to scale back Social Security benefits. According to Pratt, these organizations have become stable, developed a sense of purpose, acquired access to the political system, and gained a sense of legitimacy in the eyes of government policymakers.

A merger of the varied aging organizations is unlikely, however, because their goals, membership, and political style are so very different (Pratt, 1982). For example, the National Council of Senior Citizens tends to present the concerns of old people as an age group whereas the Gray Panthers regard themselves as "transgenerational," working for the disadvantaged, no matter what their age. The Gray Panthers support legislation to help those in need and oppose drawing up programs in terms of age. This position has been supported by some gerontologists (Neugarten and Hall, 1980) on the grounds that adequate programs cannot be funded if benefits automatically flow to the young-old who do not need them. Although age is likely to become more important in politics, the future influence of these organizations depends on the quality of the leadership (Pratt, 1982). Earlier groups sprang up, flourished, and died when their leaders or their issues faded. By 2020 the Gray Panthers could be a powerful political force or an interesting relic of the twentieth century.

AGE AND LEGAL ISSUES

Political activity reflects a person's attempt to affect the role of government, and law is the means used by government to force conformity with the social order (Weber, 1947). For thousands of years, age, law, and status have been intertwined, with the establishment of adulthood being the earliest legal use of age (Cain, 1976). Societies have found age the most efficient way to determine the assumption of responsibility, with different ages used for various privileges and obligations. For example, a 12-year-old may not drive a car, a 17-year-old may drive a car but not vote, and a 25-year-old may vote but not become president of the United States. Sometimes privileges are withheld until the brink of old age. In ancient Athens, justice was administered by a group of men who had reached the age of 60.

The sword of chronological age cuts two ways; it can be used to grant status and privileges or to withdraw them. Beginning in the nineteenth century, age began to be used to withdraw adult status from the elderly, setting them up as a group that were unable to provide for their own basic needs or denying them the right to employment (Cain, 1976). When age is used to withhold or withdraw privilege, it can be unfair to young or to old.

In the United States, a major discriminatory use of age against the young is in the field of housing, and few states or cities prohibit discrimination by landlords against families with children. Conditions vary from state to state. Although California courts have forbidden the barring of children from rental units and condominiums, in Florida the courts have supported the "no children allowed" rule, and Florida homeowners who buy houses in restricted developments as childless couples are served with eviction notices when they have children. According to the Department of Housing and Urban Development, 25 percent of all rental units in the United States ban children, and another 50 percent restrict the number and age of children that are allowed on the premises (Press, 1984). Such barriers penalize adults who assume the parental role.

Researchers (Margulis and Benson, 1982) who studied housing in the Cleveland area found that 37 percent of rental units prohibited children entirely and that nearly all buildings with a majority of tenants past the age of 40 had some sort of restriction, limiting the number of children per family, the proportions of units rented to families with children, the areas of the buildings where children could live, the ages of children that were acceptable, or the length of time a child could stay as a guest. Such regulations seriously restrict housing opportunities for families with children.

Although objections to children have generally been seen as coming from retirees, the severest restrictions were found in buildings occupied by adults between the ages of 41 and 59. Middle-aged and older tenants alike agreed that children caused high maintenance costs and used abusive language, that parents were abusive when the tenants complained about their children, and that teenagers were generally threatening. In the elderly, such feelings ran deepest among those who lived in older buildings in the central city, among blacks, and among those on welfare.

Their reactions may have been exacerbated by the spread of restrictions on children in newer buildings. With new rental housing unavailable, more families with children are pushed into older buildings within the central city, increasing the concentration of children in these buildings and making older renters increasingly apprehensive about their safety and welfare. In the Cleveland area, it was primarily the old who felt that parents could not control their teenagers and that children vandalized property.

The old discriminate against the young in housing, but the rest of society discriminates against older adults, and that discrimination is most common in employment. Laws protect federal employees of any age and other adults younger than 70 from mandatory retirement, but discrimination in hiring is widespread. Employers tell older job seekers that they are "overqualified," "unskilled," less in need of a job than a younger applicant, less reliable, or less flexible (Butler and Lewis, 1982). As we saw in Chapter 13, older workers who lose their jobs often become so discouraged that they opt for early retirement.

Until laws forbidding age discrimination by employers were passed, middle-aged workers who were not protected by seniority laws often found themselves fired for no reason other than their age. Not long ago, airline flight attendants were not allowed to fly when they approached middle age, and some department stores periodically fired middle-aged clerks and department heads in order to maintain a youthful image for the young customers they hoped to attract. Employees past 70 can still be fired without "cause." For example, a distinguished professor of philosophy was offered a position by Fordham University. After he accepted, the university discovered he was 70 years old, and withdrew the offer. The professor sued on the grounds that the university had found him highly qualified but then revoked their offer, applying an arbitrary age standard. The judge ruled against the professor on the grounds that age bore some "reasonable statistical relationship to diminished capacity" and that age ceilings on employment, though unjust, were constitutional (Cain, 1976).

In another case, the elderly fared better. A Florida-based lending agency with branches in 23 states was fined $90,000 and ordered to change its practices after the Federal Trade Commission found it had discriminated against older adults who applied for loans (*AARP News Bulletin*, 1983b). Blazer Financial Services had refused loans to elderly applicants who met other financial standards, it had refused to consider pensions or public assistance as income in deciding whether to extend credit, and it had discriminated against people receiving pensions or public assistance on the grounds that they were not employed full time. Charges were brought against the company under the Equal Opportunity Credit Act.

Other legal instances of possible discrimination can be found. For example, some states require additional vision or driving tests after a certain age in order to renew a license. Is it discriminatory to require such tests from a 65-year-old but not from a 64-year-old? If, as we have seen in earlier chapters, age is a poor predictor of physical, intellectual, or social performance in later life, is it ever fair to use chronological age as an arbitrary barrier (Neugarten, 1979a)? The discrimination can work in the opposite direction. Is it discriminatory to require a 64-year-old to pay full fare on a bus or to get into a movie, but not a 65-year-old? (The 64-year-old may be retired and living on Social Security, and the 65-year-old may have an income of $100,000 a year.)

Part of the problem is that society has incompatible definitions of old age and the way that older people fit into society. According to Douglas Nelson (1982), setting the age of 65 as the "time to retire," combining disability payments in the same program as age-related Social Security payments, and establishing housing projects for the elderly, senior citizen centers, and nutrition programs for older Americans tend to segregate older Americans from the rest of society and to equate old age with disability. Abolishing mandatory retirement, eliminating job discrimination, setting up job-development programs for older workers, and such programs as Foster Grandparents challenge the assumption that the old are disabled and combat age segregation. Nelson sees two dangers from the current situation. On the one hand, dismantling the stereotype of the old as dependent and incapacitated may be used as an excuse to eliminate or sharply restrict the in-

Programs like Foster Grandparents challenge the assumption that elderly adults are disabled. Care by this foster grandmother put an ailing child on the road back to health.

come, health, and social support programs that are absolutely necessary to many of the elderly. On the other hand, an array of programs that automatically go into effect at age 65 may maintain stereotypes of aging, reinforce the segregation of the old, and encourage ageism.

Two solutions have been offered for this dilemma. The first, discussed earlier, is to make programs based on need, not age, and to treat all citizens equally. As Bernice Neugarten has said, "When we treat all old people as if they were old-old, we reinforce the misperception of "the old" as a problem group" (Neugarten and Hall, 1980, p. 80). She urges programs for the poor, the disabled, and the isolated, maintaining that if we meet their needs, we will also have met the needs of the old-old. The second solution, proposed by Nelson (1982) is to redefine old age. He sees no reason to differentiate between the 45- to 60-year-old group and the 60- to 75-year-old group, who tend to belong to the young-old. Noting that fraility and vulnerability are more likely to develop between the ages of 75 and 80 than earlier, he suggests that the marker of old age be moved to 75. Both suggestions are controversial.

ECONOMIC DISTRIBUTION

Few young adults think seriously or often about their financial situation in old age. Aware of Social Security and probably working for a company with a pension plan, they assume that retirement will be followed by an adequate income. For many of them, however, the income will be too small to support their customary standard of living, and its inadequacy may be partly the result of decisions made earlier in life.

Throughout life people make important choices—about schooling, marriage, children, occupation, health practices. Each of these choices is made within the constraints of money, time, energy, and available information and is influenced by the "price" of the alternatives. Most of us weigh present costs and benefits against costs and benefits in the future. For example, during young adulthood we may choose to invest our resources (time and money) in education in order to reap the benefits of enhanced earnings during later life. In this instance, we are shouldering current costs for the sake of future benefits, investing our resources in human capital. We may choose to have another child or to limit family size, using the extra money for luxuries, to save for our retirement years, or to "buy" more leisure, reducing our working time (Engerman, 1978). According to economist Victor Fuchs (1983), our willingness to incur costs in money, time, or energy for the sake of some future benefit will determine many of our decisions about health, schooling, fertility, and occupation. The postponement of benefits often has a powerful effect on how long we will live and on the quality of our lives.

Despite a widespread lack of planning, the financial position of older Americans as a group has improved dramatically in the past few decades (Schulz, 1980). Social Security benefits almost doubled during the 1970s; private pension programs—and their benefits—expanded; public health programs were instituted; property tax relief laws were passed in all states; food stamp programs were established to fill the needs of low-income people of all ages; and a supplemental program ensured that older Americans would receive a minimum payment even if they had not had adequate Social Security coverage. In 1959, 35.2 percent of adults past the age of 65 had incomes below the poverty level; in 1982, the proportion had dropped to 14.6 percent. And when assistance of various kinds— food, housing, and medical care—was included, the proportion dropped again: to 3.5 percent in 1982 (Pear, 1984). The group of needy elderly could decline even further. Many poor older Americans are immigrants without education who worked at unskilled jobs, a very different group from the elderly in the year 2000 (Neugarten and Hall, 1980).

Today the percentage of older adults who are living below the poverty level is not substantially different from the percentage in other groups. In fact, young children form the largest group among the poor, with 23.8 percent of those younger than 6 living below the poverty level (Pear, 1984). For the first time, the majority of older Americans can look forward to a comfortable life after retirement. However, the attainment of health, wealth, and time to enjoy them still eludes a sizable minority of retired Americans. Some of them are newly poor, and some have been poor all their lives. Whether an older person belongs to the comfortable majority or the afflicted minority depends on the interaction of public policies, a lifetime of individual decisions—and luck (Walther, 1983).

INCOME PATTERNS ACROSS ADULTHOOD

In an industrialized society like the United States, the major source of income is wages, and the total amount received over the life course depends on productivity and the length of time worked (Kreps, 1976). In most cases, the more productive a worker, the shorter the time worked, whether in a shortened work year (fewer weekly hours, longer vacations) or in a shortened work life (lengthy education, early retirement). It is the high productivity of the United States that has allowed increases in the standard of living, the longer period of education, and the support of workers in retirement.

As a general rule, when productivity increases, whether from technological advance or the worker's increased skill and experience, wages increase. For most workers, whatever their occupation, earning power rises steadily, peaking near the end of their work life (Fig. 14.2). Education and occupation determine just when a worker reaches that peak, and the higher the level of education or skill required in a job, the older a worker will be before attaining maximum income. The effect of early investment in schooling is especially large after the age of 45, when inequalities in health, work, and income become increasingly apparent. Almost 30 percent of this inequality is due to the fact that the worker without advanced schooling collected part of his or her lifetime earnings when the college graduate had no income at all but was investing in human capital in the hope of later return (Fuchs, 1983). It takes about 7 years after entry into the labor market for the college graduate to reach the point at which those missed earnings are returned in the form of higher income.

	Women	Men
15 to 19 years	$ 6,779	$ 7,753
20 to 24 years	9,407	12,109
25 to 34 years	12,190	17,724
35 to 44 years	12,239	21,777
45 to 54 years	12,116	22,323
55 to 64 years	11,931	21,053
>64 years	12,365	17,292

FIGURE 14.2   Income across adulthood (1980).

Although income rises steadily throughout young and middle adulthood, women's income always lags behind that of men.

Source: U.S. Bureau of the Census, *Statistical Abstract of the United States, 1982–83*, 103d. ed., 1982.

Despite increased real earnings over the past few decades, about one person in five holds at least two jobs (U.S. Bureau of the Census, 1982). Whether a person is male or female, black or white, the most common reason for a second job is to meet regular expenses. However, some people take a second job simply because they enjoy the work. Among other reasons people give for doubling their work load are paying off debts, saving for the future, and buying something special (Fig. 14.3).

Working careers are affected by economic cycles, and inflation may have pushed some of these hardworking women and men into their second job. In mid-1980, when inflation was near its peak, 20,000 *Psychology Today* readers responded to a survey on money (Rubenstein, 1981). Inflation, combined with high interest rates, had affected 60 percent of the group, and those younger than 30 seemed the hardest hit. They were the most dissatisfied with their present financial situation and worried most about money. They also were more likely to have made personal sacrifices in response to rising prices. For example, 35 percent of the youngest group had postponed buying a home, compared with 28 percent of

	White		Black	
	Men	Women	Men	Women
Meet regular expenses	31.1%	32.6%	37.0%	53.3%
Pay off debts	6.7	7.2	10.9	6.7
Save for future	11.8	7.3	18.0	8.1
Get experience	8.5	6.7	6.2	1.5
Help friend or relative	3.2	6.6	1.4	1.5
Buy something special	7.6	10.9	1.4	9.6
Enjoy the work	18.8	16.1	10.9	12.6
Changed job	.4	1.5	—	3.0

FIGURE 14.3   Main reason for holding more than one job—1980 (percent).

Source: U.S. Bureau of the Census, *Statistical Abstract of the United States, 1982–83*, 103d. ed., 1982.

those in their thirties and 19 percent of those in their forties. Inflation had also caused many of them to delay a return to school, travel, savings, a job change, the birth of children, or marriage.

The effect of inflation on a person's economic position is an example of the influence of historical events. Cohort differences can have a different sort of effect. Cross-sectional studies generally indicate a drop in income after the age of 55, making the last decade in the workplace a time of declining income. But when Juanita Kreps (1976) analyzed the pattern of earnings over the life course by individual cohorts, she discovered no decline in income after the age of 55. Instead, income continued to rise until retirement, with increases during the last decade resulting from general economic growth.

THE ECONOMICS OF RETIREMENT

Once people retire, their income drops considerably. Of course, many expenses probably decrease as well. A retired couple no longer has to shoulder child-rearing expenses or the costs involved in working (commuting, meals away from home, extra clothing), and some couples find their housing costs reduced as the mortgages on their homes are paid off. Other expenses may also be smaller. For example, in 1982 the Department of Agriculture estimated that the typical couple between the ages of 20 and 54 spent approximately $55.30 each week for food whereas an older couple spent about $48.90. At the same time, a couple with two adolescent children spent $100 each week for food (U.S. Bureau of the Census, 1982).

Does the shrinkage in expenditure equal the decline in income? For a good many people it does not. After age 65, per capita income is 26 percent less than it is between the ages of 55 and 64, dropping from $9874 to $7275. However, this figure makes no allowance for sex or race and does not distinguish between the employed elderly and the retired elderly. As the median income for fully employed workers past 65 is $12,365 for women and $17,292 for men, the income of the typical retired person is likely to be considerably less. In fact, 39 percent of the men past 65 and 69 percent of the women had incomes of less than $6000 per year, and nearly 21 percent of all householders past 65 had incomes of less than $5000 per year (U.S. Bureau of the Census, 1982). (See Fig. 14.4)

Older women, especially if they are alone, black, or Hispanic, are disadvantaged in comparison with men. They amass no Social Security credits for work as homemakers, and the rising incidence of divorce puts these women's income in jeopardy. Those who remained married for 10 years are entitled to spouse's benefits when they retire (a sum equal to one half of their husband's benefits), but present laws do not consider the possibility of multiple marriages. As we saw in Chapter 13, women who work outside the home often move in and out of the labor market, a practice that reduces their own eventual Social Security benefits and often keeps them from qualifying for a private pension. (On retirement, a woman is entitled to her own earned Social Security benefits or her benefits as a

	Percent Below Poverty Level
Persons 60 or older	14.1%
Persons 65 or older	17.7
White	13.6
Black	38.1
Hispanic	30.8
In families	
Male householder	8.2
Female householder	14.0
Unrelated individuals	30.8
Males	24.4
Females	32.3

FIGURE 14.4   Poverty among the elderly (1980).

As a group, the elderly are no more likely to live in poverty than the rest of the country. Older adults who are most likely to be poor are the black, the Hispanic, and individuals who live alone.

Source: U.S. Bureau of the Census, *Statistical Abstract of the United States, 1982–83*, 103d. ed., 1982.

spouse—whichever is higher.) Because women have traditionally been paid less than men, even those who have spent their entire lives working are unlikely to receive as large a pension as men. As women become more committed to their occupations, the problem will lessen in future cohorts, but unless Social Security regulations and private pension practices are changed to account for the realities of American life, the disparity is likely to remain.

Among older Americans, Social Security benefits are the major source of income, followed by interest and dividends, other pensions, and public assistance (Fuchs, 1983). Adults whose income is below a certain minimum level are entitled to Supplemental Security Income (SSI). Money goes somewhat farther among older adults because of tax breaks, assets, and **in-kind income** (goods and services that require no expenditure). For example, under regulations that took effect in 1984, Social Security benefits are not taxed among people whose income (including Social Security) is less than $25,000. Individuals who make more than $25,000 pay taxes on one half of their Social Security benefits. All older individuals, no matter what their income, receive a double personal tax exemption on income. Property taxes are reduced, but only when taxes exceed a certain portion of annual income, generally from 3 to 7 percent, depending on the state. In addition, elderly home owners escape taxes on the first $125,000 in capital gains should they decide to sell their homes and move into a smaller house or apartment.

Most older adults own their own home. Among couples, 80 percent own their homes and nearly 65 percent of couples have no mortgages. About 40 percent of the unmarried elderly own their homes (Schulz, 1980). Such assets are not easily converted into income, but if property taxes and maintenance are less than rent, homeownership increases income. It is also possible to obtain a reverse annuity mortgage, in which the homeowner sells equity to a lending agency in return for a fixed monthly payment. When the house is sold, the lending agency receives the total of its loan plus interest.

Savings, in the form of stocks, bonds, moneymarket accounts, mutual funds, and passbook savings, provide another source of income for some elderly. For most, however, the income is negligible. In the late 1960s, about 80 percent of single older individuals and 66 percent of couples had less than $5000 in financial assets, apart from equity in their homes (Schulz, 1980). The wealthiest 1 percent of the elderly own 28 percent of all assets held by people past 65, and the wealthiest 10 percent own 63 percent of the wealth (Fuchs, 1983). (By way of contrast, the wealthiest 1 percent of the total population owned 24 percent of the wealth, down from 25.5 percent in 1958 (U.S. Bureau of the Census, 1982). The situation is not likely to improve dramatically in the near future, for 68 percent of those between the ages of 58 and 63 also reported less than $5000 in assets in the late 1960s (Schulz, 1980).

Health services are a major form of in-kind income for all elderly, with Medicare (for all) and Medicaid (for low-income elderly) picking up about two thirds of their medical expenses. Among younger individuals, only about one fourth of medical expenses are covered by the government (Schulz, 1980). However, the cost of medical care has risen so sharply that, after adjusting for inflation, the average older American spent more for medical care in 1978 than in 1965—when Medicare did not exist (Fuchs, 1983), and medical expenses remain a major problem for many older adults.

Low-income elderly are eligible for food stamps, and public transportation systems often have reduced fare schedules for older adults, no matter what their income level. A few businesses give discounts on purchases to older adults. Assistance from other family members is difficult to ascertain, but it has been estimated that about 28 percent of families headed by older adults are affected (Moon, 1977). However, the flow of funds between older families and children goes in both directions, with older families being slightly more likely to receive assistance than to give it.

It has been suggested that, in order to maintain their previous standard of living, single older adults in retirement need from 51 to 79 percent of their former income, and married couples need from 55 to 86 percent (Espenshade and Braun, 1983). (The higher the preretirement income, the lower the required rate of income in retirement.) Others (Schulz, 1980) have proposed 65 to 70 percent of gross income before retirement as an appropriate figure. By itself, in 1974 Social Security was replacing more than 60 percent of earned income for only 5 out of a hundred single men and 21 out of a hundred couples in which the wife drew the dependent's benefit of half her husband's Social Security. The median replacement rate for single men was 39 percent; and for couples, 49 percent (Fox, 1979).

PLANNING FOR RETIREMENT

The problem of providing for adequate income in retirement is not easy to solve. The person who tries to figure out just how much money should be set aside for the later years soon discovers that there is no way to know the amount that will be needed. No one knows how long he or she will live after retirement, and plans that would be generous for a 5-year span or adequate for 10 are likely to provide only a meager supplement for the person who lives long past the 80-year mark—as more and more people are doing. Future rates of inflation are unknown, and the relationship of interest to inflation—which determines whether savings grow in value, retain their real value, or shrink away—is also impossible to know. Medical care is another unknown, for Medicare makes no provision for lengthy illness or most nursing home care, and medical costs rise faster than inflation. Finally, the average person has no idea what sort of life he or she would like to lead after retirement, and the 25-year-old's vision of the good life may bear little resemblance to the desires and needs of a 65-year-old.

Without Social Security or private pensions, says economist James Schulz (1980), a person would have to save 20 percent of all income throughout his or her working life in order to live comfortably during retirement. When Social Security benefits for full-time workers are considered, the required savings rate dropped to 5.5 percent in 1972 although later regulatory changes reduced the value of this benefit by more than 5 percent. Second pensions further reduce required savings for some people, but no more than half the retired couples qualified for them in the decade of the 1970s (Fox, 1979). Because the increasing proportion of older Americans makes it unlikely that the Social Security system will be changed to provide total support in retirement, only a change in the choices made by younger Americans is likely to ensure satisfactory lives among elderly in the future.

CONSUMPTION PATTERNS ACROSS ADULTHOOD

As adults age, their buying patterns change, in part because of reduced income and in part because of changing needs. Younger adults are establishing households and rearing children. They are buying houses and furnishing them, and many are spending money on child rearing. According to the Department of Agriculture, it will cost $80,000 (in constant dollars) to rear a baby born in 1982 to the age of 18 (*The New York Times*, 1983b). Adults who do not marry may also be buying and furnishing homes, but they are likely to be heavy spenders in recreational areas as well. They have more disposable income for travel, stereos, sports cars, athletic equipment, and restaurant meals.

Older individuals generally spend a greater proportion of their income on food, housing, household operations, and medical care, with a smaller proportion going to household furnishings, transportation, personal care, clothing, and recreation (Kreps, 1976). Higher energy costs in recent years may have changed some consumption patterns. All families tend to spend about 10 percent of their gross income on energy, but among households headed by adults older than 65, more of that expenditure goes for home energy and less for gasoline than among younger adults (Walther, 1983).

Considering all older adults in a single group may skew our picture of consumption patterns, for some older individuals continue to work. When consumption patterns of retired and nonretired adults older than 60 are compared, retired adults spend significantly larger shares of their income on housing, food at home, and medical care and slightly larger shares on household operations, fuel, and utilities (McConnel and Deljavan, 1983). Older employed adults spend significantly more of their income on automobiles and restaurant meals, and slightly more on gifts and contributions. Other expenditures, such as vacations, recreation, clothing, personal care, and household furnishings make up a similar proportion of the elderly household budget, whether individuals are retired or employed. Among the 4000 households in this national sample, aftertax income was just over $5000 per year among retired families and $8000 per year among employed families. There was little indication that retired families were drawing on savings to meet their expenses, and the average family appeared to be spending slightly less than it received.

Retired adults learn to adjust their consumption patterns in order to stretch their income. For example, members of the American Association of Retired Persons share the methods they have developed to make dollars go farther (*Modern Maturity*, 1983). They clip coupons, build their meals around supermarket specials, forego prepared foods, buy vegetables in season, form car pools, and pay cash for the cheapest gasoline. Much of their leisure time is spent in time-intensive goods, services, and activities, as has been predicted by economists (Becker, 1976).

How retired adults feel about their financial situation may have little relationship with their actual income level. More important may be the comparison between their present situation and their preretirement circumstances. A drastic drop, especially if it is unexpected, can lead to a feeling of relative deprivation. An analysis of six national samples indicated that a sense of relative deprivation had a stronger influence on feelings of financial well-being than social status or current income (Espenshade and Braun, 1983). A discrepancy with their own previous situation was more likely to lead to feelings of deprivation than discrepancy with the situation of others.

Consider the case of Laura and J. G. Puchi, who both took early retirement from Lockheed Corporation in 1976. By 1981, inflation had eroded their $944 monthly combined company pension to the extent that the addition of Social Security benefits for J. G. was not enough to maintain their standard of living. They had to give up vacation trips, restaurant meals, even Christmas gifts for their grandchildren. Their savings were depleted, and J. G. had to take a part-time job as a school janitor to enable them to get by. Their situation was eased somewhat when Laura became eligible for Social Security in 1982, but they say that—given another chance—they would never choose early retirement (Sheils et al., 1981).

In the past, older adults seemed content with life at a subsistence level. Many lived with deprivation during the Great Depression, and all developed in a society that made no provision for old age. Any guaranteed pension or benefits more than met their expectations. Today retirement is seen as an earned right, and when adults retire, they are unlikely to be satisfied with a drastic reduction in living standards. As we saw earlier, increased productivity often leads to higher standards of living for workers—but unless provisions are made in retirement laws, the retired person gets no benefit from society's progress. Kreps (1976) has pointed out that when a lengthy period of retirement is paralleled by sustained economic growth, the relative position of retired people may worsen, with their standard of living becoming unacceptable by social standards. For example, living without television, telephone, or electricity is no longer acceptable although all were once considered luxuries.

American productivity is not stable. After slowing for some years, it began to decline at the beginning of the 1980s, reversing itself as the country began to emerge from recession in 1983. It has been suggested that as members of the baby boom enter their high-earning years during the decade of the 1980s, the general level of savings may increase, leading to increased capital investment and an accelerated growth in productivity (Espenshade and Braun, 1983). If that should happen, general standards of living could rise, or increased national wealth could be used to finance the lengthening period of retirement and keep the income of retired adults at an acceptable level.

HOUSING

Most Americans live in houses or apartments although some live in mobile homes or in hotels, and a few live on boats. A majority (67.7 percent) live in single-family housing, and 65.6 percent of all year-round dwelling units are occupied by the person who owns them (U.S. Bureau of the Census, 1982). Home ownership steadily increases with age, jumping from 40 percent of all families headed by people younger than 35 to 70 percent of those headed by adults older than 64 (Lawton, 1980). Both long-term and periodic economic events appear to have affected the composition of households.

TRENDS IN HOUSEHOLD FORMATION

Rising affluence has had a striking effect on the housing of young, single adults. In 1950 nearly all single men and women between the ages of 25 and 34 lived with parents, other relatives, friends, or roommates. Only 4 percent of the men and 6 percent of the women lived by themselves. Thirty years later, in 1980, 29 percent of the single men and women in that same age group lived alone. Establishing individual households is more expensive than pooling resources, but real income climbed enough in three decades to allow an enormous increase in the proportion of young people who could afford the luxury of privacy and autonomy (Michael, Fuchs, and Scott, 1980).

At least since World War II, even younger adults have been leaving the nest at an early age—although they often shared quarters with someone else. During the 1950s and 1960s, most young people had generally struck out on their own by the time they were 21. The peak was reached in 1980, when 9.4 of young adults between the ages of 14 and 24 lived alone. The effect of smaller economic cycles then became apparent. The recession of 1981 made it increasingly difficult for the young to leave home. In fact, some who left during the late 1970s returned when the recession cost them their jobs. Others who kept their positions found that inflation had whisked independence out of their grasp, at least temporarily. Anita Tarjan, a 24-year-old Wisconsin schoolteacher, expressed her feelings:

I want to strike out on my own, be independent, take care of my own affairs and have privacy. But unfortunately I can't afford to. You get out of college believing you're going to have this terrific job and then when you finally do get a job, your salary just doesn't meet your expectations. You can't survive and there you are, living at home again, just like a teenager'' (Lindsey, 1984, p. 18).

The return to the nest—or the decision to postpone the departure—has resulted in higher-than-expected vacancy rates in many American cities. Improvements in the economy can reverse such trends. As employment began to rise in 1983, the formation of new households (by single, married, or cohabiting individuals) more than tripled, up from 400,000 to 1.5 million (Lindsey, 1984).

Another trend in household formation has been toward home ownership by single adults. Traditionally, single men and women lived in rented quarters. Socialization had led most to view home ownership as inappropriate for the unwed. As more and more people have either postponed marriage or decided to remain single, sales of homes, co-ops, and condominiums to single adults have increased. Federal and state income tax laws have played some part in this trend, with the deduction of mortgage interest decreasing the cost of home ownership. Most people buy their first houses when they are about 28 years old, an age that has remained steady for several years. Again, economic cycles affect such trends, and we saw earlier that 35 percent of the young adults in one group delayed a home purchase because of inflation. Between 1975 and 1982, mortgage interest rates climbed from 8.75 percent to 15.1 percent before beginning to edge down. Such an increase escalates monthly payments and calls for large amounts of cash up front. On houses sold to first-time buyers in 1981, the average down payment was more than $15,000, and the monthly mortgage payment was $694—up from $449 just two years before (U.S. Bureau of the Census, 1982). About 64 percent of these home purchases were financed entirely from savings and investments, but in 17 percent of the cases, relatives helped provide the necessary cash.

Americans have always been a highly mobile population. Between 1975 and 1980, 45 percent of Americans moved. Although about 21 percent stayed within the same metropolitan area, the rest went to a different part of the state or country (U.S. Bureau of the Census, 1982). People in their twenties are the most likely of any to make a move, generally in connection with employment, and the greater a person's education, the more likely he or she is to move (Fig. 14.5) Migration across state lines tends to be high during the implementation and stabilization stages of career development, then slows during the consolidation period (see Chapter 13). Although it is commonly believed that frequent moves are highly stressful and may lead to illness, depression, ruptured marriages, and unhappy children, researchers are beginning to find positive aspects of executive transfers. According to Jeanne Brett (1980), when mobile executives are compared with those who do not move, the movers (both husband and wife) feel that they are more capable and that their lives are more interesting. The movers also have higher levels of marital satisfaction. However, mobile executives (but not their spouses) complain more about their health and both partners are less satisfied with their social relationships.

Older adults tend to move less frequently than do the young, with people past 65 moving only one fifth as often as people younger than 35 (Lawton, 1980). As we will see, problems may arise when the elderly move, and these moves are unlikely to be connected with employment.

HOW THE ELDERLY LIVE

The financial situation of older adults affects the quality of their housing and, as we have seen, the ownership of a house can improve the quality of life. Although we tend to think of the elderly as inhabiting nursing homes or retirement communities, these living arrangements are confined to only a handful of older Americans. No more than 5 percent of people past 65 live in any kind of institution—although one person in four will spend some time in a nursing home, a personal-care home, or a psychiatric hospital before he or she dies (Lawton, 1980). Another 5 percent live in some kind of age-segregated housing—and only a minority of these individuals live in middle-class retirement communities. That leaves 90 percent of the elderly dispersed in houses and apartments across the country, in cities, suburbs, small towns, and rural areas.

Among the 70 percent of the elderly who own their own homes, five out of six live in single-family detached or semidetached houses, but only about a fourth of elderly renters occupy this kind of housing. Just under half of the renters live in apartments—buildings with five or more units. Surveys indicate that older adults tend to live in older houses of poorer quality than those occupied by adults younger than 65, but the difference between the two age groups is not striking (U.S. Bureau of the Census, 1976). For example, 0.8 percent of younger homeowners lack complete plumbing in their houses, compared with 3.2 percent of older homeowners. In almost every instance, renters put up with more defects

Years of Schooling	Age			
	18–24	**25–29**	**30–34**	**35–44**
0 to 8	6.6%	9.1%	6.9%	4.9%
9 to 11	9.8	13.5	13.2	6.4
12	10.5	13.2	10.4	7.1
13 to 15	12.1	16.9	15.0	12.5
16	21.5	23.6	18.3	12.6
>16	27.0	30.7	23.7	16.4

FIGURE 14.5   Migration across state lines.

Percent of the population whose state of residence in 1980 was different from their state of residence in 1975. Among young and middle-aged adults, moving from one state to another is closely connected with education, and most moves are related to employment.

Source: U.S. Bureau of the Census, "Geographical Mobility, March 1975 to March 1980," *Current Population Reports*, series P-20, No. 368, Table 24.

than owners: 2.6 percent of younger renters and 7.7 percent of older renters are without basic plumbing.

Most older adults are satisfied with their housing and are less likely than younger adults to complain about inadequacies. This satisfaction remains consistent across studies; 84 percent of the elderly in a national survey rated their housing as excellent or good; and 66 percent of Philadelphia elderly, 71 percent of Delaware elderly, and 79 percent of elderly living in public housing were very satisfied (Lawton, 1980). Among older adults in small Kansas towns, housing satisfaction was a predictor of mental health, more important than marital status and second only to activity—a measure composed of activity, functional health, and mobility (Scheidt and Windley, 1983). Older Kansans who were satisfied with the lighting, temperature, space, and privacy of their homes tended to have higher levels of mental health than those who were dissatisfied. It is probable, however, that people with high levels of mental health are more likely to be satisfied than those with emotional problems. Other researchers (Kasl and Rosenfield, 1980) believe that the influence of housing on mental health is probably minor and point to national surveys in which only 35 percent of adults say that it is extremely important to have a house or apartment "you like to live in."

Older people tend to reside in metropolitan areas, in small towns, and in rural areas, with the rural elderly living in the most inferior housing. Although the old are less likely to be found in the suburbs, this distribution could change. As Bernice Neugarten (Neugarten and Hall, 1980) has pointed out, people tend to age "in place," remaining in their own homes. As homeowners in the suburbs (mostly parents with growing children) age, cities are likely to be surrounded by rings of old people.

Older Adults and Mobility

A reluctance on the part of old people to move is paralleled by the negative impact of most moves. Involuntary moves, as when redevelopment projects require relocation, can have severe consequences, and older adults may grieve over such moves for years afterward (Schooler and Reubenstein, 1980). As we saw in Chapter 2, a prospective study (Ferraro, 1983) indicated that moving from one house or apartment to another within the same community was followed by increased illness and hospitalization whether or not adults moved out of choice or were satisfied with their new housing. However, most local moves—in contrast to other moves—tend to be the result of poor health and low finances, so that their effects cannot be applied to long-distance moves (Aday and Miles, 1982).

Among a large national sample of older adults, voluntary moves tended to lead to declines in health and morale, with the decline sharper when the move had been expected (Schooler, 1980). But when the move was to improved housing or neighborhoods or when the person had a confidant with whom to share worries, the impact of the move was cushioned, and declines were slight. When voluntary moves represent decided improvements in housing, the effects can be positive. In most cases, well-being shows modest improvement, and social activity tends to improve (Kasl and Rosenfield, 1980).

The negative effect of many moves becomes understandable when we consider the function of home ownership. According to M. Powell Lawton (1980), the longtime home is the cheapest housing available for most older adults. The home is often loved, and its familiarity allows the older individual to feel competent when dealing with the environment. Finally, a longtime home has a high symbolic value connected with the rearing of a family and the work of many years required for its purchase. Although not all elderly movers are homeowners, a rented apartment or house can function in some of these ways.

There may be a great reluctance to move even when housing and the surrounding neighborhood are deteriorating. An 84-year-old woman who lived in a dying Appalachian town described her husband's attachment to their home:

This spring, my son talked. He says, "Now, Mom, you just can't stay in this house forever. You got to get a smaller place and live someplace where you can be on the level." And he took us, just by force almost, to look at mobile homes and trailers. . . . And we almost bought one. They were so beautiful. And I said, "Well, are we going to sign?" And Pop said, "Well, let's think about it till morning." So we come home, and he just sit down and started to cry. "I can't do it," he said. He lived in this house 57 or 8 years. And he said, "I just can't do it. We'll stay here" [Rowles, 1980, pp. 157–158].

If they decide to move, older adults are more likely to move a short distance than to migrate across a state line, but when they make a long distance move, it is generally to a place with a warm climate. Between 1975 and 1980, 39.7 percent of all interstate immigrants past the age of 60 moved into Florida, California, or Arizona (Collins, 1983a).

Such moves by older individuals are four times as common as they were only 20 years ago, and it is believed that increased wealth and cohort influences are responsible. The generation that fought in World War II is now reaching retirement age. Moving has been a feature of their lives—from one military base to another during the war years, to college on the G.I. Bill benefits afterward, and later many of the middle-class moved because of employment. Today's migrants tend to be in their sixties, financially independent, and married. However, researchers at the University of Miami have also noted a small countermigration trend from Florida, in which the elderly return to the Northeast and Middle West (Collins, 1983a). The migrants tend to be in their seventies, poor, and widowed; and the majority appear to be returning to the state of their birth, apparently to be near their families as they move into the ranks of the old-old (Collins, 1984).

Age-Segregated Housing

In addition to occupying houses and apartments scattered throughout the community, noninstitutionalized older adults also live in hotels, mobile homes, and various forms of age-segregated housing. The small group of elderly who live in transient hotels tend to be male, single, and older than 75; those who live in resident hotels are as likely to be female as male and are either widowed or married (Goode, Hoover, and Lawton, 1979). Although some hotels with elderly residents are expensive, others are cheap, single-residency only (SRO) hotels with inadequate—or barely adequate—facilities that cater to retired adults, welfare clients, and discharged mental patients. Some older adults, mostly men, rent rooms in private homes or live in boarding houses.

Mobile-home parks may be age integrated or limited to older adults. Since 1960 the number of mobile homes has increased fivefold, and most are owner-occupied. Mobile homes have become increasingly popular with older adults, apparently because they are inexpensive compared with other housing, and the parks provide a small, homogeneous community where residents feel secure (Carp, 1976).

Age-segregated housing may take the form of mobile parks, public housing, congregate housing, special life-care communities, or retirement communities. Whether age-segregated housing is a curse or a blessing has never been settled. Segregating old people into public housing and retirement villages reduces their contact with the young and may keep the social stereotypes of old age from crumbling under the impact of mingling with the healthy young-old. It deprives the young from any benefit that might come from the experience and wisdom of the old. And it deprives the old from the stimulation of new ideas and may tend to hasten their obsolescence. Against these drawbacks to society are the feelings of older people. Studies indicate that most individuals who live in age-segregated housing love it—even those who were uncertain about the arrangement before they moved in (Lawton, 1980). They say they are no longer bothered by noise or the boisterous behavior of the young. They feel more secure, and their fear of crime goes down. Just over 30 percent said they would like a few younger adults for neighbors—but only if they were childless. Age-segregated housing appears to increase well-being, morale, social activity, and housing satisfaction. Yet it would be premature to recommend such housing to everyone. Those who move into age-segregated arrangements have chosen to do so, and they represent a minority of older adults. When adults in the community were queried by the same researcher, the picture changed. More than 60 percent preferred age-integrated housing—something they will not get in public housing for the elderly.

Public housing for the elderly is open to adults who are at least 62 years old, along with their spouses, and to handicapped people of any age. In 1981, about 27 percent of public housing units were occupied under these rules although additional older adults were living in age-integrated public housing (U.S. Bureau of the Census, 1982). The majority of older tenants are women (78 percent) and overwhelmingly single, widowed, or divorced (83 percent) (Lawton, 1980). The experience of living in planned housing can be highly beneficial. Older adults who moved into Victoria Plaza, a housing project for the elderly in San Antonio, Texas, showed marked improvements in several aspects of their life that did not appear in applicants who were rejected (Carp, 1976). After one year, their morale was higher, their housing satisfaction increased, they liked the neighborhood better, they needed fewer outside services, and they joined more organizations and social groups, visited friends more, and had more positive self-concepts. Many of the effects persisted when the residents were restudied 8 years later. Other studies have not shown such powerful benefits from age-integrated public housing. For example, in a study (Lawton and Cohen, 1974) of five urban housing projects, tenants who were admitted to the projects showed increased satisfaction and more involvement in various activities but a decline in functional health.

The problem with such studies comes from possible differences between the project tenants and adults in the community. For example, the elderly in the Victoria Plaza study were not assigned to the project on a random basis, and the screening process may have tended to select people who would be most likely to thrive in the new environment. In addition, those who were rejected may have been so disappointed by their inability to get one of the apartments that their bitterness affected their lives. Because people interact with the environment, some will improve in a situation that will lead to a decline in others. However, most researchers believe that moving from substandard community housing into good public housing generally leads to modest improvements (Kasl and Rosenfield, 1980).

Congregate housing, in which tenants have their own apartments but eat in a common dining room, is mainly found in nonprofit housing constructed by religious organizations, labor unions, or fraternal organizations (Lawton, 1980). Such an arrangement encourages socialization among residents and permits older adults to remain independent although they may be too frail to care for themselves in isolated apartments.

Special life-care communities provide care at increasingly supportive levels and are generally expensive. After a large initial payment, a monthly maintenance fee covers food, rent, utilities, maid service, and nursing care. In some communities, residents can be as independent as they like, cooking their own meals or eating in a common dining room. The community may have nursing-home facilities for residents who grow too frail to live in apartments.

Retirement villages are inhabited by middle-income retirees, and by the mid-1970s, 69 of these villages had been constructed in the United States, some of them with more than 10,000 residents (Fitzgerald, 1983). A warm climate makes Florida, Arizona, and California the favorite sites for these communities, which tend to be walled cities that provide so many facilities that their residents rarely go outside the gates. Recreation facilities (golf, tennis, shuffleboard, swimming), shops, churches, service clubs, and an array of interest clubs and activities are available. Retirement villages tend to be inhabited by the young-old. In most, residents may be as young as 50 but may not have children younger than 18. Living in a retirement village is generally a positive experience. A comparison of retired men who had moved to Arizona indicated that those who lived in retirement communities were more satisfied with their lives than men who lived in age-integrated communities, even after researchers controlled for health and socioeconomic status (Kasl and Rosenfield, 1980).

HOUSING AND COMPETENCE IN THE ELDERLY

Most older people prefer to live in their own households, and the proportion of old people who are able to do so has been growing (Carp, 1976). This continued independence is probably a combination of better health among the elderly and a

SUN CITY CENTER

Sun City Center, a retirement village south of Tampa, Florida, has more than 8500 residents in two separate developments. The typical house costs between $60,000 and $90,000, and the average income of new residents is between $21,000 and $29,000 a year. Most of the men are retired professionals or middle-level executives, and most of the women have always been homemakers although a good many are retired schoolteachers or registered nurses.

When Frances Fitzgerald (1983) visited Sun City, she found it to be a predominantly Protestant, conservative, Republican community, whose residents came from the Northeast and the Midwest. All were white. Although the village began as a couples' community, almost one third of the women are now widowed and live alone. Most men said they lived in Sun City to be able to play golf, and most women said they were there because of the people, whom they described as "pleasant," "generous," and "a cross section of the better people in the nation." Most residents are enthusiastic about Sun City, and many describe it as the ideal place to live.

The village consists of white ranch houses surrounded by lawns, each with a single tree set in a ring of white gravel and bordered in shrubbery edged with white stones. Streets and sidewalks are spotless, and cleanliness and order dominate the community, both inside and out. The majority of residents lead active lives—golf, dances, bridge, poker, bingo, shuffleboard, volleyball, bowling, handicrafts, and clubs for amateur photographers, radio hams, dabblers in the stockmarket, stamp collectors, gardeners, and poets.

Despite the age restrictions, residents did not regard Sun City as an "old-age ghetto." Asked why she and her husband had purchased a home in an age-segregated community, Erna Krauch seemed startled and said, "Oh, I didn't feel I would just be with a lot of older people. And Sun City Center isn't like that!" (p. 79). In fact, in 1980 about a fourth of the population was younger than 65. However, a good many were in their eighties, and a few were in their nineties.

There is no cemetery at Sun City, and the topics of illness, old age, and death are generally avoided in conversation. There is, however, a volunteer emergency squad with three ambulances, set up by the residents to handle the sudden heart attack or stroke that residents fear. Such medical emergencies pose the community's major threat, the one thing, says Fitzgerald, that "bursts through the cocoon of comfort and security." Next door to Sun City is a life-care community, built after the first Sun City residents began to reach old-old age. Its 152 apartments and 60-bed nursing home make it possible for residents to remain in the vicinity when they can no longer manage their own houses.

new financial independence. Eventually, however, many older individuals can no longer adapt to failing health and increased sensory loss. As we saw in Chapter 5, adaptation depends on the interaction of individual competence and environmental press, or the demands placed on behavior by the situation. The less competent the individual (whether the competence demanded is biological health, sensorimotor functioning, cognitive skill, or ego strength), the greater the impact of environmental factors. Thus, as health fails, the same environment creates a higher level of press (Lawton, 1980). Surroundings that are comfortable for the young-old can become a burden, if not an impossible situation, for the old-old.

Altering the environment slightly can reduce press and extend a person's independence for months or even years. For example, grab bars in the bathroom, higher toilet seats, handrails, and nightlights can be added to homes and apartments, making life easier for many older people. The increasing proportion of elderly has led to the manufacture of many small gadgets, such as phone amplifiers, remote controls for lighting and appliances, and knob turners that allow arthritic hands to operate stoves, faucets, television sets, and appliances. The demand has grown to the point that mail-order businesses selling "aids for easier living" have developed.

When public housing projects for the elderly were planned, such features as grab bars, handrails, the elimination of steps, emergency call buttons, and enough space for wheelchair use were incorporated to make life easier for those with slight disabilities, but most were set up on the assumption that tenants would be able to meet a certain minimum standard of health and independence. It was assumed that as tenants aged and their failing health and increased sensory loss required more support, they would move to a setting that offered increased care. A survey of 74 housing projects in California indicated that three quarters of the projects had a written, formal policy that required a certain standard of independence and that nine out of ten had an informal policy, which was discussed with tenants when they applied (Berstein, 1982). Congregate housing extends independent life for many adults, and in Chicago such projects have been constructed to help meet the needs of residents now in age-segregated housing projects (Regnier, 1983).

Nursing homes are the typical institution for adults who require extensive care. Residents tend to be the oldest of the old: The average age of institutionalized elderly is 82, and 20 percent are at least 90 years olds (Tobin, 1980). The majority of residents are women, and most are either widowed, never married, or without living children. The typical resident is also mentally and physically impaired to the extent that independent living is either extremely difficult or impossible (Lawton, 1980). For the isolated adult, institutionalization may come before it is absolutely necessary, but for the adult with spouse or living children, it usually comes only after all other possibilities have been exhausted. Because institutions are costly and seen as undesirable by older adults and gerontologists alike, an array of supporting services has grown up to extend independent living.

Life in a nursing home leaves much to be desired. When researchers observed more than a thousand residents in 44 nursing homes, they found that over a two-day period, nearly three fourths of the residents had no social contact with any staff member (Gottesman and Bourestom, 1974). More than half the time, residents were doing nothing. The environment in most nursing homes is confined and so unstimulating that the reluctance of older adults to apply for admission is understandable.

Impact of Institutionalization

Entering an institution or moving from one institution to another is often followed by decline or even death in the elderly. Considering the unstimulating quality of the environment and the fact that such moves are rarely voluntary, negative consequences are not surprising. However, there is no way of knowing whether people who come into the institution from the community are already so seriously incapacitated that the decline after entry is due to their previous condition. For some elderly, alone, poor, and unable to care for themselves, the nursing home may be better than their former environment. Among a group of 85 adults between the ages of 68 and 93 who were studied before and after admission to a home for the aged, 18 percent were dead within a year, another 30 percent had deteriorated, 46 percent were unchanged, and 6 percent improved (Lieberman and Tobin, 1983).

Relocation from one institution to another has been more thoroughly studied, and findings are similar. Unwelcome moves tend to result in physical impairment, psychological deterioration, or death in about half of the cases. At least 40 studies have testified to the serious effects of such relocations (Horowitz and Schulz, 1983). According to Milton Lieberman and Sheldon Tobin (1983), radical environmental change poses a severe stress even for elderly individuals who are physically and psychologically healthy before the move. The stress appears to come from the quality of the new environment, a lack of fit between the individual's personality or life-style and the demands of the new environment, and the amount of discontinuity between the old and new environments. These three environmental factors were the best predictors of outcome in relocation studies involving 639 elderly individuals. Aggressiveness was the personality trait that proved to be most effective in adapting to a new institutional environment, and passivity appeared to increase the risk of deterioration. The most effective cognitive strategy for dealing with the move was the development by the elderly of the view that they had mastery and control over their lives. This sense of control also has proved effective in improving the condition of nursing-home residents.

A Sense of Control

When nursing-home residents were given the feeling that they had some control over their lives, their condition improved measurably. Judith Rodin and Ellen Langer (1977) allowed each of the residents in one group to choose a potted plant, which they were expected to care for themselves, and to select the night they would attend a movie. Members of the other group were given a plant and told the staff would care for it; they also saw a movie each week, but had no say in the night it would be shown. Within 3 weeks, residents who had been encouraged to take control of their environment were happier and more active than residents who had been encouraged to depend on the staff. Within 18 months, 15 percent of the group that had taken responsibility were dead, compared with 30 percent of the dependent group. (The normal death rate in the nursing home was 25 percent.)

Other researchers also have found improvements among nursing-home residents who have been encouraged to take responsibility for some aspects of their lives. For example, nursing-home residents who were given the responsibility for maintaining bird-feeders showed significant gains in activity, happiness, and feelings of control as compared with other residents (Banziger and Roush, 1983). As in the experiment by Rodin and Langer, nurses also rated the residents with responsibility as improved, noting that they were more alert, sociable, happy, and active; slept better; and complained less. There was, however, no difference noted in the residents' medical ratings by nurses or physicians.

These interventions are based on the view that the lack of control felt by many nursing-home residents can lead to learned helplessness, which was discussed in Chapter 6. If an intervention program is to induce permanent change, the residents must continue to feel some control over their lives. When responsibility is given and then taken away, the residents' subsequent deterioration may leave them much worse off than they were before the intervention began (Rodin, 1982).

Although this woman was injured in a fall, she is able to live in her own home because a community volunteer shops for her and keeps her from being socially isolated.

How does life in a nursing home lead to learned helplessness? It may be that once a person moves into a nursing home, he or she finds it difficult to maintain a self-concept. The routine of health-care workers tends to take away many of the decisions and responsibilities of the older person, and staff attitude may convey the idea that the residents are sick and helpless (Solomon, 1982). Life in such a setting could easily erode any sense of autonomy and control. However, simply increasing autonomy across the board is unlikely to solve the problems of nursing-home residents. According to Lawton (1980), sometimes the sense of autonomy erodes because the resident has lost much of his or her personal competence. If autonomy is increased when competence is lacking, environmental press may mount above the level that can be tolerated.

SOCIAL SERVICES

At some time in our lives, nearly all of us will need help from a community social service. Although families generally do a good job in taking care of their frail or ill members, the burden often overwhelms available resources. And some individuals may be alone in the world, with no family to turn to. As Victor Fuchs (1983) points out, families, ethnic associations, and religious communities may be able to provide a good deal of assistance within their respective groups, but only the community can ensure the flow of support across groups. Some services are completely tax-supported, some are completely staffed by volunteers, but even many of the volunteer programs rely on some sort of government aid.

COMMUNITY PROGRAMS AND PUBLIC SUPPORT

At each stage of the life cycle, some sort of social support may be needed. Certain services are used by people of all income and educational levels. Crisis hot lines provide sympathy, counseling, and comfort to alcoholics; individuals with drug problems; rape victims; battered women; runaway children; gamblers; and people who fear they may commit suicide. Additional services provide more extensive counseling and material aid to people with such problems. Unwed mothers are assisted throughout pregnancy.

Not all services are crisis-related. Many social programs provide services for the disabled, the elderly, the temporarily unemployed, or the poor. Infants and young children are taken to well-baby clinics for immunizations and routine health care. Nearly five million girls and women, 88 percent of them younger than 30, are served each year at family planning clinics (*The New York Times*, 1982). Programs provide for education, unemployment compensation, and aid to dependent children. Other programs are available in the field of nutrition, transportation, housing, and medical care.

Most of these programs have general public support, but the majority compete for tax dollars. When choices have to be made, suggests Fay Cook (1982), people appear to use four standards as a guide: (1) whether the group in need of assistance has an alternative source of help; (2) whether the program fills essential needs; (3) whether the program will increase an individual's independence, making him or her less dependent on others; and (4) whether the person in need causes the condition himself or herself. She described a survey of Chicagoans that summed up such sentiments; agreement was general across social class, gender, and racial groups. When specific types of aid were discussed, the elderly received priority in matters of income and nutrition, the disabled in transportation programs, and children and adults younger than 65 for educational aid.

There is general public support for social programs that assist the elderly, especially those who are in need. In national surveys, strong approval has consistently been shown for such tax-financed programs as medical care, Social Security, and "helping the elderly." The sentiment seems solid for maintaining existing programs, but when asked about new programs, most favor them but feel that they should aid only older adults who are in need. Among a sample of Alabama Power Company customers, replies indicated that government assistance for home energy bills should go to the elderly, favoring them over the disabled, the ill, the poor, and the unemployed (Klemmack, 1983). Customers (predominantly white, middle-aged men) rated the elderly as more in need of assistance, more deserving, more grateful for assistance, and less responsible for their predicament than any of the other groups.

The elderly seem to be favored for assistance because they are not responsible for the fact that they must retire, because taxpayers generally have older relatives who need aid, and because age is an inevitable, universal condition. In this section, we will examine in depth only programs designed to assist older adults.

SOCIAL SERVICES FOR OLDER ADULTS

From the time they retire, most older adults require some sort of financial support. As we have seen, Social Security is the major form of direct income for all older adults, with Medicare the major source of in-kind income. Medicaid, food stamps, rent supplements, and Supplemental Security Income provide additional assistance to the low-income elderly. Other special services have emerged for the elderly in the fields of nutrition, transportation, home visitation and assistance, legal services, and protective care. Where these programs are available, many older adults who would otherwise be institutionalized are able to remain in their own homes. Such programs, although they require tax funding even when manned by volunteers, are less costly and more effective than institutional care.

Only a small proportion of the elderly make use of available social services (Harbert and Ginsberg, 1979). Because older adults cannot use programs unless they know about them, **outreach services** have been established to locate older people and inform them of the various programs. Publicity in the media reaches some of the elderly, but other contacts are often more effective. Informal communication systems (such as churches, clubs, and extended families), people whose employment brings them in contact with older adults (such as grocers, pharmacists, delivery people, and mail carriers), and door-to-door canvassing may be required to find older adults. It is often the "invisible elderly," the isolated, poor, old-old individuals who are most in need of services, that are the most difficult to contact (Beattie, 1976). Once older adults are located, the outreach worker describes available social services, assesses needs, and helps individuals take whatever steps are required to obtain the appropriate services.

The responsibility of the outreach worker does not end when the isolated adult is put in contact with the appropriate agency. Unless follow-up contacts are made to see that the services have actually been obtained, the outreach effort may be ineffectual.

Health and Nutrition

In a number of programs, service is brought directly into the home. For example, nearly 4000 home health-care agencies have been certified by Medicare. These agencies, run by hospitals, physicians, businesses, or nurses, make house calls to the housebound elderly. Some home health-care services have been too expensive to be useful to many of the elderly, but others have been extremely effective. In Elmira, New York, for example, Jean Sweeney Dunn and Edith R. Reidy, two registered nurses, run a home health-care agency that serves the 10,000 area residents who are 65 or older (Freudenheim, 1983). In a group this size, between 500 and 800 at any time are likely to be housebound with some medical problem. The nurses take blood pressure, health histories, check medication, and provide information on various chronic illnesses. The team works with physicians, who step in when more extensive medical care is needed. Their service keeps many elderly out of hospitals and nursing homes and reduces Medicare expenses for health emergencies. Before the service was introduced, an individual who needed medical care had to take an ambulance to the hospital emergency room at a cost of $210. Under the health-care service, which costs $20, minor emergencies are handled on the spot, blood may be drawn for laboratory testing, and physicians will make house calls when the nurses decide they are required.

Nutrition is another problem among older persons, especially those living alone. More than 30 years ago, after high levels of malnutrition and dehydration were found among isolated elderly, voluntary organizations developed "meals on wheels" programs, in which a hot meal was brought into the home each day. Meals on wheels is still an active program, and in 1973 federal funds were made available for congregate meal services. Hot meals were served in central dining facilities, and transportation was provided to bring the elderly to central locations. Congregate meals were set up in order to encourage socialization and reduce isolation among impoverished, isolated, and minority elderly (Beattie, 1976). Meals were delivered to people who could not be transported to the center. Such programs have generally been underfunded and unable to handle all the elderly who would profit from them.

Transportation

Lack of transportation multiplies the problems of the elderly, barring them from many services because they cannot reach them. In a country that depends on the automobile, older adults who have never driven, who are no longer capable of driving, or who can no longer afford to maintain an automobile are at a disadvantage. In many areas, public transportation is sketchy or unavailable. Where extensive bus and subway lines exist, psychological and physical barriers often keep the old from utilizing them, even though they may be eligible for reduced off-peak hour fares.

The fear of crime may keep older adults from using public transportation. Walking alone to a bus stop or waiting for a bus or subway, they are at the mercy of muggers, purse snatchers, and pickpockets. The fear may make them virtual prisoners in their houses or apartments. In Chicago, 41 percent of the residents past the age of 60 believe that crime is their most serious concern (Harbert and Ginsberg, 1979). Older adults who live alone or in age-integrated communities have the greatest fear of crime. A survey of nearly 3000 older adults in Washington State indicated that not social isolation, but previous experiences with crime by themselves or their acquaintances were most closely related to fear (Lee, 1983). Healthy and well-educated adults showed the least fear, perhaps because they are more in control of their lives. Thus, it is the older adults who need social services the most who are likely to be kept inside by fear.

Physical barriers to transportation are also prevalent. Negotiating subway stairs, getting on and off a bus or subway car and maneuvering through narrow aisles are beyond the abilities of some older individuals. Although improvements in the form of "kneeling" buses and buses that will take wheelchairs have been introduced in a number of cities, many of the elderly have problems reaching bus stops, and bus routes do not always pass near desired destinations.

Yet transportation may act as an antidote for aging (Cohen, 1980). Older individuals with their own means of transportation report greater life satisfaction, are more likely to be socially integrated in the community, and are better able to sustain their life goals. Aware of the importance of mobility, communities have begun to develop transportation projects for the elderly. By 1974 more than 900 such projects were in operation. About 36 percent of these programs provided door-to-door transportation on call; 46 percent used fixed routes on a regular schedule; and 3 percent used commercial taxi companies, reimbursing them for their services. In a Chicago program, called Seniors on the Move, where vans operate on both fixed schedules and door-to-door calls, about 80 percent of trips were for shopping and about 15 percent were for health care. Among the elderly in rural Indiana, almost two thirds of the adults who needed transportation assistance lived alone, and they tended to be widowed, never married, or divorced (McGhee, 1983).

Social Supports

Older adults who live alone are sometimes socially isolated. To meet their needs, various kinds of visitation programs have been developed. Some programs simply supply "friends"; others provide help with household chores or home repairs that elderly citizens may not have the financial resources or dexterity to manage on their own. A typical friendly visitor program, the Village Visiting Neighbors program, begun in the Greenwich Village area of New York City in 1972, has developed branches in other areas of Manhattan (Alexander, 1983). Financed by private groups and community support, the Greenwich Village section sends 170 volunteers to visit 189 adults past the age of 60. Visitors provide companionship and do small services, such as reading mail or paying bills for their "neighbor." They may also act as escorts if the neighbor would like to go shopping, visit a museum, or take some other outing that seems formidable for a lone, older adult. For example, Mary Mulry, a young woman in her thirties, visits Rose Wimmer, a 94-year-old widow, every week, spending two hours over tea and conversation. Susan Dinio visits an 89-year-old widower, Samuel Freedman, up to four times each week, bringing along her two young sons. Freedman, who has no children of his own, has become a substitute grandparent to the boys, whose own grandfather lives far away. Both Mulry and Dinio feel that they get as much out of the relationship as do the older adults.

Across the country in Santa Monica, California, the Adopt-a-Grandparent program has been providing social support to the elderly by bringing together adolescents and adults in their seventies and eighties (Larronde, 1983). The teenagers, who visit weekly, get school credit for the program, which carefully matches the personality of old and young. Two adolescents are assigned to each adult, and the program has been so successful that the youngsters often continue their visits long after their "class" is over. During the past 8 years, Thelma Dry, 83, has been adopted by a series of adolescents, and she says that some of her early grandchildren still keep in touch although they have now graduated from college and are married. This sort of program not only benefits the elderly, but also provides the young with an important opportunity to get to know older individuals. The interaction and resulting friendships may dispel some of the myths and stereotypes young people often have about aging.

Other Services

A few programs provide legal services for older adults. Legal-aid offices set up to serve low-income people can help some of the elderly, but often older individuals have too much income to be eligible for legal aid but not enough to pay a lawyer. Retired attorneys, volunteers from the local bar association, and paralegals who are supervised by attorneys, assist older people with government forms, tax and pension problems, wills, and other legal problems. Another sort of legal service is the protective service, in which older adults who become mentally or emotionally impaired and unable to act in their own best interests are helped with their personal affairs (Harbert and Ginsberg, 1979). At times the assistance involves commitment to a nursing home. The purpose of such services is to see that the older person's rights are not violated and to protect his or her interests—from salespeople, collection agencies, family members, or other individuals who may be exerting pressure.

Finally, foster care programs, in which older adults who cannot live by themselves are placed in the homes of others, can keep many of the elderly out of institutions. Such programs are similar to foster parent programs. Receiving homes are inspected, regulated, and licensed by individual states. The receiving family is paid from a combination of the older person's Social Security benefits, SSI, and state funds, if necessary. For example, in Massachusetts, the elderly adult retains $78 of his or her benefits and the receiving family gets $400 (Steinhauer, 1982).

When such supportive services are successful, they increase the participation of older adults in the community, extend the use of older people's capacities, and help older people adjust to new social roles (Beattie, 1976). In the next chapter, we will investigate aging in other countries and special ethnic groups, a process that may give us a new perspective on American policies and practices.

SUMMARY

Church attendance tends to be fairly stable until the age of 65; then a decline, which appears to be health-related, appears. Cohort differences and historical time both appear to affect church attendance. Any decline in church attendance with age may be offset by private religious activities, and there seems to be an increase in the personal meaning of religion among the elderly.

Although cross-sectional studies indicate a rise in conservatism with age, education and historical circumstances appear to account for seemingly greater conservatism among older adults. Most people retain the political orientation of their youth, which is modified by general trends in society. Political activity tends to peak during the fifties, but does not decline with age, and older adults tend to vote out of proportion to their numbers. The most powerful determinant of voting is education although marital status and gender also have an effect. A politics of age has not yet developed in the United States, and the influence of organizations that lobby for the elderly is sporadic.

Age can be used to grant status and privileges or to withdraw them. Discrimination against the young is most common in housing whereas discrimination against the old is most common in employment. Because age is no longer a good predictor of capability or need, it has been suggested that (1) all social programs be based on need, not age; or that (2) the marker of old age be moved from 65 to 75.

The major source of income in the United States is wages, and earning power tends to rise steadily, peaking near the end of work life. Income generally drops after retirement, but many expenses also tend to decrease—although usually not enough to offset the drop in income. Because of Social Security and pension regulations, older women are disadvantaged in comparison with men. Assets (including home ownership), tax breaks, and **in-kind income** usually help retired adults stretch their money. Consumption patterns change across adulthood as needs and income change. Retired adults' satisfaction with their financial situation seems primarily determined by the comparison between their present situation and their preretirement circumstance, with a drastic drop leading to feelings of deprivation.

Most Americans, including the elderly, live in houses or apartments, with home ownership increasing steadily with age. Rising affluence has led a large minority of single adults to form their own households, with many buying their own home. However, economic recessions can send single adults back temporarily to their parents' households. Mobility is highest among the young and tends to be related to employment. Older adults who move tend to be financially independent, married, and in their sixties. Although only a minority of older adults live in age-segregated housing, most who have chosen such housing are quite satisfied. Moving into age-segregated public housing leads to declines in some individuals and improvements in others. **Congregate housing** encourages socialization and independence among older adults. Entering a nursing home often is followed by decline or death, in part because individuals who enter such institutions tend to be in poor health, in part because the environment is usually unstimulating, and in part because the environment seems to foster learned helplessness. Studies have shown that returning some control to residents may lessen stress, improving health and satisfaction. Older adults who are aggressive generally fare much better in institutions than those who are passive.

Social programs tend to be supported by the public when the group in need of assistance has no alternative source of help, when the program fills essential needs, when the program makes an individual less dependent on others, and when the person in need did not cause the condition. **Outreach services** attempt to locate older people and inform them of various support programs, which include health services, nutritional programs (such as Meals on Wheels), transportation services, social supports (such as visiting programs and Adopt-a-Grandparent), legal services, and foster care. Such supportive services are aimed at increasing the participation of older adults in the community, extending their capacities, and helping them adjust to new social roles.

KEY TERMS

congregate housing

in-kind income

outreach services

15

CROSS-CULTURAL PERSPECTIVES ON ADULTHOOD

Not too many years ago, anthropologist Colin Turnbull (1972) studied the Ik, a hunting tribe in the mountains of northeastern Uganda, and what he found makes us look at our own society in a new way. Instead of using bows and arrows or throwing spears at game, the Ik had always hunted in a cooperative manner. Community members spread out a large net and held it up while other members drove game into it. Almost overnight, life changed for the Ik.

Concerned about the preservation of various animal species, the central government made the Iks' traditional hunting grounds into a game preserve. The Ik were no longer permitted to hunt, but were expected to become farmers. The loss of their hunting grounds demolished the basis of Ik culture. Shared social assumptions were invalidated in the eyes of tribal members. With group pride and the concept of community destroyed, life became nasty and brutish. Altruism vanished, and it was each Ik for himself or herself. The mother-child bond was destroyed, and children were left to fend for themselves from the time they were three years old. Whether a three-year-old was eaten by a leopard, fell into a fire, or starved to death was of no concern to the child's parents. Thrown on their own devices, children survived by forming juvenile bands that foraged for food. One Ik helped another only if there was a clear and immediate reward for doing so. The other end of the life cycle became a horror, for no one respected or cared for the old. When adults were too feeble to support themselves, they were left to die. Turnbull believes that the experience of the Ik demonstrates that human values are impossible without society and that the loss of a social tradition is almost synonymous with the loss of humanity.

The Ik are an extreme case, but the thoroughness of their destruction illustrates how heavily our experience of the life cycle is influenced by the shared beliefs of society. In this chapter, we examine various cultural and ethnic patterns in the hope of gaining perspective on our own lives. We begin with a look at the different ways of dividing the life cycle. After exploring the experience of life and aging in traditional societies, we examine the effect that industrialization has on these societies. Moving from a world to a national focus, we explore ethnic differences within the United States in order to see how a variety of family relationships can alter the experience of the life span within the same society. We close with a brief consideration of the problems involved in providing social services for ethnic groups within a larger society.

CULTURAL VIEWS OF THE LIFE CYCLE

Each society has its own standards and goals for various stages of the life cycle. As we saw in Chapter 1, societies divide the cycle in various ways. The standard of full adult responsibility also varies from one society to another, as does the way of reckoning age and the timing of old age.

THE MARK OF ADULTHOOD

In a high-tech society like that of the United States, the mark of adulthood is earning a living—taking a full share of economic responsibility. In many societies, adulthood is marked by marriage. For example, among the Mbuti hunter-gatherers of northeastern Zaire, a youth is not permitted to own a hunting net until he marries, and in the eyes of the culture, marriage is dedicated to the good of society. The unmarried person is seen as not truly adult, apparently because he or she has not assumed this community responsibility.

Colin Turnbull (1983), who studied the Mbuti, reports that they reacted with surprise and disbelief to the news that he was unmarried and childless. The members of this African tribe regarded him as socially irresponsible, asking if he had no feelings about his family and his country. A somewhat similar attitude was held by ancient Chinese. According to Confucian doctrine, a man became an adult on his twentieth birthday, but he was not considered a fully participating member of society until he was married and a parent (Tu, 1978).

There are good reasons for different standards of adult responsibility. In the traditional society, the family is the economic unit, controlling both production and consumption. Disease takes a heavy toll among the young in most traditional societies, and the death rate may be so high that continuation of the culture depends on encouraging the fertility of its members. In a technological society like that of the United States, the family has no direct economic function, and marriage is not required for the assumption of a full economic role. Because most children live to maturity, it is unnecessary to encourage procreation; in fact, overpopulation is a concern in most industrialized societies.

THE MEASURE OF AGE

Although the biological course of development is similar in all cultures, the social experience varies around the world. Even age is calculated in different ways. In Western societies, a person's date of birth is socially important. Without official certification of birth, it is extremely difficult for an American to get a passport, a marriage or driver's license, or a social security card. Among many tribal societies, no one knows the exact date of his or her birth (van den Berghe, 1983). Age may be reckoned in relation to another person, to some memorable event (the year of the great earthquake), or to the passage of seasons (60 summers) (Goody, 1976). Often age is determined by membership in an **age set,** a group of individuals born within a certain span of years (usually from 7 to 15) who move together through the life cycle.

Among the Masai herding society of Kenya and Tanzania, for example, age sets cover a 15-year span, and at any time a society has five male age sets: uninitiated children; initiated warriors, generally between the ages of 15 and 30; junior elders, early middle-aged men, whose sphere is procreation and domestic affairs; senior elders, late middle-aged men, whose sphere is public affairs; and old men, who are retired (van den Berghe, 1983). Masai culture is distinctive because the members of a male age set move through life in lockstep. Warriors live together in a bachelor village. A Masai male may not marry, own cattle, or have his own home until his age set achieves junior-elder status. Although Masai women also belong to an age set, political and social roles accompany membership in the male age set. Masai women are virtually excluded from public life, and their roles are limited to those of wife and mother. However, Masai women reach adulthood earlier than men, for they marry a man from an older age set while men of their own age are still warriors, single, and without responsibilities (Fry, 1980).

THE MARK OF OLD AGE

The onset of old age varies from one society to another. In the United States, old age is generally seen as beginning at age 65, whether one is single or married, a poet or a plumber, robust or feeble, primarily because the initial requirements of the Social Security system set eligibility at that age. In contrast to our focus on chronological age, old age in most traditional societies is defined in functional terms. A person is old when he or she no longer can carry out the major roles of adulthood. This may lead to the arrival of old age at a later time for one sex than for the other. For example, among the Inuit Eskimo, a man generally becomes old at about the age of 50, when he no longer has the strength to hunt during the winter, but old age tends to come about a decade later for women, whose roles are less strenuous (Guemple, 1983). Among the Black Carib of Belize, however, women become old before men. These Central American villagers consider meno-pause the marker of old age in women and impotence the marker of old age in men. Thus, a woman may be old at 50, but a man of 65 could still be considered middle-aged (Kerns, 1980).

Not all societies use loss of function as the marker of old age. Some connect ag-ing to other transitional events in the life cycle. In India, aging is connected with the family cycle. When a person's children marry, he or she is considered to have entered old age (Vatuk, 1980). Because Indians tend to marry young, an Indian man or woman often reaches old age during the forties. The Masai mark old age by the promotion into "retirement" of an age set whose members are roughly be-tween the ages of 60 and 75 (van den Berghe, 1983). As respected old men, these retired elders have no ritual or public role; their function is limited to that of con-sultant in traditional matters, and elders from more than one retired age set may be present at any one time.

Just as each culture has its own definition of old age, so the status, and treat-ment of the old differ from one society to the next. Most of us have heard that in "the good old days" aged men and women were always held in high esteem and consulted on community matters. In some societies this was true, but the actual situation of the elderly was neither so consistent nor so simple.

AGING IN TRADITIONAL SOCIETIES

A prevalent view of aging, held by social scientists and average citizens alike, is that traditional, or "preindustrial," societies venerate the old, holding them in positions of high respect. However, even among traditional societies, the status of the old varies.

In many cultures, the old receive public marks of deference. Special foods, special forms of address, and special gestures signify the exalted position held by the old. However, unless these formal gestures are backed up by prestige-generating factors, the marks of deference have little meaning. When the prestige of the elderly is high, older adults generally are consulted by younger members, and their advice is followed; they have some control over the behavior and fortunes of the young; they retain an active role in religious, economic, or domestic spheres; and they keep the prestige of the roles held during their prime years (Press and McKool, 1972). In these societies, the emphasis tends to be on the group rather than on the individual, and the extended family is either the residential or the economic unit—or both.

According to L. W. Simmons (1945), the treatment of the old in traditional societies depends on the culture's economic basis. In hunting, gathering, and fishing societies, where there is no harvest to store and existence is often precarious, the old are a drain on the economy and may be accorded deference but harsh treatment. Among the Inuit Eskimo, for example, where few men were able to hunt after they passed 50 and where arthritis and blindness were common, the childless old were often verbally abused and grudgingly fed. Even those with children were sometimes "helped" to die, and the old cooperated in their own abandonment or strangulation (Guemple, 1983). Inuit beliefs about life and death made such decisions ethical, if not customary. However, not all hunting, gathering, or fishing societies treat their old in this manner. Some, such as the Mbuti, place the responsibility of governing the tribe in the hands of adults who are too old to hunt (Turnbull, 1983).

In stable agricultural and herding societies, the old are believed to receive the best and most consistent treatment. As we have seen, in industrialized societies, retirement from employment can strip the aging adult of his or her primary role and may lead to a feeling of loss and reduced self-esteem. In stable preindustrial societies, however, retirement from the primary economic role becomes a matter of giving up one set of responsibilities for another. Grandparents are often responsible for child care, and their presence allows women to gather or farm.

Among the Hopi, where the economy is based on herding and farming, old men who no longer can follow the flocks or work in the fields card wool, spin, knit, and make sandals. Old women care for children, mind the house, grind corn, make clay pots and bowls, and weave baskets (Simmons, 1945). Thus, there is no retirement in the American sense of the word. Each person who is not bedridden has a vital role to play.

In either hunting-gathering or agricultural societies, the elderly are often active in political or religious roles. It has been suggested that the most important con-

In a stable agricultural and herding society, like that of the Hopi, older adults play vital roles as long as they are not bedridden.

tribution to the prestige of the old in traditional societies is their association with religious rites and beliefs (Gutmann, 1980). The old of many tribes are seen as witches or wizards—and for good reason. Where disease and accident drastically shorten life expectancy, survival into old age indicates favor from the gods, supernatural power, or keen intelligence. For example, among the Kagwahiv in the Amazonian areas of Brazil, the old are the objects of awe, respected for this knowledge and for the spiritual strength seen as necessary for a long life. They are believed to have supernatural power and so much spiritual strength that they can safely violate food taboos (Gutmann, 1980).

Because their extreme old age brings them near to death, the old may be seen as close to the ancestors and perhaps so full of power that their very words can change the world (Goody, 1976). The curses of the old are to be avoided; and their blessings, to be courted. When the old hold ritual power in a society, they are likely to be high in self-esteem. Such a connection appeared in a study of Apache groups in the southwestern United States (Boyer et al., 1965). Highly traditional Apache men past the age of 50, who acted as shamans, or medicine men, and thus had special access to spiritual powers, were higher in ego strength than other Apaches.

In one sense, the words of the old in preliterate cultures *can* change the world. In a society without writing, the old are the only repository of information, and they serve as the tribal memory. It has been said that "their memories are other people's culture" (Goody, 1976, p. 128). The old know the "right way" of doing things. Their knowledge of story, myth, and legend makes them entertainers as well as historians, resolvers of conflict as well as teachers, administrators as well as councillors. Although it has been proposed that books strip the old of their informational role, a recent cross-cultural study of 95 societies (Silverman and Maxwell, 1983) indicates that the elderly continue to play an important role as a relevant source of community information until modernization is quite advanced. In this study, it was social rigidity rather than community isolation that supported the old in information-related roles. The researchers speculate that in a rigid society, the elderly provide the least threatening channel for new information. Informational roles were positively related to the social esteem enjoyed by the old in various societies, but elderly men were held in higher esteem and accorded more deference than elderly women. This relationship can be traced to the fact that one aspect of social rigidity is restrictions on the movement or behavior of women.

Another important influence on the status of the old is their control of material resources. In agricultural or herding societies, ownership of lands or flocks allows older adults to retain power after they no longer can labor in the fields. If property is handed over to a son or daughter at the time of marriage, control may be kept by the parent, or the parent may retain certain rights such as food, shelter, or a portion of the harvest. The parents may reside in the same household or in a separate house on the same land. Where there are several children, the one who stays with the parents generally receives the largest inheritance (Goody, 1976).

When older adults in agricultural societies have no living children, as is the case for about one out of every five adults, they may require community support, In some societies, the indigent old may be allowed to glean in the fields after the harvest, or younger adults may give them food, clothing, or other goods, either as a religious duty or to gain community prestige (Goody, 1976).

Although most researchers agree that the status of the elderly is high in traditional societies, there is some dispute as to their actual treatment. After examining various studies, Gordon Finley (1982) has pointed out that anthropologists have not always distinguished among professed attitudes toward the old, the status of the old in society, and their actual treatment. Most researchers generally have not distinguished between the treatment accorded the young-old and the feeble members of a traditional society. However, anthropologists tend to agree that when a traditional society begins to modernize, the status of the aged usually declines.

THE EFFECT OF INDUSTRIALIZATION

As members of modern societies have carried technology into remote societies and electronic media have blanketed the globe with radio and television broadcasts, few cultures have escaped some effect of industrialization. Some formerly traditional societies have become highly developed whereas others are just beginning to feel the effects of production lines, television, and computer chips. According to Donald Cowgill (1974), as modernization transforms a society, most aspects of life are affected, and traditional outlooks and values may crumble under the impact of plentiful power, scientific technology, highly segmented economic roles, and an emphasis on efficiency and progress.

These changes affect the position of the elderly in several ways, and, in Cowgill's view, modern medicine, technologically based economies, urbanization, and widespread literacy combine to lower the status of the old. First, modern medicine radically changes life expectancy. As infant and child mortality decline, but fertility remains high, the population explodes. Population growth generally outstrips any increased productivity, and the level of poverty rises. Although the proportion of older people in the society at first declines, over the course of a generation the presence of elderly adults becomes common. Instead of a handful of elderly to venerate, most adults have parents who live into old age, as well as a large family of children to support. Once fertility is controlled, the proportion of elderly expands enormously, as it has done in most developed countries (Fig. 15.1). Unless society develops the concept of retirement, there will be competition between the generations for available jobs. The introduction of retirement removes the old from the job market, but in the process it lowers their status.

As society shifts under the pressure of technology, the family ceases to be the basic economic unit. Instead of working on the family farm, young people get jobs making steel or assembling computers. Employment gives the young a source of power that is not under the control of the traditional community and strikes at the authority of older adults (Gutmann, 1980). At the same time, the occupational skills of older adults become obsolete, and they are forced into low-paying jobs or retirement. The culture becomes youth-oriented, and the old are seen as having nothing of value to contribute.

Young people are attracted to cities because the land no longer can support the rural population, and urban areas hold the promise of economic advancement.

	More Developed Countries		Less Developed Countries	
	1965	2000	1965	2000
Birth rate (births per 1000)	18.6	17.5	40.6	27.4
Death rate (deaths per 1000)	9.1	8.1	16.1	7.6
Growth rate (percent)	1.0	0.8	2.4	2.0
Age structure (percent)				
Younger than 15	26.8	24.9	41.4	35.2
15–64	63.5	63.7	55.3	60.3
65 and older	9.6	11.4	3.3	4.6
Average age (years)	33.0	35.0	23.0	27.0
Dependency ratio (number of dependents per 100 workers)	59.0	57.0	81.0	66.0
Youth (<15)	44.0	39.0	75.0	58.0
Aged (>64)	15.0	18.0	6.0	8.0
Life expectancy (years)	70.4	73.2	49.6	65.3
Children born (number)	2.7	2.5	5.6	3.5
Number surviving to age 20	2.6	2.4	4.6	3.3

FIGURE 15.1 Projected changes in world population, 1965–2000.
Source: Philip M. Hauser, 1976, pp. 69, 71.

With the departure of the young, the extended family breaks up. Although the extended family may not have been a residential unit, its function as an economic and social unit gave the old some control over the young and ensured support for the elderly who were unable to farm or herd.

Finally, literacy and the introduction of mass media provide the society with reliable sources of information. Now it is the young who have the valued information, and as David Gutmann (1980) has suggested, the realization that other systems exist, systems with different ideas of good and bad, possible and impossible, holy and impure, destroys the mythic status of cultural ideas. The cultural justification for the older generation's prestige as well as the power that depended on their retention and passing on of traditional knowledge is lost. As we have seen, however, mass media may not affect the status of the old until modernization is well advanced.

Studies by anthropologists have not consistently confirmed Cowgill's predictions. In some societies, the status of the old has declined with modernization, just as Cowgill predicted. In other societies, the status of the old appears to have been nearly as precarious under the traditional culture as it is with modernization. And in still other societies, the old appear to have weathered the transition to a modern society with little loss of status.

Modernization in rural western Ireland followed the course predicted by Cowgill. Farms became unproductive, and the young emigrated as fast as they could. By 1975, more than 20 percent of the population in Ballybran was older than 65. Traditionally, aged parents had wielded economic power through their ownership of the land and had been venerated for their knowledge of the ancient Celtic tradition. Today, according to anthropologist Nancy Scheper-Hughes (1983), younger adults scorn the Celtic language. They view the old with pity and contempt and often ridicule them. Many older adults are childless or left alone by emigrating children.

Irish society always had been strongly patriarchal, and it is the men who have suffered the most from the breakdown of traditional culture. Fathers, whose relationship with their children has been based on authority, duty, and respect, frequently find themselves in old-age homes, nursing homes, or mental institutions. Because the relationship between mothers and children has been based on affection, adult children are likely to feel responsible for their mothers. As the extended family has deteriorated, the young no longer feel any responsibility for distant kin, and so most of the unmarried elderly who no longer can support themselves with the aid of government pensions and grants are institutionalized.

Indian culture demands respect for the aged, but elderly Indians often felt that they lacked attention and esteem. In India, the traditional family consisted of several nuclear units living in a common household and holding all property in common. The eldest male was supposed to be the family head, to exercise full authority, and to receive respect and obedience from all younger members. However, old age in the Hindu life cycle is supposed to be a time of withdrawal from family and business affairs to concentrate on spiritual development. As a result, there was a gradual, but voluntary, relinquishment of family authority to middle-aged sons when the father reached his sixties and his grandchildren reached adolescence (Vatuk, 1980).

Several nuclear units lived together in the traditional Indian family, providing an economic security for older adults that may be threatened by modernization.

In several agricultural communities in India that had little contact with industry or technology, fewer than a third of the men past 65 still exercised family authority (Harlan, 1968). Elderly men who retained a voice in village affairs tended to be those with education and high socioeconomic status, factors that are connected with caste and land ownership. The old people in these villages rarely lived alone, but they seemed insecure and dissatisfied with their situation. Those who were ill or widowed were often treated badly. Conflict between widows and their daughters-in-law was frequent and often resulted in the humiliation of the widow. Although the culture demanded respect for the aged, the ideal bore little resemblance to community practices, practices that the researcher concluded were inherent in traditional Indian village life.

Later research in a suburb of Rayapur, an agricultural village that had been absorbed by the urban sprawl of New Delhi, indicated that modernization had not destroyed the extended family (Vatuk, 1980). None of the older Indians in the village lived by themselves, and most lived in three- or four-generation households. Among these relatively affluent Indians, the physical needs of the elderly were met, but older individuals felt that their emotional and social needs were often neglected. Despite the cultural ideal of withdrawal, both women and men were highly involved in the social life of family and village. Women continued to be involved in child care, shopping, finances, and religious activity whereas men spent their time in travel on family business, visiting, and lengthy card games.

Among Hindu families in Nepal, the extended family also has survived modernization, but living in the same household with their married sons no longer assures the economic security of the elderly (Goldstein, Schuler, and Ross, 1983). The shift from farming to salaried employment in the city of Kathmandu was accompanied by unemployment, low wages, and inflation. With the agricultural family unit no longer the basis of the economy, power passed from the landholding parent to the employed son, removing any vestige of parental control. In addition to making sons employable, education has given them new values and attitudes, fostering individualism, independence, secularism, and democracy in place of obedience, respect, and deference. Low wages make it difficult for sons to support their families.

Without exception, the elderly men and women said it was essential for old people to have their own income. One woman who lived with her married son summed up the general attitude by saying, "These days money is love" (Goldstein, Schuler, and Ross, 1983, p. 716); and a 70-year-old man said, "In our society . . . sons are with you if you have property. If not, parents are left as fleas leave a dead dog" (p. 721). In a majority of households with older adults, the elderly were responsible for all or most of the household expenses, with the money coming from renting out rooms, leasing farm land, government pensions, or savings. The situation is likely to worsen, for fewer of today's employed adults will be property owners in their old age. Older adults in traditional Hindu villages were economically secure, but full of emotional and psychological insecurity. Modernization appears to be taking away their economic security as well.

In American Samoa, modernization does not seem to have affected the status of the old. Recent studies (Holmes and Rhoads, 1983) indicate that elderly men and women retain traditional household roles and that most live in extended families. Although Samoans have begun to accept a chronological definition of old age, they do not retire but switch to less strenuous jobs. Traditionally, the elderly have been responsible for tedious but important jobs, such as braiding coconut twine and weaving, on the grounds that they have more patience than the young. When interviewed, the old said that they were obeyed and respected by the young, and researchers could see no sign that their status was threatened. The only dark cloud was the high migration rate in some areas, which could affect the future position of the elderly by drastically reducing the proportion of young people.

The prediction that modernization destroys the position of the old does not always come true. Some researchers believe that when the status of the old does decline under the impact of industrialization, the decline is only temporary. Once a society reaches the highest level of modernization, the status of the old begins to improve (Finley, 1982). According to Erdan Palmore (1976a), as the importance of agricultural labor diminishes, unemployment and retirement rise among older adults, probably helping to account for the decline in their status. As societies develop, change is rapid: life expectancy is extended, productivity increases, incomes rise, educational levels climb, and shifts from rural to urban settings accelerate. These rapid rates of change depress the status of the old in comparison with the young.

When modernization is complete, the rate of change slows, and the relative position of the old begins to rise. Palmore believes that the United States reached this point about 1967, and since then the status of the old has been improving in this country, in good part as a result of social programs. However, Palmore does not predict that older adults will regain a position of high status in relation to the rest of society. Instead, he expects society to approach a state of equality, in which the status of young and old may become virtually equal.

CHINA AND HONG KONG: TWO PATHS FOR THE ELDERLY

The traditional Chinese ideal of filial piety demands respect and deference for the old. Until 1949, the government endorsed the practice of ancestor worship, which further bolstered the position of the old with the prospect of power from beyond the grave. Among traditional Chinese, sex was valued primarily for its procreative function, and the parent-child relationship was more important than the relationship between wife and husband. Family ties were sustained, and parents expected to live out their days with a married son. (A daughter's responsibilities to provide care for her parents ended when she married and joined her husband's household in another village.) To be childless in traditional China could mean an old age spent as a beggar or a vagrant (Davis-Friedmann, 1983).

However, the Confucian ideal of the venerated elderly surrounded by a large clan of married children and grandchildren was probably limited to the well-to-do, who made up no more than 20 percent of society (Ikels, 1980). Mortality was high, and many sons migrated to escape poverty. In city and countryside alike, most old people continued to work as long as they were able in order to supplement the aid they received from

their children or—in the city—from charity.

Over the past 35 years, the Chinese in Hong Kong and those in mainland China have lived in two very different societies, one capitalistic and one communistic. The position of the old has changed in both societies, but not always in the manner we would expect.

Hong Kong is densely populated and highly industrialized. The proportion of elderly has more than tripled, and one out of ten Hong Kong residents is past the age of 60. Yet in 1981, only 13.6 percent of families included a third generation, and nearly 25 percent of older adults either lived alone or with other older people (Chow, 1983). The extended family has begun to break up, taking the modified form that characterizes American society. Most adult children establish their own households either on marriage or when their first child is born. However, the move is often just around the corner, and the two households frequently share meals. The family provides major economic support for almost 50 percent of the elderly (Chow, 1983). Because of the breakup of the kin network, however, there is no community pressure to intervene when aged parents

ETHNIC DIFFERENCES

Membership in an ethnic group within a society also imposes cultural expectations that affect the way individuals experience the life cycle, expectations that may differ from those of the larger culture. As a result, conclusions about the are neglected, and the problem is worsened by forced relocation policies that separate families (Ikels, 1980). There are no pensions, and about 36 percent of older adults rely on government assistance, which is available to those 70 or older; 25 percent are employed (Chow, 1983).

As predicted, modernization has been followed by a decline in the position of the elderly. Adherence to the virtue of filial piety is declining. More than 90 percent of Hong Kong adults told interviewers that although the family has a responsibility toward its older members, the government is responsible for seeing that the old have adequate incomes (Chow, 1983). Many elderly feel unwanted, and the demand for institutional care is growing.

Across the water, in the People's Republic of China, the fate of the elderly has been different. Perhaps unintentionally, government policies have improved the economic security of old people and helped to maintain them in a favorable position, according to Deborah Davis-Freidmann (1983), who interviewed emigrants to Hong Kong and did field work in China. Although early Party proclamations seemed to strike at the position of the old, in practice the elderly have retained much of their former status. The Party certainly subordinates the family to the state, but its need to lessen welfare burdens and reduce the demand for new housing has led it to encourage multigenerational families.

In rural China, agriculture continues to rely on manual labor, and the family is still the unit of production. The multigenerational family thrives, and the traditional pattern of living with a son is firmly established. Childless adults or those who have only daughters may live alone, but they stay within the community and are supported by the collective, which guarantees them food, fuel, clothing, burial fees, housing, and medical care, but at a subsistence level. All older adults continue to work as long as they are able, either in the fields or at home. Older adults often release the young for field work by maintaining the household; and while staying home, they are able to raise pigs, which are sold for cash.

In traditional China, there were few older adults in the city. Today urban elderly fare better than their rural counterparts, for urban incomes are much higher, and city dwellers have superior medical care, the best consumer goods, and cheap transportation. Since 1978, liberalized pensions have provided from 60 to 75 percent of the last wage earned, depending on the number of years worked. The policy of allowing a retiring worker to designate which child will assume his

course of adult development reached on the basis of studies with middle-class groups, primarily drawn from the majority culture, may not provide an adequate understanding of development within ethnic groups. An **ethnic group** may be distinguished by race, religion, or national identity. It has its own attitudes, traditions, values, and beliefs, as well as its own expectations about sex roles, child

CHINA AND HONG KONG (*Continued*)

or her job gives adults who are nearing retirement a measure of family power. Older adults live with unmarried children, with a married son, or occasionally with a married daughter in crowded apartments. Official policy is to provide two rooms for a minimum of four adults. The old do the household work and care for young children while the parents work. The sharpest change from rural life is the urban practice of sometimes choosing to live with a daughter. Modernization has had an unexpected effect on the parent-daughter relationship, making it closer and more enduring than it was in traditional China.

The effect of modernization in the People's Republic indicates that, even in its initial stages, industrialization need not weaken the position of older adults. Although the Party originally opposed filial piety, traditional family values have survived, in large part because scarcities have made the multigenerational family necessary to the state.

In the People's Republic of China, scarcities have led to a persistence of the three-generation family, in which grandparents do household chores and care for young children while parents work.

rearing, the family, and aging. Membership in an ethnic group may affect self-concept, self-esteem, and life-style. Because of their small representation in the power structure of the larger society, some ethnic groups are also considered **minorities**, a term that refers to any group excluded from full participation in society because of physical or cultural characteristics (Wirth, 1945). Although members of some white ethnic groups may face subtle discrimination, their position differs considerably from that of other minorities.

AGING AND THE FAMILY IN WHITE ETHNIC GROUPS

The dominant American culture is basically a white Anglo-Saxon Protestant (WASP) culture that was originally English, but that came to include Scottish, Scotch-Irish, Welsh, and other northern European groups that were assimilated by the majority culture. At the beginning of this century, it was generally assumed that American society was a "melting pot," that immigrants would adapt themselves to the majority culture, and that a single "American" culture would prevail. By 1940, it became clear that this melting of cultures had not taken place, primarily because immigrants tended to cluster in specific regions, allowing them to pass on their culture to new generations (Gelfand, 1982). The fact that full assimilation may not occur for centuries (if ever) can be seen in Canada, where descendants of French immigrants have retained their language, rejected the idea of assimilation, and proposed independence from English-speaking areas. The Basques of Spain have similarly refused to melt into the majority culture.

Since the eighteenth century, as each ethnic group arrived in great numbers, it faced prejudice and discrimination. Most immigrants arrived with limited skills, little money, and less English. Even a highly skilled immigrant who spoke no English generally discovered that only low-paying jobs were available. But, with time, most white ethnic groups were assimilated to the extent that they could thrive in American society, and social assimilation generally followed economic success. Whether a group was fully assimilated, to the extent that members no longer identified with their culture of origin, depended in good part on whether they intermarried with the dominant group (Gelfand, 1982).

An ethnic community that establishes itself within American society may be different in many ways from the culture of origin. The transplanted group generally tends to preserve customs and values that existed at the time they left, so that changes in the "old country" are not reflected in the ethnic subculture. In addition, contact with American society may change the transplanted culture in other ways. Yet the community may remain distinctive from the larger society despite its move into the middle class, a relocation from the city to the suburbs, and a good deal of intermarriage. By looking at a group of Italian-Americans studied by Colleen Johnson (1983), we can see how cultural values are passed on within an ethnic group.

Among these Italian-Americans in the Syracuse, New York, area, for example, nearly all families had come from southern Italy. In this region of Italy, the family is paramount, and members are expected to subjugate their own interests to the good of the family, sacrifice for the family, avoid bringing any shame on the family, respect their parents, and support male authority. When they arrived in the United States, immigrants clustered together, and because entire families did not always emigrate together, it became customary to create substitute kin out of other immigrants.

More than half of the elderly members of the Syracuse Italian-American community had been born in Italy. Among these older Italians, 70 percent had less than 8 years of schooling and 20 percent were illiterate. Nearly all the men had retired from blue-collar jobs. The majority of their middle-aged offspring had graduated from high school, and more than 40 percent were in white-collar occupations. Intermarriage was high among the second generation, with half of the middle-aged adults married to non-Italians. Friendships and occupational relationships also included non-Italians, but ethnic cohesiveness was maintained by living nearby, and only a third of the middle-aged had moved out of the area.

The family of these Italian-Americans was distinctive in several ways. Relationships among family members were interdependent, a factor that seemed to create intimacy, satisfy needs, and strengthen group allegiance. Authority and power were vested in old as compared with young and males as compared with females. This hierarchy was supported by the strong sense of respect. Authority was used to enforce social conformity to family goals, which often conflicted with the need to pursue personal interests, an American value that was being absorbed by younger family members. Emotions were expressed fully, and when conflicts arose, this freedom to vent feelings tended to keep behavior in line with family goals.

How were cultural values passed on? Supervision of children was strict, discipline was swift, and physical punishment was common. Duty and service to the family were stressed. Respect was considered part of a family role; it did not have to be earned. Parents were clearly superior to children and demanded obedience. Parents also stressed the sacrifices they had made to provide for the family until the values of respect, altruism, and self-sacrifice were thoroughly engrained in their children. These practices gave older Italians power and prestige.

Compared with a control group of Protestant non-Italians, older Italian-Americans clearly had an elevated position within the family. Family interaction was virtually nonstop: 76 percent of the elderly had contact with their children daily; 39 percent saw a grandchild daily, and 89 percent saw one weekly; 61 percent saw a sibling weekly; and 66 percent saw other relatives weekly. The effect of intermarriage on family values becomes clear when family interaction of middle-aged children who married within the Italian community family is compared with those who married non-Italians (Fig. 15.2). Marrying a non-Italian diminished social involvement with aging parents but appeared to have little effect on family values.

The centrality of the family means that older Italians in Syracuse do not feel a deep loss of roles. Women continue their maternal and domestic roles and, because family has always taken precedence over employment, men seem to regard retirement as an opportunity to intensify their involvement with the family.

Respect for the elderly seems thoroughly engrained among children and grandchildren, and the tradition of interdependence and help ensures continuity of social support in old age. However, over the years, American values have begun to creep into the community, affecting even the elderly. For example, almost half of the older Italians said they expected only companionship, not support, from their children, and more than three fourths who were not living with a relative said

	In-married Italians (*n* = 76)	Out-married Italians (*n* = 98)	Protestant non-Italians (*n* = 56)
Usually incorporate parents in leisure activities	36%	18%	7%
Unqualified rejection of nursing home	44	41	6
High amount of aid to parents	38	23	15

FIGURE 15.2   Family centrality of middle-aged children (percent).

Marrying a non-Italian increased the tendency to exclude parents from leisure activities, but had little effect on family values.

Source: C. L. Johnson, 1983, p. 97.

they would not consider moving in with a child. Those who voiced such feelings, however, seemed certain that they would never be forgotten by their well-reared children.

Whether third-generation grandchildren will form as cohesive a group as the second-generation parents is unknown. For this group, proximity seems to outweigh most of the disintegrating effects of intermarriage and ensures the retention of ethnic identity. It seems probable that as long as intense interaction and interdependence continue, family values will be passed on, and older individuals will retain their status.

ETHNIC MINORITIES

Most ethnic minorities are visible and identifiable by skin color or facial features. They confront barriers in almost every area of life: housing, employment, education, medical care, recreation, clubs, and churches. Discriminated against since their first contacts outside the family, members of minority groups may become self-conscious or uncertain about their own status, always wondering whether the news that an apartment is already rented, a job is already filled, a promotion has gone to a co-worker, or a loan application has been turned down is the result of chance, fair application of standards, or their minority status (Moriwaki and Kobata, 1983).

In the face of discrimination, the minority family has had to develop special strengths. Perhaps a look at several different minority family systems will give us a clearer understanding of how the life cycle may be experienced in minority groups. We will then be able to consider whether being a minority group member places an additional burden on the aged.

Aging and the Black Family
Black history in the United States has been dominated by the experience of slavery and afterwards by segregation. From West Africa, black slaves brought the values of cooperation, interdependence, and the collective rather than the indi-

vidual good (Tate, 1983). Under slavery, blacks were not permitted to marry, and so common-law marriage was customary. The family system that developed tended to de-emphasize legal marriage, tolerate premarital sexuality, and accept illegitimate births (Ladner, 1971).

Black cooperation and interdependence led to the development of strong kinship bonds, and families often included extra relatives—both adults and children—and sometimes unrelated children. Today many families rear their adolescent daughter's child. In older families where husband and wife are both present, a relative younger than 18 is present in 22 percent, and in families headed by older women, the proportion rises to 40 percent (Hill, 1981).

Economic and social pressures have continued to shape the black family. By 1970, only 6.4 percent of black families included three or more generations (McQueen, 1979). Although both parents were present in a majority of black families, the proportion of families headed by women was growing, up from 20.7 percent in 1960 to 30.6 percent in 1970 (Cummings, 1983). Since that time the trend has continued, with 46.5 percent of black families headed by a woman in 1980 (Fig. 15.3). The practice threatens to increase the economic burden of black families because female-headed families are twice as likely as two-parent families to be poor.

One reason for the growth in female-headed families is the dismal economic prospects of the black male. Only 57.2 percent of black men (including those who were retired or in school) had jobs in mid-1983 (down from 73.7 percent in 1965), compared with 72 percent of white men (down from 77.9 percent in 1965) (Cummings, 1983). The jobless rate is highest among the youngest black men.

When an unmarried black woman becomes pregnant, marriage to an unemployed man only increases the immediate economic burden she faces. Parents have become less likely to pressure their adolescent daughters into marriage, and today 55 percent of all black babies are born to unmarried mothers (Cummings, 1983). Divorce also increases the number of female-headed households. When black couples marry, they are more likely to divorce than any other group, and the gap between them and other groups is increasing. The high—and it is getting

	1970	1982
Married couple or male-headed households	69.4%	53.5%
Female-headed households	30.6%	46.5%
Divorced	17.0%	23.0%
Spouse absent	50.0%	28.0%
Widowed	16.0%	8.0%
Never married	18.0%	41.0%

FIGURE 15.3 The changing black family (with children younger than 18).

In little more than a decade, the proportion of female-headed black families with young children increased by more than 50 percent. The largest rise was in households headed by unmarried women.

Source: U.S. Census Bureau as reported by J. Cummings, "Breakup of Black Family Imperils Gains of Decades," *The New York Times*, November 20, 1983, p. A56.

The custom of absorbing children into grandparents' families decreases the proportion of older black adults who live alone and strengthens the bonds between young and old.

higher—divorce rate among black couples is believed to be due to poor economic circumstances, stress on couples who move up into the middle class, racism, and the tendency for black women to marry men with less education than they have (Rule, 1982).

The custom of absorbing children into older families affects the experience of aging by decreasing the proportion of elderly adults who live alone. It also strengthens the bonds between young and old. However, research has generally indicated that members of the middle generation, black adult children, have no more contact with their parents than do white adult children. In a study of inner-city adults, elderly black adults were no more likely than whites to see their children, hear from them, receive help from them, or feel close to them (Cantor, 1979). The extended family does provide fundamental support and guidance for the old, and older black individuals are more likely than whites to have contact with kin outside their original nuclear family, such as nieces and nephews or cousins. Such practices are likely to decrease any feelings of loneliness or isolation among older blacks (Tate, 1983).

Given the economic and social discrimination they face, blacks seem hopeful and optimistic. When black and white adults were asked about their eventual death, middle-aged and elderly blacks said they expected to live longer than did whites. What is more, they also *wanted* to live longer (Kalish and Reynolds, 1976). The comparatively poor health and short life expectancy of blacks make such replies mystifying to researchers although one gerontologist (Tate, 1983) has suggested that age is less of a stigma among blacks than among whites and that older adults are held in higher esteem among the black community. Another factor that might influence attitudes is the availability of role models. As we saw in Chapter 3, when blacks live past the age of 75, they tend to be in better health and to live longer than do whites, a phenomenon that has been attributed either to genetic factors or to the probability that it is only the hardiest blacks who manage to survive into late old age.

Aging and the Mexican-American Family

The nearly 15 million Hispanic Americans are a widely varied group, and each subgroup has distinctive cultural elements (U.S. Bureau of the Census, 1982). If present trends continue, Americans of Hispanic ancestry will soon become the largest ethnic minority in the United States (Maldonado, 1978). About 65 percent are Mexican-Americans, or Chicanos, who make up the largest subgroup; the rest are mostly Cuban or Puerto Rican although many Hispanics have come from other Central or South American countries. Mexican-American culture is a fusion of Spanish and Indian heritage whereas Puerto Rican culture is a fusion of African, Taino Indian, Corsican, and Spanish elements (Garcia-Preto, 1982). The majority of Mexican-Americans are either first- or second-generation, and their numbers may be much greater than official statistics indicate because of the large number of illegal Mexican immigrants.

In Mexican-American culture, children validate a marriage, and romantic love between husband and wife is secondary to the preservation of marriage and the family. The prevalence of large families, the generally late departure of children from the home, and the close relationship between most parents and adult children tend to prolong the period of parenthood and emphasize parental functions (Falicov, 1982).

In addition to the centrality of the family, Mexican-American culture traditionally has stressed male leadership, mutual aid within the family, respect for age, and the extended family. These characteristics have led to a close relationship between family membership and identity, to male dominance, to the belief that the needs of the family unit are more important than the needs of any one member, to the expectation that children will care for their aging parents, to an increase in status with age, and to multigenerational families, in which parents, married sons, and their families make up the household. In practice, as David Maldonado (1979) has pointed out, many of the cultural values have been impossible to implement. As the family became urban instead of rural, the extended family began to disappear, and it became increasingly difficult for children to provide for their elderly parents. Older men, who had been valued for their expert agricultural skills, and older women, who had been valued for their continued assistance in childrearing, began to lose their functional roles and some of their traditional au-

The move to urban areas is changing the experience of aging among Mexican American families by destroying the extended family. In response, some of the elderly have developed their own organizations that may help maintain their status and pride.

thority. However, the importance of the extended nuclear family continues, as do the expectation for mutual aid and respect for the elderly.

These changes may be making aging more difficult for Mexican-Americans than it was for their parents. Mexican-Americans tend to have relatively few social contacts outside the extended kin network (Bengston and Morgan, 1983). Although their contacts with kin are extremely high, their expectations may be even higher. As a result, the Mexican-American elderly are more likely than the elderly of other groups to be dissatisfied with the frequency of their children's and grandchildren's visits (Bengston and Morgan, 1983). Studies indicate that older couples in rural areas have significantly higher levels of morale and kin interaction than city dwellers and that only the urban elderly who manage to substitute interaction with neighbors for family contacts have high levels of morale (Becerra, 1983).

The expectation of being supported in old age may be changing, as Rosina Becerra (1983) found in a review of existing studies. More than a decade ago, 95 percent of elderly Mexican-Americans in the Denver area expected their relatives to care for them, but in a later study, less than 35 percent expected to move in with their adult children if they became unable to care for themselves. Even the belief that children have the responsibility for their aged parents appears to have declined among city dwellers, with 61 percent of the adults in a Southern California study saying that the young had no responsibility to care for the old. The results of a Texas study indicate that youth, urban residence, higher socioeconomic status, and third-generational status are related to such beliefs.

In at least one area, elderly Mexican-Americans have responded to the destruction of the extended family by developing their own subculture. In East Los Angeles, older individuals have formed their own voluntary organizations, in which they can function in terms of their previous identities, demonstrating their social competence and maintaining their status and pride (Cuellar, 1978). Perhaps such clubs can substitute for the loss of traditional roles that may follow the erosion of cultural values and traditions.

Aging and the American Indian Family

Information about Native Americans—American Indians, Aleuts, and Eskimos—is sparse, and much is believed to be inaccurate. Nearly a million and a half Native Americans were reported in the 1980 census (U.S. Bureau of the Census, 1981). Government figures are unreliable because census takers are unable to speak various Indian languages; figures from the Bureau of Indian Affairs apply only to Indians eligible for services; and, from one study to the next, the criteria for establishing that a person is an Indian change. Information about elderly Indians is even scarcer, and we have no reliable estimates as to their number (Block, 1979).

Among American Indians, there are more than 400 different tribal groups, speaking more than 250 languages (Edwards, 1983). Today they form four different major groups: reservation Indians, rural Indians, migrant Indians, and urban Indians. Each group has a different life-style that interacts with particular tribal values, so that generalizations about American Indians as a single group are generally misleading (Bloc, 1979). The fruit of the American Indians' bitter history since Europeans settled in what is now the United States has been the shortest life expectancy of any group (44 years), the poorest health, and the least money.

Aging in American Indian societies generally followed the pattern described in the section on traditional societies. Old age was defined in functional terms, and, in most tribes, the old were respected and honored. Older individuals often filled political roles, acting as councillors or leaders. People worked as long as they were able, and grandparents generally cared for the children.

As economic and social changes have transformed Indian societies, the old have lost their position of esteem in some tribes. Where they have been able to make economic or cultural contributions, older individuals have managed to retain their former position. For example, among the rural Oto-Missouri and Iowa, two former agricultural, bison-hunting Plains Indian tribes, roles within the extended kin network and at the tribal level give many of the old both power and prestige (Schweitzer, 1983). The old are in demand at the tribal level as ritual specialists, as religious specialists in the Native American church, as master of ceremonies at various tribal dances and encampments, and as repositories of language and tradition. This position has been strengthened as Indians who had earlier rejected the traditional ways have been seeking to reestablish them. Speaking of her husband, a woman in her late seventies said:

People come to him and ask him things—how to do things in the old way. [In tribal government] there is a lot of paper work and we give that to the educated ones. . . . But for lots of other things people come to the old people to find out how to do things [Schweitzer, 1983, p. 173].

Within the family, older Oto-Missouri and Iowa Indians continue to be active in childrearing, and the traditional close grandparent-grandchild relationship is still strong. According to the National Indian Council on Aging, 26 percent of all Indian elderly care for at least one grandchild (Edwards, 1983). When the old have landholdings or receive lease money, they also wield economic power. Some families follow an extended nuclear family pattern in which several related households are located close together. A younger family member often lives with an aged couple. The extended kin network provides additional support for the old. There has been some weakening of kinship ties because of migration, but the young who leave sometimes return to be near aging relatives or come back years later to spend their old age within the tribal community.

Unemployment is high among nonreservation Indians. Before the recession of 1974 began, general unemployment was fairly low, but 25 percent of Oklahoma Indians were jobless, and 32 percent had incomes below the poverty level. Their consistently precarious economic situation has led to a reliance on those among the elderly who have retirement benefits, Social Security, or veterans' pensions. In some cases, these benefits are the only steady source of income within an extended kin group. Older Indians thus have retained their role of caring for the young, but with cash instead of—or in addition to—their traditional role of childrearing (Williams, 1980). It has been estimated that 60 percent of older Indians support other family members (Edwards, 1983).

Nonreservation Indians in Oklahoma include many tribes, such as the Cherokee, Choctaw, Creek, Chickasaw, and Seminole nations. Among these Indians—whether urban or rural, age continues to be defined in functional terms, and there is no segregation of the elderly. The traditional view that the elderly are respected advisers lingers, but many Indians say that lack of respect is growing, primarily because education in white schools, the adoption of Christianity, and the influence of white values have led to a conflict between the generations. The old have given up their leadership role but continue to be consulted about cultural traditions. However, many of the older nonreservation Indians lack the knowledge sought by the young about ceremonies and old life-styles, and this inability to respond places some of the elderly under stress and tends to make them defensive. It has been suggested that the gap between the idealized view of the aged and their inability to live up to that view has contributed to their diminished respect (Williams, 1980).

In some ways, Oklahoma Indians are better off than groups in other parts of the country. Their health is better, for 10.65 percent are past the age of 62, compared with 7.27 percent of the entire American Indian population (Williams, 1980). Because a majority of elderly Indians live on reservations, serious illness creates additional stress. Few reservations have adequate medical facilities or nursing homes, so the need for institutionalization isolates the aged Indian and ruptures the kinship network, for few kin can afford to make the lengthy trips required for a visit (Block, 1979). The emotional shock of sudden isolation from tribal members combined with an immersion into the dominant culture often worsens health problems. An Indian who has aged ''successfully'' within his or her own culture may be unable to survive without the customary cultural support.

The Question of Double Jeopardy

The effect of minority status on the aging process is not entirely clear and has been strenuously debated by gerontologists. One popular view is that minority status and age combine to place an individual in **double jeopardy**. According to the reasoning behind this view, older adults fo m a highly visible group that is often stereotyped and discriminated against on the basis of age, which makes them a minority. If they also belong to an ethnic group, they receive a double dose of discrimination. Age and minority status are assumed to interact, so that aging is more negative for minorities than for whites, and older minority group members will show more psychological stress than older whites (Markides, 1983).

Other researchers (Kent, 1971) have objected to this view on the grounds that the experience of aging is so powerful that all old people face similar problems. Because the elderly encounter the same biological changes and face economic and social discrimination no matter what their ethnic background, the groups become more alike. Age is seen as a leveler that diminishes the differences among ethnic groups although it does not eradicate them.

No one denies that differences exist. As a group, minority elderly have less education, are poorer, live in worse housing, are less healthy, and die sooner than elderly whites. They tend to perceive themselves as ''old'' at earlier ages than members of other groups (Markides, 1983). However, young and middle-aged minorities are also disadvantaged in comparison with young and middle-aged whites. If double jeopardy is real, suggest James Dowd and Vern Bengston (1978), then the quality of life in old age will be worse than in earlier stages of the life cycle and the disparity between minority and white elderly will be greater than that between younger members of minority and white groups.

In an attempt to test the double-jeopardy hypothesis, Dowd and Bengston studied Mexican-American, black, and white adults between the ages of 45 and 74, looking at group differences in income, health, life satisfaction, and social interaction. The findings were mixed (Bengston and Morgan, 1983). In terms of both income and health, minority aged seemed to suffer double jeopardy. The existing income gap between middle-aged whites and minorities widened, for black income declined 55 percent among adults past 65, Mexican-American income declined 62 percent, and white income declined 36 percent. Even when researchers corrected for socioeconomic status, sex, and health differences among the groups, the income gap was significantly larger in old age than it was in middle age. Self-ratings of health showed a similar pattern, with black reports of "poor" or "very poor" health increasing 13 percent from middle to old age, Mexican-American estimates increasing 6 percent, and white estimates increasing only 2 percent.

When life satisfaction was considered, the picture was somewhat different. Elderly Mexican-Americans' satisfaction was lower in comparison to the other groups than it was among the middle-aged, supporting the double-jeopardy hypothesis; but differences between blacks and whites diminished, indicating that age acted as a leveler for these groups. Age-as-a-leveler was also supported in the area of social interaction, but in a complicated manner. Older whites and Mexican-Americans reported increased contact with children and grandchildren as compared with the middle-aged whereas older blacks reported slightly less contact. Yet Mexican-American contact was so frequent at all ages that it remained the highest of any group. Mexican-Americans appeared to focus their social interaction on kin and, at every age, showed the least contact with friends, neighbors, and acquaintances. Older Mexican-Americans were even more isolated from non-kin than the other groups, but comparisons of blacks and whites did not support the idea of double jeopardy.

Asked about the three greatest problems in their lives, a commonality of experiences emerged: All three groups said that finances and health were paramount. But double jeopardy reappeared with the third problem (Bengston and Morgan, 1983). Blacks and Mexican-Americans reported concrete problems: crime among elderly blacks and transportation among elderly Mexican-Americans. The third problem among whites was low morale, a serious factor but not one related to survival.

Dowd and Bengston did not settle the double-jeopardy question. They studied only adults in the Los Angeles area, not a national sample, and none of the individuals studied was older than 74. National samples have produced different findings. After reviewing a number of studies, Kyriakos Markides (1983) found little persuasive evidence for the double-jeopardy theory. Several nationwide studies have indicated that the health and income differences between blacks and whites are smaller in old age than in middle age, perhaps because of income-maintenance policies.

Like most research on ethnic aging, Dowd and Bengston used a cross-sectional study and so might have picked up cohort differences. Many of today's black elderly are the children of slaves and grew up under strictly enforced segregation. Although discrimination is still a burden, today's minorities have opportunities that did not exist in the precivil rights era. It has been suggested, for example, that the pension status of black workers plays an important part in the income gap between older black and white Americans. Today's retired black workers were likely to have worked in agriculture, nondurable manufacturing in the South, or other jobs that were not covered by private pensions. As a result, retired black workers are only half as likely as whites to receive pension benefits. As employment has opened up to minority members, their prospects as older adults have improved. More are covered by Social Security, civil service, and private pensions, and in approximately 20 years the income gap should narrow sharply

	Median Age (years)	Younger than 15 Years (percent)	65 Years and Older (percent)
Total population	30.3%	22.4%	11.3%
White population	31.3	21.3	12.2
Black population	24.9	28.7	7.9
Hispanic population	23.2	32.0	4.9
Native Americans	23.0	31.8	5.3

FIGURE 15.4   Age of United States citizens, 1980.

Because of lower life expectancy, there is a smaller proportion of older individuals among minority groups. Improved finances and better health care could lead to similar life expectancies in all population groups among future cohorts.

Source: U.S. Bureau of the Census, *1980 Census of the Population*, 1981.

(Snyder, 1979). This trend could reverse the effect of recent cutbacks in other government assistance programs that will disproportionately affect elderly blacks during the 1980s (Hill, 1983).

Another change with possible effects on future cohorts of the elderly is in the area of health. Health insurance coverage, unknown when today's retirees were young, has raised the level of medical care among minority members in the working and middle classes and perhaps will lead to improved health in old age. If health care becomes more nearly equal, then the gap in life expectancy between white and minority groups may shrink, and the proportion of older minority groups members may grow (Fig. 15.4).

Finally, the whites in Dowd and Bengston's study were not identified by ethnic group and may have included Jewish, Italian, Polish, Greek, and other distinctive ethnic groups along with WASPs. Clumping together several different ethnic groups could distort the findings.

Discussions of double jeopardy usually revolve about disparities in income, health, housing, and the like. Some anthropologists (Holzberg, 1982) believe that studies of minority aging too often concentrate on such socioeconomic factors and tend to neglect cultural features. The aging process in minority groups is generally discussed in terms of the undeniable socioeconomic disparities without considering the effects of customs, life-style, and the role of the elderly in their ethnic community. In some ways, aging may be easier in minority groups. For example, among Japanese- and Mexican-Americans, the role of the aged appears to be more highly valued than in society at large. Among blacks, the strength of the extended kin network and the central role of the church may provide older adults with support that is lacking in the general community. For this reason, the effect of a weakened ethnic community on older adults arouses the same concern about minorities as exists for white ethnic groups. If ethnic social and religious traditions crumble, any extra strength that supports their economic position, identity, or self-esteem may be lost. When members of ethnic minorities require support from community service organizations, special problems may arise.

PROVIDING SERVICES FOR ETHNIC MINORITIES

Most social services appear to be aimed at ethnic groups that have been completely assimilated into the majority culture. People who are the best educated and socially aware are also most likely to know about the existence of various services and to be best equipped to deal with whatever bureaucracy dispenses them. They are also less likely to need the services.

If a person cannot speak English, cannot read, and is isolated from the larger community, he or she is likely to be unaware of programs that might alleviate financial or medical problems. Whether the service is a well-baby clinic meant for youngsters, a family planning center meant for young adults, or a Meals on Wheels program meant for the elderly, the barriers are the same. Lack of proficiency in English can be responsible for failure to use a service, for misuse of it, and for duplication of care. It can also lead to unnecessary or improper institutionalization. For example, in 1983, David Tom, an elderly Chinese immigrant, was released after 31 years in a mental hospital, when it was finally discovered that he had been committed to the hospital because no one understood his dialect of Chinese (*The New York Times*, 1983c).

Language is not the only barrier to services. Members of the most cohesive ethnic communities are likely to know little about disease, to be skeptical about medical care, and to be dependent when they are ill (Wesley-King, 1983). For example, although many health care facilities exist in the area of Manhattan known as East Harlem, cultural and linguistic barriers keep most of the Puerto Rican elderly from using them (Zambrana, Merino, and Santana, 1979). When they are ill, Puerto Ricans, who often do not speak English, go to *espiritistas*, or folk healers. These healers prescribe herbal remedies, warm baths, and massage to alleviate symptoms. When older Puerto Ricans attempt to get assistance from the medical system, the ridicule they encounter because of their use of *espiritistas* often alienates them, and they never return.

According to Donald Gelfand (1982), when planning, implementing, and operating social services, those in charge need to take six factors into account. In order to reach ethnic groups, especially recent immigrants and the elderly, programs must be sensitive to group members' (1) lack of knowledge about the majority culture; (2) lack of knowledge about available services; (3) reluctance to use available services in the belief that they are accepting charity; (4) unwillingness to travel beyond neighborhood boundaries and lack of adequate transportation; (5) low expectations of services; and (6) strong preference for the maintenance of their ethnic culture, which leads them to see the nonethnic service personnel as a threat to their way of doing things. These problems can be partially alleviated by locating services within neighborhoods, using ethnic personnel, and carrying on extensive educational programs, which may have to be cast in other languages.

How long these factors will be important is not known, but they will probably linger as long as ethnic neighborhoods exist. For some groups, the ethnic neighborhood may gradually disappear because the proportion of residents of childbearing age has been dropping (Baroni and Green, 1976). Because nonwhites still face discrimination in housing, white ethnic communities are more likely to disappear. And in the final analysis, it is not culture but jobs and political power that provide the basis for ethnic cohesion. As Gelfand (1982) points out, ethnicity will not disappear when the present generation of elderly is gone. However, the way people view their ethnic heritage and its effect on social relations may change.

SUMMARY

An individual's experience of the life cycle is heavily influenced by the shared beliefs of society. In the United States, where the family has no economic function, earning a living is the mark of adulthood. In traditional societies, where the family is the economic unit, marriage generally signals the assumption of adult responsibility. In traditional societies, age is unlikely to be reckoned in chronological terms, and in some cultures, membership in an **age set** determines one's age. Old age is generally defined in functional terms although some cultures connect it to transitional events in the life cycle.

Among traditional societies, the old are likely to receive harsh treatment in hunting, gathering, and fishing societies whereas in stable agricultural and herding societies, in which the old have economic roles, they are believed to receive the best treatment. Among the factors that affect the status and treatment of the old are their political or religious roles, their informational role, and their control of material resources.

With industrialization, the status of the elderly may decline as modern medicine, technologically based economies, urbanization, and widespread literacy pervade the culture. This decline in status does not always take place, however, and when it does, the decline may be only temporary. Once modernization is complete and the rate of change in the culture slows, the position of the old may begin to rise, as it has in the United States since the late 1960s.

As a result of different cultural expectations within an **ethnic group**, members of that group may experience the life cycle in a different way from the majority culture. Once white ethnic groups achieve economic success in the United States, they may be assimilated into the dominant culture. However, when immigrant groups cluster in an area they often retain their ethnic identity even though they move into the middle class and intermarry.

Ethnic minorities face discrimination, which has led them to develop special family strengths. The black family, which has been shaped by economic and social pressures, tends to de-emphasize legal marriage, tolerate premarital sexuality, and accept illegitimate births. The tradition of black cooperation and interdependence has led to the development of strong kinship bonds outside the nuclear family. The extended family provides support and guidance for the old, which may decrease feelings of loneliness or isolation.

In Mexican-American culture, the family is central, and the culture stresses male leadership, mutual aid within the family, respect for age, and the extended family. Although the culture values multigenerational families, urbanization has made them difficult to maintain; and the change, together with the lack of social contacts outside the kin network, has led to dissatisfaction among the urban elderly.

Among the many American Indians tribes are rural Indians, reservation Indians, migrant Indians, and urban Indians; and these various life styles interact with values of a particular tribe to alter the experience of the life cycle. In some tribes, economic and social changes have caused the old to lose their position of esteem whereas in others, where they retain ritual roles or wield economic power, they have retained their position of respect.

Some gerontologists believe that belonging to an ethnic minority places an aging person in **double jeopardy** whereas others believe that age is a leveler and that the elderly in all groups become more alike. Tests of the double-jeopardy theory have been inconclusive, with some research supporting it—especially in the areas of income and health—and other studies supporting the age-as-leveler view. In recent years, Social Security and pension coverage have been extended to a larger proportion of minority groups, indicating that, in about 20 years, the income gap may narrow. Standards of medical care have also risen, which may lead to improved health among minority elderly.

Members of ethnic minorities are often unaware of available social services or fail to use the services they need. It has been suggested that in order to reach ethnic groups, programs must be sensitive to a probable lack of knowledge about the majority culture, a lack of knowledge about the services, a reluctance to depend on what is regarded as "charity," transportation problems, low expectations, and a perception of the services as a threat to their own culture.

KEY TERMS

age set

double jeopardy

ethnic group

minority

PART FIVE

EPILOGUE

16

DEATH AND DYING

I n March 1974, 81-year-old Frank Tugend died at home. Tugend suffered from chronic brain dysfunction—whether Alzheimer's disease or multi-infarct dementia is uncertain—but the immediate cause of death was his refusal to eat or drink. For three years, Tugend had been slowly deteriorating. He became disoriented, did not recognize people, and finally withdrew to his room in the family home. At last, he took out his false teeth and refused to eat or drink. No matter how the family coaxed, he rejected all nourishment, telling his daughter, "I'm just going to lay here until it happens" (Jury and Jury, 1976, p. 61).

Patiently, he waited for death on a plain bed in a plain room, but always with the hand of a family member clutched tightly in his fingers. At last he slipped into a coma and died—three weeks after he had begun his final wait. After Tugend died in his own way, his grandson Mark recalled thinking, "You pulled it off, Gramp. You really pulled it off" (Jury and Jury, 1976, p. 63).

Not many people today die as Frank Tugend did: at home, in their own bed, in continual physical contact with a family member. But Tugend's family agreed there would be no hospitalization, no intravenous feeding, no prolongation of life. They felt their husband, father, grandfather, great-grandfather would want to die as he had lived—in an independent and dignified way.

Few of us would choose organic brain dysfunction as our manner of exit from the world. But when death comes, as it must to all of us, many of us would like to have some choice in the way we meet it. In this chapter, we come to grips with death. After investigating the problem of defining death, we look at the enormous change in who dies and the implications of this shift in mortality. We next consider the conditions of death in this country, comparing them with death as it was experienced by past generations. With the social aspects of death established, we narrow our focus to the dying person, exploring the process of death and the ways people meet it. Finally, we consider the survivors, ending the chapter by investigating the stages of grief.

CONDITIONS OF DEATH

Death in twentieth-century United States is a very different experience from death in earlier centuries—or even earlier in the present century. As we will see, the public and private meaning of death has gone through several transformations since the Middle Ages. We die at different ages, from different causes, and in a different setting from our forebears, and these factors have helped to change our attitudes toward the ending of life. Before we can discuss the conditions of death, we need to define the state.

DEFINING DEATH

In old movies, deciding when someone was dead was easy. A cursory glance was usually all it took for a confident pronouncement of death. On occasion, the decision was prolonged a few seconds. A finger on the pulse, an ear to the chest tended to settle the question. If any doubt remained, someone held a mirror in front of the person's face. When the glass remained bright and unclouded by exhaled breath, it was clear that death had come.

The determination of death is not nearly so simple as drama would have it. Certainly, when breathing and heartbeat stop, people die. Without oxygen traveling through the arteries, brain cells cannot live for long, and the organism soon dies. Our modern confusion over the arrival of death has grown out of medical advances. Immediate care, in the form of mouth-to-mouth resuscitation, oxygen, adrenaline, or electric shocks, may revive a person who fails all the traditional movie tests for life. Life-sustaining equipment can keep lungs and heart functioning for months while physicians fight to reverse an underlying condition that would bring death without technological support.

In most instances, the arrival of **clinical death,** marked by the termination of spontaneous breathing and heartbeat, is sufficient to determine the end of life. In an increasing number of cases, however, a person who would otherwise be clinically dead continues to exist on life-sustaining equipment. Although the lungs and heart cannot work independently and the brain no longer functions, the body lives. This condition has led researchers and legislators to strive for new definitions of death that would allow resuscitators to be unplugged in such cases.

When the brain dies, the cortex (which controls voluntary action, thought, and memory) ceases to function first, followed by the midbrain (which controls reflexes). At that point, the person is in a coma, but continues to breathe, and, if fed intravenously, can survive indefinitely without mechanical aids (Schulz, 1978). Individuals in this state are often described as "living vegetables." The most prominent example is Karen Quinlan, the young woman in an apparently irreversible coma who continued to breathe after the court allowed disconnection of her respirator. Finally, the brain stem (which controls body functions) dies, bringing respiration and heartbeat to a stop. A respirator may be able to keep vital organs functioning, but these individuals are considered to have undergone **brain death.**

Nearly 20 years ago, the Ad Hoc Committee of the Harvard Medical School proposed that brain death be accepted as the death of the individual and set forth four criteria to define it: (1) total lack of response to any stimuli, no matter how painful; (2) failure to move for 1 hour and failure to breathe for 3 minutes when taken off a respirator; (3) no reflexes and no brain stem activity; (4) a flat EEG, indicating no cortical activity. But before the respirator could be unplugged, tests for the criteria had to be repeated after 24 hours, and physicians had to be certain that the patient was not suffering from hypothermia (a body temperature below 90°F.) or from an overdose of drugs that depress central nervous system activity

(Jeffko, 1979). These last two conditions can produce symptoms similar to brain death, but are reversible.

In television's medical shows, a flat EEG establishes death, but under the Harvard Committee's definition of brain death, the lack of electrical brain activity merely confirms the diagnosis. Their definition has been regarded as too stringent by many physicians and researchers. It requires death of the midbrain and the brain stem, as well as cortical death. Some have proposed that **cerebral death,** or the death of the cortex, should be enough to establish brain death. According to neurosurgeon William Sweet (1978), two separate studies of more than two thousand individuals have established that—except for people in drug-induced comas—no one recovers after the cortex ceases to function and electrical brain activity stops. He suggests that EEG tracings from two separate machines, repeated after six hours, provide a certain diagnosis of cerebral death. This standard would allow a person in irreversible coma to be pronounced dead. At least 18 states accept total brain death as establishing the end of life, but cerebral death has not yet become the general standard.

DEMOGRAPHICS OF DEATH

As life expectancy has increased, the time at which death generally comes has shifted. In earlier centuries, death in infancy and childhood was common. Birth rates were high, and parents expected to lose from one third to one half of their children before the age of 10. Death was associated primarily with the young, and it occurred often. During the eighteenth century, for example, as many as 400 out of every 1000 babies born in London died before they were 2 years old (McKeown and Brown, 1955). As nutrition and sanitation improved, infant and child mortality gradually was reduced, and death became associated with old age. Instead of dying young of pneumonia, tuberculosis, or gastrointestinal disease, we die old of heart attacks, cancer, or stroke. Today we regard the death of a young person as unusual and unfair.

Not only has death become associated with the old, but since 1900, the general death rate in this country also has been cut just about in half (Fig. 16.1). Instead of suddenly striking at any point in the life cycle, death is more likely to follow a degenerative disease of secondary aging. As a result, death is less likely to be unpredictable, and we tend to think less about death than our forebears did (Marshall, 1980). During the past century death has come to seem less arbitrary, easier to understand, and more under the control of human beings than it once was.

These changes in the demographics of death have had widespread effects on the entire life cycle, as we saw in earlier chapters. Families are less likely to be disrupted by the death of a parent. Among American Quaker families in the early 1800s, for example, one of the parents usually died about 10 years before the last child left home. A century later, the first parent to die died about a year after the last child left home. Today both parents generally live more than 12 years after the last child leaves home (Wells, 1973). As a result, says Victor Marshall (1980),

	1900		1950		1981	
	Men	**Women**	**Men**	**Women**	**Men**	**Women**
All ages	17.9	16.5	11.1	8.2	9.6	7.8
< 1 year	179.1	145.4	37.3	28.6	13.5	10.3
1 to 4	20.5	19.1	15.2	12.7	0.7	0.5
5 to 14	3.8	3.9	0.7	0.5	0.4	0.2
15 to 24	5.9	5.8	1.7	0.9	1.6	0.6
25 to 34	8.2	8.2	2.2	1.4	2.0	0.8
35 to 44	10.7	9.8	4.3	3.0	3.0	1.6
45 to 54	15.7	14.2	10.7	6.4	7.6	4.1
55 to 64	28.7	25.8	24.0	14.0	17.8	9.4
65 to 74	59.3	53.6	49.3	33.3	40.1	21.2
75 to 84	128.3	118.8	104.3	84.0	85.3	51.9
> 84	268.8	255.2	216.4	192.0	182.4	140.9

FIGURE 16.1   U.S. death rates, 1900 to 1981 (deaths per 1000 population).

Source: U.S. Bureau of the Census. *Statistical Abstract of the United States, 1982–83*. Figures for 1900 from U.S. National Center for Health Statistics, U.S. Public Health Service.

young children rarely think about the deaths of their parents, and parents no longer keep their children under control by holding up the prospect of early death and damnation.

Not all segments of society have profited equally from the postponement of death. As we saw in Chapter 3, blacks can expect to die at a younger age than whites. But no matter what one's race or ethnic group, socioeconomic status also affects the timing of death. Individuals with low income and little education tend to die at an earlier age than well-to-do college graduates. For example, in the United States, the death rate among nonwhite men is 31 percent higher for those who fail to complete elementary school than among those who have some high school or college. Among nonwhite women, the death rate is 70 percent higher among the poorly educated (Goldschneider, 1971).

The poor (who generally are also the poorly educated) have higher levels of illness and less access to health care than people in the working or middle class. Death rates among the poor are sharply higher than in the general population during infancy, childhood, and the young adult years whereas death among middle-class men tends to be higher than average during middle and old age (Lerner, 1970). Perhaps the medical and nutritional advantages of life in the middle class keep alive many men who are vulnerable to disease and who would die young if they lived in poverty. Or perhaps the sedentary life-style of the middle class encourages the development of degenerative disease in midlife.

In most instances, life in the working class is good for one's health. Death rates from communicable disease are low during the first part of the life cycle, and there appears to be no excess of death during midlife and old age from degenerative disease. However, pockets of inequality appear among specific occupational groups: Coal miners die prematurely from black lung, workers in the asbestos industry die prematurely from asbestosis, and workers in the plastic industry who have contact with vinyl chloride die prematurely from cancer (Harshbarger, 1975). No matter what a person's occupation, when death arrives, it is likely to be in a hospital or other institution.

THE PLACE OF DEATH

Unless we die suddenly, our chances of dying at home are small. This was not always true. Until this century, most people died at home, attended by family members or perhaps a nurse. The custom was reflected in Victorian novels, which abound with deathbed scenes, in which the family gathers for last farewells, blessings, and unravelings of plots. Such scenes are rare today, and their likelihood has been decreasing steadily for about half a century.

It is generally agreed that more than 80 percent of all deaths now take place in an institution (Bok, 1978). In 1949, approximately 50 percent of deaths were in a hospital or some other institution, such as a nursing home or a home for the aged. By 1958 the proportion of institutional deaths had climbed to 61 percent. Recent national figures are not available, but, in 1967, 73 percent of all deaths in New York City and 72 percent of all deaths in the state of Maryland occurred in institutions (Lerner, 1970). Similar trends have appeared in other industrialized countries although the proportion of deaths at home is higher in countries such as Britain (Marshall, 1980).

The chances of dying in a hospital are relatively small if death comes by accident, suicide, or homicide. Only about half of the people who die from heart disease or stroke die in hospitals, probably because death often comes suddenly. Death is more likely to occur in the home than in a hospital or institution when the cause of death is influenza, senility, or "ill-defined conditions" (Lerner, 1970).

The movement of death into the hospital has probably been the result of both medical and social change. The state of medical technology has made it possible to save lives in hospitals that might have been lost at home. It has been assumed that many past home deaths may have occurred because proper medical care was not available (Lerner, 1970). As noted earlier, medical technology can prolong life and sometimes even reverse what appears to be death.

The social reasons for the movement of death into hospitals are varied. Today families are smaller, mobility has increased, and the majority of women are in the work force. A person who dies after a lengthy illness requires continual care, and many terminal patients may have no family member who can take on such responsibility. In a study of older people who had been institutionalized before their deaths, researchers found that most either lived alone, were single or separated, or had no living children (Palmore, 1976b). The trend toward hospital deaths may also be related to what some historians and sociologists have seen as a denial of death by modern society (Stannard, 1977). By removing the dying from the home, we minimize our exposure to death and cushion its disruptive effects.

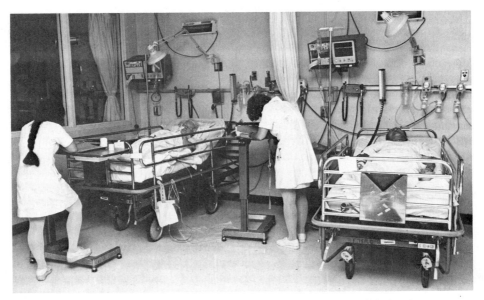

Advances in medical technology, as well as social change, are responsible for the movement of death into the hospital.

Whether this denial of death is the cause or the result of its institutionalization is uncertain. Richard Schulz (1978) believes that the tendency for Americans to avoid death may have developed because we no longer have contact with the dying process. As he points out, exposure to death used to be common and considered natural. Whether denial of death is the cause or effect of the hospitalization of death, our attitudes toward death and the dying process have changed over the years.

CULTURAL ATTITUDES TOWARD DEATH

So far as we know, human beings are the only creatures who know that they must die. This knowledge, said Ernest Becker (1973), means that fear of death is a universal human experience. Becker believed that, although we are rarely aware of it, the terror of death lies in the background of everything we do. Whether all people fear death is a matter of debate, but we do look for ways to come to terms with the inevitability of death—through religion, science, or philosophy. Two basic attitudes toward death are common in contemporary society. People generally take either the scientific perspective, in which death means the end of all existence, or the religious perspective, in which the body dies but the soul survives (Siegel, 1980).

Whichever view is held, it has been affected by society. Individual views of death are largely shaped by the belief system of a culture, which gives people a way to deal with death, reconciling them to the fact that their existence on earth must end. The strategies that have been worked out in a particular culture may change as the religion, social institutions, and economic situation of the society change (Shneidman, 1980).

STRATEGIES OF RECONCILIATION

Historian Arnold Toynbee (1968) has listed a number of strategies that have been used to come to terms with death by people in past and present cultures. One way to become reconciled to death is through the adoption of a philosophical attitude. Some become *hedonistic*, devoting themselves to enjoying life as much as possible while it lasts. They cultivate the pursuit of pleasure, and their byword is, "Eat, drink, and be merry, for tomorrow we die." The hedonistic attitude can be found in ancient Egypt, in the Old Testament, and in the Latin verse of Horace.

Others take an opposite attitude, embracing *pessimism*. In this view, life is so nasty and brutish that death is preferable. According to Toynbee, in societies pervaded by this attitude, suicide is a basic human right and to kill oneself is respectable or even a moral obligation. The pessimistic attitude can be found in Greek literature and in Hinduism and Buddhism, religions that grew out of Indian culture. In these religions, a person was fated to be reborn again and again, with each new birth seen as an additional evil to be endured.

Physical countermeasures to circumvent death have been used in many ancient societies. In ancient Egypt, for example, it was believed that the dead would continue to live as long as they were provided with the necessities of life on earth, such as food, clothing, tools, and weapons. Embalming the corpse was seen as another way of prolonging life.

Fame has been another common strategy in the battle against death. Being remembered by future generations has been seen as a sort of immortality. Rulers had statues erected to their memory and their exploits commemorated in verse. As Toynbee points out, this sort of memorial can take an ironic twist, when the poet who writes the commemorative verse achieves greater fame than the ruler or hero. Today writers, painters, and sculptors may see their works as their hope of immortality. Philanthropists may seek immortality by endowing foundations or schools that bear their names, and political leaders may be conscious that historians are the custodians of their memory. The prospect of living in the memory of others may also be used as a reconciling strategy by average citizens, who often say of the dead, "She (or he) will live as long as someone remembers her (or him)."

One of the most prevalent strategies, apparently used in every age and every culture, involves what Toynbee calls *"putting one's treasure in future generations."* Instead of stressing personal immortality, individuals see themselves as living on through their own descendants or through future generations of their own culture. This manner of reconciliation to death frees a person from self-centeredness, as does the less ethnocentric strategy of *merging the self with ultimate reality*. Buddhism and Hinduism, which took a pessimistic attitude toward life, also used this strategy of reconciliation, in which the merger with reality allows one to achieve Nirvana, thus escaping from the endless cycle of death and rebirth.

An extremely common self-centered strategy of reconciliation is the belief in *personal immortality.* A faith in the continued existence of a disembodied soul is found in ancient Sumer, Babylonia, Greece, and Egypt, as well as in most contemporary cultures. Whether the soul is believed to have existed always or to have come into existence with the birth of the earthly body, its future existence usually involves some kind of analogy with life on earth.

Connected with the belief in personal immortality is a belief in the *resurrection of the body.* Ancient Egyptians, Zoroastrians (followers of an ancient Persian religion), Christians, and Muslims are among the groups that have included an eventual reunion of soul and body in their strategies of reconciliation. Another strategy that is associated with personal immortality is the idea of final judgment—the *hope of heaven and the fear of hell.* The prospect of final judgment may fill life on earth with anxiety, but, as Toynbee points out, whatever fears of damnation exist seem generally to be offset by the hopes of reunion with departed lovers, friends, and relatives. As we trace the changes in popular attitudes toward death that have characterized Western Europe since the Middle Ages, we can observe how the use of these strategies has shifted, with first one, and then another, being stressed.

DEATH IN THE WESTERN WORLD

Over the past 8 centuries, the personal experience and collective meaning of death have changed in the Western world. Although we have tended to believe that our own feelings about death are typical of human beings everywhere and for all time, historian Philippe Aries (1981), who traced the meaning of death since the Middle Ages, found that many beliefs common in the past century or so are actually modern inventions. He proposed that as self-awareness changed and the idea of individuality developed, the experience of death altered. According to Aries, the meaning of death in predominantly Christian societies has gone through five major transformations: the tame death, the death of the self, the remote and imminent death, the death of the other, and the invisible death.

The *tame death,* which lasted until about A.D. 1200, was expected and was considered natural. Although death was frightening, people were resigned to the fact that they must die. Death was seen not as the extinction of the individual but the loss of a community member, to be accompanied by public ceremonies. The good death was the predicted death that announced its coming beforehand and gave a person time to prepare for the end. Only sudden death was terrifying, and whether a person was struck down by violence or died quietly in his or her sleep, such a death was regarded as shameful, vile, and ugly.

In the Middle Ages, people were accustomed to death. They witnessed it often, and the young were its most common victims. Death was so customary that it pervaded village life: All communal events took place in the graveyard, which adjoined the church. Fairs, public meetings, and trials were conducted in the midst of piles of disinterred bones, which had been dug up to make room for more bodies in the crowded cemetery. Because the dead were not suffering, but merely sleeping until Christ's Second Coming, there was no reason to fear them or one's own end. Any true believer was certain of final redemption.

The first great shift in public perceptions of death occurred when death came to be seen as personal extinction. Growing self-awareness, in which one's own identity became more important than the collective human destiny, led to the *death of the self,* which prevailed from about 1200 to 1600. The moment of death, once a passing into sleep, became the feared moment of judgment, and the deathbed scene changed from one of public ceremony to individual conversion. The soul was seen as separated from the body and passing immediately to its punishment or reward. The corpse became a terrible reminder of one's own fate, and bodies were sewn into shrouds so the dead face could not be seen.

By the seventeenth century, the meaning of death had changed again. Death had become integrated into life and now was both *remote and imminent.* Instead of repenting at the last moment, people thought about death and prepared for it throughout life. Life was seen as brief and vain, and although people seemed to accept the idea of mortality, the idea of their own death aroused great anxiety. With the deathbed no longer the focus of attention, a sudden death came to be preferred. Instead of burying their dead in the churchyard, many families had their own private cemetery, reserving a corner of their land for the purpose. During the previous period, the corpse had been seen as no more than a handful of dust, but now it was endowed with some sort of personality and sensibility. As this idea took hold, love became associated with death, and death was seen as romantic and erotic.

The remote death lasted for nearly 2 centuries. Then, in the early nineteenth century, importance shifted from the individual to the family. People became less concerned with their own deaths and more absorbed in the *death of the other.* This development coincided with a growth in affection for friends and family, and separation by death was a major emotional crisis. Thus, the ''other'' whose death was of concern was a loved one. Perhaps because someone else was dying, death was seen as beautiful and no longer to be feared. As romanticism developed, death was sometimes regarded a a mystical communion with infinity. The belief in hell had weakened, and instead of dwelling on the rewards of heaven, people saw the next life as a place of reunion. Attention shifted from the dead body to the soul—a disembodied spirit that roamed the earth. When a person died, he or she was believed to be attended by the souls of departed loved ones, who clustered about to ease the way into the next life. The dead were again buried in public cemeteries, and family visits to the grave became popular.

Late in the nineteenth century, the death of the other slowly gave way to the *invisible death.* It may be that as death gradually was pushed to the end of the life span, it became easier to deny its presence. For whatever reason, death became hidden. Whether to spare the dying or to avoid confronting death, the practice of concealing the gravity of a patient's condition spread. Death was removed from the family, and people were sent to hospitals to die. As medical technology grew, the medical profession took over the management of death, and undertakers assumed control of mourning. Displays of grief were avoided, and mourning was kept private. Death ceased to be regarded as a natural, inevitable event and became a failure of medicine.

Recently, said Aries, there has been a revolt against invisible death. As it became common for life to be prolonged artificially, people began to protest. An increasing number of individuals have refused to allow all possible medical intervention for dying family members, and, as we will see, some are urging that death once again be recognized and made visible. The aim is to reestablish death as an important event and to make possible a dignified death.

Although Aries has been criticized for failing to consider the impact of changing social conditions on attitudes toward death, it is generally recognized that his overview is unmatched in sweep and depth (Marshall, 1980). There is also general agreement that denial of death is widespread in society. This denial is seen most clearly when death is near and in funeral and mourning practices. How do people feel about death when its arrival is not expected for many years?

MOVING TOWARD DEATH

In a sense we are all moving toward death because each day we live brings us one day closer to the end of life. As we get older, the consciousness that time is running out may change our feelings about death and the way we think about life. This reassessment of life is at the basis of the final developmental task in Erik Erikson's (1982) theory of personality, when we attempt to forge a reconciliation out of the struggle between integrity and despair and search for meaning in life.

IMPENDING DEATH

Because death has become associated with aging, young adults may find it difficult, if not impossible, to think of death in personal terms. Their parents, even their grandparents, are probably alive; their friends are healthy. They know that death can come suddenly at any age, but its rarity make it as unlikely a threat as being struck by a bolt of lightning. In middle age, attitudes toward death change as people begin to experience it at firsthand. The death of parents and acquaintances of their own age may lead them to confront the idea of personal death. This awareness of death as a real possibility for themselves appears to lead to a change in the way they think about time. Young adults think about time as the number of years that have elapsed since their birth; by middle age, adults begin to think about time as the number of years they have left to live (Neugarten, Crotty, and Tobin, 1964).

When people enter old age, time becomes even shorter, and the awareness of impending death may change the way they organize their lives and use their remaining time (Kalish, 1976). When death is not viewed as a possibility, time stretches endlessly ahead. Everything can be done, and there is no need to establish priorities. When death is expected in a few years, choices must be made. Possessions, experiences, and relationships are perceived as transient. The words "You can't take it with you" suddenly take on new meaning. Time begins to run out, and the inclination to plan future events appears to decline slightly. Among men between the ages of 17 and 91, those older than 75 were the most likely to say that they definitely did not find themselves imagining what they would be doing a year from now (Giambra, 1977). However, the tendency was slight, with most older adults thinking about the future less often than the young, but not forgoing all plans and future daydreams. As we move closer to death, we seem to organize our lives with the end in mind. For example, when asked what they would do if they knew they would die within 6 months, adults older than 60 were less likely than younger people to say they would change their way of living radically or try to tie up the loose ends of their lives (Kalish and Reynolds, 1976). (See Fig. 16.2.)

According to Victor Marshall (1980), the awareness of impending personal death is only partially the result of age. He believes that people tend to compare themselves with other people who are like them. Age is an important cue to similarity, but not the only one used. In a study of adults between the ages of 64 and 96, Marshall found that 50 percent of adults younger than 75 believed they would live at least 10 more years, but that only 10 percent of those older than 85 thought they would live that long.

A more accurate predictor of a person's awareness of impending death, however, was family history. No matter what their age, people tended to compare themselves with their parents. Those who were older than their parents' age at death believed they had less than 5 years to live whereas those who were younger than their parents' age at death believed that they would live at least 10 additional years. Other factors that entered into a person's beliefs about his or her own life expectancy were the death of siblings, self-perceived health, and the death of friends.

If the approach of death leads us to attempt to find meaning in life, as Erikson has suggested, one way to discover that meaning is by reviewing our lives. Robert

	Age		
	20–39	40–59	>59
Change life-style markedly (travel, sex, new experiences)	24%	15%	9%
Center on inner life (read, contemplate, pray)	14	14	37
Focus concern on others, be with loved ones	29	25	12
Complete projects, tie up loose ends	11	10	3
No change in life-style	17	29	31
Other	5	6	8

FIGURE 16.2 Behavior in the face of death (percent).

If faced with imminent death, older adults are less likely than younger individuals to say that they would make radical changes in their lives or attempt to be with loved ones. They are much more likely to say that they would read, contemplate, or pray in their remaining days.

Source: R. A. Kalish and D. K. Reynolds, 1976.

Butler (1975) believes that the anticipation of death starts a process of **life review,** in which people survey, observe, and reflect on their past. In one study (Marshall, 1975), the fewer years an older person believed were left, the more frequently he or she talked with others about the past and more likely he or she was to agree that "my memories are the most important thing I own" (Fig. 16.3). People who recalled more turning points in their lives, who said more past events had turned out well, and who saw themselves in control of what had happened at the turning points tended to be satisfied with their lives and willing to live them over and to think that they had made out of their lives what they wanted. Such people were also likely to reminisce with others whereas those who were less satisfied with their lives tended to reminisce alone.

Although the life review can trigger anxiety, guilt, depression, or despair when it leads to the resurgence of unresolved conflicts, it can also end in the resolution of old conflicts and fears and provide insight into past experiences and a sense of significance to life (Butler, 1975). However, the review does not occupy all a person's remaining years. Once the process is completed and the conflicts resolved, the reviewing process recedes in importance, and the tendency to reminisce declines.

Not all reminiscence is for the purpose of giving meaning to life. People may reflect on the past to help create a continuous sense of self, to enhance self-esteem by identifying a present situation with a valued past, or to impress others. At times, reminiscence may fulfill more than one purpose (Marshall, 1980).

Questions have been raised concerning the actual function of life review. In Butler's proposal, the review is a normative process in which a person sorts out and restructures the past in an attempt to solve past conflicts. When the process is successful, it leads to serenity or integrity; when unsuccessful, it leads to turmoil or despair.

Not all researchers agree that life review functions in this manner. Morton Lieberman and Sheldon Tobin (1983) believe that instead of leading to higher ma-

	Expect to Live an Additional		
	10 or More Years	5 to 10 Years	Less than 5 Years
My memories are the most important thing I own:			
Agree	14%	10%	36%
Disagree	86%	90%	64%
I talk about things that have happened in my past life with someone else:			
At least once a week	36%	32%	62%
Less frequently	64%	68%	39%

FIGURE 16.3   Life review and the approach of death.

As individuals approach death, they are more likely to talk about the past with others, perhaps because they have completed their life review and no longer feel any conflict about their memories.

Source: V. W. Marshall, 1975, 112–129.

turity, the life review may be primarily defensive. In their study of older adults who entered homes for the aged, those who had successfully completed a life review were more serene and more satisfied with life than those who had not. However, the completion of a life review did not significantly improve an individual's ability to adapt. When the researchers considered the ability to handle stress, they found adaptive failure in 38 percent of older adults who avoided the past, 35 percent of those who were in the process of life review, and 30 percent of those who had completed life review. Instead of solving problems, say Lieberman and Tobin, the older adult is reworking the past, creating a meaningful, but mythic, image of the self that will defend his or her self-concept. They believe that a successful life review in Butler's (or Erikson's) terms, requires special skills that may not be characteristic of the majority of women and men.

Other researchers have pointed out that some sort of life review may be common today, but that it may be a relatively new development in human history (Marshall, 1980). When life expectancy was short, death came most often to the young, and its arrival was unpredictable, there may have been little time or reason for reflecting on one's past. And in the centuries before individualism developed, when each death was seen in relation to the community, a life review may have been inconceivable.

PERSONAL ATTITUDES TOWARD DEATH

Many researchers who study people's attitudes toward death assume that everyone fears it. After analyzing research on attitudes toward death, Marshall (1980) pointed out that researchers are so certain that we are all afraid of death that the fear is built into their studies. For example, in one study, the failure to make a will was considered evidence for fear of death when it could easily have been indifference, the lack of possessions, or the absence of heirs. In another study, people who avoided consulting doctors were considered to have a "latent" fear of death when they may have had a low opinion of the medical profession. When people say they are not afraid to die, the reply is frequently coded as a "denial" of their fear. Marshall believes that the assumption of a universal fear of death clouds our understanding of the meaning of death.

Research indicates that few people admit to being terrified of death. In a study of more than a thousand adults in the Los Angeles area, only 4 percent said they were "very afraid" of death, and 63 percent said they were "not at all afraid" (Bengston, Cuellar, and Ragan, 1977). When we do fear death, what aspect of it is most terrifying? Among adults of all ages, fears focus first on the dissolution of the body, then on the end of all experiences, the pain of dying, an unknown future, and the grief of their families (Diggory and Rothman, 1961). Among younger adults in another study (Shneidman, 1971), the most unpleasant aspect of death was the end of experiences, followed by the pain of dying, an unknown future, an end to personal plans, and the grief of friends and family. The dissolution of the body received almost no attention.

As people move through the life span, it seems plausible that the meaning of death is likely to change. When asked to contemplate their own deaths, the majority of young, well-educated *Psychology Today* readers were unafraid (Shneidman, 1971). They either felt resolved about their deaths or pleasure in being alive. About one in three readers felt either fearful (19 percent), discouraged (5 percent), or depressed (11 percent) at the thought of their own death. A majority also said they thought about their own death "occasionally," with 21 percent saying they never or only rarely thought about their death, and 22 percent thinking about it frequently.

Some researchers have found that fear of death is low throughout young adulthood, peaks during middle age, and then declines (Schulz, 1978). For example, people between the ages of 41 and 50 are most likely to say that "death always comes too soon" (Riley and Foner, 1968). This coincides with the time at which people first confront the idea of personal death although the response could reflect cohort differences, for these men and women were young adults during World War II, when death often came to the young.

Other researchers have found the greatest fear of death among the young. In one study (Kalish and Reynolds, 1976), 40 percent of young adults, 26 percent of middle-aged adults, and only 10 percent of older adults said that they were afraid to die. A number of studies have supported the idea that the fear of death is smallest among the old. It may seem odd that those who are about to die have the least fear of death, but several explanations have been offered for this diminished fear (Kalish, 1976). First, the older person may place less value on his or her life than the younger person. Declining health, economic problems, the loss of roles, and an awareness of mortality could combine to lower the valuation of life. Second, older people may feel they have received their allotted number of years. Most adults are aware of the typical life expectancy in their society, and once they have passed the proverbial threescore and 10, they may believe that any additional years are a bonus. Finally, older adults are socialized to their deaths. As people go through life, they see others die, and, as they deal with these deaths, they may even rehearse their own.

For some people, death may be preferable to continued life. Among adults of all ages, a strong majority say they do not want to live to be 150 (Back and Gergen, 1966). Once again, Marshall (1980) has analyzed the research and from the replies established five major reasons people might lose all fear of death—or even want to die. He found that older adults frequently describe the following situations as worse than death: total inactivity, complete uselessness, becoming a burden to one's family, losing one's mental competence, and progressively deteriorating physical health accompanied by physical discomfort. Less frequently offered reasons for welcoming death included a disgust with world conditions, the loss of all friends and contemporaries to death, and an eagerness to see what lies beyond the grave.

As adults age and come to terms with their own death, they find various supports. When older men and women are asked what comforts them when they think about death, approximately 35 percent say that religious faith sustains them

(Peterson, 1980). About 40 percent rely on their achievements in life for comfort, saying that memories of a full life give them strength in the face of death, and the remaining 25 percent rely on love from family and friends.

The absence of any fear of death does not, however, mean that people have no concern about dying. None of the studies we have examined reflects the feelings of a person who knows death is only months or days away. Once the process of dying begins, attitudes may change.

THE PROCESS OF DYING

At one time, the dying person managed his or her own death, generally choosing to end life at home, surrounded by family and close friends. Now that most of us die in hospitals, the control of the dying process has moved from the individual to the medical profession. As the invisible death progresses, there may be efforts to keep the patient from realizing the seriousness of his or her condition or a mutual pretense that death will not come. Recently, a revolt against the invisible death has led to attempts to return some control to the patient.

INFORMING THE PATIENT

Most physicians are reluctant to tell a patient that he or she has a terminal illness. Until concealment becomes impossible, the patient is kept in the dark about the condition. In one study (Oken, 1961), 88 percent of doctors surveyed said they would not tell a patient if they discovered a cancer that would probably be fatal. Honesty in such a situation, said most doctors, would be "torture" and "the cruelest thing in the world." They generally told patients that their ailment was a "growth," "lesion," "mass," "tumor," or "hyperplastic tissue." Only if they felt the patient needed a chance to plan financial affairs would they be frank about his or her chances. Yet when these same physicians were asked if *they* would want to be told, 60 percent said that they would.

Similar findings have appeared in other studies. An analysis of such research indicates that about 80 percent of physicians consistently say they deceive their dying patients, but that about 80 percent of physicians also would want to know if they were dying (Feifel, 1965). Doctors say such deception is warranted because the truth would only confuse the patient, cause unnecessary pain or discomfort, or destroy all hope. Many believe that patients do not want to know the truth (Bok, 1978).

The wisdom of withholding the news of fatal illness is not supported by studies of the general public. Among healthy people, about 79 percent say they would like to know if they were dying. Among patients with curable cancers who had been told of their condition, only 7 percent objected to the knowledge—although 19 percent denied they had ever been told. And among patients who were dying of cancer, 80 percent said that cancer patients should be told the truth (Hinton, 1967).

When patients are not told that death is near, they are robbed of the opportunity to put their affairs in order, and the chance to control the manner of their dying is destroyed. The knowledge that death is near might change such decisions as whether to enter a hospital, whether to have surgery, where the last days of life will be spent, and who will share them. Time spent with family, friends, or clergy during this terminal period will also be affected, especially if the patient is the only one who does not know the truth. In addition, informed patients appear to tolerate pain more easily, recover from surgery more rapidly, and cooperate better with therapy (Bok, 1978).

Despite efforts at concealment, most patients learn—without being told—that their illness is fatal (Glaser and Strauss, 1965; Kübler-Ross, 1969). A reluctance on the part of family, physician, or nurses to discuss the patient's condition, their facial expressions, and a tendency to avoid the patient generally reveal the situation. For example, studies have shown that nurses take significantly longer to answer calls from dying patients than from severely ill patients who are expected to recover (Kastenbaum and Aisenberg, 1972). Some patients appear never to realize that they are dying although researchers believe they may realize the truth at some level, moving back and forth from recognition to unawareness (Schulz, 1978).

Often patient, medical staff, and family are caught up in what has been called the "ritual drama of mutual pretense" (Glaser and Strauss, 1965). All parties know that death will soon come, but all pretend that recovery is certain. Staff and family operate on the rule that the impending death is not to be mentioned unless the patient initiates the conversation, and because such conversations are uncomfortable and improper in American society, the patient is unlikely to bring up the subject. Conversation with the patient focuses on "safe" topics, such as food, grooming, the weather, and minor symptoms. If the truth is inadvertently revealed, both parties involved ignore or misinterpret the exposure.

When the patient's conditions deteriorates so far that nearness to death is visible to all, the pretense breaks down, and death is acknowledged. As the researchers note, this mutual pretense can give the dying person some dignity and privacy, but only at the expense of closer relationships with family and staff at a very important time.

THE STAGES OF DEATH

As death becomes certain, a person enters the **dying trajectory,** the emotional states through which an individual travels in the weeks, days, and hours preceding death (Glaser and Strauss, 1968). The trajectory may be rapid or slow, regular or spasmodic. It can be a steady decline or a decline interrupted by plateaus, or it may take an erratic up-and-down course. The patient's basic ailment also affects the dying trajectory, so that death from leukemia, from intestinal cancer, from emphysema, and from congestive heart failure will follow different courses. The age of the patient may also affect the path toward death.

Whether patients' attitudes toward death go through a predictable series of stages during the death trajectory is uncertain. After interviewing more than two hundred dying patients, Elisabeth Kübler-Ross (1969) proposed a five-stage theory of dying that has become widely known. According to Kübler-Ross, when a patient first discovers that death is certain, the first reaction is *denial and isolation*. Almost every patient, she says, responds with, "No, not me. It cannot be true." For most people, this stage occupies a brief period although from time to time a patient may briefly lapse back into it. Denial is soon followed by *anger and resentment*. In this second stage, the patient is angry because the course of life has been interrupted; asks, "Why me?"; and is envious of healthy people. On seeing a vigorous person, the question may become, "Why couldn't it have been him?" Anger is directed randomly—at the doctor, the nurses, the family. The anger is not meant personally but is a rage against death.

From anger, the patient passes into the third stage, which consist of *bargaining*. Now effort is directed at postponing death. The patient may try to strike a bargain with God, perhaps promising to spend any remaining time in service to the church, or with the physician, promising to donate his or her body to science if the doctor can only grant a little more time. For a brief period, bargaining sustains the patient; then the fourth stage, *depression,* takes over. Kübler-Ross stresses that this is not a reactive depression that follows the loss of health, job, or some possession, but a preparatory loss, in which the patient is preparing for the loss of everything and everyone he or she loves.

Finally, if the patient has had sufficient time to work through the preceding stages, he or she will enter the final stage, *acceptance*. Now the patient is neither depressed nor angry, but begins to contemplate the end calmly and perhaps with quiet expectation. Acceptance of death does not mean that the patient now wishes to die. Even after a patient has come to accept death, says Kübler-Ross, a thin, bright thread of hope remains. In every stage, the patient hopes for a medical breakthrough, a sudden remission. Once any glimmer of hope is extinguished, death comes quickly—within 24 hours.

Popular as this portrayal of dying has become, research has generally failed to support it. Investigators find that although the patients they study may exhibit any of the attitudes described by Kübler-Ross, they do not go through the stages in any particular order and many never enter some of the stages (Shneidman, 1973). For example, in one study (Kastenbaum and Weisman, 1972), patients appeared to fall into two groups, each with a typical pattern of behavior that persisted until death. One group responded to the awareness of death with withdrawal, remaining inactive throughout their last months. The other group responded to death by intensifying activity, throwing themselves into their daily affairs with vigor, initiating new activities, and making new friends.

The demarcation of stages in Kübler-Ross's theory seems based more on intuition than on any particular pattern of responses from patients (Schulz, 1978). For example, the two hundred patients studied by Kübler-Ross have never been adequately described, her terms have not been adequately defined, and no statistical information has been provided. We do not know what percentage of patients went through all five stages. Furthermore, the theory makes no allowance for individual differences that are likely to affect the dying trajectory: nature of the disease, sex, ethnicity, personality, cognitive style, developmental levels, or immediate situation in which dying occurs (Kastenbaum, 1975). Finally, the theory is based on Kübler-Ross's observations in industrialized society. It is unlikely that a dying person in the thirteenth century, for example, who was accustomed to seeing death almost daily and who had a deep religious faith, would feel the same denial and anger that may be common today.

AN APPROPRIATE DEATH

The extension of life and the probability that death will follow some degenerative disease have increased the time of the dying trajectory. Instead of dying suddenly, most of us will spend weeks, if not months, moving toward death. This extension has made it more important to plan for death and to try to control the way in which we die (Marshall, 1980). Life-prolonging measures have led to comatose patients with no chance of recovery being kept alive by respirators and intravenous feeding. The result is a form of dying that has been called a "degradation ceremony" (Shneidman, 1980), in which people meet their deaths in an ignominious manner.

This undignified death has developed in part because of the nature of the hospital. Hospitals are devoted to the healing process, and dying patients are seen as failures. Members of the medical staff are uncomfortable around the dying and often feel guilty because they tend to wonder if some omitted or overlooked treatment might have turned dying into healing (Mauksch, 1975). And so attempts at "healing" often continue long after it is apparent that the patient has embarked on the dying trajectory.

According to Avery Weisman (1972), we should instead be striving for an **appropriate death**. An appropriate death is the sort of death a person might

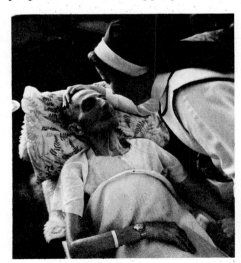

In hospices, a person may die with dignity, provided with affection and pain relief, allowed some control over important decisions, but not subjected to life-extending technology.

THE TIMING OF DEATH

From time to time, stories appear about people who either will themselves to die or else determinedly hang onto life until a long-awaited event, such as the birth of a grandchild or the return of a son from military service, occurs. In some communities, such control over the moment of death may be common. According to Murray Trelease (1975), who served as parish priest to Alaskan Indians during the 1960s, the time of dying often seemed to be chosen. In many cases, the dying individual spent several days making plans, telling his or her life story, and praying for family members. Then Trelease was called for and, a few hours after he had given Communion, the person would quietly die. Trelease cannot explain how the dying individual realized that death was close or was able to influence the time of death.

Among the Founding Fathers, two may have managed to postpone their deaths by a few days or hours. July 4, 1826, was the fiftieth anniversary of the Declaration of Independence, an important celebration in the young United States. On that momentous day both John Adams and Thomas Jefferson died. When the gravely ill Adams was asked if he knew what day it was, the former president replied, "It is the glorious Fourth of July." He then lapsed into a coma, reviving briefly to say, "Thomas Jefferson survives." A few hours later he was dead. Jefferson, whose health had been steadily declining, had been expected to die several days earlier. His pulse was barely perceptible, but just before midnight on July 3, he asked, "This is the Fourth?" Assured that it was, he died about 12 hours later (Slater and Solomita, 1980).

Intrigued by such stories, David Phillips (1972) decided to test them. He assumed that, because their celebrity drew attention to their birthdays, famous people might postpone their deaths until the day had passed. He checked the death dates of 348 noted Americans, noting how many died during the month before their birthday and how many died the following month. According to actuarial figures, 29 could be expected to die during any month. Phillips found that only 16 of these prominent people died in the month preceding their birthday, but that 36 died in the first month after their birthday, 27 in the second, and 41 in the third. In a second study, Phillips found that the more famous a person, the more

choose—if the choice were available. This means that patients would be protected from needless medical procedures that only dehumanize and demean them. An appropriate death would allow people to die with dignity and with some control over the manner of their death.

An appropriate death would allow the needs of the patients to be met. The basic needs of the dying are the control of pain, the retention of dignity, and love likely it was that his or her death was postponed until after his or her birthday. Among extremely famous people, such as Mark Twain and George Washington, there was a 78 percent drop in deaths during the month before the birthday. In people whose fame was slight, such as Nikola Tesla and Millard Fillmore, the death rate dropped only 20 percent.

At first it seemed that Phillips had shown some human control over the time of death. Then Richard Schulz and Max Bazerman (1980) noted a flaw in Phillips' study. He had forgotten to take into account the number of days before the birthday in the anniversary month, which should be included in any postponement of death. If the 31 days immediately preceding the birthday are used as the postponement period, the dip in deaths almost disappears.

Yet Schulz and Bazerman have not ruled out the possibility that human beings may be able to postpone their deaths. It may be that birthdays are not perceived as worth hanging on to celebrate. Perhaps if a similar analysis could be performed on occasions that are extremely important to individuals, such as the marriage of a child or the birth of a grandchild, we might find them preceded by a dip in deaths. Enormous obstacles stand in the way of such a study, however. The date of birth is a matter of public record, but the information required for any analysis of postponements for special events is not recorded on death certificates.

One such apparent case has been reported. According to David Jackson and Stuart Younger (1979), a 56-year-old woman with advanced cancer was in a coma. She had suffered cardiorespiratory arrest and was breathing with the aid of a respirator. The overwhelming majority of the medical staff believed that it was cruel to keep her alive and that the humane thing to do would be to disconnect the respirator, especially after she developed a urinary infection and pneumonia. But the woman seemed to have a goal; her daughter was 7 months pregnant, and she had repeatedly said that her one wish was to live long enough to see her grandchild. Slowly she recovered from her coma, and after 7 weeks in intensive care she was able to go home. She was awake, alert, and able to walk and take part in family activites. She saw her new granddaughter; spent Thanksgiving, Christmas, and New Year's with her family; and then died suddenly, 11 weeks after she had left the hospital.

and affection (Schulz, 1978). Unless pain is controlled, dignity may be threatened. One way to retain dignity is to allow patients some control over decisions that affect the course of illness. This can be done by keeping the patient informed about his or her condition. A knowledgeable patient can participate in the treatment program instead of being treated like an object to which things (tests, transfusions, intravenous feedings) are suddenly done. The patient's need for love and affection is best filled by physical contact—touching, holding—and by listening to the patient and giving assurances that he or she will not be abandoned.

The awareness that the needs of dying patients are difficult to meet in a hospital has led to the establishment of hospices. **Hospices** are institutions or wards within hospitals that use no technology to extend life but provide the dying with pain relief, attention, and affection. In 1948 the first hospice was founded in England by Dame Cicely Saunders. The movement has been growing rapidly and generally coordinates a program of home and hospice care. Under the direction of physicians, pain is relieved while leaving the patient alert. In the United States, a mixture of morphine and tranquilizers in a cherry syrup, supplemented by antidepressants, is commonly used (Lack, 1977).

Staff and volunteer aides help to fill the patient's need for love and affection, spending hours listening to the patient and providing physical contact. Visiting hours are virtually unrestricted, and the family is encouraged to spend as much time with the patient as they like. The family of the patient is seen as part of the treatment program, and after the death, the family is helped through the mourning process.

It appears that hospice treatment not only restores dignity to the patient but reduces medical costs as well. Although it is a labor-intensive program, it uses volunteers, rejects expensive medical technology, and—through coordinated home care—generally allows patients to stay at home for at least 2 weeks longer than is generally possible with standard medical care (Schulz, 1978).

Many patients at last accept death calmly and without any mental turmoil (Weisman, 1972). Many other dying patients fear not death, but the lengthy dying process, which they believe will be marked by prolonged pain, increasing weakness, helplessness, and the sense that one has become a burden (Bok, 1978). New attitudes toward dying, as exemplified in the hospice movement, may do much to reduce such fears.

BURIAL RITES AND MOURNING CUSTOMS

Once death comes, concern shifts from prolonging life to repairing the social fabric, which has been torn by death. All societies have some sort of rules and rituals regarding the disposal of dead bodies and the behavior of the survivors (Bowlby, 1980). According to anthropologist Raymond Firth (1961) funeral rites help the bereaved, maintain the integrity of society, and provide for economic exchange. They assist the bereaved by making the loss of the loved one real, by giving them a socially sanctioned opportunity to express their grief, and by defining a mourning period, which sets a date for their return to full community life. The rites maintain society by allowing other community members to take leave of a member, to express their loss publicly, and to channel their fear and anger in acceptable ways. The economic benefits involve an exchange of goods and services between families and groups, which demonstrates family cohesion and the solidarity of kin relationships, assuring community members that they can count on such assistance themselves when their own family members die.

Funeral rites are believed to be most important to a society when the death rate is high and the society is precarious. In a tribal society with an extremely high mortality rate, for example, death may be seen as threatening the cohesiveness of the group and, thus, the culture itself. Through elaborate funeral rituals, property and other rights may be transferred and the threat to community stability minimized (Marshall, 1980).

In the United States, the funeral ritual often consists of a wake, in which the embalmed body is displayed in the mortuary for viewing by friends and family; a formal funeral service at a mortuary or church; and a graveside burial service. Jewish rites omit the wake and substitute a week of formal mourning, called shivah, when prayers are said for the dead and friends call on the grieving family to pay their last respects.

The custom of viewing the body has been both praised and criticized. One of its values is the presentation of the dead person as a body, making the death real and helping survivors to accept its finality (Pine, 1975). Another value is believed to be an easing of the mourning process, with the "normal-looking" embalmed body smoothing over any suffering or covering any mutilation that might have preceded death (Parsons and Lidz, 1967). This presentation of a lifelike body has been condemned by others as an example of our denial of death, with the "slumbering" corpse seen as a rejection of bodily decay (Marshall, 1980). Such a "calming reunion" with the corpse, said Aries (1974), blurs the realization that death has occurred and banishes sadness and mourning. Survivors react in different ways to the viewing of the body. In one study of widows (Glick, Weiss, and Parkes, 1974), 52 percent found the experience unpleasant, and about 30 percent regretted having seen the corpse. Only 14 percent said they were glad they had seen the body. However, some who reported almost unbearable feelings of loss on seeing the body said such things as, "I didn't believe he was dead until I saw him in the casket" (p. 110). It is, of course, just this recognition that is seen as one of the values of funeral rites.

Some social recognitions of mourning, in the form of black dress or armbands and a specified period of mourning, have virtually disappeared in many part of American and English society. The loss of such clear social expectations is believed by some to be harmful (Gorer, 1965; Parkes, 1972). Without social guidelines, a grieving survivor may be confused and insecure, uncertain just how to express grief and when reentry into normal social roles is appropriate. As we will see, the process of grieving does not always lead to recovery.

THE PROCESS OF GRIEVING

There are at least two parties to every death—the person who dies and the survivor or survivors who mourn (Toynbee, 1968). The desolation that follows the loss of a loved one is known as **bereavement,** and it has been called the "most severe psychological trauma most people will encounter in the course of their lives" (Parkes and Weiss, 1983). The survivors' grief is so much sharper than the pain of dying, says Toynbee (1968), that people who truly love one another would choose to survive their beloved in order to spare him or her the terrible burden of grief. Despite its pain, grief may have a positive function.

THE USES OF GRIEF

The person who grieves experiences physiological and psychological symptoms. During acute grief, a person may feel tightness in the throat, shortness of breath, a choking sensation, the need to sigh, an empty feeling in the pit of the stomach, weakness, and pangs of intense distress (Lindemann, 1944). A 30-year-old widow tried to describe her feelings:

I had heard that expression, "heartache," and I had read it, but this is the only time I really knew what it feels like. It is pain inside me, physical pain, all the way up. It's very tight and I get very hurt. It's inside the heart that I hurt" [Parkes and Weiss, 1983, p. 1].

In most instances, these sensations occur periodically and may last from 20 minutes to an hour. The grieving person may be unable to sleep, eat, or carry out daily activites.

Such reactions are considered a "normal" response to the loss of a loved one. Most "normal" responses, such as the physical pain that causes us to withdraw a hand from a hot surface, have a function, and attempts to discover the function of acute grief have produced two major explanations. According to Sigmund Freud (1917), grief is a process that reflects our attempt to free ourselves from our tie to the deceased person. Although we try to withdraw from this bond, we continue to cling to it, so that the symptoms of bereavement reflect the inner struggle that results when realization of our loss conflicts with our desire to hold onto the person. In the process, our thoughts dwell on the dead person, and we go over each separate memory. In this view, mourning is useful because it detaches us from the dead and allows us to reestablish our lives in their absence.

Other theorists see the causes and function of grief differently. John Bowlby and Murray Parkes (1970) see grief as an adaptive mechanism. They believe that the outward signs of grief are primarily an attempt at reunion, and they point out that these are found in social animals as well as in human beings. When parent and child or mates are separated, both become anxious and search for the other, often crying out and attacking anyone who tries to stop them. If death is not the cause of separation, the signs of grief may reunite the pair, and this reunion may be grief's major adaptive function. In any case, obvious grieving may cause other individuals to offer aid, or it may signal that a special situation exists in which normal social rules are suspended. The grief-stricken person is treated as if ill and allowed to behave in ways that are usually considered unacceptable (Parkes and Weiss, 1983). In fact, others (Averill, 1968) have seen this secondary function of grief as its adaptive purpose because it brings the group to the aid of the bereaved, protecting the mourner and reducing his or her vulnerability.

After a time, the acute signs of grief subside, but grieving is not over at this point. It has been suggested that, when dealing with loss, most people go through a similar series of stages.

THE STAGES OF GRIEF

The process of dying has been seen as moving through a series of stages that culminate in the acceptance of loss of self. Grief has similarly been seen as a process that moves through stages of adaptation to the loss of others. The four stages of normal grief—numbness, yearning, disorganization and despair, and reorganization—are not sharply marked off, but blend into one another (Parkes, 1972). In the first stage, which usually begins a few minutes after the death, a person is shocked and may feel little emotion other than emptiness or numbness. There also may be partial disbelief or an insistence that some mistake has been made. After a few hours or days, this protective numbness gives way to yearning, the second stage of grief, in which the acute reactions described earlier flood through the person.

The survivor's yearning is characterized by tension, high arousal, restless activity, and a continual search for the lost person, in which the bereaved may cry out the dead person's name or go to locations he or she used to frequent. The survivor develops a **perceptual set**, expecting at any moment to see or hear the person. Because of this set, sounds may be interpreted as the person's voice, passersby at first appear to be the deceased person, or an illusion of the person may be seen, sitting in a favorite chair or working in the garden. Many survivors feel the presence of the dead person although they never have the illusion of any physical presence. In one study of nearly three hundred Welsh widows and widowers (Rees, 1970), 39 percent had felt the presence of their dead spouse and 14 percent had experienced hallucinations of his or her presence.

The search for the lost person is accompanied by a continual reworking of memories, especially memories surrounding the death. This is often an "if only" process, in which the survivor goes over and over the death, trying to decide what might have happened had different choices of action been taken. For example, a widower whose wife died of cancer might think, "If only I had insisted that she see a doctor sooner," or a mother whose small son had been hit by a car might think. "If only I hadn't let him go out to play." Feelings of guilt alternate with feelings of anger, in which survivors angrily blames someone else—the doctor, the hospital, God, or the deceased person—for the death and, thus, their grief.

Once the intense yearning is over, the survivor often becomes depressed. During this disorganization stage of grief, he or she may become apathetic and submissive, pervaded by a sense of defeat. A typical attitude is "You sometimes can't help wondering whether anything is worthwhile any more" (Parkes and Weiss, 1983). Widows are more likely than widowers to go through this depressive stage. Anger has not completely disappeared, but its strongest expression is over. Sometimes survivors in this third stage of grief will be filled with panic and say they would run away if they only had somewhere to go. It is still possible for pangs of grief to reoccur should a situation arise that reminds the survivor of the dead person, but such acute attacks are infrequent.

Finally, the reorganization stage begins. In order to recover from bereavement, a person must accept the loss intellectually, accept the loss emotionally, and reorganize his or her self-concept, establishing an identity and world view that reflect the new reality (Parkes and Weiss, 1983). Intellectual acceptance requires the survivor to understand the death and to see the world as continuing to make sense. Without this understanding, the survivor will live under the continual expectation of new losses. Emotional acceptance allows the survivor to find more pleasure than pain in remembering the dead person. The new identity will be based on roles that do not assume the existence of the dead person. The mother of a dead child no longer thinks of herself as "Sally's mother," and the widower no longer thinks of himself as "Mary's husband." The recovery process is generally well underway within a year, and by that time some intellectual and emotional acceptance has been reached. The process of normal grieving can be lengthy, and the new identity may not be firmly established for another two or three years. For some people, recovery may never come.

ABNORMAL PATTERNS OF GRIEF

Grief is not the same for everyone. Murray Parkes and Robert Weiss (1983) have identified three patterns of abnormal grief in which the prospects of recovery are shaky. These patterns appeared in the Harvard Bereavement Study, a longitudinal study of widows and widowers younger than 45. Survivors whose response to loss did not lead to recovery showed unanticipated grief, conflicted grief, or chronic grief.

Unanticipated Grief

When death is expected, as when a person dies after a lengthy illness, the pain of bereavement is sharp, but it tends to follow the course of normal grieving. When there is less than 2 weeks' warning that an illness is fatal and less than 3 days' warning that death is imminent, however, **unanticipated grief** develops, and chances of normal recovery shrink. Knowledge of impending death appears to

When death strikes without warning, survivors may still be anxious, lonely, and depressed for years afterward, withdrawing socially and refusing to accept the reality of their loss.

give survivors an opportunity to prepare although Parkes and Weiss believe that no anticipatory grieving takes place during this period. During the anticipatory period, they found no sign of any grieving that allowed the surviving spouse to move into the bereavement process early. However, forewarning allows both parties in the death to resolve and round off their relationships, so that the survivor is less likely to feel guilt and self-reproach. The death becomes predictable, and because it is seen as having a cause, the world continues to make sense. This predictability also allows the survivor to rehearse and prepare for the death as he or she learns to live with the prospect of the loss.

Among widows and widowers in the Harvard Bereavement Study, those whose spouses died with almost no forewarning were more likely to have trouble accepting the reality of their loss, to be filled with guilt, and to show more anger than widows and widowers who had had considerable warning. Two to 4 years after the death, about half of those with unanticipated grief still had trouble accepting the reality of the death, and even more found it inexplicable. More than half were also still anxious, lonely, depressed, and filled with self-reproach. They tended to be withdrawn socially, refused to date, and were concerned about their ability to function as a spouse, a parent, or a worker.

Conflicted Grief

Contrary to expectations, widows and widowers whose marriage had been filled with conflict and dissension faced a more difficult recovery from bereavement that those whose marriages had been happy. This connection between lack of recovery and a conflict-ridden marriage was apparent only among those who had had forewarning of the death. When there was no forewarning, participation in an unhappy marriage did not seem to pose an additional risk.

Survivors of conflict-ridden marriages went through **conflicted grief.** They tended to show little grief during the first few weeks after their spouses' death, accepting their loss and sometimes even welcoming it. Most returned early to social activities. Within a year, however, these widows and widowers often showed delayed grief. At a time when others were recovering from their grief, these survivors had become unable to accept their loss and were filled with self-reproach. Two to 4 years after the death, approximately half of this group were in poor physical health, guilty, angry, depressed, and concerned about their functioning as parent or worker. Six out of 10 had begun to yearn for the lost spouse whose death had seemingly had little effect on them, and eight out of ten were anxiety-ridden.

Why were survivors of unhappy marriages unable to put their grief behind them? The researchers suggest that most of these survivors had ambivalent relationships with their spouses and that the ambivalence left them filled with regret and self-reproach. Their grief may have been as much for the good marriage they had never had as for the empty, unhappy marriage they had endured. In addition, these widows and widowers may have wished at times that their marital partners would die and end the relationship. When that actually happened, they may have felt like murderers and begun to grieve in restitution for their mental crime.

Chronic Grief

The third abnormal grief pattern, **chronic grief,** seemed to be predicted by a marriage in which one partner was highly dependent on the other. The dependent partner felt unable to carry out ordinary roles without the presence, emotional support, or help of the other. With the partner gone, the survivor's insecurity was so great that he or she was unable to establish an autonomous existence.

Widows and widowers whose grief became chronic displayed extremely intense yearning shortly after their spouses' death. However, high yearning without dependency was not related to chronic grief. About a year afterward, they were more lonely and tearful than other survivors and still showed levels of grief that would have been considered "normal" a few weeks after the death. Two to 4 years after the loss, more than half were still anxious and said they would not care if they died the next day.

The widows and widowers in this study were comparatively young and faced with grief at a period in their lives when death is unexpected. Death that strikes at other times in the life cycle may have somewhat different effects.

OTHER FACES OF DEATH

Most studies of grief are centered on the loss of a spouse, and the majority concern young and middle-aged widows and widowers. Bereavement that involves other relationships and older age groups may follow a different course. An examination of parents' reactions to the death of a child and reactions to the death of an older spouse may help to place the study of middle-aged widows and widowers in perspective.

Grieving for a Child

In this society, infants and children are not supposed to die, and the rarity of such deaths may make them especially difficult to bear. Parents grieve not only for the infant or child they have lost but for their perceptions of the person their child would have become (Callahan, Brasted, and Granados, 1983).

When an infant dies without warning from crib death, known as sudden infant death syndrome (SIDS), the parents' immediate reaction is shock, disbelief, and anger. Because, in most cases, the child has appeared healthy or shown only minor signs of nasal congestion, the unexpectedness of the death places this bereavement on a course similar to that of widows and widowers who suffer from unanticipated grief. However, the mourning of parents of SIDS victims is complicated by two additional factors. First, the death of an infant is so unusual that people do not know how to respond to the parents. Often a conspiracy of silence develops, in which friends avoid the issue entirely (Helmrath and Sternitz, 1978). When the matter cannot be avoided, others may either try to minimize the loss, perhaps by saying, "It's all right; you have another child at home," or hint that the parents are to blame (Callahan, Brasted, and Granados, 1983). Such responses isolate the parents and increase the burden of bereavement. Second, because the causes of SIDS is unknown, it is difficult to understand the death. The lack of a scientific cause also may result in one partner's accusing the other of neglecting the child.

Despite these additional problems, most parents manage to adapt to the death, perhaps because their central roles of worker and spouse are intact. On occasion, however, the effects are permanent. Sometimes the death of an infant leads to a disruption of the marriage, especially when communication between partners already is poor. Other couples are so afraid of repeating the loss that they resolve never to have another child.

In her work with parents who have lost a child by accident, Elisabeth Kübler-Ross (Kübler-Ross and Goleman, 1976) has found that after the initial shock, a deep rage wells up that needs to be expressed before parents can come to terms with the death. She also believes that the way many hospitals handle such accidental deaths interferes with the mourning process and increases the likelihood of chronic grief. In most cases, parents are sedated as soon as the child is declared dead, a practice that only denies or postpones the necessary grief. And unless parents see the corpse of their child, they find it extremely difficult to accept the death. Five years after her child's death, one mother who had not been allowed to see the corpse still turned down the child's bed each night. Finally, Kübler-Ross recommends that the parents return to the hospital about a month after the death so they can ask the questions they were too numbed to think of at the time they received the news. This practice gives parents the sort of concrete detail that makes the death real to them.

Grieving for the Old

The death of a spouse who has lived into later adulthood may be easier on the surviving spouse than the death that strikes in young or middle adulthood. Although some older widows and widowers show abnormal grief patterns, research seems to indicate that younger widows are more likely to have health and emotional problems. (Maddison and Walker, 1967). Among the patients of eight London physicians, widows younger than 65 were more likely than older widows to complain to their physician of emotional problems. The younger widows also took seven times as much sedation in the 6 months following the death as in the 6 months preceding it and continued their consumption at almost the same rate over the second 6 months. Older widows, however, did not increase their consumption of sedatives after their husbands died (Parkes, 1972).

Two explanations have been put forth for the greater adaptability of older widows and widowers (Parkes and Weiss, 1983). Cohort effects may be responsible for some of the difference. Older adults grew up at a time when death was more common than today and when mourning customs were universally observed. If, as some psychologists and sociologists believe, such rituals lessen the burden of bereavement, the adherence of older adults to custom may help them through their grief. Experience with death and the expectation of it may also make bereavement easier for older adults to bear. Because death is expected to arrive during later adulthood, even the sudden death of an elderly spouse may not seem untimely. If this is so, then intellectual and emotional understanding may be easier and unanticipated grief less hazardous for the old.

BEREAVEMENT COUNSELING

Most people manage to adjust to the death of loved ones, but abnormal grief concerns many researchers. This concern has led to the development of programs that help people through the months after the death of a loved one. Such programs, which have been called **subvention,** or bereavement counseling, try to reduce the aftereffects of death on the survivors and help them to live more productively and with less stress than if they are left to their own devices (Shneidman, 1973). Most programs use techniques common to individual or group therapy, and survivors are encouraged to express their emotions and to develop a personal relationship with the therapist.

According to Parkes and Weiss (1983), not all survivors require bereavement counseling. Based on the results of the Harvard Bereavement Study, a Bereavement Risk Index has been developed to predict which survivors are in danger of developing one of the abnormal grief patterns. Only these high-risk survivors are offered counseling at St. Christopher's Hospice in London; indeed, Parkes and Weiss believe that low-risk survivors could be harmed, not helped, by bereavement counseling. Most of those who do need help, they say, require assistance in ending their grief, not in establishing it. Among widows and widowers, for example, they believe that further encouraging the expression of grief helps only those who have survived conflict-ridden marriages and are in danger of falling into the conflicted grief pattern.

At the University of Virgina Medical Center, a program aimed at just this group of survivors has been developed. People suffering from conflicted grief are helped by what has been called regriefing therapy. Although years have passed since the death, survivors are taken through the original grief process again in the hope that it will help them reach emotional and intellectual understanding of the death. In addition, therapists help them deal with their ambivalent love-hate feelings toward the dead person (Horn, 1974).

One counseling program uses survivors who have adjusted to their loss to assist newly bereaved individuals. In the Widow-to-Widow Program, widows who have emerged from the reorganization stage of grief contact new widows, providing advice, reassurance, assistance, and a sympathetic ear. In group meetings, practical advice, such as how to handle finances, is available (Silverman et al., 1974).

In Port Chester, New York, subvention is handled through group discussions for survivors. The program was established by a local hospital after the medical staff realized that a large proportion of their patients had recently lost someone close to them and that many survivors were turning to drugs and alcohol in an attempt to cushion the effect of their loss. In a series of six group discussions led by professional counselors, survivors learn about normal grieving, an understanding that the medical staff believes helps protect them from the physical and emotional consequences of chronic grief (Spear, 1983).

Bereavement counseling at St. Christopher's Hospice appears to have reduced the more dramatic consequences of bereavement. Survivors of patients at the hospice are rated on the Bereavement Risk Index, and trained counselors visit all ''high-risk'' widows and widowers about 10 days after the death of the spouse.

During the 8 years since the program was instituted, suicide among survivors has declined by more than two thirds (Parkes and Weiss, 1983).

Perhaps the need for bereavement counseling arises when society becomes large and impersonal. When communities were small and mobility was limited, most individuals were woven into the social network in such a way that support after bereavement was automatically provided. It may also be that our postponement of death has made bereavement more difficult. When life expectancy was short and death came early and struck often, people may have been better equipped to handle their grief than most of us are today. As noted in Chapter 1, when infant and child mortality was extremely high, the death of offspring seemed to occasion little lasting grief. The change seems well worth the risk of hazardous bereavement.

SUMMARY

Attempts to determine the moment of death have led to the development of several definitions. In most instances, the absence of spontaneous breathing and heartbeat, or **clinical death,** is sufficient. The use of medical technology to prolong respiration and heartbeat has led to the acceptance of **brain death** as establishing the end of life although some proposed that **cerebral death** is sufficient. Because of the increase in life expectancy, death has come to be associated with old age. As a result of social and medical change, most people now die in hospitals, a development that has been associated with the modern denial of death.

Individual views of death are shaped by the belief system of a culture. Among the strategies that have been used to reconcile human beings to death are hedonism, pessimism, physical countermeasures, fame, putting one's treasure in future generations, merging the self with ultimate reality, personal immortality, resurrection of the body, and the hope of heaven and the fear of hell. Over the past 8 centuries, the experience and meaning of death in the Western world have changed, and Phillipe Aries has charted the transformations as the tame death, death of the self, remote and imminent death, death of the other, and the invisible death.

An awareness of impending personal death develops as a result of age, family history, the death of siblings, self-perceived health, and the death of friends. The anticipation of death may start a process of **life review,** which may solve past conflicts and give meaning to life or rework the past in order to defend a person's self-concept. Although there are conflicting data, it appears that the fear of death is greatest among the young, with older people fearing death the least because they value their own life less, feel they have achieved typical life expectancy, and are socialized to expect death.

Patients with terminal illness often are deceived by their physicians. However, despite the concealment, most learn that their illness is fatal. Even so, the ritual drama of mutual pretense frequently lasts until it is clear that the patient will soon die. Elisabeth Kübler-Ross has proposed that the **dying trajectory** consists of five stages: denial and isolation, anger and resentment, bargaining, depression, and acceptance. However, it appears that all patients do not go through all the stages and that the stages may occur in any order. The hospitalization of death and the prolongation of the dying trajectory have led to the establishment of **hospices,** where patients may have an **appropriate death.**

All societies have some sort of funeral rites, which appear to help the bereaved, maintain the integrity of society, and provide for economic exchange. The disappearance of social recognitions of mourning may confuse survivors, leaving them uncertain about how to express their grief and when to reenter normal social roles.

Bereavement has been called the most severe psychological trauma most people ever encounter. Grief has physiological and psychological symptoms, and it has been seen as both an attempt to detach us from the dead and an adaptive mechanism that either leads to reunion after separation or brings aid from others. The stages of grief—numbness, yearning, disorganization and despair and reorganization—are not sharply demarcated. Numbness may last for days or weeks, to be followed by yearning, which is the acute stage of grief. During this stage, the survivors's **perceptual set** leads to expectations of encountering the dead person. Depression is common during the disorganization stage, and during the reorganization stage the survivor accepts the loss intellectually and emotionally, developing an identity that does not depend on the dead person. Among abnormal grief patterns are **unanticipated grief, conflicted grief,** and **chronic grief.** Parents generally are able to adapt to the death of a child, perhaps because their roles of worker and spouse are intact. Grief among older widows and widowers may not be as severe as grief among the young, perhaps because of cohort differences, an adherence to ritual, greater experience with death, and expectation of death during later adulthood. Bereavement counseling, or **subvention,** is not necessary for all survivors, but it is helpful for those who are in danger of developing one of the abnormal grief patterns.

KEY TERMS

appropriate death	**dying trajectory**
bereavement	**hospice**
brain death	**life review**
cerebral death	**perceptual set**
chronic grief	**subvention**
clinical death	**unanticipated grief**
conflicted grief	

GLOSSARY

accommodation ability of the eye to change its shape in order to focus properly

acute illness a physical disorder with a limited duration

acute brain dysfunction a reversible brain disorder characterized by disturbed metabolism throughout the brain; also known as delirium

adulthood the portion of the life span after maturity

ageism discrimination against older adults

age-irrelevant society a society in which age loses much of its meaning as a predictor of the way a person lives

age-normative influences influences that affect almost every person in a particular society at about the same point in the life span

age set a group of individuals born within a certain span of years (usually from 7 to 15) who move together through the life cycle

age-stratification a sociological model of aging in which people are viewed as living through a sequence of age-related positions or roles

alcoholism a substance abuse disorder in which dependence on alcohol interferes with health, personal relationships, occupation, and social functioning

alveoli tubes and ducts within the lung that lead to the air sacs

Alzheimer's disease the major cause of chronic brain dysfunction, known as senile dementia in older people and presenile dementia in the young; death usually comes about 5 years after diagnosis

androgynous possessing a high degree of both male and female personality traits

appropriate death the sort of death a person might choose—if the choice were available

arousal activation of the cortex and reticular formation in the brain, which generally leads to some action

arteriosclerosis thickening and stiffening of arterial walls

astrocyte glial cell within the nervous system that apparently keeps neurotransmitters from accumulating in the spaces between neurons

atherosclerosis thickening and stiffening of arterial walls, accompanied by deposit of hard, yellow, fatty plaques that can choke off the supply of blood

atropic gastritis chronic inflammation of the stomach, characterized by destruction of mucous and peptic glands; it is not caused by normal aging

average life span mean age of survival for members of any species

bereavement the grief that follows the death of a loved one

biological age the individual's position on his or her own potential life span; it is closely connected with physical health

brain death death as measured by death of the cortex, midbrain, and brain stem

canalization genetic predisposition that

guides development in a direction that is difficult to deflect and that is expressed in any natural human environment

cardiac output the volume of blood pumped by the heart in one minute

career occupation characterized by interrelated training and work experience, in which a person moves upward into a series of increasingly remunerative positions requiring additional responsibility

cataract age-related visual disorder, in which the lens becomes opaque so that light cannot penetrate it

cerebral death death as measured by death of the cortex; the midbrain and brain stem still may be functioning

chronic grief abnormal grief pattern, in which lasting grief follows the death of a partner in a relationship in which one partner was highly dependent on the other

chronic illness long-standing health problem that cannot be cured and that tends to get worse with time

chronic organic brain dysfunction an irreversible organic brain disorder that ends in death after a long decline; *see* **Alzheimer's disease, multi-infarct dementia**

chronological age elapsed time since birth

classical conditioning simple form of learning, in which an emotion or muscular response is transferred to a new stimulus

climacteric gradual decline in ovarian function known as ''change of life'' that culminates in menopause

clinical death death as measured by the termination of spontaneous breathing and heartbeat

cognitive style an individual's habitual way of attending to information, perceiving it, remembering it, and thinking about it

cohabitation an arrangement in which couples live together without legal marriage

cohort generation of people born at the same time

common-law marriage a form of marriage, legal in some states, in which a cohabiting couple's declaration of marriage is treated by the state as a legally contracted marriage

competence person's ability to respond to the demands of the environment

conflicted grief abnormal, delayed grief shown by survivor of a conflict-ridden marriage

congregate housing housing in which tenants have their own apartments but eat in a common dining room

consolidation stage career stage, beginning at about age 35, when an experienced person advances as far as possible

creative pleasures leisure activities of medium-high intensity; ''useful play''

creativity novel response that brings together previously unconnected elements in a new and unusual way

cross-linkage theory theory of aging that assumes aging results from the accumulation of cross-links between molecules, produced as a by-product of metabolism

cross-sectional design research design in which two or more age groups, each from a different cohort, are studied at one time

crystallization stage career stage, in which an adolescent explores various fields, matching needs, interests, and values with opportunities

crystallized intelligence acquired knowledge and developed intellectual skills, which reflect the application of fluid intelligence to cultural content

delirium *see* **acute brain dysfunction**

depression an affective disorder, in which a continuing despondent mood is accompanied by pessimism, low self-esteem, and feelings of foreboding

development any age-related change in body or behavior from conception to death

developmental pleasures leisure activities of medium intensity that increase physical or cognitive skills

dialectical approach a psychological view of development, in which people are assumed to interact with a continually changing environment, so that each generation presumably reaches a new level of functioning

disengagement a gradual withdrawal from social roles and a decreased involvement with others that some sociologists believed was typical of older adults

diversion leisure activies of medium-low involvement that provide a change of pace and relief from routine activities

diverticulosis a condition in which irregular pouches develop along the walls of the large intestine, often becoming obstructed, infected, and painfully inflamed

DNA-repair theory a theory of aging that proposes aging is caused when accumulated DNA damage destroys the ability of cells to function

double jeopardy the proposal that, because old people and ethnic minorities are both stereotyped and discriminated against, older adults who belong to minority groups are the victims of double discrimination, making aging more stressful and more negative for minorities than for whites

Down's syndrome a genetic disorder marked by characteristic facial features, some degree of mental retardation, and premature aging

dying trajectory the emotional states that one passes through during the process of dying

elastin the fibers of protein that make up about 30 percent of arterial walls

emphysema a lung disorder in which the walls separating the alveoli are destroyed, reducing respiratory lung surface

encode to record information in the memory system for later retrieval

environmental press demands of the environment that motivate the individual

episodic memory memory record of events, in which each memory is linked with a time and place

ethnic group any group within a society that is distinguished by race, religion, or national identity; *see* **minority**

external validity the extent to which information produced by research or testing can be applied in other situations

factor analysis statistical technique, by which researchers examine people's performance on a variety of tasks, looking for relationships between them

field dependent cognitive style, in which people find it difficult to separate a part from an organized whole and rely on surrounding stimuli when making perceptual judgments

field independent cognitive style, in which people easily separate a part from an organized whole and can ignore surrounding stimuli when making perceptual judgments

flexibility cognitive style, in which people shift easily from one activity or method to another when it becomes apparent that the previous approach is no longer useful

fluid intelligence basic cognitive processes, which are required to identify and understand relationships and to draw inferences on the basis of that understanding

formal operational thought logical, abstract thought that can be applied to hypothetical situations; in Piaget's system, it is the most advanced form of thought

free-radical theory theory of aging that proposes aging is the result of the bonding of free radicals to other molecules

functional age a person's ability to function in society; it probably reflects biological, psychological, and social age

functional mental disorder a mental disorder that is unrelated to brain deterioration and has no organic basis

generational stake personal interest in a relationship between generations

generativity ego strength of middle age in Erikson's theory; made up of procreativity, productivity, and creativity

gerontology the scientific study of aging

glaucoma visual disorder, in which a steady increase in pressure develops within the eye because fluid is unable to leave the eye by the normal channel

Hayflick limit approximate boundary to

the cell's ability to divide, which is between 40 and 60 times in human fetal tissue

history-normative influences influences that result from circumstances that exist at a particular historical moment

hospice institutions or wards within hospitals, where the dying are given pain relief, attention, and affection, but no technology is used to extend the life span

hypochrondriasis a somatoform disorder, characterized by physical symptoms that have no organic basis and an exaggerated fear of disease

hypertension high blood pressure

identity stable sense of self that is confirmed by experience, so that self-perceptions match the perception of one's self by others; in Erikson's theory, the ego strength of adolescence

immunological theory a programmed theory of aging in which the immune system loses its ability to recognize foreign substances and abnormal cells and begins to attack the body

implementation stage career stage in which a young person makes an initial commitment to a vocation and takes an entry-level position

impulsivity cognitive style, in which people scan possibilities hastily, decide quickly, and make many errors

information processing view of human cognitive functioning as a system that manipulates, stores, classifies, and retrieves information

in-kind income goods and services that require no expenditure, such as medical services covered by Medicare or food stamps

intelligence mental operations that enhance the ability to function effectively in the environment

interindividual differences differences in patterns of change across individuals

intimacy an emotional state characterized by acceptance, self-disclosure, and feelings of trust and closeness

intraindividual change changes within the individual

ischemic heart disease an age-related condition in which the heart muscle is starved for oxygen, apparently as a result of atherosclerosis

job occupation with limited upward advancement

keratoses warty skin growths, which are either dry and light-colored or greasy and dark-colored; they may appear anywhere on the body

Korsakoff's syndrome an organic brain disorder found in alcoholics that is caused by long-term vitamin B deficiencies

later adulthood the third and final period of adulthood; in this book, arbitrarily set at the portion of the life span after the age of 60

learned helplessness condition in which a person has repeatedly failed to cope with environmental stess and, feeling powerless, has ceased all attempts to cope

leisure activities freely chosen activity, so that any single activity may be obligatory for one person and leisure for another

life-cycle squeeze economic or emotional stress caused by the interaction of basic life-cycle patterns associated with work and family, as when the care of an aging parent and responsibility for children overlap

life expectancy the number of years the average person can expect to live

life review a process in which people survey, observe, and reflect upon their past, believed to be initiated by the anticipation of death

life structure underlying pattern of a person's life in Levinson's theory of development

lipofuscin an inert brown pigment that accumulates in body cells and is associated with the aging process

longevity the length, or duration, of life

longitudinal design a research design in which a group from a single cohort is studied at several ages

long-term memory unlimited capacity system, containing all the information that could possibly be available to us

maximum life span the oldest age to which any individuals in a species survive

mechanistic model psychological view of development in which people are seen as being like machines, so that development follows regular laws

melanin dark pigment in the skin that produces tanning and age spots

melanocytes pigment-containing cells in the skin

menopause cessation of menstruation, usually around the age of 50

metamemory understanding of the way the memory system works

middle adulthood the second portion of adulthood; in this book, arbitrarily set at the years between 40 and 60

midlife crisis physical and psychological distress that develops when the developmental tasks of middle age threaten to overwhelm a person's internal resources and systems of social support

minority any group excluded from full participation in society because of physical or cultural characteristics; *see* **ethnic group**

modified extended family the typical form of contemporary American families, in which the generations live apart but are linked by mutual aid and affection

multi-infarct dementia a chronic organic brain disorder apparently caused by repeated interruptions of blood supply to the brain

neurofibrillary tangles bundles of paired, helical filaments that accumulate in the brain with age, but that have not been clearly established as due to primary aging

neurosis any functional brain disorder in which the person remains in touch with reality, whether or not he or she is able to carry out normal functions

nocturnal myoclonus a sleep disorder in which the sleeper's leg muscles twitch or jerk

nonnormative influence developmental factor that is specific to an individual and does not affect all members of society or all members of any cohort

normal aging see **primary aging**

normative stability a type of constancy in which a person's individual characteristic may change but remains at the same rank in comparison with other members of his or her own cohort

old-age dependency ratio the number of people over 65 in a society divided by the number between 18 and 64

operant conditioning a form of learning in which behavior changes as a result of reinforcement

organic brain disorders mental and emotional disruptions caused by physical changes within the brain; in elderly people, the condition is commonly called senility

organismic model a psychological view of development in which people are seen as active organisms whose changes are due to interaction with the environment

osteoarthritis a painful inflammation of the joints apparently caused by the rubbing together of bone ends

osteoporosis a loss of calcium from the bone that is so pronounced that the bones become brittle and break easily

outreach services programs that are designed to inform the public about the existence of other services

paranoid disorder a functional mental disorder in which the person has either a grandiose delusion or delusions of persecution

paraphrenia a mild form of schizophrenia that makes its first appearance in older adults

parental imperative the proposal that parenthood plays a pivotal and controlling role over the life span and that basic personality differences between the sexes have evolved with the requirements of young children in mind

Parkinson's disease a chronic organic brain disorder, accompanied by a tremor and a distinctive posture and walk, which often leads to severe mental impairment

perceptual set readiness to perceive stimuli in a particular way

periodontal disease an inflammation of the gums and surrounding tissue that can cause bone loss and loosened teeth

personality consistency of thinking, feeling, and reacting within a person that accounts for similarities in his or her behavior

personality dimension related traits that are part of the structure of personality

postpartum depression a temporary depression that develops in some women following childbirth

presbycusis progessive, age-related loss of the ability to hear high-frequency sounds

presbyopia inability to focus the eyes at short range; farsightedness

presenile dementia *see* **Alzheimer's disease**

primary aging the inevitable, gradual, age-related changes that can be observed in all members of a species; also called normal aging

proactive interference disruption in learning caused when old material interferes with new material to be learned

production deficiency failure to use a skill or capacity that a person possesses

progeria an extremely rare disease that causes extreme aging in young children

programmed theories theories of aging based on the belief that aging is genetically controlled

psychological age age in terms of adaptive ability, reflecting intellectual skills, emotions, and motivation

psychometry field of mental testing

psychosis a functional brain disorder in which normal mental activity is severely impaired and the person's perception of reality is drastically distorted

psychosocial moratorium a period between childhood and adulthood when life choices can be worked on but no commitment is made

random sample a sample in which every member of a group that will be studied has an equal chance of being selected

reflection cognitive style, in which people carefully consider all possibilities, take a long time to reach a decision, and make few errors

relaxation the least intense form of leisure, including resting, daydreaming, and sleeping

retroactive interference disruption in learning caused when previously learned material interferes with material to be learned

rigidity cognitive style, in which people are unlikely to shift from one activity or method to another even when the change is beneficial

sample the group of people selected for study and who represent a larger group

schizophrenia the most common psychosis, characterized by disturbed thought, perception, and emotions and often accompanied by delusions and hallucinations

secondary aging changes associated with aging that are caused by abuse, disuse, and disease, but that are neither universal nor inevitable

self-concept organized, coherent, and integrated pattern of perceptions related to the self, encompassing self-esteem and self-image

semantic memory organized knowledge about the world and about rules for manipulating other knowledge

senile dementia *see* **Alzheimer's disease**

senile plaques patches of debris found in the cell bodies of the brain; although they seem inevitable in advanced old age, they are more common in diseased brains

sensory memory fleeting register of environmental information

sensual pleasures the most intense form of leisure activities, in which the activation of the senses provides intense pleasure, gratification, excitement, rapture, or joy

sequential design a research design that combines elements of cross-sectional, longitudinal, and time-lag designs, in either a cross-sectional or longitudinal sequence

short-term memory a limited capacity system that keeps information in consciousness

sleep apnea a sleep disorder in which the sleeper stops breathing for a least 10 seconds

social age age as determined by a person's roles and habits relative to those expected by society for particular ages

social-learning theory a psychological view of development that grew out of mechanistic models, but that sees the individual as somewhat active

socialization the process by which people absorb the attitudes, values, and beliefs of their society

specification stage career stage roughly corresponding to undergraduate college years, when an individual makes specific career decisions and takes job training

stabilization stage career stage roughly corresponding to the years between 25 and 35, when an individual becomes established in a chosen field

stimulus persistence slowness of the nervous system to recover from stimulation, a condition believed to be age-related

stress physiological and psychological responses to unpleasant or threatening stimuli

stressor an unpleasant or threatening stimulus that evokes physiological and psychological responses

subvention bereavement counseling, which attempts to reduce the aftereffects of death on the survivors

terminal drop a distinct drop in IQ scores that occurs a few years before death, no matter what a person's age

time-lag design a research design in which groups from several different cohorts are studied, but the studies are spaced so that each group is assessed at the same age

tinnitus persistent ringing, roaring, or buzzing in the ears

trait characteristic of personality; an enduring disposition of thoughts, feelings, and behavior

unanticipated grief abnormal grief that may develop in survivors when a loved one dies unexpectedly

vacuoles dense granules surrounded by fluid-filled cavities found in the cell bodies of the brain; although they are increasingly common with age, they are most prevalent in diseased brains

wear-and-tear theories theories of aging based on the belief that living damages biological systems; among the wear and tear theories of aging are the DNA-repair theory, the cross-linkage theory, and the free-radical theory

Werner's syndrome a genetic disorder that causes premature aging, beginning in the teens or early twenties

young adulthood the first portion of adulthood; in this book, arbitrarily set at the years from 20 to 40

REFERENCES

AARP News Bulletin. "Heavy Skills Lift Californian High Above Her Competition." 24 (May 1983a), 3. (chap. 4)

———. "Firm Accepts Fine, Conditions in Initial Aging Bias Credit Case." 24 (June 1983b), 3. (chap. 14)

———. "Tossing, Turning Don't Faze Longtime Pilot." 24 (June 1983c), 1 +. (chap. 7)

———. "Study Concludes Less Educated Get More from College Classes." 24 (July–August, 1983d), 3. (chap. 13)

Abbott, M., E. Murphy, D. Bolling, and **H. Abbey.** "The Familial Component in Longevity—A Study of Offspring of Nonagenarians. II: Preliminary Analysis of the Completed Study." *Johns Hopkins Medical Journal,* 134 (1974), 1–16. (chap. 3)

Abeles, R. P., L. Steel, and **L. L. Wise.** "Patterns and Implications of Life-Course Organization: Studies from Project TALENT." In P. B. Baltes and O. G. Brim, Jr. (eds.), *Life-Span Development and Behavior.* Vol. 3. New York: Academic Press, 1980, pp. 307–337. (chap. 13)

Abelson, H. I., P. M. Fishburne, and **I. Cisin.** *National Survey on Drug Abuse: 1977.* Vol. 1. DHEW Publication No. (ADM) 78-618 Washington, D.C.: U.S. Government Printing Office, 1977. (chap. 6)

Abrahams, B., S. S. Feldman, and **S. C. Nash.** "Sex Role Self-Concept and Sex Role Attitudes: Enduring Personality Characteristics or Adaptations to Changing Life Situations?" *Developmental Psychology,* 14 (1978), 393–400. (chap. 12)

Abrahamson, L. Y., M. E. P. Seligman, and **J. D. Teasdale.** "Learned Helplessness in Humans: Critique and Reformulation." *Journal of Abnormal Psychology,* 87 (1978), 49–74. (chap. 5)

Adams, B. N. *Kinship in an Urban Setting.* Chicago: Markham, 1968. (chap. 11)

Adams, R. D. "Morphological Aspects of Aging in the Human Nervous System." In J. E. Birren and R. B. Sloane (eds.), *Handbook of Mental Health and Aging.* Englewood Cliffs, N.J.: Prentice-Hall, 1980, pp. 149–160. (chap. 4)

Aday, R. H., and **L. A. Miles.** "Long-Term Impacts of Rural Migration of the Elderly: Implications for Research." *Gerontologist,* 22 (1982), 331–336. (chap. 14)

Adelson, J., interviewed by E. Hall. "Children and Other Political Naïfs." *Psychology Today,* 14 (November 1980), 56–70. (chap. 14)

Ainlay, S. C., and **D. R. Smith.** "Aging and Religious Participation." *Journal of Gerontology,* 39 (1984), 357–363. (chap. 14)

Albert, M. S., and **E. Kaplan.** "Organic Implications of Neuropsychological Deficits in the Elderly." In L. W. Poon, J. L. Fozard, L. S. Cermak, D. Arenberg, and L. W. Thompson (eds.), *New Directions in Memory and Aging.* Hillsdale, N.J.: Lawrence Erlbaum, 1980, pp. 403–432. (chap. 8)

Alexander, R. "The Village Volunteers Make a Gift of Friendship." *The New York Times*, November 28, 1983, B10. (chap. 14)

Allen, E. B., and **H. E. Clow.** "Paranoid Reactions in the Aging." *Geriatrics*, 5 (1950), 66–73. (chap. 6)

Alpaugh, P. K., and **J. E. Birren.** "Variables Affecting Creative Contributions Across the Adult Life Span." *Human Development*, 20 (1977), 240–248. (chap. 9)

Alpert, J. L., and **M. S. Richardson.** "Parenting." In L. W. Poon (ed.), *Aging in the 1980s: Psychological Issues.* Washington, D.C.: American Psychological Association, 1980, pp. 441–454. (chap. 12)

American Psychiatric Association. *Diagnostic and Statistical Manual of Mental Disorders.* 3d ed. Washington, D.C.: American Psychiatric Association, 1980. (chap. 6)

Anastasi, A. *Psychological Testing.* 4th ed. New York: Macmillan, 1976. (chaps. 9, 10, 13)

Anders, T. R., J. L. Fozard, and **T. D. Lillyquist.** "Effects of Age upon Retrieval from Short Term Memory, From 20–68 Years of Age." *Developmental Psychology*, 6 (1972), 214–217. (chap. 8)

Anderson, E. W., R. J. Andelman, J. M. Strauch, N. J. Fortuin, and **J. H. Knelson.** "Effect of Low-level Carbon Monoxide Exposure on Onset and Duration of Angina Pectoris." *Annals of Internal Medicine*, 79 (1973), 46–50. (chap. 5)

Anderson, J. E. "Dynamics of Development: Systems in Process." In D. B. Harris (ed.), *The Concept of Development.* Minneapolis: University of Minnesota Press, 1957, pp. 25–46. (chap. 1)

Andres, R., and **J. D. Tobin.** "Endocrine System." In C. E. Finch and L. Hayflick (eds.), *Handbook of the Biology of Aging.* New York: Van Nostrand Reinhold, 1977, pp. 357–378. (chap. 4)

Angleitner, A. "Changes in Personality Observed in Questionnaire Data from the Riegel Questionnaire on Rigidity, Dogmatism, and Attitude Toward Life." In H. Thomae (ed.), *Patterns of Aging: Findings from the Bonn Longitudinal Study of Aging.* Basel: Karger, 1976. (chap. 10)

Angres, S. "Intergenerational Relations and Value Congruence between Young Adults and Their Mothers." Doctoral dissertation, University of Chicago, 1975. (chap. 12)

Ankarloo, B. "Marriage and Family Formation." In T. K. Hareven (ed.), *Transitions: The Family and the Life Course in Historical Perspective.* New York: Academic Press, 1978, pp. 113–134. (chap. 11)

Arenberg, D. "Comments on the Processes That Account for Memory Declines with Age." In L. W. Poon, J. L. Fozard, L. S. Cermak, D. Arenberg, and L. W. Thompson (eds.), *New Directions in Memory and Aging.* Hillsdale, N.J.: Lawrence Erlbaum, 1980, pp. 67–71. (chap. 9)

———. "Changes with Age in Problem Solving." In F. I. M. Craik and S. Trehub (eds.), *Aging and Cognitive Processes.* New York: Plenum, 1982, pp. 221–236. (chap. 8)

———, and **E. A. Robertson-Tchabo.** "Learning and Aging." In J. E. Birren and K. W. Schaie (eds.), *Handbook of the Psychology of Aging.* New York: Van Nostrand Reinhold, 1977, pp. 421–449. (chap. 8)

Aries, P. *Centuries of Childhood: A Social History of Family Life.* New York: Vintage Books, 1962. (chap. 1)

———. *Western Attitudes toward Death.* Baltimore: Johns Hopkins University Press, 1974. (chap. 16)

———. *The Hour of Our Death.* New York: Knopf, 1981. (chap. 16)

Arlin, P. K. "Adolescent and Adult Thought: A Search for Structures." Paper presented at meetings of the Piaget Society. Philadelphia, June 1980. (chap. 9)

Arvidson, K. "Location and Variation in Number of Tastebuds in Human Fungiform Papillae." *Scandinavian Journal of Dental Research*, 87 (1979), 435–442. (chap. 7)

Ash, P. "Pre-Retirement Counseling." *Gerontologist*, 6 (1966), 97–99. (chap. 13)

Aslan, A., A. Vrabiescu, C. Domilescu, L. Campeanu, M. Costiniu, and S. Stanescu. "Long-Term Treatment with Procaine (Gerovital H₃) in Albino Rats." *Journal of Gerontology*, 20 (1965), 1–8. (chap. 3)

Atchley, R. C. *The Sociology of Retirement*. New York: Halstead Press, 1976. (chap. 13)

_____, L. Pignatiello, and E. Shaw. "The Effect of Marital Status on Social Interaction Patterns of Older Women." Oxford, Ohio: Scripps Foundation, 1975. (chap. 11)

Athanasiou, R., P. Shaver, and C. Tavris. "Sex." *Psychology Today*, 4 (July 1970), 37–52. (chap. 11)

Atkinson, R. C., and R. M. Shiffrin. "The Control of Short-Term Memory." *Scientific American*, 224 (1971), 82–89. (chap. 8)

Auerbach, O., L. Garfinkel, and E. C. Hammond. "Relation of Smoking and Age to Findings in Lung Parenchyma: A Microscopic Study." *Chest*, 65 (1974), 29–35. (chap. 4)

Averill, J. R. "Grief: Its Nature and Significance." *Psychological Bulletin*, 6 (1968), 721–748. (chap. 16)

Azrin, N. H. *The Job-Finding Club as a Method for Obtaining Employment for Welfare-Eligible Clients: Demonstration, Evaluation, and Counselor Training*. U.S. Department of Labor, Report No. DLMA-51-17-76-04, 1978. (chap. 13)

Babchuk, N., and A. P. Bates. "The Primary Relations of Middle-Class Couples: A Study in Male Dominance." *American Sociological Review*, 28 (1963), 377–384. (chap. 11)

Back, K. W., and K. J. Gergen, "Personal Orientation and Morale of the Aged." In I. H. Simpson and J. C. Mc-Kinney (eds.), *Social Aspects of Aging*. Durham, N.C.: Duke University Press, 1966, pp. 296–305. (chap. 16)

Bailey, M. B., P. W. Haberman, and H. Alksne. "The Epidemiology of Alcoholism in an Urban Residential Area." *Quarterly Journal of Studies in Alcoholism*, 26 (1965), 19–40. (chap. 6)

Baltes, P. B. "Life-Span Developmental Psychology: Some Converging Observations on History and Theory." In P. B. Baltes and O. G. Brim, Jr. (eds.), *Life-Span Development and Behavior*. Vol. 2. New York: Academic Press, 1979, pp. 255–279. (chap. 1)

_____, and L. R. Goulet. "Status and Issues of a Life-Span Developmental Psychology." In L. R. Goulet and P. B. Baltes (eds.), *Life-Span Developmental Psychology: Research and Theory*. New York: Academic Press, 1970, pp. 3–21. (chap. 1)

_____, H. W. Reese, and L. P. Lipsitt. "Life-Span Developmental Psychology." In *Annual Review of Psychology*. Vol. 31. Palo Alto, Calif.: Annual Reviews, 1980, pp. 65–110. (chaps. 1, 2)

_____, _____, and J. R. Nesselroade. *Life-Span Developmental Psychology: Introduction to Research Methods*. Monterey, Calif.: Brooks/Cole, 1977. (chaps. 1, 2)

_____, and S. L. Willis. "Toward Psychological Theories of Aging and Development." In J. E. Birren and K. W. Schaie (eds.), *Handbook of the Psychology of Aging*. New York: Van Nostand Reinhold, 1977, pp. 128–154. (chap. 2)

_____, and _____. "Plasticity and Enhancement of Intellectual Functioning in Old Age." In F. I. M. Craik and S. Trehub (eds.), *Aging and Cognitive Processes*. New York: Plenum, 1982, pp. 353–389. (chap. 9)

Bandura, A. *Social-Learning Theory*. Englewood Cliffs, N.J.: Prentice-Hall, 1977. (chap. 2)

Bank, S., and M. D. Kahn. "Intense Sibling Loyalties." In M. E. Lamb and B. Sutton-Smith (eds.), *Sibling Relation-*

ships: Their Nature and Significance Across the Lifespan. Hillsdale, N.J.: Lawrence Erlbaum, 1982, pp. 251–266. (chap. 11)

Banziger, G., and **S. Roush.** "Nursing Homes for the Birds: A Control-Relevant Intervention with Bird Feeders." *Gerontologist,* 23 (1983), 527–531. (chap. 14)

Barasch, M. *Breaking 100: Americans Who Have Lived Over a Century.* New York: Quill, 1983. (chaps. 5, 7, 9)

Barfield, R. E., and **J. N. Morgan.** *Early Retirement: The Decision and the Experience and a Second Look.* Ann Arbor, Mich.: University of Michigan Press, 1975. (chap. 13)

Baron, S. A., L. Jacobs, and **W. R. Kinkle.** "Changes in Size of Normal Lateral Ventricles During Aging Determined by Computerized Tomography." *Neurology,* 26 (1976), 1011–1013. (chap. 4)

Baroni, G., and **G. Green.** *Who's Left in the Neighborhoods.* Washington, D.C.: National Center for Urban Ethnic Affairs, 1976. (chap. 15)

Barron, F. "The Dream of Art and Poetry." *Psychology Today,* 2 (December 1968), 18–23 + . (chap. 9)

Barrows, C. H., Jr., and **L. M. Roeder.** "Nutrition." In C. E. Finch and L. Hayflick (eds.), *Handbook of the Biology of Aging.* New York: Van Nostrand Reinhold, 1977, pp. 561–581. (chap. 3)

Bartus, R. T., R. L. Dean III, B. Beer, and **A. S. Lippa.** "The Cholinergic Hypothesis of Geriatric Memory Dysfunction." *Science,* 217 (1982), 408–417. (chap. 6)

Baruch, G., R. Barnett, and **C. Rivers.** *Life Prints: New Patterns of Love and Work for Today's Women.* New York: McGraw-Hill, 1983. (chaps. 10, 11, 12, 13)

Beattie, W. M., Jr. "Aging and the Social Services." In R. H. Binstock and E. Shanas (eds.), *Handbook of Aging and the Social Sciences.* New York: Van Nostrand Reinhold, 1976, pp. 619–642. (chap. 14)

Becerra, R. M. "The Mexican-American: Aging in a Changing Culture." In R. L. McNeely and J. L. Cohen (eds.), *Aging in Minority Groups.* Beverly Hills, Calif.: Sage, 1983, pp. 108–118. (chap. 15)

Beck, A. In H. London and R. E. Nisbett (eds.), *Thought and Feeling.* Chicago: Aldine, 1974, pp. 127–140. (chap. 7)

Beck, S. H. "Adjustment to and Satisfaction with Retirement." *Journal of Gerontology,* 37 (1982), 616–624. (chap. 13)

Becker, E. *The Denial of Death.* New York: Free Press, 1973. (chap. 16)

Becker, G. *The Economic Approach to Human Behavior.* Chicago: University of Chicago Press, 1976. (chap. 14)

Bell, A. P., and **M. S. Weinberg.** *Homosexualities: A Study of Diversity Among Men and Women.* New York: Simon & Schuster, 1978. (chap. 11)

Bell, B., E. Wolf, and **C. B. Bernholz.** "Depth Perception as a Function of Age." *Aging and Human Development,* 3 (1972), 77–88. (chap. 7)

Bell, R. Q., and **L. V. Harper.** *Child Effects on Adults.* Hillsdale, N.J.: Lawrence Erlbaum, 1977. (chap. 12)

Bell, R. R. "Friendships of Women and of Men." *Psychology of Women Quarterly,* 5 (1981), 402–417. (chap. 11)

Bellucci, G., and **W. J. Hoyer.** "Feedback Effects on the Performance and Self-Reinforcing Behavior of Elderly and Young Adult Women." *Journal of Gerontology,* 30 (1975), 456–460. (chap. 8)

Belt, E. "Leonardo da Vinci's Study of the Aging Process." *Geriatrics,* 7 (1952), 205–210. (chap. 4)

Benbow, C. P., and **J. C. Stanley.** "Sex Differences in Mathematical Ability: Fact or Artifact?" *Science,* 210 (1980), 1262–1264. (chap. 9)

Bengston, V. L., J. E. Cuellar, and **P. K. Ragan.** "Stratum Contrasts and Similarities in Attitudes toward Death." *Journal of Gerontology,* 32 (1977), 76–88. (chap. 16)

————, and **N. E. Cutler.** "Generations and Intergenerational Relations: Perspectives on Age Groups and Social Change.'' In R. H. Binstock and E. Shanas (eds.), *Handbook of Aging and the Social Sciences*. New York: Van Nostrand Reinhold, 1976, pp. 130–159. (chap. 12)

———, and **L. A. Morgan.** "Ethnicity and Aging: A Comparison of Three Ethnic Groups." In J. Sokolovsky (ed.), *Growing Old in Different Societies*. Belmont, Calif.: Wadsworth, 1983, pp. 157–167. (chap. 15)

———, and **J. Treas.** "The Changing Family Context of Mental Health and Aging." In J. E. Birren and R. B. Sloane (eds.), *Handbook of Mental Health and Aging*. Englewood Cliffs, N.J.: Prentice-Hall, 1980, pp. 400–428. (chap. 12)

Bergler, R. "Selbstbild und Alter." In R. Schubert (ed.), *Berich I. Kongress Deutsche Gesellschaft für Gerontologie*. Darmstadt: Steinkopff, 1968, pp. 156–159. (chap. 10)

Berkowitz, B. "Changes in Intellect with Age: IV. Changes in Achievement and Survival in Older People." *Journal of Genetic Psychology*, 107 (1965), 3–14. (chap. 9)

Bernard, J. *The Future of Marriage*. New York: Bantam, 1973. (chap. 11)

Bernardo, F. M. "Survivorship and Social Isolation: The Case of the Aged Widower." *Family Coordinator*, 19 (1970), 11–25. (chap. 11)

Bernstein, J. "Who Leaves—Who Stays: Residency Policy in Housing for the Elderly." *Gerontologist*, 22 (1982), 305–313. (chap. 14)

Bhanthumnavin, K., and **M. M. Schuster.** "Aging and Gastrointestinal Function." In C. E. Finch and L. Hayflick (eds.), *Handbook of the Biology of Aging*. New York: Van Nostrand Reinhold, 1977, pp. 709–723. (chap. 4)

Binet, A., and **T. Simon.** "Méthodes Nouvelles pour le Diagnostic du Niveau Intellectuel des Arnormaux." *Annee Psychologique*, 11 (1905), 191–244. (chap. 9)

Birren, J. E. "Increment and Decrement in the Intellectual Status of the Aged."

Psychiatric Research Reports, 23 (1968), 207–214. (chap. 9)

———. "Psychophysiology and Speed of Response." *American Psychologist*, 29 (1974), 808–815. (chap. 9)

———, and **V. J. Renner.** "Research on the Psychology of Aging: Principles and Experimentation." In J. E. Birren and K. W. Schaie (eds.), *Handbook of the Psychology of Aging*. New York: Van Nostrand Reinhold, 1977, pp. 3–38. (chap. 1)

———, and **D. S. Woodruff.** "Human Development over the Life Span through Education." In P. B. Baltes and K. W. Schaie (eds.), *Life-Span Developmental Psychology: Personality and Socialization*. New York: Academic Press, 1973, pp. 305–337. (chap. 13)

Bishop, J. E. "Medical Science Helps Prolong the Life Span and the Active Years." *Wall Street Journal*, February 24, 1983. (Chap. 5)

Bjorksten, J. "Crosslinkage and the Aging Process." In M. Rockstein, M. L. Sussman, and J. Chesky (eds.), *Theoretical Aspects of Aging*. New York: Academic Press, 1974, pp. 43–59. (chap. 3)

Blau, E. " 'Taking My Turn' Takes Positive View of Aging." *The New York Times*, July 27, 1983, C18. (chap. 10)

Blazer, D., and **E. Palmore.** "Religion and Aging in a Longitudinal Panel." *Gerontologist*, 16 (1976), 305–313. (chap. 14)

Bleuler, M. E. "The Long Term Course of Schizophrenic Psychoses." In L. C. Wynne, R. L. Cromwell, and S. Matthyse (eds.), *The Nature of Schizophrenia: New Approaches to Research and Treatment*. New York: Wiley, 1978. (chap. 6)

Block, M. R. "Exiled Americans: The Plight of the Indian Aged in the United States." In D. E. Gelfand and A. J. Kutzik (eds.), *Ethnicity and Aging: Theory, Research, and Policy*. New York: Springer, 1979, pp. 184–192. (chaps. 3, 15)

Blum, J. E., E. T. Clark, and **L. F. Jarvik.** "The New York State Psychiatric Institute Study of Aging Twins." In L. F. Jarvik, C. Eisdorfer, and J. E. Blum (eds.), *Intellectual Functioning in Adults: Psychological and Biological Influences.* New York: Springer, 1973, pp. 13–20. (chap. 9)

Blythe, R. *The View in Winter.* New York: Harcourt Brace Jovanovich, 1979. (chaps. 9, 11)

Boffey, P. M. "Longer Lives Seen as Threat to Nation's Budget," *The New York Times*, May 31, 1983, C3. (chap. 3)

Bok, S. *Lying: Moral Choice in Public and Private Life.* New York: Pantheon, 1978. (chap. 16)

Bondareff, W. "Neurobiology of Aging." in J. E. Birren and R. B. Sloane (eds.), *Handbook of Mental Health and Aging.* Englewood Cliffs, N.J.: Prentice-Hall, 1980, pp. 75–99. (chap. 4)

Booth, A., and **E. Hess.** "Cross-Sex Friendships." *Journal of Marriage and the Family*, 36 (1974), 38–47. (chap. 11)

Bootzin, R. R. and **J. R. Acocella.** *Abnormal Psychology.* 3d ed. New York: Random House, 1980. (chap. 6)

Borkan, G. A., D. E. Hults, S. G. Gerzof, A. H. Robbins, and **C. K. Silbert.** "Age Changes in Body Composition Revealed by Computed Tomography." *Journal of Gerontology*, 38 (1983), 673–677. (chap. 4)

Boswell, J. *The Life of Samuel Johnson.* Vol. 1. New York: Heritage Press, 1963 (orig. pub. 1791). (chap. 1)

Botwinick, J. *Aging and Behavior.* New York: Springer, 1973. (chaps. 7, 8)

————. "Intellectual Abilities." in J. E. Birren and K. W. Schaie (eds.), *Handbook of the Psychology of Aging.* New York: Van Nostrand Reinhold, 1977, pp. 580–605. (chap. 9)

Bower, D. W., and **V. A. Christopherson.** "University Student Cohabitation: A Regional Comparison of Selected Attitudes and Behavior." *Journal of Marriage and the Family*, 39 (1977), 447–453. (chap. 11)

Bowlby, J. *Attachment and Loss.* Vol. III. *Loss: Sadness and Depression.* New York: Basic Books, 1980. (chap. 16)

————, and **C. M. Parkes.** "Separation and Loss." in E. J. Anthony and C. Koupernik (eds.), *The Child in His Family.* Vol. 1. New York: Wiley, 1970. (chap. 16)

Bowles, N. L., and **L. W. Poon.** "An Analysis of the Effect of Aging on Recognition Memory." *Journal of Gerontology*, 37 (1982), 212–219. (chap. 8)

Boyer, B., B. Kopper, R. Boyer, F. Brawer, and **H. Kawai.** "Effects of Acculturation on the Personality Traits of the Old People of the Mescalero and Chiricahua Apaches." *International Journal of Social Psychiatry*, 11 (1965), 264–272. (chap. 15)

Boyer, J. L., and **F. W. Kasch.** "Exercise Therapy in Hypertensive Men." *Journal of American Medical Association*, 21 (1970), 1668–1671. (chap. 5)

Brett, J. In C. Cooper and R. Payne (eds.), *Current Concerns in Occupational Stress*, 1980. (chap. 14)

Brim, O. G., Jr., and **J. Kagan.** "Constancy and Change: A View of the Issues." in O. G. Brim, Jr., and J. Kagan (eds.), *Constancy and Change in Human Development.* Cambridge, Mass.: Harvard University Press, 1980, pp. 1–25. (chap. 1)

Brinley, J. F., T. J. Jovick, and **L. M. McLaughlin.** "Age, Reasoning, and Memory." *Journal of Gerontology*, 29 (1974), 182–189. (chap. 9)

Britton, J. H., and **J. O. Britton.** *Personality Changes in Aging: A Longitudinal Study of Community Residents.* New York: Springer, 1972. (chap. 10)

Brody, E. M., P. T. Johnsen, M. C. Fulcomer, and **A. M. Land.** "Women's Changing Roles and Help to Elderly Parents: Attitudes of Three Generations." *Journal of Gerontology*, 38 (1983), 597–607. (chap. 12)

Brody, H., and **N. Vijayashankar.** "Anatomical Changes in the Nervous System." In C. E. Finch and L. Hayflick (eds.), *Handbook of the Biology of Aging.* New

York: Van Nostrand Reinhold, 1977, pp. 241–261. (chap. 4)

Brody, J. E. *The New York Times Guide to Personal Health.* New York: Times Books, 1982. (chaps. 5, 7)

_____. "Personal Health: Guiding Children to Reduce the Risks of Heart Disease." *The New York Times*, July 20, 1983a. (chap. 5)

_____. "Divorce's Stress Exacts Long-Term Toll." *The New York Times*, December 13, 1983b, C1 +. (chap. 11)

Bronson, W. C. "Adult Derivatives of Emotional Expressiveness and Reactivity Control: Developmental Continuities from Childhood to Adulthood." *Child Development*, 38 (1967), 801–817. (chap. 1)

Brown, G. W., and **T. O. Harris.** *Social Origins of Depression.* New York: Free Press, 1978. (chap. 12)

Bruner, J. S. "The Course of Cognitive Growth." *American Psychologist*, 19 (1964), 1–15. (chap. 3)

Brunner, L. S., and **D. S. Suddarth.** *Textbook of Medical-Surgical Nursing.* New York: Lippincott, 1975. (chap. 7)

Buchholz, M., and **J. E. Bynum.** "Newspaper Presentation of America's Aged: A Content Analysis of Image and Role." *Gerontologist*, 22 (1982), 83–88. (chap. 1)

Buell, S. J., and **P. D. Coleman.** "Dendritic Growth in Aged Human Brain and Failure of Growth in Senile Dementia." *Science*, 206 (1976), 854–856. (chap. 4)

Bulcke, J. A., J.-L. Termote, Y. Palmers, and **D. Crolla.** "Computed Tomography of the Human Skeletal Muscular System." *Neuroradiology*, 17 (1979), 127–136. (chap. 4)

Burkitt, D. P. "The Link between Low-Fiber Diets and Disease." *Human Nature*, 1 (December 1978), 34–41. (chap. 5)

Burnside, I. M. "Alzheimer's Disease: An Overview." *Journal of Gerontological Nursing*, 5 (August 1979), 14–20. (chap. 6)

Buss, A. R. "Dialectics, History, and Development: The Historical Roots of the Individual-Society Dialectic." In P. B. Baltes (ed.). *Life-Span Development and Behavior.* Vol. 1. New York: Academic Press, 1979, pp. 313–333. (chaps. 2, 10)

Busse, E. W., and **C. Eisdorfer.** "Two Thousand Years of Married Life." in E. Palmore (ed.), *Normal Aging: Reports from the Duke Longitudinal Study, 1955–1969.* Durham, N.C.: Duke University Press, 1970, pp. 266–269. (chap. 11)

Butler, R. N. *Why Survive? Being Old in America.* New York: Harper & Row, 1975. (chaps. 1, 16)

_____, and **M. I. Lewis.** *Aging and Mental Health.* 3d ed. St. Louis: C. V. Mosby, 1982. (chaps. 3, 4, 5, 6, 14)

Butters, N. "Potential Contributions of Neuropsychology to Our Understanding of the Memory Capacities of the Elderly." in L. W. Poon, J. L. Fozard, L. S. Cermak, D. Arenberg, and L. W. Thompson (eds.), *New Directions in Memory and Aging.* Hillsdale, N.J.: Lawrence Erlbaum, 1980, pp. 451–460. (chap. 8)

Cain, L. D. "Aging and the Law." In R. H. Binstock and E. Shanas (eds.), *Handbook of Aging and the Social Sciences.* New York: Van Nostrand Reinhold, 1976, pp. 342–368. (chap. 14)

Calearo, C., and **A. Lazzaroni.** "Speech Intelligibility in Relationship to the Speed of the Message." *Laryngoscope*, 67 (1957), 410–419. (chap. 7)

Callahan, E. J., W. S. Brasted, and **J. L. Granados.** "Fetal Loss and Sudden Infant Death: Grieving and Adjustment for Families." In E. J. Callahan and K. A. McCluskey (eds.), *Life-Span Developmental Psychology: Nonnormative Events.* New York: Academic Press, 1983, pp. 145–166. (chap. 16)

Cameron, P. "Mood as an Indicant of Happiness: Age, Sex, Social Class, and Situational Differences." *Journal of Gerontology*, 30 (1975), 216–224. (chap. 10)

_____, **D. Robertson,** and **J. Zaks.** "Sound Pollution, Noise Pollution, and Health: Community Parameters." *Jour-*

nal of Applied Psychology, 56 (1972), 67–74. (chap. 5)

Campbell, A. "Politics through the Life Cycle." *Gerontologist*, 11 (1971), 112–117. (chap. 14)

————. *The Sense of Well-being in America: Recent Patterns and Trends*. New York: McGraw-Hill, 1979. (chap. 5)

————, **P. Converse,** and **W. Rodgers.** *The Quality of American Life: Perceptions, Evaluations and Satisfactions*. New York: Russell Sage Foundation, 1976. (chap. 13)

Campbell, D. P. *Handbook for the Strong-Campbell Interest Inventory*. Stanford, Calif.: Stanford University Press, 1974. (chap. 13)

Canestrari, R. "Paced and Self-Paced Learning in Young and Elderly Adults." *Journal of Gerontology*, 18 (1963), 165–168. (chap. 8)

Cantor, M. H. "The Informal Support System of New York's Inner City Elderly: Is Ethnicity a Factor?" In D. E. Gelfand and A. J. Kutzik (eds.), *Ethnicity and Aging: Theory, Research, and Policy*. New York: Springer, 1979, pp. 153–174. (chap. 15)

Card, J. J., and **L. L. Wise.** "Teenage Mothers and Teenage Fathers: The Impact of Early Childbearing on the Parents' Personal and Professional Lives." *Family Planning Perspectives*, 10 (1978), 199–204. (chap. 13)

Cargan, L., and **M. Melko.** *Singles: Myths and Realities*. Beverly Hills, Calif.: Sage, 1982. (chap. 11)

Carp, F. M. "Housing and Living Environments of Older People." In R. H. Binstock and E. Shanas (eds.), *Handbook of Aging and the Social Sciences*. New York: Van Nostrand Reinhold, 1976, pp. 244–271. (chaps. 2, 14)

Cartwright, L. K. "Personality Changes in a Sample of Women Physicians." *Journal of Medical Education*, 52 (1977), 467–474. (chap. 13)

Cattell, R. B. *Abilities: Their Structure,*

Growth, and Action. Boston: Houghton Mifflin, 1971. (chap. 9)

Cavanaugh, J. C. "Comprehension and Retention of Television Programs by 20- and 60-Year-Olds." *Journal of Gerontology*, 38 (1983), 190–196. (chap. 2)

Chalke, H. D., J. R. Dewhurst, and **C. W. Ward.** "Loss of Sense of Smell in Old People." *Public Health*, 72 (1958), 223–230. (chap. 7)

Charles, D. C. "Historical Antecedents of Life-Span Developmental Psychology." In L. R. Goulet and P. B. Baltes (eds.), *Life-Span Developmental Psychology: Research and Theory*. New York: Academic Press, 1970, pp. 23–52. (chap. 1)

Cherlin, A. "A Sense of History: Recent Research on Aging and the Family." In M. W. Riley, B. B. Hess, and K. Bond (eds.), *Aging in Society: Selected Reviews of Recent Research*. Hillsdale, N.J.: Lawrence Erlbaum, 1983, pp. 5–24. (chap. 12)

Chester, N. L. "Pregnancy and the New Parenthood: Twin Experiences of Change." Paper presented at the meeting of the Eastern Psychological Association. Philadelphia, 1979. (chap. 12)

Children's Defense Fund. *Employed Parents and Their Children*. Washington, D.C.: Children's Defense Fund, 1982. (chap. 12)

Chiriboga, D., and **L. Cutler.** "Stress and Adaptation: Life Span Perspectives." In L. W. Poon (ed.), *Aging in the 1980s: Psychological Issues*. Washington, D.C.: American Psychological Association, 1980, pp. 347–362. (chap. 5)

————, and **M. Thurnher.** "Concept of Self." In M. Lowenthal, M. Thurnher, and D. Chiriboga (eds.), *Four Stages of Life*. San Francisco: Jossey-Bass, 1976. (chap. 10)

Chow, N. W.-S. "The Chinese Family and Support of the Elderly in Hong Kong." *Gerontologist*, 23 (1983), 584–588. (chap. 15)

Chown, S. "Age and the Rigidities."

Journal of Gerontology, 16 (1961), 355–362. (chap. 9)

Cicirelli, V. G. "Categorization Behavior in Aging Subjects." *Journal of Gerontology*, 31 (1976), 676–680. (chap. 9)

_____. "Interpersonal Relationships of Siblings in the Middle Part of the Lifespan." Paper presented at the Biennial Meeting of the Society for Research in Child Development. Boston, April 1981. (chap. 11)

_____. "Sibling Influence throughout the Lifespan." In M. E. Lamb and B. Sutton-Smith (eds.), *Sibling Relationships: Their Nature and Significance Across the Lifespan*. Hillsdale, N.J.: Lawrence Erlbaum, 1982, pp. 267–284. (chap. 11)

Clark, M., and **R. Henkoff.** "A Strange Sort of Therapy." *Newsweek*, October 20, 1980, 65–66. (chap. 5)

Clark, W. C., and **L. Mehl.** "Thermal Pain: A Sensory Decision Theory Analysis of the Effect of Age and Sex of d', Various Response Criteria, and 50 percent Pain Threshold." *Journal of Abnormal Psychology*, 78 (1971), 202–212. (chap. 7)

Clausen, J. A. "Men's Occupational Careers in the Middle Years." In D. H. Eichorn, J. A. Clausen, N. Haan, M. P. Honzik, and P. Mussen (eds.), *Present and Past in Middle Life*. New York: Academic Press, 1981, pp. 321–351. (chaps. 10, 13)

_____, **P. H. Mussen,** and **J. Kuypers.** "Involvement, Warmth, and Parent-Child Resemblances in Three Generations." In D. H. Eichorn, J. A. Clausen, N. Haan, M. P. Honzik, and P. Mussen (eds.), *Present and Past in Middle Life*. New York: Academic Press, 1981, pp. 299–319. (chap. 12)

Clayton, V. P., and **J. E. Birren.** "The Development of Wisdom Across the Life Span: A Reexamination of an Ancient Topic." In P. B. Baltes and O. G. Brim, Jr. (eds.), *Life-Span Development and Behavior*. Vol. 3. New York: Academic Press, 1980, pp. 103–135. (chap. 9)

Clendinen, D. "Testing the Waters before Retirement." *The New York Times*, October 27, 1983, C1+. (chap. 13)

Clingempeel, W. G. "Quasi-Kin Relationships and Marital Quality in Stepfather Families." *Journal of Personality and Social Psychology*, 41 (1981), 890–901. (chap. 12)

Cohabitation Research Newsletter, 4 (June 1974), 2. (chap. 11)

Cohen, C. I., D. Cook, and **H. Rajkowski.** "What's In a Friend?" Paper presented at the 33d Annual Scientific Meeting of the Gerontological Society. San Diego, November 1980. (chap. 11)

Cohen, S. H. "Multiple Impacts and Determinants in Human Service Delivery Systems." In R. R. Turner and H. W. Reese (eds.), *Life-Span Developmental Psychology: Intervention*. New York: Academic Press, 1980, pp. 125–148. (chap. 14)

Cohler, B. J., and **H. U. Grunebaum.** *Mothers, Grandmothers, and Daughters.* New York: Wiley-Interscience, 1981. (chap. 12)

Coleman, L. M., and **T. C. Antonucci.** "Impact of Work on Women at Midlife." *Developmental Psychology*, 19 (1983), 290–294. (chaps. 10, 13)

Coles, R. *The Old Ones of New Mexico.* Albuquerque: University of New Mexico Press, 1973. (chaps. 8, 14)

_____. "Work and Self-Respect." In E. H. Erikson (ed.), *Adulthood*. New York: Norton, 1978, pp. 217–226. (chap. 13)

Collins, G. "Many More of Elderly Migrate to New States." *The New York Times*, December 9, 1983a, A20. (chap. 14)

_____. "Long Distance Care of Elderly Relatives a Growing Problem." *The New York Times*, December 29, 1983b, A1+. (chap. 12)

_____. "Increasing Numbers of Aged Return North from Florida." *The New York Times*, March 15, 1984. (chap. 14)

Colvez, A., and **M. Blanchet.** "Disability

Trends in the United States Population 1966–76: Analysis of Reported Causes.'' *American Journal of Public Health*, 464 (1981), 71. (chap. 5)

Comfort, A. ''Sexuality in Later Life.'' In J. E. Birren and R. B. Sloane (eds.), *Handbook of Mental Health and Aging.* Englewood Cliffs, N.J.: Prentice-Hall, 1980, pp. 885–892. (chap. 4)

Conrad, C. C. ''When You're Young at Heart.'' *Aging*, 258 (1976), 11–13. (chap. 5)

Cook, F. L. ''Public Support for Services to Older People,'' *National Forum*, 62 (Fall 1982), 223–225. (chap. 14)

Coomb, L. C., R. Freedman, J. Friedman, and **W. F. Pratt.** ''Premarital Pregnancy and Status Before and After Marriage.'' *American Journal of Sociology*, 75 (1970), 800–820. (chap. 11)

Corby, N., and **R. L. Solnick.** ''Psychosocial and Physiological Influences on Sexuality in the Older Adult.'' in J. E. Birren and R. B. Sloane (eds.), *Handbook of Mental Health and Aging.* Englewood Cliffs, N.J.: Prentice-Hall, 1980, pp. 893–921. (chap. 4)

————, and **J. M. Zarit.** ''Old and Alone: The Unmarried in Later Life.'' In R. B. Weg (ed.), *Sexuality in the Later Years: Roles and Behavior.* New York: Academic Press, 1983, pp. 131–145. (chap. 11)

Corso, J. F. ''Auditory Perception and Communication.'' In J. E. Birren and K. W. Schaie (eds.), *Handbook of the Psychology of Aging.* New York: Van Nostrand Reinhold, 1977, pp. 535–553. (chap. 7)

Costa, P. T., Jr., and **R. R. McCrae.** ''Objective Personality Assessment.'' In M. Storandt, I. C. Siegler, and M. F. Elias (eds.), *The Clinical Psychology of Aging.* New York: Plenum Press, 1978. (chap. 10)

————, and ————. ''Still Stable after All These Years: Personality as a Key to Some Issues in Adulthood and Old Age.'' In P. B. Baltes and O. G. Brim, Jr. (eds.),

Life-Span Development and Behavior. Vol. 3. New York: Academic Press, 1980, pp. 65–102. (chap. 10)

Cowan, P., C. Cowan, J. Coie, and **L. Coie.** In L. Newman and W. Miller (eds.), *The First Child and Family Formation.* Durham, N.C.: University of North Carolina Press, 1978. (chap. 12)

Cowan, W. M. ''The Developing Brain.'' *Scientific American*, 241 (1979), 88–133. (chap. 1)

Cowgill, D. O. ''Aging and Modernization: A Revision of the Theory.'' In J. F. Gubrium (ed.), *Late Life: Communities and Environmental Policy.* Springfield, Ill.: Charles Thomas, 1974, pp. 123–146. (chap. 15)

Cowley, M. *The View from 80.* New York: Viking, 1980. (chaps. 1, 4)

Coyle, J. T., D. L. Price, and **M. R. De-Long.** ''Alzheimer's Disease: A Disorder of Cortical Cholinergic Innervation.'' *Science*, 219 (1983), 1184–1190. (chap. 6)

Coyne, A. C., S. K. Whitbourne, and **D. S. Glenwick.** ''Adult Age Differences in Reflection—Impulsivity.'' *Journal of Gerontology*, 33 (1978), 402–407. (chap. 9)

Craik, F. I. M. ''An Observed Age Difference in Response to a Personality Inventory.'' *British Journal of Psychology*, 55 (1964), 453–462. (chap. 10)

————. ''Age Differences in Human Memory.'' In J. E. Birren and K. W. Schaie (eds.), *Handbook of the Psychology of Aging.* New York: Van Nostrand Reinhold, 1977, pp. 384–420 (chaps. 2, 8)

————, and **M. Byrd.** ''Aging and Cognitive Deficits: The Role of Attentional Resources.'' In F. I. M. Craik and S. Trehub (eds.), *Aging and the Cognitive Processes.* New York: Plenum, 1982, pp. 191–212. (chap. 8)

————, and **E. Simon.** ''Age Differences in Memory: The Roles of Attention and Depth of Processing.'' In L. W. Poon, J. L. Fozard, L. S. Cermak, D. Arenberg, and L. W. Thompson (eds.), *New Directions in Memory and Aging.* Hillsdale,

N.J.: Lawrence Erlbaum, 1980, pp. 95–112. (chap. 8)

Crook, M. A., and **F. J. Langdon.** "The Effects of Aircraft Noise in Schools around London Airport." *Journal of Sound and Vibration*, 34 (1974), 222–232. (chap. 5)

Crosson, C. W., and **E. A. Robertson-Tchabo.** "Age and Preference for Complexity among Manifestly Creative Women." *Human Development*, 26 (1983), 149–155. (chap. 9)

Cuber, J. F., and **P. B. Harroff.** *Sex and the Significant Americans.* Baltimore: Penguin, 1965. (chap. 11)

Cuellar, J. "El Señor Citizen Club: The Older Mexican-American in the Voluntary Association." In B. Myerhoff and A. Simic (eds.), *Life's Career-Aging: Cultural Variations on Growing Old.* Beverly Hills, Calif.: Sage, 1978. (chap. 15)

Cumming, E., and **W. E. Henry.** *Growing Old: The Process of Disengagement.* New York: Basic Books, 1961. (chaps. 2, 10, 13)

Cummings, J. "Breakup of Black Family Imperils Gains of Decades." *The New York Times*, November 20, 1983, A1+. (chap. 15)

Curtiss, S. *Genie: A Psycholinguistic Study of a Modern Day "Wild Child."* New York: Academic Press, 1977. (chap. 11)

Cutler, N. E. "Age and Political Behavior." In D. S. Woodruff and J. E. Birren (eds.), *Aging: Scientific Perspectives and Social Issues.* 2d ed. Monterey, Calif.: Brooks/Cole, 1983, pp. 409–442. (chap. 14)

Cutler, R. G. "Life-Span Extension." In J. L. McGaugh and S. B. Kiesler (eds.), *Aging: Biology and Behavior.* New York: Academic Press, 1981, pp. 31–76. (chap. 3)

Cutler, S. J., and **R. L. Kaufman.** "Cohort Changes in Political Attitudes: Tolerance of Ideological Nonconformity." *Public Opinion Quarterly*, 39 (1975), 63–81. (chap. 14)

Cytrynbaum, S., L. Blum, R. Patrick, J. Stein, D. Wadner, and **C. Wilk.** "Midlife Development: A Personality and Social Systems Perspective." In L. W. Poon (ed.), *Aging in the 1980s: Psychological Issues.* Washington, D.C.: American Psychological Association, 1980, pp. 463–474. (chap. 10)

Dalderup, L. M., and **M. L. C. Fredericks.** "Colour Sensitivity in Old Age." *Journal of the American Geriatric Society*, 17 (1969), 388–390. (chap. 7)

Damon, A., C. C. Seltzer, H. W. Stoudt, and **B. Bell.** "Age and Physique in Healthy White Veterans at Boston." *Aging and Human Development*, 3 (1972), 202–208. (chap. 4)

Daniel, C. W. "Cell Longevity: *In Vivo.*" In C. E. Finch and L. Hayflick (eds.), *Handbook of the Biology of Aging.* New York: Van Nostrand Reinhold, 1977, pp. 122–158. (chap. 3)

Dapcich-Miura, E., and **M. F. Hovell.** "Contingency Management of Adherence to a Complex Medical Regimen in an Elderly Heart Patient." *Behavior Therapy*, 10 (1979), 193–201. (chap. 8)

Davies, M. J., and **A. Pomerance.** "Quantitative Study of Aging Changes in the Human Sinoatrial Node and Internodal Tracts." *British Heart Journal*, 34 (1972), 150–152. (chap. 4)

Davis, J. M., N. L. Segal, and **G. K. Spring.** "Biological and Genetic Aspects of Depression in the Elderly." In L. R. Breslau and M. R. Haug (eds.), *Depression and Aging: Causes, Care, and Consequences.* New York: Springer, 1983, pp. 94–113. (chap. 6)

Davis, M. A., and **E. Randall.** "Social Change and Food Habits of the Elderly." In M. W. Riley, B. B. Hess, and K. Bond (eds.), *Aging in Society: Selected Reviews of Recent Research.* Hillsdale, N.J.: Lawrence Erlbaum, 1983, pp. 199–218. (chap. 5)

Davis-Friedmann, D. *Long Lives: Chinese Elderly and the Communist Revolution.* Cambridge, Mass.: Harvard University Press, 1983. (chap. 15)

de Beauvoir, S. *The Coming of Age.* New York: Putnam, 1972. (chap. 10)

Denney, N. W. "Classification Abilities in the Elderly." *Journal of Gerontology,* 29 (1974), 309. (chap. 9)

_____. "Problem Solving in Later Adulthood: Intervention Research." In P. B. Baltes and O. G. Brim, Jr. (eds.), *Life-Span Development and Behavior.* Vol. 2. New York: Academic Press, 1979, pp. 38–66. (chap. 9)

_____, and **D. R. Denney.** "The Relationship Between Classification And Questioning Strategies Among Adults." *Journal of Gerontology,* 37 (1982), 190–196. (chap. 9)

_____, and **J. A. List.** "Adult Age Differences in Performance on the Matching Familiar Figures Test." *Human Development,* 22 (1979), 137–144. (chap. 9)

Dennis, W. "Creative Productivity between the Ages of 20 and 80 Years." In B. L. Neugarten (ed.), *Middle Age and Aging.* Chicago: University of Chicago Press, 1968, pp. 106–114. (chap. 9)

deVries, H. A. "Physiology of Exercise and Aging." In D. S. Woodruff and J. E. Birren (eds.), *Aging: Scientific Perspectives and Social Issues.* 2d ed. Monterey, Calif.: Brooks/Cole, 1983, pp. 285–304. (chaps. 3, 4, 5)

_____, and **G. M. Adams.** "Electromyographic Comparison of Single Doses of Exercise and Meprobamate as to Effects on Muscle Relaxation." *American Journal of Physical Medicine,* 51 (1972), 130–141. (chap. 5)

Diggory, J., and **D. Rothman.** "Values Destroyed by Death." *Journal of Abnormal and Social Psychology,* 63 (1961), 205–210. (chap. 16)

Dohrenwend, B. S., and **B. P. Dohrenwend.** "Some Issues in Research on Stressful Life Events." *Journal of Nervous and Mental Disease,* 166 (1978), 7–15. (chap. 5)

Donosky, L. "Keeping Your Work Clothes On." *Newsweek,* November 1, 1982, 58. (chap. 5)

Douglas, K., and **D. Arenberg.** "Age Changes, Cohort Differences, and Cultural Change on the Guilford-Zimmerman Temperament Survey." *Journal of Gerontology,* 33 (1978), 737–747. (chap. 10)

Douvan, E., and **R. Kulka.** "The American Family: A Twenty-Year View." In J. E. Gullahorn (ed.), *Psychology and Women: In Transition.* New York: Wiley, 1979, pp. 83–93. (chap. 11)

Dowd, J. J., and **V. L. Bengston.** "Aging in Minority Populations: An Examination of the Double Jeopardy Hypothesis." *Journal of Gerontology,* 33 (1978), 427–436. (chap. 15)

Drachman, D. A. "An Approach to the Neurology of Aging." In J. E. Birren and R. B. Sloane (eds.), *Handbook of Mental Health and Aging.* Englewood Cliffs, N.J.: Prentice-Hall, 1980, pp. 501–519. (chap. 6)

Dullea, G. "When Parents Work on Different Shifts." *The New York Times,* October 31, 1983, B12. (chap. 12)

Edwards, E. D. "Native-American Elders: Current Social Issues and Social Policy Implications." in R. L. McNeely and J. L. Cohen (eds.), *Aging in Minority Groups.* Beverly Hills, Calif.: Sage, 1983, pp. 74–82. (chap. 15)

Eichorn, D. H., J.A. Clausen, N. Haan, M. P. Honzik, and **P. H. Mussen.** *Present and Past in Middle Life.* New York: Academic Press, 1981. (chap. 5)

_____, **J. V. Hunt,** and **M. P. Honzik.** "Experience, Personality, and IQ: Adolescence to Middle Age." In D. H. Eichorn, J. A. Clausen, N. Haan, M. P. Honzik, and P. H. Mussen (eds.), *Present and Past in Middle Life.* New York: Academic Press, 1981, pp. 89–116. (chap. 9)

Eisdorfer, C. "Arousal and Performance Experiments in Verbal Learning and a Tentative Theory." In G. A. Talland (ed.), *Human Aging and Behavior.* New York: Academic Press, 1968, pp. 189–216. (chap. 8)

_____. "Conceptual Modes of Aging:

The Challenge of a New Frontier." *American Psychologist*, 38 (1983), 197–202. (chap. 1)

———, **J. Nowlin**, and **F. Wilkie**. "Improvement of Learning in the Aged by Modification of Autonomic Nervous System Activity." *Science*, 170 (1970), 1327–1329. (chap. 8)

———, and **B. A. Stotsky**. "Intervention, Treatment, and Rehabilitation of Psychiatric Disorders." In J. E. Birren and K. W. Schaie (eds.), *Handbook of the Psychology of Aging*. New York: Van Nostrand Reinhold, 1977, pp. 724–748. (chap. 6)

———, and **F. Wilkie**. "Intellectual Changes." In E. Palmore (ed.), *Normal Aging: II*. Durham, N.C.: Duke University Press, 1974, pp. 95–102. (chap. 9)

———, and ———. "Stress, Disease, Aging, and Behavior." In J. E. Birren and K. W. Schaie (eds.), *Handbook of the Psychology of Aging*. New York: Van Nostrand Reinhold, 1977, pp. 251–275. (chap. 5)

Eisner, D. "The Effect of Chronic Organic Brain Syndrome upon Concrete and Formal Operations in Elderly Men." Unpublished manuscript. William Patterson College of New Jersey, 1973. (chap. 9)

Ekerdt, D. J., R. Bosse, and **J. S. LoCastro**. "Claims that Retirement Improves Health." *Journal of Gerontology*, 38 (1983), 231–236. (chap. 13)

Eklund, L. "Aging and the Field of Education." In M. W. Riley, J. W. Riley, Jr., and M. E. Johnson (eds.), *Aging and Society*. Vol. 2. *Aging and the Professions*. New York: Russell Sage Foundation, 1969, pp. 324–351. (chap. 13)

Elahi, V. K., D. Elahi, R. Andres, J.D. Tobin, M. G. Butler, and **A. H. Norris**. "A Longitudinal Study of Nutritional Intake in Men." *Journal of Gerontology*, 38 (1983), 162–180. (chap. 5)

Elder, G. H., Jr. *Children of the Great Depression*. Chicago: University of Chicago Press, 1974. (chap. 1)

———. "Family History and the Life Course." In T. K. Hareven (ed.), *Transitions: The Family and the Life Course in Historical Perspective*. New York: Academic Press, 1978, pp. 17–64. (chap. 12)

Elsayed, M., A. H. Ismail, and **R. S. Young**. "Intellectual Differences of Adult Men Related to Age and Physical Fitness Before and After an Exercise Program." *Journal of Gerontology*, 35 (1980), 383–387. (chap. 8)

Engen, T. "Method and Theory in the Study of Odor Preferences." In A. Turk, J. W. Johnston, and D. G. Moulton (eds.), *Human Responses to Environmental Odors*. New York: Academic Press, 1974. (chap. 7)

———. "Taste and Smell." In J. E. Birren and K. W. Schaie (eds.), *Handbook of the Psychology of Aging*. New York: Van Nostrand Reinhold, 1977, pp. 554–561. (chap. 7)

Engerman, S. "Economic Perspectives on the Life Course." In T. K. Hareven (ed.), *Transitions: The Family and the Life Course in Perspective*. New York: Academic Press, 1978, pp. 271–286. (chap. 14)

Ensor, R. E., J. L. Fleg, Y. C. Kim, E. F. deLeon, and **S. M. Goldman**. "Longitudinal Chest X-Ray Changes in Normal Men." *Journal of Gerontology*, 38 (1983), 307–314. (chap. 4)

Epstein, S. "Traits Are Alive and Well." In D. Magnusson and N. S. Endler (eds.), *Personality at the Crossroads: Current Issues in Interactional Psychology*. Hillsdale, N.J.: Lawrence Erlbaum, 1979. (chap. 10)

Ericksen, J. A., W. L. Yancey, and **E. P. Ericksen**. "The Division of Family Roles." *Journal of Marriage and the Family*, 41 (1979), 301–313. (chap. 12)

Erikson, E.H. *Childhood and Society*. New York: Norton, 1950. (chap. 1)

———. *Young Man Luther*. New York: Norton, 1962. (chap. 10)

———. *Identity: Youth and Crisis*. New York: Norton, 1968. (chap. 13)

———. *Gandhi's Truth*. New York: Norton, 1969. (chap. 10)

_____. *Identity and the Life Cycle*. Reissue. New York: Norton, 1980a. (chaps. 1, 10, 11, 13)

_____. "On the Generational Cycle: An Address." *International Journal of Psycho-Analysis*, 61 (1980b), 213–223. (chap. 9)

_____. *The Life Cycle Completed*. New York: Norton, 1982. (chaps. 9, 10, 14, 16)

_____, and **J. M. Erikson.** "On Generativity and Identity: From a Conversation with Erik and Joan Erikson." *Harvard Educational Review*, 51 (1981), 249–269. (chap. 10)

_____, interviewed by **E. Hall.** "A Conversation with Erik Erikson." *Psychology Today*, 17 (June 1983), 22–30. (chaps. 1, 10)

Espenshade, T. J., and **R. E. Braun.** "Economic Aspects of an Aging Population and the Material Well-Being of Older Persons." In M. W. Riley, B. B. Hess, and K. Bond (eds.), *Aging in Society: Selected Reviews of Recent Research*. Hillsdale, N.J.: Lawrence Erlbaum, 1983, pp. 25–51. (chap. 14)

Everitt, A.V., and **C. Y. Huang.** "The Hypothalamus, Neuroendocrine, and Autonomic Nervous Systems in Aging." In J. E. Birren and R. B. Sloane (eds.), *Handbook of Mental Health and Aging*. Englewood Cliffs, N.J.: Prentice-Hall, 1980, pp. 100–133. (chap. 4)

Falbo, T., and **L. A. Peplau.** "Power Strategies in Intimate Relationships." *Journal of Personality and Social Psychology*, 38 (1980), 618–628. (chap. 11)

Falicov, C. J. "Mexican Families." In M. McGoldrick, J. K. Pearce, and J. Giordano (eds.), *Ethnicity and Family Therapy*. New York: Guilford, 1982, pp. 134–141. (chap. 15)

Featherman, D. L. "The Life-Span Perspective in Social Science Research." Prepared for the Social Science Research Council. Unpublished paper. University of Wisconsin, 1981. (chaps. 1, 2)

_____, and **T. M. Carter.** "Discontinuities in Schooling and the Socioeconomic Life Cycle." In W. H. Sewell, R. M. Hauser, and D. L. Featherman (eds.), *Schooling and Achievement in American Society*. New York: Academic Press, 1976. (chap. 13)

Feifel, H. "The Function of Attitudes Toward Death." In *Death and Dying: Attitudes of Patient and Doctor*. New York: Group for the Advancement of Psychiatry, 1965, pp. 632–641. (chap. 16)

Feldman, R. M., and **S. N. Reger.** "Relations Among Hearing, Reaction Time, and Age." *Journal of Speech and Hearing Research*, 10 (1967), 479–495. (chap. 7)

Feldman, S. S., and **B. Aschenbrenner.** "Impact of Parenthood on Various Aspects of Masculinity and Feminity: A Short-Term Longitudinal Study." *Developmental Psychology*, 19 (1983), 278–289. (chap. 12)

_____, **Z. C. Biringen,** and **S. C. Nash.** "Fluctuations of Sex-Related Self-Attributions as a Function of Stage of the Family Life Cycle." *Developmental Psychology*, 17 (1981), 24–35. (chaps. 10, 12)

Ferraro, K. F. "The Health Consequences of Relocation Among the Aged in the Community." *Journal of Gerontology*, 38 (1983), 90–96. (chaps. 2, 14)

Ferretti, F. "Older Collegians Make Up for Lost Time." *The New York Times*, May 27, 1983. (chap. 8)

Finley, G. E. "Modernization and Aging." In T. M. Field, A. Huston, H. C. Quay, L. Troll, and G. E. Finley (eds.), *Review of Human Development*. New York: Wiley-Interscience, 1982, pp. 511–523. (chap. 15)

Firth, R. *Elements of Social Organization*. 3d ed. London: Tavistock, 1961. (chap. 16)

Fiske, M. "Tasks and Crises of the Second Half of Life: The Interrelationship of Commitment, Coping, and Adaptation." In J. E. Birren and R. B. Sloane (eds.), *Handbook of Mental Health and Aging*. Englewood Cliffs, N.J.: Prentice-Hall, 1980, pp. 337–373. (chaps. 5, 10)

Fitzgerald, F. "A Reporter at Large: Interlude—Sun City Center," *The New Yorker*, 59 (April 25, 1983), 54–109. (chap. 14)

Foner, A. "The Polity." In M. W. Riley, M. Johnson, and A. Foner (eds.), *Aging and Society*, Vol. 3. *A Sociology of Age Stratification*. New York: Russell Sage Foundation, 1972, pp. 115–159. (chap. 14)

_____, and **K. Schwab.** *Aging and Retirement*. Monterey, Calif.: Brooks/Cole, 1981. (chap. 13)

Fox, A. "Earnings Replacement Rates of Retired Couples: Findings from the Retirement History Study." *Social Security Bulletin*, 42 (January 1979), 17–39. (chap. 14)

Fozard, J. L., and **S. J. Popkin.** "Optimizing Adult Development: Ends and Means of an Applied Psychology of Aging." *American Psychologist*, 33 (1978), 975–989. (chap. 7)

_____, and **J. L. Thomas.** "Psychology of Aging: Basic Findings and Their Psychiatric Applications." In J. G. Howells (ed.), *Modern Perspectives in the Psychology of Old Age*. New York: Brunner-Mazel, 1975, pp. 107–169. (chap. 7)

_____, **E. Wolf, B. Bell, A. McFarland,** and **S. Podolsky.** "Visual Perception and Communication." In J. E. Birren and K. W. Schaie (eds.), *Handbook of the Psychology of Aging*. New York: Van Nostrand Reinhold, 1977, pp. 497–534. (chap. 7)

Francher, J.S., and **J. Henkin.** "The Menopausal Queen: Adjustment to Aging and the Male Homosexual." *American Journal of Orthopsychiatry*, 43 (1973), 670–674. (chap. 11)

Frank, E., C. Anderson, and **D. Rubinstein.** "Frequency of Sexual Dysfunction in 'Normal' Couples." *New England Journal of Medicine*, 299 (1978), 111–115. (chap. 11)

Freeman, J. T. "The Old, Old, Very Old Charlie Smith." *Gerontologist*, 22 (1982), 532–536. (chap. 3)

Freemon, F. R. "Evaluation of Patients with Progressive Intellectual Deterioration." *Arch. Neurol.*, 33 (1976), 658–659. (chap. 6)

Freud, S. "On Psychotherapy." *Collected Papers*. Vol. 1. London: Hogarth Press, 1924. (chap. 6)

_____. "Mourning and Melancholia." In *Collected Papers of Sigmund Freud*. Vol. 4. London: Hogarth Press, 1953, pp. 152–170 (orig. pub. 1917). (chap. 16)

Freudenheim, M. "Home Health Unit Thrives Upstate, *The New York Times*, November 10, 1983, B2. (chap. 14)

Friedman, M., and **R. H. Rosenman.** *Type A Behavior and Your Heart*. New York: Knopf, 1974. (chap. 5)

Fries, J. F., and **L. M. Crapo.** *Vitality and Aging*. San Francisco: W. H. Freeman, 1981. (chaps. 3, 5)

Frieze, I. H., J. E. Parsons, P. B. Johnson, D. N. Ruble, and **G. L. Zellman.** *Women and Sex Roles: A Social Psychological Perspective*. New York: Norton, 1978. (chap. 10)

Fry, C. L. "Cultural Dimensions of Age: A Multidimensional Scaling Analysis." In C. L. Fry (ed.), *Aging in Culture and Society*. New York: Praeger, 1980, pp. 42–64. (chap. 15)

Fuchs, V. R. *How We Live: An Economic Perspective on Americans from Birth to Death*. Cambridge, Mass.: Harvard University Press, 1983. (chaps. 13, 14)

Furchgott, E., and **J. K. Busemeyer.** "Heart Rate and Skin Conductance During Cognitive Processes as a Function of Age." Paper presented at the Meeting of the Gerontological Society, 1976. (chap. 8)

Furstenberg, F. F., Jr. "Conjugal Succession: Reentering Marriage after Divorce." In P. B. Baltes and O. G. Brim, Jr., (eds.), *Life-Span Development and Behavior*. Vol. 4. New York: Academic Press, 1982, pp. 107–146. (chap. 11)

Gagnon, J. H. "Review of *Homosexualities: A Study of Diversity among Men and*

Women.'' Human Nature, 2 (March 1979), 20–24. (chap. 11)

———, and **C. S. Greenblatt.** *Life Designs: Individuals, Marriages, and Families.* Glenview, Ill.: Scott-Foresman, 1978. (chap. 11)

Gaiter, D. J. "10% of U.S. Elderly Have Problem with Alcohol, Congressmen Told." *The New York Times*, June 11, 1983. (chap. 6)

Gaitz, C. M., and **D. E. Baer.** "Characteristics of Elderly Patients with Alcoholism." *Archives of General Psychiatry*, 24 (1971), 372–378. (chap. 6)

Garcia-Preto, N. "Puerto Rican Families." In M. McGoldrick, J. K. Pearce, and J. Giordano (eds.), *Ethnicity and Family Therapy.* New York: Guilford, 1982. (chap. 15)

Gardner, E. G., and **R. H. Monge.** "Adult Age Differences in Cognitive Abilities and Educational Background." *Experimental Aging Research*, 3 (1977), 337–383. (chap. 9)

Gardner, H. *Frames of Mind: The Theory of Multiple Intelligences.* New York: Basic Books, 1983. (chap. 9)

Garfinkel, R. "By the Sweat of Your Brow." In T. M. Field, A. Huston, H. C. Quay, L. Troll, and G. E. Finley (eds.), *Review of Human Development.* New York: Wiley-Interscience, 1982, pp. 500–507. (chap. 13)

Garn, S. M. "Bone Loss and Aging." In R. Goldman, M. Rockstein, and M. Sussman (eds.), *The Physiology and Pathology of Human Aging.* New York: Academic Press, 1975, pp. 39–57. (chap. 4)

Gebhard, P. H. "Postmarital Coitus Among Widows and Divorcees." In P. Bohannon (ed.), *Divorce and After.* Garden City, N.Y.: Doubleday, 1970, pp. 81–96. (chap. 11)

Gelfand, D. E. *Aging: The Ethnic Factor.* Boston: Little, Brown, 1982. (chap. 15)

Gelfand, S. "The Relationship of Experimental Pain Tolerance to Pain Threshold." *Canadian Journal of Psychology*, 18 (1964), 36–42. (chap. 7)

Gelman, R. "Complexity in Development and Development Studies." In W. A. Collins (ed.), *Minnesota Symposia on Child Psychology.* Vol. 15. *The Concept of Development.* Hillsdale, N.J.: Lawrence Erlbaum, 1982, pp. 145–154. (chap. 1)

Gendreau, P., and **M. D. Suboski.** "Intelligence and Age in Discrimination Conditioning of Eyelid Response," *Journal of Experimental Psychology*, 89 (1971), 379–382. (chap. 8)

Georgakas, D. *The Methuselah Factors: Strategies for a Long and Vigorous Life.* New York: Simon & Schuster, 1980. (chap. 3)

George, L. K., G. G. Fillenbaum, and **E. Palmore.** "Sex Differences in the Antecedents and Consequences of Retirement." *Journal of Gerontology*, 39 (1984), 364–371. (chap. 13)

Geyer, R. F. *Bibliography Alienation.* 2d ed. Amsterdam: Netherlands Universities' Joint Social Research Centre, 1972. (chap. 13)

Giambra, L. M. "A Factor Analytic Study of Daydreaming, Imaginal Process, and Temperament: A Replication on an Adult Male Life-Span Sample." *Journal of Gerontology*, 32 (1977), 675–680. (chap. 16)

Gilbert, J. G. "Thirty-Five Year Follow-up Study of Intellectual Functioning." *Journal of Gerontology*, 28 (1973), 68–72. (chap. 8)

Gilligan, C. *In a Different Voice: Psychological Theory and Women's Development.* Cambridge, Mass.: Harvard University Press, 1982. (chap. 10)

Glaser, B. G., and **A. L. Strauss.** *Awareness of Dying.* Chicago: Aldine, 1965. (chap. 16)

———, and ———. *Time for Dying.* Chicago: Aldine, 1968. (chap. 16)

Glenn, N. D. "Psychological Well-Being in the Postparental Stage: Some Evidence from National Surveys." *Journal of Marriage and the Family*, 37 (1975), 105–110. (chap. 12)

————. "Values, Attitudes, and Beliefs." In O. G. Brim, Jr., and J. Kagan (eds.), *Constancy and Change in Human Development.* Cambridge, Mass.: Harvard University Press, 1980, pp. 596–640. (chaps. 1, 2, 14)

Glick, I. O., R. S. Weiss, and **C. M. Parkes.** *The First Year of Bereavement.* New York: Wiley, 1974. (chap. 16)

Glick, P. C. "Updating the Life Cycle of the Family." *Journal of Marriage and the Family*, 39 (1977), 5–13. (chap. 12)

————. "Future American Families." *The Washington COFO MEMO*, 2 (Summer/Fall, 1979), 2–5. (chap. 11)

————. "Remarriage: Some Recent Changes and Variations." *Journal of Family Issues*, 1 (1980), 455–478. (chap. 11)

Gold, D., and **D. Andres.** "Developmental Comparisons between Ten-Year-Old Children with Employed and Unemployed Mothers." *Child Development*, 49 (1978a), 75–84. (chap. 12)

————, and ————. "Relations between Maternal Employment and Development of Nursery School Children." *Canadian Journal of Behavioural Science*, 10 (1978b), 116–129. (chap. 12)

Goldman, R. "Aging of the Excretory System: Kidney and Bladder." In C. E. Finch and L. Hayflick (eds.), *Handbook of the Biology of Aging.* New York: Van Nostrand Reinhold, 1977, pp. 409–431. (chap. 4)

Goldschneider, C. *Population, Modernization, and Social Structure.* Boston: Little, Brown, 1971. (chap. 16)

Goldstein, M. C., S. Schuler, and **J. L. Ross.** "Social and Economic Forces Affecting Intergenerational Relations in Extended Families in a Third World Country: A Cautionary Tale from South Asia." *Journal of Gerontology*, 38 (1983), 716–724. (chap. 15)

Goode, C., S. L. Hoover, and **M. P. Lawton.** *Elderly Hotel and Rooming-House Dwellers.* Philadelphia: Philadelphia Geriatric Center, 1979. (chap. 14)

Goody, J. "Aging in Nonindustrial Societies." In R. H. Binstock and E. Shanas (eds.), *Handbook of Aging and the Social Sciences.* New York: Van Nostrand Reinhold, 1976, pp. 117-129. (chap. 15)

Gordon, C., C. M. Gaitz, and **J. Scott.** "Leisure and Lives: Personal Expressivity Across the Life Span." In R. H. Binstock and E. Shanas (eds.), *Handbook of Aging and the Social Sciences.* New York: Van Nostrand Reinhold, 1976, pp. 310–341. (chap. 13)

Gorer, G. *Death, Grief, and Mourning.* New York: Doubleday, 1965. (chap. 16)

Gottesman, L. E., and **N. C. Bourestom.** "Why Nursing Homes Do What They Do." *Gerontologist*, 14 (1974), 501–506. (chap. 14)

Gould, R. L. "Adult Life Stages: Growth toward Self-Tolerance." *Psychology Today*, 8 (February 1975), 74–78. (chap. 10)

————. *Transformations: Growth and Change in Adult Life.* New York: Simon & Schuster, 1978. (chap. 10)

Granick, S., K. M. Kleban, and **A. D. Weiss.** "Relationships between Hearing Loss and Cognition in Normally Hearing Aged Persons." *Journal of Gerontology*, 31 (1976), 434–440. (chap. 7)

Gray, D. "A Job Club for Older Job Seekers: An Experimental Evaluation." *Journal of Gerontology*, 38 (1983), 363–368. (chap. 13)

Grenville, T. N. E. *U.S. Decennial Life Tables for 1969–1971.* Washington, D.C.: U.S. Public Health Service, 1976. (chap. 5)

Groffman, K. J. "Life-Span Developmental Psychology in Europe: Past and Present." In L. R. Goulet and P. B. Baltes (eds.), *Life-Span Developmental Psychology: Research and Theory.* New York: Academic Press, 1970, pp. 53–68. (chap. 1)

Grossman, F. K., L. S. Eichler, and **S. A. Winickoff.** *Pregnancy, Birth, and Parenthood.* San Francisco: Jossey-Bass, 1980. (chap. 12)

Grove, G. L., and **A. M. Kligman.** "Age-

Associated Changes in Human Epidermal Cell Renewal.'' *Journal of Gerontology*, 38 (1983), 137–142. (chap. 2)

Gruenfeld, L. W., and **A. E. MacEachron.** ''Relationship between Age, Socioeconomic Status, and Field Independence.'' *Perceptual and Motor Skills*, 41 (1975), 449–450. (chap. 9)

Grzegorczyk, P. B., S. W. Jones, and **C. M. Mistretta.** ''Age-Related Differences in Salt Taste Acuity.'' *Journal of Gerontology*, 34 (1979), 834–840. (chap. 7)

Guemple, L. ''Growing Old in Inuit Society.'' In J. Sokolovsky (ed.), *Growing Old in Different Societies*. Belmont, Calif.: Wadsworth, 1983, pp. 24–28. (chap. 15)

Guilford, J. P. ''Theories of Intelligence.'' In B. B. Wolman (ed.), *Handbook of General Psychology*. Englewood Cliffs, N.J.: Prentice-Hall, 1973, pp. 630–643. (chap. 9)

Gurin, J. ''Chemical Feelings.'' *Science 80*, 1 (November/December 1979), 28–33. (chap. 7)

Gutmann, D. ''Parenthood: A Key to the Comparative Study of the Life Cycle.'' In N. Datan and L. H. Ginsberg (eds.), *Life-Span Developmental Psychology: Normative Life Crises*. New York: Academic Press, 1975, pp. 167–184. (chap. 12)

———. ''Observations on Culture and Mental Health in Later Life.'' In J. E. Birren and R. B. Sloane (eds.), *Handbook of Mental Health and Aging*. Englewood Cliffs, N.J.: Prentice-Hall, 1980, pp. 429–447. (chap. 15)

Haan, N. ''Common Dimensions of Personality Development: Early Adolescence to Middle Life.'' In D. H. Eichorn, J. A. Clausen, N. Haan, M. P. Honzik, and P. H. Mussen (eds.), *Present and Past in Middle Life*. New York: Academic Press, 1981, pp. 117–153. (chap. 10)

Hacker, H. M. ''Blabbermouths and Clams: Sex Differences in Self-Disclosure in Same-Sex and Cross-Sex Friendship Dyads.'' *Psychology of Women Quarterly*, 5 (1981), 385–401. (chap. 11)

Hagestad, G. O. ''Patterns of Communication and Influence Between Grandparents and Grandchildren in a Changing Society.'' Paper presented at the World Conference of Sociology. Upsala, Sweden, August 1978. (chap. 12)

———. ''Problems and Promises in the Social Psychology of Intergenerational Relationships.'' In R. W. Fogel, E. Hatfield, S. B. Kiesler, and E. Shanas (eds.), *Aging*. Vol. 3. *Stability and Change in the Family*. New York: Academic Press, 1981, pp. 11–46. (chap. 12)

———. ''Parent and Child: Generations in the Family.'' In T. M. Field, A. Huston, H. C. Quay, L. Troll, and G. E. Finley (eds.), *Review of Human Development*. New York: Wiley-Interscience, 1982, pp. 485–499.(chap. 12)

Hall, E., M. E. Lamb, and **M. Perlmutter.** *Child Psychology Today*. New York: Random House, 1982. (chaps. 1, 9)

Hall, G. S. *Senescence: The Last Half of Life*. New York: Appleton, 1922. (chap. 1)

Halstead, B. ''Woman for All Ages Voices Plight of Elderly.'' *AARP News Bulletin*, 24 (May 1983), 2 + . (chap. 1)

Hamburger, V. ''The Concept of 'Development' in Biology.'' in D. B. Harris (ed.), *The Concept of Development*. Minneapolis: University of Minnesota Press, 1957, pp. 49–58. (chap. 1)

Hammond, C.B., and **W. S. Maxon.** ''Current Status of Estrogen Therapy for the Menopause.'' *Fertility and Sterility*, 37 (1982), 5–25. (chap. 4)

Hammond, E. C., L. Garfinkel, and **H. Seidman.** ''Longevity of Parents and Grandparents in Relation to Coronary Heart Disease Associated Variables.'' *Circulation*, 43 (1971), 31–44. (chap. 3)

Hammond, P. E. ''Aging and the Ministry.'' In M. W. Riley, J. W. Riley, Jr., and M. E. Johnson (eds.), *Aging and Society*. Vol. 2. *Aging and the Professions*. New York: Russell Sage Foundation, 1969, pp. 293–323. (chap. 14)

Harbert, A. S., and **L. H. Ginsberg.** *Hu-*

man Services for Older Adults: Concepts and Skills. Belmont, Calif.: Wadsworth, 1979. (chap. 14)

Hareven, T. K. "The Last Stage: Historical Adulthood and Old Age." In E. H. Erikson (ed.), *Adulthood.* New York: Norton, 1978, pp. 201–215. (chap. 13)

Harlan, W. "Social Status of the Aged in Three Indian Villages." In B. L. Neugarten (ed.), *Middle Age and Aging.* Chicago: University of Chicago Press, 1968, pp. 469–475. (chap. 15)

Harman, D. "Free Radical Theory of Aging: Effect of Free Radical Reaction Inhibitors on the Mortality Rate of Male LAF¹ Mice." *Journal of Gerontology*, 23 (1968), 476–482. (chap. 3)

Harris, L., and **Associates.** *The Myth and Reality of Aging in America.* Washington, D.C.: National Council on the Aging, 1975. (chap. 13)

———. *Aging in the Eighties: America in Transition.* Washington, D.C.: National Council on the Aging, 1981. (chap. 13)

Harshbarger, D. "Death and Public Policy: A Research Inquiry." In N. Datan and L. H. Ginsberg (eds.), *Life-Span Developmental Psychology: Normative Life Crises.* New York: Academic Press, 1975, pp. 299–307. (chap. 16)

Hatfield, E., D. Greenberger, J. Traupmann, and **P. Lambert.** "Equity and Sexual Satisfaction in Recently Married Couples." *Journal of Sex Research*, 18 (1982), 18–32. (chap. 11)

Hauser, P. M. "Aging and World-Wide Population Change." In R. H. Binstock and E. Shanas (eds.), *Handbook of Aging and the Social Sciences.* New York: Van Nostrand Reinhold, 1976, pp. 58–116. (chap. 3)

Havighurst, R. J. "The Nature and Values of Meaningful Free-Time Activity." in R. Kleemeier (ed.), *Aging and Leisure.* New York: Oxford University Press, 1961. (chap. 13)

Hawley, I., and **F. Kelly.** "Formal Operations as a Function of Age, Education, and Fluid and Crystallized Intelligence."

Paper presented at the Annual Meeting of the Gerontological Society. Miami, Florida, November 1973. (chap. 9)

Hayflick, L. "The Cellular Basis for Biological Aging." In C. E. Finch and L. Hayflick (eds.), *Handbook of the Biology of Aging.* New York: Van Nostrand Reinhold, 1977, pp. 159–186. (chap. 3)

Haynes, S. G., M. Feinleib, N. Scotch, and **W. B. Kannel.** "The Relationship of Psychosocial Factors to Coronary Heart Disease in the Framingham Study. II. Prevalence of Coronary Heart Disease." *American Journal of Epidemiology*, 107 (1978), 384–402. (chap. 5)

Hebb, D. O. *Organization of Behavior.* New York: Wiley, 1949. (chap. 9)

———. "Drives and the CNS." *Psychological Review*, 62 (1955), 243–253. (chap. 8)

———. "On Watching Myself Get Old." *Psychology Today*, 12 (November 1978), 15–23. (chap. 9)

Heglin, H. J. "Problem-Solving Set in Different Age Groups." *Journal of Gerontology*, 11 (1956), 310–317. (chap. 9)

Heisel, M. A., and **A. O. Faulkner.** "Religiosity in an Older Black Population." *Gerontologist*, 22 (1982), 354–358. (chap. 14)

Helmrath, T. A., and **E. M. Sternitz.** "Death of an Infant: Parental Grieving and the Failure of Social Support." *Journal of Family Practice*, 6 (1978), 785–790. (chap. 16)

Hennig, M. "Career Development of Women Executives." Doctoral dissertation, Harvard Business School, 1970. (chap. 13)

———, and **A. Jardim.** "Women Executives in the Old-Boy Network." *Psychology Today*, 10 (January 1977), 76–81. (chap. 13)

Hess, B. "Friendship." In M. W. Riley, M. Johnson, and A. Foner, *Aging and Society.* Vol. 3. *A Sociology of Age Stratification.* New York: Russell Sage Foundation, 1972, pp. 357–393. (chap. 11)

Heston, L. L., and **A. R. Mastri.** "The Genetics of Alzheimer's Disease: Associations with Hemalologic Malignancy and Down's Syndrome." *Archives of General Psychiatry*, 34 (1977), 976–981. (chap. 6)

Hetherington, E. M., M. Cox, and **R. Cox.** "Stress and Coping in Divorce: A Focus on Women." In J. E. Gullahorn (ed.), *Psychology and Women: In Transition*. New York: Wiley, 1979, pp. 95–128. (chap. 12)

Heyman, D. K., and **F. C. Jeffers.** "The Influence of Race and Socioeconomic Status upon the Activities and Attitudes of the Aged." In E. Palmore (ed.), *Normal Aging*. Durham, N.C.: Duke University Press, 1970, pp. 310–318. (chap. 13)

Hickey, T. *Health and Aging*. Monterey, Calif.: Brooks/Cole, 1980. (chaps. 1, 3, 5)

Higgins, J. "Effects of Child Rearing by Schizophrenic Mothers: A Follow-up." *Journal of Psychiatric Research*, 13, (1976), 1–9. (chap. 6)

Hill, R., N. Foote, J. Aldous, R. Carlson, and **R. Macdonald.** *Family Development in Three Generations*. Cambridge, Mass.: Schenkman, 1970. (chaps. 11, 12)

_____, and **P. Mattessich.** "Family Development Theory and Life-Span Development." In P. B. Baltes and O. G. Brim, Jr. (eds.), *Life-Span Development and Behavior*. Vol. 2. New York: Academic Press, 1979, pp. 161–204. (chap. 12)

Hill, R. B. "The Economic Status of Black Americans." In J. D. Williams (ed.), *The State of Black America*. New York: National Urban League, Inc., 1981. (chap. 15)

_____. "Income Maintenance Programs and the Minority Elderly." In R. L. McNeely and J. L. Cohen (eds.), *Aging in Minority Groups*. Beverly Hills, Calif.: Sage, 1983, pp. 195–211. (chap. 15)

Hinton, J. *Dying*. Harmondsworth, Eng.: Penguin, 1967. (chap. 16)

Hirsch, B. B. *Living Together: A Guide to the Law for Unmarried Couples*. Boston: Houghton Mifflin, 1976. (chap. 11)

Hoffman, L. "Maternal Employment, 1979." *American Psychologist*, 34 (1979), 859–865. (chap. 12)

Hogan, D. P. "The Transition to Adulthood as a Career Contingency." Paper presented at the meeting of the Rural Sociological Society. Burlington, Vermont, August 1979. (chap. 13)

Holahan, C. J. *Environmental Psychology*. New York: Random House, 1980. (chap. 5)

Holland, J. L. *Making Career Choices: A Theory of Careers*. Englewood Cliffs, N.J.: Prentice-Hall, 1976. (chap. 13)

Holmes, L., and **E. Rhoads.** "Aging and Change in Samoa." In J. Sokolovsky (ed.), *Growing Old in Different Societies*. Belmont, Calif.: Wadsworth, 1983, pp. 119–211. (chap. 15)

Holmes, O. W. *The Autocrat at the Breakfast Table*. New York: Heritage Press, 1955 (orig. pub. 1858). (chap. 5)

Holmes, T. H., and **R. H. Rahe.** "The Social Readjustment Rating Scale." *Journal of Psychosomatic Research*, 11 (1967), 213–218. (chap. 5)

Holzberg, C. S. "Ethnicity and Aging: Anthropological Perspectives on More Than Just Minority Elderly." *Gerontologist*, 22 (1982), 249–257. (chap. 15)

Hooper, F. H., and **N. W. Sheehan.** "Logical Concept Attainment during the Aging Years." In W. F. Overton and J. M. Gallagher (eds.), *Knowledge and Development*. Vol. 1. *Advances in Research and Theory*. New York: Plenum, 1977, pp. 205–254. (chap. 9)

Horn, J. "Regrieving: A Way to End Pathological Mourning." *Psychology Today*, 7 (May 1974), 104. (chap. 16)

Horn, J. L. "The Theory of Fluid and Crystallized Intelligence in Relation to Concepts of Cognitive Psychology and Aging in Adulthood." In F. I. M. Craik and S. Trehub (eds.), *Aging and Cognitive Processes*. New York: Plenum, 1982, pp. 237–278. (chap. 9)

Hornblum, J., and **W. Overton.** "Area and Volume Conservation Among the Elderly: Assessment and Training." *Developmental Psychology*, 12 (1976), 68. (chap. 9)

Horowitz, M. J., and **R. Schulz.** "The Relocation Controversy: Criticism and Commentary on Five Recent Studies." *Gerontologist*, 23 (1983), 229-234. (chap. 14)

House, J. S., and **C. Robbins.** "Age, Psychosocial Stress, and Health." In M. W. Riley, B. B. Hess, and K. Bond (eds.), *Aging in Society: Selected Reviews of Recent Research.* Hillsdale, N.J.: Lawrence Erlbaum, 1983, pp. 175-198. (chap. 5)

Houser, B. B., and **L. J. Beckman.** "Background Characteristics and Women's Dual-Role Attitudes." *Sex Roles*, 6 (1980), 335-366. (chap. 12)

Hoyenga, K. B., and **K. T. Hoyenga.** *The Question of Sex Differences: Psychological, Cultural, and Biological Issues.* Boston: Little, Brown, 1979. (chap. 10)

Howell, S. C. "Environments as Hypotheses in Human Aging." In L. W. Poon (ed.), *Aging in the 1980s: Psychological Issues.* Washington, D.C.: American Psychological Association, 1980, pp. 424-432. (chap. 5)

Hubbard, L. "In Search of 40 Winks." *Modern Maturity*, (April/May, 1982), 72-74. (chap. 4)

Hudson, R. B., and **R. H. Binstock.** "Political Systems and Aging." In R. H. Binstock and E. Shanas (eds.), *Handbook of Aging and the Social Sciences.* New York: Van Nostrand Reinhold, 1976, pp. 369-400. (chap. 14)

Hunt, M. *Sexual Behavior in the 1970's.* New York: Dell, 1974. (chap. 11)

Huston-Stein, A., and **A. Higgins-Trenk.** "Development of Females from Childhood Through Adulthood: Career and Feminine Role Orientations." In P. B. Baltes (ed.), *Life-Span Development and Behavior.* Vol. 1. New York: Academic Press, 1978, pp. 257-296. (chap. 13)

Hutchinson, I. W., III. "The Significance of Marital Status for Morale and Life Satisfaction Among Lower-Income Elderly." *Journal of Marriage and the Family*, 37 (1975), 287-293. (chap. 11)

Huyck, M. H. "From Gregariousness to Intimacy: Marriage and Friendship over the Adult Years." In T. M. Field, A. Huston, H. C. Quay, L. Troll, and G. E. Finley (eds.), *Review of Human Development.* New York: Wiley-Interscience, 1982, pp. 471-484. (chap. 11)

Hyde, J. S., and **D. E. Phillis.** "Androgyny across the Life Span." *Developmental Psychology*, 15 (1979), 334-336. (chap. 10)

Ikels, C. "The Coming of Age in Chinese Society: Traditional Patterns and Contemporary Hong Kong." In C. L. Fry (ed.), *Aging in Culture and Society.* New York: Praeger, 1980, pp. 80-100. (chap. 15)

Jackson, D. and **P. R. J. Burch.** "Dental Caries as a Degenerative Disease." *Gerontologia*, 15 (1969), 203-216. (chap. 4)

Jackson, D. L., and **S. Younger.** "Patient Autonomy and 'Death with Dignity': Some Clinical Caveats." *New England Journal of Medicine*, 301 (1979), 404-408. (chap. 16)

Jaco, E. G. *The Social Epidemiology of Mental Disorders.* New York: Russell Sage Foundation, 1960. (chap. 6)

Jarvik, L. F. "Discussion: Patterns of Intellectual Functioning in the Later Years." In L. F. Jarvik, C. Eisdorfer, and J. E. Blum (eds.), *Intellectual Functioning in Adults: Psychological and Biological Influences.* New York: Springer, 1973, pp. 65-67. (chap. 9)

————. "The Impact of Immediate Life Situations on Depression: Illnesses and Losses." In L. D. Breslau and M. R. Haug (eds.), *Depression and Aging: Causes, Care, and Consequences.* New York: Springer, 1983, pp. 114-120. (chap. 6)

Jeffko, W. G. "Redefining Death." *Commonweal*, July 6, 1979, 394-397. (chap. 16)

Jernigan, T. L., L. M. Zatz, I. Feinberg, and **G. Fein.** "The Measurement of Cerebral Atrophy in the Aged by Computed Tomography.'' In L. W. Poon (ed.), *Aging in the 1980s*. Washington, D.C.: American Psychological Association, 1980, pp. 86–94. (chap. 4)

Johnson, C. L. ''Interdependence and Aging in Italian Families.'' In J. Sokolovsky (ed.), *Growing Old in Different Societies*. Belmont, Calif.: Wadsworth, 1983, pp. 92–103. (chap. 15)

Johnson, E., and **B. Bursk.** ''Relationships Between the Elderly and Their Adult Children.'' *Gerontologist*, 17 (1977), 90–96. (chap. 12)

Johnson, H. R. ''Education in an Aging Society.'' *National Forum*, 62 (Fall 1982), 19–21. (chap. 13)

Johnston, L., and **S. H. Anderson.** ''New York Day by Day: A Sense of History.'' *The New York Times*, June 9, 1983. (chap. 8)

Johnstone, J. W. C., and **R. J. Rivera.** *Volunteers for Learning*. Chicago: Aldine, 1965. (chap. 13)

Jones, H. B. ''A Special Consideration of the Aging Process, Disease and Life Expectancy.'' In J. H. Lawrence and J. G. Hamilton (eds.), *Advances in Biological and Medical Physics*. Vol. 4. New York: Academic Press, 1956, pp. 281–337. (chap. 3)

Jones, L. Y. *Great Expectations: America and the Baby Boom Generation*. New York: Coward McCann & Geoghegan, 1980. (chaps. 1, 2)

Jordan, W. D. ''Searching for Adulthood in America.'' In E. H. Erikson (ed.), *Adulthood*. New York: Norton, 1978, pp. 189–200. (chap. 2)

Jury, M., and **D. Jury.** *Gramp*. New York: Grossman, 1976. (chap. 16)

Kahana, B., and **E. Kahana.** ''Grandparenthood from the Perspective of the Developing Grandchild.'' *Developmental Psychology*, 3 (1970), 98–105. (chap. 12)

Kakar, S. ''Images of the Life Cycle and Adulthood in Hindu India.'' In E. J. Anthony and C. Chiland (eds.), *The Child in His Family*. Vol. 4. *Children and Their Parents in a Changing World*. New York: Wiley-Interscience, 1978, pp. 319–332. (chap. 1)

Kalish, R. A. ''Death in a Social Context.'' In R. H. Binstock and E. Shanas (eds.), *Handbook of Aging and the Social Sciences*. New York: Van Nostrand Reinhold, 1976, pp. 483–507. (chap. 16)

———, and **D. K. Reynolds.** *Death and Ethnicity: A Psycho-Cultural Study*. Los Angeles: University of Southern California Press, 1976; reprinted, Farmingdale, N.Y.: Baywood Publishing Co., 1981. (chaps. 15, 16)

Kallman, E. J., and **L. F. Jarvik.** ''Individual Differences in Constitution and Genetic Background.'' In J. E. Birren (ed.), *Handbook of Aging and the Individual*. Chicago: University of Chicago Press, 1959, pp. 216–263. (chap. 3)

Kanter, R. M. ''Why Bosses Turn Bitchy.'' *Psychology Today*, 9 (May 1976), 56–59+. (chap. 13)

Kaplan, M. ''The Issue of Sex Bias in DSM-III: Comments on the Articles by Spitzer, Williams, and Kass.'' *American Psychologist*, 38 (1983), 802–803. (chap. 6)

Kare, M. R. ''Changes in Taste with Age—Infancy to Senescence.'' *Food Technology*, (August 1975), 78. (chap. 7)

Kasl, S. V., and **S. Rosenfield.** ''The Residential Environment and Its Impact on the Mental Health of the Aged.'' In J. E. Birren and R. B. Sloane (eds.), *Handbook of Mental Health and Aging*. Englewood Cliffs, N.J.: Prentice-Hall, 1980, pp. 468–498. (chap. 14)

Kastenbaum, R. ''Is Death a Life Crisis? On the Confrontation with Death in Theory and Practice.'' In N. Datan and L. H. Ginsberg (eds.), *Life-Span Developmental Psychology: Normative Life Crises*. New York: Academic Press, 1975, pp. 19–50. (chap. 16)

———, and **R. Aisenberg.** *The Psychology of Death*. New York: Springer, 1972. (chap. 16)

———, and **A. D. Weisman.** ''The Psychological Autopsy as a Research Procedure in Gerontology." In D. P. Dent, R. Kastenbaum, and S. Sherwood (eds.), *Research Planning and Action for the Elderly*. New York: Behavioral Publications, 1972. (chap. 16)

Kasworm, C. E. "The Older Student as an Undergraduate." *Adult Education*, 31 (1980), 30–47. (chap. 13)

Kausler, D. H. *Experimental Psychology and Human Aging*. New York: Wiley, 1982, (chap. 9)

Kay, B., and **J. N. Neelley.** "Sexuality and the Aging: A Review of Current Literature." *Sexuality and Disability*, 5 (1982), 38–46. (chap. 4)

Keating, D. P., and **L. V. Clark.** "Development of Physical and Social Reasoning in Adolescents." *Developmental Psychology*, 16 (1980), 23–30. (chap. 9)

Keating, N., and **B. Jeffrey.** "Work Careers of Ever Married and Never Married Retired Women." *Gerontologist*, 23 (1983), 416–421. (chap. 13)

Kelly, J. "Cosmetic Lib for Men." *The New York Times Magazine*, September 25, 1977. (chap. 4)

Kenshalo, D. R. "Age Changes in Touch, Vibration, Temperature, Kinesthesis, and Pain Sensitivity." In J. E. Birren and K. W. Schaie (eds.), *Handbook of the Psychology of Aging*. New York: Van Nostrand Reinhold, 1977, pp. 562–579. (chap. 7)

Kent, D. P. "The Negro Aged," *Gerontologist*, 11 (1971), 48–51. (chap. 15)

Kerns, V. "Aging and Mutual Support Relations Among the Black Carib." In C. L. Fry (ed.), *Aging in Culture and Society*. New York: Praeger, 1980, pp. 112–125. (chap. 15)

Kimble, G. A., and **H. W. Pennypacker.** "Eyelid Conditioning in Young and Aged Subjects." *Journal of Genetic Psychology*, 103 (1963), 283–289. (chap. 8)

Kimmel, D. C. "Adult Development and Aging: A Gay Perspective." *Journal of Social Issues*, 34 (1978), 113–130. (chap. 11)

_____, **K. F. Price,** and **J. W. Walker.** "Retirement Choice and Retirement Satisfaction." *Journal of Gerontology*, 33 (1978), 575–585. (chap. 13)

Kinsey, A. C., W. B. Pomeroy, C. E. Martin, and **P. H. Gebhard.** *Sexual Behavior in the Human Female*. Philadelphia: Saunders, 1953. (chap. 11)

Kivnick, H. Q. "Grandparenthood: An Overview of Meaning and Mental Health." *Gerontologist*, 22 (1982), 59–66. (chap. 12)

Kleemeier, R. W. "Intellectual Change in the Senium." *Proceedings of the Social Statistics Section of the American Statistical Association*, 1962, pp. 290–295. (chap. 9)

Klemmack, D. L. "Public Support for Government Energy Assistance Payments to Older Persons." *Gerontologist*, 23 (1983), 307–312. (chap. 14)

Klerman, G. L. "Problems in the Definition and Diagnosis of Depression in the Elderly." In L. D. Breslau and M. R. Haug (eds.), *Depression and Aging: Causes, Care, and Consequences*. New York: Springer, 1983, pp. 3–19. (chap. 6)

Kline, D. W., D. M. Ikeda, and **F. J. Schieber.** "Age and Temporal Resolution in Color Vision: When Do Red and Green Make Yellow?" *Journal of Gerontology*, 37 (1982), 705–709. (chap. 7)

_____, **F. J. Schieber, L. C. Abusamra,** and **A. C. Coyne.** "Age, the Eye, and the Visual Channels: Contrast Sensitivity and Response Speed." *Journal of Gerontology*, 38 (1983), 211–216. (chap. 7)

_____, and **J. Szafran.** "Age Differences in Backward Monoptic Masking." *Journal of Gerontology*, 30 (1975), 307–311. (chap. 7)

Klocke, R. A. "Influence of Aging on the Lung." In C. E. Finch and L. Hayflick (eds.), *Handbook of the Biology of Aging*. New York: Van Nostrand Reinhold, 1977, pp. 432–444. (chap. 4)

Knox, A. B. *Adult Development and Learning*. San Francisco: Jossey-Bass, 1978. (chap. 8)

Kogan, N. "Creativity and Cognitive Style: A Life-Span Perspective." In P. B. Baltes and K. W. Schaie (eds.), *Life-Span Developmental Psychology: Personality and Socialization.* New York: Academic Press, 1973, pp. 145–178. (chap. 9)

_____. "Cognitive Styles in Older Adults." In T. M. Field, A. Huston, H. C. Quay, L. Troll, and G. E. Finley (eds.), *Review of Human Development.* New York: Wiley-Interscience, 1982, pp. 586–601. (chap. 9)

Kohlberg, L. "Continuities in Childhood and Adult Moral Development Revisited." In P. B. Baltes and K. W. Schaie (eds.), *Life-Span Developmental Psychology: Personality and Socialization.* New York: Academic Press, 1973, pp. 179–204. (chap. 9)

Kohn, M. L. "Job Complexity and Adult Personality." In N. J. Smelser and E. H. Erikson (eds.), *Themes of Work and Love in Adulthood.* Cambridge, Mass.: Harvard University Press, 1980, pp. 193–210. (chap. 13)

Kohn, R. R. *Principles of Mammalian Aging.* Englewood Cliffs, N.J.: Prentice-Hall, 1971. (chap. 3)

_____. "Heart and Cardiovascular System." In C. E. Finch and L. Hayflick (eds.), *Handbook of the Biology of Aging.* New York: Van Nostrand Reinhold, 1977, pp. 281–317. (chap. 4)

Kolata, G. "Lowered Cholesterol Decreases Heart Disease." *Science,* 223 (1984), 381–382. (chap. 5)

Kozma, A., and **M. J. Stones.** "Predictors of Happiness." *Journal of Gerontology,* 38 (1983), 626–628. (chap. 10)

Kreppner, K., S. Paulsen, and **Y. Schuetze.** "Infant and Family Development: From Triads to Tetrads." *Human Development,* 25 (1982), 373–391. (chap. 12)

Kreps, J. M. "The Economy and the Aged." In R. H. Binstock and E. Shanas (eds.), *Handbook of Aging and the Social Sciences.* New York: Van Nostrand Reinhold, 1976, pp. 272–285. (chap. 14)

Krier, B. A. "He Hopes Life in the Fasting Lane Will Be Long." *Minneapolis Tribune,* July 18, 1982, 3F. (chap. 5)

Kübler-Ross, E. *On Death and Dying.* New York: Macmillan, 1969. (chap. 16)

_____, **interviewed by D. Goleman.** "The Child Will Always Be There: Real Love Doesn't Die." *Psychology Today,* 10 (September 1976), 48–52. (chap. 16)

Labouvie-Vief, G. V. "Discontinuities in Development from Childhood to Adulthood: A Cognitive-Developmental View." In T. M. Field, A. Huston, H. C. Quay, L. Troll, and G. E. Finley (eds.), *Review of Human Development.* New York: Wiley-Interscience, 1982, pp. 447–455. (chap. 9)

_____, and **M. J. Chandler.** "Cognitive Development and Life-Span Developmental Theory: Idealistic versus Contextual Perspectives." In P. B. Baltes (ed.), *Life-Span Development and Behavior.* Vol. 1. New York: Academic Press, 1978, pp. 182–210. (chaps. 2, 9)

_____, and **J. N. Gonda.** "Cognitive Strategy Training and Intellectual Performance in the Elderly." *Journal of Gerontology,* 31 (1976), 327–331. (chap. 8)

_____, **W. J. Hoyer, P. B. Baltes,** and **M. M. Baltes.** "Operant Analysis of Intellectual Behavior in Old Age." *Human Development,* 17 (1974), 259–272. (chap. 9)

Lachman, J. L., and **R. Lachman.** "Age and the Actualization of World Knowledge." In L. W. Poon, J. L. Fozard, L. S. Cermak, D. Arenberg, and L. W. Thompson (eds.), *New Directions in Memory and Aging.* Hillsdale, N.J.: Lawrence Erlbaum, 1980, pp. 285–311. (chap. 8)

Lack, S. "I Want to Die While I'm Still Alive." *Death Education,* 1 (1977), 165–176. (chap. 16)

Ladner, J. L. *Tomorrow's Tomorrow: The Black Woman.* New York: Doubleday, 1971. (chap. 15)

Lair, C. V., W. H. Moon, and **D. H. Kausler.** "Associative Interference in the

Paired-Associate Learning of Middle-Aged and Old Subjects.'' *Developmental Psychology*, 1 (1969), 548–552. (chap. 8)

Lamb, M. E., and **M. A. Easterbrooks.** ''Individual Differences in Parental Sensitivity: Origins, Components, and Consequences.'' In M. E. Lamb and L. R. Sherrod (eds.), *Infant Social Cognition*. Hillsdale, N.J.: Lawrence Erlbaum, 1981, pp. 127–154. (chap. 12)

Langone, J. *Long Life: What We Know and Are Learning About the Aging Process*. Boston: Little, Brown, 1978. (chap. 3)

Langway, L. et al. ''Growing Old, Feeling Young.'' *Newsweek*, November 1, 1982, 56–65. (chap. 5)

LaPorte, R. E., R. Black-Sandler, J. A. Cauley, M. Link, C. Bayles, and **B. Marks.** ''The Assessment of Physical Activity in Older Women: Analysis of the Interrelationship and Reliability of Activity Monitoring, Activity Surveys, and Caloric Intake.'' *Journal of Gerontology*, 38 (1983), 385–393. (chap. 5)

Larronde, S. ''Adopt-a-Grandparent.'' *Modern Maturity*, 26 (August–September 1983), 50–51. (chap. 14)

Larson, R. ''Thirty Years of Research on the Subjective Well-Being of Older Americans.'' *Journal of Gerontology*, 33 (1978), 109–125. (chap. 10)

Lasch, C. *Haven in a Heartless World: The Family Besieged*. New York: Basic Books, 1977. (chap. 12)

Laslett, P. ''Mean Household Size in England Since the Sixteenth Century.'' In P. Laslett (ed.), *Household and Family in Past Time*. Cambridge: Cambridge University Press, 1972, pp. 125–158. (chap. 2)

Laudenslager, M. L., S. M. Ryan, R. C. Drugan, R. L. Hudson, and **S. F. Maier.** ''Coping and Immunosuppression: Inescapable but Not Escapable Shock Suppresses Lymphocyte Proliferation.'' *Science*, 221 (1983), 568–570 . (chap. 5)

Laurence, M. W., and **A. J. Arrowood.** ''Classification Style Difference in the Elderly.'' In F. I. M. Craik and S. Trehub (eds.), *Aging and Cognitive Processes*. New York: Plenum, 1982, pp. 213–220. (chap. 9)

LaVoie, J. C. ''Ego Identity Formation in Middle Adolescence.'' *Journal of Youth and Adolescence*, 5 (1976), 371–385. (chap. 10)

Laws, J. L., and **P. Schwartz.** *Sexual Scripts: The Social Construction of Female Sexuality*. Hinsdale, Ill.: Dryden Press, 1977. (chap. 12)

Lawson, C. ''Broadway.'' *The New York Times*, September 23, 1983, C2. (chap. 10)

Lawton, M. P. ''Impact of the Environment on Aging and Behavior.'' In J. E. Birren and K. W. Schaie (eds.), *Handbook of the Psychology of Aging*. New York: Van Nostrand Reinhold, 1977, pp. 276–301. (chap. 5)

————. *Environment and Aging*. Monterey, Calif.: Brooks/Cole, 1980. (chap. 14)

————, and **J. Cohen.** ''The Generality of Housing Impact on the Well-Being of Older People.'' *Journal of Gerontology*, 29 (1974), 194–204. (chap. 14)

Layde, P. M., H. W. Ory, and **J. J. Schlesselman.** ''The Risk of Myocardial Infarction in Former Users of Oral Contraceptives.'' *Family Planning Perspectives*, 14 (1982), 78–80. (chap. 5)

Lee, G. R. ''Social Integration and Fear of Crime Among Older Persons.'' *Journal of Gerontology*, 38 (1983), 745–750. (chap. 14)

Lee, J. A., and **R. H. Pollack.** ''The Effects of Age on Perceptual Problem-Solving Strategies.'' *Experimental Aging Research*, 4 (1978), 37–54. (chap. 9)

————, and ————. ''The Effects of Age on Perceptual Field Dependence.'' *Bulletin of the Psychonomic Society*, 15 (1980), 239–241. (chap. 9)

Leech, S., and **K. L. Witte.** ''Paired Associate Learning in Elderly Adults as Related to Pacing and Incentive Conditions.'' *Developmental Psychology*, 5 (1971), 180. (chap. 8)

Lehman, H. C. ''The Creative Production Rates of Present versus Past Generations of Scientists." In B. L. Neugarten (ed.), *Middle Age and Aging*. Chicago: University of Chicago Press, 1968, pp. 99–105. (chap. 9)

Leiblum, S., G. Bachmann, K. Kemmann, D. Colburn, and **L. Swartzman.** "Vaginal Atrophy in the Post-Menopausal Woman: The Importance of Sexual Activity and Hormones." *Journal of the American Medical Association*, 249 (1983), 2195–2198. (chap. 4)

Leon, G. R., B. Gillum, R. Gillum, and **M. Gouze.** "Personality Stability and Change over a 30-Year Period—Middle Age to Old Age." *Journal of Consulting and Clinical Psychology* [in press]. (chap. 10)

Lerner, M. "When, Why, and Where People Die." In O. G. Brim, Jr., H. E. Freeman, S. Levine, and N. A. Scotch (eds.), *The Dying Patient*. New York: Russell Sage Foundation, 1970. (chap. 16)

Lerner, R. M. "Nature, Nurture, and Dynamic Interactionism." *Human Development*, 21 (1978), 1–20. (chap. 2)

————, and **N. A. Busch-Rossnagel.** *Individuals as Producers of Their Own Development*. New York: Academic Press, 1981. (chap. 14)

Leroux, C. *A Silent Epidemic*. Chicago: Alzheimer's Disease and Related Disorders Association, 1981. (chap. 6)

LeVine, R. "Culture, Context, and the Concept of Development." In W. A. Collins (ed.), *Minnesota Symposia on Child Psychology*. Vol. 15. *The Concept of Development*. Hillsdale, N.J.: Lawrence Erlbaum, 1982, pp. 162–166. (chap. 2)

Levinson, D. J., C. N. Darrow, E. B. Klein, M. H. Levinson, and **B. McKee.** *The Seasons of a Man's Life*. New York: Knopf, 1978. (chaps. 10, 11, 13)

Levy, R. I., and **J. Moskowitz.** "Cardiovascular Research: Decades of Progress, a Decade of Promise." *Science*, 217 (1982), 121–129. (chap. 5)

Levy, S. M., L. R. Derogatis, D. Gallagher, and **M. Gatz.** "Intervention with

Older Adults and the Evaluation of Outcome." In L. W. Poon (ed.), *Aging in the 1980s: Psychological Issues*. Washington, D.C.: American Psychological Association, 1980, pp. 41–61. (chap. 6)

Lewin, T. "A New Push to Raise Women's Pay." *The New York Times*, January 1, 1984, B1 + . (chap. 13)

Lieberman, M. A. "Social Contexts of Depression." In L. D. Breslau and M. R. Haug (eds.), *Depression and Aging: Causes, Care, and Consequences*. New York: Springer, 1983, pp. 121–133. (chap. 6)

————, and **S. Tobin.** *The Experience of Old Age*. New York: Basic Books, 1983. (chaps. 14, 16)

Lindemann, E. "Symptomatology and Management of Acute Grief." *American Journal of Psychiatry*, 101 (1944), 141–148. (chap. 16)

Lindsey, R. "A New Generation Finds It Hard to Leave the Nest." *The New York Times*, January 15, 1984, 18. (chap. 14)

Litsky, F. "At 43, an Athlete Starts Over." *The New York Times*, July 2, 1983, 29. (chap. 4)

Litwak, E. "Reference Group Theory, Bureaucratic Career and Neighborhood Primary Group Cohesion." *Sociometry*, 23 (1960), 72–84. (chap. 12)

Livson, F. B. "Paths to Psychological Health in the Middle Years: Sex Differences." In D. H. Eichorn, J. A. Clausen, N. Haan, M. P. Honzik, and P. H. Mussen (eds.), *Present and Past in Middle Life*. New York: Academic Press, 1981, pp. 195–222. (chap. 10)

Livson, N. "Developmental Dimensions of Personality: A Life-Span Formulation." In P. B. Baltes and K. W. Schaie (eds.), *Life-Span Developmental Psychology: Personality and Socialization*. New York: Academic Press, 1973, pp. 97–122. (chap. 10)

Loftus, E. *Memory*. Reading, Mass.: Addison-Wesley, 1980. (chap. 6)

Longo, V. G. *Pharmacological Review*, 18 (1966), 965. (chap. 6)

Lopata, H. Z. *Widowhood in an American City.* Cambridge, Mass.: Schenkman, 1973. (chap. 11)

_____. "Widowhood: Societal Factors in Life-Span Disruption and Alternatives." In N. Datan and L. H. Ginsberg (eds.), *Life-Span Developmental Psychology: Normative Life Crises.* New York: Academic Press, 1975, pp. 217–234. (chap. 11)

_____. *Women as Widows: Support Systems.* New York: Elsevier-North Holland, 1979. (chap. 11)

_____. "The Widowed Family Member." In N. Datan and N. Lohmann (eds.), *Transitions of Aging.* New York: Academic Press, 1980, pp. 93–118. (chap. 11)

Lowenthal, M. F. "Toward a Sociopsychological Theory of Change in Adulthood and Old Age." In J. E. Birren and K. W. Schaie (eds.), *Handbook of the Psychology of Aging.* New York: Van Nostrand, 1977, pp. 116–127. (chap. 2)

_____, and **D. Chiriboga.** "Transition to the Empty Nest: Crisis, Challenge, or Relief?" *Archives of General Psychiatry*, 26 (1972), 8–14 (chap. 12)

_____, **M. Thurnher,** and **D. Chiriboga.** *Four Stages of Life.* San Francisco: Jossey-Bass, 1975. (chap. 11)

Luria, A. R. *Cognitive Development: Its Cultural and Social Foundations.* Cambridge, Mass.: Harvard University Press, 1976. (chap. 9)

Maccoby, E. E. "Commentary and Reply." In G. R. Patterson, "Mothers: The Unacknowledged Victims," *Monographs of the Society for Research in Child Development*, 45, no. 5 (1980), Whole No. 186, 56–63. (chap. 12)

Mackinodan, T. "Immunity and Aging." In C. E. Finch and L. Hayflick (eds.), *Handbook of the Biology of Aging.* New York: Van Nostrand Reinhold, 1977, pp. 379–408. (chap. 4)

Macklin, E. D. "Review of Research on Nonmarital Cohabitation in the United States." In B. I. Murstein (ed.), *Exploring Intimate Life Styles.* New York: Springer, 1978, pp. 197–243. (chap. 11)

_____. "Nontraditional Family Forms: A Decade of Research." *Journal of Marriage and the Family*, 42 (1980), 905–922. (chap. 11)

Madden, D. J. "Aging and Distraction by Highly Familiar Stimuli during Visual Search." *Developmental Psychology*, 19 (1983), 499–507. (chap. 8)

Maddison, D. C., and **W. L. Walker.** "Factors Affecting the Outcome of Conjugal Bereavement." *British Journal of Psychiatry*, 113 (1967), 1057. (chap. 16)

Maddox, G. L. "Persistence of Life Style Among the Elderly." In E. Palmore (ed.), *Normal Aging.* Durham, N.C.: Duke University Press, 1970, pp. 329–331. (chaps. 10, 13)

_____, and **E. B. Douglass.** "Self-Assessment of Health." In E. Palmore (ed.), *Normal Aging II.* Durham, N.C.: Duke University Press, 1974, pp. 49–54. (chap. 5)

_____, and **J. Wiley.** "Scope, Concepts, and Methods in the Study of Aging." In R. H. Binstock and E. Shanas (eds.), *Handbook of Aging and the Social Sciences.* New York: Van Nostrand Reinhold, 1976, pp. 3–34. (chap. 1)

Maher, B. In H. London and R. E. Nisbett (eds.), *Thought and Feeling.* Chicago: Aldine, 1974, pp. 85–103. (chap. 7)

Maldonado, D., Jr. "Aging in the Chicano Context." In D. E. Gelfand and A. J. Kutzik (eds.), *Ethnicity and Aging: Theory, Research, and Policy.* New York: Springer, 1979, pp. 175–183. (chap. 15)

Mancini, J. A., and **D. K. Orthner.** "Recreational Sexual Preference among Middle-Class Husbands and Wives." *Journal of Sex Research*, 14 (1978), 96–106. (chap. 13)

Marcia, J. E. "Identity Six Years After: A Follow-Up Study." *Journal of Youth and Adolescence*, 5 (1976), 145–160. (chap. 10)

Margulis, H. L., and **V. M. Benson.** "Age-Segregation and Discrimination

Against Families with Children in Rental Housing." *Gerontologist*, 22 (1982), 505–512. (chap. 14)

Markides, K. S. "Aging, Religiosity, and Adjustment: A Longitudinal Analysis." *Journal of Gerontology*, 38 (1983), 621–625. (chap. 14)

_____. "Minority Aging." In M. W. Riley, B. B. Hess, and K. Bond (eds.), *Aging in Society: Selected Reviews of Recent Research*. Hillsdale, N.J.: Lawrence Erlbaum, 1983, pp. 115–137. (chap. 15)

Marks, L. E., and J. C. Stevens. "Measuring Sensation in the Aged." In L. W. Poon (ed.), *Aging in the 1980s: Psychological Issues*. Washington, D.C.: American Psychological Association, 1980, pp. 592–598. (chap. 7)

Marsh, G. R., and L. W. Thompson. "Psychophysiology of Aging." In J. E. Birren and K. W. Schaie (eds.), *Handbook of Mental Health and Aging*. New York: Van Nostrand Reinhold, 1977, pp. 219–248. (chap. 4)

Marshall, H., and M. H. Oden. "The Status of the Mature Gifted Individual as a Basis for Evaluation of the Aging Process." *Gerontologist*, 2 (1962), 301–306. (chap. 14)

Marshall, V. W. "Age and Awareness of Finitude in Developmental Gerontology." *Omega*, 6 (1975), 113–129. (chap. 16)

_____. *Last Chapters: A Sociology of Aging and Dying*. Monterey, Calif.: Brooks/Cole, 1980. (chap. 16)

Marx, J. L. "Hormones and Their Effects in the Aging Body." *Science*, 206 (1979), 805–806. (chap. 4)

Maslow, A. H. *Motivation and Personality*. New York: Harper & Row, 1954. (chap. 11)

Masters, W. H., and V. E. Johnson. *Human Sexual Response*. Boston: Little, Brown, 1966. (chap. 4)

Matsuyama, S. S., and L. F. Jarvik. "Genetics and Mental Functioning in Senescence." In J. E. Birren and R. B. Sloane (eds.), *Handbook of Mental Health and Aging*. Englewood Cliffs, N.J.: Prentice-Hall, 1980, pp. 134–148. (chap. 3)

Matthews, S. H., and J. Sprey. "The Impact of Divorce on Grandparenthood: An Exploratory Study." *Gerontologist*, 24 (1984), 41–47. (chap. 12)

Mauksch, H. O. "The Organizational Context of Dying." In E. Kübler-Ross (ed.), *Death: The Final Stage of Growth*. Englewood Cliffs, N.J.: Prentice-Hall, 1975, pp. 7–24. (chap. 16)

Mazess, R. B., and S. H. Forman. "Longevity and Age Exaggeration in Vilacabamba, Ecuador." *Journal of Gerontology*, 34 (1979), 94–98. (chap. 3)

McCarthy, J. "A Comparison of the Probability of the Dissolution of First and Second Marriages." *Demography*, 15 (1978), 345–359. (chap. 11)

McConnel, C. E., and F. Deljavan. "Consumption Patterns of the Retired Household." *Journal of Gerontology*, 38 (1983), 480–490. (chap. 14)

McConnell, S. R. "Retirement and Employment." In D. S. Woodruff and J. E. Birren (eds.), *Aging: Scientific Perspectives and Social Issues*. 2d ed. Monterey, Calif.: Brooks/Cole, 1983, pp. 333–350. (chap. 13)

McCrae, R. R., and P. T. Costa, Jr. "Aging, the Life Course, and Models of Personality." In T. M. Field, A. Huston, H. C. Quay, L. Troll, and G. E. Finley (eds.), *Review of Human Development*. New York: Wiley-Interscience, 1982, pp. 602–613. (chap. 10)

_____, and _____. "Psychological Maturity and Subjective Well-Being: Toward New Synthesis." *Developmental Psychology*, 19 (1983), 243–248. (chap. 10)

McGhee, J. L. "Transportation Opportunity and Rural Elderly: A Comparison of Objective and Subjective Indicators." *Gerontologist*, 23 (1983), 505–511. (chap. 14)

McKain, W. C., Jr. *Retirement Marriage*. Storrs, Conn.: University of Connecticut Agriculture Experiment Station, 1969. (chap. 11)

McKeown, T. "Determinants of Health." *Human Nature*, 1 (April 1978), 60–67. (chap. 3)

——, and **R. G. Brown.** "Medical Evidence Related to English Population Changes in the Eighteenth Century." *Population Studies*, 9 (1955). (chap. 16)

McQueen, A. J. "The Adaptations of Urban Black Families: Trends, Problems, and Issues." In D. Reiss and H. A. Hoffman (eds.), *The American Family: Dying or Developing*. New York: Plenum, 1979, pp. 79–102. (chap. 15)

Mead, G. H. *Mind, Self and Society*. Chicago: University of Chicago Press, 1934. (chap. 11)

Mead, M. *Culture and Commitment*. Rev. ed. Garden City, N.Y.: Anchor Books, 1978. (chap. 12)

Medvedev, Z. A. "Caucasus and Altay Longevity: A Biological or Social Problem." *Gerontologist*, 14 (1974), 381–387. (chap. 3)

Melvin, T. "Ruling Awaited on Paternity Leave." *The New York Times*, October 23, 1983, WC6. (chap. 12)

Melzack, R. *The Puzzle of Pain*. New York: Basic Books, 1973. (chap. 7)

Michael, R. T., V. R. Fuchs, and **S. R. Scott.** "Changes in the Propensity to Live Alone: 1950–1976." *Demography*, 17 (February 1980), 39–56. (chap. 14)

Miernyk, W. H. "The Changing Life Cycle of Work." In N. Datan and L. H. Ginsberg (eds.), *Life-Span Developmental Psychology: Normative Life Crises*. New York: Academic Press, 1975, pp. 279–286. (chap. 13)

Mihal, W. L., and **G. V. Barrett.** "Individual Differences in Perceptual Information Processing and Their Relation to Automobile Accident Involvements." *Journal of Applied Psychology*, 61 (1976), 229–233. (chap. 9)

Milbrath, L. W., and **M. L. Goel.** *Political Participation*. 2d ed. Chicago: Rand McNally, 1977. (chap. 14)

Miller, B. D., and **D. Olsen.** "Typology of Marital Interaction and Contextual Characteristics: Cluster Analysis of the I.M.C." Unpublished paper available from D. Olsen, Minnesota Family Study Center, University of Minnesota, 1978. (chap. 11)

Miller, F. T. "Measurement and Monitoring of Stress in Communities." In L. W. Poon (ed.), *Aging in the 1980s: Psychological Issues*. Washington, D.C.: American Psychological Association, 1980, pp. 383–388. (chap. 5)

Miller, G. A. "The Magical Number Seven, Plus or Minus Two: Some Limits on Our Capacity to Process Information." *Psychological Review*, 63 (1956), 81–97. (chap. 8)

Miller, J., C. Schooler, M. L. Kohn, and **K. A. Miller.** "Women and Work: The Psychological Effects of Occupational Conditions." *American Journal of Sociology*, 85 (1979), 66–94. (chap. 13)

Miller, M. "Geriatric Suicide: The Arizona Study." *Gerontologist*, 18 (1978), 488–496. (chap. 6)

Miller, P. Y., and **W. Simon.** "The Development of Sexuality in Adolescence." In J. Adelson (ed.), *Handbook of Adolescent Psychology*. New York: Wiley-Interscience, 1980, pp. 383–407.

Mischel, W. *Introduction to Personality*. 3d ed. New York: Holt, Rinehart and Winston, 1981. (chap. 10)

Moberg, D. O. "Religiosity in Old Age." In B. L. Neugarten (ed.), *Middle Age and Aging*. Chicago: University of Chicago Press, 1968, pp. 497–508. (chap. 14)

Modern Maturity. "They Show How to Live on Less," 26 (June–July 1983), 94. (chap. 14)

Moncrieff, R. W. *Odour Preferences*. New York: Wiley, 1966. (chap. 7)

Money, J. "The American Heritage of Three Traditions of Pair-Bonding: Mediterranean, Nordic, and Slave." In J. Money and H. Musaph (eds.), *Handbook of Sexology*. New York: Elsevier/North Holland Biomedical Press, 1977, pp. 497–504. (chap. 11)

Monge, R., and **D. Hultsch.** "Paired Associate Learning as a Function of Adult Age and the Length of Anticipation and Inspection Intervals." *Journal of Gerontology*, 26 (1971), 157–162. (chap. 8)

Moon, M. *The Measurement of Economic Welfare—Its Application to the Aged Poor.* New York: Academic Press, 1977. (chap. 14)

Moore, L. M., C. R. Nielsen, and **C. M. Mistretta.** "Sucrose Taste Thresholds: Age-Related Differences." *Journal of Gerontology*, 37 (1982), 64–69. (chap. 7)

Morgan, L. A. "Intergenerational Financial Support: Retirement-Age Males, 1971–1975." *Gerontologist*, 23 (1983), 160–166. (chap. 12)

Moriwaki, S. Y., and **F. S. Kobata.** "Ethnic Minority Aging." In D. S. Woodruff and J. E. Birren (eds.), *Aging: Scientific Perspectives and Social Issues.* Monterey, Calif.: Brooks/Cole, 1983, pp. 52–71. (chap. 15)

Morrow, R. S., and **S. Morrow.** "The Measurement of Intelligence." In B. Wolman (ed.), *Handbook of General Psychology.* Englewood Cliffs, N.J.: Prentice-Hall, 1973, pp. 656–672. (chap. 9)

Mortimer, J. T., M. D. Finch, and **D. Kumka.** "Persistence and Change in Development: The Multidimensional Self-Concept." In P. B. Baltes and O. G. Brim, Jr. (eds.), *Life-Span Development and Behavior.* Vol. 4. New York: Academic Press, 1982, pp. 263–313. (chap. 10)

Moss, H. A., and **E. J. Susman.** "Longitudinal Study of Personality Development." In O. G. Brim, Jr., and J. Kagan (eds.), *Constancy and Change in Human Development.* Cambridge, Mass.: Harvard University Press, 1980, pp. 530–595. (chaps. 1, 10)

Murcer, B. "A Happy Yankee Career That Spanned Generations." *The New York Times*, June 26, 1983, p. 2S. (chap. 4)

Murphy, C. "Age-Related Effects on the Threshold, Psychophysical Function, and Pleasantness of Menthol." *Journal of Gerontology*, 38 (1983), 217–222. (chap. 7)

Murphy, G. E., and **E. Robins.** "The Communication of Suicidal Ideas." In H. L. P. Resnik (ed.), *Suicidal Behavior.* Boston: Little, Brown, 1968. (chap. 6)

Murphy, M. D., R. E. Sanders, A. S. Gabriesheski, and **F. A. Schmitt.** "Metamemory in the Aged." *Journal of Gerontology*, 36 (1981), 185–193. (chap. 8)

Murstein, B. I. "Mate Selection in the 1970s." *Journal of Marriage and the Family*, 42 (1980), 777–792. (chap. 11)

Mussen, P. H., and **N. Haan.** "A Longitudinal Study of Patterns of Personality and Political Ideologies." In D. H. Eichorn, J. A. Clausen, N. Haan, M. P. Honzik, and P. Mussen (eds.), *Present and Past in Middle Life.* New York: Academic Press, 1981, pp. 391–409. (chap. 14)

Nagel, E. "Determinism and Development." In D. B. Harris (ed.), *The Concept of Development.* Minneapolis: University of Minnesota Press, 1957, pp. 15–24. (chap. 1)

Nahemow, L., and **M. P. Lawton.** "Toward an Ecological Theory of Adaptation and Aging." In H. M. Proshansky, W. H. Ittelson, and L. G. Rivlin (eds.), *Environmental Psychology: People and Their Physical Settings.* 2d ed. New York: Holt, Rinehart and Winston, 1976, pp. 315–321. (chap. 5)

National Center for Educational Statistics. *Participants in Adult Education.* Washington, D.C.: National Center for Educational Statistics, 1978. (chap. 13)

Neimark, E. D. "Toward the Disembedding of Formal Operations from Confounding with Cognitive Style." In I. Sigel, D. Brodzinsky, and R. Golinkoff (eds.), *Piagetian Theory and Research: New Directions and Applications.* Hillsdale, N.J.: Lawrence Erlbaum, 1981, pp. 177–190. (chap. 9)

_____. "Cognitive Development in Adulthood: Using What You've Got." In

T. M. Field, A. Huston, H. C. Quay, L. Troll, and G. E. Finley (eds.), *Review of Human Development*. New York: Wiley-Interscience, 1982, pp. 435–446. (chap. 9)

Neisser, U. "Academic and Artificial Intelligence." In L. B. Resnick (ed.), *The Nature of Intelligence*. Hillsdale, N.J.: Lawrence Erlbaum, 1976a, pp. 135–144. (chap. 9)

————. *Cognition and Reality*. San Francisco: Freeman, 1976b. (chap. 8)

Nelson, D. W. "The Meanings of Old Age for Public Policy." *National Forum*, 62 (Fall 1982), 27–30. (chap. 14)

Neugarten, B. L. "Adult Personality: Toward a Psychology of the Life Cycle." In B. L. Neugarten (ed.), *Middle Age and Aging*. Chicago: University of Chicago Press, 1968, pp. 137–147. (chap. 1)

————. "Adaptation and the Life Cycle." *Journal of Geriatric Psychiatry*, 4 (1970), 71–87. (chaps. 5, 12)

————. "Personality Change in Later Life: A Developmental Perspective." In C. Eisdorfer and M. P. Lawson (eds.), *The Psychology of Adult Development and Aging*. Washington, D.C.: American Psychological Association, 1973, pp. 311–338. (chap. 10)

————. "Age Groups in American Society and the Rise of the Young-Old." *Annals of the American Academy of Political and Social Science*, 415 (1974), 187–198. (chap. 14)

————. "The Future and the Young-Old." *Gerontologist*, 15 (1975), 4–9. (chap. 1)

————. "Personality and Aging." In J. E. Birren and K. W. Schaie (eds.), *Handbook of the Psychology of Aging*. New York: Van Nostrand Reinhold, 1977, pp. 626–649. (chap. 10)

————. "Policy for the 1980s: Age or Need Entitlement?" In National Journal Issues Book, *Aging: Agenda for the Eighties*. Washington, D.C.: *The National Journal*, November 1979a, pp. 48–72. (chap 14)

————. "Time, Age, and the Life Cycle." *American Journal of Psychiatry*, 136 (1979b), 887–894. (chap. 10)

————, and **L. Brown-Rezanka.** "A Midlife Woman in the 1980s." In U.S. House of Representatives. Select Committee on Aging and Subcommittee on Retirement Income and Employment, *Women in Midlife—Security and Fulfillment*. Part 1. Washington, D.C.: U.S. Government Printing Office, 1978, pp. 24–38. (chaps. 11, 12)

————, **W. Crotty,** and **S. Tobin.** "Personality Types in an Aged Population." In B. L. Neugarten (ed.), *Personality in Middle and Late Life: Empirical Studies*. New York: Atherton, 1964, pp. 159–187. (chap. 16)

————, **interviewed by E. Hall.** "Acting One's Age: New Rules for Old." *Psychology Today*, 13 (April 1980), 66–80. (chaps. 1, 8, 13, 14)

————, and **K. K. Weinstein.** "The Changing American Grandparent." *Journal of Marriage and the Family*, 26 (1964), 199–204. (chap. 12)

Newton, N., and **C. Modahl.** "Pregnancy: The Closest Human Relationship." *Human Nature*, 1 (March 1978), 40–49. (chap. 12)

New York Times, The. "Birth Clinic Visits Rose During 1980." June 23, 1982. (chap. 14)

————. "Census Bureau Finds Women Are Planning Fewer Children." May 8, 1983a. (chap. 12)

————. "Bringing Up a Child Now Costs $80,000." May 27, 1983b. (chap. 14)

————. "Man Who Spent 31 Years in Hospital Is Freed." December 30, 1983c, A10. (chap. 15)

————. "Activist, in 70's, Says Age Distinguishes Her." March 12, 1984a, D15. (chap. 14)

————. "Study Shows Births Up in Women in Their 30's." May 9, 1984b, C8. (chap. 12)

Nicak, A. "Changes in Sensitivity to Pain

in Relation to Postnatal Development in Rats." *Experimental Gerontology*, 6 (1971), 111–114. (chap. 7)

Nichols, M., and **S. R. Leiblum.** "Lesbianism as Personal Identity and Social Role: Conceptual and Clinical Issues." Unpublished article. Rutgers University, 1983. (chap. 11)

Norris, A., C. Mittman, and **N. W. Shock.** "Lung Function in Relation to Age: Changes in Ventilation with Age." In L. Cander and J. H. Moyer (eds.), *Aging of the Lung*. New York: Grune and Stratton, 1964, p. 138. (chap. 4)

Nunnally, J. C. "Research Strategies and Measurement Methods for Investigating Human Development." In J. R. Nesselroade and H. W. Reese (eds.), *Life-Span Developmental Psychology: Methodological Issues*. New York: Academic Press, 1973, pp. 87–109. (chap. 2)

Offenbach, S. I. "A Developmental Study of Hypothesis Testing and Cue Selection Strategies." *Developmental Psychology*, 10 (1974), 484–490. (chap. 9)

Ohlsson, M. "Information Processing Related to Physical Fitness in Elderly People." *Reports from the Institute of Applied Psychology*, 71 (1976), 1–12. (chap. 8)

Ohta, R. J., M. F. Carlin, and **B. M. Harmon.** "Auditory Acuity and Performance on the Mental Health Status Questionnaire in the Elderly." *Journal of the American Geriatrics Society*, 29 (1981), 476–478. (chap. 7)

Oken, D. "What to Tell Cancer Patients." *Journal of the American Medical Association*, 175 (1961), 1120–1128. (chap. 16)

Okudaira, N., H. Fukuda, K. Nishihara, K. Ohtani, S. Endo, and **S. Torii.** "Sleep Apnea and Nocturnal Myoclonus in Elderly Persons in Vilcabamba, Ecuador." *Journal of Gerontology*, 38 (1983), 436–438. (chap. 4)

Olton, D. S., and **W. A. Feustle.** *Experimental Brain Research*, 41 (1981), 380. (chap. 6)

Omenn, G. S. "Behavior Genetics." In J. E. Birren and K. W. Schaie (eds.), *Handbook of the Psychology of Aging*. New York: Van Nostrand Reinhold, 1977, pp. 190–218. (chap. 3)

Oppenheimer, V. K. "The Changing Nature of Life-Cycle Squeezes: Implications for the Socioeconomic Position of the Elderly." In R. W. Fogel, E. Hatfield, S. B. Kiesler, and E. Shanas (eds.), *Aging: Stability and Change in the Family*. New York: Academic Press, 1981, pp. 47–82. (chap. 12)

Orbach, H. L. "Aging and Religion: A Study of Church Attendance in the Detroit Metropolitan Area." *Geriatrics*, 16 (1961), 119–121. (chap. 14)

Ostrow, A. C. "Physical Activity as It Relates to the Health of the Aged." In N. Datan and N. Lohmann (eds.), *Transitions of Aging*. New York: Academic Press, 1980, pp. 41–56. (chap. 5)

Overton, W. F., and **V. Clayton.** "The Role of Formal Operational Thought in the Aging Process." Unpublished manuscript. State University of New York, Buffalo, 1976. (chap. 9)

_____, and **H. W. Reese.** "Models of Development: Methodological Implications." In J. R. Nesselroade, and H. W. Reese (eds.), *Life-Span Developmental Psychology: Methodological Issues*. New York: Academic Press, 1973, pp. 65–86. (chap. 2)

Owens, W. A. "Age and Mental Abilities: A Second Adult Follow-up," *Journal of Educational Psychology*, 57 (1966), 311–325. (chap. 9)

Palmore, E. B. "The Effects of Aging on Activity and Attitudes." In E. Palmore (ed.), *Normal Aging*. Durham, N.C.: Duke University Press, 1970, pp. 332–341. (chap. 13)

_____. "Health Practices and Illnesses." In E. Palmore (ed.), *Normal Aging II*. Durham, N.C.: Duke University Press, 1974, pp. 49–55. (chap. 15)

_____. "The Future Status of the Aged." *Gerontologist*, 16 (1976a), 297–302. (chap. 15)

———. "Total Chance of Institutionalization among the Aged." *Gerontologist*, 6 (1976b), 504–507. (chap. 16)

———, **L. K. George,** and **G. G. Fillenbaum.** "Predictors of Retirement." *Journal of Gerontology*, 37 (1982), 733–742. (chap. 13)

Panek, P. E., G. V. Barrett, H. L. Sterns, and **R. A. Alexander.** "Age Differences in Perceptual Style, Selective Attention, and Perceptual-Motor Reaction Time." *Experimental Aging Research*, 4 (1978), 377–387. (chap. 9)

Papalia, D. "The Status of Several Conservation Abilities across the Life Span." *Human Development*, 15 (1972), 229–243. (chap. 9)

Parker, E. B., and **W. J. Paisley.** *Patterns of Adult Information Seeking.* Final Report on USOE Project No. 2583. Stanford, Calif.: Stanford University Press, 1966. (chap. 8)

Parker, E. S., and **E. P. Noble.** "Alcohol Consumption and Cognitive Functioning in Social Drinkers." *Journal of Studies on Alcohol*, 38 (1977), 1224–1232. (chap. 6)

Parkes, C. M. *Bereavement: Studies of Grief in Adult Life.* New York: International Universities Press, 1972. (chap. 16)

———, and **R. S. Weiss.** *Recovery from Bereavement.* New York: Basic Books, 1983. (chap. 16)

Parlee, M. B. "The Friendship Bond." *Psychology Today*, 13 (October 1979), 43–54 + . (chap. 11)

Parr, J. "The Interaction of Persons and Living Environment." In L. W. Poon (ed.), *Aging in the 1980s: Psychological Issues.* Washington, D.C.: American Psychological Association, 1980, pp. 393–406. (chap. 5)

Parsons, T., and **V. M. Lidz.** "Death in American Society." In E. S. Shneidman (ed.), *Essays in Self-Destruction.* New York: Science House, 1967, pp. 133–140. (chap. 16)

Pastalan, L. A., R. K. Mautz, and **J. Merrill.** "The Simulation of Age-Related Sensory Losses: A New Approach to the Study of Environmental Barriers." In W. F. E. Preiser (ed.), *Environmental Design Research.* Stroudsberg, Pa.: Dowden, Hutchinson & Ross, 1973, pp. 383–392. (chap. 7)

Pear, R. "Census Bureau Finds Turnout in Federal Elections Is Rising." *The New York Times*, November 22, 1983, A23. (chap. 14)

———. "Rise in Poverty from '79 to '82 Is Found in U.S.," *The New York Times*, February 24, 1984, A1 + . (chap. 14)

Peplau, L. A. "What Homosexuals Want in Relationships." *Psychology Today*, 15 (March 1981), 28–38. (chap. 11)

Perlmutter, M. "What Is Memory Aging the Aging of?" *Developmental Psychology*, 14 (1978), 330–345. (chap. 8)

———. "Age Differences in Adults' Free Recall, Cued Recall, and Recognition." *Journal of Gerontology*, 34 (1979), 533–539. (chap. 8)

———. "Learning and Memory Through Adulthood." In M. W. Riley, B. B. Hess, and K. Bond (eds.), *Aging in Society: Selected Reviews of Recent Research.* Hillsdale, N.J.: Lawrence Erlbaum, 1983, pp. 219–241. (chap. 8)

———, and **J. A. List.** "Learning in Later Adulthood." In T. M. Field, A. Huston, H. C. Quay, L. Troll, and G. E. Finley (eds.), *Review of Human Development.* New York: Wiley-Interscience, 1982, pp. 551–568. (chap. 8)

———, and **D. B. Mitchell.** "The Appearance and Disappearance of Age Differences in Adult Memory." In F. I. M. Craik and S. Trehub (eds.), *Aging and Cognitive Processes.* New York: Plenum, 1982, pp. 127–144. (chap. 8)

Perone, M., and **A. Baron.** "Age-Related Effects of Pacing on Acquisition and Performance of Response Sequences: An Operant Analysis." *Journal of Gerontology*, 37 (1982), 443–449. (chap. 8)

Peterson, J. A. "Social-Psychological Aspects of Death and Dying and Mental Health." In J. E. Birren and R. B. Sloane (eds.), *Handbook of Mental Health and*

Aging. Englewood Cliffs, N.J.: Prentice-Hall, 1980, pp. 922–942. (chap. 16)

Pfeiffer, E. "Psychopathology and Social Pathology." In J. E. Birren and K. W. Schaie (eds.), *Handbook of the Psychology of Aging.* New York: Van Nostrand Reinhold, 1977, pp. 650–671. (chap. 6)

_____, and **G. Davis.** "Use of Leisure Time in Middle Life." In E. Palmore (ed.), *Normal Aging II.* Durham, N.C.: Duke University Press, 1974, pp. 232–243. (chap. 13)

Phillips, D. "Deathday and Birthday: An Unexpected Connection." In J. M. Tanner (ed.), *Statistics: A Guide to the Unknown.* San Francisco: Holden-Dong, 1972. (chap. 16)

Piaget, J. *Six Psychological Studies.* New York: Random House, 1967. (chap. 9)

_____. *"Biology and Knowledge.* Chicago: University of Chicago Press, 1971. (chap. 1)

_____. "Piaget's Theory." In P. H. Mussen (ed.), *Handbook of Child Psychology.* 4th ed. Vol. 1. W. Kessen (ed.), *History, Theory, and Methods.* New York: Wiley, 1983, pp. 103–128. (chap. 9)

_____, and **B. Inhelder.** *The Psychology of the Child.* New York: Basic Books, 1969. (chap. 9)

Pine, V. R. *Caretaker of The Dead: The American Funeral Director.* New York: Irvington, 1975. (chap. 16)

Plath, D. W. "Contours of Consociation: Lessons from a Japanese Narrative." In P. Baltes and O. Brim, Jr. (eds.), *Life-Span Development and Behavior.* Vol. 3. New York: Academic Press, 1980, pp. 287–305. (chap. 12)

Pollack, R. H., and **B. M. Atkeson.** "A Life-Span Approach to Perceptual Development." In P. B. Baltes (ed.), *Life-Span Development and Behavior.* Vol. 1. New York: Academic Press, 1978, pp. 85–109. (chap. 7)

Poon, L. W., and **A. T. Welford.** "Prologue: A Historical Perspective." In L. W. Poon (ed.), *Aging in the 1980s: Psychological Issues.* Washington, D.C.: American Psychological Association, 1980, pp. xiii–xvii. (chap. 1)

Post, F. "Paranoid, Schizophrenia-like, and Schizophrenic States in the Aged." In J. E. Birren and R. B. Sloane (eds.), *Handbook of Mental Health and Aging.* Englewood Cliffs, N.J.: Prentice-Hall, 1980, pp. 591–615. (chaps. 6, 7)

Pratt, H. J. "The 'Gray Lobby' Revisited," *National Forum,* 62 (Fall 1982), 31–33. (chap. 14)

Press, A. "Suffer the Little Children." *Newsweek,* January 2, 1984, 47. (chap. 14)

Press, I., and **M. McKool.** "Social Structure and Status of the Aged: Toward Some Valid Cross-Cultural Generalizations." *Aging and Human Development,* 3 (1972), 297–306. (chap. 15)

Prial, F. J. "More Women Work at Traditional Male Roles." *The New York Times,* November 15, 1982, 1+. (chap. 13)

Punch, J. L., and **F. McConnell.** "The Speech Discrimination Function for Elderly Adults." *Journal of Auditory Research,* 9 (1969), 159–166. (chap. 7)

Quetelet, A. *A Treatise on Man and the Development of His Faculties.* Edinburgh: William and Robert Chambers, 1842. (chap. 1)

Quinn, J. F. *The Early Retirement Decision: Evidence from the 1969 Retirement History Study.* U.S. Department of Health, Education, and Welfare, Social Security Administration, Office of Research and Statistics (Staff Paper No. 29). Washington, D.C.: U.S. Government Printing Office, 1978. (chap. 13)

_____. "Wage Determination and Discrimination among Older Workers." *Journal of Gerontology,* 34 (1979), 728–735. (chap. 13)

Rabbitt, P. "An Age-Decrement in the Ability to Ignore Irrelevant Information." *Journal of Gerontology,* 20 (1965), 233–238. (chap. 8)

_____. "Changes in Problem Solving Ability in Old Age." In J. E. Birren and

K. W. Schaie (eds.), *Handbook of the Psychology of Aging*. New York: Van Nostrand Reinhold, 1977, pp. 606–625. (chap. 9)

———. "Breakdown of Control Processes in Old Age." In T. M. Field, A. Huston, H. C. Quay, L. Troll, and G. E. Finley (eds.), *Review of Human Development*. New York: Wiley-Interscience, 1982, pp. 540–550. (chap. 9)

Rabinowitz, J. C., B. P. Ackerman, F. I. M. Craik, and J. L. Hinchley. "Aging and Metamemory: The Roles of Relatedness and Imagery." *Journal of Gerontology*, 37 (1982), 688–695. (chap. 8)

Ragozin, A. S., R. B. Basham, K. A. Crnic, M. T. Greenberg, and N. M. Robinson. "Effects of Maternal Age on Parenting Role." *Developmental Psychology*, 18 (1982), 627–634. (chap. 12)

Rapoport, R., and R. Rapoport. *Leisure and the Family Life Cycle*. Boston: Routledge and Kegan Paul, 1976. (chap. 13)

Rebok, G. W., and L. R. Offermann. "Behavioral Competencies of Older College Students: A Self-Efficacy Approach." *Gerontologist*, 23 (1983), 428–432. (chap. 13)

Reedy, M. N. "Personality and Aging." In D. S. Woodruff and J. E. Birren (eds.), *Aging: Scientific Perspectives and Social Issues*. 2d ed. Monterey, Calif.: Brooks/Cole, 1983, pp. 112–136. (chap. 10)

———, J. E. Birren, and K. W. Schaie. "Age and Sex Differences in Satisfying Love Relationships Across the Adult Life Span." *Human Development*, 24 (1981), 52–56. (chap. 11)

Rees, J. N., and J. Botwinick. "Detection and Decision Factors in Auditory Behavior of the Elderly." *Journal of Gerontology*, 26 (1971), 133–136. (chap. 7)

Rees, W. D. "The Hallucinatory and Paranormal Reactions of Bereavement." M.D. thesis. Cited in C. M. Parkes. *Bereavement*. New York: International Universities Press, 1970. (chap. 16)

Regnier, V. "Housing and Environment." In D. S. Woodruff and J. E. Birren (eds.), *Aging: Scientific Perspectives and Social Issues*. 2d ed. Monterey, Calif.: Brooks/Cole, 1983, pp. 351–369. (chap. 10)

Reid, G. "Job-Search and Effectiveness of Job-Finding Measures." *Industrial and Labor Relations Review*, 25 (1972), 479–495. (chap. 13)

Reinert, G. "Prolegomena to a History of Life-Span Developmental Psychology." In P. B. Baltes and O. G. Brim, Jr. (eds.), *Life-Span Development and Behavior*. Vol. 2. New York: Academic Press, 1979, pp. 205–254. (chap. 1)

Renner, V. J., and J. E. Birren. "Stress: Physiological and Psychological Mechanisms." In J. E. Birren and R. B. Sloane (eds.), *Handbook of Mental Health and Aging*. Englewood Cliffs, N.J.: Prentice-Hall, 1980, pp. 310–336. (chap. 5)

Renwick, P. A., and E. E. Lawler. "What You Really Want from Your Job." *Psychology Today*, 11 (May 1978), 53–65 + . (chap. 13)

Resnik, L. B. "Introduction: Changing Conceptions of Intelligence." In L. B. Resnick (ed.), *The Nature of Intelligence*. Hillsdale, N.J.: Lawrence Erlbaum, 1976, pp. 1–10. (chap. 9)

Riegel, K. F. "Toward a Dialectical Theory of Development." *Human Development*, 18 (1975), 50–64. (chap. 2)

———. "History of Psychological Gerontology." In J. E. Birren and K. W. Schaie (eds.), *Handbook of the Psychology of Aging*. New York: Van Nostrand Reinhold, 1977, pp. 70–102. (chaps. 1, 10)

Riegel, P. S. "Athletic Records and Human Endurance." *American Scientist*, 69 (1981), 285–290. (chap. 4)

Riley, M. W., and K. Bond. "Beyond Ageism: Postponing the Onset of Disability." In M. W. Riley, B. B. Hess, and K. Bond (eds.), *Aging in Society: Selected Reviews of Recent Research*. Hillsdale, N.J.: Lawrence Erlbaum, 1981, pp. 243–252. (chap. 5)

———, and A. Foner. *Aging and Society*.

Vol. 1. *An Inventory of Research Findings.* New York: Russell Sage Foundation, 1968. (chaps. 11, 12, 13, 14, 16)

_____, M. Johnson, and A. Foner (eds.). *Aging and Society.* Vol. 3. *A Sociology of Age Stratification.* New York: Russell Sage Foundation, 1972. (chap. 2)

Rinke, C. L., J. J. Williams, K. E. Lloyd, and W. Smith-Scott. "The Effects of Prompting and Reinforcement on Self-Bathing by Elderly Residents of a Nursing Home." *Behavior Therapy.* 9 (1978), 873–881. (chap. 8)

Rizzato, G., and L. Marazzini. "Thoracoabdominal Mechanics in Elderly Men." *Journal of Applied Physiology*, 28 (1970), 457–460. (chap. 4)

Roach, M. "Another Name for Madness." *The New York Times Magazine*, January 16, 1983, 22–31. (chap. 6)

Robertson, J. "Significance of Grandparenthood: Perceptions of Young Adult Grandchildren." *Gerontologist*, 16 (1976), 137–140. (chap. 12)

Rockstein, M., J. Chesky, and M. Sussman. "Comparative Biology and Evolution of Aging." In C. E. Finch and L. Hayflick (eds.), *Handbook of the Biology of Aging.* New York: Van Nostrand Reinhold, 1977, pp. 3–34. (chap. 3)

_____, and M. Sussman. *Biology of Aging.* Belmont, Calif.: Wadsworth, 1979. (chaps. 3, 4, 7)

Rodin, J. "Managing the Stress of Aging: The Role of Control and Coping." In S. Levine and H. Ursin (eds.), *Coping and Health.* New York: Plenum, 1980, pp. 171–202. (chap. 5)

_____. "Aging, Control and Health." Presidential address, Eastern Psychological Association. Baltimore, April 1982. (chap. 14)

_____, and E. J. Langer. "Long-Term Effects of a Control-Relevant Intervention with the Institutionalized Aged." *Journal of Personality and Social Psychology*, 35 (1977), 879–902. (chap. 14)

Rohlen, T. P. "The Promise of Adulthood in Japanese Spiritualism." In E. H. Erikson (ed.), *Adulthood.* New York: Norton, 1978, pp. 121–148. (chap. 2)

Rollins, B. C., and R. Galligan. "The Developing Child and Marital Satisfaction of Parents." In R. M. Lerner and G. B. Spanier (eds.), *Child Influences on Marital and Family Interaction.* New York: Academic Press, 1978, pp. 71–105. (chap. 12)

Romalis, C. "Taking Care of the Little Woman: Father-Physician Relations During Pregnancy and Childbirth." In S. Romalis (ed.), *Childbirth: Alternatives to Medical Control.* Austin: University of Texas Press, 1981, pp. 92–121. (chap. 12)

Romaniuk, J. G., and M. Romaniuk. "Participation Motives of Older Adults in Higher Education: The Elderhostel Experience." *Gerontologist*, 22 (1982), 364–368. (chap. 13)

Rosen, B. "Management Perception of Older Employees." *Monthly Labor Review*, 101 (1978), 33–35. (chap. 13)

Rosen, R. C., and E. Hall. *Sexuality.* New York: Random House, 1984. (chaps. 4, 11, 12)

Rosenman, R. H. "The Role of Behavior Patterns and Neurogenic Factors in the Pathogenesis of Coronary Heart Disease." In R. S. Eliot (ed.), *Stress and the Heart.* New York: Futura, 1974, pp. 123–141. (chap. 5)

Ross, H. G., and J. I. Milgram. "Important Variables in Adult Sibling Relationships: A Qualitative Study." In M. E. Lamb and B. Sutton-Smith (eds.), *Sibling Relationships: Their Nature and Significance Across the Lifespan.* Hillsdale, N.J.: Lawrence Erlbaum, 1982, pp. 225–250. (chap. 11)

Rossi, A. S. "Aging and Parenthood in the Middle Years." In P. B. Baltes and O. G. Brim, Jr. (eds.), *Life-Span Development and Behavior.* Vol. 3. New York: Academic Press, 1980, pp. 137–205. (chap. 12)

Rossman, I. "Anatomic and Body Composition Changes with Aging." In C. E. Finch and L. Hayflick (eds.), *Handbook of the Biology of Aging.* New York: Van Nostrand Reinhold, 1977, pp. 189–221. (chap. 4)

Rovee, C. K., R. Y. Cohen, and **W. Shlapack.** "Life Span Stability in Olfactory Sensitivity." *Developmental Psychology,* 11 (1975), 311–318. (chap. 7)

Rowles, G. D. "Growing Old 'Inside': Aging and Attachment to Place in an Appalachian Community." In N. Datan and N. Lohmann (eds.), *Transitions of Aging.* New York: Academic Press, 1980, pp. 153–170. (chap. 14)

Rubenstein, C. "Survey Report: How Americans View Vacations." *Psychology Today,* 13 (May 1980), 62–76. (chap. 13)

_____. "Survey Report: Money &." *Psychology Today,* 15 (May 1981), 29–44. (chap. 14)

_____, **P. Shaver,** and **L. A. Peplau.** "Loneliness." *Human Nature,* 2 (February 1979), 58–65. (chap. 11)

Rubin, L. *Women of a Certain Age: The Midlife Search for Self.* New York: Harper & Row, 1979. (chaps. 11, 12)

Rubin, Z. *Liking and Loving: An Invitation to Social Psychology.* New York: Holt, Rinehart and Winston, 1973. (chap. 11)

Rubner, M. "Probleme des Wachstums under der Lebensdauer." In *Gesellschaft fur Innere Medizin und Kinderheilkunde.* Vol. 7. Vienna: Mitteilungen, Beiblat, 1908. (chap. 3)

Rule, S. "Black Divorces Soar; Experts Cite Special Strain." *The New York Times,* May 24, 1982, A17. (chap. 15)

Sabatini, P., and **G. Labouvie-Vief.** "Age and Professional Specialization: Formal Reasoning." Paper presented at the Annual Meeting of the Gerontological Society. Washington, D.C., November 1979. (chap. 9)

Sacher, G. A. "Life Table Modification and Life Prolongation." In C. E. Finch and L. Hayflick (eds.), *Handbook of the Biology of Aging.* New York: Van Nostrand Reinhold, 1977, pp. 582–638. (chap. 3)

Salthouse, T. A. *Adult Cognition.* New York: Springer-Verlag, 1982. (chap. 1, 8, 9)

_____. "Why Is Typing Rate Unaffected by Age?" Paper presented at the Annual Scientific Meeting of the Gerontological Society. San Francisco, October 1983. (chap. 9)

_____, and **B. L. Somberg.** "Isolating the Age Deficit in Speeded Performance." *Journal of Gerontology,* 37 (1982), 59–63. (chap. 8)

Saltin, B., G. Blomquist, J. H. Mitchell, R. L. Johnson, K. Wildenthal, and **C. B. Chapman.** "Response to Exercise after Bed Rest and after Training." *American Heart Association Monograph.* No. 23. New York: American Heart Association, 1968. (chap. 5)

Sanadi, D. R. "Metabolic Changes and Their Significance in Aging." In C. E. Finch and L. Hayflick (eds.), *Handbook of the Biology of Aging.* New York: Van Nostrand Reinhold, 1977, pp. 73–98. (chap. 3)

Santrock, J. W., R. Warshak, C. Lindbergh, and **L. Meadows.** "Children's and Parents' Observed Social Behavior in Stepfather Families." *Child Development,* 53 (1982), 472–480. (chap. 12)

Satariano, W. A., and **S. L. Syme.** "Life Changes and Disease in Elderly Populations: Coping with Change." In J. L. McGaugh and S. B. Kiesler (eds.), *Aging: Biology and Behavior.* New York: Academic Press, 1981, pp. 311–327. (chap. 5)

Scanzioni, L., and **J. Scanzioni.** *Men, Women and Change: A Sociology of Marriage and the Family.* New York: McGraw-Hill, 1976. (chap. 11)

Scarr, S. *Race, Social Class, and Individual Differences in I.Q.* Hillsdale, N.J.: Lawrence Erlbaum, 1981. (chap. 1)

Scarr, S., and **R. A. Weinberg.** "Attitudes, Interests, and IQ." *Human Nature,* 1 (April 1978), 29–36. (chap. 12)

Schaie, K. W. "Rigidity—Flexibility and Intelligence: A Cross-Sectional Study of the Adult Life Span from 20 to 70

Years." *Psychological Monographs*, 72 (1958), 9 Whole No. 462, 1–26. (chap. 9)

_____. "Methodological Problems in Descriptive Developmental Research on Adulthood and Aging." In J. R. Nesselroade and H. W. Reese (eds.), *Life-Span Developmental Psychology: Methodological Issues*. New York: Academic Press, 1973, pp. 253–280. (chaps. 1, 2)

_____. "Quasi-Experimental Research Designs in the Psychology of Aging." In J. E. Birren and K. W. Schaie (eds.), *Handbook of the Psychology of Aging*. New York: Van Nostrand Reinhold, 1977, pp. 39–58. (chap. 2)

_____. "The Primary Mental Abilities in Adulthood: An Exploration in the Development of Psychometric Intelligence." In P. B. Baltes and O. G. Brim, Jr. (eds.), *Life-Span Development and Behavior*. Vol. 2. New York: Academic Press, 1979, pp. 67–115. (chap. 9)

_____. "The Seattle Longitudinal Study: A Twenty-One Year Exploration of Psychometric Intelligence in Adulthood." In K. W. Schaie (ed.), *Longitudinal Studies of Adult Psychological Development*. New York: Guilford Press, 1982. (chap. 1)

_____. "Age Changes in Adult Intelligence." In D. S. Woodruff and J. E. Birren (eds.), *Aging: Scientific Perspectives and Social Issues*. 2d ed. Monterey, Calif.: Brooks/Cole, 1983, pp. 137–148. (chap. 9)

_____, and **C. Hertzog.** "Fourteen-Year Cohort-Sequential Analyses of Adult Intellectual Development." *Developmental Psychology*, 19 (1983), 531–543. (chap. 9)

_____, and **G. Labouvie-Vief.** "Generational Versus Ontogenetic Components of Change in Adult Cognitive Behavior." *Developmental Psychology*, 10 (1974), 305–320. (chap. 9)

_____, and **I. A. Parham.** "Stability of Adult Personality: Fact or Fable?" *Journal of Personality and Social Psychology*, 36 (1976), 146–158. (chap. 10)

Scheidt, R. J., and **P. G. Windley.** "The Mental Health of Small-Town Rural Elderly Residents: An Expanded Ecological Model." *Journal of Gerontology*, 38 (1983), 472–479. (chap. 14)

Scheper-Hughes, N. "Deposed Kings: The Demise of the Rural Irish Gerontocracy." In J. Sokolovsky (ed.), *Growing Old in Different Societies*. Belmont, Calif.: Wadsworth, 1983, pp. 168–178. (chap. 15)

Schiffman, S. "Food Recognition by the Elderly." *Journal of Gerontology*, 32 (1977), 586–592. (chap. 7)

_____, and **M. Pasternak.** "Decreased Discrimination of Food Odors in the Elderly." *Journal of Gerontology*, 34 (1979), 73–79. (chap. 7)

Schlenkar, E. D., J. S. Feurig, L. H. Stone, M. A. Ohlson, and **O. Mickelsen.** "Nutrition and Health of Older People." *American Journal of Clinical Nutrition*, 16 (1973), 1111–1119. (chap. 5)

Schneirla, T. C. "The Concept of Development in Comparative Psychology." In D. B. Harris (ed.), *The Concept of Development*. Minneapolis: University of Minnesota Press, 1957, pp. 78–108. (chap. 1)

Schonfield, A. E. D. "Learning, Memory, and Aging." in J. E. Birren and R. B. Sloane (eds.), *Handbook of Mental Health and Aging*. Englewood Cliffs, N.J.: Prentice-Hall, 1980, pp. 214–244. (chap. 8)

_____, **H. Davidson,** and **H. Jones.** "An Example of Age-Associated Interference in Memory." *Journal of Gerontology*, 38 (1983), 204–210. (chap. 8)

Schonfield, D. "Who Is Stereotyping Whom and Why?" *Gerontologist*, 22 (1982), 267–272. (chap. 1)

Schooler, K. K. "Response of the Elderly to Environment: A Stress-Theoretic Perspective." In M. P. Lawton, P. G. Windley, and T. O. Byerts (eds.), *Aging and the Environment: Directions and Perspectives*. New York: Garland STPM Press, 1980. (chap. 14)

_____, and **D. I. Rubenstein.** "The Impact of the Planned Environment on the Elderly." In R. R. Turner and H. W.

Reese (eds.), *Life-Span Developmental Psychology: Intervention.* New York: Academic Press, 1980, pp. 103–124. (chap. 14)

Schram, S. F., and D. F. Osten. "CETA and the Aging." *Aging and Work*, 1 (1978), 163–174. (chap. 13)

Schrank, H. T., and J. M. Waring. "Aging and Work Organizations." In M. W. Riley, B. B. Hess, and K. Bond (eds.), *Aging in Society: Selected Reviews of Recent Research.* Hillsdale, N.J.: Lawrence Erlbaum, 1983, pp. 53–70. (chap. 13)

Schulz, J. H. *The Economics of Aging.* 2d ed. Belmont, Calif.: Wadsworth, 1980. (chap. 14)

Schulz, R. *The Psychology of Death, Dying, and Bereavement.* Reading, Mass.: Addison-Wesley, 1978. (chap. 16)

_____. "Emotionality and Aging: A Theoretical and Empirical Analysis." *Journal of Gerontology*, 37 (1982), 42–51. (chap. 10)

_____, and M. Bazerman. "Ceremonial Occasions and Mortality: A Second Look." *American Psychologist*, 35 (1980), 253–261. (chap. 16)

Schwab, D. P., and H. G. Heneman II. "Effects of Age and Experience on Productivity." *Industrial Gerontology*, 4 (1977), 113–117. (chap. 13)

Schweitzer, M. M. "The Elders: Cultural Dimensions of Aging in Two American Indian Communities." In J. Sokolovksy (ed.), *Growing Old in Different Societies.* Belmont, Calif.: Wadsworth, 1983, pp. 168–178. (chap. 15)

Scott-Maxwell, F. *The Measure of My Days.* New York: Penguin, 1979. (chap. 10)

Sears, P. S., and A. H. Barbee. "Career and Life Satisfaction Among Terman's Gifted Women." In *The Gifted and the Creative: Fifty-Year Perspective.* Baltimore: Johns Hopkins University Press, 1978. (chap. 10)

Sears, R. R. "Sources of Life Satisfaction of the Terman Gifted Men." *American Psychologist*, 32 (1977), 119–128. (chap. 10)

Seashore, S. E., and J. T. Barnowe. "Collar Color Doesn't Count." *Psychology Today*, 6 (August 1972), 53–54+. (chap. 13)

Self, P. A. "The Further Evolution of the Parental Imperative." In N. Datan and L. H. Ginsberg (eds.), *Life-Span Developmental Psychology: Normative Life Crises.* New York: Academic Press, 1975, pp. 185–190. (chap. 12)

Selmanowitz, V. J., R. I. Rizer, and N. Orentreich. "Aging of the Skin and Its Appendages." In C. E. Finch and L. Hayflick (eds.), *Handbook of the Biology of Aging.* New York: Van Nostrand Reinhold, 1977, pp. 496–509. (chaps. 3, 4)

Shah, I. *World Tales.* New York: Harcourt Brace Jovanovich, 1979. (chap. 2)

Shanan, J., and R. Sagiv. "Sex Differences in Intellectual Performance during Middle Age." *Human Development*, 25 (1982), 24–33. (chap. 9)

_____, and M. Sharon. *Adjustment Patterns of Immigrant Students (Hebrew).* Jerusalem: Hebrew University of Jerusalem and Ministry of Absorption and Immigration, 1971. (chap. 9)

Shanas, E. "Social Myth as Hypothesis: The Case of the Family Relations of Old People." *Gerontologist*, 19 (1979), 3–9. (chap. 12)

_____, and G. L. Maddox. "Aging, Health, and the Organization of Health Resources." In R. H. Binstock and E. Shanas (eds.), *Handbook of Aging and the Social Sciences.* New York: Van Nostrand Reinhold, 1976, pp. 592–618. (chap. 3)

Sheehy, G. *Passages: Predictable Crises of Adult Life.* New York: Dutton, 1976. (chap. 10)

Sheils, M., M. Hager, C. Leslie, and D. Foote. "Can You Afford to Retire?" *Newsweek*, June 1, 1981, 24–34. (chap. 14)

Shields, E. A. "Rigidity in the Aged." Ph.D. dissertation, Northwestern University, 1957, *Dissertation Abstracts*, 18 (1958), 668–669. (chap. 9)

Shneidman, E. S. "You and Death," *Psychology Today*, 5 (June 1971), 43–45+. (chap. 16)

_____. *Deaths of Man*. New York: Quadrangle, 1973. (chap. 16)

_____. *Death: Current Perspectives*. 2d ed. Palo Alto, Calif.: Mayfield, 1980. (chap. 16)

_____, and **N. L. Farberow.** "Attempted and Completed Suicide." In E. S. Shneidman, N. L. Farberow, and R. E. Litman (eds.), *The Psychology of Suicide*. New York: Science House, 1970. (chap. 6)

Shock, N. W. "Biological Theories of Aging." In J. E. Birren and K. W. Schaie (eds.), *Handbook of the Psychology of Aging*. New York: Van Nostrand Reinhold, 1977a, pp. 103–115. (chap. 2)

_____. "Systems Integration." In C. E. Finch and L. Hayflick (eds.), *Handbook of the Biology of Aging*. New York: Van Nostrand Reinhold, 1977b, pp. 639–665. (chap. 4)

Siegel, R. K. "The Psychology of Life after Death." *American Psychologist*, 35 (1980), 911–931. (chap. 16)

Siegler, I. C. "The Terminal Drop Hypothesis: Fact or Artifact?" *Experimental Aging Research*, 1 (1975), 169–185. (chap. 8)

_____, and **P. T. Costa, Jr.** "Health Behavior Relationships." In J. E. Birren and K. W. Schaie (eds.), *Handbook of the Psychology of Aging*. 2d ed. New York: Van Nostrand Reinhold [in press]. (chap. 5)

_____, **L. K. George,** and **M. A. Okun.** "A Cross-Sequential Analysis of Adult Personality." *Developmental Psychology*, 15 (1979), 350–351. (chap. 10)

Sieman, J. R. "Programmed Material as a Training Tool for Older Persons." *Industrial Gerontology*, 3 (1976), 183–190. (chap. 8)

Silverman, P., and **R. J. Maxwell.** "The Significance of Information and Power in the Comparative Study of the Aged." In

J. Sokolovsky (ed.), *Growing Old in Different Societies*. Belmont, Calif.: Wadsworth, 1983, pp. 43–55. (chap. 15)

Silverman, P. R., D. MacKenzie, M. Pettipas, and **E. Wilson.** *Helping Each Other in Widowhood*. New York: Health Sciences, 1974. (chap. 16)

Simmons, L. W. *The Role of the Aged in Primitive Society*. New Haven, Conn.: Yale University Press, 1945. (chap. 15)

Simon, A. "The Neuroses, Personality Disorders, Alcoholism, Drug Use and Misuse, and Crime in the Aged." In J. E. Birren and R. B. Sloane (eds.), *Handbook of Mental Health and Aging*. Englewood Cliffs, N.J.: Prentice-Hall, 1980, pp. 653–670. (chap. 6)

Simon, E. W., R. A. Dixon, C. A. Nowak, and **D. F. Hultsch.** "Orienting Task Effects on Text-Recall in Adulthood." *Journal of Gerontology*, 37 (1982), 575–580. (chap. 8)

Sinex, F. M. "The Molecular Genetics of Aging." In C. E. Finch and L. Hayflick (eds.), *Handbook of the Biology of Aging*. New York: Van Nostrand Reinhold, 1977, pp. 37–62. (chap. 3)

Skinner, B. F. "Intellectual Self-Management in Old Age." *American Psychologist*, 38 (1983), 239–244. (chap. 8)

Skodol, A. E., and **R. L. Spitzer.** "Depression in the Elderly: Clinical Criteria." In L. D. Breslau and M. R. Haug (eds.), *Depression and Aging: Causes, Care, and Consequences*. New York: Springer, 1983, pp. 20–29. (chap. 6)

Skolnick, A. "Married Lives: Longitudinal Perspectives on Marriage." In D. H. Eichorn, J. A. Clausen, N. Haan, M. P. Honzik, and P. H. Mussen (eds.), *Present and Past in Middle Life*. New York: Academic Press, 1981, pp. 269–298. (chap. 11)

Skre, H. "Neurological Signs in a Normal Population." *Acta Neurologica Scandinavia*, 48 (1972), 575–606. (chap. 7)

Slater, S., and **A. Solomita.** *Exits*. New York: Dutton, 1980. (chap. 16)

Sloane, R. B. "Organic Brain Syndrome." In J. E. Birren and R. B. Sloane (eds.), *Handbook of Mental Health and Aging*. Englewood Cliffs, N.J.: Prentice-Hall, 1980, pp. 554–590. (chap. 6)

Snyder, P. C. "Future Pension Status of the Black Elderly." In D. E. Gelfand and A. J. Kutzik (eds.), *Ethnicity and Aging: Theory, Research, and Policy*. New York: Springer, 1979, pp. 291–307. (chap. 15)

Social Security Administration. "OASDI Cash Benefits—Table Q-6." *Social Security Bulletin*, USDHEW, 43 (1980), 75. (chap. 13)

Soergel, K. H., F. F. Zboralske, and **J. R. Amberg.** "Presbyesophagus: Esophageal Motility in Nonagenarians." *Journal of Clinical Investigation*, 43 (1964), 1472–1479. (chap. 4)

Solnick, R. L., and **J. E. Birren.** "Age and Male Erectile Responsiveness." *Archives of Sexual Behavior*, 6 (1977), 1–9. (chap. 4)

————, and **N. Corby.** "Human Sexuality and Aging." In D. S. Woodruff and J. E. Birren (eds), *Aging: Scientific Perspectives and Social Issues*. 2d ed. Monterey, Calif.: Brooks/Cole, 1983, pp. 202–224. (chap. 4)

Solomon, K. "Social Antecedents of Learned Helplessness in the Health Care Setting." *Gerontologist*, 22 (1982), 282–287. (chap. 14)

Soumerai, S. B., and **J. Avorn.** "Perceived Health, Life Satisfaction, and Activity in the Urban Elderly: A Controlled Study of the Impact of Part-Time Work." *Journal of Gerontology*, 38 (1983), 356–362. (chap. 13)

Spanier, G. B., and **R. A. Lewis.** "Marital Quality: A Review of the Seventies." *Journal of Marriage and the Family*, 42 (1980), 825–839. (chap. 11)

Spear, L. "Treatment of Grief Explored." *The New York Times*, November 6, 1983, WC9. (chap. 16)

Spearman, C. *The Abilities of Man*. New York: Macmillan, 1927. (chap. 9)

Spence, J. T. "Traits, Roles, and the Concept of Androgyny." In J. E. Gulla-horn (ed.), *Psychology and Women: In Transition*. New York: Wiley, 1979, pp. 167–188. (chap. 10)

Spencer, R. F. "Evolution and Development: A View of Anthropology." In D. B. Harris (ed.), *The Concept of Development*. Minneapolis: University of Minnesota Press, 1957, pp. 214–223. (chap. 2)

Springer, K. J., and **H. E. Dietzmann.** "Correlation Studies of Diesel Exhaust Odor Measured by Instrumental Methods to Human Odor Panel Ratings." Paper presented at Odor Conference at the Korlinska Institute. Stockholm, Sweden, 1970. (chap. 7)

Srole, L., and **A. K. Fischer.** "The Mid-Manhattan Longitudinal Study vs. 'The Mental Paradise Lost' Doctrine." *Archives of General Psychiatry*, 37 (1980), 209–221. (chap. 6)

Staiano-Coico, L., Z. Darzynkiewicz, J. M. Hefton, R. Dutkowski, G. J. Darlington, and **M. E. Weksler.** "Increased Sensitivity of Lymphocytes from People over 65 to Cell Cycle Arrest and Chromosomal Damage." *Science*, 219 (1983), 1335–1337. (chap. 3)

Stannard, D. E. *The Puritan Way of Death*. New York: Oxford University Press, 1977. (chap. 16)

Starr, B. D., and **M. B. Weiner.** *The Starr-Weiner Report on Sex and Sexuality in the Mature Years*. New York: Stein and Day, 1981. (chap. 4)

Stein, B., A. Cohen, and **H. Gadon.** "Flextime: Work When You Want To." *Psychology Today*, 10 (June 1976), 40–43 + . (chap. 13)

Stein, P. "Singlehood: An Alternative to Marriage." *Family Coordinator*, 24 (1975), 489–505. (chap. 11)

Steiner, G., interviewed by E. Hall. "The Freakish Passion." *Psychology Today*, 6 (February 1973), 56–69. (chap. 13)

Steinhauer, M. B. "Geriatric Foster Care: A Prototype Design and Implementation Issues." *Gerontologist*, 22 (1982), 293–300. (chap. 14)

Stenback, A. "Depression and Suicidal

Behavior in Old Age." In J. E. Birren and R. B. Sloane (eds.), *Handbook of Mental Health and Aging*. Englewood Cliffs, N.J.: Prentice-Hall, 1980, pp. 616–652. (chap. 6)

Sterns, H. L., and **R. E. Sanders.** "Training and Education of the Elderly." In R. R. Turner and H. W. Reese (eds.), *Life-Span Developmental Psychology: Intervention*. New York: Academic Press, 1980, pp. 307–330. (chaps. 8, 9, 13)

Stinnett, N., J. Collins, and **J. E. Montgomery.** "Marital Need Satisfaction of Older Husbands and Wives." *Journal of Marriage and the Family*, 32 (1970), 428–434. (chap. 11)

Stix, H. "Elders in Residence—Bridging the Generation Gap." *Los Angeles Times*, March 16, 1981, V1 + . (chap. 8)

Storck, P., W. Looft, and **F. H. Hooper.** "Interrelationships among Piagetian Tasks and Traditional Measures of Cognitive Abilities in Mature and Aged Adults." *Journal of Gerontology*, 27 (1972), 461–465. (chap. 9)

Stoudt, H. W., A. Damon, R. A. McFarland, and **J. Roberts.** *Weight, Height and Selected Body Measurements of Adults. United States, 1960–1962*. U.S. Public Health Service Publication No. 1000, Series 11, No. 8. Washington, D.C.: U.S. Government Printing Office, 1965. (chap. 4)

Streib, G. F., and **C. J. Schneider.** *Retirement in American Society: Impact and Process*. Ithaca, N.Y.: Cornell University Press, 1971. (chap. 13)

Stroud, J. G. "Women's Careers: Work, Family, and Personality." In D. H. Eichorn, J. A. Clausen, N. Haan, M. P. Honzik, and P. H. Mussen (eds.), *Present and Past in Middle Life*. New York: Academic Press, 1981, pp. 353–390. (chap. 13)

Stuckey, M. F., P. E. McGhee, and **N. J. Bell.** "Parent-Child Interaction: The Influence of Maternal Employment." *Developmental Psychology*, 18 (1982), 635–644. (chap. 12)

Super, D. E. *The Psychology of Careers*. New York: Harper & Row, 1957. (chap. 13)

Sussman, M. B. "The Family Life of Older People." In R. H. Binstock and E. Shanas (eds.), *Handbook of Aging and the Social Sciences*. New York: Van Nostrand Reinhold, 1976, pp. 218–243. (chap. 12)

Sweet, W. H. "Brain Death." *New England Journal of Medicine*, 299 (1978), 410–411. (chap. 16)

Swensen, C. H. "A Respectable Old Age." *American Psychologist*, 38 (1983), 327–334. (chap. 13)

Talbert, G. B. "Aging of the Reproductive System." In C. E. Finch and L. Hayflick (eds.), *Handbook of the Biology of Aging*. New York: Van Nostrand Reinhold, 1977, pp. 318–356. (chap. 4)

Tate, N. "The Black Aging Experience." In R. L. McNeely and J. L. Cohen (eds.), *Aging in Minority Groups*. Beverly Hills, Calif.: Sage, 1983, pp. 95–107. (chap. 15)

Tavris, C., and **C. Offir.** *The Longest War: Sex Differences in Perspective*. New York: Harcourt Brace Jovanovich, 1977. (chap. 10)

Tellis-Nayak, V. "The Transcendent Standard: The Religious Ethos of the Rural Elderly." *Gerontologist*, 22 (1982), 359–363. (chap. 14)

Tennov, D. *Love and Limerence: The Experience of Being in Love*. New York: Stein and Day, 1979. (chap. 11)

Terkel, S. *Working*. New York: Pantheon, 1974. (chap. 13)

Tesch, S. A. "Review of Friendship Development Across the Life Span." *Human Development*, 26 (1983), 266–276. (chap. 11)

Thomae, H. "The Concept of Development and Life-Span Developmental Psychology." In P. B. Baltes and O. G. Brim, Jr. (eds.), *Life-Span Development and Behavior*. Vol. 2. New York: Academic Press, 1979, pp. 281–312. (chap. 1)

———. "Personality and Adjustment to Aging." In J. E. Birren and R. B. Sloane (eds.), *Handbook of Mental Health and Aging*. Englewood Cliffs, N.J.: Prentice-Hall, 1980, pp. 285–309. (chap. 10)

Thomas, E., and **K. Yamamoto.** "Attitudes Toward Age: An Exploration in School-Age Children." *International Journal of Aging and Human Development*, 6 (1975), 117–129. (chap. 1)

Thomas, P. D., W. C. Hunt, P. J. Garry, R. B. Hood, J. M. Godwin, and **J. S. Goodwin.** "Hearing Acuity in a Healthy Elderly Population: Effects on Emotional, Cognitive, and Social Status." *Journal of Gerontology*, 38 (1983), 321–325. (chap. 7)

Thompson, G. B. "Work Versus Leisure Roles: An Investigation of Morale Among Employed and Retired Men." *Journal of Gerontology*, 28 (1973), 339–344. (chap. 10)

Thurow, L. *The Zero-Sum Society*. New York: Penguin, 1980. (chap. 13)

Thurstone, L. L. *Vectors of Mind*. Chicago: University of Chicago Press, 1935. (chap. 9)

Tiger, L. *Men in Groups*. New York: Random House, 1969. (chap. 11)

Time. "Victims of Heat: The Poor and the Old (65 Plus)." September 1, 1980, p. 55. (chap. 5)

Tobin, S. S. "Institutionalization of the Aged." In N. Datan and N. Lohmann (eds.), *Transitions of Aging*. New York: Academic Press, 1980, pp. 195–211. (chap. 14)

Tolstoy, L. *Anna Karenina*. 2 vol. New York: P. F. Collier & Son, 1917 (orig. pub. 1875). (chap. 11)

Tonna, E. A. "Aging of Skeletal-Dental Systems and Supporting Tissue." In C. E. Finch and L. Hayflick (eds.), *Handbook of the Biology of Aging*. New York: Van Nostrand Reinhold, 1977, pp. 470–495. (chap. 4)

Toynbee, A. *Man's Concern with Death*. New York: McGraw-Hill, 1968. (chap. 16)

Tracy, N. M. "Woman, 27, Deals with Isolating Horror of Progeria." *Minneap-olis Tribune*, July 10, 1983, 1F +. (chap. 3)

Tramer, R. R., and **E. H. Schludermann.** "Cognitive Differentiation in a Geriatric Population." *Perceptual and Motor Skills*, 39 (1974), 1071–1075. (chap. 9)

Traupmann, J., E. Eckels, and **E. Hatfield.** "Intimacy in Older Women's Lives." *Gerontologist*, 22 (1982), 493–498. (chap. 11)

Treas, J. "Aging and the Family." In D. S. Woodruff and J. E. Birren (eds.), *Aging: Scientific Perspectives and Social Issues*. 2d ed. Monterey, Calif.: Brooks/Cole, 1983, pp. 94–109. (chaps. 11, 12)

———, and **A. VanHilst.** "Marriage and Remarriage Rates Among Older Americans." *Journal of Gerontology*, 16 (1976), 132–136. (chap. 11)

Trelease, M. L. "Dying Among Alaskan Indians: A Matter of Choice." In E. Kübler-Ross (ed.), *Death: The Final Stage of Growth*. Englewood Cliffs, N.J.: Prentice-Hall, 1975, pp. 33–37. (chap. 16)

Troll, L. E. "Grandparenting." In L. W. Poon (ed.), *Aging in the 1980s: Psychological Issues*. Washington, D.C.: American Psychological Association, 1980a, pp. 475–481. (chap. 12)

———. "Intergenerational Relations in Later Life: A Family System Approach." In N. Datan and N. Lohmann (eds.), *Transitions of Aging*. New York: Academic Press, 1980b, pp. 75–91. (chap. 12)

———, **S. J. Miller,** and **R. C. Atchley.** *Families in Later Life*. Belmont, Calif.: Wadsworth, 1979. (chaps. 11, 12)

Tu Wei-Ming. "The Confucian Perception of Adulthood." In E. H. Erikson (ed.), *Adulthood*. New York: Norton, 1978, pp. 113–120. (chap. 15)

Tulving, E. "Episodic and Semantic Memory." In E. Tulving and W. Donaldson (eds.), *Organization of Memory*. New York: Academic Press, 1972. (chap. 8)

Turnbull, C. M. *The Mountain People*. New York: Simon & Schuster, 1972. (chap. 15)

_____. *The Human Cycle.* New York: Simon & Schuster, 1983. (chap. 15)

Turner, B. "The Self Concept of Older Women." *Research on Aging,* 1 (1979), 464–480. (chap. 10)

Tversky, A., and **D. Kahneman.** "Judgment Under Uncertainty: Heuristics and Biases." *Science,* 185 (1974), 1124–1131. (chap. 9)

_____, and _____. "The Framing of Decisions and the Psychology of Choice." *Science,* 211 (1981), 453–458. (chap. 9)

Twain, M. *The Adventures of Tom Sawyer.* New York: Heritage Press, 1936 (orig. pub. 1876). (chap. 13)

Uhlenberg, P. "Changing Configurations of the Life Course." In T. K. Hareven (ed.), *Transitions: The Family and the Life Course in Perspective.* New York: Academic Press, 1978, pp. 65–98. (chap. 12)

Ullmann, L. P., and **L. Krasner.** *A Psychological Approach to Abnormal Behavior.* 2d ed. Englewood Cliffs, N.J.: Prentice-Hall, 1975. (chap. 6)

U.S. Bureau of the Census. *Annual Housing Survey.* Washington, D.C.: U.S. Government Printing Office, 1976. (chap. 14)

U.S. Bureau of the Census. *1980 Census of the Population.* Washington, D.C.: U.S. Government Printing Office, 1981. (chap. 15)

U.S. Bureau of the Census. *Statistical Abstract of the United States, 1982–83.* 103d edition. Washington, D.C.: U.S. Government Printing Office, 1982. (chaps. 1, 2, 3, 4, 5, 6, 11, 12, 13, 14, 15)

U.S. Bureau of the Census. *American Women: Three Decades of Change.* Washington, D.C.: U.S. Government Printing Office, 1983a. (chap. 11)

U.S. Bureau of the Census. *Estimates of the Population of the United States, by Age, Sex, and Race: 1980–82,* P-25, No. 929. Washington, D.C.: U.S. Government Printing Office, 1983b. (chap. 3)

U.S. Public Health Service. *Alzheimer's Disease: Q & A.* NIH Pub. No. 80-1646. Washington, D.C.: U.S. Government Printing Office, 1980. (chap. 6)

U.S. Public Health Service. *Healthy People: The Surgeon General's Report on Health Promotion and Disease Prevention.* DHEW Pub. No. 79-55071. Washington, D.C.: U.S. Government Printing Office, 1979. (chap. 5)

Vaillant, G. E. *Adaptation to Life: How the Best and Brightest Came of Age.* Boston: Little, Brown, 1977. (chaps. 10, 13)

van den Berghe, P. "Age Differentiation in Human Societies." In J. Sokolovsky (ed.), *Growing Old in Different Societies.* Belmont, Calif.: Wadsworth, 1983, pp. 72–81. (chap. 15)

Vatuk, S. "Withdrawal and Disengagement as a Cultural Response to Aging in India." In C. L. Fry (ed.), *Aging in Culture and Society.* New York: Praeger, 1980, pp. 126–148. (chap. 15)

Vecsey, G. "Mrs. King in a Familiar Spot." *The New York Times,* June 28, 1983, A25. (chap. 4)

Verba, S., and **N. Nie.** *Participation in America: Political Democracy and Social Equality.* New York: Harper & Row, 1972, (chap. 14)

Verillo, R. T. "Age-Related Changes in the Sensitivity to Vibration." *Journal of Gerontology,* 35 (1980), 185–193. (chap. 7)

Veroff, J., E. Douvan, and **R. Kulka.** *The Inner American: A Self-Portrait from 1957 to 1976.* New York: Basic Books, 1981. (chap. 11)

_____, and **S. Feld.** *Marriage and Work in America: A Study of Motives and Roles.* New York: Van Nostrand Reinhold, 1970. (chap. 11)

Visintainer, M. A., J. R. Volpicelli, and **M. E. P. Seligman.** "Tumor Rejection in Rats after Inescapable or Escapable Shock." *Science,* 216 (1982), 437–439. (chap. 5)

Vygotsky, L. S. *Mind in Society.* Cambridge, Mass.: Harvard University Press, 1978. (chap. 1)

Waddell, K. J., and **B. Rogoff.** "Effect

of Contextual Organization on Spatial Memory of Middle-Aged and Older Women." *Developmental Psychology*; 17 (1981), 878–885. (chap. 8)

Walford, R. L. *Maximum Life Span*. New York: Norton, 1983. (chaps. 1, 3, 4, 5)

———, R. H. Weindruch, S. R. S. Gottesman, and C. F. Tam. "The Immunopathology of Aging." In C. Eisdorfer, B. Starr, and V. J. Cristofalo (eds.), *Annual Review of Gerontology and Geriatrics*. Vol. 2. New York: Springer, 1981, pp. 1–48. (chap. 3)

Wallach, M. A., and N. Kogan. *Modes of Thinking in Young Children*. New York: Holt, Rinehart and Winston, 1965. (chap. 9)

Wallerstein, J. S., and J. B. Kelly. *Surviving the Break-Up: How Children Actually Cope with Divorce*. New York: Basic Books, 1980. (chap. 12)

Walsh, D. A. "The Development of Visual Processes in Adulthood and Old Age." In F. I. M. Craik and S. Trehub (eds.), *Aging and Cognitive Processes*. New York: Plenum, 1982, pp. 99–125. (chap. 7)

———. "Age Differences in Learning and Memory." In D. S. Woodruff and J. E. Birren (eds.), *Aging: Scientific Perspectives and Social Issues*. 2d ed. Monterey, Calif.: Brooks/Cole, 1983, pp. 149–177. (chap. 8)

Walsh, R. P., and C. L. Connor. "Old Men and Young Women: How Objectively Are Their Skills Assessed?" *Journal of Gerontology*, 34 (1979), 561–568. (chap. 1)

Walther, R. J. "Economics of Aging." In D. S. Woodruff and J. E. Birren (eds.), *Aging: Scientific Perspectives and Social Issues*. 2d ed. Monterey, Calif.: Brooks/Cole, 1983, pp. 370–390. (chap. 14)

Wang, H. S., and E. W. Busse. "EEG of Healthy Old Persons—A Longitudinal Study: I. Dominant Background Activity and Occipital Rhythm." *Journal of Gerontology*, 24 (1969), 419–426. (chap. 4)

———, W. D. Obrist, and E. W. Busse. "Neurophysiological Correlates of the Intellectual Function of Elderly Persons Living in the Community." *American Journal of Psychiatry*, 126 (1970), 1205–1212. (chap. 4)

Wanner, R. A., and L. McDonald. "Ageism in the Labor Market: Estimating Earnings Discrimination against Older Workers." *Journal of Gerontology*, 38 (1983), 738–745. (chap. 13)

Wantz, M. S., and J. E. Gay. *The Aging Process: A Health Perspective*. Cambridge, Mass.: Winthrop, 1981. (chaps. 4, 5, 7)

Washburn, S. L. "Longevity in Primates." In J. L. McGaugh and S. B. Kiesler (eds.), *Aging: Biology and Behavior*. New York: Academic Press, 1981, pp. 11–29. (chap. 3)

Waterman, A. S. "Identity Development from Adolescence to Adulthood: An Extension of Theory and a Review of Research." *Developmental Psychology*, 18 (1982), 341–358. (chap. 10)

Waugh, N. C., and R. A. Barr. "Encoding Deficits in Aging." In F. I. M. Craik and S. Trehub (eds.), *Aging and Cognitive Processes*. New York: Plenum, 1982, pp. 183–190. (chap. 8)

Webb, W. B. "Sleep in Older Persons: Sleep Structure of 50- to 60-Year-Old Men and Women." *Journal of Gerontology*, 37 (1982), 581–586. (chap. 4)

Weber, F., R. J. Barnard, and D. Roy. "Effects of a High-Complex-Carbohydrate, Low-Fat Diet and Daily Exercise on Individuals 70 Years of Age and Older." *Journal of Gerontology*, 38 (1983), 155–161. (chap. 3)

Weber, M. *The Theory of Social and Economic Organization*. New York: Oxford University Press, 1947. (chap. 14)

Weg, R. B. "Changing Physiology of Aging: Normal and Pathological." In D. S. Woodruff and J. E. Birren (eds.), *Aging: Scientific Perspectives and Social Issues*. 2d ed. Monterey, Calif.: Brooks/Cole, 1983, pp. 242–284. (chaps. 3, 4, 5)

Weingartner, H., J. Grafman, W. Boutelle, W. Kaye, and P. R. Martin. "Forms of Memory Failure." *Science*, 221 (1983), 380–382. (chap. 6)

Weisman, A. D. *On Dying and Denying: A Psychiatric Study of Terminality*. New York: Behavioral Publications, 1972. (chap. 16)

Weisman, S. R. "Reagan Begins to Wear a Hearing Aid in Public." *The New York Times*, September 8, 1983, A14. (chap. 7)

Weiss, L., and M. F. Lowenthal. "Life-Course Perspective on Friendship." In M. F. Lowenthal, M. Thurnher, and D. Chiriboga (eds.), *Four Stages of Life*. San Francisco: Jossey-Bass, 1975, pp. 48–61. (chap. 11)

Weiss, R. S. *Going It Alone: The Family Life and Social Situation of the Single Parent*. New York: Basic Books, 1979. (chap. 12)

Weissman, M. M. "The Myth of Involutional Melancholia." *Journal of the American Medical Association*, 242 (1979), 742–744. (chap. 6)

Welford, A. T. *Ageing and Human Skill*. London: Oxford University Press, 1958. (chap. 8)

Wells, R. V. "Demographic Change and the Life Cycle of American Families." In T. K. Rabb and R. I. Rotberg (eds.), *The Family in History*. New York: Harper & Row, 1973, pp. 85–94. (chap. 16)

Wesley-King, S. "Service Utilization and the Minority Elderly." In R. L. McNeely and J. L. Cohen (eds.), *Aging in Minority Groups*. Beverly Hills, Calif.: Sage, 1983, pp. 241–249. (chap. 15)

West, R. L., R. D. Odom, and J. R. Aschkenasy. "Perceptual Sensitivity and Conceptual Coordination in Children and Younger and Older Adults." *Human Development*, 21 (1978), 334–345. (chap. 9)

Whitbourne, S. K., and A. S. Waterman. "Psychosocial Development During the Adult Years: Age and Cohort Comparison." *Developmental Psychology*, 15 (1979), 373–378. (chap. 10)

White, S. E., and K. Reamy. "Sexuality and Pregnancy: A Review." *Archives of Sexual Behavior*, 11 (1982), 429–443. (chap. 12)

Wiersma, W., and H. J. Klausmeier. "The Effect of Age upon Speed of Concept Attainment." *Journal of Gerontology*, 20 (1965), 398–400. (chap. 9)

Wilensky, H. L. *Work and Leisure*. New York: Free Press, 1962. (chap. 13)

Wilkie, F., and C. Eisdorfer. "Intelligence and Blood Pressure." In E. Palmore (ed.), *Normal Aging: II*. Durham, N.C.: Duke University Press, 1974a, pp. 87–94. (chap. 9)

———, and ———. "Terminal Changes in Intelligence." in E. Palmore (ed.), *Normal Aging: II*. Durham, N.C.: Duke University Press, 1974b, pp. 103–115. (chap. 9)

Williams, G. C. "Warriors No More: A Study of the American Indian Elderly." In C. L. Fry (ed.), *Aging in Culture and Society*. New York: Praeger, 1980, pp. 101–111. (chap. 15)

Williams, R. B., J. D. Lane, C. M. Kuh, W. Melosh, A. D. White, and S. M. Schanberg. "Physiological and Neuroendocrine Response Patterns During Different Behavioral Challenges: Differential Hyperresponsivity of Young Type A Men." *Science*, 218 (1982), 483–485. (chap. 5)

Willis, S. L., and P. B. Baltes. "Intelligence in Adulthood and Aging: Contemporary Issues." In L. W. Poon (ed.), *Aging in the 1980s: Contemporary Issues*. Washington, D.C.: American Psychological Association, 1980, pp. 260–272. (chap. 9)

Windley, P. G., and R. J. Scheidt. "Person-Environment Dialectics: Implications for Competent Functioning in Old Age." In L. W. Poon (ed.), *Aging in the 1980s: Psychological Issues*. Washington, D.C.: American Psychological Association, 1980, pp. 407–423. (chaps. 5, 7)

Wingrove, C. R., and J. P. Alston. "Cohort Analysis of Church Attendance, 1939–1969." *Social Factors*, 53 (1974), 324–331. (chap. 14)

Winikoff, B. "Changing Public Diet." *Human Nature*, 1 (1978), 60–65. (chap. 5)

Winograd, E., A. D. Smith, and **E. W. Simon.** "Aging and the Picture Superiority Effect in Recall." *Journal of Gerontology*, 37 (1982), 70–75. (chap. 8)

Wirth, L. "The Problem of Minority Groups." In R. Linton (ed.), *The Science of Man in the World Crisis.* New York: Columbia University Press, 1945. (chap. 15)

Wiswell, R. A. "Relaxation, Exercise, and Aging." In J. E. Birren and R. B. Sloane (eds.), *Handbook of Mental Health and Aging.* Englewood Cliffs, N.J.: Prentice-Hall, 1980, pp. 943–958. (chap. 5)

Wohlwill, J. F. *The Study of Behavioral Development.* New York: Academic Press, 1973. (chaps. 1, 2)

Wolfinger, R. E., and **S. J. Rosenstone.** *Who Votes?* New Haven, Conn.: Yale University Press, 1980. (chap. 14)

Wood, V., and **J. Robertson.** "The Significance of Grandparenthood." In J. F. Gubrium (ed.) *Time, Roles, and Self in Old Age.* New York: Human Sciences Press, 1976. (chap. 12)

Woodruff, D. S. "Physiology and Behavior Relationships in Aging." In D. S. Woodruff and J. E. Birren (eds.), *Aging: Scientific Perspectives and Social Issues.* 2d ed. Monterey, Calif.: Brooks/Cole, 1983, pp. 178–201. (chap. 7)

———, and **J. E. Birren.** "Age Changes and Cohort Difference in Personality." *Developmental Psychology*, 6 (1972), 252–259. (chaps. 1, 2, 10)

Wright, P. H. "Men's Friendships, Women's Friendships and the Alleged Inferiority of the Latter." *Sex Roles*, 8 (1982), 1–20. (chap. 11)

Wyatt, R. J., interviewed by R. Young. "A Conversation with Richard Jed Wyatt." *Psychology Today*, 17 (August 1983), 30–41. (chap. 6)

Yankelovich, D. *New Rules.* New York: Random House, 1981. (chaps. 2, 11, 12, 13)

Yarrow, M. R., P. Scott, L. De Leeuw, and **C. Heinig.** "Childrearing in Families of Working and Nonworking Mothers." *Sociometry*, 25 (1962), 122–140. (chap. 12)

Yerkes, R. M. "Psychological Examining in the United States Army." *Memoirs of the National Academy of Sciences*, 15 (1921), 1–890. (chap. 9)

Yesavage, J. A., T. L. Rose, and **G. H. Bower.** "Interactive Imagery and Affective Judgments Improve Face-Name Learning in the Elderly." *Journal of Gerontology*, 38 (1983), 197–203. (chap. 8)

Yin, P., and **Kwok Hung Lai.** "A Reconceptualization of Age Stratification in China." *Journal of Gerontology*, 38 (1983), 608–613. (chap. 15)

Zabarsky, M. "The Patriarch of a Commune." *Newsweek*, November 1, 1982, 62. (chap. 11)

Zacks, R. T. "Encoding Strategies Used by Young and Elderly Adults in a Keeping Track Task." *Journal of Gerontology*, 37 (1982), 203–211. (chap. 8)

Zaks, P. M., and **G. Labouvie-Vief.** "Spatial Perspective Taking and Referential Communication Skills in the Elderly: A Training Study." *Journal of Gerontology*, 35 (1980), 217–224. (chap. 8)

Zambrana, R. E., R. Merino, and **S. Santana.** "Health Services and the Puerto Rican Elderly." In D. E. Gelfand and A. J. Kutzik (eds.), *Ethnicity and Aging: Theory, Research, and Policy.* New York: Springer, 1979, pp. 308–319. (chap. 15)

Zarit, S. H. *Aging and Mental Disorders: Psychological Approaches to Assessment and Treatment.* New York: Free Press, 1980. (chap. 6)

———, **J. M. Zarit,** and **K. E. Reever.** "Memory Training for Severe Memory Loss: Effects on Senile Dementia Patients and Their Families." *Gerontologist*, 22 (1982), 373–377. (chap. 6)

Zimbardo, P. G. "The Age of Indifference." *Psychology Today*, 14 (August 1980), 71–76. (chap. 13)

———, **S. M. Andersen,** and **L. G. Kabat.** "Induced Hearing Deficit Generates Experimental Paranoia." *Science*, 212 (1981), 1529–1531. (chap. 7)

Zivian, M. T., and **R. W. Darjes.** "Free Recall by In-School and Out-of-School Adults: Performance and Metamemory." *Developmental Psychology*, 19 (1983), 513–520. (chap. 8)

Zubin, J. "Foundations of Gerontology—History, Training, and Methodology." In C. Eisdorfer and M. P. Lawton (eds.), *The Psychology of Adult Development and Aging.* Washington, D.C.: American Psychological Association, 1973, pp. 3–10. (chap. 1)

PHOTO CREDITS

PAGE	CREDIT

Chapter 1:

Opener	Owen Franken/Stock, Boston
5	Owen Franken/Stock, Boston
11	Dan Budnik/Woodfin Camp
20	Ld/Ezio–UPI/Bettmann Archives
20	Alan Carey/The Image Works
17	AP/Wide World Photos
23	Mark Antman/The Image Works

Chapter 2:

Opener	Randolph Falk/Jeroboam
36	Bruce Flynn/Picture Group
39	Frank Siteman/Taurus Photos
44	Suzanne Szasz/Photo Researchers
44	George Bellerose/Stock, Boston

Chapter 3:

Opener	Carrie Boretz/Archive Pictures
62	Harvey Stein
67	Alex Webb/Magnum
69	Stephen Shames/Black Star
72	Judy Griesedieck

Chapter 4:

Opener	AP/Wide World Photos
85	Frank Siteman/Jeroboam
86	Ken Sakamoto/Black Star
90	Cheryl A. Traendly/Jeroboam
112	Alan Carey/The Image Works

Chapter 5:

Opener	Gilles Peress/Magnum
128	Elizabeth Crews
135	James R. Holland/Stock, Boston
139	Kathryn Dudek
145	Fredrik D. Bodin/Picture Group

Chapter 6:

Opener	Ilka Hartman/Jeroboam
163	Robert V. Eckert, Jr./EKM-Nepenthe
167	Jeff Albertson/Stock, Boston
169	Abigail Heyman/Archive Pictures

Chapter 7:

Opener	Billy E. Barnes/Jeroboam
181	Barbara Alper/Picture Group

AUTHOR INDEX

SUBJECT INDEX